140161
20
AE038103
Discard from
Hartwick College

IIS ISSUE IS DEVOTED TO:
IE CHURCH AND POLITICS IN LATIN AMERICA
est editor DANIEL H. LEVINE

Vol. 21 No. 1
February 1979

# OURNAL OF INTERAMERICAN STUDIES

172421

# ınd WORLD AFFAIRS

A Publication of the Center for Advanced International Studies,
The University of Miami

SAGE PUBLICATIONS

*Journal of INTERAMERICAN STUDIES and WORLD AFFAIRS*

**EDITORIAL STAFF:**

John P. Harrison—Editor
Jan Peter Wogart—Associate Editor
Gerry Machovec—Editorial Assistant

**BOARD OF EDITORS:**

Orlando Albornoz, Universidad Central de Venezuela
D. A. Brading, Cambridge University
David Chaplin, Western Michigan University
Tom E. Davis, Cornell University
Malcolm Deas, St. Antony's College, Oxford, England
Isaac Kerstenetzky, Instituto Brasileiro de Geografia e Estatistica, Brazil
Celso Lafer, Universidade de São Paulo
Vaughan A. Lewis, University of the West Indies, Mona, Jamaica
Abraham Lowenthal, Woodrow Wilson International Center for Scholars
Robert McNicoll, University of Miami, emeritus
Carmelo Mesa-Lago, University of Pittsburgh
James J. Parsons, University of California, Berkeley
Clark Reynolds, Stanford University
Richard Schaedel, University of Texas, Austin
Hanns-Albert Steger, Universitat Erlangen-Nurnberg, Germany
Alfred Stepan, Yale University
Evelyn P. Stevens, Case Western Reserve University
Victor L. Urquidi, El Colegio de Mexico

The editors and publisher wish to acknowledge with gratitude the assistance and encouragement of the Center for Advanced International Studies, University of Miami, in providing ancillary services and support for this journal.

*Journal of*
INTERAMERICAN
STUDIES
*and* WORLD AFFAIRS

Vol 21
No. 1
February
1979

# CONTENTS

THIS ISSUE IS DEVOTED TO:
## THE CHURCH AND POLITICS IN LATIN AMERICA
Guest Editor DANIEL H. LEVINE

*Introductory Note* 3

*Religion and Politics, Politics and Religion: An Introduction*
DANIEL H. LEVINE 5

*From Medellín to Puebla: Notes for Reflection*
RENATO POBLETE, S.J. 31

*The Christian Left in Latin American Politics*
MICHAEL DODSON 45

*The Church and the Doctrine of National Security*
ROBERTO CALVO 69

*Churches and Human Rights in Latin America: Recent Trends in the Subcontinent*
BRIAN H. SMITH, S.J. 89

*Women Religious, the Poor, and the Institutional Church in Chile*
SISTER KATHERINE ANNE GILFEATHER, M.M. 129

*Salvation through Christ or Marx: Religion in Revolutionary Cuba*
MARGARET E. CRAHAN 156

SAGE PUBLICATIONS / *Beverly Hills* *London*

**POLICY: THE JOURNAL OF INTERAMERICAN STUDIES AND WORLD AFFAIRS** reflects the interests of the scholarly community and interested public concerned with the social, economic, political, and cultural aspects of life in Latin America (including the Caribbean); particularly in those instances where the subject is of concern to more than one of the traditional disciplines. As these concerns change, so will the content of the journal.

**ARTICLES** which have special relevance for interrelationships between American nations and of those nations with the rest of the world will be given special consideration. An effort will be made to include occasional articles that state an unusual or even discordant position on a subject of broad interest to be supplemented by critical comments of authorities representing differing positions on the topic. The editors continue to welcome articles by scholars from all parts of the world.

**MANUSCRIPTS** should be submitted in duplicate to: Editor, JOURNAL OF INTER-AMERICAN STUDIES AND WORLD AFFAIRS, Box 24-8134, University of Miami, Coral Gables, Florida 33124. Manuscripts should be typewritten, double-spaced, with footnotes, references, tables, and charts on separate pages, and should follow the current journal style. A brief biographical paragraph describing each author's current affiliation, research interests, and recent publications should accompany the manuscript.

**CORRESPONDENCE** regarding book reviews should be sent directly to: Book Review Editor, JOURNAL OF INTERAMERICAN STUDIES AND WORLD AFFAIRS, Box 24-8134, University of Miami, Coral Gables, Florida 33124.

---

**JOURNAL OF INTERAMERICAN STUDIES AND WORLD AFFAIRS** is published four times annually—in February, May, August and November. Copyright © 1979 by Sage Publications, Inc. All rights reserved. No portion of the contents may be reproduced in any form without written permission of the publisher.

**Subscriptions:** Regular institutional rate $28.00. Individuals may subscribe at a one-year rate of $15.00. Add $1.00 per year for subscriptions outside the United States. Orders from U.K., Europe, the Middle East, and Africa should be sent to the London office (address below). Noninstitutional orders **must** be paid by personal check.

Second-class postage paid at Beverly Hills, California.

**Inquiries:** Address all correspondence and permissions requests to SAGE PUBLICATIONS, INC., 275 South Beverly Drive, Beverly Hills, California 90212. Inquiries and subscriptions from U.K., Europe, the Middle East, and Africa should be sent to SAGE PUBLICATIONS LTD, 28 Banner Street, London EC1Y 8QE, England. Other orders should be sent to the Beverly Hills office.

**Advertising:** Current rates and specifications may be obtained by writing to the Advertising Manager at the Beverly Hills office (address above).

This journal is abstracted or indexed in **Historical Abstracts, Human Resources Abstracts, Sage Urban Studies Abstracts, International Political Science Abstracts, Public Affairs Information Service, Current Contents, Social Sciences Citation Index, Social Sciences Index, ABC POL SCI** and **United States Political Science Documents.**

**Back Issues:** Information about availability and prices of back issues may be obtained from the publisher's order department (address above). Write to London office for sterling prices.

**Claims for undelivered copies** must be made no later than three months following month of publication. The publisher will supply missing copies when losses have been sustained in transit and where the reserve stock will permit.

**Change of Address:** Six weeks' advance notice must be given when notifying of change of address. Please send old address label along with the new address to insure proper identification. Please specify name of journal.

**JOHN P. HARRISON**
*University of Miami*
*P.O. Box 248134*
*Coral Gables, Florida 33124*

# *INTRODUCTORY NOTE*

This special issue of the *Journal of Interamerican Studies and World Affairs* covers a topic which the editors have had under consideration for three years. Its realization at this opportune time, together with the cohesion and breadth of coverage, is the work of Guest Editor Daniel H. Levine whose own research in the field has brought him into close contact with scholars concerned about and writing on the role of the Church and religion in the contemporary politics of Latin America. Preliminary versions of the articles appearing in this issue were presented at a two-day session on the topic held at the Smithsonian Institution in Washington, D.C., under the sponsorship of the Woodrow Wilson Center's Latin American Program directed by Abraham F. Lowenthal. The sessions were effectively cochaired by Alexander Wilde and Daniel Levine. Many specialists from government, the press, and religious organizations, in addition to scholars in and out of universities, were in active attendance. The final versions of each contribution benefited from the questions and observations of the participants, as well as the organizational and critical acumen of the guest editor. Many of the sources on which the articles are based are not readily available for editorial verification. Mrs. Gerry Machovec, the Journal's editorial assistant, wishes to thank the contributors who cooperated fully with her in an effort to make all citations verifiable by readers, especially those not easily accessible.

The impact of the Council of Latin American Bishops (CELAM) on contemporary life and politics in the Western Hemisphere is inherent to much of what follows, with particular reference to its second conference held in Medellín, Colombia, in 1968. The extent to which its conclusions have been implemented and absorbed by the hierarchy of the Church, as indicated by preparation for CELAM's third conference in Puebla, Mexico, in October 1978, is the subject of Father Poblete's article.

Journal of Interamerican Studies and World Affairs, Vol. 21 No. 1, February 1979, 3-4
© 1979 Sage Publications, Inc.

The May 1979 issue of the *Journal of Interamerican Studies* will contain a critical review of the articles in this issue by Alexander Wilde, who will have the opportunity to draw upon his own extensive research on the Church and religion in Latin America. He will also comment on the discussion in Washington and the developments from that time to the inauguration by Pope John Paul II of the Third General Council of Latin American Bishops in Puebla, Mexico, which is scheduled to begin on January 27, 1979.

—*John P. Harrison*
Editor

**DANIEL H. LEVINE**
*Department of Political Science*
*University of Michigan*
*5601 Haven Hall*
*Ann Arbor, Michigan 48109*

# *RELIGION AND POLITICS, POLITICS AND RELIGION*
## *An Introduction*

Religion and politics have depended on and influenced one another since the origins of what we know as Latin America. Their relation is both mutual and multifaceted; mutual because religion and politics have evolved together over the years, taking material and symbolic support from one another, and multifaceted because it embraces interinstitutional conflict and accommodation (e.g., the "church-state" relations which dominated earlier scholarship) as well as more subtle and elusive exchanges whereby religious and political orders gave legitimacy and moral authority to one another. In this process, religious notions of hierarchy, authority, and obedience reflected and reinforced the pattern of existing social and political arrangements to such an extent that the two orders often seemed indistinguishable.

Historically it is true that the weight of Catholic influence (both material and symbolic) has gone to reinforce existing social arrangements in Latin America. *But this is not a necessary relation.* For it is not religion per se which produces conservative effects, but rather a particular set of historically determined concepts, traditions, and organizational commitments. As these change, we may expect new models of social and political action to arise in association with them. In the same measure, change in the political order, leading to new concepts and forms of action, will necessarily alter the impact of politics on religion, providing new pressures, problems, and models for action.

These potentialities are now being realized throughout Latin America, as both religion and politics undergo profound and far-reaching changes. These parallel and often explicitly related processes give voice to a general sense of crisis and uncertainty which

Journal of Interamerican Studies and World Affairs, Vol. 21 No. 1, February 1979, 5-29
© 1979 Sage Publications, Inc.

has stimulated a search for new ideals, understandings, and forms of action. This convergence of change in a traditionally dominant church with societies themselves undergoing rapid marches and countermarches has produced a setting uniquely geared to conflict, innovation, and self-questioning.

Such is the setting of our inquiry. Now, as in the past, religion and politics are closely related in Latin America. Indeed, a great deal of the conflict so visible in Latin American Catholicism in recent years has centered precisely over a struggle to redefine the meaning of religious symbols, and in this way redirect the social and political thrust of the Church as an institution and of Catholicism as a set of religious beliefs, practices, and motivations.[1] The intense interest in and concern for politics which lies at the heart of this process has in fact made the relation of religion and politics, if anything, closer and more dynamic in recent years than ever before.

The articles presented here all touch on one or another aspect of this process. In introducing them to the reader, I want to stress the importance of keeping religion and politics in a dynamic and dialectical balance, giving full and equal weight to each in our analysis.[2] Both religion and politics must be taken seriously as sources of motivation and guiding ideas. In this relation, action and meaning cannot be simply deduced from either side of the equation. Rather, these are empirical questions. Therefore, it is necessary to trace out the sociological linkages between religious and political themes in particular contexts and problems, for the transformation of religious ideas poses new problems and dilemmas for politics, while at the same time the pattern of political change raises new problems and dilemmas for religion.

Religion and politics are thus both analytically and empirically related—*the two cannot and should not be separated.* This position differs considerably from that taken in much recent work on "development," "modernization," and the role of religion in these processes.[3] In general, such writings see increasing functional specialization and institutional differentiation as both inevitable and good. In this view, no single institution can embrace all human activity or provide valid frameworks for its significance. Rather, spheres of competence are marked off and the whole is best represented by the metaphor of a marketplace—an arena in which different interests interact and work out changing codes of mutual coexistence.

This is a view of society with deep roots in the Protestant Reformation and its aftermath in Liberal and Utilitarian thought. The insistence on increasing secularization and differentiation common to much of this work often leads to a stance which strips religious institutions and leaders of most activities and functions not "explicitly religious," (e.g., concerned with cult, ritual, or salvation) turning these over to other institutions. To put it crudely, in this view preachers should preach, leaving politics and the care of the social order in general to the "experts."

Elsewhere I have argued that this perspective is a poor guide to the study of religion and politics in general (Levine, 1978; Levine and Wilde, 1977). In the specific case of Latin America, these authors totally failed to anticipate and understand the dramatic reemergence of political themes in Catholicism, especially (although not only) on the "Left." By arguing for a neat separation of spheres of action, their approach assumes that a parallel separation is possible in the minds of the actors themselves. But if religion really *is* a source of powerful motivations and lasting orientations in many areas of life, then the problem for analysis is to trace out the real links between religion and those actions—not simply to seek a dividing line.

In any case, the line which separates religion and politics is not as clear and sharp as these theories would have us believe. It all depends on what is meant by the terms. So far, I have used both "religion" and "politics" in a conventional way, with no attempt at more precise definition. "Religion" has referred to those activities surrounding church institutions (centered on cult and ritual), while "politics" has been identified implicitly with government or actions affecting government in some way. But these conventional usages are not sufficient, for, as I suggested earlier, an important part of the dynamic relation between religion and politics in contemporary Latin America rests on the expanded and altered meaning of the terms themselves. Consider, then, the potential scope of each.

For our puroses, a working definition of religion should help isolate a set of beliefs and motivations and shed light on the way they generate regular patterns of action. Thus, we need a concept linking beliefs to action. For Catholicism, "pastoral action" provides such a concept. The idea of pastoral action, of course, derives from the biblical metaphor of a shepherd caring for his flock. Traditionally this "care" has been centered on charity, moral suasion, and tending to the needs of the sick and lonely. But pastoral action can mean many things, and in Latin America today it is an open question as to just how far, and in what direction, it extends. Is it limited to the provision of comfort, solace, and charity? May it encompass testimony, bearing witness to and sharing the conditions of peoples' lives as a sign of human solidarity? Need it include denunciation of those social conditions which make a fully human and moral life impossible, such as extreme poverty and oppression? Or must it be developed further to provide a basis for action to change society, making religious communion a part of social and political reconstruction? These issues are all alive in the Church today.

In much of Latin America, the Catholic hierarchy's response to pressures for greater political involvement has been to emphasize what the bishops see as "pastoral" (and hence, "non-political") actions.[4] But if the scope of the "pastoral" is expanded along the lines suggested above, it is hard to see how such actions can be kept out of politics. This becomes particularly difficult as the meaning of politics itself is stretched beyond the confines of government or partisan conflict, for, like pastoral action, "politics" can also be broadened to include denunciations of injustice. This brings new issues to the agenda of national life, or massive community action, such as land invasions, which seek to redress grievances and change the structure of power and opportunity in daily life. Such activities, while not political in a narrowly partisan or official sense, are nevertheless essentially political, as they raise basic issues of power, authority, legitimacy, and distribution.[5]

If both pastoral action and politics are expanded in this way, they flow easily together, and the distinction of religious from political roles and functions loses much of its presumed sharpness. Moreover, when these evolving concepts are tied to institutions, the potential for new and complex forms of action is enormous. This is particularly so in Catholicism, whose extraordinary development of hierarchical structures linking local, national, and international actors and resources provides a uniquely dense and complex context for action. Here, actions undertaken out of pastoral motives at the local level may be funded by international agencies working through the structures of the Church, with considerable repercussions on the national political scene. This process is particularly visible where, in the face of growing authoritarian rule, the Catholic Church has become, for all practical purposes, the only public voice of opposition (Smith, this issue).

While religion has long been considered a problem for politics, it is important to note that politics presents no less a problem for religion. Traditionally, the problems religion poses to the political order in Latin America have been seen in terms of "church-state" conflicts, centering over the control of schools, the regulation of marriage and divorce, birth control, and the like. The traditional problems politics has posed for religion in Latin America are the mirror image of these—the threat of growing secularization and the expansion of the state into areas previously left to religious guidance and control.

Although this kind of conflict persists in many areas, I would argue that it is no longer of central importance, especially in Latin America. Rather, with the changes noted above, religion now poses a problem for politics above all as a source of motivation for radical action and as an institutional shield for dissent from authoritarian rule. This new stance implies that politics and social life in general bring new problems to religion. The following section explores three basic aspects of this situation: (1) changing images of the Church and their impact on the way religious faith leads to social and political activism; (2) new perspectives on change and transformation (as opposed to static models) for understanding the world; and (3) in this context, the meaning of power, force, and violence, and the related issue of the church's stance on social division and class conflict in general.

These issues take form in the development of a series of groups and positions concerned with the proper relation of the Church and of religion in general to social and political change in Latin America. Three broad positions, on Left, Right, and Center will be discussed below:[6] first, on the "Left," the example of Camilo Torres and the development of Liberation Theology, combining new theological positions with a commitment to social and political revolution; second, on the "Right," the emergence of groups like the Societies for the Defense of Tradition, Family, and Property now spreading throughout the region, which combine an extremely traditional religious stance with reactionary social and political positions closely tied to the ideologies of national security being elaborated by military regimes in the area; and finally, in the "Center," a growing group of bishops and key Catholic institutions striving to maintain the unity of the Church against fierce pressures from Right and Left alike, while still hoping to respond in some creative way to the demands of contemporary social and political life.

### *Basic Issues*

Much of the motive force of recent changes in the Latin American Catholic Church has come in the gradual working out of the impact of the Second Vatican Council (Vatican II) and the subsequent Second General Conference of Latin American Bishops held in Medellín, Colombia, in 1968 (Medellín). A fresh look at those key events is particularly appropriate now, for while the articles in this issue were being prepared (early and mid-1978), preparations were underway for a Third General Conference of Latin American Bishops to be held in Puebla, Mexico, in late 1978. The Puebla meeting was organized to review and evaluate the decade since Medellín, while charting a course for the future (Poblete, this issue). Such a review brings out the enormous stimulus to change in the Latin American Church which came from Vatican II and Medellín. Let us consider, then, the content, direction, and impact of the changes begun there.

Vatican II marked a major attempt to rethink the nature of the Church, the world, and the proper relation between the two. Alongside the traditional model of the Church as an institution, which had stressed eternal, unchanging aspects of belief, structure, and hierarchy, the Council elaborated a vision of the Church as a "Pilgrim People of God"—a living, changing community of the faithful making its way through history. Viewing the Church as a "Pilgrim People of God" thus means, in a very basic sense, accepting the importance of historical change, both as a *fact* and as a powerful source of changing values.[7] This acceptance of change, as opposed to more traditional insistence on stasis and permanence, has had far-reaching and (one suspects) unanticipated consequences for the Church. Let me suggest several.

If situations and institutions are historically determined, then no particular social form is necessary—all change with time and new conditions. From this perspective, it is then no longer possible to be certain about the proper relation of individuals and groups within society, or even within the Church. Moreover, attention to the historical sources of change leads quite readily to a concern for understanding how societies developed as they did. Once this step is taken, the Church is decisively freed (at least in potential) from its previous identification with conservative forces and existing structures. Societies change as a matter of course, and they can be changed by human will, and not simply endured in hopes of a better life to come.

The Council's emphasis on the Church as a Pilgrim People of God also had profound impact on the structure and meaning of authority in the Church—the kinds of authority, activity, and obedience seen as necessary and legitimate. By laying such great stress on the historical experience of change, this model helped move emphasis within the

Church away from a predominant concern with roles, rank, and juridically defined hierarchy, and towards testimony and witness (in the biblical sense of solidarity through shared experience) as sources of authority and models for action (Levine, 1978). This new emphasis is of central importance, for if authority is grounded in testimony and witness, then the holders of authority (bishops, for example) are moved to action and expected to act as a necessary expression of their religious roles.

The link of authority to action also has had a major impact on the scope and meaning of obedience within the Church. The expectation of relatively automatic obedience has been called into question increasingly by priests, nuns, and laity alike who feel that for authority to have a legitimate claim to obedience, its holders must act to promote social justice. Moreover, the stress on action and shared experience, by putting the bases of authority and obedience on a more egalitarian, community-oriented footing, has contributed to important pressures for making collegiality and power-sharing a reality within the ecclesiastical institution itself. The often glacial pace of movements on this dimension has led to great frustration among key groups in the Church, particularly religious women (sisters), whose implications for the future are still uncertain (Gilfeather, this issue).

This renewed emphasis on shared experience, solidarity, and action draws heavily on biblical (especially Old Testament) images which stress the role of God as an active presence in the world. In this view, belief and authentic faith are seen as most completely expressed in actions to promote social justice (Migúez Bonino, 1976; Miranda, 1974). Moreover, activism itself has a different focus, because with the pervasive emphasis on historical experience, it is no longer a simple matter of applying known doctrine to the case at hand. Rather, as we shall see, the process begins with social analysis, searching in society for the "signs of the times"—events and situations which stimulate and enrich religious reflection.

These new perspectives were amplified by the Council's more general reevaluation of the meaning of social action, which gave it new autonomy and status in the Catholic scheme of things. Several dimensions are central to this process, most notably: (1) an opening to secular disciplines, particularly in the social sciences, as sources of valid knowledge about the world; and (2) related to this, a recognition of the autonomous validity of temporal values and of the possibility of drawing religious lessons and meaning from the problems and experiences of daily life. Let me review these briefly.

Vatican II stimulated the incorporation of many ideas and categories of analysis from contemporary social science into Catholic thinking about society. This began in a mild way, with general sociological analysis and a broad concern for "development." But, as we shall see, this small opening quickly expanded, above all in Latin America, to encompass new ideas about violence, "structural change," and essentially Marxist notions of economic dependency, praxis, and revolution. The possibility of drawing valid values from the world is related, for it implies a basic reorientation of Catholic activism. While earlier approaches (traditional, Catholic Action, and Christian Democratic alike) all in some measure sought to transform the world in accord with the principles of a known body of Christian doctrine, these new perspectives lead in a different direction.

The starting point here is social, not religious. Thus, rather than form specifically or exclusively "Christian" groups, those inspired by religious faith, in this view, join with others sharing their social goals, be they Christian or not. In Latin America, this perspective led quickly to the development of extensive and often controversial Christian-Marxist alliances—alliances whose goals were derived not from authorized expressions of Catholic social doctrine, but rather from a searching look at society, a look increasingly taken in the light of Marxist categories of analysis.

Of course, the Council's impact did not reach so far all at once. The first fruits of these changes came rather in a flurry of interest for "development" and a series of development projects of Christian inspiration. This orientation peaked in the early years of Christian Democratic rule in Chile, when it seemed as if that party might indeed make development a reality within this framework. But by the time of Medellín, this optimism had all but disappeared, and the appeal of Christian Democracy had soured in a rash of divisions, conflicts, and disappointments. At Medellín, the bishops took quite a new tack, and their conclusions (Conference of Latin American Bishops, 1970) mark without a doubt the single most important milestone in the recent development of Latin American Catholicism.

Like Vatican II, Medellín provided a broad reconsideration of all aspects of religious life, locating them with specific reference to the contemporary transformation of Latin America. For our purposes, Medellín is particularly important for its treatment of the key issues of force and violence, and the related question of social division and class conflict.

The matter of violence was put in perspective at Medellín by Pope Paul's comments during his visit to Colombia condemning violence as antievangelical and un-Christian. While supporting efforts at social change, the Pope thus ruled out violence as a legitimate tool of social transformation. The bishops differed, arguing, basically, that many kinds of violence exist. Thus, violence cannot be identified with only individual or even collective acts of aggression, but must be recognized as well in the day-to-day operations of unequal, unjust, and oppressive social structures. This was defined as "institutionalized violence." The distinction of "institutionalized violence" from more overt forms of aggression was a major step, for it opened the way to justifying counter-violence—violent acts intended to undo the inherent, institutionalized violence of the established order, replacing it with a more just society.

This social analysis was placed in a broader context of religious belief by the bishops' discussion of sin. Conventionally considered to refer to personal situations and individual morality, sin was extended here to characterize entire social systems whose injustice, oppression, and institutionalized violence were sinful, because they imposed social conditions which made a fully moral and decent life impossible. Once this kind of connection is made, it is clearly a short and relatively easy step to argue that if oppressive social, economic, and political structures are sinful, and hence prevent the full realization of human potential, then religious liberation, which involves freedom from sin, is in some measure tied to change in these structures—by revolution if necessary.

Finally, the Church's attention was focused once again, at Vatican II and at Medellín, on the poor, and more generally on the sources and meaning of poverty.[8] Of course, the Catholic Church has long paid considerable attention to the poor. But in social terms, most of this concern was expressed in welfare programs—aid to the poor within the bounds of existing social, economic, and political arrangements. Moreover, poverty was largely seen as a result of individual failings: hence, charity and job training were stressed. With the new orientations just described, however, poverty can be seen in a new light, as a structural (not an individual) problem. From this perspective, the misery of poverty and the injustice which causes it can never be resolved through individual charity alone. Rather, the structures which cause poverty must be changed—and this is a matter of power and political action.

More is at stake here than the simple reorientation of policies and programs, for a large part of the post-Medellín debates in the Latin American Church has involved attempts to reinterpret the symbolic meaning of poverty as well. For proponents of change, poverty need no longer be simply endured in the hopes of greater rewards in Heaven. Action and change are necessary and legitimate. Indeed, the phrase "the poor shall inherit the earth" is often taken in a much more direct and literal sense than has hitherto been the case. Moreover, the "poor" of the Gospels have often been transformed, among radical Catholics, into the working class or proletariat, and action to promote the coming of the Kingdom of God identified for all practical purposes with revolutionary struggle.

This renewed and transformed concern with poverty has also been expressed in a growing movement by priests and especially religious women to share the life and experiences of the poor—living with them, working with them, joining with them in the goals, frustrations, and general activities of daily life. As Dodson and Gilfeather note in their contributions here, this experience has often had a profound effect on the individuals involved. By bringing them into direct contact with the full misery and injustice of the life of the poor, it has made them more aware of the need for change, and served in this way as a spur to the organization of movements for social and political change by priests in several countries.

The impact on religious women has been particularly profound. As Gilfeather points out, because of a general scarcity of clergy, sisters in Chile (and elsewhere) increasingly have taken on duties and responsibilities hitherto reserved for priests. The experience of these responsibilities, coupled with the impact of living with the poor, has led to a profound transformation in religious values and a high degree of radicalization in and frustration with the structures of the Church. The sisters are restive within the institutional structures of the Church, which, while giving them greater burdens and responsibilities, nevertheless clings to a tradition of male-dominated authority structures which drastically restrict the recognition and rewards available to the sisters for their labors. In this case, new models of the Church, transformed authority structures, and the symbolic struggle over the meaning of poverty come together in a fascinating and potentially explosive mixture.

This brief sketch of the impact of Vatican II and Medellín indicates the depth and extent of change. A predominant concern with stasis was replaced by an emphasis on change. Social conflict and division were openly recognized, and a beginning made towards a full and open commitment to the poor. Finally, at least tentative steps were taken towards the legitimation of violence.[9] How have these ideas and initiatives been expressed in Latin America? No single, unified response is visible. Instead, several alternatives stand out, and the next section examines these in closer detail.

## *Cases: Left, Right, and Center*

The case of Camilo Torres is a good place to begin, for in many ways Torres was a precursor, exemplifying in his own brief career all of the elements of change just discussed.[10] Torres entered the priesthood under the influence of French social Catholicism as espoused by Dominican priests then living in Colombia. His vocation was thus strongly influenced by a particular dedication to social reform through Christian action. This orientation was reinforced by his advanced clerical education, which took him to Louvain University in Belgium. In the mid-1950's, Louvain was a center for reform-minded Latin American Catholics and a source of much Christian Democratic thinking. Thus, when he returned to Colombia in late 1958, Torres came inspired by ideas of development through Christian action.

But he soon grew frustrated with elite persuasion, reformist methods, and with the very assumption that some uniquely Christian solution to social problems existed. His career evolved rapidly, and in 1965 he founded a movement, the United Front, intended to bring together all progressive forces in the pursuit of political change. These activities led to conflict with the ecclesiastical heirarchy, which ended with Torres' voluntary "reduction" to lay status to devote himself full time to politics. Events moved swiftly: the United Front was formed in May, 1965; Torres left the priesthood in June; he entered a guerrilla front in October; and he was killed in early 1966 in a skirmish with an army patrol.

This brief but spectacular career raises at least three issues for Latin American Catholicism, all of which were taken up and treated more systematically in later years: first, the relation of religious faith to action in the world; second, the status of power, force, and violence; and third, the proper relation between Catholics and other (specifically Marxist) groups in the promotion of change.

Camilo Torres clearly believed that authentic religious faith required action to transform an unjust world. Religion was not simply "spiritual," a disembodied faith brought out only on Sundays. Rather, it was an integral part of life. Hence, genuine faith could only achieve full expression in a just and equitable society. In his words, "When circumstances impede men from devoting themselves to Christ, the priest's proper duty is to combat these circumstances . . . the revolutionary struggle is a Christian and priestly struggle" (1972: 264-265).

It is important to be clear about this issue. Torres did not oppose politics in religion, or somehow put politics before religion. Rather, he saw the two as intimately and necessarily joined, and looked for the way religious commitments required action to make them effective. In his view, a true Christian was obliged to be political, for only in this way could love of neighbor, the key Christian precept, be made effective. Individual acts of kindness and charity were negated by the unjust structures of society. And since these structures were founded on power, only power (not appeals to conscience or good will alone) could change them. The rapid turn to politics and guerrilla action flowed directly from these understandings. Once one recognized the fact of social division, and became aware of the full implications of phrases like "love thy neighbor," then the use of power and even violence as means to a more just society was legitimate.

Finally, Torres anticipated the extraordinary development of Marxist-Christian dialogue and cooperation, for as he moved away from Christian (and Christian Democratic) reformism and its concern for building church-related programs, he came logically to value alliances with any and all groups dedicated to the cause of revolution.

The career of Camilo Torres is important, for it was not a fluke or a chance aberration, but rather responded to many growing pressures for change in church and society alike. These pressures and new perspectives have been developed most systematically in Latin America in what has come to be known as Liberation Theology. A brief look at Liberation Theology will thus round out our view of the Left's response to change in church and society. As the name implies, Liberation Theology is concerned with the meaning of religion for social and political liberation, and vice versa. It has evolved in recent years as a distinctively and self-consciously Latin American approach to the relation of religion and politics.

The Latin American focus of these writings is significant in itself, for it reflects a deliberate effort to root the understanding of religious faith in the particular experiences of contemporary Latin America. Theology is thus placed in the context of real social experience, and this once cloistered and abstract discipline is transformed into a reflection on concrete historical situations and struggles.[11] In this way, the methodology of Liberation Theology begins with a look at concrete social problems, drawing themes and imperatives for action from this analysis. The central problem for religion is thus no longer atheism, indifference, or even hostility to religion per se, but rather social and political transformation. Gutiérrez, a leading Peruvian theologian, states the issue sharply:

> Much contemporary theology seems to start from the challenge of the *non-believer.* He questions our *religious world* and faces it with a demand for profound purification and renewal. . . . This challenge in a continent like Latin America does not come primarily from the man who does not believe, but from the *man who is not a man,* who is not recognized as such by the existing social order: he is in the ranks of the poor, the exploited; he is the man who is systematically and legally despoiled of his being as a man, who scarcely knows that he *is* a man. His challenge is not aimed first at our religious world, but at our *economic, social, political and cultural world;* therefore it is an appeal for the revolutionary transformation of the very bases of a dehumanizing society. The question is not therefore how to speak of God in an adult world, but how to proclaim him as a Father in a world that is not human [1974: 69].

Liberation Theology faces the issues of power, force, and violence quite directly, building them into its analysis of the nature of authentic religious commitment. Like Camilo Torres, Gutiérrez argues that Christians must look at society realistically, giving full weight to the struggle and conflict so visible everywhere. Traditional Catholic positions which oppose class struggle in the name of an ideal of Christian love and unity are rejected. Real Christian love, Gutiérrez argues, is founded on commitment to a more just society and action to bring it about (1973: 278).

The influence of contemporary social science, and particularly of Marxist thought,[12] is notable in the adoption of a perspective of continuous change, the identification of the working class as the motor of this change, and a deep concern with the fusion of theory and action in an authentic revolutionary *praxis.* Let me review these briefly.

The recognition of change is central to Liberation Theology, and fits well with a view of the Church as Pilgrim People of God. From this perspective, writers like Assmann (1971), Dussel (1976), Gutiérrez (1973), or Segundo (1973, 1976) illuminate the kinds of problems faced by religious people as they seek social and political change. Above all, they want to avoid any rigid identification with the present, and thus keep Catholic thought and action open to change. Assmann says it well:

> The transcendence of God rests on the fact that he is always before us, on the frontiers of the future. God is provocative, that is, he calls us ahead, and can only be met as one who moves forward with his people in a continuous dismantling of structures [1971: 21].

For Liberation Theology, change is both permanent and ultimately rooted in social conflict. This point of view stems in large measure from the disillusionment already noted with "development" as practiced in Latin America. "Development" was originally seen as a non-revolutionary path to progress and broad social benefits through economic growth and industrialization in a capitalist framework. But for radical Catholics, such "development" has masked a reality of increasing poverty, misery, and inequality. Rejecting "development," these writers have turned for orientation to the theories of "dependency" which have emerged in Latin America in recent years.[13]

From dependency theory, Liberation Theology acquired an explanation of the Latin American situation and a set of categories which strengthened and gave focus to the social and economic concerns so central to its religious analysis. Even a minimal glance at the vast body of writings on dependency suggests the reasons for their attractiveness to radical Catholics. To dependency theory, the inequality and misery associated with capitalist development in Latin America are not accidental, but rather are a necessary consequence of the subordination of Latin American societies and economies to the interests of dominant world capitalist powers. *Their* development depends on the continued exploitation of Latin America and other "underdeveloped" regions. Moreover, their policies and programs are implemented by local allies in control of social, cultural, economic, and political institutions. The solution, for dependency theory and Liberation Theology alike, lies not in more of the same (that is, more "development") but in the construction of a new social order.

What finally is "liberation"? Basically, liberation involves freedom from bondage of all kinds—the bondage of ignorance, alienation, poverty, and oppression. Such liberation is neither wholly spiritual nor wholly material. Rather, it is the fusion of the two which gives this perspective its unique and compelling force. Religious and political liberation go together: "purely religious" actions, limited to the institutional Church, are rejected as a false consciousness; while "pure politics" lack meaning in the cosmic scheme of things. In this view, the key role of religious action is to join the two planes, removing traditional religious legitimation of the social order while channeling religious energies and motivations toward its transformation.

Religion is linked to politics through the emphasis on *praxis* which runs through these writings. Praxis refers to a course of action so theoretically informed and self-aware that the activity itself expresses consciously the insights which logical study and reflection provide. Liberation Theology stresses both individual and collective praxis of this kind, making action, in effect, a necessary consequence of authentic faith—a kind of validation of the reality of that faith. This concern for conscious, self-aware action has received two notable expressions in recent years: first, in the work of Paolo Freire, the Brazilian educator; and second, in programs for cooperation and joint action with Marxists. Consider Freire first.

Paolo Freire (1968, 1974) has had an enormous influence on Latin American Catholicism. He argues that education must do more than impart skills. Each student must acquire an active role in creating his own awareness of the surrounding world. This process (*concientización* in Spanish) is intended to develop in each person a critical awareness of society as a human, and therefore changeable, product. To Freire, the first and most basic step in change is liberating people from the oppressors they have internalized, for he argues that the dominated absorb the dominators' vision of them. Thus, the poor believe themselves to be "lazy" and "stupid." Only when the social order is demythologized, through the development of critical consciousness, can people proceed to liberate themselves. In this process, the transformation of religious concepts plays a major role. If religious symbols can also be demythologized and freed of their ties to the existing social order, then a major step toward psychological and cultural liberation will have been taken.

A more directly political path has been followed by Catholic radicals pursuing dialogue, cooperation, and open political alliances with Marxists. These initiatives have appeared all over Latin America since

Medellín, evolving furthest in Chile during the Allende regime. The evolution of Christians for Socialism in Chile is important, for it raised in practical terms most of the issues under consideration here. Thus, questions of activism, power, the meaning of politics for religious action, and the proper role for Christians (particularly priests and religious) in politics all came to the surface in sharp and controversial forms (Eagleson, 1975). Shortly before the overthrow of Allende, the movement was condemned by Chile's bishops, who feared that Christianity's central religious message was being swamped in an overwhelming political commitment. To the bishops, Christians for Socialism made bad policy and poor theology as well: bad policy by aggravating political divisions within the Church and commiting its survival to the fortunes of the socialist regime; and poor theology by reducing the Church's dynamic plane to an exclusively political one. If the Church were to become political, the mission of salvation might be lost:

> The Church is meant to be the salt of the earth. "And if salt becomes tasteless, how is its saltiness to be restored?" (Mt. 5:15) If the Church is turned into a political or temporal faction, who will save us? [Eagleson, 1975: 224]

With the fall of socialism in Chile, many in the Church have drawn back from full political commitment. The reaction of Chile's bishops has been echoed broadly in the region (Conferencia Episcopal de Colombia, 1976). But in dealing with the issues of politics and political commitment raised so sharply by Liberation Theology and Christians for Socialism, leaders of the Latin American Church are in a difficult situation, for they face concerted and often bitter opposition from all sides.

Considerable attention has been given here to the evolution of what is generally called the Christian Left. It is important to realize, however, that other equally vigorous positions exist. Indeed, as radical Catholics moved to more open political commitments, their activism has been matched, if not exceeded, on the Right, most notably by the Societies for the Defense of Tradition, Family, and Property (TFP) which have emerged in many countries.[14] Moreover, the weight of these groups on the Right has been reinforced in several key Latin American military establishments by the development of attitudes deeply hostile to the Church, rooted in the armed forces' views on "national security."

TFP and the military both reject the postconciliar and especially the post-Medellín changes in the Church as a betrayal of the religion they were brought up to honor, revere, and defend. The basic TFP world view combines very traditional forms of Catholic religious practice (the Latin mass, continued veneration of discarded saints, the ostentatious display of lachrymose religious images, and the like) with a strong commitment to reactionary social, economic, and political positions. TFP members see themselves as part of a general counterrevolutionary offensive, and explicitly attribute most of the ills of the modern world to the aftereffects of the French Revolution (Corrêa de Oliveira, 1970). The most notable aspect of their social doctrine is a belief in the absolute sanctity of private property (De Castro Mayer et al, 1971) combined with an appreciation of the healthy virtues of social inequality. Naturally enough, they reject any dialogue with non-Catholic groups as the opening wedge of communist infiltration—a clever tactic for weakening the defenses of western, Christian civilization (Corrêa de Oliveira, 1971).

The reaction of the military is less specifically religious in tone and inspiration, but also reveals a deep hostility toward the contemporary Latin American Church. The military's views are grounded in their doctrine of "national security," according to which there is no real distinction between war and peace (Comblin, 1976, and Calvo, this issue). Because the natures of war and conflict have changed, *all* times are now times of war. As a result, national security itself can no longer be confined to the external defense of secure frontiers, but now requires *internal* unity and discipline to counter the social conflict and subversion which impede national progress. Since unity must be enforced and subversion combatted at every turn, the role of the state and especially of its security apparatus is greatly enhanced, while traditional civil liberties and representative institutions are eliminated.

The military see their struggle as part of the general defense of western, Christian civilization against communism. Hence, no contradiction is perceived between their position and "Christian principles," and extensive use is made of Christian images, symbols, and alliances wherever possible. But given the developments in the Church already described, and the ambiguities of "pastoral action" which have been noted here, the generals are continuously faced with "Christian" actions, which in their eyes amount to simple subversion. Moreover, the problem is not limited to "radicals," for as Calvo and Smith will point out later, the very leaders of the institutional Church, the bishops, instead of supporting the military's defense of "Christian values," have gradually moved into opposition over issues of human rights, social justice, and in the simple attempt to defend priests, nuns, and lay people engaged in pastoral action who are arrested as subversives. The net result has been growing tension and strain between the Church and the military regimes which now hold power in many countries.

The central institutions of the Church, led by the bishops, are caught in the middle. Since the late 1950s, their general goal has been withdrawal from partisan politics and concentration of energies on internal renewal and pastoral action. But, as we have seen, this position is full of ambiguities. Quite apart from its inherent difficulties, however, it is also under attack from many sides. The Left rejects it as hypocritical and unrealistic, while the Right calls the bishops to decisive action against communism. Caught in the center, the bishops are trying to hold the Church and the Catholic community together in the face of enormous divisive pressures, while retaining maximum possible autonomy from governments and political groups alike.

In many cases, this central position has been reached after a series of ups and downs concerning politics and political action. The enthusiasm of the late 1960s for development, social action, and internal Church reform was quickly tempered by reaction to what a number of bishops saw as the excesses of Liberation Theology and Christian-Marxist alliances. But in the shadow of the growing wave of authoritarian, "national security" regimes (most notably in the Southern Zone countries of Brazil, Argentina, Chile, and Uruguay), many Church leaders have been forced to take a new look at the issues as politics, this time in the form of the military, intrudes once again on the life of the Church.

The evolving position of the Chilean bishops is a good example of this process, for although Chile is an extreme case, it nevertheless encapsulates and concentrates many of the issues seen in fragmented form elsewhere. As we have seen, the hierarchy originally condemned Christians for Socialism in Chile because they feared (1) a relativization of the Christian message and its subordination to political goals, (2) the implications of any political division of the Church whereby different groups would each claim the mantle of Church authority for their positions, and (3) the reduction of transcendental commitments to the level of political ideologies. Thus they argued it is not true that everything is ultimately political, or that politics need be a primary form of commitment. Limits and distinctions were required. The Gospel does not depend on political action for its effectiveness, the Church in any case takes no particular political model as its own (transcending all), and finally, Church action is basically different *in kind* from political action, as force and power (so central to politics) are set aside (Eagleson, 1975: 179-228).

But by 1977 the tables had been turned. The Allende regime was no more. Gone with it were not only the activists on the Left (in Church and society alike), but also the entire apparatus of Chile's civil society and juridical, republican traditions. In 1973, a number of bishops were willing to legitimize the military regime, seeing it at the least as a respite from turmoil and constant conflict. But by 1977 the conflict had not gone away. Rather, the "internal" war continued, with the Church itself now coming under attack (Sanders and Smith, 1976). The Church's response has taken many forms. On the public scene, in 1977 the bishops issued a collective pastoral entitled *Our Life as a Nation* which explicitly took issue with the doctrine of national security, reaffirming the values of democracy, pluralism, and openness. They rejected the regime's attempt to cast itself as the defender of Christian values, noting that

> we do well to recall the teaching of the Church. She strongly upholds legitimate pluralism in the realm of ideas and socio-political groups, while also pointing out the need for national unity and the proper way to obtain it.
>
> The road to peace and unity cannot be reached through imposition. Unity, like truth (including religious truth), cannot be imposed by force. It must be proposed to people so that it can be accepted on the basis of inner conviction and a personal decision [Chilean Episcopal Conference, 1977: 8-9].

In Chile, as elsewhere in Latin America, the bishops are groping for ways to preserve the unity[15] and autonomy of the Church while maintaining its ability to contribute creatively to the welfare of the community through social and pastoral action. In this regard, as Smith shows in this issue, the Church's great organizational flexibility has been of crucial importance. While it cannot change authoritarian regimes on its own, nevertheless the Church has managed to organize and finance institutions to help the victims of oppression while keeping alive the hope for a different kind of future. In many cases, church organizations (particularly at the local level) have in effect become surrogates for the social and political participation and interchange no longer permitted in society at large. This real potential for serving as an institutional shield, a shelter for activities prohibited by the government, makes the hierarchy's deep concern for preserving the unity of the institution of the Church all the more understandable. The full impact of these developments on the life of the Church is still unclear, but it seems inevitable that this growing, direct involvement *with* the poor and weak *against* the power of the state, which finds the Church itself becoming a victim in many cases, will affect the institution's future stance toward the issues and choices we have thus far considered.

## *Conclusions*

Throughout the course of events considered here, the ecclesiastical hierarchy has generally resisted attempts to push it along exclusively political tracks.[16] In this regard, it is important to note that both Christians for Socialism and the TFP-military position emphasize political action as legitimate and necessary for the Church. Each wants to harness the moral authority of Catholicism to its own image of the good social and political order. Each defends a different image of the Church, and calls it to combat in a different cause.

The bishops resist "politics" as such, but politics clearly lies at the core of all these disputes. In a basic sense, politics is a crucial field of action for controlling, delimiting, and defining the activities of the institutional Church and its agents. More generally, politics is a crucial field of action as it is the arena in which individual moral choices are brought together with collective consequences. Finally, politics is a crucial field of action because of its close, dialectical relation with religion. Believers feel compelled to political action as an expression of their religious faith, and their actions manifest a general kind of commitment within which it is difficult to disentangle religion from politics at all.

Their mutual centrality is not surprising. Politics, after all, deals at the most general level with the organizing principles and symbols of the entire society. Religion, in turn, provides values which give meaning to human life, placing any given set of social or political events in a broader framework of significance. In Latin America today, religion is a problem for politics, and politics no less a problem for religion, as each gropes for new understandings of itself and of its relation to the other.

Finally, politics is a crucial field of action, for while the churches and the faithful act in and on politics, at the same time political forces impinge powerfully on them, shaping the challenges they face and the constraints and opportunities within which they must work. Thus, the problems and possibilities of the Catholic Church in Chile, Brazil, Argentina, or El Salvador now differ sharply from those of earlier years, just as the Chilean situation at any of these times is far removed from the context of contemporary Honduras, Colombia, or Cuba.

These issues are considered from different perspectives and in different contexts in the articles which follow. Poblete analyzes the process of change within the Latin American Church leading up to the Third General Conference of Latin American Bishops in Puebla. He documents elements of continuity and change in this process, while shedding light on the sources and ramifications of division and conflict within the Latin American Church. The transformation of concepts of religion and politics and their implication for action are explored for the Catholic Left by Dodson, who examines the origins and development of radical Catholicism as both an innovative religious theology and a new political theory, and shows how these new insights led to the formation of religiopolitical movements to promote change in several countries.

As we have seen, a major element shaping the context within which the Latin American Church acts is the new ideology of national security elaborated by military regimes throughout the region. Calvo examines the sources and key elements of these ideas, while laying out the main lines of the Church's analysis and doctrinal response. On a more direct, practical level, Smith looks at the Church's defense of human rights in Latin America today. He explores the developing organizational basis of Church response to authoritarian rule, and its implications for the future. He further analyzes the way in which the very concept of human rights has broadened beyond traditional civil liberties to include demands for more just social, economic, and political structures.

I have stressed the importance of experience, both within new models of the Church and also as a major factor in transforming the outlook of Church personnel. Gilfeather's analysis of the experiences of religious women living in marginal areas in Chile brings out very sharply the impact of experience on these sisters, particularly with respect to the content of their religious life and the nature of their role within the institutional Church. Her article suggests the enormous potential such new experiences have for transforming the inner life of the Church as a community. But she documents as well the high degree of frustration these women find in the Church, as their new experiences generate modes of perception, belief, and action which find little or no expression within the formal structures of the ecclesiastical institution.

What is the response of the churches to change within society at large? How do they react to major social upheavals and transformations? In contemporary Latin America, Cuba since 1959 offers a fascinating laboratory of change, and Crahan provides a synthetic view of the impact of revolutionary change on the weak and backward churches (both Protestant and Catholic) of Cuba. Her analysis sheds considerable light on the way in which institutional transformation and changes in the sheer volume and meaning of religious affiliation and practice go together.

## NOTES

1. Good reviews of recent Latin American developments include Smith, 1975, and Comblin, 1977.

2. This point is more fully developed in Levine, 1978.

3. Two quite different examples of this tendency, among many, are Vallier, 1970, and Silvert, 1967.

4. In this vein, Msgr. Alfonso López Trujillo, Secretary General of CELAM argues that political neutrality is an essential precondition for the Church's pastoral independence. He refers, above all, to neutrality in partisan politics (1975).

5. See Levine and Wilde, 1977, for a full discussion of the various meanings of pastoral action and of politics.

6. Since they are derived from political alignments, terms like Left, Right, and Center often fail to capture the dimensions of religious orientation which underly positions taken. I am using the terms here in accord with conventional understandings, with full awareness of their ambiguous and sometimes misleading character. The text should make the meaning of these terms clear in each particular case. There is a long-standing tendency in Catholicism to search for a "third position," opposing both left (communism) and Right (capitalism). This stance is severely criticized in Dussel, 1978.

7. For a fuller account of Vatican II, see Hebblethwaite, 1975 or O'Dea, 1968. The implications of new models of the Church in Latin America are discussed more fully in Levine, 1978 and Smith and Sanks, 1977. As both Smith and Gilfeather point out in their contributions to this issue, the emergence of new models of the Church can also be seen on a different, though related dimension. Traditionally, Catholicism has taken a very broad view of its membership. As a universal *church,* it was open to all who met only minimal requirements for entry. Thus, Catholicism traditionally rejected the (Protestant) model of *sects*, which looks to an elite core of members, highly motivated, aware, and knowledgeable. There is considerable evidence in Latin America now that many Catholics

are moving to a view of the Church which stresses greater knowledge, more conscious commitment, and high levels of participation, all sect-like qualities, with important implications for the authority structure of the Church and for the relations of groups within it.

8. Turner (1974, 265-267) suggests that a concern for the meaning of poverty is typical of periods of intense cultural crisis and reorientation, what he calls liminal periods." His analysis fits the current Latin American scene well.

9. For a complete discussion of the difficulties the Church faces in legitimizing violence in the specific case of Colombia, see Levine and Wilde, 1977.

10. On Torres, see particularly Broderick, 1975.

11. As Dussel states (1976: 145), the text for theological reflection is not a set of abstract categories, but rather a social situation.

12. The great attraction of Marxist thought to Latin American Catholic radicals has been criticized sharply by the North American Jesuit, Coleman, in these terms: "As a social scientist, I have often been puzzled, if not irritated, by the almost religious importance many Latin American theologians of liberation give to the writings and analysis of Karl Marx. At times, Marxist thought (albeit with a revisionary attempt to extrapolate a 'scientific' Marx from Marx the materialist, atheistic philosopher) is identified *tout court* with social scientific analysis. Such an approach does not accord with the anti-dogmatic stance of a social science" (1976: 133).

13. The literature on dependency is enormous. Kahl (1976) provides a good introduction to the issues and a useful discussion of their development in Latin America.

14. The first TFP nuclei were founded in Brazil in the years preceding the military coup of 1964. TFP militants played a major role in organizing public opposition to the Goulart regime. Later, in Chile, TFP was active in the opposition to Allende, often forming the core of such right-wing groups as *Patria y Libertad.*

15. They hope to maintain the unity of the Catholic community around the Church's central ecclesiastical institutions. Hence, they reject those who, like Torres or Liberation Theology writers, argue that the Church's unity requires the construction of a new social order (López Trujillo, 1975).

16. The bureaucratic politics of this process are yet to be studied in full. There have been important struggles over the control and orientation of CELAM, and attempts to curtail Liberation Theology through restrictions on funding by international, particularly German, Church agencies (Metz et al., 1978).

## REFERENCES

ASSMANN, H. (1971) Opresión-Liberación Desafío a los Cristianos. Montevideo: Tierra Nueva.

BRODERICK, W. J. (1975) Camilo Torres. Garden City, NY: Doubleday.

CELAM [Council of Latin American Bishops] (1970) The Church in the Present Day Transformation of Latin America in the Light of the Council. Bogotá: CELAM.

COMBLIN, J. (1977) "The Church in Latin America after Vatican II," LADOC 7 (January-February): 1-18.

——— (1976) "Theology of captivity: Christianity and the national security system." Harvard University. (unpublished)

CHILEAN EPISCOPAL CONFERENCE (1977) "Our life as a nation." LADOC 7 (July-August): 1-14.

COLEMAN, J. (1976) "Civil religion and liberation theology in North America," pp. 113-138 in S. Torres and J. Eagleson [eds.] Theology in the Americas. Maryknoll, NY: Orbis.

CONFERENCIA EPISCOPAL DE COLOMBIA (1976) Identidad Cristiana en la Acción Por la Justicia. Bogotá: SPFC.

CORRÊA DE OLIVEIRA, P. (1971) Trasbordo Ideologico Inadvertido y Dialogo. Madrid: C.I.O.

——— (1970) Revolución y Contra-Revolución. Buenos Aires: Tradición, Familia, y Propiedad.

DE CASTRO MAYER, A., G. DE PROENÇA SIGAUD, P. CORRÊA DE OLIVEIRA, and L. MENDONÇA DE FREITAS (1971) Reforma Agraria, Cuestión de Conciencia. Bogotá: Asociación Colombiana Para la Defensa del Derecho Natural.

DUSSEL, E. (1978) "El tercerismo eclesial (Táctica Política y Mecanismo Ideológico)," in E. Tamez and S. Trinidad [eds.] Capitalismo y Anti-Vida La Opresión de Las Mayorías y la Domesticación de los Dioses, Tomo I. San José, Costa Rica: EDUCA.

——— (1976) History and the Theology of Liberation: A Latin American Perspective. Maryknoll, NY: Orbis.

EAGLESON, J. [ed.] (1975) Christians and Socialism: Documentation of the Christians for Socialist Movement in Latin America. Maryknoll, NY: Orbis.

FREIRE, P. (1974) Las Iglesias, la Educación, y el Proceso de Liberación Humana en la Historia. Buenos Aires: Asociación Editorial La Aurora.

——— (1968) Pedagogy of the Oppressed. New York: Seabury.

GUTIERREZ, G. (1974) "Liberation, theology, and proclamation," pp. 57-77 in C. Geffré and G. Gutiérrez [eds.] The Mystical and Political Dimensions of the Christian Faith. New York: Herder & Herder.

——— (1973) A Theology of Liberation History, Politics, and Salvation. Maryknoll, NY: Orbis.

HEBBLETHWAITE, P. (1975) The Runaway Church Post Conciliar Growth or Decline. New York: Seabury.

KAHL, J. (1976) Modernization, Exploitation, and Dependency in Latin America. New Brunswick, NJ: Transaction Books.

LEVINE, D. (1978) "Authority in Church and society: Latin American models." Comparative Studies in Society and History 20: 4.

——— and A. WILDE (1977) "The Catholic Church, 'politics,' and violence: the Colombian case." Review of Politics 39 (April): 220-239.

LOPEZ TRUJILLO, A. (1975) "El Compromiso Político del Sacerdote." Tierra Nueva (Bogotá) 14 (July): 17-53.

METZ, J. B., et al. (1978) "Memorandum de Teologos de la República Federal Alemana Sobre La Campaña Contra la Teología de la Liberación." Diálogo (Guatemala) 38 (March): 31-35.

MIGUEZ BONINO, J. (1976) Christians and Marxists: The Mutual Challenge to Revolution. Grand Rapids: Eerdmans.

MIRANDA, J. (1974) Marx and the Bible: A Critique of the Philosophy of Repression. Maryknoll, NY: Orbis.

O'DEA, T. (1968) The Catholic Crisis. Boston: Beacon.

SANDERS, T. and B. SMITH (1976) "The Chilean Catholic Church during the Allende and Pinochet regimes." American Universities Field Staff Reports, West Coast South America Series 23: 1.

SEGUNDO, J. L. (1976) The Liberation of Theology. Maryknoll, NY: Orbis.

——— (1973) The Community Called Church. A Theology for Artisans of a New Humanity. Maryknoll, NY: Orbis.

SILVERT, K. H. [ed.] (1967) Churches and States: The Religious Institution and Modernization. New York: American Universities Field Staff.

SMITH, B. (1975) "Religion and social change: classical theories and new formulations in the context of recent developments in Latin America." Latin American Research Rev. 10 (Summer): 3-34.

——— and T. SANKS (1977) "Liberation ecclesiology: praxis, theory, and praxis." Theological Studies 38 (March): 3-38.

TORRES, C. (1972) Father Camilo Torres Revolutionary Writings. New York: Harper Colophon.

TURNER, V. (1974) Dramas, Fields, and Metaphors: Symbolic Action in Human Society. Ithaca, NY: Cornell Univ. Press.

VALLIER, I. (1970) Catholicism, Social Control, and Modernization in Latin America. Englewood Cliffs, NJ: Prentice-Hall.

*Daniel H. Levine, the Guest Editor of this issue, is Associate Professor of Political Science at the University of Michigan. He has recently completed a larger study which deals with the issues raised in this article, as well as with related questions in the study of religion, the Catholic Church, and politics in Latin America.*

**Publisher's Note:** The following information is printed in accordance with U.S. postal regulations: Statement of Ownership, Management and Circulation (required by 39 U.S.C. 3685). 1. Title of Publication: JOURNAL OF INTERAMERICAN STUDIES AND WORLD AFFAIRS. 1A. Publication No.: 958920. 2. Date of Filing: September 22, 1978. 3. Frequency of Issue: Quarterly. 3A. No. of Issues Published Annually: 4 (four). 3B. Annual Subscription Price: institutions, $28.00; individuals, $15.00. 4. Location of Known Office of Publication: 275 South Beverly Drive, Beverly Hills (Los Angeles), California 90212. 5. Location of the Headquarters or General Business Offices of the Publishers: 275 South Beverly Drive, Beverly Hills (Los Angeles), California 90212. 6. Names and Complete Addresses of Publisher, Editor, and Managing Editor: Publisher: Sara Miller McCune, 1102 Oakhurst Drive, Los Angeles, California 90035; Editor: John P. Harrison, Box 248134, University of Miami, Coral Gables, Florida 33124; Managing Editor: None. 7. Owner (If owned by a corporation, its name and address must be stated and also immediately thereunder the names and addresses of stockholders owning or holding 1% or more of total amount of stock. If not owned by a corporation, the names and addresses of the individual owners must be given. If owned by a partnership or other unincorporated firm, its name and address, as well as that of each individual must be given.): Sage Publications, Inc., 275 South Beverly Drive, Beverly Hills, California 90212; Sara Miller McCune, 1102 South Oakhurst Drive, Los Angeles, California 90035; Marvin Sirot, Mohawk Lane, Greenwich, Connecticut 06830; Gustave Sirot, Wingate Road, Guilford, Connecticut 06340; John B. Hurford, 220 East 63rd Street, New York, New York 10021; Albert L. Zesiger, 1125 Fifth Avenue, New York, New York 10028; Judith C. Zesiger, 1125 Fifth Avenue, New York, New York 10028. 8. Known Bondholders, Mortgagees, and Other Security Holders Owning or Holding 1% or More of Total Amount of Bonds, Mortgages or Other Securities: None. 9. For Completion by Nonprofit Organizations Authorized to Mail at Special Rates (Section 132.122, PSM): Not Applicable.

| | Av. No. Copies Each Issue During Preceding 12 Months | Actual No. of Copies of Single Issue Published Nearest to Filing Date |
|---|---|---|
| 10. Extent and Nature of Circulation | | |
| A. Total no. copies printed (net press run) | 1632 | 1666 |
| B. Paid circulation: | | |
| 1. Sales through dealers and carriers, street vendors and counter sales | 133 | 55 |
| 2. Mail subscriptions | 1234 | 1237 |
| C. Total paid circulation (sum of 10B1 and 10B2) | 1362 | 1292 |
| D. Free distribution by mail, carrier or other means: samples, complimentary, and other free copies | 48 | 42 |
| E. Total distribution (sum of C & D) | 1415 | 1334 |
| F. Copies not distributed: | | |
| 1. Office use, left-over, unaccounted, spoiled after printing | 217 | 332 |
| 2. Returns from news agents | — | — |
| G. Total (sum of E, F1 and 2—should equal net press run shown in A) | 1632 | 1666 |

11. I certify that the statements made by me above are correct and complete. (Signed) Gary Polinsky, Manager. 12. 39 U.S.C. 3626 provides in pertinent part: "No person who would have been entitled to mail matter under former section 4359 of this title shall mail such matter at the rates provided under this subsection unless he files annually with the Postal Service a written request for permission to mail matter at such rates." In accordance with the provisions of this statute, I hereby request permission to mail the publication named in item 1 at the reduced postage rates presently authorized by 39 U.S.C. 3626. (Signed) Gary Polinsky, Manager.

**RENATO POBLETE, S.J.**
*Centro Bellarmino*
*Casilla 10445*
*Santiago, Chile*

# *FROM MEDELLÍN TO PUEBLA*
## *Notes for Reflection*

Ten years ago the Latin American Catholic Bishops held their Second General Conference in Medellín, Colombia. The conference had a great influence not only within the Catholic Church, but also on the formation of socioeconomic and political issues in Latin American countries. At the time of this writing, we are in the midst of preparations for the Third General Conference taking place in Puebla, Mexico, in October 1978. Therefore, this seems a good opportunity to reflect on the general processes of change in the Church leading to Puebla and their implications for the future.

Medellín and Puebla constitute two privileged moments in the life of the Latin American Church. History will consider them as two expressions of ecclesial discernment in which not only the bishops take part, but all people of God in Latin America. Both events mark the culmination of a process of intraecclesial maturation concerning the nature of the Church's evangelizing task in the different areas in which she carries out her mission.

But while both events can be considered as end points, they can also be seen as beginnings. In effect, Medellín is the product of the life of the Latin American Church. One cannot understand it without reference to that life, which marks it with a dynamic characteristic to be analyzed later in this paper.

Ten years after Medellín, Puebla has been called upon to perform a similar function. The Church ponders over its rightful mission, which has a permanent and universal character but which must also be considered in certain historical, economic, social, political, and cultural contexts. Therefore, from the standpoint of the Faith, temporal realities are analyzed so that the Church's mission will respond more fully to

Journal of Interamerican Studies and World Affairs, Vol. 21 No. 1, February 1979, 31-44
© 1979 Sage Publications, Inc.

its proper identity and its own being, simultaneously resulting in greater service to the people of Latin America.

When discussing Latin America, consideration must be given to its dual dimension of unity and diversity. Different economic, political, social, cultural, ethnic, and religious conditions make it difficult to issue valid general judgments. Latin America is, and must be considered, a complex and differentiated unit. Each local church has its own characteristics derived from the richness of its particular history and varied local challenges. Consequently, our reflection must never ignore this dual character—the union of history and destiny, and the diversity and complexity arising from local conditions. Neither must we forget that other problems exist, such as arms races and the juridical solution of existing conflicts, which must be approached and understood in common. The Latin American episcopate's announcements on these matters will undoubtedly have a greater impact than those from individual churches alone.

In the following reflections we are specifically interested in considering the maturation process of the Church concerning the exigencies of its evangelizing mission in the face of temporal facts. Medellín and Puebla are approached with this perspective in mind—as two moments in the process of doctrinal clarification and renewed commitments on the part of the Church—in the face of challenges to Christian conscience and action presented by the social, economic, and political characteristics of Latin America.

## *The Latin American Church Before Medellín*

It is a mistake to assume that the social action of the Latin American Church started in Medellín. Awareness of the social projection of the gospel and the Church's commitment to the demands of the gospel is older. This is made evident not only by statements from the various episcopates, but also by important actions undertaken in the fields of social and political work carried on by Catholic laymen.

Documents issued by diverse hierarchies reveal that with each succeeding occasion, the bishops have become increasingly certain that the social relations peculiar to the different aspects of life must be ruled by "Justice" as a *sine qua non* of the righteous practice of charity. In this manner, the mentality which looked to "charity" and "resignation" as a solution for social injustice is finally overcome. Two examples are found in the documents of the Chilean Episcopal Conference, "The Church and Chilean Peasant," issued in 1962, and "The Social and Political Duties of Catholics in the Present Time," issued in 1964. Another example is found on the Latin American level, when in 1966 CELAM (Council of Latin American Bishops) prepared the declaration of the Latin American episcopate gathered at Mar del Plata on "The Church and Latin American Intregration." These are eloquent examples of the decided good will of the Church in contributing to the temporal liberation of all men and countries as part of its evangelizing task.

Prior to Medellín and with the wisdom of the Universal Church, the Second Vatican Council, through publication of the Conciliar Constitution *Gaudium et Spes* and Paul VI's 1967 *Enciclica Populorum Progressio,* contributed to the enlightenment of the doctrinal reflection and action already undertaken by the Latin American Church.

Pre-Medellín documents insist not only on the practice of charity or welfare, which has always been part of the Church's work, but also on progressively making the church take into account the need for structural reforms to overcome injustice. It is no longer enough to provide immediate solutions of social assistance (always necessary) or to appeal only to the conversion of the heart of man, but rather it is necessary to uproot the profound causes of social evil through the promotion of structural reforms. These reforms, which are means and not ends in themselves, must lead to the integral development of the whole man and all men.

In accordance with the above, many national churches—those of Brazil, Chile, Venezuela, Colombia, Ecuador and Costa Rica—have supported the creation of movements of Christian inspiration such as cooperatives, trade unions, and projects for human promotion. The Church also helped create political parties of Christian inspiration.

Structural reforms, particularly agrarian reform, received decisive help from churches such as those in Chile and Ecuador which symbolically and actually contributed to the accelaration of the process by surrendering their own lands. The Church has also provided technical aid to the peasants through, for example, the Institute of Agrarian Promotion (INPROA).

It was precisely in the field of the promotion of structural reforms that the first serious disagreements arose within the social and political movements of Christian inspiration. Sharing the profound conviction of the need for structural change to pass from unjust situations to more just ones, disagreements developed regarding the proper speed of change and the best strategy to promote it effectively. The divisions which arose undoubtedly were more at the level of the "thinking elite" and leaders rather than that of the *"comunidad de bases,"*[1] but the impact of these splits and the loss of energy they signified seriously damaged the effectiveness of what would have been a joint and sustained action on the part of Christians.

The impact of the Cuban revolution in its first period, together with the personality and activity of its principal leaders, attracted the sympathy of many Christian groups. In fact, during the 1960s and 1970s a number of Christians, disillusioned with reformism, started to speak about revolution. They adopted Marxist categories and methods of analysis, Marxist thought, and finally adopted Marxist strategy.

Until approximately 1965 the social doctrine of the Church constituted the fount of inspiration for the social and political actions of Christians. They not only searched for ethical orientation as such, but even thought that a finished model of a new society could be offered. This model, obtained through a series of social reforms, was to be an alternative to the intrinsic contradictions of liberal capitalism.

To a certain extent the Conciliar Constitution *Gaudium et Spes* frustrated the expectations of more committed groups in Latin America. It emphasized the autonomy of the temporal, proposed more of an anthropology than a model, and insisted that the mission of the Church be strictly religious. Thanks to the intervention of certain Latin American bishops, an addendum was made in No. 42: "But, from that precisely religious mission, functions, lights and energies are generated which can serve to establish the human community as per Diving Law."

It is perhaps during that decade that secular ideologies began to replace the Church's social doctrine. They rejected the mediation function of the social doctrine between faith and the social and political compromise, and attempted to subordinate faith to ideology and political commitments.

Critical groups within the Church reacted, charging that the social doctrine of the Church was abstract, ahistorical, static, and identified with a particular political and social movement—Christian Democracy. From their point of view, Christian Democracy had shown itself incapable of promoting a real revolution and a definitive break with liberal capitalism and imperialism. Other Christian groups more receptive to the Church's social thinking were so busy with tasks emanating from their urgent political responsibilities that they neglected doctrinal formation. They perceived, not without disillusion, that the Church was neither proposing models nor identifying herself with any of them, even though they were Christian-inspired. Consequently, the Church's social doctrine was eventually forgotten by some of these groups.

Medellín marked the beginning of a reevaluation of the Church's social doctrine. With the conference acting parallel to the consolidation of Liberation Theology, vast Catholic sectors supported more strongly the alternative position outlined previously.

## *The Significance of Medellín*

From the standpoint of its immediate significance in the life of the Church, the 1968 meeting of the Latin American episcopate in Medellín deeply affected the living forces of the Church. It helped consolidate the bishops' consideration of the temporal dimension of the Church's evangelizing task and guaranteed its commitment in the fight for justice. It also gave Christian legitimization to many changes begun a decade ago, when it was thought that all structural changes emanated from Marxist groups. The Christian sectors realized the value of ecclesial ratification of their just aspirations. In addition, Medellín deeply and thoroughly analyzed the reality of Latin America and, from the standpoint of faith and with the moral authority belonging to the Church, denounced injustices in extremely vigorous language.

Together with the legitimation of the change process, this denunciation morally compelled many Latin American episcopates to take a more positive stand and renew their commitments in evangelizing and promoting justice and peace in Latin America.

The doctrinal horizon of the deliberations and conclusions of Medellín is based on the *Enciclical Populorum Progressio,* the Conciliar Constitution *Gaudium et Spes,* and Paul VI's 1968 speech in Bogotá. Its doctrinal scope must be understood in the frame of reference provided by these documents.

The meeting was structured around three fundamental topics: human promotion by the reaffirmation of justice and peace; evangelization and growth in faith; and finally, reflection on the visible Church and its structures.

A notable characteristic of the Medellín documents is the urgency of the call to immediate action. The document on "Justice" tells us that "It is necessary to work. It has not ceased to be the hour of speech but it has come to be, with an even more dramatic *urgency,* the hour for *action"* (CELAM, 1970: Justice 1, 3).[2] The same urgency was expressed in the document on "Peace" which states that the "static vision of the situation becomes even more intolerable when projected into the future," for a multiplication of problems and tensions is foreseen (Peace 2, 7).

The principles emphasized in these documents include *concientización;* that is, the awakening of the masses to consciousness so that through their participation in the realization of change and in the common effort to create a new society, they may become the true agents of their own liberation. This process of making the masses conscious is, in fact, an effort to enable them to assume their responsibilities in civic and political life. *Conscientización* is, then, a means of achieving *liberation.*

The word liberation is very frequently used in the Medellín texts to indicate the process of helping man free himself from the oppressiveness in which the majority of Latin Americans find themselves. "Our peoples desire their liberation and growth in humanness . . . they are filled with longing for total emancipation, liberation from all slavery, for personal maturity, and collective integration." The documents state that the laity is faced with the challenge of a liberating and humanizing commitment: to "liberate men from cultural, social, economic, and political slavery, all of which oppose our development" (Justice 1, 4, 7).

Another key concept in the documents is *participation.* The document on "Peace" states "that men should be the agents of their own history" (Peace 2, 14a), and declares that "justice, and therefore peace, are won through the dynamic action of the awakening and organization of the popular sectors of society which are capable of pressing action by public officials who are often impotent in the carrying out of their social projects without popular support" (Peace 2, 18).

Some of the central ideas which will cause greater repercussions in the future are the concepts of the liberation of man from all servitude, and the denunciation of established violence in structures of sin.

The reforms proposed by Medellín specifically reject approval of violent revolution and the violent activities of some groups, for in the majority of cases they only engender a spiral of more violence, repressive violence, kidnapping, torture, and terrorism.

## *The Latin American Church After Medellín*

Medellín signified a revitalization of ecclesial conscience and behavior in the face of social commitment required by the gospel, with the majority of episcopates writing pastoral letters on the theme of Medellín. Here the hierarchy increasingly exercised social criticism—the denunciation of injustice in all its forms.

As the Church is simultaneously universal and local, transcendental and historical, the general orientation of her preaching and activity responds to the most serious problems presented at any given moment. In the period before Medellín, stress was placed on seeking justice in human relations and gradually on the urgency of structural reforms. Since then, the changes taking place in the political order, with a proliferation of military regimes and economic models which imply a high social cost, have matured the ecclesial conscience, to the point of awareness that the greatest threat to justice lies in the increasing violation of human rights, the negation of many fundamental public liberties, recourse to torture as generalized practice, delay of the just aspirations of the most needy, and denial of any right to participate in politics—all well-known instances of this process.

The Church is not an opportunist in its fight for human rights: Pius XII focused his maximum concern and interest on this subject, and in John XXIII's 1963 encyclical *Pacem in Terris,* he asserts that if human rights are not respected, there is no possibility of peace for humanity.

In ecclesial reflection since Medellín, human rights comprise the basic requirement of an integral *development* of all men as the goal of economic activity. What is needed is civic coexistence based on majority consensus expressed in juridical, organizational, and governmental structures which are genuinely *democratic.* It may even be said that in the Church's view, there is no respect for human rights without integral development in the economic sphere and democracy in the political sphere. Denunciation of violations of human rights must accompany denunciations of violence in all its forms: terrorism, kidnapping, torture, extortion, and so on.

The Church's revitalization following Medellín signified a renewal of its commitment to the fight for justice, but also led to growing divisions among Christians concerning the pace of change and the most effective strategies to promote it. A new element surfaced to make this debate more disagreeable: the possibility of resorting to subversive violence as the only means to end the "institutionalized violence" which had been condemned in such hard terms at Medellín. Many impatient groups felt the condemnation of institutionalized violence and structures of sin expressed at Medellín justified returning to subversive violence or exclusively accepting those social processes which could result in a total change in the forms of human coexistence. Thus, many members of groups such as the Montoneros and Tupamaros have been formed in Catholic circles. At least originally, they seek in the Medellín declarations inspiration and orientation for their activities.

Added to this concern with violence was the effort to reduce the liberation praised by Medellín to a purely economic and political dimension. Economically, this meant the rupture of dependence; politically, it meant the abolition of all political power considered oppressive in nature.

The more general views of reality were also affected by this tendency and led many Christians to equivocal positions in social action to reduce the Church or people of God to the level of the social and economic poor. The massive presence of extreme poverty in Latin America exacerbated this position.

As a result of the increasing intraecclesial tension arising from different perceptions of the Church's temporal task and current historical commitment, at least three Catholic trends have emerged with distinct doctrinal and pastoral conceptions and divergent political positions. They are: (1) Catholic *integralism* of the political right wing; (2) Catholic progressivism, inspired by the official Papal documents and by those of the Latin American hierarchy; and (3) a current created around the Theology of Liberation, one manifestation being the movement called "Christians for socialism." In addition to these three categories, there is a great variety of common Christians indifferent to a more sophisticated reflection, who practice a traditional Catholicism expressed in popular religion and who have been but superficially touched by the debate taking place among the more enlightened elite.

The Theology of Liberation is strengthened as a method of analysis and as a language capable of striking at the consciences of Christians to the extent that it is presented with biblical images. This gives it an evangelical character and a more directly religious tone than that of the social teaching of the Church. At the same time, it takes reality and historical practice as a privileged place from which thought must emanate in the light of faith, life, and destiny of man in general and the people of Latin America in particular.

To explain the causes of the socioeconomic prostration of Latin America, some branches of Liberation Theology use the theory of dependency to identify it as the cause of all evils in Latin America. This relates it to the Marxist diagnosis, in vogue for over a decade, and leads to consensus over the necessary strategy for breaking the chain of dependency from the capitalist system and in creating conditions for the liberation of men from all servitude. For them, this road can be offered only by socialism. However, they neglect to mention which form of socialism is offered, or what the real possibilities are for its establishment. Here, the answers are not clear. Meanwhile, this internal division continues to weaken the Church's task and its pledge for justice in Latin America.

It is important to point out a major fact in the life of the Church, especially for its lay members: the diminishing influence of the social and political groups of Christian inspiration in Latin America. Paradoxically, however, these same groups have again started to value doctrinal formation and appreciate the potential contribution of the social teaching of the Church. Dialogue with them, which for historical reasons became tense or impossible, has now been reestablished.

Neither the Church itself nor these groups now expect a model of organization of human coexistence to come from the social teaching. Both have learned that the value of this discipline and its special contribution to everyday life will have to be found in the explication of values and principles which must be respected in any model or system which seeks to order social relations. Lay Christians can elaborate their own model. The Church, as such, has none, but does have something to say to each of the models. In this measure social teaching becomes a fount of inspiration, an inducement, and sometimes even a utopia.

Finally, the Church has lost considerable influence in economic and political processes. Elites cannot ignore the presence and activity of the Church, but they have closed their ears to her word. The denunciation of injustice, whose most cruel expression is the violation of human rights, constitutes the primordial task of the Church in present historical circumstances. She has assumed this task with all the gravity that is required, exposing herself to the consequences. Thus, with the Church interpreting the feelings of vast majorities in Latin America, her moral prestige has grown in a sustained manner and she has truly become "the voice of those who have no voice." She finds herself, as never before, in the best situation for fulfilling her evangelizing task.

## *The Pre Document of Puebla*

The main points of the Medellín documents dealing with the relation of the Church and society have been presented. Judging from the tone of the Pre Document,[3] we shall now attempt to demonstrate that the meeting in Puebla will follow the same course as that of Medellín.

The Pre Document of Puebla cannot be compared with that of Medellín. It is a working document to be criticized, modified, or even rejected. Of course, it is not an episcopal document of prophetic style, as was Medellín. This Pre Document for Puebla is partly the result of suggestions made during the four regional meetings of the various Latin American episcopates which took place during July and August 1977. Documentation covered over 300 pages. Minutes and suggestions reflecting the ongoing concerns of the bishops were compiled and later put in order.

On the topic of concern to us here, the relation of the Church to social problems, the Pre Document makes a social, economic, and political diagnosis while listing important points on the Church's social thinking. The diagnosis attempts to avoid comprehensive theories on the problems of underdevelopment and prostration in Latin America. Since the injustices are so evident in themselves and with different theories still not proven, the bishops did not want to set forth any one theory. Primarily, the Pre Document recognized that not only on the continent as a whole, but also in each country, there has been considerable *economic* progress over the last ten years (CELAM, 1978: para. 135). The central point repeated throughout the document (para. 135, 153) is that in spite of economic progress, the gap between rich and poor has widened in all countries (para. 140, 141) and the problem of *extreme poverty* remains one of the most important challenges (para. 142, 145).

These two facts present the greatest challenge to evangelization and to the true meaning of being a Christian. Although there is more poverty in Africa and Asia, these are non-Christian continents. To what extent can Latin America be considered Christian when justice and solidarity are not present and when life is not lived in a more fraternal society (para. 146)?

In the Pre Document this diagnosis binds the theme of extreme poverty with the problem of unemployment (para. 150) and other conditions of life which illustrate the great state of prostration. On the other hand, the possibilities of popular organization and mobility reportedly are weak, trade unionism is hampered, and the violation of union rights continues (para. 159). Furthermore, necessary structural reforms such as tax, agrarian, and judicial reform have not been carried out or are easily flouted (para. 162, 169). The political scene is characterized by a proliferation of military regimes to the detriment of civil participation (para. 173).

The concept of authority and the high concentration of power which are characteristic of regimes inspired by the ideology of national security have caused a wave of violation of human rights. This phenomenon is part of the rise of violence made more acute in relation to political order: subversion and countersubversion, insurrection and counter-insurrection, terrorism and kidnapping, repression and torture (para. 176).

Instead of leading to coexistence, political behavior is no longer integrated and becomes exclusionist without seeking political consensus, negotiation, or arbitration (para. 177). Pressure groups (para. 178) are then analyzed; the military sector, university students, trade unions, and so on. Among these groups, those with economic power stand out, their influence in government having increased during recent years. In accruing major advantages from national economic progress and foreign investments, they have become separated from the rest of the population. They also frequently control the social communication media.

One point of dispute in this Pre Document involves the causes of the state of prostration which affect great masses (para. 187). The causes are multiple, since numerous factors converge: historical, ethnic, cultural, economic, and political. Some are related to the problem of international justice, but it is difficult to solve them within Latin America unless there is greater integration of the countries or greater powers of negotiation. Economic dependence is pointed out as one of the most serious factors (para. 189), but not the only one. Others are imbalances in commerce, foreign debt, overdeveloped laws on the part of developed countries, and high royalties. In short, technological and scientific dependence are also important. All through history economic development of the developed countries has been accomplished through exploitation of the underdeveloped (para. 192). This dependence is also a cause of underdevelopment, tax evasion, and the flight of profits. Great emphasis is also placed on the grave problem of arms races, and military expenditure in general (para. 193).

The document implies the need for a real cultural revolution, as most Latin American problems are related to a cultural ethos in which work, honesty, austerity, and saving are considered of little value (para. 196). Perhaps not enough emphasis has been placed on the need for solidarity. Many problems are due to corruption, venality, and public and private immorality which not only disintegrate social relations, but also comprise unjust means of acquiring riches.

The other part of the Pre Document is related to several doctrinal problems. The social teachings of the Church insist on the theme of the community of goods and proper use of wealth for the common good (para. 723): "Property in its essential social projection cannot be a fount of privilege or of oppression, but of freedom and fraternity."

The theme of integral liberation which embraces the diverse dimensions of human existence is presented (para. 732). Liberation must lead everyone to participate in the same condition and enjoy the same rights and liberties, as well as favor fraternal communion with other men and with God (para. 734).

It defends the mission of the Church, which cannot be confined to a religious field alone, but also must be interested in temporal problems (para. 737). Among the doctrinal orientations, it insists that evangelization, integrally conceived, must be a fount of animation for the social presence of the Church (para. 745). Action for justice is thus a constitutive element or, better yet, an integral part of evangelization.

Some ideologies which have special standing in Latin America are analyzed, among them liberalism and various forms of socialism. There is criticism of the individualistic ideology of capitalism, inspired by the interests of a social class (the bourgeoisie) which applies the principle of freedom with serious contradictions, makes property an absolute right, and accepts social legislation only with great difficulty. Its fundamental motive is profit (para. 763). The document defines different socialisms and states that if a type of socialism respecting liberty, guaranteeing human rights, and ensuring a fraternal and truly democratic coexistence were fostered in Latin America, there would be no contradiction with Christianity.

In its criticism of Marxism, the Pre Document asserts that Marxist analysis cannot be disassociated from dialectical materialism. Capitalism, like collectivism, is a form of the sin of riches. Both systems, limiting their horizon to the economic, produce similar effects, generating forms of oppression and repression which spring from idolatry—an idolatry of material goods. Each in its own way is materialistic and atheistic, practically or theoretically (para. 787).

The Pre Document criticizes the theory of National Security and its connection with totalitarian theories and the submission of all human activity to the aims of the state. The document condemns not only rightist integralism, which instrumentalizes the faith and social teaching of the Church to restore old systems, but also leftist integralism, which instrumentalizes the faith in order to establish a revolutionary system, normally of the Marxist type.

The Pre Document suggests certain goals in the construction of a new society: (1) mechanisms to give voice to those who have no voice and to give form to desires which cannot be expressed (one has to act through them so that no one is marginal in the new society, and one must be able to work with those who are the most needy (para. 824); (2) formation of a community of goods for a society without privilege in which sufficient property gives everyone a necessary space for autonomy (para. 826), with emphasis on the social dimension of property, the common destiny of possession (para. 830), and the destruction of all "social domination" (para. 829); and (3) the construction of a true democracy.

Division of power is stressed, contrary to the practice of totalitarian regimes which tend to accumulate all power within the state. Democracy must be political, juridical, economical, and social—simultaneously. All intermediate groups are important and democracy should learn to live with them fully (para. 834-842).

Finally, the doctrinal portion describes as a necessary goal the discovery of a new way of life not limited to the possibilities available within the present model alone, but further implying austerity, especially on the part of those who own more, so that everyone's basic needs can be satisfied.

The Pre Document has had an extremely wide circulation, having been reprinted and discussed in almost all Latin American nations. During April and May 1978, each National Conference of Bishops prepared comments and sent them to the Council of Latin American Bishops. At CELAM a group of bishops representing the four regions into which Latin America had been divided, for practical reasons, together with a small group of experts, analyzed all contributions. Bearing in mind the most important points emphasized by the bishops, they then wrote the Basic Document of the Puebla meeting.

The Basic Document, shorter than the Pre Document, corrects some deficiencies of the older document and serves as the working paper for

Puebla. It contains the same concerns, and its socioeconomic and political analyses are similar to those of the Pre Documents.

Judging from the amount of preparation and analysis of the desires of all bishops attending the Latin American Conference of Bishops, one can certainly forecast that the Third Assembly of Puebla will be a step forward from the meeting held at Medellín.

## NOTES

1. The popular level activities of the *comunidades de bases* are dealt with more fully in the Gilfeather and Smith articles in this issue.

2. While there is a 1973 English version of the Medellín document (CELAM) published by the U.S. Catholic Conference entitled "The Church in the Present-Day Transformation of Latin America in the Light of the Council," quotations in this article are English translations by the author from the Spanish original. The first number in these citations refers to the general category, and the second number refers to the numbered sections in that category.

3. The full title is "La Evangelizacion en el presente y en el futuro de America Latina . . . Documento de consulta a las Conferencias Episcopales."

## REFERENCES

CELAM [Consejo Episcopal Latino americano] (1978) La Evangelización en el presente y en el futuro de América Latina. Puebla, Mexico, 1978. Preparación. Documento de consulta a las Conferencias Episcopales. III Conferencia General del Episcopado Latinamericano. Bogotá: General Secretariat of CELAM.

——— (1970) "The Church in the present day transformation of Latin America in the light of the Council." Second General Conference of Latin American Bishops. Bogotá: General Secretariat of CELAM.

*Renato Poblete is a Jesuit priest and sociologist affiliated with the Centro Bellarmino in Chile. The author of numerous works on Latin American society, he is also Executive Secretary for the Social Action Department of CELAM.*

**MICHAEL DODSON**
*58 North Stanworth Drive*
*Princeton, New Jersey 08540*

# *THE CHRISTIAN LEFT IN LATIN AMERICAN POLITICS*

After decades of neglect, interest in the political significance of Latin American Catholicism increased sharply in the late 1960s when it began to appear that the Church might have unimagined potential for promoting social change, particularly in a continent plagued by social upheaval and political instability (Drekonja, 1971: 59-65). In both word and deed, the postconciliar Church manifested a changing social orientation which entailed open involvement in political issues on behalf of the poor. In fact, by August 1968 and the convening of the Council of Latin American Bishops (CELAM) in Medellín, Colombia, the Church seemed to be changing its social and political attitudes so profoundly that reports of a revolutionary Church began to accompany discussions of the political situation in Latin America. Since Medellín, an important literature has evolved from efforts to understand this change in Latin American Catholicism. The experience sent students of the Church back to the question first posed by Marx and Weber: can traditional religious institutions be a source of energy for changing society (Silvert, 1967; Smith, 1975)?

The search for an answer to this question has resulted in a variety of perspectives and arguments about the relationship of religion to social change in Latin America. Depending on which country one studied and at what point in time, writers have seen the Church as a dynamic force for social change (D. Smith, 1970; Sanders, 1970; Drekonja, 1971; Williams, 1969, 1973; Turner, 1971; Vallier, 1967, 1970), a moderate force for social change (B. Smith, 1975, 1976; Levine and Wilde, 1977), a mild obstacle to social change (deKadt, 1967, 1970, 1971), and a serious obstacle to social change (Mutchler, 1969; Vekemans, 1964).[1] Such diverse points of view are not necessarily contradictory because the postconciliar Church has spawned a wide range of groups possessing

Journal of Interamerican Studies and World Affairs, Vol. 21 No. 1, February 1979, 45-68
© 1979 Sage Publications, Inc.

an array of strategies for political action. There is, however, a strong tendency in the literature to explain and judge the entire range of groups and points of view from a single interpretive framework. Until recently the predominant conceptual approach to the study of the Latin American Church and its role in social change was drawn directly from the developmental paradigm which informed the broader study of comparative politics in the 1960s.[2] Thus, there is more overlap in the interpretations mentioned above than first meets the eye.

In sifting through the literature, one is struck by the tendency of many North American writers to generalize about the "progressives" who changed the Church in the aftermath of Vatican II. Although the word "revolutionary" is sometimes used, it usually serves as a synonym for progressive. The impression thus developed is that progressives have been the dynamic force in changing Latin American Catholicism and have effectively defined the Church's viable range of sociopolitical options. The right and left have received far less attention. Both conservatives and radicals are either ignored in the theoretical writings, or assigned a negative, counterdevelopmental role. This article questions the assumption on which that orientation rests and examines the case of the radicals, whose explicit goal is to make the Church an agent of social change.

The article examines three writers who have been prominent among the students of the Latin American Church. I explicate briefly the framework of interpretation they have used to criticize and evaluate the political behavior of progressives and radicals in the Church. It is important, I believe, to clarify how the developmentalist perspective shapes the way in which these writers distinguish the progressives from the radicals. (Later I will show how the distinction looks from the point of view of the radicals.) Analysis will be based on a comparison of religious change in two countries—Argentina and Chile—where struggle and innovation in the Church has been notably intense. In each country both progressive and radical groups have emerged among the clergy, becoming sufficiently organized to have an impact in the political arena. Through comparison of the Argentine Movement of Priests for the Third World and the Chilean Christians for Socialism, I will evaluate the strengths and weaknesses of the developmentalist approach to the study of the Church and social change in Latin America.

A second issue guiding this analysis follows logically from the first. What intellectual framework is employed by the left to explain and criticize the Latin American Church's role in social change? The answer to this question entails an implicit critique of the development paradigm. Hence, I propose to examine the way recent church involvement in social change looks from the point of view of the left. Of course, the radicals themselves must be criticized, but in relation to *their own* intellectual frame of reference and normative goals as well as those of development theory.

## *Developmentalism and the Study of the Christian Left*

Religious innovation raised high expectations that the Church might assume a constructive role in promoting social change and political development. Imbued with the hope and optimism which pervaded the "decade of development," North American writers were attracted to the prospect that so traditional and conservative an institution as the Roman Catholic church would embrace and promote the values of modernization. With the Church at least nominally commanding the loyalty of over 90% of the Latin American people, a visible shift on its part in a modernizing direction was envisioned as a great stimulus to the "nation builders." The case of the Chilean Church stood out among the national churches of the region; indeed, it became a model in the minds of North American observers. Just as United States policy makers looked to Chile as a test case of political development, so prominent students of the Church looked to Chile as a test case of "religious system development" (Vallier, 1967: 466). It is no coincidence, then, that the bulk of this literature on religion and social change shares so fully in the language, concepts, and perspectives of the broader development literature (Almond and Powell, 1966; Pye, 1966; Huntington, 1968, 1971).

Several authors have conceived modernization in the Church as a process of reformulating religious values to promote a natural social consensus and heightened integration. The Church has always promoted value consensus, of course, but the new consensus would allow for innovation while at the same time helping "to minimize the competition between the old and new elites and [also] to avoid unnecessary and counterproductive conflict" (Williams, 1969: 334-335). This language and conceptual framework are based on a view of Chile in the mid-1960s, which set a reform-minded Church in a pluralistic society. Williams labels this church "prophetic," but ignores entirely the possibility that religious change (and prophetic values) might clash with developmentalism, as he sees it, or be accompanied by social conflict. One finds a similar, though more discriminating analysis, in the work of Einaudi et al., (1969), who also focus on the Christian Democratic experience in Chile and the early liberalization of the Church there. Einaudi's conception of a "prophetic church" also envisions a reformist or modernizing Church dedicated to the building of western, pluralist democracy. He recognizes that change-oriented members of the Church have diverse orientations, and that no single, homogeneous, progressive Church emerges from Vatican II and Medellín. So he distinguishes between prophetic *liberals* who seek to transcend "partisan politics," promoting nation-building through social harmony and consensus, and prophetic *radicals* who engage in "movements" or in partisan politics which generate conflict and disunity (Einaudi et al., 1969: 48-50). The latter are dismissed as utopian and counterproductive.[3]

This general perspective is most fully elaborated in the work of Vallier (1967, 1970, 1972). Vallier built a model of Church development in which the Church initiates and sponsors "a framework of order" relevant to "injustice" and "a generalized need for rapid and deep changes in the institutional system." Vallier's developed Church, in fact, represents "a new conception of order." His theory requires that Church development produce "symbols and normative principles that legitimate fundamental change but in such ways that continuity with certain elements can be observed" (1967: 466). Achieving this objective requires the *avoidance* of "partisan politics." Success promotes social integration and political stability, which in turn enable the Church to remain above partisan politics. Remarkably, Vallier's developed religious system is to promote "fundamental" social change without ever soiling itself with what one writer has called the "messiness" of politics. The Church exercises its religious power in socially relevant ways without exercising political power.

Vallier is aware that Medellín stimulated many approaches to religious innovation, and he captures this diversity by distinguishing "pastoral" from "clerical" radicals (1972). His virulent criticism of the clerical radicals typifies the normative framework of the developmental approach. Here he shows clearly what was only implicit in his earlier work as well as that of Williams and Einaudi—that a prophetic "modernizing" church is not radical but liberal and, indeed, apolitical. Taking Chile and Colombia as polar types of Church political involvement, Vallier expounded the differences between "pastoral radicalism" and "clerical radicalism" as seen from a developmental perspective. In pastoral radicalism the priest avoids using his religious office as a basis for building up social and political authority. He carefully side-steps all partisan political involvement or identification. In his pastoral activity "the religious floor is a generalized source of certainty and identity for other roles in society, but it is not the base on which all choices are made" (1972: 22). The religious norms fostered by the priest are suprapartisan in this model, transcending specific political options and therefore rising above political conflict. Thus, pastoral radicals can promote the "Christian revolution," while at the same time helping to "depoliticize" society and foster "civic development" and "nation-building."

The clerical radicals present a sharp contrast. By stressing the Colombian example, Vallier generalizes the case of Camilo Torres, the well-known guerrilla priest who died in a skirmish with government troops in February 1966, into a prototype of clerical radicalism. By doing so he identifies the Christian left with Camilismo, guerrilla warfare, and in his words, violent "assaults on the establishment." In Vallier's view, the clerical radicals are politically "retrogressive" (counterdevelopmental) for several reasons. First, they engage in direct political action through religiopolitical movements of the left: they try to "lead the social revolution." Since such activity is partisan, it must be conflictual in its impact and therefore retrogressive with respect to nation-building which is conceived in terms of harmonious integration. Second, they organize their religious roles from the perspective of a "comprehensive closed religious framework." Like the protagonists of the Protestant Reformation, the clerical radicals are fanatical men who define all issues in terms of a single, unchangeable religious perspective. Third, Vallier charges the clerical radicals with having a unidimensional and dogmatic religious perspective *because* they utilize Marxist social analysis, which is intrinsically dogmatic. Finally, the clerical radicals make a "traditionalizing demand" for the laity to "defend" the Church's institutional structures and dominance in society, or to augment the corporate interests of the religious institution (1972: 22-23). The analysis which follows examines this dichotomy between pastoral and clerical radicals, measuring it against the actual experience of the religiopolitical movements of the left in Argentina and Chile. I will try to determine the extent to which these characteristics do in fact appropriately describe the Christian left. Are the clerical radicals uniformly committed to

Camilismo? Vallier's approach prejudges these issues, for within the theoretical framework of developmentalism there is no place for the left. For this reason we must judge the left in terms of its own goals, and then relate our findings back to the charges made by Vallier.

The terminology, then, which has been used to describe Church change in Latin America has been too broad. Some writers have lumped everything from Chilean Christian Democracy to Camilo Torres under the label "progressivism," suggesting that a single, homogeneous, change-oriented Church has evolved in Latin America. The developmentalists have been guilty of this, but have in fact systematically excluded the radical left from their analysis. Indeed, I contend that their intellectual framework leads students of the Church away from the study of priest groups consciously organized for direct political action. Such groups have appeared in most countries in Latin America, yet they have scarcely been noticed by North American writers preoccupied with the search for agents of development.[4]

In this regard, it is important to be clear on the composition of the "Christian Left." In my view, an effective definition of the Christian left lies between the two extremes of Christian Democracy, which represents a liberal progressivism, and Camilismo, which represents a fully developed revolutionary position. A significant field of Christian radicalism lies between these positions and is notable for its rejection of both reformism and violent revolution, along with the unstated assumption that these are the only options Latin Americans possess. The fact is that the religiopolitical movements discussed here look extremist only when compared to the Christian Democrats and when evaluated in terms of developmental criteria; when compared to Camilismo the Third World Priests look moderate, while the Christians for Socialism, though more radical than the Third World Priests, hardly appear to be a band of guerrilla revolutionaries. The Christian left is united by a common political theory, the theology of liberation, which encompasses a radical theology, a radical social analysis borrowed largely from the neo-Marxist literature on dependency, and a radical, but not revolutionary, political program of democratic socialism. Therefore, the Christian left does include those who have engaged in direct political action and who utilize Marxist analysis, as Vallier contended. But it remains to be seen whether this has made their activities inherently retrogressive.

## *Liberation Theology: The Normative Criteria for Religiopolitical Action*

It is essential to examine the relationship between thought and practice in the study of the Latin American Christian left. Below, I discuss briefly the crisis in the Church with respect to development which occurred after 1965 and the subsequent turning away from the capitalist model toward socialism. This crisis in perspective made necessary the creation of new "prophetic" clerical roles, "prophetic" roles which seemed to require the organization of individual ministries into religiopolitical movements of the left. Let us examine this process and the liberation values which inform the political programs of two such movements.

Officially, the Catholic Church acknowledged that capitalism as well as socialism produced detrimental social consequences as early as 1891 with the publication of Pope Leo XIII's encyclical *Rerum Novarum.* But as recently as 1960, the Latin American church had shown no inclination to condemn capitalist expansion in Latin America because it failed to improve the lives of the vast majority of people. Only in Chile (Sigmund, 1973) and Brazil (deKadt, 1970) had criticisms of capitalism been clearly voiced within the Church. In the case of Chile, the Christian Democratic movement attempted to carve out a "third way" between capitalism and socialism. With the election of Eduardo Frei to the presidency in 1964, Chilean Christian Democrats got a chance to demonstrate that a "third position" could transform social structures and bring real change for the better in the lives of the poor. In power, Christian Democracy became closely identified with the reformist position of the Alliance for Progress, a position supported by the United States and based on capitalist development. Frei's "revolution in liberty" meant reform within capitalist economic structures and formally democratic electoral processes; it excluded the more profound change implied in socialism.

The general failure of the Alliance for Progress, and the specific failure of the Frei regime to bring about land reform, to "denationalize" the Chilean economy, or to raise the living standard of the great mass of poor, undercut the appeal of a reformist path to development. Indeed, these failures led to a rethinking of the very concept of development and a gradual rejection of its premises. Activist clergy began to sense that capitalist development implied not progress, but deepening poverty in their countries and *less* likelihood that democratic institutions of a participatory nature would flourish. Gradually there emerged in the Church (as in society at large) a perspective which saw "development" as exploitation, benefiting the rich nations and select elites in Latin America at the expense of the great majority of ordinary people. From this changing awareness came the development of a theology of liberation, which adopted a conflict model of social analysis to replace the consensus model of the developmentalists and attempted to articulate a vision of the good society quite different from that presented by western capitalism. Let us turn first to the prophetic ministry which is developed to meet the exigencies of a conflictual social order; then we will examine the political alternative envisioned in liberation theology.

When seen from the vantage point of the poor, Latin America's social order appeared laden with "structural" obstacles to change. Thus, poverty was less a function of individual failure than "systemic" failure. The political interests and policies of both local and foreign elites seemed to become not only inconsistent with, but diametrically opposed to, those of the Latin American masses. This appraisal of the social order recalled the prophetic ministry of Old Testament gospels: that ministry had been fashioned precisely to meet a condition of captivity, exploitation, and oppression. Priests adopting this new perspective found it necessary to revise both their theology and their ministry in terms of the ancient prophetic tradition in order to struggle against "structural sin" (Schillebeeckx, 1970: 27).

Moving out of a purely confessional role and into the public domain brought with it the need to clarify the priests' social role. Two broad themes evolved. First, for radical priests a prophetic ministry involves the interpretation of the gospel in light of social conflict and exploitation, not with an eye to transcending or avoiding such conflict for the sake of some "higher" consensus. A prophetic ministry interprets the "signs of the times," an activity with two dimensions—one negative, the other positive. Negatively, a prophetic ministry calls for the denunciation of structural sin. This means attempting, through social analysis, to determine where the chain of exploitation begins, and requires exposure and criticism of its social roots. Radical clergy see this as "desacrilizing" or delegitimizing the current social order. Obviously, Christian radicalism differs sharply from Christian reformism. The latter has no provision at all for a denunciatory role, for it is not imagined that the social and political orders could require "desacrilization" (Williams, 1969, 1973; Vallier, 1967, 1970).

Second, the tearing down of unjust structures must be accompanied by the building up of a new order. Hence, radical clergy also have assumed a role of community leadership by attempting to organize their followers for political action, guided by a vision of the Christian eschatology and a "hope" for the future that is both spiritual and temporal, and therefore political. Liberation theology (theory) and priests organizing for social change (praxis) are bound together in a single prophetic action.

Finally, as to the social goals which inform this prophetic Christian vision, two themes lie at the core of liberation theology. First, liberationists argue that meaningful social change in Latin America implies the full participation of ordinary people in the shaping of their own lives. Profound dependence and passivity must give way to an equally profound participation. Second, social structures must be reordered to promote human cooperation and to redistribute social values in a more egalitarian fashion. Participatory democracy and humanist socialism thus go together.[5]

In this vein, it is clear that radical Latin American clergy follows the democratic tradition associated with the name of Rousseau rather than the more cautious and skeptical tradition deriving from Locke (Sabine, 1952). The "freedom" each tradition espouses is quite different. Lockean concepts of freedom are based on a model of "bourgeois" social relations (MacPherson, 1964) appropriate to a market society which rewards egocentrism, individualism, and competition. Such a society is inherently conflictual, and its core value of freedom is "freedom from" norms imposed by the collectivity (Berlin, 1967). In the eyes of radical clergy this view of freedom corresponds to the social conditions of liberal democracies and implies materialism, social conflict, and exploitation. They opt instead for an egalitarian approach to freedom, which seeks not to protect individuals from the collectivity, but rather to enable them to be free within it. Liberation theology thus emphasizes a "positive" kind of liberty, a "freedom to," which stresses participation, self-determination, and the creation of social conditions to make both available to all citizens. Following Rousseau, liberationists stress the value of equality, making it inseparable from freedom.

The attempt to join the values of freedom and equality has led radical priests to promote socialism as well. For in practice, the stress on structural sin noted earlier means that capitalist social and political institutions are the chief obstacles to the fulfillment of democratic values. The only way to expand the range of choice within which poor and exploited peoples can identify and meet their own goals is to replace capitalism with socialism. Míguez Bonino's views are representative of liberation theology here:

> Humanization is for capitalism an unintended by-product, while it is for socialism an explicit goal. Solidarity is for capitalism accidental, for socialism it is essential. In terms of their basic ethos, Christianity must critique capitalism radically, in its fundamental intention, while it must critique socialism functionally, in its failure to fulfill its purpose [1976: 115].

## *Case Studies*

### *THE FORMATION OF RADICAL MOVEMENTS*

Radical priest movements seemed to burst on the Latin American scene quite suddenly in the late 1960s. In fact, however, a major factor which led to their creation had been developing for nearly a decade. The worker-priest experiment thrust priests into factory jobs to share the daily life of the working class as early as 1960 in Argentina. In Chile priests entered the *poblaciones* in the first years of the Frei government. In each case direct contact with the poor was a catalyst in politicizing clergy during the '60s. Although initially supported by the hierarchy as a move to revive the working class' declining interest in the Church, such experiments evolved rapidly as immersion in the life of working people brought priests face to face with massive poverty, social dislocation, and individual alienation. Worker-priests in Argentina discovered a large rift in the working class between a labor aristocracy and a mass a unemployed or underemployed workers for whom "development" brought no improvement in standard of living. Between the conclusion of Vatican II in 1965 and CELAM in 1968, worker-priests in virtually all countries of Latin America began to interpret this pattern as the inevitable consequence of "dependent" capitalist development.[6]

Thus, in Argentina and Chile the rejection of developmentalism and the turn to a liberation perspective evolved over nearly a decade, rooted in informal exchanges among priests with similar experiences. An early issue was how to acquire within the existing organizational structure of the Church the latitude necessary for effective social commitment. How far would the hierarchy permit activists to go? In Argentina radicalized priests found it necessary to expand their social role with little or no support from the hierarchy. In many areas of the country the hierarchy not only resisted the leftward drift of the clergy, but sought to crush such a move by suspending priests, moving them to remote parishes, and even collaborating with the government to deport foreign clergy. In Chile a more dynamic climate of Christian activism and a more liberal hierarchy made early efforts to work among the poor seem more fruitful in that country. As we shall see below, however, this did not mean that the Christian left would be in the long run more successful there. Before turning to that issue, let us take a closer look at the factors which fostered the transition from loose networks of social-activist priests to organized, nationwide movements of politically committed clergy.

In Argentina two factors stand out. The first is the maturity of the worker-priest experiment as discussed above. By May 1968, when the Movement of Priests for the Third World was formally created at Córdoba, the worker-priest experiment was a decade old. In urban, industrialized Argentina this meant that a "pooling" of highly motivated priests with common, radicalizing experiences had taken place. These priests were politicized to a working-class political culture heavily influenced by the legacy of Peronism. The result was a strongly unified perspective which gave a large measure of coherence to their movement even in its early stages. The second factor is the important, but changing, Argentine hierarchy. On the one hand, the obdurate resistance of certain bishops to the activities of radical priests in their dioceses and the heavy-handed penalties meted out by such bishops pushed the radicals to one another's defense. Priests expelled from one diocese were welcomed in another. Moreover, the complicity of government authorities in several such incidents made it seem all the more essential for priests to band together. Mutual assistance led to collective action and finally to the construction of an organizational apparatus. On the other hand, there were bishops in Argentina who openly supported radical priests when they needed that support most. As early as 1965, Bishops Antonio Quarracino, Alberto Devoto, and Jeronimo Podestá attended meetings of radical priests and gave them public support. In 1967 Bishop Podestá lost his diocese as a result of promoting social activism and worker organization (Dodson, 1972: 62), and thereby became a potent symbol to the fledgling Third World Priest movement. After the movement's formation in 1968, a small number of bishops gradually moved to open support for the Third World priests, including the influential Archbishop of Santa Fe, Vicente Zaspe. In short, both with resistance and with support, the Argentine hierarchy played an important role in the formation of the Third World Priest movement.

In turning to the Chilean experience we must recall that the developmentalist approach outlined above did not anticipate the appearance of *any* radical priest movement in Chile. In fact, however, a numerous and diverse Christian left emerged in Chile during the half-decade between 1968 and the military coup in September 1973 which halted all political activity. The Christian left in Chile included the Young Church, the Movement of Unified Popular Action (MAPU), Christian Left, The Eighty, The 200, and the Christians for Socialism. In part this broad range of groups represents the fragmentation of the left which occurred during the period, and in part it merely represents the evolution of groups with significantly overlapping memberships. Let us briefly examine the origins of these groups with the purpose of seeing how the largest and most radical of the groups, the Christians for Socialism, came to be formed.

It is important, first of all, to mention the prominent role played by Christian Democracy in Chilean political life prior to 1968. The existence of a lay political party of Catholic inspiration simply made clergy more aware of political issues than was the case in Argentina and other countries of Latin Amerca. In addition, the well-funded Jesuit research center, Centro Bellarmino, constantly publicized issues of social reform. Other Catholic orders in Chile also sponsored research and teaching centers, designed primarily to promote efforts at "development." In the crisis of Christian Democratic government discussed earlier, these centers also helped focus attention on underdevelopment. The Jesuit Latin American Institute for Doctrine and Social Studies (ILADES), for example, made the interpretation of the Church's social doctrine in relation to underdevelopment the central theme of its investigation. Its director in the late 1960s, Gonzalo Arroyo, became a leading figure in the Christians for Socialism.

In Chile the crucial year in the emergence of the Christian left was 1968. Until that year Christian activism had found its expression through Christian Democracy and a "pastoral movement" centered in the *poblaciones.* But the growing sense of the failure of Christian Democratic reform programs, together with the gradual mobilization and politicization of the working-class prior to the 1970 elections, began to draw these social activists leftward. A "rebel" wing developed in the Christian Democratic party. Then, on August 11, 1968, a group of radicalized Christians, including nine priests and about 200 lay people, occupied the Cathedral in Santiago, using the occasion to denounce both social injustice and the inadequacy of efforts by the institutional Church to alleviate it. This brief occupation of the Cathedral, timed to coincide with the Eucharistic Congress in Bogotá which inaugurated the CELAM meetings, received wide publicity in Chile and became a focal point for gathering discontent within the Church. The "Young Church" movement grew out of the occupation. The Young Church movement itself was only a stage, albeit a crucial one, in the transition to left political militancy within the Church. Although it managed to hold a national meeting in October 1970, to affirm its "complete support of the Government of Popular Unity," it did not remain the focal point of Christian left activism (Epica, 1973: 4-8). On the one hand, some early members of the movement helped to form MAPU in 1969, which became part of the united front of the Popular Unity coalition. For these members, direct involvement in secular party politics became the outlet for their social commitment. Others in the Young Church movement, particularly clergy who chose to focus their efforts at internal Church reform and pushing the institutional Church toward direct political action, subsequently formed a series of new movements culminating in the formation of Christians for Socialism. In retrospect, the major significance of the Young Church is that it represented, first, a crystallization of the shift to the left in the church, and second, "a moment of cleavage," a dividing point at which some Christians moved into secular party politics, some stayed within the parameters of official church doctrine, and some began the effort to build up a "'parallel' Church" which would ally the institutional church with the struggle for socialism (Rojas and Vanderschueren, 1977: 25).

The Christians for Socialism movement grew out of the April 1971 meeting of 80 priests whose common background was very like that of the members of the Third World Priests in Argentina. The Eighty, as they were initially called, issued a strong declaration urging cooperation among Christians and Marxists, calling for the mobilization of the working class, and asserting that criticism of the Popular Unity government must come from "within the revolutionary process" (Rojas and Vanderschueren, 1977: 42). By November 1971, the Eighty, which was composed primarily of priests from Santiago, had created the larger Christians for Socialism movement.

*POLITICAL ACTION STRATEGIES*

Let us turn now to the question of strategies for political action adopted by these movements. They can be compared in terms of the two roles outlined above, denunciation and organization, and further as to the degree of militancy taken with respect to radical social change. Of course, neither movement was ever fully united over a single strategy or level of militancy, so I will be speaking of general tendencies which predominated.

The Movement of Priests for the Third World brought itself national attention through effective exercise of the denunciatory role. Indeed, their skill in publicizing social problems and the ineptitude of the Onganía regime in dealing with them was remarkable. From the "Rebel Christmas" of 1968, in which Third World Priests organized a nationwide protest tied to the symbols of one the year's major religious seasons, through the coup of June 1970, the movement was a constant thorn in the side of the regime, as well as a perpetual goad to the Church hierarchy. The movement showed a great ability to become associated with workers' strikes, student demonstrations, barrio protests, and peasant mobilizations without alienating the hierarchy sufficiently to move it to active collaboration with the regime. Criticisms of the regime often hit home in telling ways. The Third World Priests publicized the government's neglect of the working class at a time when inflation was wreaking havoc with workers everywhere in the country. The jailing of priests along with union leaders heightened public awareness of the costs of proscribing political parties. In addition, the priests carefully cloaked all their actions in the rhetoric of Vatican II, Medellín, and statements of Latin American bishops from Helder Camara to their own Eduardo Pironio. Thus, when the government counterattacked, it seemed to attack the church as a whole. This tended to drive a wedge between regime and Church. Gradually, individual bishops, their own consciousness raised by the wide range of publications and activities of the Third World Priests in their dioceses, began to speak out in support of the movement; perhaps more significantly in the short run, a growing number joined their voices to the chorus of antiregime protest which originated with the Third World Priest movement.

Although this denunciatory role was notably effective at the national level, direct political organization was confined largely to the parish level. In this area, the movement's greatest effectiveness was clearly among shanty-town dwellers and rural workers. The industrial working class had its own organizations in the Peronist movement. After 1970 the movement's major organizational thrust was in linking the unorganized working-class poor to the Peronist movement.

Clearly, the Third World Priests followed a relatively moderate political strategy during the crucial early years, in spite of the radical character of their theology and social analysis. They became identified with the extreme left only in the eyes of a small minority of the public. Between 1969 and 1972 the movement served as the focal point of protest against the repressiveness and austerity of military rule. It bore a striking resemblance, through its peaceful protest, to the civil rights movement in the United States under Martin Luther King. By 1972 the Third World Priests were also a center of the movement for a return to electoral politics and full participation by Peronists in national political life (Dodson, 1974b: 63-67).

When the Christian left in Chile is compared with that of Argentina, the later and more rapid evolution of a radicalized movement in Chile is evident. This difference seems to be accounted for at least in part by the more open, fluid, and rapidly changing political context of Chilean society as a whole. Two factors will be stressed in the following discussion. The first is the bitterly contested nature of Chilean elections in 1970 and 1973, which involved all sectors of society, as compared with the very controlled and limited nature of political activity under military rule in Argentina. The second is the role of the hierarchy in relation to the radical movement in the Church and in relation to the existing regime. Let me briefly compare these in more detail, with an eye to assessing the appropriateness of the political action strategy adopted by each movement within its particular political and religious context.

We saw above how the Argentine Third World Priest movement comprehended both the limitations and the opportunities which their immediate political and religious environment provided them. They correctly perceived the existence of very widespread, but latent support for Peronism throughout the country. They skillfully linked their own denunciations of the Onganía and Lanusse governments to this grassroots Peronism in such a way as to become a highly visible source of political opposition to an increasingly unpopular regime from 1968 to 1973. Such a strategy not only gave them significant political credibility in the eyes of the working classes, but also helped to give them unprecedented influence with the hierarchy. At no point did the Third World Priests seek to establish a priestly authority independent of the hierarchy. They did not call on their hierarchy publicly to commit itself to Peronism. They did, however, mount attacks against certain individual bishops who clearly were guilty of imposing excessive limitations or harsh punishments on activist priests. By isolating such bishops within the hierarchy, while gradually gaining the outspoken support of other bishops, they were able to influence the highest levels of the hierarchy to take public positions against military rule and for political programs which met the needs of the poor.

The Chilean case offers an interesting contrast. In 1968 there was no ban on the political participation of any group; in fact, there was active, effective participation on the left, center, and right of the political spectrum. Moreover, in the wake of Christian Democratic government, the active political participation of Christians and the identification of the Church with political programs was uniquely strong. As was suggested above, a Christian left was forming in Chile at this time because of growing disenchantment with the failure of Christian Democratic reformism. A large number of these left Christians, persons of primarily middle-class background, joined MAPU and became part of the Unidad Popular. Within that larger political coalition, their own development as a distinctly Christian voice for radical social change was inhibited. As part of a secular political movement which openly competed for and then held power, MAPU could not play the highly visible, prophetic role of social criticism (denunciation) which the Third World Priests played in Argentina. As we shall see, MAPU was also outflanked on its own left by the more militant members of the Young Church movement who formed The Eighty and Christians for Socialism.

The latter two groups, which formed after the election of the Unidad Popular government, more closely resembled the Third World Priests. Composed primarily of clergy, they exercised the prophetic role in the fashion of an interest group rather than as part of a coalition, and focused much of their concern on persuading the church to become an agent of social change. These similarities, however, mask important differences in the political strategies pursued by the religiopolitical movements in the two countries. Like MAPU, the Christians for Socialism supported the UP in the early stages of its administration. What distinguished them was the latter's conscious effort to link the entire institutional Church to the socialist program of the UP. Indeed, although much of the movement's public efforts focused on the same denunciatory role which so distinguished the Third World Priests, it became increasingly preoccupied after 1971 with transforming the entire Church from within. Thus, as Christians for Socialism grew in membership and developed the organizational apparatus which made it resemble the Third World Priests, it in fact pursued a strategy which diverged sharply from that of the Argentine movement. It moved increasingly toward what Smith (1978: chap. 8) has called a "parallel magisterium" within the Church.

An extremely significant difference emerges here between the political and religious contexts of Argentina and Chile. In Argentina the radical priests could criticize the government, publicize unjust policies, voice the demands of the poor, and even criticize the church for inaction, without seriously implicating the hierarchy as a whole or appearing to challenge its authority. It was much easier for the Argentine hierarchy to follow the lead of the Third World Priests in a country with widespread popular unrest and virtually no political freedom, then for the Chilean hierarchy to accede to the demand of Christians for Socialism that they explicitly ally the Church to the UP government *in power* and against the very large number of Chileans who opposed that government. The strain this put on the relationship between Christians for Socialism and the hierarchy was further heightened by the former's continuous move leftward between 1971 and September 1973. In this period the Movement went considerably to the left of the UP. As that government came increasingly under attack from both left and right, as it sought compromise solutions to which the Church hierarchy lent its own prestige, the Christians for Socialism urged more intense revolutionary commitment by Christians and by the Church as a whole. An impasse was reached by early 1973, when the hierarchy began to distance itself from the beleaguered regime and moved to sanction the Christians for Socialism by banning participation in their movement. The military coup of September 11, 1973 preempted a final confrontation between the two.

The Movement of Priests for the Third World set out in 1968 to make their Church a voice and an instrument for social change, and they achieved notable short-run success. Their greatest success was in gaining a hearing within the institutional Church for a liberation point of view. The hierarchy's declaration at San Miguel in May 1969 bore the influence of the Third World Priests and provided a strong veil of legitimacy which the priests were able to utilize successfully over the next five years. Further, the movement helped force an open break between the Church and the regime of Onganía, and the loss of this ally certainly hastened Onganía's demise. The movement also turned the Church around from open hostility toward Peronism to a cautious acceptance, helping to pave the way for the return of elections and of Peronists to active political participation. Thus, the Third World Priests helped to change their Church, were a strong voice of protest during a period of national political crisis, assisted materially in discrediting military rule, and helped to promote a return to democratic politics.

But in their very strength lay a serious weakness for which there is a striking parallel in the experience of the Chilean Christians for Socialism. As the movement evolved, most of its members became convinced that the road to socialism and participatory democracy lay in Peronism. After 1972 they actively promoted Peronism and forged an alliance with the Peronist movement at a variety of levels. But, like many Argentines, they placed too much hope in the healing powers of the Peronist movement. They failed to recognize the serious splits latent in Peronism and overestimated the degree to which Perón would be willing or able to change Argentine society according to the norms of liberation theology. Once on the scene, Perón soon turned away from the masses to whom the priests were linked and, in his famous May 1, 1974 speech, read the left, including the Third World Priests, out of his movement. The disillusionment which followed revealed that the priests had failed to lay the foundation for grassroots organization which would enable the movement to retain its coherence through this crisis. With Perón's death and the erosion of Peronism leading to the military coup of March 1976, the Third World Priest movement declined and returned to a pre-1968 stage of loose-knit, individualized ministries at a local level, bound together only by a common dedication to the poor. Today many Third World Priests are in hiding or in exile, and the Argentine Church is a muted voice of resistance to authoritarian rule.

Like the Third World Priests, the Christians for Socialism became closely identified with one segment of a much broader political spectrum and overestimated the popular appeal and political efficacy of that segment. In their early phase they identified strongly with UP policies, then gradually moved to the left of the regime and toward closer identification with the position of the MIR on the extreme left. This precluded any influence they might have had with the government (just as the Third World Priests lost influence with Perón's government in early 1974), and also drove a further wedge between them and the hierarchy. Had the coup not intervened, it is likely that pressure from the Church hierarchy would have had the same effect of breaking up the Christians for Socialism movement in Chile that government pressure had in disrupting the Argentine Third World Priest movement.

Two final weaknesses of the Christian for Socialism attempt at living out a "prophetic" Christianity may be mentioned and compared briefly to the Argentine case. It has been suggested already that the membership of MAPU was largely middle-class in origin and outlook. The Christians for Socialism were also middle-class people whose backgrounds tended to be university oriented rather than popularly based. Although the Third World Priest movement had its share of middle-class professors, it seemed also to have a much higher proportion of active members who were working in "villas miserias," who had lengthy backgrounds as worker-priests, and whose political contacts were strongly rooted in the working class. By comparison, the Christians for Socialism were a more elitist group in the sense that they lacked these *direct* ties with the masses whom they sought to help. They did not create opportunities to build practical alliances with working class groups either within or without the Church. By their own admission, they failed to tap into the strong base of popular religiosity in Chile where the base communities are functioning today. The Third World Priests were less elitist and more successful at uniting popular religious and political expression through Peronism.

The other point of comparison involves the extent to which each movement pursued a strategy which promoted unity or division within the Church as a whole. Obviously, both movements had their detractors within the Church. But, on balance, the Christians for Socialism promoted far greater discord within the Church than did the Third World

Priests. While alienating a few of the most reactionary bishops, the latter managed to promote considerable unity and a closing of ranks *against* an unpopular government. Although some tension between movement and hierarchy always existed, far better rapport, mutual understanding, and restraint characterized their relationship than that of the Chilean hierarchy and Christians for Socialism. While part of the disparity can be attributed to differing political contexts as described above, part of the reason also lies with the separate political strategies chosen by the two movements.

## *Conclusions*

Clearly, the Christian left does not conform very closely to the description implicit in development analyses. The Third World Priests in Argentina were less radical theologically and politically than Vallier (1972) imagined, and were more successful in uniting the Church around a program calling for social change and the return of democratic politics. On the other hand, the Christian Democratic experience in Chile was hardly the nonpartisan, socially integrating movement that development theory expected it to be. Nor can the political and religious fragmentation of the late 1960s and early 1970s be blamed only on the left. All political sectors were "partisan" and the extensively documented record of the efforts by the center and the right to prevent the left from achieving victory *within* the boundaries of the electoral process belie claims of the developmentalists to the contrary. In this respect a major accomplishment of the Christians for Socialism, in terms of liberation norms, was the forceful way in which they dispelled the illusion that the Church was neutral in politics if only it avoided *direct* partisan commitments. It can be argued, of course, that in making their own political choice to move toward the extreme left of the political spectrum, they made the *wrong* political choice.

It is also important to bear in mind the place of these movements within the institutional Church and their relation to its perceived needs. The Argentine case is instructive here. It shows that when it is in the Church's corporate interests (as seen by the hierarchy, not the left) to disassociate itself from the regime, an alliance between the left (which gives the Church linkages at the grass roots), and the hierarchy, however informal, can be effective in mounting a powerful campaign of denunciation. Clearly, both elements of the Church are pursuing a political strategy in such a case. Vallier saw the importance of disassociating Church and regime, but he denied that it was a political option and his theory prevented him from seeing the possibility which developed in Argentina of a radical left movement providing the energy to bring about such disassociation and making the Church a prominent voice for social change.

Let us close by returning to the developmentalist critique of the Christian left. On the basis of the data presented here, I would argue the following points. First, the distinction between pastoral and clerical radicals breaks down in the actual experience of any church attempting to bring about social change. The cases of Argentina and Chile bear this out, the latter quite dramatically with Christian Democracy spawning a plethora of politically activist Christian groups. On the other hand, Christians for Socialism did tend in practice to make their particular interpretation of the historically correct political option the only one acceptable for the entire church, as Vallier had feared they would. I do not find that the Third World Priests did this, and on Vallier's analysis they would have been more likely to than the Christians for Socialism because of the "undeveloped" character of the Argentine Church. Second, clerical radicalism does not lead to demands by clergy that the laity defend the Church's corporate interests. The hierarchy will look after the Church's institutional interests in any case. This is one important reason why the bishops came to support the Third World Priests in Argentina and to oppose the Christians for Socialism in Chile.

## NOTES

1. Of the five writers who see the Church as a dynamic force for social change three had worked in Chile during the 1960s. Of those who see the Church as a moderate force for change, one (Smith) had looked at the Chilean case in 1974 after the fall of Allende. Levine and Wilde studied Colombia in the 1970s. Writers who focused on the Church as an obstacle to social change had studied the Brazilian case, where Catholic radicals were crushed after the military coup of 1964 (de Kadt), or they studied the Church from a frame of reference in which radicalism was institutionally (Mutchler) or ideologically (Vekemans) precluded.

2. The structure and evolving nature of the development paradigm can best be seen in the essay by Huntington (1971). Very recent writings on the Church have avoided the simplistic adaptation of a development model, and therefore do not come under the

criticisms presented in this article. See Bruneau (1974), Levine and Wilde (1977), and B. Smith (1976, 1977). However, in the newer literature there is not yet any comparative study of the Christian left, which was ignored or deprecated in the earlier literature.

3. Other writers who have made a similar argument include de Kadt (1970) and Sanders (1973). Much of the difficulty with this approach lies in the narrow understanding of politics which characterizes it. Levine and Wilde (1977) provide a good critical discussion of this issue.

4. There are two brief studies of the Christian left in Peru, neither of which has been published. They are Macauly (1972) and Mooney (1976). Two very recent studies of the Christian left in Chile are by Rojas and Vanderschueren (1977) and B. Smith (1978). None of these studies attempt systematic comparison of the Christian left across countries.

5. The political theory of liberation theology is treated at much greater length in Dodson (1974a). See especially Chapter Three.

6. Major works in the dependency literature are summarized and criticized in two recent essays: James and Bath (1976) and Fagen (1977). Dependency theory is a "given" in liberation theology.

## REFERENCES

ALMOND, G. and B. POWELL (1966) Comparative Politics: A Developmental Approach. Boston: Little, Brown.

BERLIN, I. (1967) "Two concepts of liberty," pp. 141-152 in A. Quinton [ed.] Political Philosophy. Oxford Eng.: Oxford Univ. Press.

BRUNEAU, T. C. (1974) The Political Transformation of the Brazilian Catholic Church. London: Cambridge Univ. Press.

de KADT, E. (1971) "Church, society and development in Latin America." J. of Development Studies (October): 23-41.

——— (1970) Catholic Radicals in Brazil. Oxford: Oxford Univ. Press.

——— (1967) "Paternalism and populism: Catholicism in Latin America." J. of Contemporary History 2: 89-106.

DODSON, M. (1974a) "Religious innovation and the politics of Argentina: a study of the movement of priests for the third world." Ph.D. dissertation. Indiana University.

——— (1974b) "Priests and Peronism: radical clergy in Argentine politics." Latin American Perspectives 1: 63-67.

——— (1972) "The Catholic Church in contemporary Argentina," pp. 57-67 in A. Ciria [ed.] New Perspectives on Modern Argentina. Bloomington, IN: Latin American Studies Program, Indiana University.

DREKONJA, G. (1971) "Religion and social change in Latin America." Latin American Research Rev. 6: 53-72.

EINAUDI, L. et al. (1969) Latin American Institutional Development: The Changing Catholic Church. Santa Monica, CA: Rand Corporation.

Epica (1973) "Christians for socialism." (September): 4-8.

FAGEN, R. (1977) "Studying Latin American politics: some implications of a 'dependencia' approach." Latin American Research Rev. 12, 2: 3-26.
HUNTINGTON, S. (1971) "The change to change: modernization, revolution and politics." Comparative Politics 3: 283-322.
——— (1968) Political Order in Changing Societies. New Haven, CT: Yale Univ. Press.
JAMES, D. and C. R. BATH (1976) "Dependency analysis of Latin America." Latin American Research Rev. 11, 3: 3-54.
LEVINE, D. and A. WILDE (1977) "The Catholic Church, 'politics,' and violence: the Colombian case." The Rev. of Politics 39: 220-249.
MACAULY, M. G. (1972) "Ideological change and internal cleavages in the Peruvian Church: change, status quo and the priest: the case of ONIS." Ph.D. dissertation. University of Notre Dame.
MacPHERSON, C. B. (1964) The Theory of Possessive Individualism. Oxford Eng.: Oxford University Press.
MIGUEZ-BONINO, J. (1976) Christians and Marxists. Grand Rapids: Eerdmans.
MOONEY, M. H. (1976) "The role of the church in Peruvian political development." M. A. thesis. University of Windsor.
MUTCHLER, D. (1969) "Adaptations of the Roman Catholic Church to Latin American development: the meaning of internal church conflict." Social Research 36: 231-252.
PYE, L. (1966) Aspects of Political Development. Boston: Little, Brown.
ROJAS, J. and F. VANDERSCHUEREN (1977) "The Catholic Church of Chile: from 'social Christianity' to 'Christians for socialism'" LARU Studies 2, 14-59.
SABINE, G. (1952) "The two democratic traditions." The Philosophical Rev. 61: 451-474.
SANDERS, T. (1973) "The theoloy of liberation: Christian utopianism." Christianity and Crisis. 33: 167-173.
——— (1970) "The church in Latin America." Foreign Affairs (Spring): 289-299.
SCHILLEBEECKX, E. (1970) "El majisterio y el mundo politico." Enlace 13: 27.
SIGMUND, P. (1973) "Latin American Catholicism's opening to the left." The Rev. of Politics. 35: 61-77.
SILVERT, K. (1967) Churches and States: The Religious Institution and Modernization. New York: American Universities Field Staff.
SMITH B. (1978) "The Catholic church and political change in Chile, 1925-1975." Ph.D. dissertation. Yale University.
——— (1975) "Religion and social change: classical theories and new formulations in the content of recent developments in Latin America." Latin American Research Rev. 10: 3-34.
——— and T. SANDERS (1976) "The Chilean Catholic church during the Allende and Pinochet regimes." American Universities Field Staff 23: 1-25.
——— and T. SANKS (1977) "Liberation ecclesiology: praxis, theory, praxis." Theological Studies 38: 3-38.
SMITH, D. (1970) Religion and Political Development. Boston: Little, Brown.
TURNER, S. (1971) Catholicism and Political Development in Latin America. Chapel Hill: Univ. of North Carolina Press.
VALLIER, I. (1972) "Radical priests and the revolution," pp. 15-26 in D. Chalmers [ed.] Changing Latin America: New Interpretations of its Politics and Society. Montpelier, VT.: Capital City Press.
——— (1970) Catholicism, Social Control and Modernization in Latin America. Engle-

wood Cliffs, NJ: Prentice-Hall.
——— (1967) "Church Development in Latin America: a five-country comparison." J. of Developing Areas 1: 461-476.
VEKEMANS, R. (1964) "Economic development, social change, and cultural mutation in Latin America," pp. 129-142 in W. d'Antonio and F. Pike [eds.] Religion, Revolution and Reform: New Forces for Change in Latin America. New York: Praeger.
WILLIAMS, E. (1973) "The emergence of the secular nation-state and Latin American Catholicism." Comparative Politics 5: 261-277.
——— (1969) "Latin American Catholicism and political integration." Comparative Political Studies 2: 327-348.

*Michael Dodson, Assistant Professor of Political Science at Texas Christian University, is a Visiting Fellow at Princeton University for the academic year 1978-1979, where he is working on the contributions of Christian thought to the development of democratic and constitutional ideas. His current interests are in Latin American politics, with a focus on the relationship of religion and social change. He has published in* Latin American Perspectives *and the* Journal of Latin American Studies.

ROBERTO CALVO

# THE CHURCH AND THE DOCTRINE OF NATIONAL SECURITY

In a book which has circulated rather widely in Latin America (Lieuwen, 1960), it was stated that, with the passage of time, Latin American military men would intervene less and less in politics. This was not an altogether mistaken belief, considering that in 1961 Paraguay was a "military island" in a sea of Latin American civilian governments. Today the situation has radically changed in many ways. On the one hand, more than half the population of Latin America lives under military regimes; on the other, military domination has a different cast: it is no longer a caudillo who takes over, but the armed forces, which have institutionalized their access to the government. Linked to the foregoing is the emergence of an authoritarian ideological platform—the military call it a doctrine of national security—which provides the armed forces with the necessary rationale for their political activities.

This new form of gaining political power has not been free of tensions or conflicts with institutions dedicated to a democratic concept of political life. At the present time, the strained and difficult relationship between the Church and the military state is of major concern in Latin America. In the context of this concern, this paper will present an analysis embracing three aspects. The first describes the historical-sociological-political background of the military-regime problem in order to help explain it. The second summarizes the most important features of the doctrine of national security. The third discusses certain elements of the doctrine, beginning with the criticisms leveled by the Church.

Journal of Interamerican Studies and World Affairs, Vol. 21 No. 1, February 1979, 69-88
© 1979 Sage Publications, Inc.

## *I. The Historical-Sociological-Political Background Of The Military Phenomenon in Latin America*

For purposes of analysis, it seems necessary to distinguish between two types of problems related to present military governments and the doctrine of national security. There is not only the problem of explaining the background of military intervention, but also the problem of defining the characteristics assumed by the military regimes which base themselves on national security.[1]

The first type of problem presents two aspects: the objective situation of the politicoinstitutional crisis (nation-state crisis) which detonates the political intervention of the military; and the perception by the military of the crisis and the role played by this perception in the doctrine of national security.

The second type of problem deals with the behavior of the military in power. It has any number of aspects, all of them associated with the nature of the military institution (the "total" professional socialization of military institutes, and the like) and the so-called contextual characteristics (the economy, culture, and the like).[2] Owing to lack of space, only the first type of problem in this complex situation will be discussed.

One of the most popular interpretations of the nation-state crisis (Germani, 1969) declares that because the processes of change are unsynchronized and conflictive, they make interventions more likely. Using the same approach (Cuellar, 1971), the Great Depression of the 1930s and the Second World War are linked with the rupture of the "oligarchical pact" in Latin America and the emergence of populist forms derived from the breakdown of traditional patterns of legitimacy or from the hegemonic crisis. The economic scheme of "inward development" based on import-substituting industrialization, which emerged with these new forms of domination, was nearly exhausted by the 1960s and had a negative impact on the rest of the social system. Frustrated aspirations and expectations, problems of capital accumulation, and widespread use of ideologies were elements of this crisis which has led to military intervention.

Although this interpretation has some diagnostic validity, it is rather one-sided in giving major importance to infrastructural factors, which are assumed to be closely linked to external factors—for example, imperialism and dependency—in the structural origin of the crisis. The problem has much deeper, historicocultural roots, which can by no means be reduced to simply an economic stage in Latin American history and which cannot be ignored in any attempt at interpretation. Two kinds of historical events are related to the present Latin American crisis and to "suspension" of this crisis by the military.

There is, first, the objective fact that military participation in politics is a constant found throughout Latin American history.[3] The military presence is simultaneous with and even predates the birth of Latin American states, which achieved political independence in the early part of the nineteenth century. "In those times," writes Beltrán (1970), "there was a mingling of political and military roles. The revolutionary sectors had few professional military men, and often the same people were simultaneously political leaders and soldiers."

During periods which varied from country to country, the military appeared on the national political scene—playing a "moderating" role—at times when the politicoideological battles of the civilians (or in some cases, of the military) threatened the stability of the national state.[4] This is precisely the type of evidence adduced by some authors (Cuellar, 1971) for their argument that the "directive" participation of the military in politics takes place in moments of hegemonic crisis, which may occur at any time in the development of a society.

No less important in the problem under study is the professionalization of the armed forces which, along with the state, seem to be relatively consolidated. "Military professionalization—that is, the existence of people who make war their sole occupation—is in keeping with rationalization of the state and the consequent specialization of functions" (Beltrán, 1970). The findings of authors like Putnam (1967) and Needler (1966) furnish some evidence for belief that the appearance of an ideological platform like the doctrine of national security is associated with the degree of professionalization and/or institutionalization of the armed forces.

The second kind of events refers to the continuous failure of the Latin American societies—that is, all the social conglomerates: classes, groups, institutions, ideologies, and so on—to constitute themselves as nation-states, in order to create a viable political system leading to formation of a broad and participatory social base.[5] Historically, this failure is connected, on the one hand, with the economic, cultural, and political characteristics of Iberian colonization and, on the other, with the sociocultural characteristics of the preexisting Indian populations. Both elements fused to create a rigidly dualist society, dominated by an exclusivist and predatory oligarchy. As is pointed out by Jaguaribe (1972: 49), Latin American societies remained underdeveloped until the early part of the twentieth century because they had become dualist societies in which the top priority given to the goals of the elite was not compatible with the interests of the masses. These countries were thus prevented from integrating, with the result that a social system unfit for development was established.

National development, spurred by industrialization through the import substitution which began with the depression of the 1930s, accelerated from the end of the Second World War until the early 1950s. Afterward, however, the structural limitations of Latin America's internal markets did not permit self-sustained growth of the economy.

In political terms, the economic scheme of import-substituting industrialization was stimulated and reinforced by the so-called populist plan, under which the progressive forces promoted political modernization by mobilizing the masses. Briefly, populism gave rise to pressing political questions which focused on the need for social participation and for power structure in accord with the mobilization and democratization of the masses. As Huntington (1972: 16) has stated, the changes implied in these questions tend "to undermine traditional foundations, and they complicate the problems of creating new bases of political association and institutions that combine legitimacy and effectiveness. The rates of social mobilization and political participation are high; the rates of political organization are low." Countries which have experienced this process have a history of instability, disorder, social insecurity, economic deterioration, and political polarization and violence, ranging from the armed left of Maoists and Castristas to traditional conservatism, whose factions also arm themselves, and spanning all the centrist parties.[6]

Within this sociopolitical framework, obviously very simplified, the military turn out to be the only social group with a broad national organization and perspective and which is sufficiently unified and powerful to impose its regime.

## *II. The Doctrine of National Security*

The systematic elaboration of this doctrine has been centered essentially in Brazil and Chile, where it was followed by military takeovers.

General Carlos de Meira Mattos (1975) eloquently explains the genesis of the doctrine and its influence on the politicoadministrative action of Brazil:

> In the fourteen years from 1949 to 1964, the National War College had little influence on government decisions. During this period, it formulated its doctrine of national security and thoroughly researched the field of development. It trained civilian and military elites qualified to think objectively about Brazil as a whole, to draft a policy of using national power for purposes of security and to further explore attempts to choose development strategies. At the time of the 1964 revolution, the doctrine of the National War College was already formulated and had been discussed in workshops and classrooms. The leader of the revolution, President Castelo Branco, and his chief advisors Golbery do Couto e Silva, Ernesto Geisel, Juárez Távora, and Cordeiro de Farias—who were all ex-military men and had actively shared in drawing up this doctrine when they were members of the cadres of the National War College— found it easy to transform into government policy this doctrine that was the result of fourteen years of preparation in the São Jóao Fortress.

Some time later than Brazil, the Chilean military had attempted a systematic elaboration of the doctrine of national security. The military takeover of September 11, 1973 launched a production of literature about this doctrine comparable only to that of Brazil (Calvo, 1977: 51).[7]

An analysis of what has been written on this doctrine reveals it rigorously systematized presentation. Like an institutional organization chart, its constituent parts are ordered in a relatively logical and coherent whole. Some see in the doctrine an expression of the technical specialization and educational curriculum received by the military during their training.[8] It becomes clear with analysis that the doctrine reflects a predominantly military vision of society, the economy, and culture. The basic elements of society are seen through the world view of the professional soldier.

The doctrine contains concepts derived from the social sciences, especially from political science and geopolitics, which the military believe make it scientific, technical, and therefore neutral.[9] Some military men (Medina, 1976) claim that it is not ideological because it deals with a government function encompassing almost all national activities.

The military divide their doctrine into two major parts: its conceptual elements, and the security system it proposes.

## *BASIC CONCEPTS OF THE DOCTRINE*

The doctrine rests on five key concepts: national security, the state, war, national goals, and national power.

### *The Concept of National Security*

Various definitions of national security are provided by Brazilians, Chileans, and Argentines. They are all similar in content and do not differ appreciably in their bases. Perhaps the most widespread definition is that of the Brazilian Amaral Gurgel (1976): "National security is the guarantee given by the state to achieve or defend national goals against existing hostilities and pressures."[10]

The following characteristics of national security can be deduced from this definition: it is the ability of sovereign states to maintain themselves and survive; its existence is subject to the "weight" of national power; it is expressed in permanent political, economic, pyschological, social, military, and diplomatic actions; its purpose is to stabilize and strengthen the vital interests of the nation; it is aimed at guarding against and overcoming the effects of internal disturbances, natural catastrophes, and outside aggression; and it must ensure the national goals set by the government.

This concept of national security is novel to the uninitiated, for it goes beyond the traditional concept of national defense. According to advocates of the doctrine, national defense is part of national security, inasmuch as the latter acts in the national sphere and the former only in the field of warfare. National security acts through national power, whether in domestic or foreign affairs, and it is administered by the head of the state. National defense, however, acts through military power and is directed by the armed forces.

### *The State and National Security*

The state is the legal manifestation of the nation, and it is dedicated to the common good of all members of society.[11] Social order requires that the state, by virtue of its authority, guarantee obedience of the law to all members of society. The state is the broadest legal grouping and it contains in itself all the means necessary for maximum fulfillment of the human being. To be stable, it requires a population settled in a specific and exclusive territory with precise borders, within which authority can be exercised independently of other states and which also delimits the areas of competence among them. Pinochet (1974), drawing an analogy with the organic, defines the state "as an organic component, produced by a combination of a part of humanity settled on a portion of territory, both of which are united under the idea of a state. Like any existing reality, the state had a structure and a goal."

The state is the agent which has national survival as its essential and ultimate goal. This means that it maintains public order, both legal and institutional, and ensures the free exercise of sovereignty and socio-economic development; in other words, it provides security and development. Security consists in protecting the nation from threats of any kind—war, internal disturbances, natural catastrophes, and so on. In the theoretical schema of the national security doctrine of the Latin American military regimes, the first two threats are given special importance.

*War and Subversion*

According to the military, national defense was initially intended only to prevent or cope with external threats. This concept had to be revised and linked with internal security because of a new form of aggression which appeared in several countries—the so-called subversion, or warfare, waged by guerrillas and irregulars.

This new form of war was the expression not only of conflicts in those countries which sought independence of the great powers and/or a change of government, but also of the conflict between the United States and the Soviet Union. Regarding the latter, General Castelo Branco says that "with the impossibility of a direct nuclear confrontation, hostilities between the great powers were channeled into peripheral wars like a 'war of liberation,' a 'revolutionary war,' or a 'local war' " (Mattos, 1975: 64).[12]

"As a general rule—states Chilean General Alejandro Medina (1976), "It was evident that the Marxist countries provided funds, training, and political orientation, as well as a concerted attack in the international organizations and the media, even using front agencies with the same ideological inspiration."[13] Faced with this threat, the state must mobilize all its natural power to resist it.

### *National Goals*

National goals, as guideposts in the life of a nation, result from the balance existing between the means available to the country and the obstacles standing in the way of realizing aspirations and natural interests. Therefore, because only the government can assess the national situation, it has to set the goals.

The military use various criteria to classify goals. The most usual is one which distinguishes between permanent natural goals and eventual goals. The first category represents a living and very real tradition of natural interests, combining the aspirations of the nation in three basic aspects—self-determination, greater integration, and prosperity—which are manifested in the exercise of sovereignty, economic independence, and socioeconomic development. The second category of goals is that of unsatisfied aspirations and needs, but it is believed that their attainment is within the scope of national power, and that eventually they will become available within a given period of time.[14]

### *National Power*

To exist fully, the state requires two elements: national power and national security. There is no national security without national power.

According to General Pinochet in his *Geopolítica,* national power "is a social factor capable of influencing the sentiment, thought, and will of the human masses in both the internal and external spheres" (1974). In the internal sphere, there is no power similar to that of the state; but this is not true in the external sphere, for the power of the state may be subjugated by another, greater, power.

Several factors increase national power. Since they are numerous, we mention only those significant in geopolitics.

National power is constituted by the territory, population, national character of the population, national spirit, renewable and nonrenewable natural resources, industrial capacity, capacity for scientific and technological development, military might, form of government, popular support, economic policy, quality of diplomacy, education and culture, communications systems, internal legislation, and sovereignty. Essentially, they are the same elements which make up the state.

National power is very dynamic as a consequence of the variations always affecting the elements which constitute it. It may therefore be increased or dangerously diminished to the benefit or detriment of the sovereignty of the state.

## *THE NATIONAL SECURITY SYSTEM*

The security of a nation depends basically on the existence and execution of a national security system, both in a doctrinal and operational sense. This system is a harmonious whole, organized and functional, which should comprise the following basic elements: national goals, the national security doctrine, national security policies, the organic structure of the system, and a national security strategy. Some of these elements will be discussed in further detail.

The security system should encompass, channel, and direct all national activities: those directly related to internal policies, including the activities of political parties and pressure groups; those related to external policies; those related to the economic-financial complex; those related to the psychosocial field; and those activities specifically of the armed forces.

The system also has the following characteristics: it is unified and national; it is totally shared by the "living forces" of the nation, as consistent with national security; it is above politics ("national security is a lofty activity that pursues the supreme goals of the fatherland. For this reason, neither its direction nor execution should be subject to the pressures of organized political groups in special situations, since only the vital and higher interests of the nation should be taken into account"); and it changes and grows according to the variability of the nation's potential.

### *National Security Policy*

National security policy consists of the lines of action, orientation, and programming established by the government and guided by the national security doctrine. National security policy is conditioned by internal and external factors. The most important of the internal factors is present economic and social development. Whereas the cultural aspect gives vitality to the national security policy, economic development is the sine qua non of this security. "There can be no security without development, just as there can be no development without security," says Villegas (1968), an Argentine general who has been interested in the relationship between development and security. On the one hand, insufficient development cannot provide the minimum resources needed for an adequate degree of security; on the other, development without security cannot be successful in the long run, since insecurity will eventually jeopardize prospective development.

Social development influences the national security policy because social and economic disparities create internal tensions which result in increased domestic security measures to prevent possible threats.

The basic external factor in the national security policy is the evolution of the international situation in terms of changes in the balance of power between the great powers and the consequent influence of the latter on other countries.

Given these features, the national security policy can be characterized as follows: it is based wholly on the spirit and letter of the national security doctrine; it is directed toward attaining the political goal of national security; it is national in that it covers all areas and agencies of the state; it is flexible, for it depends on external and internal variables; and it is closely influenced by development in all its aspects—political, economic, social, and cultural.

### *The Organic Structure of the System*

This refers to the group of agencies which are organized in a harmonious and hierarchical way to be responsible for carrying out national security. Its constituent principles are the same as those which characterize the system as a whole. The functions of these agencies are to direct, advise, plan, and implement in the various fields of action—internal (economic, defense, psychosocial, and so on) and external (diplomatic).

### *National Strategy*

Strategy is the science and art in using all national resources, including the armed forces, in order to provide effectively for the attainment of the nation's vital goals, safeguarding against any kind of potential or presumed enemy.

The strategy, therefore, consists in applying national power—political, economic, psychosocial, and military—to attainment of the national goals determined by policy when these goals are confronted with hostilities from the national power of other states. It is as important in peacetime as in war. It conditions, coordinates, and directs the sectors in charge of the resources and activities of the state in their implementation of the various strategies derived from the national strategy. Furthermore, the formulation and execution of national strategy are the responsibilities of the government. There are as many strategies—political, economic, psychosocial, and military—as there are spheres of action.

## *III. The Church and the Doctrine of National Security*

The previous section attempted to present an objective synthesis of the doctrine without injecting value judgments and/or interpretations. We thereby hoped to avoid the mistakes of some critical studies which, owing to their complete lack of objectivity, have distorted the doctrine, transforming it into an "entelechy" and attributing to it every event in countries under military governments. We do not, however, wish to conceal the fact that the excesses of this doctrine have been the object of valid criticism which has come mainly from the Church and which will be broadly discussed in this section.

The Church reacts strongly against established political power when it becomes evident that there is a violation of human rights and persecution of both civilians and the clergy. There are several kinds of Church documents which cast serious doubts on the Christian character of the national security doctrine. One type of Church document presents philosophical, economic, and political reasons. This category includes for example, "La Seguridad Nacional, condición del bien común" (National Security as a condition of the common good) by Msgr. J.M. Santos (1976), Bishop of Valdivia (Chile), and "Doctrina de la Seguridad Nacional a la luz de la doctrina de la Iglesia" (The National Security Doctrine in the light of Church doctrine) by Msgr. C. Padin (1968), Bishop of Bauru (Brazil). A second type of criticism, supplemented by elements of the first type, presents religious and theological reasons. Such documents as "Comunicacão pastoral au povo de Deus" (A pastoral message to God's people) of the Episcopal Conference of

Brazil (1977), "Nuestra Convivencia Nacional" (Our National Coexistence) of the Episcopal Conference of Chile (1977), and "Reflexion Cristiana para el Pueblo de la Patria" (Christian Reflections for the People of the Fatherland) of the Episcopal Conference of Argentina (1977) belong to this category.

The content of these documents centers on some key concepts about man, society, and history. Let us examine some of the criticisms they raise.

### *CRITICISMS OF THE NATIONALISM AND AUTHORITARIANISM OF THE DOCTRINE*

One of the principle criticisms contained in the above-mentioned documents is aimed at the nationalist bias of the national security doctrine. It is a fact that this doctrine makes loyalty to the nation an imperative for all its citizens, which requires that the real interests of a nationality be placed above all other interests. Understood in this way, nationalism inspires, motivates, and influences all policy formulation and strategy conception of these regimes.

In this respect, Msgr. Jorge Hourton, Auxiliary Bishop of Santiago, recalls the teachings of Pius XII on nationalism just at the time when the national security doctrine burst on the Chilean scene with unprecedented force.

> It has been too quickly forgotten that the nationalist state has been responsible for the sacrifice of an enormous number of lives and property and that it has imposed oppressive economic and spiritual burdens. The substance of the error consists in confusing national life as such with nationalist policies. The former is the right and glory of a people, and it should be fostered; the latter is the germ of infinite evils, and it can never be sufficiently rejected. National life is, by itself, the operating whole of all those values of civilization that are peculiar to and characteristic of a given group and that serve as the link spiritually uniting this group. At the same time, this life enriches, through its own contribution, the culture of all humanity. In essence then, national life is not political. This reality is so true that, as history and experience demonstrate, national life can develop alongside others, within the same state, just as it can also transcend the political confines of the state. National life did not become a starting point for the dissolution of the community of man until it began to be used as a

> tool for political ends—that is, when the ruling and centralized state made nationality the basis of its expansionist drive. Then the nationalist state—seed of rivalries and incentive for discord—was born [Hourton, 1976].

This criticism of nationalism has led to criticism of another aspect which, according to Chilean and Brazilian bishops, is central to the present formulation of military nationalism: the triple identification of "nation, state, and military government" and its corrolary, the subservience of individual to state. The Brazilian bishops write:

> In the humanist and Christian vision, the nation is the sum of all the forms of association of its people. The right of free association should be recognized, respected, and encouraged by the state—that is, by the government. To be nationalist, therefore, does not mean sacrificing a faith, a belief, ideas, or values that may appear to be harmful to or incompatible with the interests and attitudes of the prevailing political system.
>
> Also, from a humanist and Christian standpoint, the nation is not synonymous with the state. It is not the state that grants liberties and human rights, which existed long before the nation itself. It does, however, behoove the state to recognize, defend, and foster the human rights of each and every one of its citizens.
>
> Those holding power are also tempted to confuse the people's duty to be loyal to the nation with their duty to be loyal to the state—that is, the government. To place the state, the government, above the nation, means that the security of the state is overvalued and individual security is debased. This is to reduce the people to silence and a climate of fear [Episcopal Conference of Brazil, 1977].

The nation-state identification denounced by the Brazilian bishops becomes even more reprehensible when the military sector assumes the right to be the only depository of the interests and values of the nation.[15] As has been pointed out in a recent study, "the idealized vision of military groups that they are above ideological, political, economic, and social disputes has logically resulted in reaffirmation of their claim to be the most suitable interpreters of national goals." From this perspective, those in power regard all dissenting voices, criticisms, and denunciations of the military regimes as attacks on the nation itself (Vicaria de la Solidaridad, 1977).[16]

The Chilean, Brazilian, and Argentine bishops have not overlooked the basic inconsistency between theoretical formulation of the national security doctrine and political practice of the military regimes. The military say they hold to a Christian concept of the individual, society, and state. Nonetheless, by their extreme concentration of power, violation of human rights, and restraint of freedom, they contradict this concept. Thus, Chilean and Brazilian episcopates have constantly stressed the social teachings of the Church in this matter.

The subservience of individual to state and his reduction to the role of nothing but citizen, violate the Christian concept of person and state. Man as man—that is, endowed with intelligence and will—has certain inalienable rights. In this anthropophilosophical concept of man as a person, as having a spiritual nature, as a center of freedom and knowledge, man himself is more a whole than a part, more an end than a means. But, as one writer comments, "the human person—if he is defined in terms of himself, if he is a being—cannot become complete and final except in intimate fulfillment with another person" (Moreno, 1977). Man, as a person, requires society *per abundantiam*; as an individual, he requires it *per indigentiam*. The Second Vatican Council states that "the social disposition of a man shows that the development of the human person and the development of society itself condition one another, because the beginning, the subject, and the end of social institutions are and should be the human person who, by his very nature, absolutely requires social life." Society appears, therefore, not only as a means, providing the person with the conditions of existence and development he needs, but also as an instrument of personalization. The Thomist doctrine declares that "each person is to the community as the part is to the whole," but at the same time, "man in his totality and in all his characteristics is not structured for the sake of political society." The national security doctrine would seem to contradict this principle in asserting "all in the state, nothing against the state, nothing outside the state."

"National interest" in the Brazilian military, "common good" in the Chilean, are two widely used concepts. In its Declaration of Principles, the Government of Chile states unequivocally that "the goal of the state is the general common good, defined . . . as the ensemble of social conditions that permits each and every Chilean to reach full personal fulfillment."

This definition would appear to be objectionable not for what it expresses, but for what it does not express. In correct doctrine, the common good is the goal and task of society. It is not the simple sum of private individual good; rather, it encompasses all the good that society can transmit and that reverts to the person through justice. In order to be vitiated, the common good entails and requires recognition of the fundamental rights of the person. It therefore embraces right, justice, liberty, and material prosperity.

It can again be demonstrated, as has the Church in Chile and Brazil, that the military declarations are a dead letter. There is no common good in Brazil (Episcopal Conference of Brazil, 1977: 12), where the power of the state is indifferent to the persecution of laymen, priests, and bishops, where it tolerates terrorist attacks on those who have raised their voices for innocent people in prison, and where there is no justice for the poor. Nor is there a common good in Chile (Episcopal Conference of Chile, 1977), where the state of siege has become a permanent situation, where certain human rights are systematically violated, and where economic recovery is being accomplished at an intolerable cost to the impoverished majorities.

### *CRITIQUE OF THE CONCEPT OF SECURITY*

Another of the biases found in the national security doctrine is the exaggerated importance given to the concept of security, to the point of turning it into an end in itself. The Brazilian bishops are very clear in their denunciation of this attitude: "The ideology of national security placed above personal security is spreading throughout the Latin American continent, as has happened in the Soviet countries . . . this doctrine leads regimes that rule by force to incur the characteristics and practices of the communist regimes—the abuse of power by the state, arbitrary imprisonment, torture and suppression of freedom of thought" (Episcopal Conference of Brazil, 1977). In this regard, the doctrinal reflections of Msgr. Santos are relevant. He writes that national security does not constitute an end in itself. It is intended to be a means by which the person can fully realize himself, a means which contributes to attainment of the common good of society. This is its norm, its unit of measurement, and its standard of evaluation; this must be used to judge its procedures. "Everyone," says John XXIII, must act according to his own decision, conviction, and responsibility, and not be moved by coercion or pressures that almost always derive from force, because a society that is based solely on force has to be characterized as inhumane. In such a society, man is, in fact, deprived of his freedom, rather than feeling encouraged to improve his life and perfect himself."

The more cohesive a community is internally, the less need there is to use force to unite it. "It would be foolish to think that a nation does not need to protect its existence by means of the instruments appropriate to national security, but it would be equally foolish to think that national security can be placed above the human person without safeguarding the legitimacy of its procedures and consideration of the common good."

Another pernicious effect of overvaluing security is its manipulation by certain social groups. Frequently, protecting essential rules is confused with maintaining the status quo, chiefly by the action of interested groups who view any change or tendency to change as a threat to basic rules, even calling these changes subversive. Since national security regimes have generally lost touch with a large part of their social base, they easily become victims of such a confusion.

The consequences of this confusion are reflected in what one critic (Orrego, 1976; CISEC, 1977) has referred to as "the logic of total security": the security doctrine is founded on the belief that conflict is a real possibility and that it must be prevented. Because there are numerous causes which may generate a conflict, security tends to be all-embracing, seeking to control all foreseeable situations. At the beginning, the military fought armed extremists, but since this was not sufficient to achieve "total security," not only are the Marxist political parties proscribed, but also those parties which are "easy prey" for the Marxists—in the case of Chile, the radical parties and the Christian Democrats. This, however, is still not enough. Total security becomes like a snowball rolling downhill, continually growing in size with those who are "infiltrated" by Marxism. Union, members and professionals are added to the proscribed parties, and finally the Church itself. In their search for total security, national security regimes end by marginalizing the majority of a society which will never be secure enough for those in power.

In this connection, Brazilian bishops have protested that "inspired (by the national security doctrine), the military regimes, in the name of their battle against communism and for economic development, declare an 'anti-subversion war' against all those who do not agree with the authoritarian vision of the organization of society" (Episcopal Conference of Brazil, 1977).

# NOTES

1. It is hardly necessary to stress that the national security doctrine does not appear in a monolithic form in all Latin American countries. The countries can provisionally be classified according to the degree to which this doctrine has been systematized and conceptualized and according to the prevailing national security system. In first place are the countries under military regimes with a high degree of doctrinal systematization and conceptualization (Brazil and Chile); next are the countries under military regimes with doctrines that are not very systematized (Argentina, Bolivia, and Uruguay) and those with governments controlled by the military (Ecuador, Peru, and some Central American countries); and finally, there are a few countries with formal democracies where their military groups possess the doctrine but without the objective and subjective conditions which exist in the preceding countries.

It should be made clear that this is an elementary classification which does not pretend to cover all the different versions of the national security doctrine. There are other equally relevant variables and criteria, such as the various national goals set by countries and the various forms of alliances, and of social influence entered into by military and civilian groups.

2. It should be mentioned here that this study is based on a theoretical-methodological premise. The social reality of the countries of the region, their different and contradictory political experiences, and the speed of their sociopolitical changes are usually beyond the interpretive scope of theoretical schemes. As Aron says, "there is no primary cause, no principal cause. The different orders of events constantly act and react on one another, and there is no evidence that a given order of events will exercise the same action in all societies" (1956: 170).

3. At present, as Lowenthal (1976) points out, the Latin American military institutions exercise their political influence either directly or openly as rulers or indirectly as a specially privileged pressure group. In no country of Latin America—with the possible exception of Costa Rica, where the officers' corps is almost completely disbanded with every presidential election—do the armed forces play a minor political role or even one limited to policing and national defense.

4. The socialization of the military takes into account the central role played by this group in the development of Latin American societies.

5. Deutsch and Foltz (1966) have pointed out that the nation is characterized by: (1) its independence—that is, the fact that its affairs are not directed from abroad; (2) its relatively secure and stable cohesiveness; (3) its political organization, in the sense that the "nation" provides the administrative, legal, and enforcement means to enable the government to effectively control public affairs; (4) its autonomy—that is, the ability of the government to generate the necessary support and consensus to maintain its control; and (5) its legitimacy, which is the mechanism that helps maintain a high level of loyalty to the nation.

6. The periods of President Goulart in Brazil, Perón in Argentina, and Allende in Chile are almost paradigms of the situation described.

7. In 1974 General Pinochet republished his *Geopolítica*, which he had written in 1968 when he was still an army colonel, a specialist on the general staff, and professor of geopolitics in the army's War Academy. A year earlier, in 1973, a collection of essays had appeared under the title "Fuerzas Armadas y Seguridad Nacional" (The Armed Forces

and National Security), edited by the Institute of General Studies and published three weeks after the September 1973 takeover. (These essays had been written and were already available some time earlier.) In September 1975, Colonel Gerardo Cortés Rencoret gave a lecture on this subject to the faculty and students of the Austral University of Valdivia. This lecture was reprinted in the newspaper *Mercurio* of Santiago, in the *Cuadernos* of the Political Science Institute of the Catholic University of Chile, and in the collected work "Nuestro Camino" (Our Path), distributed by the Government Information Office.

In December, 1975, the Economics Department of the University of Chile organized a seminar on the "Strategy of Economic Development for Chile," in which one of the participants was General Agustín Toro Davilá, rector of that university and director of the National Security Academy.

In addition, other actions were taken to systematize study of the doctrine and make it better known. The National Security Academy was established as an advanced institute of the branches of the armed forces. Courses were offered in the army's War Academy to specialized journalists and in the Catholic University of Chile, while they were made compulsory in the Catholic University of Valparaíso and in the fourth year of the social science programs of secondary schools.

July 1976 marked the first appearance of a journal called "Seguridad Nacional" (National Security) in Latin America (Calvo, 1977: 51-52).

8. In the case of Brazil, the worship of technology by the military elite is rooted in the positivism of Saint-Simon, influential during the early years of the Republic (Ríos, 1970: 151).

9. An illustration of this is the comment of General De Meira Mattos: "The national security policy is formulated under a rigorous process of scientific reasoning: it is divided into a system, a structure, and a technique that constitute the instruments of an ordered and consistent rationale leading to policies and strategies that will efficiently achieve the desired goals" (1975).

10. The Chilean military have formulated the following definition: National security is the structuring of the potential of a country so that the latter can carry out its development in complete control of its sovereignty and independence, both internal and external.

11. A concept widely used by the Chilean military.

12. The Latin American military have adopted the North American geopolitical concept of a world divided into two opposing blocs of power: "communist world" and "free world." The Latin American countries are members of the so-called free world, which is threatened both within and without by "international communism."

Under the ideological division of labor during the cold war, the United States had the task of discouraging and generally counteracting the military force of international communism. The Latin Americans' mission was to prevent subversive activities in their countries. Whereas North American leaders have significantly modified this concept, the Latin American military have stubbornly insisted on maintaining it unchanged.

13. One of the most striking features of the right-wing authoritarian regime is its militant anticommunism. Where does it come from? The answer, which is a complicated one, can be only partial and therefore provisional. Literature on the subject indicates that it lies in the almost total politicomilitary dependency of the Latin American armies on the U.S. army. This dependency stems from the latter's provision of not only arms and technicomilitary training, but also, to a considerable extent, of continual ideological indoctrination.

14. Brazil and Chile, it would seem, do not differ substantially in their national goals as may be appreciated in the available literature. General Golbery Do Couto e Silva states that for Brazil, the goals are "national integration, self-determination and sovereignty, well-being, and progress" (1967). The Chileans have the same framework of reference.

15. This position, in the case of Chile, is clearcut. Decrees one and two of the constituent act of the governing junta state "(1) that the public force which under the constitution is composed of the Army, Navy, Air Force, and Police, has been organized by the state to safeguard and defend its moral and physical integrity and its historical and cultural identity, and (2) that, therefore, its supreme mission is to ensure above all else the survival of the superior and permanent realities and values of the Chilean nationality. . ."

16. Again, the case of Chile is dramatically paradigmatic, as is evidenced by the controversy surrounding the letter sent to the OAS by five Chilean lawyers protesting the violation of human rights in Chile (Calvo, 1977: 63).

## REFERENCES

AMARAL GURGEL, J. A. (1976) Segurança e democracia. Rio de Janeiro: José Olympio.

ARON, R. (1956) Recherches et débats. Paris: Centre catholique des intelectuels français.

BELTRÁN, V. R. (1970) "Estrategia, armas y cambio social en America latina," pp. 27-51 in V. R. Beltrán [ed.] El papel político y social de las Fuerzas Armadas en América latina. Caracas: Monte Avila.

CALVO, R. (1977) "Seguridad nacional y temas conexos." Tierra Nueva 23: 47-70.

CISEC (1977) Hacia un estatuto para la paz en Chile. Santiago: CISEC.

CUELLAR, O. (1971) "La participación política de lost militares en América latina," pp. 13-69 in L. M. Vega et al Fuerzas Armadas, poder y cambio. Caracas: Tiempo Nuevo.

DEUTSCH, K. and W. J. FOLTZ [eds.] (1966) Nation-Building. New York: Atherton.

Episcopal Conference of Argentina (1977) "Reflexión cristiana para el pueblo de la patria." Criterio 1764: 267-269.

Episcopal Conference of Brazil (1977) "Comunicacao pastoral au povo de Deus." Cadernos de CEAS 47: 5-14.

Episcopal Conference of Chile (1977) "Nuestra convivencia nacional." Solidaridad 15.

GERMANI, G. (1969) Sociología de la modernización. Buenos Aires: Paidós.

HOURTON, J. (1976) Iglesia y democracia: La ensenanza de Pío XII. Santiago: Ediciones Aconcagua.

HUNTINGTON, S. (1972) El orden político en las sociedales en cambio. Buenos Aires: Paidós.

JAGUARIBE, H. (1972) Crisis y alternativas de América latina: reforma o revolución. Buenos Aires: Paidós.

LIEUWEN, E. (1960) Armas y política en América latina. Buenos Aires: Sur.

LOWENTHAL, A. (1976) "Ejercitos y política en América latina." Estudios Internacionales 35: 38-64.

MATTOS, C. de Meira (1975) Brasil: Geopolítica e destino. Rio de Janeiro: José Olympio.

MEDINA, A. (1976) "Teoria de la Seguridad Nacional—Su orientacíon en Chile." Seguridad Nacional 2 (Septiembre): 99-108.

MORENO, F. (1977) Democracia y desarrollo. Santiago. (mimeografiado)

NEEDLER, M. (1966) "Political Development and Military Intervention in Latin America." American Political Science Review 60: 616-626.

ORREGO, F. (1976) "Libertad y seguridad nacional," pp. 123-150 in G. Arriagada, Seguridad nacional y bien común. Santiago: Corporación.

PADIN, C. (1968) "La doctrine de la sécurité nationale à la lumière de la doctrine de l'Eglise." SEDOC 431: 432-444.

PINOCHET, A. (1974) Geopolítica. Santiago: Andrés Bello.

PUTNAM, R. (1967) "Toward explaining military intervention in Latin American Politics." World Politics 20: 83-110.

RIOS, J. A. (1970) "Los militares y el poder en Brasil," pp. 147-160 in V. R. Beltrán [ed.] El papel político y social de las Fuerzas Armadas en América latina. Caracas: Monte Avila.

SANTOS, J. M. (1976) "La seguridad nacional, condición del bien común," pp. 87-119 in G. Arriagada et al. Seguridad Nacional y bien común. Santiago: Corporación.

SILVA, Do Couto e, G. (1967) Geopolítica do Brasil. Rio de Janeiro: José Olympio.

Vicaria de la Solidaridad del Arzobispado de Santiago (1977) Estudio sobre la doctrina de la seguridad nacional y régimen militar. Santiago (mimeografiado)

VILLEGAS, O. G. (1968) "Seguridad, política, estrategia." Temas Militares 4.

*Roberto Calvo is the pen name of a sociologist, university professor, specialist in Latin American affairs, and author of several scientific monographs and articles.*

**BRIAN H. SMITH, S.J.**
*Woodstock Theological Center*
*Georgetown University*
*Washington, D.C. 20057*

# *CHURCHES AND HUMAN RIGHTS IN LATIN AMERICA*
## *Recent Trends in the Subcontinent*

Over the past fifteen years the military have seized power in most major South American countries, leaving only Colombia and Venezuela with democratic regimes. The armed forces claim that only they are capable of controlling the domestic violence and social disruptions which accompanied the rapid political and economic changes of the 1960s. This process of social conflict and subsequent military intervention has been especially notable in the countries of the subcontinent region—Brazil, Bolivia, Chile, Argentina, Peru, and Uruguay.

Military rule, however, has not led to a decline in violence; indeed, most of these governments have resorted to extremely repressive measures in pursuing their objectives. In responding to the problems which brought them to power (labor unrest, inflation, societal polarization, and the growth of Marxist parties or guerrilla movements), the military have employed severe measures to restore order and promote more stable economic growth. These efforts have involved placing strict controls on organized labor, student groups, and political parties, suspending constitutional guarantees and processes, and offering generous incentives to domestic producers and foreign investors. Power has been consolidated by effective mobilization of the forces of physical coercion (the armed forces and the police) and by the appeal to traditional emotion-laden symbols such as anticommunism, nationalism, and protection of private property (Comblin, 1977; Methol Ferré, 1977).[1] Although guerrilla activity has declined and inflation rates have slowed in some places, these military regimes, in the process of promoting stability, have systematically violated a whole gamut of human rights as guaranteed by the two United Nations covenants—the International Covenant on Civil and Political Rights and the

Journal of Interamerican Studies and World Affairs, Vol. 21 No. 1, February 1979, 89-128
© 1979 Sage Publications, Inc.

International Covenant on Economic, Social, and Cultural Rights (Amnesty International, 1975-1976a: 84).[2]

Amidst this atmosphere of repression, churches have become important actors in the struggle to counter these abuses of state power in the subcontinent. At the international level, church networks have become one of the most reliable sources of information to the outside world on the extent of rights violations inside these countries. In turn, the international network of the churches has provided considerable financial and material support to groups working to defend and promote human rights in the southern tier of Latin America.

At the national level, the Catholic bishops of these Latin churches have increased their public condemnations of abuses of power. In so doing, they not only have denounced such crimes as murder, torture, and denial of habeas corpus and fair trial, but also have pointed to what they believe are the deeper underlying causes precipitating the rapid increase of such systematic violations of human rights—unjust economic structures, maldistribution of land and wealth, lack of effective social participation by the poor, and the pervasiveness of an ideology of national security which subjugates all rights of the person to the expediency of the State (Mitchell, 1977).[3]

Several of the most recent pastoral letters of the bishops of Brazil, Chile, and Argentina, for example, have clearly emphasized that there is a connection between violation of classic civil rights and the desire upon the part of wealthy elites to preserve their economic power. They point to a clear relationship between abuse of persons (especially the poor) and a refusal to respect basic economic and social rights in society by those who benefit from military rule (USCC, 1977a, 1977b, 1976d). They also call upon existing governments as well as landed and industrial elites to make profound changes in the economic and social systems as a necessary step to guarantee the full panoply of human rights as defined by the international covenants of the United Nations.

Most of these episcopal letters have urged secular leaders to make such changes as greater distribution of land and other economic resources, respect for independent labor unions, effective social participation by the poor in decisions affecting their lives, and fair application of law to limit government power. In these documents, the bishops also commit the organizational network of the Church to a vigorous defense of those whose rights are being violated and to a more profound identification with the plight of the poor (CELAM, 1970).[4] This general concern for human rights and new commitment to the oppressed have legitimized the setting up of a whole new series of social and pastoral programs in Latin American churches over the past decade, including new Church-sponsored organizations concerned with the promotion of human rights. Since the early 1970s, churches in Chile, Brazil, Paraguay, Bolivia, and Argentina (Lernoux, 1977; Culhane, 1975; Latinamerica Press, 1975, 1977b)[5] have created new religious and social structures to respond to the needs of the poor who have borne the brunt of repression in these respective countries.

While the documents of the hierarchies in these countries have been widely publicized both in South America as well as in Western Europe and North America, to date there has been little research done on these newly emerging human rights commissions and lay leadership programs functioning at lower levels of the churches. The activities of these new organizations have expanded rapidly in the last several years, and they not only have provided substantial assistance to those suffering human rights violations, but also have precipitated serious conflict between Church and state and at times tension within the respective churches themselves.

It is, therefore, important to study these new organizations in greater detail in order to assess the Church's real capacity to promote the structural changes the bishops see as a necessary basis for the observance of all human rights. Such information is also important to assess what contradictions are emerging for churches as a whole in this work and whether they can continue to make an active promotion of human rights an essential part of their religious mission.

This paper will focus on the learning experiences and accomplishments of Church-sponsored human rights commissions and other pastoral programs which have emerged since the early 1970s in Chile, Brazil, Paraguay, Bolivia, and Argentina. I shall analyze (1) under what conditions, and with what type of support, these programs have emerged, (2) what range of activities they have undertaken to promote civil, political, social, and economic rights, and (3) what impact they have had both on the political system and on the respective national churches themselves.

I shall give brief descriptive overviews of the activities of each of these churches in the area of human rights using the three above questions as organizing components for the available empirical data. In a concluding section I will offer a comparative analysis of all five cases as to what they reveal regarding the capacities and limitations of churches as complex organizations in protecting and promoting the full gamut of human rights.

## *I. Chile: The Committee of Co-operation for Peace, the Vicariate of Solidarity, and the Base Communities*

Within three weeks of Chile's military coup of September 11, 1973, Catholic, Protestant, and Jewish leaders moved to establish emergency committees to assist refugees and also families of those who had been killed or jailed or who had disappeared. There are several reasons why church leaders acted so quickly and with government acquiescence. In previous years, all church leaders had been forced to take the social concerns of the poor more seriously due to the steady movement to the left in the political system since the early 1960s. During both Frei's and Allende's presidencies, many church groups focused more efforts on identifying with problems of the poor, and the Catholics had begun to establish small basic communities in working class areas to evangelize the poor more effectively. The churches also maintained fairly cordial relations with the Marxist government, and established closer communication with one another in the process. When the coup occurred, by and large major church leaders publicly remained neutral. The Permanent Committee of the Catholic Conference even issued a mildly critical declaration two days after the coup, lamenting the bloodshed and calling upon the military to respect all gains made by the working classes during the last decade (Oviedo Cavada, 1974: 174).

In the aftermath of the coup, when thousands were being tortured, murdered, or put in large concentration camps, the persecuted turned in droves to the churches for help. All other major social and political organizations were placed under strict controls, and the past performance, current neutrality, and existing organizational network of the churches (especially the Catholic Church) made them ready channels of assistance. Furthermore, the particularly brutal nature of the repression shocked international public opinion, and Protestant and Catholic Church groups in Western Europe and North America were most willing to provide immediate financial and material assistance to Chilean Church leaders attempting to help those in need. The new military regime acquiesced reluctantly to church efforts to assist those being persecuted, seeking religious legitimation for having overturned the longstanding democratic traditions of the country, and because it had no effective mechanism to handle the human casualties of its own brutality.

Finally, due to the long and vigorous history of political participation and multiparty competition in the country, many civilian leaders were anxious and willing to do something to counter the repression and assist those being persecuted. Many, especially in parties associated with the Christian left—MAPU and "Izquierda Cristiana"—had formerly been active in church-sponsored educational or social programs in the 1960s and found no difficulty in moving back into church structures to carry out humanitarian programs.

All of these political and religious factors in the context of sudden and brutal repression led to the formation of the Committee of Cooperation for Peace by seven major religious denominations in the country.[6] Over the next two years, the Committee established a whole range of services for Chileans suffering the effects of the coup—legal aid, assistance to workers arbitrarily dismissed from their jobs, medical programs in areas where public health clinics had been suspended, small self-help projects for the unemployed, and soup kitchens in urban working-class areas for starving children. The Committee also established regional offices in 15 of the 25 provinces where similar projects were begun. By 1975 over 300 full-time lawyers, social workers, and medical personnel were working in various parts of the country, and the annual budget (over $2 million) was provided mainly by Protestant and Catholic sources in North America and Western Europe and some nonconfessional agencies (U.S. Congress, House, 1976: 59).[7]

In December 1975, General Pinochet demanded the churches disband the Committee of Peace for having assisted many Chileans sought by the secret police (DINA) to leave the country. The government also argued that many civilians formerly associated with the Allende government were using the Committee to continue their political activities under Church auspices. Thus, under severe pressure both from Pinochet and the government-controlled press, church leaders agreed to close the Committee in late December. However, Cardinal Silva immediately moved to incorporate many of the activities and personnel of the former Committee of Peace into a new organization under Catholic auspices—the Vicariate of Solidarity—established in late January 1976. Over the past two years this Vicariate has established offices in the majority of Chile's 25 dioceses. These offices provide legal and health services, manage between 40 and 50 farm cooperatives in rural areas, and support soup kitchens for hungry children and adults in major urban areas. The Vicariate also issues a biweekly bulletin ("Solidaridad") from its Santiago headquarters which publishes accounts of its various projects as well as data on malnutrition, unemployment, and disappeared persons. Its budget is somewhat larger than that of the Committee for Peace, though funds are drawn mainly from the same foreign sources as supported that group. The Protestant churches have also continued to support, on their own, self-help worker enterprises with assistance from West European sources (Vicaría de la Solidaridad, 1977).

In addition to the work of the Committee for Peace and its successor, the Vicariate, the small base communities established in most of the 25 Catholic dioceses of the country have taken on new vitality and importance since the coup. During the Frei and Allende years these groups did not attract significant numbers of people due to the expanding activities of social and political organizations associated with parties. But since 1973, these neighborhood groups have become the only opportunities for Chileans (especially in working-class areas) to meet and discuss their problems. These communities are subdivided into three or four sectors, each focusing on different religious or social issues—bible study, catechetical training, prayer, and self-help social services. Thus far there has been no systematic study of these groups, but it was estimated in 1975 that there were approximately 20,000 active leaders of these communities and 10,000 more (almost exclusively women) who have received extensive training as catechists (Gilfeather, 1976).[8]

Taken together, the activities of all of these programs and structures operating under Church auspices in contemporary Chile have dealt with the effects of violations of a broad range of civil, social, and economic rights. So far, their impact on changing the political and economic structures which cause such violations has, however, been minimal. Official repression continues, with almost no opportunity for effective participation or distribution of resources in favor of the poor. In fact, the policies of the junta have rolled back most of the working-class gains made under Frei and Allende—labor unions are under government surveillance, wages are limited, agrarian reform organizations are being dismantled, and speculators are permitted to amass wealth and buy up enterprises formerly owned by the government. Arrests and tortures have subsided since 1974 and 1975, but the courts only very recently have begun to act with any independence and accept the Vicariate's legal requests to investigate lists of disappeared persons.

Despite their inability to affect direct change, the work of the Committee for Peace and the Vicariate have had an impact in other important ways. These committees have amassed well-documented evidence on civil rights violations. Based upon these reports and other sources (e.g., early on-site inspections and some newspaper stories in Chile), international organizations have been able to publicize continuing rights violations in the country. The Committee for Peace and the Vicariate have also provided survival assistance to thousands who would have perished or despaired, and thus have kept alive a spirit of hope. In addition, the small base communities have nourished a sense of solidarity and critical awareness among working classes, while serving as surrogate training grounds for future political leaders if and when the military relinquishes control of the country.

The impact of these activities on the Church has been considerable, but also not without tensions for the Church itself. For the first time in its history, the Chilean Catholic Church is beginning to penetrate the culture of the poor, and urban workers and slum dwellers are identifying with the Church now much more than ever before. But both the upper class and the military are disillusioned with the Church and view it as naive or as an obstacle to their current plans for the country. Right wing Catholics have also publicly attacked the Church for being infiltrated by Communists (Sociedad Chilena de Defensa de la Tradición, Familia y Propiedad, 1976). Since the coup, nearly 200 priests (mainly foreigners) have been expelled or urged to leave the country. Criticisms of foreign sources of support for church programs have also appeared in the press, such as the attempt to discredit the Inter-American Foundation by *El Mercurio* in January 1978 (El Mercurio, 1978).

Although the hierarchy has occasionally criticized the government for its general economic and political policies, their public documents have been very cautious and usually include some concessions to the government. For example, in their 1975 pastoral letter, "Gospel and Peace," the bishops thanked the military for having saved the country from Marxism, and praised the actions of the wives of the military for helping the poor (Comité Permanente del Episcopado de Chile, 1975). In their document, "Our Life as a Nation," they said that some abuses of power or unwarranted actions are inevitable and that there is an international campaign to discredit Chile's reputation organized by Marxists abroad (USCC, 1977b). Furthermore, in the four and one-half years since the coup, the bishops have seldom critized the government publicly for torture, and have only expressed sharp criticisms (or threatened excommunication) when the authority or person of bishops themselves have been attacked.

This ambiguous stance and selective public criticisms are due to divisions of opinion within the hierarchy as to the merits of the government, to their desire to maintain communication with the military, to an unwillingness to precipitate an all-out war with the state, and to a fear of affecting a more serious public division than already exists among the bishops and faithful alike. As a result, the prophetic role of the bishops has been exercised with extreme caution. But, while at times they have acquiesced to government demands regarding Church-sponsored programs, on the whole their cautious stance has made it possible for the whole new network of human rights activities at lower levels of the church to continue with some degree of effectiveness, under implicit Church protection.

## *II. Brazil: Small Base Communities, Justice and Peace Commissions, and Land Commissions*

The reaction of the churches to the Brazilian military coup of March 1964 was not as swift or dramatic as in Chile. Moreover, new church structures to promote human rights in Brazil have not been able, so far, to mobilize with the same degree of effectiveness and coordination as in Chile. Nevertheless, some new programs have begun to operate in the past few years affecting civil, social and economic rights, and small base communities are now mushrooming in many rural areas of the country and perform similar critical roles as in Chile.

There are many reasons for this relatively slow reaction to an authoritarian regime by the Brazilian Church. First, when the coup occurred, the great majority of the hierarchy acquiesced in hopes that the new government would be able to control the social turmoil of the Goulart administration, and carry out its own announced plan for stable and effective economic development (Bruneau, 1974: 66, 93, 181).[9] Furthermore, the immediate aftermath of the Brazilian coup was not as brutal and repressive as in Chile. The military did not immediately resort to widespread torture or mass murder, nor did they close Congress and suppress all forms of social participation. In addition, although the Brazilian Church, like the Chilean, had begun to involve itself in social issues in the early 1960s (paralleling the new awakening of social consciousness in the universal Church reflected by Vatican II), neither the hierarchy as a whole nor the laity were strongly committed to this option. A small core of bishops centering around Dom Helder Camara were urging a more active social commitment by the Church, but, by 1964, they had lost influence in the National Conference of Brazilian Bishops [CNBB] (Bruneau, 1974: 124). Many Catholic Action lay leaders active in promoting social change in rural areas in the pre-1964 period moved away from the Church by 1965, when the bishops attempted to exercise stricter controls on their programs and eliminate all activities with political repercussions (Bruneau, 1974: 126). Hence, in the aftermath of the coup, the leadership of the CNBB favored cooperation with what seemed to be a moderate regime, and in any case the Church lacked the organizational capacity or network to oppose official policies.

In 1968, however, the government began to impose more repressive measures to curb escalating opposition and eliminate growing leftist guerrilla activities. Habeas corpus was suspended, all civilian control over security forces was eliminated, the Congress, the courts, and the press were severely curtailed, and the use of torture became systematic and widespread. These repressive policies also began to affect the Church itself, as church publications, radio stations and pastoral programs in rural areas were placed under close surveillance and some church personnel (especially in rural areas) harassed, imprisoned or expelled.[10]

In such an atmosphere of controlled and systematic repression which also touched the institutional church itself, bishops as a group began to criticize the regime, and new church structures at the local level (base communities and self-help social programs) emerged as alternate forms of social participation and humanitarian assistance for the poor. In May 1970, the Episcopal Conference published its first major public criticism, denouncing the use of torture and lack of fair trials and expressing the need for greater social participation and respect for legitimate criticism of government policies (CNBB, 1970: 415).[11]

At this time several dioceses began to implement some of the new pastoral orientations of Medellín—formation of small base communities, lay leadership training, and social action favoring the poor. In the northeast of Brazil, for example, where the repressive political and economic policies of the regime have been the most severe (and where harassment of clergy first began), both base communities and social programs run by lay leaders began to take root by the late 1960s (Hope, 1975: 46).[12] Small base religious communities also sprang up in the early 1970s in the center-west and in several urban areas, such as São Paulo. They emerged in response to the elimination of other forms of social participation. Although these communities are in the beginning stages of development and face problems due to long-standing patterns of personalistic piety, the rootlessness of migrants, and lack of well-trained personnel, they have mushroomed throughout Brazil over the past five years.

No systematic study of these groups has yet been done, but it is estimated that about 50,000 such centers are operating at the present (Bono, 1977: 1). The Episcopal Conference in 1976 issued a document outlining the focus and purpose of such base communities. Included in the desired activities of these groups is the development of critical social and political awareness among the participants (Estudos de CNBB, 1976a). The political sensitivity of these orientations has led to increasing numbers of arrests of lay leaders and technical experts assisting these communities, and many have been tortured (Hope, 1975: 54; Bono, 1977: 20).

In addition to these new grassroots self-help programs and religious communities, the National Episcopal Conference in 1972 authorized the establishment of Justice and Peace Commissions, both at the national level as part of the CNBB itself and in several dioceses. The purpose of these commissions is to conduct study projects of socio-economic needs of various regions and provide assistance to prisoners and their families. Due to the lack of staff and the weak structural development of the Church in many areas of the country, these commissions have not yet begun to function effectively.

In the archdiocese of São Paulo, however, with the largest concentration of population in the country (over ten million people) and one of the most outspoken of the Brazilian bishops, Cardinal Evaristo Arns, the Justice and Peace Commission over the past few years has inaugurated several programs pertaining to violations of civil, social, and economic rights. In 1975 it published two books on the link between private death squads and security forces in the early days of the government and on the maldistribution of income and economic resources in the archdiocese (Szulc, 1977: 19). Lists of disappeared persons were also printed in the archdiocesan newspaper, *O São Paulo,* based on documented evidence brought to the Commission by private individuals and church personnel. In 1977 the Commission received grants from the Inter-American Foundation and from Catholic organizations in West Germany. With some additional local contributions, the Commission expanded its personnel to provide emergency relief for prisoners, ex-prisoners, and their families, offer legal and social services to the labor sector, disseminate information on the Commission activities, and assist other dioceses in the creation of similar Commissions.

In addition to Justice and Peace Commissions, the bishops of the Amazon region have started programs for Indians and small landholders who are being displaced by government development projects and large national and international agrobusiness enterprises. Under the auspices of the National Justice and Peace Commission and the CNBB's Commission of Missionary Action, meetings were held in June 1975 by prelates and technicians in these areas to discuss the dispossession of peasants and to begin legal aid and educational programs to help protect their land claims (Estudos de CNBB, 1976b).[13] Since then, similar programs have been inaugurated by several Amazon dioceses but, as with the base communities, large numbers of participants have been harassed, arrested, or murdered.

While not as well organized or funded as the Chilean Church's activities for human rights, these new programs in Brazil have attempted to promote and defend a whole range of civil, social, and economic rights of the oppressed. Their impact so far on government and business policy has not been dramatic. While the number of cases of torture and disappearances has decreased since 1974 and the Congress has been reopened and censorship bans have been lifted on several publications, no effective political participation exists for the vast number of citizens. Nor has the government changed its economic strategy of development which allows industrialists and agricultural enterprises to amass great wealth and land at the expense of workers, peasants, and Indians.[14]

As in the Chilean case, one of the most effective but limited contributions of these new programs has been the provision of alternate forms of social participation for the poor and powerless. While not affecting significant changes in economic and political structures, these at least have provided opportunities for some self-help and for the nurturing of a critical awareness and sense of dignity among them.

The impact of these structures on the Church, however, has been very notable since 1970, for the government has increased its surveillance and harassment of participants in these small base communities, self-help projects, Justice and Peace Commissions, and land commissions. In addition, paramilitary death squads and security forces have murdered several priests, and even kidnapped a bishop for a short period of time in 1976. More persecution of church personnel is occurring in Brazil than in Chile. This not only has solidified church identity with the oppressed, but also has stimulated the hierarchy as a group to issue more decisive denunciations of the government. In this way, the equilibrium of the institutional Church is now clearly on the side of the lower classes. Thus, in November 1976, and again in February 1977, the National Conference of Brazilian Bishops issued strongly worded documents condemning the murder of priests and Indians, attacking policies which absolutize national security, and bluntly stating that the present model of Brazilian development is characterized by injustice and promotes institutionalized violence (USCC, 1977c, 1976d). Both of these documents are far more consistent and critical of the government than comparable statements by the Chilean hierarchy. It is also clear that a consensus now exists among higher and lower leaders in the Brazilian Church that opposition to the government is necessary, since the state itself has singled out the Church for special repression as a subversive organization (Barbosa, 1978: 27).[15]

The Church has suffered both external limitation and increasing internal tensions as a result of its human rights programs and the prophetic stance of its bishops. For example, the Church is heavily dependent on the state for maintaining its schools, universities, radio stations, and hospitals, and since the late 1960s the government has curtailed funding for these operations and levied taxes on church properties. Increasing numbers of foreign priests are being expelled from the country, and the archdiocesan newspaper of São Paulo is one of the few remaining newspapers subject to censorship prior to publication. In late 1976 the Church was also ordered to withdraw some of its personnel from mission territories where murder and dispossession of Indians and peasants are occurring, although later the order was reversed.

Right-wing Catholics belonging to the "Tradition, Fatherland and Family" movement also have increased their public attacks on the Church as being infiltrated by communists. One bishop who belongs to this organization (and who owns a considerable amount of land),

Archbishop Geraldo Sigaud of Diamantina, in February 1977, publicly accused two fellow bishops of being communists—Bishop Pedro Casaldáliga of São Felix and Bishop Tomáz Balduino of Goias Velho (USCC, 1978b: 15). Both of the accused have been active in defending the land claims of peasants and Indians in rural areas. The government mounted a major public campaign to discredit these two prelates and gave Archbishop Sigaud's accusation widespread circulation in the government-controlled media. Only strong pressure by the Vatican and the Episcopal Conference kept the Minister of the Interior from expelling Casaldáliga (a Spaniard) from the country. All of these events, however, point to continual Church-state conflicts in the near future and further external pressures by the government to circumscribe human rights activities by Catholic religious and lay leaders.

Unlike the Chilean Church, the Brazilian Church's official concern with human rights originated from a direct attack on the Church itself, and as this attack has intensified so have the efforts of many bishops, priests, and lay leaders to promote civil, social, and economic rights of the poor. The institutional infrastructure of the Brazilian Church and the amount of foreign support for its human rights programs are both far less developed than is the case in Chile. The bishops attempt to offset this institutional weakness through more aggressive public denunciations than the Chilean bishops, but this in turn precipitates stronger official repression of local action programs. The institutional power of the Church to blunt the authoritarian policies of the regime is therefore limited, but as repression continues the whole character of the Church is gradually changing and its mission to the poor more consciously felt and affirmed.

## *III. Paraguay: Peasant Leagues, Small Base Communities, and the Committee of Churches for Emergency Assistance*

The oldest continuous dictatorship in South America exists in Paraguay, where Alfredo Stroessner has held power since 1954. In this highly personalistic regime, almost all social institutions in the country (unions, professional associations, courts, universities, business organizations) are controlled or infiltrated by Stroessner sympathizers. A powerful police force (operating under continuous state-of-siege conditions) maintains "order," and the system as a whole is held together by a highly pervasive pattern of corruption supported by profits from institutionalized smuggling (Dominguez, 1975: 95-96).

Between 1958 and 1975 there were five brief but intense waves of arrests and torture involving political opponents to the regime—students, labor leaders, dissident members of the Colorado Party (Stroessner's official group), suspected members of a small communist party. In April and May 1976, however, a new and more widespread wave of repression occurred aimed particularly at members of the Protestant and Catholic clergy and peasant and Indian leaders associated with church programs, especially in rural areas. Over 1,000 men and women were arrested at this time and many were subjected to torture and other forms of cruel and inhuman treatment in 13 detention centers in various parts of the country. In addition, 32 of Paraguay's 34 foreign Jesuit priests were expelled from the country (Stephansky and Alexander, 1976: 161).

Although the government claimed that these programs were supporting guerrillas and planning violent revolution, no substantial proof was provided to justify these claims, nor is there any significant terrorist activity in the country (Stephansky and Alexander, 1976: 174). The real reason for the repression of church personnel was the fact that both Catholic and Protestant Church organizations have set up independent structures for both social and religious participation outside government control. In the aftermath of Vatican II (1962-1965) and Medellín (1968), the Catholic Church began to concentrate more effort on evangelizing hitherto neglected groups in Paraguay—peasants and Indians in the interior of the country who constitute two-thirds of the population. Foreign missionaries (especially Spanish Jesuits) have been most active since the mid-1960s in establishing peasant leagues in rural areas which include credit unions and small agricultural cooperatives. Money for these projects has been provided by foreign church agencies (such as Catholic Relief Services in the United States, and Adveniat and Misereor in West Germany). Some of the activities of these leagues have included teaching peasants and Indians their legal rights and helping them pressure the government to apply its own agrarian reform and labor laws more fairly. Parallel to these Catholic peasant leagues have been similar organizations sponsored by the Disciples of Christ from the U.S. These also provide credit to small landholders and train peasants in the rudiments of government and law as these effect their interests (Stephansky and Alexander, 1976: 180).

Such organizations have enabled peasants and Indians to be more aware of their civil and economic rights under existing law, while stimulating them to become spokespersons to represent directly their own interests without reliance upon any of the organizations asociated with the government. Even though most of the leagues purposely chose peasants publicly known as members of the ruling Colorado Party, the government was most concerned that they were being trained in independent organizations outside its control. Furthermore, since these cooperatives and credit unions were able to bypass intermediary agents in marketing their produce, they were able to receive fairer prices for their goods. Large landholders and financial and commercial institutions saw their socioeconomic dominance threatened, and therefore actively opposed these new programs. All of these factors led to the harsh crackdown of mid-1976 with massive arrests, torture, and deportations of clergy and laity active in the leagues.

The reaction of the churches to this repression has occurred on several fronts. First, small base communities and deacon training programs for the laity have taken on new vitality now that the leagues are more circumscribed. These pastoral programs have begun to flourish in almost all major regions in the interior. They involve small groups of 40 to 50 people (mostly men) and combine bible study and catechetical training with frank discussions of agrarian and social problems, such as the legal right of peasants and Indians to seek redress of grievances and form self-help organizations. These new base communities have also been subject to similar harassment by police forces, but lay leaders are determined to continue their activities despite risk to their lives.[16]

The Catholic hierarchy reacted swiftly and strongly to the mid-1976 wave of arrests which also was accompanied by a press campaign charging communist infiltration in the Church. On June 15, 1976, all eleven Catholic bishops in Paraguay issued a pastoral letter that was read in churches at Sunday Mass. They unequivocally denounced the use of violence and torture to eliminate subversion (even terrorism) and demanded an end to arbitrary procedures, massive arrests, intimidation of entire peasant villages, confiscation of goods, and prolonged holding of people incommunicado. They also emphasized the need for an efficient and respectable judiciary to administer justice fairly (USCC 1976b: 7, 9, 10, 11). The bishops condemned the government's campaign of defamation and persecution against the Church, emphasizing that only church leaders can judge what truly conforms to the Gospel.

Finally, they affirmed the "inalienable responsibility of the Church in the promotion of activities which are inherent to it," and renewed their "decision to carry them forward at whatever cost in terms of sacrifice" (USCC 1976b: 14; Stephansky and Alexander, 1976: 209).[17]

The third and final effort to promote and defend human rights by churches in the aftermath of the most recent wave of repression has been the formation of the Committee of Churches for Emergency Assistance. On June 28, 1976, representatives of the Catholic and Lutheran Churches and the Disciples of Christ announced the establishment of a new ecumenical organization to help prisoners and their families (USCC, 1976c: 19). The Committee operates out of the chancery office of the Episcopal Conference of Paraguay and provides food and medicines to prisoners, economic and rehabilitation assistance to families of prisoners, ex-prisoners, or the disappeared, runs a documentation and information service, and offers legal aid to those charged with crimes (Stephansky and Helfield, 1977: 4). The Committee has received financial and material support from the World Council of Churches, Catholic Relief Services (U.S.), Misereor (West Germany), Christian Aid (England), Christian Church (U.S.), and the Catholic Justice and Peace Commission in Holland. Catholic and Protestant leaders in human rights working in other parts of Latin America, North America, and Western Europe have also visited the Committee on several occasions over the past two years to give it moral support and international visibility (Wilde, 1977, 301; Comité de la Iglesias, 1977b, 6; 1977c, 6).[18]

The Committee has achieved some important results over the past two years. It has been given daily visiting rights to Emboscada prison (where most of the prisoners are now incarcerated), and the living conditions there have improved significantly due to food and medicines the Committee has brought in. Literacy training programs and artisan cooperatives have been set up in the prison under the Committee's direction. The sale of artisan products, such as woodcarvings and woven baskets, serves not only to raise additional relief funds, but also circulates public reminders in society at large that there are people in prison.

Lists of prisoners also have been prepared and presented to the International League of Human Rights during its two visits to Paraguay in 1976 and 1977. The government has allowed 45 of these prisoners to be processed in civilian courts, and the Committee has provided lawyers for the defense of 40 of them. The government has also released over 200 prisoners since September 1976, so that by December 1977 there were only 179 remaining in Emboscada. (The whereabouts of many who have disappeared, however, is still not known and many people are now imprisoned for shorter periods, thus maintaining a climate of fear.) The bulk of the Committee's budget (more than one-half of its funds) is spent on relief programs for families of prisoners or persons who have disappeared in the countryside. To date 177 projects (assisting 224 families) have been set up. These include not only food and clothing, but also help to establish or continue self-help projects in farming, artisan work, or husbandry (Comité de las Iglesias, 1977a: 3-4).

In this way, the work of the new ecumenical committee has contributed to some significant changes on behalf of legal rights and care of prisoners and survival aid for their families. Furthermore, self-help projects similar to cooperatives begun by Catholic and Protestant churches ten years ago are being reformed with aid from this Committee. But the basic structures of political and economic power of the country have not changed significantly. Stroessner is still in complete control and in early February 1978 was given yet another term in office in a controlled election. The economy has been bolstered by recent financial agreements allowing both Brazil and Argentina to build hydroelectric dams in Paraguayan territory (Vidal, 1978), and no major changes have occurred in the concentration of land and wealth in the country.

The government has made concessions by releasing some prisoners, allowing civil trials for others, and permitting various social and economic improvement programs by the Committee of Churches. These concessions, however, have been due not only to Church denunciations, but more importantly to pressure from various international human rights organizations and from the U.S. government, to which General Stroessner is particularly sensitive. There is no major internal threat to Stroessner's power at present and he can afford, under prodding by Washington, Amnesty International, and the International League of Human Rights, to loosen the repression a bit in order to maintain U.S. economic and military aid (Barbosa, 1977: 302; Stephansky and Helfeld, 1977: 12).[19]

Both the peasant leagues and the small base communities which have been badly crippled but still function, and the Committee of Churches (moving cautiously but swiftly with strong international support during this latest period of decompression), have all had much more impact on the churches themselves than on the political and economic system. Church leaders and personnel now sense the impact of the repressive nature of the Stroessner regime more than in previous periods, since the most recent attacks have been directed primarily at their own institutions and at clerical and lay personnel. The Catholic hierarchy has clearly committed itself to continue these new social and religious programs as integral parts of the mission of the church, and in so doing are making the institution more credible than before in the eyes of the vast majority of poor in the country.

The peasant leagues and cooperatives may be smashed, and this fate could also await the new Committee of Churches if Stroessner feels it is getting out of hand and when the recent focus of international attention on Paraguay subsides. The small base communities, bible study groups, and catechetical and deacon training programs, however, will probably be defended more vigorously by the churches since they are easier to justify on specifically religious grounds, and also receive very little foreign financial support compared to the other social projects. As in Chile and Brazil, these small groups are breeding grounds for future local leaders who learn to exercise their rights of social participation in surrogate fashion under church auspices. The sense of dignity and critical awareness of poor people is being kept alive, and in the long run this is far more deleterious to Stroessner's totalitarian regime than food, clothing, medicines, or legal aid programs sponsored by foreigners.

## *IV. Bolivia: Justice and Peace Commission and Permanent Assembly of Human Rights*

Official Church opposition to the military regime in Bolivia since 1971, as in the case of Brazil, has been slow in developing. In many ways religious opposition to the Bolivian government is similar to the Chilean case, where far more significant action on behalf of human rights has occurred at lower levels of the Church and in an ecumenical context.

When General Hugo Banzer overthrew the populist-leftist military government of General Juan José Torres in August 1971, the Catholic bishops accepted the new regime with relative calm. They lamented the killing, arrests, and deportations which occurred, but expressed hope that the new government would restore order, and affirmed that church buildings were rightful places of asylum for politically persecuted persons (CEP, 1976: 22). But throughout 1972 the military did not respect this ancient right of asylum in churches, and on several occasions houses of bishops, priests, and nuns were searched, and persons there seeking help were arrested. In addition, 18 foreign priests and three Protestant pastors were expelled from the country. Several bishops on their own expressed public criticism of the government for raiding church buildings, but the 22-man Episcopal Conference (half of whom are foreigners themselves[20]) said nothing.

Although political parties, labor unions, and the press were not as severely repressed in Bolivia in the immediate aftermath of the coup as they were in Chile, during 1972 there were countless number of arrests (especially in mining, working-class, and union organizations), and torture and detentions without charge were widespread. After a Jesuit priest was arrested in January 1973, a public letter was signed by 99 priests, nuns, and Protestant pastors strongly attacking the government for these abuses of power, and also criticizing the Catholic hierarchy for their silence as a group in regard to these violations (CEP, 1976: 53). At about the same time, a group of Catholic laity and priests convinced the bishops to set up a Justice and Peace Commission (similar to the one begun in Brazil in 1972). This organization was endorsed by the Bolivian Episcopal Conference, but not constituted as an official organ of the Church. Rather, it was to be primarily the work of the laity. Dr. Luis Aldolfo Salinas, the last civilian to hold the office of president of the country in 1969, was named its first president (CEP, 1976: 67).[21]

Although originally established primarily as a reflection group to study social and economic questions in the light of the Church's social teachings, this group quickly moved into human rights work as a result of popular needs and pressures. It was soon inundated with petitions for legal aid by families seeking the whereabouts of kin who had been arrested or had disappeared. As a result, over the next two years the Justice and Peace Commission expanded its activities to include habeas corpus petitions to the courts for missing persons and material relief for their families. It also established offices in five regions outside La Paz and received financial assistance from Church-sponsored organizations in the U.S. and Western Europe. In turn it became the most reliable source of information on violations occurring within Bolivia upon which international human rights groups (such as Amnesty International) have based their reports.

In addition, it also engaged in other activities affecting sensitive political issues embarrassing to the government. It published over 301 articles in the press on human rights and pressured the government to issue a general amnesty for political prisoners. Public prayer vigils and fasts in criticism of government policies were also organized (CEP, 1976: 150). Furthermore, in February 1975, the Commission published a book recounting a massacre of 100 peasants near Cochabamba perpetrated by the military one year before.

This occurred three months after a major new wave of repression. In November 1974, the government issued a decree outlawing all public political activities and strikes, placing parties in recess, removing current leaders of all labor, professional and student organizations, postponing elections scheduled for 1975, and imposing mandatory public service on all citizens over 21 years of age. In the face of this repression, the Justice and Peace Commission stood out as the last remaining critical public voice against the government. The military expelled two foreign priests working closely with the Commission and threatened the bishops with possible expulsion of 14 more foreign clerics if they did not reorganize the Justice and Peace Commission to stop its involvement in political affairs. Although a committee of the Episcopal Conference had criticized the November decrees as "totalitarian" and contrary to the social principles of the church regarding basic human rights (CEP, 1976: 132), as a group the bishops acquiesced to official demands. The government had closed down a church-operated radio station in the mining region in January, and had also conducted further raids on bishops' houses in La Paz and Santa Cruz. In the context of this mounting attack on Church-affiliated organizations and personnel and in light of the heavy dependence of the Church on foreign clergy, the bishops opted for a strategy of conciliation with the military and placed the Justice and Peace Commission in a state of recess (CEP, 1976: 161).[22]

Throughout 1975 mounting student and labor unrest and mining strikes occurred despite the government ban on political activities. The Conference of Religious Orders of Men and Women in Bolivia petitioned the bishops to assist the striking miners who had been fired, and in April in their monthly bulletin published an analysis of the loss of purchasing power and real income by miners, workers and peasants due to currency devaluation, inflation, and controls on wages (CEP, 1976: 95, 186). In late July three foreign nuns were expelled from the country for purportedly engaging in subversive political activity.

Finally, in December 1976, the Episcopal Conference issued its first collective public criticism of the Banzer government. It criticized the very skewed distribution of wealth and unfair wage policies of the regime which made the poor bear a disproportionate part of the cost of development. The bishops also attacked the model of the state being constructed by the military which prolonged economic injustices by not allowing for adequate social participation by miners, peasants, and workers (Centro de Proyección Cristiana, 1977: 22).

In the same month, representatives of the Lutheran and Methodist Churches and a priest from the Conference of Religious Orders of Men and Women met with several lay persons to form the Permanent Assembly of Human Rights in Bolivia. This ecumenical organization included in its stated goals the sensitizing of public opinion regarding human rights, the circulation of documents of reflection on statism and national security, and the defense of structures of participation (parties, unions, workers' and peasants' organizations) (Asamblea Permanente, 1976; USCC, 1978a). The Assembly received the blessing of both Cardinal Maurer of Sucre and Archbishop Manrique of La Paz, although it was not formally tied to Catholic and Protestant church structures. It immediately moved to establish financial ties with Protestant funding agencies in Europe, and by August 1977, had set up legal aid service for prisoners and their families, as well as for miners fired from their jobs for striking and union activities. Similar to the former Justice and Peace Commission, it established regional offices in several other cities of the country, but with more financial assistance and staff than its predecessor. In its publications it listed names of those killed in the last six years and has cited documented evidence of violations of such basic rights as the right to work, the right to education, the right to organize unions, the right to habeas corpus, and a fair trial (Asamblea Permanente de los Derechos Humanos de Bolivia, 1977). It also has urged general amnesty for all political prisoners and those in exile.

One major reason the Permanent Assembly has been able to continue its activities is that General Banzer in late 1977 announced that there would be general elections in July 1978. Banzer has been conscious of U.S. interest and pressure to see democratic procedures reestablished in the country. This has made it harder for the government to repress dissent with the same amount of force as in 1975. In addition to the Permanent Assembly, many political, labor, and professional organizations have been active recently in pressuring the government to allow political exiles to return to the country for the election campaign. In late December six miners' wives, whose husbands are among this group (which numbers over 15,000), began a hunger strike in the Chancery of the Archdiocese of La Paz. The strike soon spread to student, professional, and labor organizations in more than nine cities of the country totaling more than 1,000 people (Latin America Political Report, 1978d: 12; Lucha, 1978: 21).

The Permanent Assembly provided material support for the strikers and publicized their demands in newspaper ads (Asamblea Permanente de los Derechos Humanos de Bolivia, 1978).[23] Many of the participants gathered in churches in various dioceses. When troops invaded several of these buildings in La Paz and arrested clerical and lay participants of the movement, Archbishop Manrique threatened to place the archdiocese under a three-day interdict and excommunicate those conducting the attacks (Latin America Political Report, 1978c: 29). On January 18th General Banzer gave in to the demands of the hunger strike. He announced amnesty for all political exiles and prisoners. He also said he would make no reprisals against hunger strikers or their supporters, would release the 200 people already under arrest for having taken part in the movement, and lift the ban on trade union activities. Public attention focused on preparing for the July elections and the hope for a civilian victory at the polls.[24]

Thus, church activities for human rights since 1971 in Bolivia have been variegated and at times less than consistent. Only when the property or religious personnel of the institution have been under direct attack have the bishops been willing to confront the state openly, and then only on certain occasions. The traditional conservative orientation of the bishops, the lack of strong social commitment before the military coup and the heavy dependence on foreign clergy have all made the hierarchy rather cautious in their defense of civil, social, and economic rights.

However, the clerics and religious at lower levels of the Catholic Church, especially in combination with lay Catholic and Protestant groups, have been able to mount some effective opposition to repression. Precisely because there is significant international pressure (particularly from the United States) on the regime (Latin America Political Report, 1978a),[25] as well as some effective domestic secular opposition to the government, the strategies of the Permanent Assembly and other church leaders have been able to make some gains for civil and social rights.

The impact of those activities of the former Justice and Peace Commission and the current Permanent Assembly has perhaps been as problematic for the churches as for the government. Some Catholic bishops supported the efforts of the Permanent Assembly in the hunger strike, but these involved direct attacks on the churches themselves, and the government was in a much weaker position than before due to domestic and international pressures. The past record of the bishops, however, provides little evidence to believe the hierarchy will now become a consistent defender of civil, social, and economic rights of oppressed miners and peasants.

Furthermore, the actions of both the Justice and Peace Commission and the Permanent Assembly have precipitated some public divisions in the Catholic Church. In 1974, in 1977, and most recently during the 1978 hunger strike, a small group of diocesan clergy (predominantly Bolivians) issued public criticisms of religious order priests (overwhelmingly of foreign origin) for becoming involved in politics and importing foreign ideology into the country. In addition, after the hunger strike a representative of the Latin American Anti-Communist Confederation (a right-wing Catholic organization headquartered in Mexico) visited Bolivia. In a press conference he accused Archbishop Manrique of being responsible for communist infiltration in the Bolivian Catholic Church. The government media gave considerable attention to these incidents, although the number of both diocesan clergy and conservative laity ready to assist in this campaign against church leaders and foreign priests involved in human rights activities in the country is relatively small (El Diario, 1978a, b).

Finally, unlike the churches in Chile, Brazil, and Paraguay, the Bolivian Church does not yet enjoy a significant network of small base communities which can act as training grounds for indigenous lay leaders. This means that the church must still depend heavily on foreign clergy to run its pastoral programs in the near future. This makes it particularly vulnerable to government attack. It also means that it cannot serve as an instrument for social participation and consciousness-raising at the local level with the same effectiveness as do several other national churches in the subcontinent.

For all of these reasons, although some significant changes have occurred (especially in recent years), chronic structural weaknesses and contradictions persist in the Bolivian Church. These severely limit its capacity to act as a consistent force promoting human rights, except in certain crisis situations.

## *V. Argentina: The Ecumenical Movement for Human Rights and the Permanent Assembly for Human Rights*

Church responses to human rights violations in Argentina since the military coup in 1976 have been somewhat different from other countries in the southern region. Although church leaders have spoken out against abuse of power and formed or participated in ecumenical organizations to promote human rights, their actions to date have been more circumscribed and their effectiveness more limited than that of their counterparts in neighboring countries. This is due mainly to the distinctive political situation and climate of insecurity which still prevails in the country.

In the late 1960s and early 1970s armed leftist movements emerged to oppose the military regime which took power in 1966—for example, the Montoneros and the People's Revolutionary Army (ERP). Through ransom from kidnappings, money stolen from banks, and assistance from abroad, these organizations formed the best equipped and most effective guerrilla movement in Latin America by 1973. The withdrawal of the military from power in March 1973, and the subsequent return of Juan Perón, proved a disillusionment for the left. Two months after his death they resumed their armed struggle in September 1974. During the year-and-a-half rule of Isabel Perón, the country experienced severe economic difficulties, with inflation reaching an annual rate of 700% by March 1976. After 1974, however, a state of siege was also imposed with more than 3,000 persons placed in preventive detention. Private death squads, some of which were financed or assisted by the government itself, began to operate with impunity and were responsible for a large proportion of the 1,500 assassinations which occurred during the eighteen months following Perón's death. The most infamous of these groups is the Argentine Anti-Communist Alliance (AAA), which has very close ties to the police and is responsible for over 300 murders in 1974 alone (Amnesty International, 1976b: 7).

Given this climate of terror, insecurity, and economic disruption, many Catholic bishops publicly welcomed and promised support to the government which took power in March 1976 (CELADEC, 1977: 40). The Church itself had suffered serious internal divisions during the late 1960s and early 1970s, when a group of several hundred priests actively opposed the former military regime and publicly urged major structural changes in the direction of a socialist economy. This movement had some positive impact on several bishops, but clashed with others (Dodson, 1973).[26] By 1974 the organization had disbanded (itself suffering some of the attacks by the right wing death squads), and the leadership of the Episcopal Conference was under the control of conservatives who welcomed the return of the military.

In the months following the March coup, however, several events precipitated action by church leaders on behalf of civil and political rights. The waves of killings and disappearances continued, and by November 1976 the deaths totaled over 1,200 (CELADEC, 1977: 34). These were perpetuated by both the left and the right. Many of those being persecuted and fired from their jobs flocked to churches for assistance and provided clear evidence to church personnel of systematic use of torture by the military to extract information. By the end of the year at least 25 Catholic and Protestant clergy had been arrested and ten others assassinated by right-wing death squads (Argentina Outreach, 1977: 16). Bishop Enrique Angelelli of La Rioja was killed mysteriously while collecting evidence concerning the deaths of two priests in his diocese who had been active in programs assisting the poor (Catholic Institute for International Relations, 1976: 5).[27]

Amidst this continuing violence and persecution of the churches themselves, the Catholic hierarchy issued a pastoral letter in May 1976 condemning abuses of power. The bishops denied that the welfare of the state was above the rights of individuals, and criticized the government for prolonged detentions, torture, denial of habeas corpus, and firing of workers for political reasons. They also stated that forcing others to go hungry "in order to gain unreasonable profit" was wrong, and that halting inflation too hurriedly at the expense of workers was a cardinal sin. The bishops, however, gave recognition to the delicate situation of the country and also condemned revolutionary uprising and "Marxist solutions to our problems" (USCC, 1976a: 18-19).

Two months later representatives of Catholic and Protestant churches formed the Ecumenical Movement for Human Rights (MEDH), an organization established to aid families of kidnapped persons and assist all those suffering the effects of "political and economic terrorism and indiscriminate repression." It included in its stated goals the preparation of documents concerning human rights violations, the formation of a body of lawyers to provide legal aid to those arrested and families of the disappeared, and the communication with prisoners and other detainees (Movimiento Ecuménico por los

Derechos Humanos, 1976). It also has sought some financial assistance from international Catholic and Protestant organizations, but not to the extent as similar committees in Bolivia, Paraguay, and Chile. In Argentina, any group with large amounts of outside funding is suspected of being a siphon for guerrilla support.

In addition to this ecumenical group, another organization to defend human rights was established in late 1975 by some Protestant and Catholic leaders along with intellectuals, professionals, and party representatives. This committee, known as the Permanent Assembly for Human Rights (APDH), documents cases of disappearances, presents legal petitions to the courts on behalf of those detained, and writes public letters to General Videla seeking investigations as to the whereabouts of those who are missing (Brewin et al., 1976).[28] It has neither sought, nor received, substantial amounts of international funding for its activities.

To date, the accomplishments of these two Church-related organizations have not been nearly as effective or publicized as the activities of ecumenical committees in Chile, Paraguay, and Bolivia. The Permanent Assembly has gathered well-documented evidence on cases of disappeared persons and the use of torture, and has sought redress for victims of repression in the courts and from Videla himself (Buenos Aires Herald, 1977: a, b; Latinamerica Press, 1977a). The Ecumenical Movement has, in addition to offering legal aid, provided access to emergency relief for families of prisoners and the disappeared. There has been, however, very little response on the part of the courts and the government to legal petitions or requests by church leaders for investigations (Latin America Political Report, 1978b: 38).[29] There is good reason to believe that Videla himself does not wield effective control of the military and that strong right-wing elements in the armed forces and police act independently to perpetrate murder and torture. Conservative business groups seem to support these elements, and very repressive economic measures continue against workers and unions.

Furthermore, guerrilla activities also continue and Videla uses this argument to justify further repression. In addition, over 60 lawyers have been assassinated since 1974, along with countless union and party leaders and those engaged in social programs assisting the poor. This in turn has forced Church-sponsored human rights organizations to act with extreme caution and keep a relatively low profile.

The impact of these new Church-sponsored organizations has sensitized church leaders to the chronic problem of repression, and has provided them with substantial documentation that kidnapping, murder, and torture originate more from government security forces than from guerrilla action. The hierarchy issued a second pastoral letter in May 1977, partly as a result of this information, condemning these abuses by the government and criticizing violations of workers' rights to work, to health care, and to education. While reaffirming their rejection of Marxism, the bishops also stated that this does not justify branding as Marxists all who work for justice on behalf of the poor (USCC, 1977a: 26, 27, 29).

Work for civil and political rights or for basic social assistance to the poor has precipitated continued attacks on church personnel. By December 1977 some 30 priests were in jail in Argentina, and at least 17 have been murdered by security forces (Latin America Political Report, 1977). In this sense, the Argentine situation resembles the Brazilian case of direct frontal attack on the churches themselves. The Argentine bishops, however, have been far more willing to communicate with the government and try to exercise influence behind the scenes than have their Brazilian counterparts. They still have hopes for Videla (a devout Catholic), they fear further reprisals from right-wing security forces, and are aware of the continued presence of guerrilla activities in the country. The Catholic Church in Argentina has not yet established a firm network of small base communities for evangelization and social participation which characterize the Chilean, Brazilian, and Paraguayan churches.

For all these political and religious reasons, the impact to date on human rights activities by Argentine churches has been the least effective of all other church groups in the subcontinent. The Catholic Church remains a weak and underdeveloped institution, with no past history of strong social commitment by the hierarchy. While it is slowly becoming sensitized to human rights issues as these directly affect its clergy and laity, the present prospects for the Church promoting civil, social, and economic rights are modest at best.

## *VI. Conclusions*

Although there are characteristics peculiar to each of these new church pastoral and social organizations in the five countries, some common patterns can be identified. These pertain to the three issues raised in the introduction to this paper: (1) how and why churches have become involved in human rights activities in the subcontinent; (2) the scope and extent of their work; and (3) the impact of these new structures both on society and the churches themselves.

All five cases indicate that church programs for human rights are basically reactive strategies, responding to unforeseen crises in secular society. The policy of promoting human rights (although legitimized in the Medellín documents of 1968) did not become a conscious priority of any of the national hierarchies until they were stimulated to act by pressures from below in their own churches or from outside the ecclesiastical institutions. In some cases the killing of clergy moved the bishops to set up emergency programs; in others, direct attacks on already existing church programs benefiting the poor moved them. In many situations, however, the response came from general public pressure, as many people had nowhere else to go for help and the churches were the last remaining organizations with any relative degree of freedom to act.

In all these countries the international linkages of the churches gave them an important capacity for action. Access to finances and material support in both Western Europe and the United States enabled them to begin humanitarian projects to assist the persecuted. In turn, the information on rights violations to which religious personnel had access by direct experience could be effectively and swiftly communicated through the international network of the churches themselves. Without such ability to transfer money, material, and information across national borders, these new Church-sponsored programs could not have been begun nor sustained.

Some of these churches are clearly learning from one another and making efforts to share experiences and strategies within the southern tier region itself. This process is facilitated by the growing network of communication and exchange of religious and lay personnel across national borders, which makes churches one of the few effective private transnational actors in the region capable of counteracting the international reach of the military. The growing ecumenical cooperation between Catholics and Protestants in Latin America also enhances the structural capacities of all Christian denominations to combine efforts and promote rights activities. In fact, much of the financing for these new human rights committees in Catholic countries comes from Protestant sources in Western Europe and North America.

Regarding the scope and extent of activities of these new programs, it is clear that most of the aid they provide goes for the defense of classic civil rights—the right of habeas corpus, the right to a fair trial, the right to be protected against torture. A broad consensus exists on the legitimacy of these individual rights—especially among funding agencies in Europe and the United States. The programs are also able to perform humanitarian functions, such as allowing prison visits, improving the living situation in jails, enhancing communication between those detained and their families, and providing food, clothing, and health care for families. In some instances (such as the Chilean, Brazilian, and Paraguayan cases), churches have been able to promote some social and economic rights; for example, the right to work or the right to participate in social organizations of one's own choice.

In no case, however, have churches been able by themselves to affect major changes in the political and economic structures underlying or causing the violations of civil, social, and economic rights. Where changes have occurred in patterns of repression (e.g., in Paraguay), they have been due primarily to pressures by foreign governments, or in conjunction with foreign pressure and activity by both religious and secular domestic forces within the countries themselves (e.g., in Bolivia). Even in such cases, it is too soon to predict whether a fundamental reorientation of political and economic institutions will occur, or whether this "decompression" is merely a transitory concession. Furthermore, where military regimes are strongly entrenched and unyielding to foreign and domestic opposition to their policies (e.g., in Chile and Brazil), not even momentary amelioration has been achieved by the churches.

What these human rights committees and other new pastoral programs of the churches among the poor have accomplished over the past several years, however, is to sensitize many bishops, clergy, and religious to the close relationship between the existing unequal arrangement of economic and political power and the systematic violation of civil rights of individuals and groups. In almost all of the major episcopal documents on human rights originating from the subcontinent recently, there has been a strong appeal for changes in basic institutional structures and more equitable distribution of wealth and resources in order to remove the causes of murder, torture, and kidnapping.

The bishops see very clearly that those being persecuted are predominantly spokespersons for the poor or working-class leaders themselves. A major reason for their being attacked, claim the bishops, is their demand that society meet the basic human needs of their people in a more just fashion—employment, housing, education, and health care. Now that guerrilla activity has subsided significantly throughout the region, the primary reason for repression is that the poor are demanding social and economic rights. The hierarchies, therefore, emphasize the necessity to affect changes in economic development models based on national security ideology and manipulated by elites toward other strategies of development, which include more equitable distribution of land and income as they proceed. They also stress the importance of allowing intermediary structures of social and political participation (e.g., labor unions, political parties, civic and professional associations or neighborhood groups) between the state and the individual, both to affect such changes and to provide accountability of power.

Despite these arguments on the close interrelationship of defense of civil rights, fulfillment of human needs, and responsible uses of power, there is no indication that the bishops' words are, or will be, taken seriously in the near future by those controlling economic resources or wielding coercive authority. But such pronouncements nevertheless are important because they provide an alternative moral perspective and force which challenges the legitimacy and pervasiveness of national security ideology underlying all of these rights violations. An important power of the Church, therefore, lies at the deeper ideological and spiritual level. The influence is potentially very great, since Christianity is deeply embedded in Latin American culture, and people, even if they do not practice their religion regularly, still have emotional ties to the Church. This is particularly true for middle class groups and the poor themselves. Not only have the hierarchies refused to give complete legitimation to national security regimes (as they often did to earlier authoritarian or oligarchic governments in Latin America), but the latent moral force of the church (which is most notable in crisis situations) is helping to prevent the values and symbols of this new secular ideology from gaining complete public acceptance.

In addition to this moral contribution to the defense of human rights in the subcontinent, the other most significant accomplishment by the Church at the domestic level has been to provide alternate forms of participation which can nourish a critical consciousness as well as a spirit of resistance among Indians, peasants, and workers. The new small communities and other lay training programs in the churches are acting as social incubators for future generations of leaders of the poor, and are providing them with a sense of hope and solidarity. These organizations are counterproductive to the efforts by dictatorial regimes attempting to construct a new model of society and new type of person completely dominated by state power and terror. In the long run, these are probably the most significant contributions Latin American churches are making to affect eventual structural transformations and return to democratic procedures. In the very least, they are blunting the impact of repression generated both by the military and economic elites to maintain their power.

In an immediate sense, the impact of these new programs on the churches themselves has been profound. In some instances the programs have precipitated outright persecution which reaches the highest level of church leadership. This has helped to sensitize many bishops to the plight of the lower clergy, religious, and working-class laity in a way that otherwise would not have been possible. Further, these experiences are making them aware, for the first time, that the real threat to the institutional interests of the Church comes from the right and not the left. It is shifting the priorities of the Church to a closer identification with the poor, since these people make the most pressing demands on the Church's time and resources, while showing the greatest willingness to participate in its new evangelical efforts.

Serious internal tensions and contradictions have resulted from these new directions in the Church which place important limits on how far efforts to defend human rights can go. Upper-middle-class groups, reactionary Catholics, and military officers are by and large outraged at this betrayal by church leaders of their interests. These groups wield considerable influence not only in secular society but within the church itself, since they still provide significant financial support for other Church-sponsored activities—schools, hospitals, charity funds, and the like. They can also mount effective terror campaigns against church personnel (as witnessed by TFP activities in Chile, Brazil, and Argentina), while exploiting internal divisions in the hierarchy and clergy.

A primary Catholic concern (reinforced strongly by the Vatican) is to maintain the public unity of the institution at all possible costs, while remaining open to minister to the spiritual needs of all classes of people. The Catholic Church has traditionally opted for a church rather than sect model of religious development, and this places theological limitations on its prophetic capacities as well as on its ability to represent the interests of any one social group forcefully and consistently. Both political and religious factors, therefore, influence the official policies of churches as articulated by bishops. They do not want to alienate elite groups any more than necessary, and are not likely to write them off on behalf of human rights programs which bring an all-out conflict between the Church and secular power.

Furthermore, as was seen in the case of Bolivia in relation to the clergy, and in Chile and Argentina in regard to money, international sources of support for human rights programs create some problems for the Church at the domestic level. Not only are some indigenous groups within the local churches suspicious of those with access to resources (and therefore, power) from abroad, but the military governments of these countries are sensitive to foreign influences due to their exaggerated sense of nationalism. While this dependency of the churches has not yet become a major limitation on church programs, it certainly has caused tension. It is also probable that this vulnerability in terms of foreign personnel and finances will be another factor keeping bishops from allowing an all-out confrontation between Church and state on behalf of human rights.

Finally, despite recent commitments to the interests of the poor and new working-class receptiveness to church activities and participation, all of the churches in the southern region have only begun the process of penetrating and understanding lower-class culture. Small base communities are just beginning to take root, and the vast majority of poor still have very little formal contact with the churches. Churches are, on the whole, very underdeveloped institutions in this area. It will be some time before new communities can function effectively and autonomously sufficient to withstand sustained frontal attacks on their personnel by repressive governments.

The important factor, however, is that these new programs have started to operate. Moreover, given the clear intentions of the military to stay in power for a long time, the programs analyzed here are more than short-term emergency efforts. If both international pressure and cautious diplomacy by the bishops can prevent prolonged Church-state confrontations, they may very well grow stronger. Such new grassroots structures could be important instruments for bringing about long-term change in both Church and society. The Church, therefore, while not a consistent or strong defender of rights, provider of needs, or instrument of power, does wield some crucial moral and structural influence in this region of the continent—influence which may be quite significant for the future direction of these societies.

## NOTES

1. The protection of national security has been emphasized by these military regimes in their attempts to provide themselves with a sense of legitimacy and justification for systematic repression. National security ideology includes among its major components anti-Marxism, patriotism, technocratic value-free planning, and the subordination of personal rights to the interests of the state.

2. Several international organizations have documented these violations on the basis of on-site fact-finding investigations and personal testimonies of individuals or groups within these Latin American countries. Included are Amnesty International, the International League of Human Rights, the International Commission of Jurists, the Commission on Human Rights of the United Nations Economic and Social Council, and the Inter-American Commission on Human Rights. Amnesty International, for example, it its 1975-1976 annual report, indicated that 80% of all reported incidents of serious torture to date have occurred in Latin America.

3. Two very useful collections of 14 of these documents have recently been published in English by the Latin American Documentation Service of the U.S. Catholic Conference. See references for individual citations in the LADOC "Keyhole" Series.

Mitchell (1977) provides an excellent summary of the general analysis and principles laid out in these documents regarding the interrelationship of human rights, human needs, and political and economic power.

4. This new emphasis in the Church towards service of the world, especially the poor, was officially endorsed in the documents of the Second Vatican Council (1962-1965), as well as by the Latin American bishops themselves in their second General Conference held in Medellín, Colombia, in August 1968. At this meeting, representatives of every episcopal conference in Latin America committed the Church to act as a "catalyst in the temporal realm in an authentic attitude of service." As pastors they dedicated themselves "to denounce everything which, opposing justice destroys peace," "to defend the rights of the poor and oppressed," and "to encourage and favor efforts of the people to create and develop their own grass-roots organizations for the consolidation of their rights and the search for justice."

5. Although Paraguay has not recently come under military rule, the twenty-four-year-old military government of General Stroessner in the last two years has escalated its repressive measures considerably against *campesino* leaders. The Paraguayan churches responded to this recent increase in terror by setting up an Emergency Committee on Human Rights.

Despite systematic violation of human rights by the Uruguayan government since the 1973 civil-military coup, religious groups have not been able to establish programs to promote human rights comparable to those in sister churches in other areas of the Southern Cone. The reasons for this are due to the long-standing weakness of the Uruguayan Church, the heavily secularized culture in Uruguay, and the effective neutralization of the Church by an alliance among conservative Catholics, the press, and the military.

In Peru, the military have not been guilty of violations of human rights (especially civil rights) to the same degree as their counterparts in Brazil, Chile, Argentina, Paraguay, Bolivia, and Uruguay. In the last two years, however, very repressive social and economic measures (particularly against workers in the form of wage controls and restrictions of union activities) have occurred. While the Church has not felt it necessary to establish human rights committees specifically to meet the needs of prisoners or families of disappeared persons, the bishops have begun to criticize severely the economic policies of the government along the same lines as the hierarchies in Brazil, Chile, and Argentina.

6. Two bishops were responsible for inaugurating this commission—Auxiliary Bishop Fernando Ariztía of the Western Zone of the Catholic Archdiocese of Santiago and Bishop Helmut Frenz of the Lutheran Church of Chile. Both men had been particularly active in programs helping poor before the coup and had been exposed to many cases of cruelty against their people in the days immediately following September 11th. Frenz was also a German and had direct access to immediate funding from Western Europe, including the World Council of Churches in Geneva. Both of these men urged other Catholic, Protestant, and Jewish leaders to join them (including Cardinal Silva), and together they formally established the Committee of Cooperation for Peace on October 6, 1973. Ariztía and Frenz served as cochairpersons.

7. Between October 1973 and December 1975, the various projects sponsored or assisted by funds coming through the Committee for Peace reached over 100,000 persons needing legal, medical, or economic assitance in addition to those workers assisted by 126 small enterprises set up in various parts of the country (U.S. Congress, House, 1976: 59).

8. Many of the self-help projects in these local communities (e.g., soup kitchens) are also assisted by the Vicariate of Solidarity.

9. Not only did high inflation, corruption, and incompetence characterize the democratic regime of Joaõ Goulart between 1961 and 1964, but many in the country felt that communists had a strong possibility of taking over the country as a result of this turmoil. With the exception of Chile and Cuba, the Brazilian left was the best organized Marxist movement in Latin America in the early 1960s, especially in rural areas of the northeast.

10. Between 1966 and 1971 several conflicts between the government and some bishops and priests occurred when the latter began to criticize publicly the economic policies of the government, which favored industrial development at the expense of social programs to assist the poor in interior regions. By 1969 eleven foreign priests had been expelled (of over 5,000 in the country) and one priest closely associated with Dom Helder Camara had been assassinated.

11. An English translation of the section dealing with repression and torture appears in LADOC Volume I, No. 13 (June, 1970).

12. "Operation Hope," begun by Dom Helder Camara, is one of the best-known examples of grassroots self-help programs in Northeastern Brazil. Begun in 1967, it has sponsored projects in literacy training, housing, health, and recreation in 13 urban and rural communities in the Recife-Olinda diocese. Materials and salaries for specialists are provided by the West German bishops, but most of the participants are volunteers. In addition to basic humanitarian aid, there has been a consistent emphasis on raising the social consciousness of the people. Small group discussions of community problems, identification of desirable social and economic objectives, and petitions to local authorities for better services have all become integral parts of this program.

13. Thousands of Indians and peasants have been living on these lands for years and therefore qualify by law for ownership. Nevertheless, they have never obtained legal titles from the government and now are being evicted, and in some cases murdered, by both security forces and private land developers.

14. This situation of "decompression," begun after President Ernesto Geisel took office in 1974, was only in part due to urging by the Church. The accumulated effects of rapid economic growth (primarily favoring the upper- and middle-income sectors) and organized terrorism since 1968 have solidified the power of the government. The present administration could easily afford to ease up on some of the repression and make concessions, as none of these changes would create a serious threat to military power, and tight control is still maintained over the major decision-making centers of society.

15. Security dossiers are now prepared on bishops and priests identified with these new Church-sponsored communities and programs. Among the questions included in the two-page questionnaire to be completed by police agents are: Does the bishop or priest try to disfigure the person of Christ? Does he try to disfigure the person of God? Does he talk about *comunidades de base?*

16. A priest with first-hand knowledge of deacon programs told me of his admiration for the men training to be deacons who return to groups time and time again even after being arrested and tortured.

17. One of the key government strategies used to discredit the churches is to accuse priests and ministers of betraying their ministry and acting as guerilla priests and ministers of betraying their ministry and acting as guerilla agents. The chief of the security police, Pastor Coronel, made a report to the Colorado Party in 1976 naming several missionaries as conspirators in a clandestine movement known as the OPM (Organización Político Militar). In addition, the government has produced a number of popular pamphlets and catechisms to be used in religious classes in public schools in which communism is presented as the cardinal sin for Christians, and images and activities of "bad priests" are sketched and rejected as being against true religion (Ministerio de Educación y Culto, 1977a, b).

18. In February, 1977, Cardinal Evaristo Arns of São Paulo, Brazil, personally visited the office of the Committee of Churches for Emergency Aid in a spirit of fraternal solidarity, only the third Roman Catholic Cardinal ever to visit the country. He held a press conference with Archbishop Rolon of Asunción, and both praised the committee publicly for its important work.

Other Protestant and Catholic church persons from Western Europe and North America have also visited the committee over the past two years, and thus have added to its reputation as being internationally supported in the eyes of the Paraguayan government.

19. Stephansky and Helfield in their latest report for the International League of Human Rights conclude that:

> Notwithstanding the indications of amelioration, we found no compelling evidence of change either in the overall gravity of the human rights crisis or in the character of the basic institutions underlying that crisis.
>
> Most importantly, the institutions that are at the root of the repressions of last year remain unchanged.
>
> What our mission encountered was an interlude of amelioration, a welcome one to be sure, but nevertheless an interlude to an uncertain future. There have been interludes before, of the kind we encountered, for example, in the periods that preceded episodes of repression of 1958-1959, of 1965 and of 1969, as well as the period that preceded the most recent repressions of 1975-1976. Whether the present interlude will end with another repressive episode in a continuing cycle of repression and

alleviation, or whether it can mark the beginning of an era of more durable government, will depend on governmental decisions yet to be taken [1977: 12, 17, 18].

20. Bolivia has one of the highest percentages of foreign-born priests of all Latin American churches, with 80% of the clergy coming from abroad.

21. I am most grateful to Rev. Eric de Wasseige, O.P., for much of this information on the Justice and Peace Commission of Bolivia. He worked on this commission for two years before being expelled from Bolivia in March 1975, and is now with the Washington Office on Latin America (WOLA), a Church-sponsored organization in Washington, D.C., set up by Protestant denominations in the United States to monitor human rights violations in Latin America.

22. The Commission was later reopened but placed under the direct control of the hierarchy and was constituted by a more conservative group of laity and clerics than its predecessor.

23. As the hunger strike spread, so did the demands of the participating groups. These included a withdrawal of military personnel from mining villages, restoration of union rights, and the rehiring of miners fired for strike activities.

24. Several civilian candidates competed in the July 1978 elections against the hand-picked candidate of Banzer, General Pareda Asbún. The latter won the election, but, according to reports by international observer teams, only with the help of massive fraud. Amidst mounting domestic and international pressures for a new election, a week later General Pareda Asbún engineered a counter-coup (very possibly at Banzer's suggestion). Hence, once more democratic procedures were thwarted, despite strong efforts by both domestic and international groups to the contrary.

25. Some observers in Bolivia believe that the really effective check on Banzer in early 1978 was a public remark made by the U.S. AID Director in Bolivia at that time: "President Carter believes that the Bolivian electoral process in 1978 is very important, not only for Bolivia, but for the whole of Latin America."

26. The best account of the origins and development of this organization, known as "Movement of Priests for the Third World," has been written by Dodson (1973).

27. The deaths occurred in an area of the country where the right-wing Catholic organization, "Tradition, Family and Fatherland," is active, and after Bishop Angelelli had spoken against the military coup.

28. Bishop Carlos Gattinoni of the Methodist Church was chosen as the first president of the Permanent Assembly, and Monsignors Jaime de Nevares and Enrique Angelelli (died 1976) also became members of the coordinating committee when the Assembly was formed.

29. In January 1978, the government did acknowledge that it was holding 3,700 persons and began to release some of their names. This concession, however, seems to have been the result of international pressure by the governments of France and the United States more than domestic church appeals. The French government increased diplomatic pressure in Argentina after two French nuns were kidnapped in December 1977. U.S. Secretary of State Vance made a trip to Argentina in late 1977 and also expressed this country's extreme concern over the human rights situation in Argentina. President Carter, during his visit to France in December 1977, stated publicly: "The Argentine situation is the most serious in our continent."

# REFERENCES


Amnesty International (1976a) The Amnesty International Report, 1975-1976. London: Amnesty International Publications.

——— (1976b) "Report of an Amnesty International mission to Argentina." Amnesty International Publications 6 (November 15): 7-10.

Argentina Outreach (1977) "Church members under attack." No. 2 (January-February): 16.

Asamblea Permanente de los Derechos Humanos de Bolivia (1978) "20 días de huelga de hambre!" Presencia (January 15). La Paz.

——— (1977) La declaración universal de los derechos humanos y la represión en Bolivia (October). La Paz.

——— (1976) Primera reunión de la Asamblea Permanente de los derechos humanos en Bolivia 22 (Deciembre). La Paz.

BARBOSA, R. (1978) "Issue of communism in church-state relations in Brazil." LADOC 8 (January-February): 24-27.

——— (1977) "New hope for Paraguay's prisoners." Christian Century 94 (March 30): 301-302.

BONO, A. (1977) "Cross vs. sword: Catholic aid to poor in Brazil is worsening conflict with military." Wall Street Journal (June 2): 1, 20.

BREWIN, A., L. DUCLOS and D. McDONALD (1976) "One gigantic prison." Inter-Church Committee on Chile (November). Toronto. (mimeo)

BRUNEAU, T. C. (1974) The Political Transformation of the Brazilian Catholic Church. London: Cambridge Univ. Press.

Buenos Aires Herald (1977a) "APDH seeks disappearance probe." (August 12).

——— (1977b) "Human rights assembly petitions the president." (March 23).

Catholic Institute for International Relations (1976) Death and Violence in Argentina. London: Catholic Institute for International Relations.

CELADEC [Comisión Evangélica Latinoamérica de Educación Cristiana] (1977) Iglesia Argentina: Fidelidad al evangelio? Lima: CELADEC.

CELAM [Council of Latin American Bishops] (1970) "Peace," p. 80 in Vol. 2 of The Church in the Present Day Transformation of Latin America in the Light of the Council. Bogotá: General Secretariat of CELAM.

Centro de Proyección Cristiana (1977) "Documento del episcopado Boliviano sobre la misión de la Iglesia ante la sociedad histórica del país," in Los Derechos Humanos hoy en Latinoámerica: las declaraciones y documentos de la Iglesia universal y las Naciones Unidas. Lima: Centro de Proyección Cristiana.

CEP [Centro de Estudios y Publicaciones] (1976) Bolivia: 1971-1976; Pueblo, Estado, Iglesia. Lima: CEP.

COMBLIN, J. (1977) "La doctrina de la seguridad nacional," in Dos ensayos sobre seguridad nacional. Two volumes. Santiago: Vicaría de la Solidaridad.

Comité de las Iglesias (1977a) Boletín Informativo (Asunción) (Septiembre): 1-6.

——— (1977b) Boletín Informativo (Julio): 1-6.

——— (1977c) Boletín Informativo (Mayo): 1-6.

Comité Permanente del Episcopado de Chile (1975) "Evangelio y paz." Mensaje Volume 24 (Octubre): 462-473. Santiago.

CNBB [Conferencia Nacional dos Bispos do Brasil] (1970) "Documento pastoral do

Brasilia." Revista Eclesiastica Brasiliera Volume 30 (Junho): 415-425. Brasilia.

CULHANE, E. K. (1975) "Strange alliance in Uruguay." America 17 (May).

El Diario (1978a) "Clero diocesano pronuncia sobre la misión de la Iglesia." 29 (Enero). La Paz.

——— (1978b) "Relaciones sobre la infiltración comunista en la Iglesia Boliviana." 7 (Febrero).

DODSON, M. (1973) "Religious innovation and the politics of Argentina: a study of the movement of priests for the Third World." Ph.D. dissertation. Indiana University.

DOMINGUEZ, J. (1975) "Smuggling." Foreign Policy No. 20 (Fall): 87-96, 161-164.

Estudos de CNBB (1976a) Pastoral Social, No. 10 São Paulo: Ediçaoes Paulinas.

GILFEATHER, K. (1976) "Women in ministry." America 2 (October): 191-194.

HOPE, M. (1975) "The people's priest." Lithopinion [New York] (Spring): 46-55.

Latin America Political Report (1978a) "Bolivia: delaying tactics." (February 10): 46.

——— (1978b) "Argentina: whose balloon?" 12 (February 3): 37-38.

——— (1978c) "Bolivia: the will of the people." 12 (January 27): 29-30.

——— (1978d) "Bolivia: heavens above." 12 (January 13): 12-13.

——— (1977) "Argentina: war of words." 11 (December 3): 397-399.

Latinamerica Press (1977a) "Armed band seizes members of Argentina multichurch group." 9 (December 22): 1-2.

——— (1977b) "Bishops challenge Peru's economic policies." 9 (July 21): 3, 4, 8.

——— (1975) "Government bars bishops' letter on violence in Uruguay." 7 (October 16): 1.

LERNOUX, P. (1977) "Church cowed by Uruguayan military." Report to Alicia Patterson Foundation (January 18): 8-page memo.

Lucha (1978) "Bolivian hunger strike." (January-February): 21-24. South Bend, In.

El Mercurio (1978) "La Inter-American Foundation y sus programas en Chile." 25 (Enero): 24. Santiago.

METHOL FERRE, A. (1977) "Sobre la actual ideología de la seguridad nacional," in Dos Ensayos Sobre Seguridad Nacional. Two volumes. Santiago: Vicaría de la Solidaridad.

Ministerio de educación y Culto (1977a) "Estudiano felices sin comunismo." Asunción: Ministerio de educación y culto. (mimeo)

——— (1977b) "Las verdades anticomunistas de hoy." Asunción: Ministerio de educación y Culto. (mimeo)

MITCHELL, R. A. (1977) "Latin American bishops speak: human rights, needs and power." Washington D.C.: Woodstock Theological Center. (unpublished)

Movimiento Ecuménico por los Derechos Humanos (1976) "Documento Base." 9 (Junio). Buenos Aires. (mimeo)

OVIEDO CAVADA, C. [ed.] (1974) "Declaración de comité permanente del episcopado sobre la situación del país," p. 174 in Documentos de Episcopado Chile, 1970-1973. Santiago: Ediciones Mundo.

Sociedad Chilena de Defensa de la Tradición, Familia y Propiedad (1976) La Iglesia del Silencio en Chile. Santiago: Edunsa.

STEPHANSKY, B. S. and R. J. ALEXANDER (1976) "Report of the Commission of Enquiry into human rights in Paraguay of the International League for Human Rights, July 6-15, 1976." U.S. Congress, House Subcommittee on International Organizations of the Committee on International Relations, Human Rights in Uruguay and Paraguay, 94th Congress, 2nd session: 161-218.

STEPHANSKY, B. S. and D. M. HELFELD (1977) "Denial of human rights in Paraguay: report of the second commission of enquiry of the international league for human rights." (December): 4-5. New York.

SZULC, T. (1977) "'Recompression' in Brazil." New Republic 7 (May): 19-21.

USCC [United States Catholic Conference] (1978a) "Bolivians seek democracy and freedom." LADOC (Washington, D.C.) 8, 3 (January-February): 44-47.

——— (1978b) "Sigaud versus Casaldaliga and Balduino." LADOC Volume 8, 3 (January-February): 15-23.

——— (1977a) "The Common Good and the Present Situation." Argentina Episcopal Conference. LADOC Keyhole Series 16: 23-29.

——— (1977b) "Our life as a nation." Chilean Episcopal Conference. LADOC Keyhole Series 15: 41-54.

——— (1977c) "Christian requirements of a political order." National Conference of Brazilian Bishops. LADOC Keyhole Series 16: 54-67.

——— (1976a) "A Christian reflection for the people of Argentina." LADOC Keyhole Series 15: 16-20.

——— (1976b) "Amidst persecutions and consolations." Episcopal Conference of Paraguay. LADOC Keyhole Series 15: 6-15.

——— (1976c) "Paraguay churches unite their efforts." LADOC 6, 65 (July-August): 19.

——— (1976d) "Pastoral message to the people of God." National Conference of Brazilian Bishops. LADOC Keyhole Series 15: 21-35.

U.S. Congress, House Subcommittee on International Organizations of the Committee on International Relations (1976) "Prepared statement of Jose Zalaquett Daher, chief legal council, committee of cooperation for peace in Chile," p. 59 in Chile: The Status of Human Rights and Its Relationship to U.S. Economic Assistance Programs. 94th Congress, second session.

Vicaría de la Solidaridad (1977) "Vicaría de la solidaridad: un año de labor." (Santiago) (Enero). Santiago. (mimeo)

VIDAL, D. (1978) "Paraguay enjoys old siestas and the new boom." New York Times 18 (February): 6.

WILDE, M. D. (1977) "Paraguayans savor Christian solidarity." The Christian Century 94 (March 30): 302.

*Brian H. Smith is Research Associate at the Woodstock Theological Center, Georgetown University. He has published articles on the contemporary church in Latin America and is completing his doctoral dissertation in political science at Yale University on the Chilean Catholic Church and political change from 1925 to 1978.*

**SISTER KATHERINE ANNE GILFEATHER, M. M.**
*Maryknoll Sisters*
*Maryknoll, New York 10545*

# *WOMEN RELIGIOUS, THE POOR, AND THE INSTITUTIONAL CHURCH IN CHILE*

The Church in Chile, in its efforts to reach and evangelize the poor, crippled by a gradually diminishing clergy, has over more than a decade come to place extraordinary emphasis on the presence of religious personnel in marginal urban and rural areas. This pastoral priority has induced considerable numbers of religious women to leave their original works (especially education) to take part in the direct apostolate in marginal areas, while the majority of foreign religious women who have recently arrived have opted to follow their example.

The style of life chosen by these women is simple, often in the extreme, but is in all cases a brusque change from their previous standard of living. Though these changes were necessary to achieve the desired identification with the poor, nevertheless, there have been secondary effects of this pastoral approach which require consideration and some form of evaluation at this moment in the history of the Chilean Church. It is our opinion that these women present a microcosmic reflection of the Church itself and its sincere struggle to remain faithful to its interior dynamism, which is the Spirit working through human history.

The New Testament itself gives proof that the first Christian women were proficient scholars of sacred scripture and that they assumed roles of considerable leadership; it was not, however, a participation without problems. Although the New Testament reflects a Judaic theological and sociological frame of reference with respect to women, the Pauline theology of "equality in Christ" offered a new religiousocial framework for man-woman relations in the Christian community—a truly revolutionary approach whose implications were not then understood.

Perhaps the major source of information on the status of women in the first Christian communities is found in the Acts of the Apostles. The first clue we find which throws light on the status of women in these

Journal of Interamerican Studies and World Affairs, Vol. 21 No. 1, February 1979, 129-155
© 1979 Sage Publications, Inc.

communities is contained in the story of Paul's conversion. He had asked and was given permission to arrest members of the new Church, women as well as men (Acts 9: 1-2). If women had been secure, under the dominion of their husbands in private and silenced in the churches in public, there would have been no need to persecute them. The punishment and confinement of men would have been sufficient. We see the same situation in Antiochia, Thyatira, and Beroea, where women enjoyed great influence in Christian communities. They were designated as prophets; others received authority to dedicate themselves to teaching and interpreting the central concepts of the faith. Acts abounds with data concerning the participation of early Christian women in the affairs of the community and its cultic life. There is no doubt that this participation was significant in attracting other women from every social class who became active at all levels of the institutional life of the Church.

However, the concept of "equality in Christ" was obscured in the later writings of St. Paul; what he understood as a temporal ethic of the status quo in the context of the "last days" became, two generations later, moral orientations to conserve the same status quo. Having lost the vision of an imminent kingdom, the Church was deprived also of the theology which had helped it to live in that Spirit. As a consequence, we have inherited two diverse messages: the theology of our "equality in Christ," and the day-to-day practice of the subordination of women. Efforts at reconciling these opposing concepts have brought the Church to an ambiguous position of maintaining the status quo on the one hand by a subordination of women on the social level, and an affirmation of the concept of equality as functional in the "world to come" on the other. The effect of this almost Gnostic dualism has been confusion, distortion, and the consequent elimination of feminine influence from the Church's public sphere. She might aspire to sainthood, to martyrdom, to being a teacher in the community, but could never intrude beyond the clerical pale. Women have thus been excluded from roles of equal responsibility with men in the institutional, theological, and spiritual lives of the Church, thereby impoverishing it and debilitating its pastoral action.

With the above as a statement of the situation to date, we focused our research precisely on the pastoral action of the Church in Chile and upon the most numerous sector of pastoral personnel—religious women (Catholic sisters). We chose what we felt to be a particularly creative group of these women, those living and working in marginal areas, in order to evaluate the consequences of their identification with the poor for their own lives and for the Chilean Church as a whole. Our choice created, in turn, a need to face the frustrations of these women in many areas and at all levels, and to relate this to "structures" operative in their institutional-Church relations, congregational ties, previous formation, vocational commitment, doctrinal stance, planning, schedules, and even in their attitudes toward work and play. Having described the basic content of this paper, we would now like to explore the historical evolution of the problem.

## *The Problem in its Historical Dimension*

When we speak of the dynamic of history, whether with respect to the Church or to humanity in general, we are speaking in sociological terms of social change. We would like to stress four dimensions of change—individualization, innovation, concern with power, and secularization—(Nisbet, 1970: 370-394) which we feel are basic to any discussion of social change, but seem particularly applicable to the area under discussion. The first of these is "emergence of the individual" as a focus and concern, thereby replacing the restrictive social codes and traditional communities of long duration. This poses serious challenges to the individual's relationship to religion, and to the institution of the Church, which has traditionally offered a buffer in man's relations with the larger world. The person seeking refuge against a loss of identity in that world has several options: (a) a position which affirms the world and sustains dialogue with the environment, offering the possibility of a redemptive experience; (b) a sectarian stance in search of a group whose philosophy contradicts the actual values of society in a dramatic form (Marty, 1960: 125-132); and (c) the "community" solution, which offers support rather than isolation. Experience proves that the first position is difficult; religious energies tend to be dissipated and identify with the very upheaval the individual seeks to escape. The second stance is attractive but ultimately dangerous in the light of its tendency to escapism. Only the third option offers its members mutual support, helping them achieve the goal of the first position without falling into its inherent traps. It appears to offer the shock absorber absent in the traditional institutionalized bureaucratic Church.

This option is found within the Church in Basic Christian Communities, in numerous orientation and formation groups grounded structurally on small homogeneous communities of mutual support, and also among religious communities. In great part these have rejected traditional concepts and the restrictions of antiquated and dysfunctional structures in order to search for new forms of community life in circumstances more in accord with their Gospel values. A graphic example is the case of religious women working in apostolates among marginal groups, particularly those living in urban *poblaciónes* or "shanty-towns." Their rejection of traditional structures is apparently rooted in their search for something more radical, more authentic—a simple life style in an atmosphere of mutual support. Their search has led them to ongoing innovation, which is our second dimension of change.

Over the centuries, the Church, like all institutions, has repeatedly faced the need to change in order to carry out its divine-human role and function. This need of functioning in a world in flux among men and women whose needs are profound and diverse has brought the Church to innovation, not as a *structure*, but rather through the brotherhood of its members. These people, moved by a genuine desire to make the message of Christ known and understood and, in part, by a rebellion against the dysfunctionality of Church structures and the alienation of its hierarchy from contemporary reality, have begun a voyage toward the future in search of something better. They have made new discoveries along the way simply because they were looking for "something." The place of "luck" or coincidence in the development of new concepts—that is to say, "innovation"—has been called "serendipity" among sociologists and the action of the Spirit among Christians. It is the discovery of valid results not deliberately sought, a happy surprise.

Acceptance of the essential concepts of Vatican II and of the Medellín Documents is the acceptance of the necessity of getting used to "change" as a constant in our lives. It requires a certain elasticity which would make possible the acceptance of changing circumstances without losing the sense of continuity and essential integrity. The effort to achieve this balance has been costly for the Church and its personnel. Faced with the necessity of making the Good News understandable, above all to the poor and marginal, it became obvious that many structures and methods had lost their meaning in the light of actual circumstances, and it is the responsibility of pastoral agents, religious women and priests, to confront and solve pastoral dilemmas. The investigation under consideration was begun to observe the innovations of a group of religious women who aspire to reach the marginal sectors of society through a close identification with all aspects of that lifestyle. The changes which this determination brought about in their lives, their spirituality, and their general attitude toward the Church and its structures, are the focus of this study. One such change in attitude can be observed with respect to power/authority structures in the Church.

Although Christian authority has always been based on "service," there does exist an ecclesiastical power structure which has been, up to the present, carefully limited. We have spoken for centuries of "clergy" and "laity," of "pastors" and their "flocks" which follow the voice of the Church. Vatican II restored the dignity of the lay role in a definitive form and, although implementation has been uneven throughout the Church, the importance of this role is growing steadily. Historic circumstances have placed the Church in a pastoral dilemma. Lacking clergy, she has sought among laity and religious replacements in various aspects of the priestly office. Religious women (sisters), above all in Latin American countries, carry immense responsibilities in pastoral work without enjoying even the most minimal participation in the ecclesistical power structure.

There is an ever-growing movement in the Church which insists on a more profound study of the concept of "power," which is seen as coming from God and not from the institution. Thus, the "extension of power" as a dominant consideration, the third dimension of change, has now come to be a reality in the Catholic Church. Religious personnel in close contact with pastoral problems and in charge of actual "innovations" to make the Good News vibrant can perhaps best understand and describe the ecclesiastical power structure in practice, as they are the ones who live out the consequences and feel the limitations which this structure engenders. The religious women under consideration, by their very style of life and identification with the most marginal social groups, offer a particularly interesting case study for our observation.

The last aspect of social change, secularization, is the best known. I prefer to use the Weberian concept of secularization as rationalization for the purpose of this analysis, with emphasis on the influence of rationality over the merely traditional. Above all, "secularization" is seen as the source of those values and attitudes which lead to (1) the rejection of old norms of submission, (2) a heightened esteem for the earth and matter in the context of a future life, (3) respect for the individual and for the individual and collective well-being, (4) control of the environment rather than a passive submission before it, and (5) most important, a preoccupation with the welfare of men and women here and now and not only in their transcendental dimension.

These characteristics of secularization are amply demonstrated in the pastoral action of the Chilean Church. Through the exercise of its prophetic role, in confrontation with an environment hostile to the exercise of human rights, the Church has been "the voice of those without a voice" and the hope of the masses who live in misery and hunger. The hundreds of "dining rooms" for children, only one example of the Church's social action, are in the hands of religious and other dedicated lay women. However, this preoccupation with the human condition, with suffering and despair, has its repercussions among individuals who live and work in constant contact with these groups. These are the repercussions which we probe in the lives of those religious dedicated to the marginal groups in our society—the economically deprived.

## *The Problem in its Historical-Ecclesiastical Dimension*

Even before the Vatican Council II (1961-1962), the Chilean Episcopate had begun to meet with experts and technicians in the elaboration of a Pastoral Plan for the country. This plan initiated a series of changes which even the Bishops themselves could not have foreseen.

Lamenting the lack of a global pastoral plan, the document underscored the ignorance and divorce from reality which existed within the Church, declaring that

> There is an even greater ignorance of the mission of the Church to a world in the process of rapid changes. Our generation feels called to the construction of a new temporal world and the Church is not sufficiently aware of or present to this great labor. It is ignorant of it for the most part and frequently assumes a hostile attitude toward it. The great problems of vital interest to men today do not appear to preoccupy the Church at all [Centro Bellarmino, 1962].

Nevertheless, the document insisted that "the objective of the apostolate of the Church is man and that this man lives in the world by the will of

God and for this reason must dedicate himself to the world." In the section "Guideline for Action" the document affirms:

> The most fundamental aspect of a reorganization of the apostolate in accord with actual conditions is not primarily the elaboration of a plan for the convenient management of available resources, but rather a cultural mutation, a change of attitude and of spirituality which would be directed toward a continuous theological revision based on a sociological understanding of the reality. Only in this way could rational planning be given a soul [Centro Bellarmino, 1962].

The document stressed the need for penetrating the world, above all the most abandoned sectors. This penetration was seen to require a direct confrontation with socioeconomic problems, if they were serious about giving preference to the laboring class.

Among the priorities mentioned, the plan included a general mission for the entire country during 1963. It was called the "Gran Misión" and it reached the most distant corners of the land and the most abandoned of its people through the recruiting of hundreds of religious women, seminarians, priests, and dedicated laymen and women. An anticipated consequence of this process was the conscientization of great numbers of religious for whom a hitherto unknown world had been opened. The majority, who had been dedicated to education and were largely unaware of the problems of pastoral work among the poor, now found themselves enriched by their experience, and many were convinced of a new direction in their lives.

At the same time, the Second Vatican Council had a major impact. In the third session, beginning in 1964, the Council had stated firmly that in the Gospel and in the traditional doctrine of the Church "the poor" occupied a place of preference with respect to the announcement of the message of Salvation. The texts considered at this time were among those most discussed, "The Church and the Modern World," "The Missions," "The Religious Life," and so on. These texts were received with enthusiasm and widely promulgated. Study of and reflection on these texts was very common during those years; the great majority of religious had their own copies of the Council Documents and used them for private meditation and reading.

In our opinion it was the conjunction of the Chilean Episcopal concern expressed in the Pastoral Plan (Centro Bellarmino, 1962), the experience of the Gran Misión of 1963, and the strong impact of the results of the Vatican Council II, which prepared the way for the first "experiments" with small communities of religious in the marginal areas of Santiago. Later the Medellín Documents (CELAM, 1969) would lend further support to this new innovation.

With time it was possible to perceive a growing consciousness of the poverty and misery oppressing the masses, of the structural factors perpetuating that situation, and of the urgent need for change. One could observe clear indications of a growing tendency among many religious congregations to commit themselves and their individual members to the interests of the poor, of urban and rural laborers, and to reject former commitments to the dominant and favored minorities of society. This was only a beginning, but the profound significance of this beginning would be apparent only with the passage of time and the accumulation of human experience. It was, nevertheless, a response to the challenge of Medellín directed to religious communities with respect to their mode of service:

> The particular mandate of the Lord to evangelize the poor should bring us to a distribution of our resources and apostolic personnel in such a way that effective preference is given to those sectors that are most in need, economically poor and segregated for whatever cause [CELAM, 1969; author's translation].

## *Women Living on the Margin of the Institutional Framework*

### *I. WHO SHALL BE INCLUDED?*

Our initial desire was to investigate only a sample of those religious working in *poblaciónes* and in rural apostolates throughout the country (Gilfeather, 1978). However, early in the preparations it was decided to include all of these religious with only one condition—that they live as well as work in these marginal areas. This would, of course, greatly limit the numbers involved and keep the study focused on its prime objective. A list was drawn up of 45 small communities in the Santiago area. Personal visits to each group resulted in the elimination of 13 communities whose style of living did not coincide with our criteria for a marginal situation. Thus, 32 small communities became the basis of our investigation in Santiago. Following the same procedure, 58 small communities in 18 dioceses throughout the country were contacted and the purpose of the study explained. Of this number, 50% coincided with our objectives, bringing the total number of small communities under investigation to 61. "Small communities" consisted of, on the average, three persons per house. The total number of individuals involved was 136.

### *II. THE INSTRUMENT*

Initially, our plan included private interviews with each religious woman, but preliminary visits to *poblaciónes* led us to abandon this approach. The varied schedules of these women would have meant three or four visits to each small community in order to interview each member. Time and expense factors led us to choose a more functional approach in a questionnaire which, along with two personal trips to each house for the purpose of coming to know the women, their works, and their situations, became the basis of our study.

It may be well at this point to clarify the meaning of "marginal." As used here, marginal refers to those areas inhabited by the very poor who do not enjoy the normal conveniences of those living in better neighborhoods (light, water, gas, and so on). The situation would be similar to the worst slum areas. The term has also been used to describe works or apostolates outside the normal institutional framework of the Church. As used in Chilean ministerial documents, "marginal" has been reserved for those *poblaciónes* or slum areas without any conveniences (light, water, and so on). We have been less strict here, since we feel that the concept of marginality is very relative. We refer to the effects of an all-pervasive environment, rather than to the absence or presence of certain commodities. (Anyone with first-hand knowledge of life in a *población* is well aware that one can theoretically have water but not be able to get a drop throughout the major part of a day.) In the case of rural Chile, not only are normal commodities and conveniences absent, but most cultural and recreational facilities are also lacking.

In order to determine the real level of poverty of the women in our study, it is necessary to keep in mind that we are looking at the situation from their point of view and most of them come from middle- or upper-middle classes; thus the environment of any *población* would be a serious and drastic change from their normal life situation.

## *III. THE WOMEN AND THEIR ENVIRONMENT*

Sixty two percent of these religious lived in small groups of from two to four persons, with three being the more usual size of a community. Seventy-one percent were from 30 to 50 years of age, a relatively young group except when one considers the rigors of this style of life. Education levels were especially high, as almost 70% had university degrees or at least Normal School diplomas. The majority were foreigners and 67% of them had spent less than 10 years in the country.

The largest portion of responses came from those in urban marginal sectors (69.2%), while 30.8% lived in rural areas. Over 60% had lived in a marginal sector from one to six years, while only 30% had been there longer. It is interesting to compare the years in which the majority of religious began to live in marginal areas with possible factors of influence. These coincide with the publication of the first reflections on the Medellín Documents (CELAM, 1969) and the letters and Pastoral Plan of the Chilean hierarchy (Centro Bellarmino, 1962). These last designated work among marginal sectors as top priority in the allocation of pastoral resources (1970-1974). The years of greatest influx into the marginal areas coincide with a political period which gave emphasis to the promotion of the laborer and the marginal in general, penetrating society with the mystique of the "New Man." After 1974 there is a notable decline in the number of religious women going to live in marginal areas.

It was rather more complex to identify the principal work of these women. The majority worked at more than one type of job, often combining a profession with part-time pastoral activities. Financial factors are responsible for a good part of this complexity; many religious are forced to take on remunerative work to defray the expenses which the small allotment from the diocese cannot begin to cover.

Together with the size, placement, and activities of the community, we should consider the history of the group—the path followed by each member as they came together. Only 8.8% were assigned to their present situation by superiors, while 91.2% were living in marginal areas by their own choice. It is clear that religious women are particularly sensitive to the voice of the hierarchy in Chile in the selection of apostolic activities, and ecclesiastical priorities as expressed in letters and pastoral plans had a major impact in their decisions.

This is extremely positive from the position of the institutional Church, but it is important to remember that new priorities may have unanticipated consequences, such as unwittingly damaging other works which also have their place in the pastoral life of the Church. An overly simplistic type of focus can give exaggerated emphasis to one area, making others appear old-fashioned and unworthy of approval. This seems to have been the case with the marginal apostolate: many religious decided to go out to marginal areas to be in accord with the stated pastoral priorities of the Church, without any real calling or capacity for this style of life. What better setting for later frustration?

Along with a strong desire to identify with the poor and abandoned, almost a third of our sample specified that they were led by a desire to live a more radically evangelical lifestyle in a small supportive community. This stated desire convinced us of the importance of investigating the type of spirituality present in these small groups and the potential they offer in creative planning for the religious life of the future.

What exactly is a marginal area like? Here we draw on our experiences in Santiago, Concepción, and Talca. Most houses are similar, mainly constructed of wood (very few of concrete) and quite small, with combined livingroom-dining areas, and a kitchen which is often visible as one enters. Bedrooms are extremely small, but in most cases private. In many small houses we saw the efforts of religious to keep a small room apart for meetings or visitors so that the occupants of the house might enjoy some privacy. However, this was not always possible, due to the lack of space. Furniture is extremely simple and sparse, usually of cane or cheap wood of the type found in lower-middle-class or laborers' homes. The presence of small touches of color, rag rugs or knitted cushions, plants, and colorful posters gave evidence of the interest taken in raising the morale of family members and refusal to be dominated by the depressing effect of extreme poverty. Since the houses in marginal areas are placed close together, there are no real gardens, trees, or shade; only the everpresent flower boxes in the windows and a few plants at the front gate offer a touch of green to an otherwise bleak atmosphere. For this reason, most religious women try to spend at least one day a week away from their marginal areas, seeking the recreation, fresh air, and green grass they must live without all week. The streets are unpaved and become a morass of mud and puddles during the winter season and a sea of fine dirt that fills the air and the houses in summer. Many women assured us that the daily struggle to keep themselves, the house, and the washing clean took far more time than ever before. The obvious lack of privacy was even more astounding after conversing with these women. Accustomed to a life which had contained periods of silence and tranquility, they had had to resign themselves to the noise of the *población,* the radios playing incessantly at high volumes, the crying and screams of children, the ever-present *cantinas* (bars) and their clientele; in short, to number less inconveniences which come from having to live on top of each other in conditions of extreme poverty.

## *Tensions and Frustrations*

A search for the source of tensions and frustrations in the lives of these religious women constituted one of the essential dimensions of the investigation. It was our conviction that these women were among the most highly frustrated of Church personnel. We further hypothesized that this frustration would have its roots in the misery of their environment (above all in urban settings), in their style of life, in the absence or presence of structures in their community life, in their congregational ties, and, of most interest to us here, in their relations with the institutional Church.

Our data show that the urban-rural factor is of great importance in determining the level and quality of frustration. Three Frustration Indexes showed that religious in urban marginal areas suffered in a much more exaggerated form of frustration than their rural sisters in all of the following areas: the environment and all its aspects, congregational ties and interpersonal relations, the Church (its treatment of women and the lack of sufficient financial help) the lack of structures in all aspects of life (privacy, rest, recreation, prayer, and so on), and, finally, from the rigidity of their previous spiritual formation. These women were both more conscious of and more anxious for solutions to these problems than religious women in rural areas. They felt more confronted by their environment and more obliged to give an adequate response to that confrontation. As a result, this confrontation with abject misery, unjust structures in operation, and personal impotence produced tension and the tension engendered even more frustration. Not only was the frustration level higher, but its quality was distinct. Whereas both urban and rural groups suffer from ill health, physical and mental, deficiencies in formation and professional preparation, tiredness and lack of time, only the urban group had become more highly conscious of the necessity for structures in their lives and the consequences of their absence whether with respect to prayer, recreation, or rest, and the relation of all this to their own frustration. In the rural groups frustration appeared to be more diffuse in its origins.

The relationship between frustration and structures was one of the most revealing of the study. The immense importance of such factors as overworking, exhaustion, rest, recreation, and their effects on all areas of life was clearly demonstrated by the women's responses. All these factors either required structures for their protection, or were symptoms of the lack of these structures. The previous formation of these women often made life almost impossible and added to their already rising frustration level. Religious in urban settings felt themselves judged and confronted by their own environment; they felt forced to question all the elements of their consecrated life; their poverty appeared a sham in the face of such misery, their celibacy, as previously understood, an obstacle to healing friendship. The following is an expression of the feelings of a large group of urban religious:

> Unhappily, our formation does not offer a healthy policy that would enable us to enjoy recreation and rest. There are many who think that it is less agreeable to the Lord to give oneself free time, indeed, many look down upon a sister who takes a free day for herself. For this reason we live in anxiety and nervous tension [Gilfeather, 1978].

The lack of preparation was highly correlated with frustration, and we can see the cause rather clearly with respect to a group that is so highly educated but whose education has little or nothing to do with the exigencies of the environment. As we see the numbers of religious women going out to marginal areas seriously diminishing in the past few years, we need to ask if there has been sufficient reflection upon the experience of women in the field and if their experience has been used to enrich the preparation of new candidates. Only in this way can the original traumatic situations be avoided. Without serious reflection in this area, others will be condemned to repeat the mistakes of their sisters.

### *THE INSTITUTIONAL CHURCH AND ITS CONTRIBUTION TO FRUSTRATION*

The sources of frustration with the institutional Church are varied and multiple. Central is the economic factor which is intimately related to the quality of ties between religious women and the Church. This was expressed in the following hypothesis: "The lack of concrete interest and adequate financial support on the part of the institutional Church is an added source of tension and frustration for religious in marginal situations" (Gilfeather, 1978). The data show that 92% of these religious, both from urban as well as rural areas, stated categorically that they suffer from a lack of sufficient financial support.

In the pastoral action of the Church in Chile, women have many and profound responsibilities. Nevertheless, access to levels of real authority in the ecclesiastical pyramid remains closed to them. This will be discussed in a later section, but it suffices here to emphasize that this situation is, without doubt, one of the prime sources of frustration for these religious women and one which resists all rationalizations and arguments to the contrary. Women, both religious and lay, carry heavy pastoral burdens of great responsibility but the exercise of real authority, symbolized by the priesthood, is beyond their reach.

Based on responses to our questionnaire, an Index of Frustration with the Church was constructed. Upon joining the two highest levels of frustration, we found that 75.9% of these religious felt frustration with the institutional Church. Most lived in urban marginal areas, a fact which corresponds with our original hypothesis. We also found that the younger religious were more highly frustrated than their older sisters, while the level of frustration rose steadily with the level of education. Taking nationality into consideration, North American religious were the most highly frustrated (87.5%), followed closely by the Europeans. The Spanish and other Latin Americans felt relatively lower degrees of frustration (60%), while the Chilean religious occupied an intermediate position (78%).

We have noted some correlation between the frustration of the women and their relations with the institutional Church. Let us take a closer look at this relationship.

## *Religious and the Institutional Church: Responses*

Experience is the key to human relations, and we see a clear expression of this fact in the relations between the religious women under observation and the Chilean hierarchy. Although we have already mentioned briefly some aspects of this relationship, there is one dimension not often taken into account: the indifference toward women, perhaps unconscious, but nonetheless notable in the official documents of the Church. For example, the Medellín Documents mention women only once as part of a multitude of groups seeking justice throughout the continent. In his well-known book *Theology of Liberation* (1973), Gustavo Gutiérrez writes that his work is based on the Gospel and the experiences of men and women in Latin America. But there is no mention of the intrinsically unjust position of women in Latin American society, and much less of their secondary position in the Catholic Church. Some argue that injustice affects so many dimensions of life in Latin America and is such a common component in all structures that it is not worthwhile stressing a mere symptom of a more pervasive problem. It is important to bear in mind that people respond to their environment in accord with their previous experience. If this experience has been liberating, responsible, and creative, the response will be a healthy one which should enrich personal fulfillment. But if this experience has been limited, restricted, bitter, and dependent, the response will be immature, irresponsible, and inconsequential for personal fulfillment. The latter has been the real experience of Latin American women. How can they be expected to contribute in a liberated, creative fashion to the development of a free continent?

The reader will recall that the actual pastoral priorities of the Catholic Church in Chile led to changes in structures and proceedings, which in turn led to new roles for women in pastoral action. Thus, women have been incorporated on a number of different levels of pastoral planning into roles of administrators of parishes in many dioceses of Chile. Many works traditionally reserved to priests are now in the hands of women. The importance of this work is such that not a few congregations have closed some of their schools in order to give their personnel the liberty to dedicate themselves to this new pastoral dimension. Despite the ample horizons offered in positions of leadership and responsibility, we still find that almost 76% of our sample felt frustrated with the institutional Church.

The pastoral experience offered to the Chilean women, particularly the religious women, is both varied and profoundly responsible. Nevertheless, this experience has proven itself to be a double-edged sword. Although her responsibility grows, this has the unanticipated consequence of making her more conscious of her secondary position in the Church, her lack of real authority in ecclesiastical structures, and her totally limited role in the area of cult. Our data show that more than 28% of these women felt abandoned by the institutional Church; 37% felt they had no way to give an accounting of their labors to the institutional Church, nor did they see any apparent desire on the part of the Church that they should do so; 56% felt that the pastoral work of the Church was highly inadequate in the areas of catechetics, sacramentalization, and youth, but likewise felt unable to communicate this to policy makers. The factors which caused the highest frustration are the following:

(1) Many positions of great responsibility are already in the hands of women but positions of ecclesiastical authority remain beyond their reach .........79.4%

(2) The position of the hierarchical Church with regard to the ordination of women is both illogical and inadmissible........69.2%

(3) Financing on the part of the institutional Church is totally inadequate in the face of our needs........61% (A second "control" question revealed that 92% suffer from a "lack of financial support.")

In a recent study of women working in the Church in Chile, we find an interesting contrast to those data. Asked if they felt that lay and religious women were given works of lesser responsibility than men, 66% were emphatically negative. Their reasons can be summarized as follows:

> Women are sharing at least equally with, if not outdistancing men with respect to burdens of responsibility in the Church's pastoral programs. We are likewise talking about real responsibility, not the possession of clerical titles or status [Galilea, et al., 1976].

There are substantial differences between that group and the present sample which help account for the contrary opinions. In the 1976 study the great majority of women involved lay women, not religious. Their educational level was far lower, and the extent of their dedication much more limited, ranging from two or three hours to a few days weekly of pastoral service. The present sample deals with highly educated women, completely dedicated to the ideal of service, identified by their very role with the institutional Church, and therefore highly vulnerable with respect to its policies and deficiencies. To put it succinctly, they have more to lose.

The religious woman engaged in pastoral action in Chile knows her own capacity, her professional preparation, and the success she has enjoyed in exercising responsibility for the People of God. At the same time she is becoming more and more conscious of the lack of theological and psychological bases for those restrictions which have reduced her to a secondary position in the Church. This gap between ecclesiastical structures and changing cultural mores continues to produce enormous tensions among these women, particularly those most dedicated to pastoral action who are more vulnerable to the experience of two coexisting realities in constant warfare.

### *I. THE FINANCIAL PROBLEM*

We have already alluded to this problem in the discussion on frustration. Here we would like to analyze in greater detail what lies behind the statement by 92% of the sample that they are receiving inadequate financial support. Aside from the fact that many are already receiving help from their own congregations to supplement the monthly stipend received from the Chancery (Administrative offices of the Church), 42.2% feel obligated to work in some remunerative field which in many cases takes them out of the marginal area and seriously limits the time dedicated to pastoral work. We are here faced with the fact of "pastoral efficiency." If the Church is concerned with forming its personnel, helping them to renew their religious dedication, and orienting their pastoral labors, it seems somewhat myopic to destroy their efficiency by not providing the necessary means to do the job well. However, there is a strong possibility that many religious prefer to work in this fashion as a proof of their identification with the environment, or because they feel guilty if they do not face the same risks and sufferings of their neighbors. Reflecting on the questionnaire data and also on our conversations with these women, we are led to formulate several questions in this regard. Are these women being realistic with regard to their needs? Is there a frank and open dialogue with ecclesiastical superiors or, on the contrary, does there exist a tendency to "angelism" on the part of one side or both? Is it possible that they have adopted certain aspects of this style of life without having accomplished a total identification and, for this reason, feel themselves deprived of resources to which they had access in another context? In any case, is it really possible to give up one's standard of living entirely? Is it indeed even realistic to hope to do so? Are they aware of the effect which this factor might produce not only among those who already live in marginal areas, but also among those who are considering this possibility and are perhaps vacillating in the face of the effects of this financial problem?

If the Church continues to emphasize the same priorities in the future, it will have to confront the conditions in which many of its personnel in marginal areas are living, and they, in turn, will be forced to evaluate their style of life and work in the light of their own personal and community limitations.

## *II. IMAGE OF THE CHURCH*

With respect to the Church model preferred by these women, they were presented with a selection in two different areas. The first included a type of "universal Church" to which all could aspire to belong, with different levels of commitment. Along with this was included an "elite Church" model which would exact a profound commitment from its members and would, for this reason, be a "minority Church." The majority 57.7%, chose the elite Church model, only 11.6% chose the universal model, while 22.2% chose a combination of both concepts in which the minority would influence the formation of the masses.

Taking into consideration the position of the Church in society, the sample was presented with a second selection. The first Church model offered was that of a "conformist Church" which would adapt to any type of society in order to protect its institution and its liberty of action. The second model was that of a "critical Church," one more prophetic in its approach to injustice despite any problems which this stance might occasion. Over 88% of the religious women chose a critical Church model. The 6.8% which chose "another model" were referring to a critical model based on charity and wisdom. None chose a conformist Church model.

### *III. THE RELATIVE IMPORTANCE OF PASTORAL PROBLEMS*

With respect to opinions on the highest priority problems in the Church, we asked our sample to rank the problems they considered most urgent for the Church. With a total of nine choices, responses were scattered, but the most frequent choices were the following: primarily "the need to build strong effective primary communities" (Comunidades de Base)—38.3%; secondarily "the protection of human rights in society"—24.4%.

In the 1976 study, these same pastoral priorities were evaluated and compared with the responses of the Chilean bishops, (Smith, 1978) to the same question. The results were extremely revealing. The most frequent first and second choices for these women was the need to build strong effective primary communities (Comunidades de Base), while the bishops chose as the most urgent problem the lack of vocations to the priesthood and, in second place, the need to augment pastoral personnel with well-prepared laymen. This emphasizes certain tendencies already detected among the bishops, most notably their strong preoccupation with personnel problems such as the rapidly disappearing clergy and how to fill in the gaps thus created—that is, a preoccupation with "means." The women in both samples face the pastoral problem itself—the "ends"—evangelization of society. Perhaps they are less concerned with means because they are so personally involved at the grass-roots level. The bishops, on the other hand, are limited by their very ecclesiastical role.

With respect to the religious women under study, their choice of evangelization through small communities of mutal support and their emphasis on the protection of human rights brings to mind those new values necessary for building a more humanized society. Even in the case of their pastoral priorities, these women are faithful to their humanizing vocation in the Church as well as in society.

### *IV. FORMS OF DOCTRINAL COMMITMENT*

One of the principal hypotheses of our study was that "the experience of women working and living in marginal areas would make them more critical of the institutional Church and would lead them to a less literal position with respect to its teachings." The assessment of doctrinal positions, never an easy task, becomes extremely difficult through a questionnaire, for as an individual becomes less literal and rigid in religious perspectives, the structure of the questionnaire becomes less useful. It offers no other alternative but to present the individual as "less religious" because of low scores in scales of doctrinal affirmations and practices of traditional interpretation. A solution was sought and found in the use of a scale (Hunt, 1972) offering three possible positions:

(1) *A Literal interpretation*: the individual accepts the affirmation as true without questioning it in any form. This position seems to imply that the individual has not reflected upon the relationship of this affirmation to other areas of life.
(2) *An Antiliteral interpretation*: the individual rejects the Christian orientation as without value in itself. This attitude is based on an ingenuous, literal and pseudoscientific interpretation of religion, and seems to reflect a rebellion against the rigid teachings of childhood or against those who have presented onerous restrictions on personal life.
(3) *A Mythological interpretation*: the individual reinterprets the religious affirmation in order to find the profound symbolic meaning which exists beyond a literal interpretation. This type of person has a more complex religious frame of reference and is capable of assimilating both the intention of orthodox religion and the realities of the contemporary world. This level of commitment is considered the most mature.

The Hunt scale adapted for our study was composed of ten affirmations, with three possible responses for each—each alternative corresponding to one of the above interpretations. The sum of the individual responses and the resulting scale gave us an Index of Doctrinal Commitment Position. It is important to emphasize here that the Index represents only an orientation or tendency; nevertheless, the results seem valuable enough for careful reflection.

While more than 66% of the religious in our sample took a mythological stance with regard to doctrinal commitment, less than 23% possessed a literal interpretation and barely 10% could be classified as antiliteral. A literal interpretation was most frequent among older women, while the mythological interpretation was most common among younger religious. The higher the level of education, the more probable was the presence of a mythological position, while a literal interpretation was most common among religious with less education. In terms of nationality, North Americans were strongly mythological, Europeans (with the exception of the Spaniards) offered the only antiliteral position, while Latin Americans (with the exception of Chileans) and Spaniards were most representative of the literal position. Interestingly enough, the group possessing a mythological position showed itself most frustrated with the institutional Church.

The group was highly mature with respect to its doctrinal position, having demonstrated a marked tendency to reinterpret religious affirmations in search of a more profound symbolic meaning rather than the absolutism of total blind acceptance or total rejection. This display of maturity in the area of doctrinal commitment can be evaluated only adequately as part of the larger dimension of personal spirituality, of which it is both an aspect and an indication. Thus, we are led to expect a reflective spirituality on the part of these women, one which goes beyond the surface, a personal freedom unfettered and creative in its confrontation with the environment. The following section will analyze their spirituality and its profound relationship to the marginal experience.

## *Changes in Spirituality Patterns*

The response of these women to the frustrations of life is rather unique in its blend of rebellion with innovation *within* and continuing commitment *to* institutional structures. They look for new ways to achieve their goals; they question those goals institutionalized by society and even by the Church. Their very style of life is counter to the material goals of success and comfort of their own society. The values they stress—compassion, mutual affirmation, respect for life, creativity, dialogue, and the like—are in fact those most needed in our alienated society which speaks incessantly of "community" without knowing how to achieve it. It is our belief that religious women possess the most adequate response to the present societal frustration. The very apostolic experience which they have chosen demonstrates an openness to the search for more functional means and methods; for this reason we hoped to find the same search in the realm of spirituality, the same "rebellion" and "innovation" we have come to expect in their day-to-day living. We expressed this in the following hypothesis: "The experience of these women has the potential to enrich and deepen their spirituality" (Gilfeather, 1978). Due to the limitations of space, we will consider only some of the traditional components of spirituality.

*A. Prayer.* One factor which must be considered in any discussion of prayer is the context in which it takes place. The presence or absence of a small chapel or oratory can enrich or impoverish that context and is an indication of the importance given to prayer in the community. The fact that 90% of the sample live in small communities where space is extremely limited but which possess a small chapel or oratory speaks eloquently of the priority given to prayer by these religious. Looking at the content of their prayer, we find three principal orientations: 53% pray the Divine Office in common (psalms and readings from Old and New Testament and the Fathers of the Church); 49% participate in free, shared prayer with others; while over 17% prepare paraliturgical ceremonies in the absence of a priest. These orientations are not exclusive but overlap in various combinations of activities. The importance of the Divine Office, which is the Church's official prayer, reveals the spirituality of these women. They seek bonds of union with the universal prayer of the Church. Their shared vocal prayer provides a firm basis for mutual support and understanding. The frequency of paraliturgical ceremonies, directed by the sisters themselves, clearly shows that they are learning to detach themselves from a total dependence upon the clergy for spiritual development and opening themselves to receive what is necessary from their sisters.

To what can we ascribe these orientations in their prayer life? Were these orientations always present? Over 90% declared that their prayer life had experienced great changes since their coming to live in a marginal area; thus their spirituality clearly has been affected by their marginal experience. A closer look at their responses indicated the extent and content of this change. The terms they use reveal that from a rational, theoretic, structured, private prayer, it has come to be "affective, evangelical, down to earth, communal, intimate, interiorized, and based on life." In this way the religious themselves evaluate the effect of the environment upon their prayer and the development of new modes of prayer and of being present to the Lord as well as to one's brother and sister.

*B. Meditation.* One of the classic activities of the spirituality of religious life is meditation, and despite what we would expect from a group which is often plagued with constant calls for service and little free time, over 90% dedicate time each day to this exercise. The terms used to describe changes in their meditation are very similar to those used for prayer: "done with more regularity, less theoretic, less structured, more profound, more effective, based more on daily life, done with greater pleasure and for longer periods."

*C. Devotion to the Virgin Mary.* Considered one of the oldest and dearest devotions in the Church and deeply related to the life of the religious, devotion to Mary has become a rather ambiguous aspect of the spirituality of many of these religious. A quarter of our women stated that their devotion to the Virgin Mary had either diminished or no longer existed. The majority, almost 60%, expressed their veneration on one or another level, but of that group, over 38% stated that their devotion had been enriched profoundly by their marginal experience. They spoke of the Virgin Mary as having become a "real person" to them, nearer and more of a woman like themselves. She was no longer the powerful Mother of God, but rather the "poor virgin," the "woman of faith" who accompanied them in their labors for a suffering people. It is possible that those who felt their devotion had diminished or disappeared were rejecting an image of Mary which no longer holds meaning in the face of their experience or the context of their lives.

*D. Revision of Life.* This refers to an evaluation of an individual's life in the light of the Gospel and in common with the members of his or her community. The purpose is to grow in Gospel values with the support of the entire primary group. Fully 68% of our sample take part weekly in this type of evaluation, and from their responses it is clear that their marginal experience has enriched and deepened this activity. The terms they use recall those mentioned for meditation and prayer. Thus, their revision of life has become "more demanding, it exacts more effort and commitment, it opens new horizons and areas before untouched, it is more down to earth, more evangelical, more sincere, more supportive, based on real life, I get much more out of it."

*E. Spiritual Direction.* Traditionally considered essential in the religious life, spiritual direction by a priest has become a luxury for most religious in areas with few priests. Only 28.7% of our sample enjoys some form of spiritual direction, "although unsatisfactory," while 50% feel the deprivation of direction keenly and hope to find help "someday." The most realistic attitude was expressed by over 23% of the sample, who found a substitute among friends or the members of their own primary community. This new form of spiritual orientation deserves our attention not only because it satisfies a need and offers a substitute for priestly direction, but also because it constitutes an integral form of human and spiritual growth that is at least as sound, if not sounder, than traditional forms of direction. A well-established group where sincerity, openness, and a desire to mature in the Lord are dominant provides the best context for personal growth. Interestingly, the great majority of those who had chosen this type of orientation in their lives live in urban marginal areas. Throughout our observation of these women it became obvious that those living in urban areas were more creative in their search for solutions. This creativity may be the fruit of a more deeply felt need than that experienced by their rural sisters.

*F. Sharing the Faith Experience.* From earliest times, the Christian community has been based on a sharing of the faith experience. Although such sharing is essential to the Christian commitment, Christians have for too long been formed in a contrary type of spirituality stressing independence and detachment from others. This has been particularly true in the religious life. It was all the more surprising, then, to find that over 95% of the sample expressed a strong desire to share their faith experience with their sisters and others. Almost 67% find it easy to do so, while a third complain of obstacles which are, in great part, difficulties in interpersonal relationships. The resulting lack of communication and the climate of conflict created make sharing impossible. What interests us here is the perception of need for mutual sharing of one's faith experience in Christ. If this conviction is strong enough solutions will be sought to problems, be they lack of time, exhaustion, or personal conflicts. Clear goals and strong motivation can help cut through the thick curtain of obstacles which can smother life in common, leaving only an attitude of tolerance in a boarding-house atmosphere.

*G. The Vows.* As these are so essential to the life of a religious, we wished to evaluate their relevance in the lives of our group. Over 85% of those living in urban marginal areas declared their vows to be more relevant today than ever; 72% of their rural sisters agreed. The reasons recall those given for changes in prayer, meditation, and revision of life. Those who feel most "questioned" by their environment (the urban sisters) are those whose vows are more relevant than ever. Their vows have opened up a new liberating dimension which supports rather than limits their commitment.

The vow receiving the greatest coverage in writings on the religious life today is poverty; it was, likewise, of most interest to our group. In speaking of changes in their living out of the vow, the sisters used terms which express the values they prize most highly: "the vow (poverty) gives me greater liberty, it permits real solidarity with my people, it frees me for service, I feel it is a source of liberation for me, it helps me to be more open to others, I am drawn to share more of what I am, I feel that it leads me to question myself and my motives, through it I am learning to accept myself as I am." If, as we suggested previously, one's participation in human affairs depends upon one's experience, then the contribution of these women to the future Latin American society should be a most positive and humanizing one, for their vision of the vow of poverty emphasizes a liberating dimension which enriches rather than impoverishes the human spirit.

Their style of life gives concrete evidence of the importance given not only to the vow, but also to the consequences of their identification with the poor. For this reason we asked them if the vow could be lived with sincerity in a different type of social context, in a less demanding style of life. Their responses reveal considerable ambiguity. Almost 40% denied the possibility of living the vow with sincerity in a more comfortable style of life. Those who showed more tolerance were from rural areas. It would appear that the tensions of a life of extreme simplicity, amidst the general misery of urban marginal sectors, influence the relative strength of opinions originating there. A danger is inherent in this intransigent attitude with respect to the vow of poverty. The great majority of religious women in Chile do not live in urban or rural marginal sectors. For this reason a judgment with respect to the "sincerity" of their mode of life, and particularly their living out of the vow of poverty, is questionable and, moreover, is symptomatic of an attitude of "exclusiveness" with respect to a particular style of life. These are the false dichotomies which cause divisions among personnel and damage pastoral efforts.

## *Conclusions*

The above data may or may not point to a "new spirituality," but the foregoing facts are indicative of the multiple changes experienced by these women since coming to live in marginal areas.

The responses of religious women living in marginal areas reveal attitudes and values which have only a secondary place in our society. They have developed a way of life (or spirituality) based on values, qualities, and attitudes which have been repeated over and over again in the analysis: "authenticity, liberation, solidarity, compassion, sensitivity, openness, sharing, confrontation, self-acceptance, respect for life." These are human as well as Christian values, humanizing factors which at least partially define Christian existence and should inform the action of the Church. Their "spirituality" reflects definite interests, motives and options—it takes sides with the oppressed, the marginal, the poor in general, and for that very reason is based on praxis, solidarity, and shared experience.

These women do not express themselves in terms of abstract analysis or in intellectual discussion, but in the use of a wide gamut of human expression—art, music, dialogue, solidarity, compassion, and openness. They do not separate the sacred from the profane, the religious dimension from daily living. On the contrary, the content of their liturgy, prayer, and meditation is a reflection of the reality of their life situation. Through these same activities they give expression to their fears, frustrations, and feelings of oppression, but, above all, to their hope for a new society where justice and humanity will prevail.

Just as experience has shaped their spirituality, so too it has altered their values and attitudes as witnessed in responses to structures at all levels and in all areas of their lives: relations with the institutional Church, vocational commitment, work, recreation, planning, prayer, even their doctrinal stance have all been deeply affected by the marginal experiment. The four dimensions of social change have thus come full circle in the fertile ground of the *población* environment. To the extent that the emergence of the individual, innovation, the power controversy, and secularization become prevalent in an environment, whether singly or in conjunction, tensions inevitably result. We have seen evidence that the situations of these women point to a high degree of tension, and that the data suggest the urgency of dealing with the problem and seeking creative solutions if the Church continues to avail itself of their dedication. The institutional Church appears, in many instances, to be cautious of these women, of their growing self-awareness and the resulting conflictual relationship between institution and personnel. It is an uneasy courtship and we might ask ourselves what, in fact, sustains them. To a great extent, it appears to be their spirituality which overrides their frustrations and tensions. It likewise offers a surety that, despite a possible (or probable) continued environment of frustration and tension, these women will, unlike so many disillusioned political ideologists, remain in marginal areas.

This identification with the "broken ones" of society which has engendered such unexpected purpose, strength, and creativity in these women, has the potential to enrich the religious life of the entire Chilean Church.

"Being rich He became poor that He might enrich us."
(II Cor. viii.9.)

## REFERENCES


CELAM [Council of Latin American Bishops] (1969) "Poverty of the Church." Second General Conference of Latin American Bishops, Bogotá: General Secretariat of CELAM.

Centro Bellarmino (1962) Pastoral Plan of the Chilean Episcopate, 1961-1962. Santiago, Chile: Centro Bellarmino.

GALILEA, C., K. GILFEATHER and J. PUGA (1976) Las Mujeres que Trabajan en la Iglesia: La Experiencia Chilena. Santiago, Chile: Centro Bellarmino.

GILFEATHER, K. (1978) Religiosas en Apostolados Marginales. Santiago, Chile: Centro Bellarmino.

GUTIÉRREZ, G. (1973) Theology of Liberation. History: Politics and Salvation. Maryknoll, NY: Orbis.

HUNT, R. (1972) "Mythological-symbolic religious commitment: the LAM scales." J. for the Scientific Study of Religion 2 (March).

MARTY, M. (1960) "Sects and cults." Annals of the American Academy of Political and Social Science 332 (November): 125-134.

NISBET, R. (1970) The Social Bond. New York: Alfred A. Knopf.

SMITH, B. (1978) "The Catholic Church and political change in Chile, 1925-1975." Ph.D. dissertation. Yale University.


*Katherine Gilfeather, Maryknoll sister and sociologist, is a member of the staff of the Bellarmino Center for Research and Social Action in Santiago, Chile. She has lived and worked in Chile for almost 25 years.*

**MARGARET E. CRAHAN**
*Woodstock Theological Center*
*Georgetown University*
*Washington, D. C. 20057*

# *SALVATION THROUGH CHRIST OR MARX*
## *Religion in Revolutionary Cuba*

Unlike churches in the rest of Latin America, those in Cuba did not embark at the outset of the 1960s on a period of liberalization and innovation in theology, pastoral forms, lay participation and political strategies. Rather, the coming to power in 1959 of a revolutionary government and the initiation of substantial societal restructuring reinforced conservatism within the churches. Strong challenges to the legitimacy of the government by the churches from 1959 through 1961 were not effective due largely to institutional limitations and their identification as bulwarks of prerevolutionary structures. Hence, in spite of a marked increase in participation and contributions, the churches' counterrevolutionary stance had limited impact. Contributing to this was the exodus of many religious activists to the United States and Spain, and a turning in upon themselves by the churches which came to serve as refuges from change. During a period of religious ferment in the rest of Latin America, the Cuban churches entered a period of stasis from which they only began emerging in the late 1960s, challenged by the consolidation of the revolution and by international developments.

The crisis which the Cuban churches underwent was the result primarily of institutional and theological conservatism which sprang largely from the nature of their own and Cuba's historical development. While the churches were weak, Christianity was a pervasive cultural presence which encouraged negative reactions to the introduction of socialism. This helps explain why resistance to the revolution based on religious motives was greater than the low levels of participation in church services and activities in prerevolutionary Cuba would suggest.

After a period of retreat and quiescence from 1963 to 1968, the Catholic and Protestant churches began exploring the possibilities of rap-

Journal of Interamerican Studies and World Affairs, Vol. 21 No. 1, February 1979, 156-184
© 1979 Sage Publications, Inc.

prochement with the government and experimentation with new theological definitions and pastoral programs better adapted to the reality of Christians living in a socialist society. This process has proceeded slowly and with more caution than comparable activities in other areas of Latin America, partly the result of the fact that, rather than having the opportunity to react and adapt gradually to rapid change, the Cuban churches were swept up in a period of turbulence in which many of their basic premises were directly challenged. Hence, it was only in the early 1970s that Cuban churchpeople really began exploring the implications of such developments as liberation theology, increased lay participation in ecclesiastical decision-making, and other innovations. To a considerable extent, the Cuban revolution, rather than transforming the Cuban churches, reinforced traditional policies and behavior, making the churches today less open and innovative than those in most other Latin American countries.

In order to better understand the distinct nature of the Cuban churches as compared to those in other Latin American countries, this essay will analyze religious affiliation, practice, and attitudes in Cuba through an examination of the evolution of the protestant and Catholic churches principally since 1959. Institutionalized rather than Afro-Cuban religion (santería) will be emphasized, as the former appears to have been more directly affected by the revolution, and more empirical studies have been undertaken concerning it. Due to the absence of survey data regarding Cuban Judaism, it will not be included. The data available consists of some dozen studies dating from 1940 to the present dealing with both national and subnational samples (Cepeda, 1966; Davis, 1942; de la Huerta Aguiar, 1960; Echevarría Salvat, 1971; El Equipo Diocesano de Jovenes de Camagüey, 1967; Noguiera Rivero, 1962; Rochon, 1967; Universidad Central "Marta Abreu" de las Villas, 1959; Torroella, 1963). These include the results of a survey of some forty Cuban church leaders, both clerical and lay, resident in Cuba, Europe, and the United States, whom I interviewed in 1973, 1974, and 1976. The interviews were in-depth explorations of both prerevolutionary and postrevolutionary conditions designed to elicit not only individual attitudes, but also evaluations of general trends within institutions.[1] Since the surveys are not generally fully comparable, the data available are suggestive rather than definitive and are most revealing in the context of other sources. In addition, given the high degree of ideological permeation of both Catholic and Protestant belief systems, no attempt has been made to isolate religious from ideological factors. Indeed, the presence or absence of change in Cuban religious attitudes is more comprehensible if one regards them in the context of ideological developments.

## *I. Prerevolutionary Background*

It is widely held that religion in general and the Catholic Church in particular were relatively weak in prerevolutionary Cuba (Aguilar, 1974: 21-22; Davis, 1942: 49; Dewart, 1963: 93-99; Nelson, 1970: 268; Houtart and Rousseau, 1971: 113-114; and Ruiz, 1968: 162). This opinion is based primarily on the nominal nature of many Cubans' commitment to Catholicism, the numerical weakness of Protestants and Jews, and the noninstitutional nature of the Afro-Cuban sects. Other factors include the urban concentration of Catholic and Protestant personnel and institutions and their consequent scarcity in rural areas, emphasis on institution-building and elite education rather than pastoral duties, higher percentage of female over male formal participation, limited number of Cuban vocations, and the image of the churches as foreign institutions—the Catholic Church being tied to Spain and the Protestant churches to the United States.

While all this is true, certain cautions should be kept in mind. Although throughout Latin America the frequency of attendance at services traditionally has been low and the institutional churches often the object of considerable hostility, Christianity exerts a predominant influence which in moments of crisis can result in a reassertion of loyalty to the churches. The Cuban case is an apt demonstration of this, for while the vast majority of Catholics in the prerevolutionary period rarely practiced their religion according to standard indicators, many Cubans rejected the revolution, in part, because of the strong animosity toward Marxism which socialization in a predominantly Christian society encouraged. The appearance of weakness on the part of the Catholic Church was stimulated, in part, by the fact that Cuba was the object of the most intense proselytizing efforts by U.S. Protestants in all Latin America. In addition, the importation of substantial numbers of Africans as slaves up through the mid-nineteenth century resulted in the proliferation of spiritist beliefs which became mingled with Christian ones. The presence of Protestant, Jewish, and Afro-Cuban religions not only provided competition for the Catholic Church, but also gave Cuba perhaps the most diverse religious scene in all Latin

America, particularly in the post-World War II period.

The presence of a multitude of denominations and sects contributed to a degree of flexibility and casualness toward religion that was reinforced by the increasing secularization of Cuban society. Nevertheless, even in rural areas most Cubans identified themselves as Christians, though they may never have had any contact with a church. Such individuals can be found among those who adduce religious motives for leaving Cuba after 1959. The so-called weakness of religion in prerevolutionary Cuba was primarily institutional rather than cultural and, to a degree, due to the nature of the historical evolution of the Catholic Church in the island.

Catholicism was introduced into Cuba with the arrival of Columbus. The transformation of the island into a way-station or staging area for expeditions to the more heavily populated mainland colonies meant that it became of secondary, or even tertiary, importance to colonial authorities both civil and ecclesiastical. By the nineteenth century decay in the Catholic Church was pronounced. Increasingly the island was populated by miscreant peninsular clerics exiled to Cuba for punishment or conservative priests and religious fleeing from the newly independent mainland Spanish colonies. This combination contributed to the development of reactionary attitudes within the Church and lax observance of clerical duties. The conservatism of the Catholic Church was demonstrated by the hierarchy's strong opposition to Cuba's breaking away from Spain. Yet even after independence, when the Catholic Church's prestige was very low, the influence of the values it encouraged was evident. In 1900, for example, 80 of 107 Cuban municipalities, three of six provincial governors, and all but one judge of the first instance opposed the legalization of civil marriage (Ruiz, 1968: 161). This reflected the fact that the religious values of Cubans and the opinions and actions of church personnel were not necessarily identified as one by the general populace. Generalized religious belief and esteem for religion continued in spite of unpopular political and social positions taken by the churches.

The temporal and spiritual poverty of the Catholic Church in Cuba at the outset of the twentieth century provided opportunities for more liberal and populist competitors, such as the U.S. Protestants, as well as political movements, such as the socialists. This stimulated an internal reevaluation of Catholic strategies and by the 1920s the Church had recouped somewhat and was beginning to reassert its political clout. Part of its strategy derived from a belief in the desirability of maintaining an alliance with secular power and extracting from it financial benefits and a guarantee of a religious monopoly. The Cuban Catholic Church became aware of pressures for modernization, particularly among the urban bourgeoisie—the prime source of its vocations and local financial support. In an effort to cultivate the loyalty of this group, lay organizations were expanded and given a more activist orientation. In the late 1920s Catholic Action, aimed at keeping the bourgeoisie active in the Church while helping Catholics adapt to changing times, was introduced from Spain. This organization opened up decision-making to limited lay input and tended to focus energies on the creation of an idealistic new Christendom which bore little relevance to the Cuban reality.

The challenge of socioeconomic injustice in Cuba, as well as competition from secular groups such as political parties and labor unions, was also felt by the Protestant churches in the 1920s and 1930s resulting in increased emphasis on social welfare activities, particularly in the unevangelized rural areas. There was also a rise in interest in *santería* and pentecostalism, which provided a more direct sense of participation and a supportive community wherein problems of daily life were dealt with. Increased resources and the appearance of greater relevance resulted in more widespread religious activity in Cuba in the 1940s and 1950s. This encouraged a sense of optimism within the churches (Crahan, 1977, 1978). There was an upsurge of involvement not only in nontraditional organizations, but also in traditional ones such as Hijas de María and Caballeros Católicos. These groups reduced the possibilities of integrating churchpeople into secular movements, a factor which contributed to the churches' marginalization during the 1950s conflict between the forces of Fulgenico Batista and Fidel Castro.

Prior to 1959 the Catholic Church, and to a degree the Protestant denominations, largely adhered to a policy which Levine (1973) has defined as "traditional interventionism," which emphasized the cultivation and manipulation of elite secular ties. Such tactics are characteristic of highly stratified societies in which power is concentrated in the hands of a few who hold sway over a relatively noncomplex institutional order. In such situations the Church benefits as a result of the strength of allied structures more than from its own actions or those of its membership. Given the weakness of secular institutions in Cuba, due primarily to the heavy influence of the United States in the prerevolutionary period, the civil-ecclesiastical linkages which existed did not provide the churches with the degree of influence resulting from this strategy in other Latin American countries. The dependency of Cuban political and economic structures on the United States and the fact that the Catholics and Protestants received most of their funding and personnel from abroad caused the churches to suffer from a double dependency. Dominance first by Spain and later by the United States undercut the development of strong national institutions. This encouraged political instability and contributed to the turning to strongmen, such as Gerardo Machado and Fulgencio Batista. Most churches attempted to build links with these regimes even in the face of corruption, repression, and maintenance of acute socioeconomic injustices. This further contributed to the low esteem Cubans held for the institutional churches.

The strategy recommended by Vallier (1970) that Latin American churches build an independent base for themselves as articulators of universal values would have been unworkable in Cuba given the substantial gap between social classes. This meant that goals would have to be, and were, defined in terms so general as to have little possibility of implementation. This helps explain the difficulty clerics encountered in proselytizing among the urban and rural poor, who tended to identify the churches as bulwarks of the status quo. Notable is the degree to which religious values did permeate Cuban society. Such penetration of Christian beliefs, including Afro-Cuban versions, has been repeatedly attested to in the anthropological and other literature (Barnet, 1968: 56-57, 84-86).[2] The depth of the roots of generalized religious belief helps explain the negative reaction of many ostensibly nonreligious Cubans as the revolution became increasingly Marxist.

Within six months of the establishment of the Castro government, many churches, particularly the Catholic, experienced growth in membership and activities as they became the prime institutional opponents of the revolution. Attendance at Mass and other services increased and there was an influx of new members and contributions to such groups as Agrupación Católica, while 1,000,000 Cubans turned out in Havana for the National Catholic Congress in November 1959, a gathering which previously had attracted about 10,000. In this period the traditionally low levels of formal participation were reversed and the churches became highly politicized (Crahan, 1976). Growth was not sustained to a considerable extent as a result of the emigration of a substantial proportion of the faithful, as well as 70% of the Catholic priests and 90% of Catholic religious, together with 50% or better of

Protestant clerical and lay leaders.[3] It was this exodus more than any other single factor which threw the Cuban churches into crisis.

## *II. Religious Affiliation*

Church estimates of the number of nominal Catholics in prerevolutionary Cuba cluster around 70-75% of the total population (@7,500,000), while estimates for the 1970s range from 60-65% of 9-10,000,000 people. In the pre-1959 period there was approximately one priest for every 10,000 Cubans, and since the mid-1960s one for every 40,000. In 1970 it was reported that two-thirds of the population were still being baptized and buried in Catholic ceremonies, as compared with 95% for the rest of Latin America (Hageman and Wheaton, 1971: 30-31; López Oliva, 1970: 180). The number of currently practicing Catholics is well under a million (IH 4731191).

In a 1957 survey of 4,000 agricultural workers throughout Cuba, 52.1% claimed to be Catholic, while 96.5% expressed belief in God. More than half (53.5%) claimed never to have seen a parish priest and only 7.8% admitted having any dealings with one. A substantial proportion (41.4%) of rural workers insisted they had no religion whatever (Echevarría Salvat, 1971: 14-15; Domínguez, 1975: 16-17). A 1958 survey of rual youths in Las Villas province, where there was a relatively high concentration of clerics, revealed a far smaller percentage professing no religion—13% of the males and 11.3% of the females, 84.8% of the men and 83.3% of the women asserting they were Catholics (Universidad Central, 1959: 29-30). Two years later, in 1960, a survey of 4,000 Cubans in all six provinces revealed that 72.5% claimed to be Catholic and 19% professed no religion. The same investigation reported that in Bayamo in rural Oriente only 48% were Catholic, while 30% had no religion (de la Huerta Aguiar, 1960: 45-47). These figures highlight the concentration of Catholics in urban areas and the resultant weakness of the Church in the countryside. Nevertheless, the vast majority identified themselves as Christians.

In both prerevolutionary and revolutionary Cuba not only was there a scarcity of pastors, but they were distributed very unequally throughout the island. In 1972 there were 211 priests in Cuba: 102 in Havana Province, 36 in Oriente, 25 in Las Villas, 18 in Camagüey, 17 in Matanzas, and 13 in Pinar del Río. An equal number of nuns was distributed with like disproportion—176 located in Havana Province, while 32 of 37 male religious were there (Wallace, 1973: 5). This compares with 232 priests in urban Havana in 1953, 200 of whom were teaching in private schools (Houtart and Rousseau, 1971: 115). There were also approximately 3,000 Catholic religious in Cuba at that time, mainly in the cities engaged in nonpastoral work. As a consequence, there were rural areas and even some urban neighborhoods which were virtually unevangelized or, at most, superficially so. This helps explain the loose hold of the institutional church over the bulk of the population, as well as its identification with the urban bourgeoisie.

In 1958 Protestant officials claimed from 150,000 to 250,000 adherents. This was substantial growth from a 1940 estimate of 40,000 to 50,000 by U.S. sociologist Davis, who surveyed Cuba's 440 organized Protestant churches. Davis believed there were 35,000 Protestants in ten main groups (Northern Baptist, Church of God, Society of Friends, Protestant Episcopal Church, The Methodist Church, Presbyterian Church, Salvation Army, West Indies Mission, Southern Baptist, and Seventh Day Adventist), with 5,000 more in small independent congregations. Active membership constituted one percent of the total Cuban population of 4,200,000. Annual Protestant growth was 10.5 new members per church (Davis, 1942: 52, 62-63), which if maintained would have added 83,160 to the Protestant rolls by 1959 for a total of 123,160. Given the repeated references to membership increases and expansion of the number of churches in the late 1940s and 1950s, an estimate of 150,000 Protestants in Cuba by the time of the revolution does not seem exaggerated.[4] Data from the 1950s, however, indicate more substantial increases. A 1957 survey of 4,000 agricultural workers reported 3.3% of the respondents were Protestant, while a 1958 survey of Las Villas reported 3.1%. A 1960 study claimed the somewhat inflated figure of 6% (Echevarría Salvat, 1971: 14; Universidad Central, 1959: 29-30; de la Huerta Aguiar, 1960: 45).

Recent estimates of Protestant strength range from 25,000 to 65,000.[5] Evidence from most Protestant churches supports substantial declines as exemplified by the Methodists, who constituted the largest non-Catholic denomination in 1960.

CHANGES IN METHODIST MEMBERSHIP, 1957-1974*

| *1957* | *1960* | *1972* | *1974* |
|---|---|---|---|
| 7,847 | 10,347 | 2,629 | 2,478 |

*(Lewis, 1960; United Methodist Information, 1972: 1; Ordoñez, 1974).

Losses resulted primarily from migration abroad, particularly prior to 1970. A 1969 survey of Catholic parishes in urban Havana projected that by 1972, 50% to 70% of their prerevolutionary membership would have left the island (Jover, 1974: 27). A small Baptist church in Oriente lost 49 of its 80 members from 1960 to 1969, nine of them in the period 1961 to 1964 because the pastor was not sympathetic to the revolution. Some of these became members of the Communist party, although most did not (García Franco, 1970: 6-8).

Other congregations reflected such declines. The Reformed Presbyterian Church of Luyano reported a drop from 266 members in 1959 to 94 in 1970, in spite of 142 new members having been received during that period. The prime reasons were departure from Cuba of 105 members or loss of commitment by 129. The average age of Luyano members or aspirants in 1970 was 45.5 years, with 60.6% over 50 and 48% having six years of education or less. Thirty-eight percent were housewives, 28% workers, 14% retired males, with an equal percentage of students, while the remainder was unclassified (Wallace, 1973: 6). These and other data confirm that churchgoers in contemporary Cuba are often individuals who reached their majority before the revolution, with a continued heavy proportion of females, children and older persons, rather than adult males. There are exceptions, such as the Catholic parish of San Juan del Monte in a working-class neighborhood in Havana. In the prerevolutionary period it was quite active and has suffered fewer losses than, for example, the wealthier parishes of Vedado. Baptist congregations in Oriente have also held firm, aided by the fact that almost none of their pastors migrated abroad.

Davis' 1940 data concerning the occupations of Protestants identified approximately 29% as housewives, 20% as workers, 1% as retired, and 23% as students. A comparision with Luyano thirty years later reveals some changes precipitated by the revolution. The drop in student membership suggests that the ideological transformation prompted by revolutionary education was having its impact on Cuban youth. Proportionally more housewives and retirees participated in 1970, indicating less integration into revolutionary society, as well as more leisure time for these groups. Such comparisons can only be hypothetical without further data and consideration of other variables.

Overall, the Catholic Church and the less populist Protestant denomiations (Methodist, Presbyterians, and Episcopalians) suffered the greatest losses of membership and pastors. Groups whose appeal

TABLE 1
Occupations of Protestant Faithful in 1940 and 1970

| OCCUPATIONS | PERCENTAGES | |
|---|---|---|
| | NATIONWIDE 1940* | LUYANO 1970** |
| Housewives | 29 | 38 |
| Workers | 20 | 28 |
| Students | 23 | 14 |
| Unemployed | 13 | 0 |
| Retired | 1 | 14... (males only) |
| Unclassified | 14 | 6 |

* Davis, 1942: 74
** Wallace, 1973: 6

was traditionally to the poor and which were more adaptable were better able to weather the ferment of the 1960s in Cuba. The Baptist Convention of Western Cuba, for example, reported in 1971 that the denomination was "alive and growing" with 7,000 members, 319 having joined in 1970 and 22 students enrolled in a four-year seminary course. They also claimed that there were 9,000 Baptists in the Eastern Convention (Religious News Service, 1971: 7; Ordoñez, 1974: 11). This would make them, together with the Jehovah's Witnesses, the most rapidly growing denomination in Cuba. Statistics on the Jehovah's Witnesses and Seventh Day Adventists are difficult to obtain. Estimates by officials of the Cuban Council of Evangelical Churches place their strength at 20,000 to 35,000 with an increasing number in Havana, although prior to the revolution they were concentrated in the rural areas (IH 47413; IH 471119; IH 3703212). Such groups, as well as other fundalmentalist sects, provide alternative communities for those who resist integration into the socialist society being built in Cuba. Individuals, for example, who oppose universal military service, public education, and the collectivization of small privately held farms, find reinforcement among the Jehovah's Witnesses. For those who wish to publicly express their disaffection from the present government, membership in such groups is an obvious means.

The limited evidence available suggests that there has been less of a decline in adherence to Afro-Cuban beliefs than to institutional religion. Prior to 1959 *santería* was identified primarily with the rural lower class and did not exclude formal affiliation with an institutional church. While only one percent claimed spiritism as their religion in a 1957 survey of agricultural workers and in a 1960 national sample, other evidence indicates that one-quarter of the Cuban people engaged in spiritist practices (Echevarría Salvat, 1971: 14; de la Huerta Aguiar, 1960: 45, 48). Given the syncretic nature of Afro-Cuban beliefs, their adaptability to changing conditions in Cuba appears greater than that of the more institutionalized religions.

## *III. Religious Practice*

Afro-Cuban religious services, as well as Catholic and Protestant ones, have remained substantially unchanged since 1959. Those adaptations which have occurred are as much the result of international factors, including Vatican II and new theological formulations, as Cuban circumstances. This is not to say that the revolution has not stimulated attempts to make religion responsive to the challenges posed by contemporary Cuba. The tremendous membership losses most churches suffered, however, encouraged passivity and left many congregations without a critical mass to generate new programs and strategies. Only in the late 1960s, and more especially the 1970s, have serious efforts been undertaken to make the churches consonant with their existential situation.

Nonetheless, a frequently expressed opinion of current church leaders in Cuba is that their congregations are stronger, having been purified of members whose commitments were superficial. As one patriarch of the Presbyterian Church expressed it:

> Before, many became members of the church precisely to take advantage of the benefits of the primary schools and of the colleges, to be a candidate for a scholarship in the United States, to receive help—social and economic—from the church. There were 600,000 unemployed in Cuba before the triumph of the Revolution—it was a society of crisis, no? You can imagine how a pastor

> could be of influence, can't you? But people come to church now because of a profound religious conviction; we have members of greater quality [Wallace, 1973: 7].

Consequently, the decline in membership does not upset some pastors and, as in the prerevolutionary period, there is considerable variation in the level of activity almost always related to the vitality of a particular congregation's leadership, as well as the services rendered.

According to a 1966 survey of agricultural workers, only 0.7% of the 4,000 Catholic and non-Catholic respondents had attended church four or more times a year; 93.5% had not attended at all. Of professed Catholics, 88.8% reported not having attended Mass in a year, with 4.3% attending three or more times (Echevarría Salvat, 1971: 15-16). A 1958 study of Las Villas Province revealed that only 3.8% of 201 male Catholic respondents had attended Mass in the previous month, while 5.1% of the females had. Close to 90% of the females and 92.6% of the males had not attended any sort of church service (Universidad Central, 1959: 32). Nine years later, a 1967 survey of the diocese of Camagüey revealed that 3,597 of the province's residents, some 0.6% of its population, were attending Mass regularly.[6] This included 1,618 children, and with the exception of the city of Camagüey, most of those attending were children. For the entire diocese, 49% of those frequenting Mass were 24 or younger. A comparison of these results with 1965 diocesan statistics reveals that the socioeconomic status of those who attended Mass remained essentially the same, with housewives constituting one-half and students one-fifth. Workers and professionals amounted to 3% and 9% respectively. Of those who attended Mass, 12% never received communion, while 10% received only once a year. Forty-seven percent received communion occasionally. The most frequent communicants were in Camagüey, Ciego de Avila and Morón—urban centers with 100,000 populations. This implies that the greater availability of church facilities and personnel in cities continued to influence the level of religious activity (El Equipo Diocesano, 1967: 12-14).

In 1940 Davis reported that only 25% of Cuban Protestants were active in their respective churches, with the remainder neither attending services nor contributing financially (Davis, 1942: 56, 63). Close to two decades later Protestant attendance in Las Villas was 82% of those males claiming to be Protestants and 88% of the females, a substantial increase. This confirmed frequent reports in the 1950s of increasing fervor on the part of congregations (Universidad Central, 1959: 32). In the Luyano Presbyterian Church in 1970, 48% of the 130 members interviewed regularly attended services, 33% irregularly, and 19% never. It was also reported that a good number of young people were beginning to attend services (Wallace, 1973: 6). In the same year a 33-member Baptist Church in Oriente claimed 42% of the congregation were regular attendees, 33% rarely, and 25% never (García Franco, 1970: 5-6, 10). The growth of Protestantism in Cuba begun in the 1950s was obviously shortcircuited by the turmoil precipitated by the revolution, as was the level of participation in church activities of all denominations.

Attendance at religious instructions in the Catholic diocese of Camagüey in 1967, for example, was 1.1%, or 1,641 of all elementary school age children. Fifty-five percent of the Catholic children were receiving instruction at home. Religious instruction for adults was emphasized beginning in 1962, with 50% of the Catholic faithful having some type of formal instruction between 1962 and 1967. This would seem to have been partly an effort to counteract the ideological inroads of Marxism-Leninism. Nine percent of the Catholic adults who were active in the diocese served as catechists, while 7% helped prepare liturgies, and 6% participated in discussion groups. Such activities were concentrated in Camagüey city where the greatest number of trained leaders were, as well as the strongest tradition of church involvement (El Equipo Diocesano, 1967: 10-21).

The continued urban concentration of militant Catholics and church activitists in Havana, Santa Clara, Santiago and Camagüey, in the face of difficulties with the government in the 1960s, was ascribed by the former Catholic Action leader, Mateo Jover (1974: 23), to the more flexible attitudes of civil officials in urban areas. No doubt the relatively greater strength of church people in these areas also helped. This is linked to greater access to means of religious formation, including more contact with clerics.

Reforms stimulated by both domestic Cuban conditions and international factors such as Vatican II were implemented slowly and with some tension between those who regarded the church as a refuge from change and those who looked to reform as a means of making the church more relevant to the existing situation. The pattern is similar in the Protestant churches, which shared a preoccupation with encouraging and maintaining religious loyalty, particularly among young people, in order to guarantee the churches' institutional futures.

Prior to the revolution, lay activists and priests, ministers, and other religious were frequently recruited through the church schools. The nationalization of private schools in 1961 elminated that source. With one exception, the present and former church leaders I interviewed had all attended such schools. This was in spite of the fact that approximately 60% of them came from families which were not formally religious, illustrating the phenomenon that the chief appeal of church schools was their reputation for quality education. The departure from Cuba of a high proportion of the teachers in such schools meant a vacuum was created in the early 1960s with respect to the religious formation of youth. Traditional groups, such as Catholic Action and the Protestant Student Christian Movement, also suffered.

By 1962 the churches were counteracting or responding to Marxism with catechetical instruction and discussion groups which met to explore the relevance of Christian faith to their daily lives (El Equipo Diocesano, 1967: 10; IH 5771112). Such groups would later raise basic questions concerning the goals and functions of the churches, and served in some instances as stimuli for internal reforms and liberalization of church attitudes toward the revolution. Perhaps the most basic was whether or not church people should continue to oppose the government, since it was making some headway in remedying such chronic socioeconomic ills as unemployment and poverty, particularly in rural areas. This prompted explorations of whether a Christian might at times support a political system traditionally condemned by the churches. As such discussions progressed, a liberal minority began to argue that one achieved salvation not simply through rectitude in one's own life, but also through struggle to achieve socioeconomic justice in one's community. These conclusions combined with the development of liberation theology in the rest of Latin America to stimulate increased questioning of traditional theological formulations, hierarchical authority, and pastoral strategies by a minority of Cuban Christians.

## *IV. The Churches in Prerevolutionary and Revolutionary Cuba as seen by Cuban Christians*

In spite of continuing traditionalism among most church people in contemporary Cuba, all 40 of the clerical and lay Catholic and

Protestant church leaders I interviewed residing both within and without the island were critical of their institutions in the prerevolutionary period. Some held that radical changes were and still are needed, while others supported more limited measures which were essentially adaptive, not just to changing conditions in Cuba, but also to trends within the international ecclesial community. Progressivism was stronger among Protestants than Catholics, but in both cases reformers have recently captured high positions within their institutions. The result is that church leadership is sometimes more liberal than the faithful. The trauma of the radical changes initiated by the revolution and the political and economic isolation of Cuba instigated by the United States helped insulate Cuban Christians from liberalizing currents which were present in the rest of Latin America in the 1960s. Receptivity to the policies of the progressive leadership has consequently been somewhat limited. Beyond this, an almost exclusive dependence on theologies developed in response to European and North American circumstances left the churches with few resources to bring to bear on their actual situation.

Major criticisms of the churches in pre-1959 Cuba were elitism, lack of concern with socioeconomic justice, autocracy, over-preoccupation with financial matters, using charitable gestures to avoid confronting the structural bases of poverty and exploitation, cowardice in the face of political repression and corruption, overdependency on foreign and domestic political and economic elites, and failure to assume a prophetic role in a highly inegalitarian society. In addition, the churches were scorned for racism, pietism, pacifism, triumphalism, enclavism, puritanism, paternalism, individualism, and escapism.[7]

The charge of racism sprang from the fact that some church schools and organizations were unwilling to admit blacks. In addition, the predominantly Spanish Catholic clergy harbored attitudes of superiorty which, at times, depreciated Cuban culture as well as Cuban capacity to administer church institutions. Something akin to this existed in most of the U.S.-dominated Protestant churches. Among both Catholics and Protestants there was a pietistic emphasis on devotional aspects of religion and individual regeneration as the means to salvation. This permitted Christians to limit their responsibility for those less fortunate to occasional acts of charity. Given the widespread emphasis on misfortune as the "will of God," religion in prerevolutionary Cuba served to encourage acceptance of the status quo. For the poor the churches alleviated some of the pain of everyday existence by promising a reward in the hereafter. As the conflict between the forces of Batista and Castro escalated in the 1950s most churches maintained themselves aloof from the struggle, although some individual churchpeople assumed partisan roles. It is illuminating to note that one cleric who distinguished himself for his social activism in the 1950s and who subsequently left Cuba as a result of fear of communism, estimated that only 1.5% of Cuban churchpeople were seriously engaged in attacking endemic socioeconomic problems in the prerevolutionary period (IT 57311). He and other churchpeople concede that they did little to transform Cuba in pre-1959 period to conform more closely with Christian ideals. This would appear to be supported by the opinion of several thousand agricultural workers in a 1957 survey in which only 3.4% of them expressed any belief that the Catholic Church would be of any assistance in improving their lot (Echevarría Salvat, 1971: 25).

Belief by religious leaders that to change society it was necessary simply to change the individual and his or her values has changed somewhat since the revolution, with progressive and liberal sectors accepting the necessity of structural change and rejecting the notion of the churches as neutral or apolitical. There has also been a move away from the position that one can separate a church from the political, social, and economic contexts in which it exists. This has resulted in a push to abandon the role of the Church as primarily a consoler of the suffering and protector from divine wrath. In its place is offered the concept of a Christian community totally compromised in the struggle for socioeconomic justice.

While a prime impetus for this has been the revolution, the majority of Cuba's Christians did not conceive of the possibility of far-reaching changes resulting from the triumph of the 26th of July Movement. In reality the support of churchpeople for Castro's movement prior to 1959 sprang largely from opposition to Batista.[8] Hence the widespread reaction, both within and without the churches as radical changes began to be introduced, that the revolution was being betrayed. Such feeling was particularly strong within reformist groups such as Catholic Action and the Young Christian Workers, together with the Student Christian Movement. Castro's declaration of his Marxism-Leninism strengthened the sense of having been duped, an opinion which continues to hold sway among some Cuban churchpeople.[9]

This was reinforced by the loss of church personnel through emigration, the marginalization that retreat into religion as a refuge from change caused, and divisions within the churches. Further, the Catholic Church had no long-range strategy of response, nor did it appear to comprehend the realities of the situation (Jover, 1974: 20-21). The Protestant churches, less obviously counterrevolutionary than the Catholic, followed a policy of neither supporting nor opposing the revolution, but rather placing emphasis on Christian witness and opposition to atheism. They were also concerned with dissociating themselves from the counterrevolutionary image of Catholicism. Yet their greater identification with the United States presented its own problems given the anti-American turn of the revolution (United Methodist Information, 1972: 3; IH 471191; ISM 472115).

A 1964-1965 survey of Protestant youth found that the turn toward socialism was generally considered a betrayal which resulted in replacing one dictatorship with another. Some said they had expected it and that it was the fault of U.S. policy which drove Castro into the arms of the Soviet Union. A minority held it was a natural and logical step and in reality the only option. Pietism came into play with those who felt that, since God had permitted it, then it was all for the best. Some believed it was a challenge to proselytize the communists (Cepeda, 1966: 25-26). Reactions among Catholics were generally negative, with a good proportion feeling that opposition to the revolution was a moral responsibility.

Even prior to Castro's declaration of his Marxism-Leninism, disaffection had been growing over agrarian reform, nationalization of businesses, and executions of Batistianos and active counterrevolutionaries. For many Christians the agrarian reform law of 1959 was a violation of what they regarded as the Christian principle of the sanctity of private property (Dewart, 1963: 147-148; Rivas, 1971: 6). However, by 1965 a majority of Christian youth surveyed felt that it had been a pressing necessity and an unavoidable step, although some objected to what they regarded as injustices resulting from it. Support for the government's nationwide literacy campaign in the early 1960s was also strong, although 6% regretted what they felt was its ultimate objective—communist indoctrination. The reaction to the 1961 closing of the church schools was very negative—87.2% still opposing it in 1964 and 1965, although 81% approved of the nationalization of industries and businesses. This latter was a far more liberal stance than that of older churchpeople. Finally, 100% of the Protestant youths surveyed opposed the official executions which occurred in the early years of the revolution (Cepeda, 1966: 25). These youths must be regarded as atypical, as a national survey in the early 1960s revealed that only 3.5% of Cuban young people wanted to emulate Jesus Christ, and most regarded piety as an indication of a weak individual (Torroella, 1963: 21-22, 38-39, 45).

Church youth in the mid-1960s essentially contented themselves with being Christian witnesses, while minorities were either fervently prorevolutionary or antirevolutionary (Cepeda, 1966: 22). More recently there has been a small number of young people from nonreligious backgrounds who have been attracted to the churches in the hopes of finding solutions to some of the transcendental questions which they do not find satisfactorily answered by Marxism-Leninism (Jover, 1974: 29; Wallace, 1973: 6-7). Most Cuban youths, however, continue to be relatively unattracted to religion.

Overall, the reaction of the Cuban churches was more direct and less complex than that of the Chilean churches to Salvador Allende's attempted introduction of parliamentary socialism from 1970 to 1973. Religious, political, and economic changes throughout Latin America in the 1960s reduced the traditional hostility toward Marxist options, and there was within Chile a vocal minority of Christians who strongly supported this development. The very correct relations between the Chilean episcopacy and Allende's government are in contrast to the early responses of most Cuban church leaders. The differences between the Cuban and Chilean reactions highlight the diminishing of cold war tensions in the 1960s and the growing diversity of political analysis within the churches, although the leadership continues by and large to emphasize institutional preservation via traditional strategies.

## *V. The Churches in Revolutionary Cuba*

The revolution precipitated crises within the churches not simply as a result of the official adoption of Marxism-Leninism, but also because of tremendous losses in the ranks of the laity and the emigration or expulsion of priests, ministers, and other religious. Voluntary departures caused sometimes acrimonious debate within the churches and served to emphasize the differences between those who supported the revolution, those who argued it was the responsibility of the individual to stay and bear Christian witness, and those who felt their only recourse was to leave Cuba.[10] The reaction of Protestant youth to pastors and lay leaders who left ranged from acceptance to criticism of what they considered the abandonment of the flock in the face of the wolf (Cepeda, 1966: 27-28).

In the mid-1960s some clerics and laypersons were drafted into the Military Units to Aid Production (UMAP), a short-lived manual labor program for tramps, pimps, homosexuals, common criminals, and others regarded as deviants. A few pastors were jailed for counterrevolutionary activities and some 30 Baptist ministers for dealing with blackmarket currency. The reaction of Protestant youths to this was unanimous: if the pastors or lay leaders were imprisoned for counterrevolutionary activities and no other reason, then it was justified. However, if the actions considered counterrevolutionary were simply the preaching of the Gospel or the free exercise of their beliefs, then prison was deemed unjust (Cepeda, 1966: 28). Of significance is the fact that those of my informants who had been in jail or in UMAP all made the point that the most painful thing had been their sense of having been abandoned by their churches. The shock of doing manual labor alongside individuals they normally would not have come into contact with occasioned for some a reevaluation of the meaning of religion in their lives, while for others it resulted in a further retreat into traditional views. Furthermore, all resumed their church activities upon their release, some being greeted warmly as martyrs, while others were regarded with some disconfort (García Franco, 1966; IM 5771112; IH 4701181; IH 377221).

The loss of substantial proportions of their staffs resulted in opening the way for increased lay participation in the churches, which combined with international currents to stimulate reform. Pressure for change resulted in some liberalization, most notably in the Presbyterian, Methodist and Baptist churches and less so among the Catholics, Episcopalians, Seventh Day Adventists, and Jehovah's Witnesses. Within the Catholic Church it precipitated a crisis which came to a head in the late 1960s just prior to the issuing of the conciliatory pastoral letters of 1969 which broke the silence maintained since the early 1960s. In a 1972 article, "Cuban Catholics and Castro," the Cuban emigrée political scientist, Jorge Domínguez, ascribes the issuance of the conciliatory April 10, 1969 document to four factors: a desire for "political reinsertion or breathing space in the prevailing system"; "doctrinal reintegration into the post-conciliar church"; "transnational interaction within the Church"; and "ecumenical dialogue" (Domínguez, 1972: 25). A fifth factor was the struggle within the Church over internal liberalization.

Prior to this time the reforms envisioned by Vatican II had been ignored and unrealized in Cuba, due in large measure to the resistance to change which a sense of being beleaguered encouraged. Catholic theology and seminary training adhered to prerevolutionary forms and the theology of liberation made only slight inroads. This was in spite of strong lay support for reforms in the manner of saying Mass—94% in the diocese of Camagüey in 1965 and again in 1967; reception of communion—72% in 1965 and 75% in 1967; and reduction of the number of statues in churches—65% in 1965 and 58% in 1967 (El Equipo, 1967: 17).

By the late 1960s three main groups emerged among Catholic activists: conservatives who were not enthusiastic about liturgical and other reforms promoted by Vatican II and the 1968 Latin American bishops meeting at Medellín, Colombia, and who in general supported a passive witnessing church; the pragmatists who favored tight episcopal control of any move toward rapprochement with the government and were lukewarm toward substantial increases in lay participation; and the reformers, who included some of the most militant advocates of lay participation and who felt that dialogue with the government should proceed only if the Church recognized its obligation not only to support the government for its positive accomplishments, but also to criticize it. The episcopacy's argument that relatively uncritical support was first necessary to win the confidence of the government in view of past difficulties was rejected by both conservatives and reformers. The precise nature of the Catholic Church as critic was detailed by the ex-president of Cuban Catholic Action Youth, Mateo Jover, in a 1969 seminar in New York. Jover suggested the initiating of dialogue between Christians and Marxists at the grass-roots level. The feedback to government cadres which would result from this, he felt, would help open them up to Christian opinions to a greater extent than if the dialogue was limited to the upper echelons of church and state (Jover, 1974). Clearly, the presumption was that both institutions would better reflect the attitudes of the bulk of their adherents if this path was followed.

The Cuban bishops rejected both the reformist and conservative positions, publishing on August 10 and September 3, 1969, pastoral letters appealing for the lifting of the U.S. trade embargo of Cuba and emphasizing support for national developmental goals and the need to respect the atheistic position. These letters precipitated internal crises. The reformers objected to what they regarded as the episcopacy's failure to balance support for the government with the raising of critical issues, and the conservative majority regarded the declarations as evidence of the treason or cowardice of the bishops. A good number of Catholic activists left the Church at this point, and a papal emissary was sent from Rome in an effort to ameliorate some of the divisions.

One hundred lay leaders and an equal number of priests met in Havana in October 1969 to discuss Church-State relations and reform within the Church. An alliance of clerics and lay conservatives held sway against the calls for substantial lay participation in decision-making relating not only to internal Church matters, but also to relations with the government. In the aftermath of this meeting, some new Christian communities were formed by the disaffected, a few of which emphasized charismatic practices (IM 5771112). While relations with the government did improve after 1969, in some respects the divisions within the Church became more pronounced. Rapprochement with the government was favored, however, by the positive impression Castro obtained when he met with progressive Christians in Chile in 1971 and increased contacts of Cuban churchpeople with such progressives throughout Latin America. Episcopal strategy since the late 1960s has been marked by caution. Current emphasis is on pastoral renewal and spiritual regeneration.

Comparable but less severe struggles occurred within some of the Protestant churches. Here, too rapprochement with the government was actively pursued by most churches beginning in the late 1960s. This reflected the increasing consolidation of the progovernment left in positions of leadership, in spite of the fact that many Protestants continued to oppose the revolution. As late as the mid-1960s many Protestant youths who were generally more liberal than their elders continued to be against their churches taking a public stance for or against the revolution—44% against; 17% in favor; 39% no opinion (Cepeda, 1966: 27). Most local churches regarded political involvements as taboo, although the national leadership of such denominations as the Presbyterians and Methodists and the Cuban Council of Evangelical Churches increasingly took stands on national and international issues in favor of government policies. This was the result of a desire to insert themselves into revolutionary society not only as the most pragmatic course, but also as the most prophetic.

The majority of Cuban church people, however, continued into the 1970s to be negatively disposed toward the revolution, a fact which one minister noted condemned the churches to be constituted largely of social outcasts. Those changes which had occurred within the churches he deemed inadequate.[11] A World Council of Churches official, a frequent visitor to Cuba, estimated in 1971 that 95% of Cuba's Protestants seemed ill-at-ease in their own society. In addition, he found a tendency in them to idealize the past and to look to emigration as the solution to their discomfort (Tschuy, 1971: 4). This was especially true of the more middle-class congregations, whereas the rural, lower-class churches were less inclined toward inner or exterior migration and more open to the possibilities offered by the revolution. Overall, the churches attracted a fairly high proportion of the disaffected, with indications that those groups least integrated into contemporary Cuba, such as the Jehovah's Witnesses, were the fastest growing (IH 47413; IH 471191). Today the churches as institutions provide some shelter for those who do not accept the revolution, while within the marginalized religious community those churches which are most conservative provide reinforcement and justification for dissatisfaction with the current system.

Those who desire to substantially change the values and opinions of churchpeople look to the conscientization of the Cuban Christian through new pastoral programs, revised educational materials, and more prophetic theological formulations. As Cuba's leading theologian, Dr. Sergio Arce Martínez, phrases it, the future of the churches in Cuba "will depend greatly on the way we are able to get a wide biblical-theological education and create serious Cuban theology that is adequate to our specific situation.[12] This attitude is shared by the former papal nuncio in Cuba, Archbishop Cesare Zacchi, who was instrumental in the period between 1963 and 1975 in bettering relations with Castro's government. Zacchi holds that Catholics should integrate themselves into the revolution through the mass organizations. Such action, the nuncio feels, would produce a beneficial interchange between Christians and Marxists which could result in the introduction of Catholic ideals into the revolution (López Oliva, 1970: 63; IH 4714111). Such positions run into opposition from those who feel, as does Jover, that at the level of systems legitimation and values an absolute impermeability exists between the Catholic Church and the revolutionary government. Unlike Arce and Zacchi, Jover feels that Marxist-Christian agreement over national virtues and objectives does not imply any fundamental agreement over values. Hence, he and others continue to urge the Catholic Church to work toward a situation where "there will be a pluralism of systems of legitimacy and permeability on the level of both values and norms" (Jover, 1974: 28). Given the manifold weaknesses of the churches in Cuba, such a strategy has limited viability.

Resistance to change within the Cuban churches can be explained, in part, by the fact that the impulse for renewal has come primarily from the leadership rather than the base resulting in limited involvement of the laity. The outcome has been a degree of resentment on their part towards church officials. In the early 1970s this resulted in the defeat of some progressives in Protestant church elections, as well as a period of quiescence and reassessment within the Catholic Church. By 1974 the progressives were again gaining strength and consolidating their position. There was also some movement toward the formation of fundamentalist and charismatic groups within and without the church. Thus, in terms of religious beliefs and resultant actions, the strongest tendency is toward the continuance of prerevolutionary patterns, although some are expressed in new forms. What is new is the slow increase in progressive leaders and the theological conceptualizations they promote.

The most essential of these is a new definition of salvation which deemphasizes other-worldly elements in favor of the responsibility of the Christian to seek the kingdom of God on earth. Influenced by liberation theology, the emphasis is on the obligation to struggle for socioeconomic justice and collaborate with those movements which appear most likely to achieve it. Stress is laid on the integration of one's Christian commitment and one's socioeconomic contribution to an equitable society, even if it involves the overthrow of existing secular as well as ecclesial structures. This position conflicts with the division many Cuban Christians continue to make between the spiritual and the secular. In 1967 forty percent of the Catholics in the diocese of Camagüey felt that one's religious life and secular life are independent entities. In addition, the notion of divine intervention remained strong, with 37% regarding God as the one to turn to for solutions to problems (El Equipo, 1967: 18-21). These attitudes set them apart from the majority of Cubans who were strongly imbued with secularism well before the revolution (Torroella, 1963: 14-28). New theological definitions to date have failed to transform the world view of most Cuban Christians.

## *VI. Conclusion*

Religion in prerevolutionary Cuba appeared to be weaker than in the rest of Latin America due to the institutional limitations of the churches and their reliance on a dependent national bourgeoisie and foreign sources of funding and personnel. This, combined with a relatively high degree of secularism in Cuban society, tended to relegate the churches to a marginalized position. These weaknesses resulted in the churches' power being less feared than in some other Latin American countries, which may, in part, explain the revolutionary government's apparent lack of deep concern even in the tense early years of 1960. Yet Cuba was a strongly Christian country which had been evangelized not only by Spanish Catholics, but also by U.S. Protestants, which resulted in the widespread dissemination of certain cultural values and norms even among those Cubans who never had any contact with formal religion.

The generalized Christian orientation of Cuban society contributed to a negative reaction to the revolution as it became more socialist. The situation was compounded by strong anticommunism among elements of the Spanish Catholic clergy and the U.S.-linked Protestant churches. While involvement in the churches was greater on the part of the urban bourgeoisie, the nature of religious certitude resulted in counterrevolutionary reactions on the part of strong believers from all classes, even when they were not frequent practitioners. Hence, even among the rural poor who were, by and large, the prime beneficiaries of such revolutionary programs as the expansion of public health and educational facilities, upgrading of housing, and elimination of unemployment, there were those who believed that support of the Castro government was totally inimical to their duties as Christians. Since the Church proclaimed itself the center of value and source of all meaning in life, the government's attempt in the early 1960s to capture the ultimate loyalty of all Cubans was regarded as antireligious. Under threats to its existence both from within and without Cuba, the government was suspicious of churches whose ultimate allegiance was to a source of meaning and values which had temporal links to western capitalism. As mutual hostility receded, in part as a result of the migration of the more negatively disposed church personnel and laity abroad, the churches turned in upon themselves in response to a desire for refuge from turmoil.

For some the revolution reinforced commitment to traditional religious practices, and there was a general tendency to escape into pietism. However, government mobilization of the population, particularly in programs aimed at dealing with traditional societal ills, prompted some positive response by a minority of churchpeople. In instances where there was enough latitude within the individual's church to allow for the operation of a dual commitment, there was the possibility of remaining one of the faithful. This was not the case with many churches, and between 1962 and 1968 there was considerable attrition in church membership beyond that caused by emigration. Increasingly in the late 1960s and early 1970s, losses appear to have resulted from conflicts within the churches. The possibility of the disintegration of the churches as constituted stimulated reflection aimed at rooting the churches firmly in their existential context, a task which required major theological reformulations and structural modifications. This process is more advanced in some Protestant churches than in the Catholic, in part because of the more flexible authority structures of the former.

As the churches were exposed to foreign explorations of Marxist-Christian dialogue and cooperation, they became more open. Church leadership was stimulated to join with the government in identifying problems of mutual concern and cooperating in such areas as education, health care, and the establishment of ethical goals. The churches were, in fact, challenged by the government's successes in eliminating such chronic problems as gambling, prostitution, and begging. Individuals began to voice their feelings that the churches' only means of survival was to integrate into the revolution. The definition of this process resulted in tensions between those who urged the churches to establish themselves as both supporters *and* critics of the government. Since the revolutionaries feel the only valid criticism is that which comes from within the process, such a strategy requires greater integration into the revolutionary process than that desired by many churchpeople.

A continuing problem has been doubts within the churches that they have the spiritual, intellectual, and emotional resources to assume a prophetic role in society. A majority of Protestant youth surveyed in the mid-1960s did not think their institutions possessed such abilities (Cepeda, 1966: 26). The attitude within the Catholic Church is pessimistic too; only six of 100 young activists from Santa Clara in 1970 were still with the church in 1975 (IM 5771112). Some Christians hope for a change in the government's ideological stance, but the increasing institutionalization of the revolution and the orthodoxy of the Party Congress in December 1975 does not encourage this. The Constitution adopted at that gathering provides for freedom to practice one's religion, although the government officially supports atheistic materialism. There is also some possibility that the greater democratization mandated by this document, particularly the establishment of nationwide representative assemblies under a program known as Popular Power, may result in more diversity within the revolution which could encourage increased integration of Christians.

The consolidation and institutionalization of the revolution, however, will probably result in increased ideological pressure on Christians, as well as on those who harbor Afro-Cuban beliefs. Given the small minority of Cubans presently affiliated with churches, such pressure over the long term could have substantial impact on the churches as institutions. Furthermore, changes outside Cuba may very well reduce the ability or willingness of international ecclesial structures to support them.

The beliefs of Cuban churchpeople are not changing rapidly enough to cause them to incorporate themselves into the revolution in any number, nor would this necessarily secure the future of the churches given the ideological distance between Marxism and Christianity. Even those who are most positively disposed toward the revolution and who accept Marxist economic analysis do not accept the materialist explanation of life. This is the most profoundly disturbing dilemma for those progressives I interviewed. If they maintain a belief in a transcendental explanation of life, there will always be the possibility of conflict of goals with the government. Revolutionary change in Cuba has already had a tremendous effect on the churches as temporal institutions. Only if substantial numbers of Cubans feel a strong need for an otherworldly explanation of life is there a likelihood that the churches will recuperate. Even then, it is probable that believers will seek to change their churches substantially to meet their specific needs in a socialist society. This portends even greater upheavals for the Cuban churches in the future than those already experienced.

## NOTES

1. These interviews are subsequently identified throughout the paper by a series of numbers beginning with IH, IT, ISM and IM. Since they are privileged in nature, further information is not available. Therefore, they are not listed in the reference section.

2. Pertinent studies not listed in the references include the works of Fernando Ortiz, Lydia Cabrera, and John Dumoulin.

3. Approximately 550 of 800 Catholic priests left and 2,700 of some 3,000 religious. Of these, approximately 8% were expelled by the Cuban government for alleged counter-revolutionary activities. Beginning in 1963 some Cuban and Spanish priests returned, joined by a few French and Belgian clerics. In the late 1960s the government indicated its willingness to grant residence permits to some 100 foreign religious if they could be recruited. This process has been slow (Houtart and Rousseau, 1971: 124; IH 4714111). The mainline Protestant denominations were hit particularly hard, losing as much as 50%

or more of their congregations and 80% to 90% of their ministers. More populist groups, such as the Baptists and Pentecostals, were less severely affected (United Methodist Board of Missions, 1971b: 3; Tschuy, 1971; Rivas, 1971: 7).

4. This is the sum claimed by Cepeda (1966: 11) and Hageman and Wheaton (1971: 31), while the Libro de Cuba (Anonymous, 1954: 747) reports 400,000 active Protestants.

5. Hageman and Wheaton (1971: 31) estimated 50,000 in 1970, when membership appeared to be stabilizing. Wallace reiterates that number two years later (Wallace, 1973: 10).

6. The study included parishes in Camagüey, Ciego de Avila, Morón, Florida, Nuevitas, Guaimaro, Santa Cruz del Sur, Jatibónico, Amancio Rodríguez, Vertientes, and Esmerelda.

7. Such criticisms have been reiterated by Tschuy, former Latin American Secretary of the World Council of Churches, and in evaluations by some U.S. churches of their prerevolutionary operations in Cuba (Rivas, 1971: 4; United Methodist Board of Missions, 1971a).

8. Of 50 Christian youths interviewed in the mid-1960s, 24% claimed to have been members of anti-Batista clandestine organizations. Only 2% claimed to have been pro-Batista (Cepeda, 1966: 25). Of the 33 Methodist ministers in Cuba in the 1950s, 15% were nonviolent anti-Batista activists; 60% passive opponents, and 25% claimed neutrality (Rivas, 1971: 5).

9. For a perceptive analysis of the impact of Castro's declaration, see Dewart (1963).

10. For the impact of the Cuban emigrées on the U.S. churches, see Cuban Research Center newsletters, 2 and 4. More recently there has been some liberalization among these individuals as attested to by the formation of progressive groups such as the Florida-based Cuban Christians for Justice and Freedom, which supports the end to the U.S. embargo of Cuba and encourages the resumption of diplomatic relations.

11. Reverend Israel Batista as quoted in Hageman and Wheaton (1971: 53).

12. Arce as quoted in Hageman and Wheaton (1971: 171).

## REFERENCES

AGUILAR, L. (1974) Cuba, 1933: Prologue to Revolution. New York: W. W. Norton.

Anonymous (1954) Libro de Cuba. Habana: no publisher.

BARNET, M. [ed.] (1968) The Autobiography of a Runaway Slave: Esteban Montejo. New York: Pantheon.

CEPEDA, R. (1966) "La juventud evangélica y la iglesia: estudio sobre Cuba." (unpublished).

CRAHAN, M. E. (1978) "Protestantism in Cuba," forthcoming in R. Millett, [ed.] Protestantism in Latin America. Grand Rapids: Eerdmans.

——— (1977) "Penetracao religiosa e nacionalismo em Cuba: atividades metodistas norte-americanas, 1898-1958." Religiao e Sociedale 1, 1 (Maio): 81-103.

——— (1976) "Testimony." Hearings before the Subcommittee on International Organizations of the Committee on International Relations, House of Representatives, Ninety-Fourth Congress, First Session, H.R. 6382. Washington: U.S. Government Printing Office: 274-288.

DAVIS, J. M. (1942) The Cuban Church in a Sugar Economy. New York: International Missonary Council.

DE LA HUERTA AGUIAR, R. F. (1960) "Espiritismo y otras supersticiones en la ponlación cubana." Revista del Hospital Psiquiátrico de la Habana 2, 1 (Enero-Marzo): 44-48.

DEWART, L. (1963) Christianity and Revolution: The Lesson of Cuba. New York: Herder & Herder.

DOMÍNGUEZ, J. (1975) Unpublished manuscript excerpts.

——— (1972) "Cuban Catholics and Castro." Worldview 15 (February): 24-29.

ECHEVARRA SALVAT, O. A. (1971) La Agricultura Cubana, 1934-1966: Régimen Social, Productividad y Nivel de Vida del Sector Agrícola. Miami: Ediciones Universal.

EL EQUIPO DIOCESANO DE JOVENES DE CAMAGÜEY (1967) "Estadistica socio-religiosa de la Diocesis de Camagüey." (unpublished).

GARCÍA FRANCO, R. (1970) "Estudio socio-religioso de una iglesia pequeña." (unpublished).

——— (1966) "Pastores en la U.M.A.P.: diálogo en la U.M.A.P." October 2. (unpublished)

HAGEMAN, A. L. and P. E. WHEATON [eds.] (1971) Religion in Cuba Today: A New Church in a New Society. New York: Association Press.

HOUTART, F. and A. ROUSSEAU (1971) The Church and Revolution. Maryknoll, NY: Orbis.

JOVER, M. (1974) "The Cuban church in a revolutionary society." LADOC 4, 32 (April): 17-36.

LEVINE, D. H. (1973) "The meaning of politics to Catholic elites in Latin America." Paper presented at IX World Congress of the International Political Science Association, August 19-25, 1973, Montreal.

LEWIS, B. H. [ed.] (1960) Methodist Overseas Mission, 1960: Gazetteer and Statistics. New York: Board of Missions of the United Methodist Church.

LÓPEZ OLIVA, E. (1970) Los Catolicos y la Revolucion Latinoaméricana. Habana: Instituto del Libro.

NELSON, L (1970) Rural Cuba. New York: Octagon.

NOGUEIRA RIVERO, G. (1962) "El sincretismo religioso como causa desencadenante y lo determinante de sindromes neuróticos y pseudo-psicóticos en el niño cubano." Revista del Hospital Psiquiátrico de la Habana 3, 1 (Enero-Marzo): 37-46.

ORDOÑEZ, J. (1974) "Informe sobre una visita a Cuba, 20 a 28 de junio 1974." Panamá. (unpublished)

Religious News Service (1971) Press release. March 18.

RIVAS, G. (1971) Minutes of the Cuba Sub-Group, Latin American Methodist Task Force. March 1.

ROCHON, L. (1967) "La sociedad agropecuaria 'Jesús Feliú': un caso de cambio en el medio rural bajo un régimen socialista de transición." Etnología y Folklore 4 (Julio-Diciembre): 23-37.

RUIZ, R. E. (1968) Cuba: The Making of a Revolution. Amherst: Univ. of Massachusetts Press.

TORROELLA, G. (1963) Estudio de la Juventud Cubana. La Habana: Comisión Nacional Cubana de la UNESCO.

TSCHUY, T. (1971) "Responses to questions in Mr. Davis' letter of February 11, 1971, Tannay, Switzerland." (unpublished)

UNITED METHODIST BOARD OF MISSIONS (1971a) Minutes of May 14 meeting. Cuba Sub Group, Latin American Task Force.

——— (1971b) Minutes of March 1 meeting. Cuba Sub Group, Latin American Task Force.

UNITED METHODIST INFORMATION (1972) News Release. July 25.

UNIVERSIDAD CENTRAL "MARTA ABREU" DE LAS VILLAS (1959) La Educación Rural en Las Villas: Bases para la Redacción de Unos Cursos de Estudios. Santa Clara: Universidad Central.

VALLIER, I. (1970) Catholicism, Social Control, and Modernization in Latin America. Englewood Cliffs, NJ: Prentice-Hall.

WALLACE, J. (1973) "Christians in Cuba." Cuba Resource Center Newsletter 3, 1 (April): 3-11.

*Margaret E. Crahan is currently Associate Professor of History at Herbert H. Lehman College, City University of New York, and John Courtney Murray Fellow at the Woodstock Theological Center. She has published on religion and politics in Hapsburg, and in Peru, on colonial administrative history, and on twentieth-century Cuba. Presently she is writing a study of U.S. missionaries in Cuba and has just completed editing with Franklin W. Knight* Africa and the Caribbean: Legacies of a Civilization, *to be published by Johns Hopkins University Press. Research for the present essay took her to Cuba in 1973-1974, 1976, and 1977.*

# Advertising Supplement: Journal of Interamerican Studies and World Affairs

This supplement has been prepared especially for our readers to bring them information and announcements of professional interest. By placing advertisements in the pages of this journal, our advertisers have indicated a desire to communicate with our readers. We hope our readers will acknowledge their indirect support of the journal and its purposes by mentioning the journal in correspondence with advertisers.

172421

SOCIAL FORMATIONS AND POWER
IN LATIN AMERICA

edited by **JORGE GRACIANRENA and ROLANDO FRANCO,**
*United Nations Economic Commission for Latin America, Santiago, Chile*

Two perspectives are presented concerning the political development of Latin America over the last three decades—the political process in relation to inherent values and ideological frames of reference, and as it has been reflected in the social sciences—through a discussion of regional contributors.

**A special issue of CURRENT SOCIOLOGY, Spring 1978**
**266 pages / Individual $4.00 / Institutional $7.50**

**SAGE PUBLICATIONS, INC.**
**275 South Beverly Drive**
**Beverly Hills, California 90212**

**SAGE PUBLICATIONS LTD**
**28 Banner Street**
**London EC1Y 8QE, England**

# LATIN AMERICA AND WORLD ECONOMY: A Changing International Order

edited by **JOSEPH GRUNWALD**

How do nations of Latin America interact with other countries in the world community? This anthology approaches the region's relations with the outside world from both an economic and a political perspective, examining Latin America's desire to integrate with the world economy, as well as its struggle for self-reliance. Latin American and non-Latin American contributors discuss a range of subjects including the character of the "special relationship" between Latin America and the United States, and the ambiguous nature of Latin America's relations with other countries of the Third World.

**CONTENTS**

Preface
1. Reflections on Latin America in the World Economy, JOSEPH BRUNWALD

**Part I. Economic Relations with Industrial Countries**
2. The Mature Neighbor Policy: A Proposal for A United States Economic Policy for Latin America, ALBERT FISHLOW
3. Britain's Economic Relations with Latin America, LAURENCE WHITEHEAD
4. The Economic Relations between Germany and Latin America and the significance of the European Community, ALBRECHT von GLEICH
5. Latin America's Opening to the Pacific, CLAUDIO VELEZ

**Part II. Mexico and Brazil**
6. The External Sector of the Mexican Economy, LEOPOLDO SOLIS
7. The Determinants of Brazil's Foreign Economic Policy, WERNER BAER, CARLOS von DOELLINGER

**Part III. Regional Integration and Economic Relations with the Third World**
8. The Andean Pact: A Model of Economic Integration for Developing Countries, RICARDO FFRENCH-DAVIS
9. Fissures in the Volcano? Centeral American Economic Prospects, CLARK W. REYNOLDS
10. Latin America and the Third World, FELIPE HERRERA

**Part IV. Two Major Issues: Financing Development and the Multinational Corporation**
11. Problems of External Financing in Latin America, LUIS ESCOBAR
12. Mexico and Multinational Corporations: An Explanation of State Action, DOUGLAS BENNETT, MORRIS J. BLACHMAN, KENNETH SHARPE

**Part V. Commentary**
**The Good Neighbor Policy Revisite**

**Part V. Commentary**
The Good Neighbor Policy Revisited, BRYCE WOOD
Notes on SELA, GABRIEL VALDES S.

*"As long as the notion persists that Latin America is unimportant for the United States and other developed countries, it will be difficult to persuade Latin American countries that they are living in an interdependent world. One-sided importance creates a one-sided dependency relationship. Such a perseption results in demands, not cooperation. Cooperation for development becomes meaningful only when there is a recognition of interdependence on both sides of the North-South relationship."*

*— from Chapter 1*

***Sponsored by the Center for Inter-American Relations**
**Latin American International Affairs, Volume 2**

| | | | |
|---|---|---|---|
| **1978** | **ISBN 0-8039-0864-4** | **hardcover** | **$18.50** |
| **320 pages** | **ISBN 0-8039-0966-7** | **softcover** | **$ 8.95** |

**SAGE** PUBLICATIONS, INC.
275 South Beverly Drive
Beverly Hills, California 90212

**SAGE** PUBLICATIONS LTD
28 Banner Street
London EC1Y 8QE, England

Please mention Journal of Interamerican Studies and World Affairs when writing advertisers.

Vol. 21 No. 2
May 1979

# JOURNAL OF INTERAMERICAN STUDIES

# and WORLD AFFAIRS

A Publication of the Center for Advanced International Studies.

The University of Miami

SAGE PUBLICATIONS

*Journal of INTERAMERICAN STUDIES and WORLD AFFAIRS*

**EDITORIAL STAFF:**

John P. Harrison—Editor
Jan Peter Wogart—Associate Editor
Gerry Machovec—Editorial Assistant

**BOARD OF EDITORS:**

Orlando Albornoz, Universidad Central de Venezuela
D. A. Brading, Cambridge University
David Chaplin, Western Michigan University
Tom E. Davis, Cornell University
Malcolm Deas, St. Antony's College, Oxford, England
Isaac Kerstenetzky, Instituto Brasileiro de Geografia e Estatistica, Brazil
Celso Lafer, Universidade de São Paulo
Vaughan A. Lewis, University of the West Indies, Mona, Jamaica
Abraham Lowenthal, Woodrow Wilson International Center for Scholars
Robert McNicoll, University of Miami, emeritus
Carmelo Mesa-Lago, University of Pittsburgh
James J. Parsons, University of California, Berkeley
Clark Reynolds, Stanford University
Richard Schaedel, University of Texas, Austin
Hanns-Albert Steger, Universitat Erlangen-Nurnberg, Germany
Alfred Stepan, Yale University
Evelyn P. Stevens, Case Western Reserve University
Victor L. Urquidi, El Colegio de Mexico

The editors and publisher wish to acknowledge with gratitude the assistance and encouragement of the Center for Advanced International Studies, University of Miami, in providing ancillary services and support for this journal.

*Journal of*
INTERAMERICAN
STUDIES
*and* WORLD AFFAIRS

Vol. 21
No. 2
May
1979

# CONTENTS

*A Trudeau Decade: Canadian-Latin American Relations 1968-1978*
J.C.M. OGELSBY 187

*Leonardo Ruiz Pineda: Leader of the Venezuelan Resistance, 1949-1952*
CHARLES AMERINGER 209

*From "Color" to "Rainbow": U.S. Strategic Planning for Latin America, 1919-1945*
JOHN CHILD 233

*Industrialist in the Wilderness: Henry Ford's Amazon Venture*
JOHN GALEY 261

**BOOKS RECEIVED** 291

SAGE PUBLICATIONS / *Beverly Hills* *London*

**POLICY: THE JOURNAL OF INTERAMERICAN STUDIES AND WORLD AFFAIRS** reflects the interests of the scholarly community and interested public concerned with the social, economic, political, and cultural aspects of life in Latin America (including the Caribbean); particularly in those instances where the subject is of concern to more than one of the traditional disciplines. As these concerns change, so will the content of the journal.

**ARTICLES** which have special relevance for interrelationships between American nations and of those nations with the rest of the world will be given special consideration. An effort will be made to include occasional articles that state an unusual or even discordant position on a subject of broad interest to be supplemented by critical comments of authorities representing differing positions on the topic. The editors continue to welcome articles by scholars from all parts of the world.

**MANUSCRIPTS** should be submitted in duplicate to: Editor, JOURNAL OF INTERAMERICAN STUDIES AND WORLD AFFAIRS, Box 24-8134, University of Miami, Coral Gables, Florida 33124. Manuscripts should be typewritten, double-spaced, with footnotes, references, tables, and charts on separate pages, and should follow the current journal style. A brief biographical paragraph describing each author's current affiliation, research interests, and recent publications should accompany the manuscript.

**CORRESPONDENCE** regarding book reviews should be sent directly to: Book Review Editor, JOURNAL OF INTERAMERICAN STUDIES AND WORLD AFFAIRS, Box 24-8134, University of Miami, Coral Gables, Florida 33124.

---

**JOURNAL OF INTERAMERICAN STUDIES AND WORLD AFFAIRS** is published four times annually—in February, May, August and November. Copyright © 1979 by Sage Publications, Inc. All rights reserved. No portion of the contents may be reproduced in any form without written permission of the publisher.

**Subscriptions:** Regular institutional rate $28.00. Individuals may subscribe at a one-year rate of $15.00. Add $1.00 per year for subscriptions outside the United States. Orders from U.K., Europe, the Middle East, and Africa should be sent to the London office (address below). Noninstitutional orders **must** be paid by personal check.

Second-class postage paid at Beverly Hills, California. ISSN 0022-1937

**Inquiries:** Address all correspondence and permissions requests to SAGE PUBLICATIONS, INC., 275 South Beverly Drive, Beverly Hills, California 90212. Inquiries and subscriptions from U.K., Europe, the Middle East, and Africa should be sent to SAGE PUBLICATIONS LTD, 28 Banner Street, London EC1Y 8QE, England. Other orders should be sent to the Beverly Hills office.

**Advertising:** Current rates and specifications may be obtained by writing to the Advertising Manager at the Beverly Hills office (address above).

**This journal is abstracted or indexed in Historical Abstracts, Human Resources Abstracts, Sage Urban Studies Abstracts, International Political Science Abstracts, Public Affairs Information Service, Current Contents, Social Sciences Citation Index, Social Sciences Index, ABC POL SCI and United States Political Science Documents.**

**Back Issues:** Information about availability and prices of back issues may be obtained from the publisher's order department (address above). Write to London office for sterling prices.

**Claims for undelivered copies** must be made no later than three months following month of publication. The publisher will supply missing copies when losses have been sustained in transit and where the reserve stock will permit.

**Change of Address:** Six weeks' advance notice must be given when notifying of change of address. Please send old address label along with the new address to insure proper identification. Please specify name of journal.

*J.C.M. OGELSBY*
*Department of History*
*University of Western Ontario*
*London, Canada*

# *A TRUDEAU DECADE*
## *Canadian-Latin American Relations 1968-1978*

Pierre Elliot Trudeau became leader of Canada's Liberal Party and Prime Minister of Canada in April 1968. Almost immediately he promised an effort to take new directions in Canada's external relations. One of the regions he focused attention on was Latin America (Dobell, 1972: 115).

That Trudeau was interested in Latin America appears natural for an intellectual raised in Quebec. There has long been a certain sympathy with the concept of *latinité*. French-Canadian intellectuals often believed that they had much in common with Latin Americans, because of their religions or cultural heritage, and felt a pull from that region even if they had never visited it. Trudeau had been editor of a leading Quebec journal, *Cité Libre,* and that journal occasionally had editorial comment on events in Latin America. Indeed, Trudeau established his position on political involvement in the Inter-American system in that journal and he has not wavered from that position since then (Octobre 1964; and his recent statement in *International Canada,* 1976).

Trudeau was not alone in pushing for closer relations with Latin America. One of his closest friends and a member of his Cabinet was Gérard Pelletier. Pelletier had not only traveled as far south as Argentina during the Perón years but had demonstrated his desire to improve Canadian knowledge of Latin American affairs by posting a correspondent to the region when he became editor of Canada's largest French language newspaper, *La Presse.* Unfortunately he found, as others have found, that the post cost too much and that it was too difficult for one man to handle the responsibility of such a vast area. His second major

Journal of Interamerican Studies and World Affairs, Vol. 21 No. 2, May 1979, 187-208
© 1979 Sage Publications, Inc.

contact with Latin America came in 1967 when he was serving as Parliamentary Secretary to Paul Martin, the Secretary of State for External Affairs in the Cabinet of Lester Pearson.

Martin was not a man to let his Parliamentary Secretaries (a virtually powerless position that provides some experience to potential cabinet ministers at the discretion of the minister) have much influence in the formulation of foreign policy (Dobell, 1972: 12-13; Thordarson, 1972: 22-27). Pelletier in discussion with me showed that he found the post frustrating and appeared relieved that he was going to be allowed to make a trip to Latin America, one of the areas of his "responsibility." At least he would be able to see for himself the activities of Canada's representatives there.

The embassies that Pelletier visited existed in isolation from the mainstream of Canadian foreign policy. The posts were, like most of Canada's minor embassies of the time, small. The staffs, while willing to do their duty, more often than not probably recognized that they would have preferred to be elsewhere. There was little interest in them at home and generally staff limitations meant that the officers spent more time in routine administrative duties rather than in the more stimulating political and economic ones.

The one issue that dominated Canadian thinking concerning Latin America was whether or not to join the Organization of American States (OAS). Martin was committed to that goal but could neither move the Cabinet nor the country toward full membership. Canada had been satisfied to join several bodies within the OAS,[1] but refrained from joining any that would be too costly, such as the Pan American Health Organization. Cost factors had traditionally weighed heavily in any decisions regarding Latin America and the mid-1960s would prove no exception (Ogelsby, 1976a: 44). Pelletier, committed as he was to improving the contact between Canada and Latin America, learned from his three and one-half week visit to seven countries, and much of what he learned probably had an influence on the new government. As one of the two or three men closest to Trudeau and the individual with the most recent experience in Latin America,

Pelletier had confirmed impressions that there was much to be done in improving Canadian-Latin American relations. In my two conversations with him before he became a Minister of the Crown, and in a very brief meeting shortly after his appointment to Cabinet, it was clear that he thought Canada could do more in terms of bilateral contact at the diplomatic, commercial, development assistance, and cultural levels. He was not committed to full membership in the OAS, but he was convinced that Canada should clarify its position with regard to the region, so it is not surprising to find that Pelletier and others close to Trudeau were anxious to review Canada's role in Latin America (Dobell, 1972: 12-13; Thordarson, 1972: 115). To begin that review, Trudeau announced there would be a mission leaving in the autumn of 1968.

The 1968 mission to nine Latin American republics was the largest ever sent to the region. It could have gone the way of its predecessors and been just another mission, whose members had returned to Canada full of enthusiasm but who all too quickly had become embroiled in more pressing matters (Ogelsby, 1976a: 9-36). But it did not. Its preliminary report was but a prelude for a more intensive study which culminated in one of the six booklets published in 1970 as part of the Trudeau government's foreign policy review: *Foreign Policy for Canadians.* The booklet, *Latin America,* and the government's actions since 1968 bear the stamp of Trudeau and Pelletier: Canada would not seek full membership in the OAS at the moment but would seek closer links with the organization; it would be prepared to participate in several more OAS bodies although it would not join the Inter-American Development Bank (BID); it would increase bilateral contacts in the areas of trade, investment, culture, and development assistance.[2]

Some staunch Latin Americanists were not too sure what this all meant especially after the government had closed its embassies in the Dominican Republic, Educador, and Uruguay in late 1969, but the closures were in line with the government's intentions to expand its role in francophobic Africa and to open a mission at the Vatican. Pelletier had seen no reason to have missions everywhere in Latin America, especially if it meant spreading the personnel too thinly and thus reducing Canadian effectiveness. As it was, the closures affected only those embassies handled by chargé d'affaires subordinate to ambassadors in Caracas, Bogotá, and Buenos Aires. This must have seemed the easiest way to deal with closures, but it certainly did not take into account Canadian interests, especially in the Dominican Republic (Sokol, 1970).

The publication of *Foreign Policy for Canadians* still did not guarantee that the Trudeau government would make a serious effort toward Latin America, but it gave rise to speculation that there would be some initiatives as the government was obviously seeking closer ties to Europe, Latin America, and the western Pacific—to counter the overwhelming presence of the United States. This attempt to find counterweights to the United States has since become known as "The Third Option." The government published a position paper (Sharp, 1972) which indicated that it conceived that Canada had three options open to it with regard to the United States: ultimate absorption; the status quo; or a more aggressive attempt to diversify and deepen Canada's ties outside North America. This last proposal differs very little from the one suggested in 1866 when the Fathers of Confederation sought closer commercial ties with Latin America and the Caribbean.

Once again Canadians would be pushing for closer links with Latin American countries usually prone to ignore Canada unless Canadians pushed Latin Americans to notice them. Canada is obscured from Latin America by the presence of the United States. If Latin Americans come to Canada, it is usually after having spent some time in the United States and as part of a pilgrimage to see Niagara Falls or, perhaps, events such as Expo 67 or the Olympic Games. Prior to 1970 few senior Latin American statesmen had come to Ottawa at their own initiative. Indeed, there is a direct parallel between the Canadian and Latin American experience. Both regions have concentrated their efforts on contacts with the United States and Europe and the former, rather than the latter, has been the chief focus of these contacts.

In 1970, then, Canada was taking the initiative once again, although this time Latin America was not going to be the primary focus of attention and would have to share the effort with other regions of the world. It might be expected that Canada, as a relatively small country of 23 million people, would not have the personnel to carry out a worldwide effort, but Canada was at the time a relatively rich country, with a highly educated population, and the government had the determination and the blueprint.

The first order of business after the tabling of *Foreign Policy for Canadians* in the House of Commons on 25 June was to take advantage of an OAS General Assembly meeting on 30 June to have a Parlimentary Secretary to the Minister for External Affairs attend the assembly in order to announce that Canada wished to become a "Permanent Observer" to the organization. Rather than seek full membership, the government had decided to undertake "a systematic strengthening" of bilateral relations and to work "through agencies of the Inter-American system and the UN" in order to improve "Canadian knowledge and understanding of those [Latin American] countries and their regional institutions" so that a better informed Canada could, "at some future date, opt for full participation" in the OAS (Canada, 1970: 32). This resolution was in line with the Trudeau view. It was also in keeping with a general Canadian desire to avoid political involvement; while the majority of Canadians have had no interest in the OAS, it is probably fair to say that most Canadians have a negative "gut" feeling about the organization. A "Permanent Observer" was just that—an observer—and thus the government avoided awakening a visceral response that might have proved embarrassing.

The following April another Parliamentary Secretary headed the Canadian delegation to an OAS General Assembly at San José, Costa Rica. It was at this meeting that the OAS approved the idea of a "Permanent Observer" role. The way was clear for Canada, and on 2 February 1972 Canada's Minister for External Affairs, Mitchell Sharp, made his first public appearance on the issue. He announced in Ottawa that the OAS had accepted the Canadian application. Two and one-half months later the government appointed Alfred Pick, an experienced Foreign

Service Officer, to head its Permanent Observer Mission to the OAS. It is one of the smallest missions in Canada's foreign service and is now headed by Pick's successor, Dr. Arthur Blanchette.

Membership in the OAS has been the dominant issue in Canada's on-again, off-again flirtation with Latin America (Miller, 1948; Harbron, 1963; Ogelsby, 1968). For years that debate obscured Canada's relations with the area. The Trudeau government appears to have avoided that trap and has maneuvered very skillfully. But using Parliamentary Secretaries rather than the External Affairs Minister, the chief government spokesman, it indicated that the issue had a low priority. And yet the government gained an additional source of information and established closer contact with regional representatives that may prove useful over the years.

Canada moved relatively quickly to join OAS-affiliated bodies. It joined the Pan American Health Organization (1971) and the Inter-American Institute of Agricultural Sciences (1972). More significantly, and surprisingly, Canada, after announcing in *Latin America* that it would not seek membership in the Inter-American Development Bank (BID), did so in early 1972. Canada had been reluctant to join because it believed that BID would require too high a percentage of Canada's aid funds, but this move can probably be accounted for in several ways. For one thing Trudeau government has consistently been increasing Canada's development assistance allotment until it now stands at over $1 billion. Thus the initial fear of a large financial commitment to this multilateral organization had dissipated. For another, one of the government's initial goals had been to move development assistance away from bilateral to multilateral assistance in order to weaken the "tied-aid" apsects. Other reasons could include dissatisfaction at the way Canada's annual $10,000,000 contributions (since 1964) had been handled. Canada had had no control over the initial selection of projects and had had little opportunity to express its philosophy or explain its system of development assistance to the bank or its borrowers. And then there was also the shadow of possible commercial intelligence that membership might provide to further Canadian-Latin American trade links. Besides, Canada liked to receive recognition for its efforts.

Canada committed $100,000,000 over an initial three-year period to BID and had another $202,000,000 on call. Five years later Canada continued to have more than $400,000,000 committed to the BID (Inter-American Development Bank, 1978).

In April 1978 there was a little more publicity than usual about BID in Canada, because the BID held its annual meeting in Vancouver, British Columbia. This permitted the current Minister of Finance, Jean Chretien, to obtain exposure for his government in a possible election year, though his publicists may have gone a little far when they described him in his role as host as having "a longstanding interest in Latin America." Chretien made several trips there in his previous short-lived tenure as Trade Minister, but unlike Pelletier and Trudeau he had not appeared to be attracted to the region prior to the 1970s. Nevertheless he made an enthusiastic impression and even expressed "grave concern" over the United State's $265 million arrears *(Globe and Mail,* 18 April 1978). Having once joined an organization, Canadians like to participate and sometimes can be surprising.

One of the reasons given for not joining the OAS has been a fear of getting caught on one side or another of arguments between Latin America and the United States. Canada's membership in the BID has at least twice publicly shown Canada prepared to take a position that disturbed those used to "quiet diplomacy." Chretien's "grave concern" statement may have startled some, but Canadians have shown they can take positions as in the 1973 BID meeting when the Canadian representative objected to using the "BID as a lever and a whip to punish recipient countries involved in 'bilateral' disputes over expropriation and compensation." The specific problem was Allende's Chile and its disagreement with the United States, and the Washington correspondent of the *Financial Post* saw the Canadian position as possibly damaging to Canadian-United States relations (Solomon, 1973). He was obviously wrong.

The Trudeau government's steps toward the Inter-American system created very little stir in Canada, but its relations with Chile did. The September 1973 coup d'état that deposed President Salvador Allende and his government was not ignored in Canada. This was unusual because Canadians do not normally take much interest in a Latin American change of government, but Chile was not just another Latin American government. It was a freely elected one that pursued Marxist goals. This, of course, guaranteed that Chile would receive heavy international news coverage. And so Canadians, whose newspapers rely heavily upon United States, British, and French news agencies, were not unaware of the situation.

One of the paradoxes of the situation was that the Department of External Affairs did not appear particularly concerned about the Allende election and its implications. Canada's embassy there had traditionally been small and unimportant; it continued to be so. The fact that Chile was a focus of world attention and that the political aspects of the post in these circumstances would be demanding seems to have escaped External Affairs, which faced with a need to economize decided not to bolster the embassy staff at the political level. As it was, for much of the Allende period only the ambassador was involved in political reporting at a time when even the Australians had assigned two diplomats to the task. When External Affairs later sent an additional officer and thus permitted two staff members to concentrate on political matters, the staff, as all but the plotters, was not prepared for a coup (the ambassador was in Argentina on personal business). If the 11 September coup was a surprise to Chile, the impact of the coup was a surprise to the Trudeau government. Part of the problem was the fact that the government was a minority one and thus had to move more circumspectly than otherwise. There were two issues involved: recognition of the military government and asylum for refugees. In the face of the considerable opposition from organizations sympathetic to Marxist solutions and from organizations concerned with human rights, the government chose to follow its normal policy of recognizing a government when it is convinced that the particular government is in control of affairs. Canada maintains that recognition does not necessarily mean approval of the recognized government's policies (Canada 1973: 6667). It recognized the junta on 23 September.

The refugee issue (Hanff, 1977) was a more prolonged matter. Canada had gained an image as a sanctuary for refugees by opening its doors to refugees in the 1950s and 1960s. The refugees had largely been from Communist countries and it had been easy to justify. Now there wre those who demanded consistency and the government had to consider admitting Marxists. Under considerable pressure the government did decide to admit refugees, but its policy reflected an awareness of the divisions in Canada over the issue. Hence it was cautious in terms of numbers—it has so far offered to take about 7,000 refugees. For the some 5,000 admitted it has usually provided heads of families and single adults with language training and an opportunity to find a place in the country. Unfortunately, the refugees arrived in Canada at a time when the economic situation was deteriorating, so that their settlement has not always been satisfactory. The government has been cautious about admitting extremists. Although this upsets those few sympathetic to an extremist viewpoint, the government reflects the wishes of the majority of Canadians. The issue became less trying when the government achieved a majority in July 1974 and regained greater control of its affairs. Hence, it has resisted demands from Marxist or human rights groups to take positions against the Chilean government or to pressure Canadian businesses involved in Chile.

The next major diplomatic exposure for the Trudeau government was the Prime Minister's trip to Mexico, Cuba, and Venezuela in January 1976. Trudeau had traveled widely in his first seven years in power, but he had not made an official visit to any Latin American country. The 1976 visit received considerable publicity. Unlike the 1968 misison and the 1977 mission of his Secretary of State for External Relations to Latin America, the Canadian press and television gave the trip extensive coverage, especially the Cuban aspect of the trip.[3] Trudeau and Castro were news and much was made of the fact that Trudeau was the first head of government of a NATO country to visit Cuba. Also there was the attraction of viewing two of the Americas' leading political personalities. Paradoxically, although the two leaders appeared to enjoy the meeting, Cuban-Canadian relations, which had been warming up considerably before the mission, have tended to return to the staid, formal aspects of the period prior to 1970 (Ogelsby, 1975). In Canada there was considerable opposition to Cuba's African adventures and the government faced strong questioning in the Commons over its development assistance to a country engaged in combat abroad. That assistance has been phased down. However, there has been considerable effort to capitalize on the Prime Minister's meeting with the Mexicans and the Venezuelans, especially at the economic level.

It is at the economic level that Canadian governments have traditionally put their greatest effort toward Latin America.[4] The Trudeau government has been no exception. Trade and investment received a prominent place in *Foreign Policy for Canadians* and the government has, as a result, stimulated Canadian efforts but has also instituted programs to help Latin Americans gain knowledge of the Canadian market.

One important innovation has been the establishment of Joint-Ministerial Committees. The first such committee had its origins during the 1968 mission's visit to Mexico. Mitchell Sharp announced on 22 November that Canada and Mexico had agreed to meet regularly to discuss matters of mutual concern. It was three years before the committee finally met in October 1971. That Ottawa meeting saw itself as a "new phase" in relations between the two countries although both were trying to overcome old problems such as easier access of Mexican fruits and vegetables and the importance of the United States. However, there was a genuine effort to establish a continuing dialogue (Canada, 1971) and it was left up to the Mexican government to decide when it would be held again. Mexico, anxious to sell its growing manufactured products abroad, began to take some initiative in the relationship and sent a large trade mission to Canada in 1972, its President came in 1973, and the Ministers did meet again, in Mexico, in January 1974. The latest meeting, 22 November 1977, was well attended by senior officials on both sides and clearly the governments had more to talk about and more to be positive about than during the first tentative attempts at a reasonably regular gathering. As the final joint communique noted, "during the six years since the First Meeting of the Committee, Mexican-Canadian trade has nearly tripled and a significant number of concrete steps have been taken to extend and diversify the range of contacts between the Canadian and Mexican people as well as between respective governments and business communities" (Canada, 1977b).

The general satisfaction with the "Joint-Committee" concept has led to the establishment of joint economic committees with Cuba in 1975 and with Brazil in 1976. The private business sector has also taken up the idea and since 1971 there has been an annual meeting of the Canada-Mexico Businessmen's Committee. Its own summaries of the meetings indicate that it is more than just an opportunity for its members to travel.

The Brazil-Canada Chamber of Commerce came into existence in December 1973. The drive behind its establishment came from Brascan, Canada's largest overseas corporation and a company which has been a major presence in Brazil since the turn of the century (Ogelsby, 1976a: 126-142); Massey-Ferguson and Alcan joined in the effort to make the Canadian business community more aware of Brazil. The chamber of commerce, located in Toronto, now has more than 40 members and has its counterpart in Brazil. Its monthly newsletter keeps members and interested parties informed of Canadian-Brazilian relations in the business and cultural affairs.[5]

Brascan was also instrumental in organizing the establishment of the Canadian Association Latin-America (CALA). Founded in 1969, CALA was first led by Michael Lubbock, an Englishman of extraordinary talent who had been in charge of railways in Peru and had previously served as a director of the Bank of London and South America. Lubbock worked with a limited budget to build membership—it has grown from 62 corporate members in 1970 to 141 in 1977—and through his contacts in Latin America to bring leading Latin Americans in the public and private sector to CALA's annual conferences. It was hoped that

CALA's efforts would increase Canadian-Latin American trade in both directions, but for all its efforts CALA has not been able to stand as a private organization. Since 1973 it has had to carry out its activities with the help of government funding. In 1976 and 1977 the government supplied about half of CALA's budget. It is a measure of the government's recognition that CALA does provide a service that has enabled the organization to survive; indeed, when Lubbock, then in his seventies, retired in early 1976, government seconded one of its experienced trade officials to the organization.

It is one of the paradoxes of the Canadian experience that government and private enterprise tend to pool their resources and interests. One would think that 140 of Canada's major companies could support an active office dedicated to finding markets (CALA's 1977 budget, excluding the Executive Director's government salary, was $142,000). But not in Canada. Businesses tend to become interested in overseas markets to the extent that the government does and it seems reasonable to conclude that Canadian business involvement with Latin America depends very much on the efforts and funds provided by government. Hence the Canadian taxpayer has become used to supporting both a bureaucracy (in this case its trade commissioners in Latin America) and private enterprise (CALA, 1977).

Canada's trade with Latin America has increased in dollar volume since 1967. In that year Canada exported goods worth over $335 million and Latin American imports were valued at more than $416 million. Ten years later the figures had risen five-fold. Inflation and the increase in the price of oil probably explain a good portion of the larger figures. Venezuelan oil accounted for 62% of Canada's imports. In terms of world trade, however, Canada and Latin America continued to find that their trade hovered around 4% of their international markets, though this is a modest increase over the slightly more than 3% of the early 1960s.

After much effort and considerable discussion at the Ministerial level, Canada has been able to increase its exports to Venezuela, the one Latin American country that has managed to maintain a

TABLE 1
Canadian-Latin American Trade ($ millions)

| COUNTRY | 1967 EXPORTS TO | 1967 IMPORTS FROM | 1977 EXPORTS TO | 1977 IMPORTS FROM |
|---|---|---|---|---|
| Argentina | 33.3 | 5.1 | 104.7 | 22.8 |
| Bolivia | 2.2 | .5 | 3.9 | 11.2 |
| Brazil | 27.5 | 31.4 | 275.6 | 213.9 |
| Chile | 17.7 | 1.7 | 37.0 | 22.6 |
| Colombia | 18.1 | 13.3 | 60.8 | 63.6 |
| Costa Rica | 4.1 | 7.2 | 13.8 | 25.9 |
| Cuba | 42.3 | 6.3 | 184.0 | 45.3 |
| Dominican Republic | 4.7 | .9 | 25.3 | 24.7 |
| Ecuador | 3.1 | 8.1 | 20.4 | 68.0 |
| El Salvador | 4.4 | 2.0 | 13.4 | 14.8 |
| Guatemala | 2.9 | 2.4 | 16.2 | 23.3 |
| Haiti | 1.1 | .9 | 15.9 | 3.4 |
| Honduras | 1.1 | 11.6 | 8.9 | 18.6 |
| Mexico | 49.2 | 29.5 | 217.4 | 194.2 |
| Nicaragua | 2.8 | 1.8 | 9.1 | 14.4 |
| Panama | 4.6 | 14.7 | 18.7 | 12.9 |
| Peru | 32.5 | 2.2 | 46.9 | 37.5 |
| Uruguay | 2.9 | .4 | 8.2 | 4.2 |
| Venezuela | 82.0 | 276.3 | 542.4 | 1,361.0 |
| TOTALS | 336.5 | 416.3 | 1,622.6 | 2,182.3 |

Source: Dominion Bureau of Statistics (1967) and Statistics Canada (1977).

favorable balance of trade with Canada for almost half a century. A Canadian decision in the 1950s to purchase cheaper Venezuelan oil for the provinces east of Ottawa, rather than pipe Alberta oil there, has made Canada dependent on that oil. This did not matter much before OPEC raised prices. Now Canada is trying harder to penetrate the Venezuelan market and the Trudeau visit and the trade missions of 1975 and 1976 have helped. Canada increased the value of its 1977 exports to almost $200 million over 1976's $355 million trade. This left Canada, which had only a $227 million deficit in its 1970 Venezuelan trade, with an $820 million one in 1976. Prior to 1973 Canada could make up that deficit through her trade with the rest of Latin America. Since OPEC, that has not been the case.

Canada's major Latin American trading partners are themselves no longer willing to suffer unfavorable trade balances. Mexico, Brazil, and Cuba are anxious to improve their own trade position with Canada. These countries, with Venezuela, comprise 80% of Canada's Latin American market, and they have not been particularly happy with Canada's determination to protect its textile and shoe industries or, in the case of Cuba, to prefer South African over Cuban sugar. Canadians on the other hand, have not always found it easy to break through the tariff and bureaucratic walls in those countries. What is noticeable now is that the countries are more willing to talk about the issues on a regular basis rather than, as has been done in the past, make rhetorical statements about the problem and then file them away to be brought out when the next mission passes through.

Prior to the Trudeau decade, "mission diplomacy" was an occasional happening (Canada, 1977a). Now it seems to be a regular approach in the transaction of Canadian-Latin American relations. Even the provincial governments and federal agencies have discovered that the "flight of the snowbirds" is available to them at taxpayers' expense. The period 1973-1977 saw more than 25 Canadian missions, usually to the four major markets, between October and May, and even though it is possible to be cynical about the timing of these missions, the missions reflect the government's determination to develop strong bilateral relations with a few Latin American countries. This is in keeping with the experience of the successful businessmen and investors who gained access to and an understanding of particular countries. The scattergun approach and the quick visits to a number of republics rarely have produced firm economic ties.

Canadians have always felt somewhat superior (and perhaps very guilty) about the quality of their economic, spiritual, and social life. Hence, they have exhibited an urge to improve the lives of less fortunate peoples.[6] The first Canadian missionaries arrived in 1853. In 1968 there were over 2,000 missionaries in Latin America, 1,952 were Catholic and the majority of them were in Haiti, Bolivia, Chile, Honduras, and Peru. By 1977 the numbers of Catholic missionaries had declined to 1,288 with serious reductions in several of the countries: Haiti (406 to 331); Brazil (320 to 210); Bolivia (131 to 59); Chile (209 to 67), and Peru (409 to 257; Canadian Conference of Catholic Bishops, 1969;

1978). One reason for this decline in numbers is the decrease in the number of Canadians choosing such a vocation; another is that in certain countries, particularly Bolivia and Chile, the military rulers tended to see the Canadians as social activists.

Canadian Protestants are usually dispersed among several North American missionary efforts. The longest sustained Canadian Protestant mission has been the Baptist one in Bolivia, which began to phase itself out before the decade began. Where there has been a decline in missionary presence, there has been an increase in secular activity through the Canadian University Service Overseas (CUSO) or through grants and personnel provided by the Canadian International Development Agency (CIDA). In 1976-1977 there were about 200 CUSO and CIDA people in the region. CIDA also funds missionary activities centered on development through its Non-Governmental Organizations budget.

Latin America is not a major focus of development assistance activity because Canada concentrates its main effort on the 40 most needy nations. In 1968-1969, Latin America received less than 6% of the $288.9 million designated for external aid. In 1970, CIDA established a bilateral development assistance program in addition to its BID commitment, but that program "was to transfer know-how and skills rather than capital, to permit Latin America to use its own physical and human resources to the fullest extent possible" (Canada, 1975). This meant that in 1976-1977, CIDA disbursed $26.4 million out of a world total of $447.7 million of its bilateral commitment. Almost one-third of this disbursement went to support projects involved with agriculture, fisheries, and forestry (Canada, 1976: 56).

It is worth noting that the bilateral thrust evidenced in the trade and investment effort continues in the CIDA and CUSO programs. But it is possible to see a mix as a result of previous missionary and business activity. Canada's traditional strong economic ties with Mexico, Brazil, and Cuba and the strong missionary ties with Brazil, Cuba, Peru, and Haiti are reflected in its present activities. The largest recent bilateral disbursements have gone to those countries, Colombia, and the republics of Central America. All in all about 15 countries have received some form of Canadian assistance however modest it has been. This assistance has often meant that Canadian industries or Canadian experts have benefited by participation in specific projects, and it appears that the struggle within Canada led by concerned humanitarians to "untie" aid funding has been defeated. Canada's $1.2 billion commitment to development in 1978, at a time when there are almost one million Canadians unemployed, has raised questions. Canadians, who normally have accepted the government's aid commitments, apparently are concerned about its impact on Canada. This has forced CIDA recently to confirm the concept of "tied-aid" and to stress the benefits of that aid expenditure to Canadian industry.

Canada's development commitment will continue to serve donor and recipient save in the International Development Research Centre (IDRC), established in 1970. The IDRC receives government financial support, but the government exercises no control over it. Its Board of Governors and staff are from various parts of the world and it has a regional office in Bogota. The IDRC has directed its efforts in Latin America toward agricultural and livestock research. It is seen as a major and unique organization (Randall, 1977: 216-218).

At the intellectual and cultural level significant strides were made at the beginning of the decade, perhaps not as much a result of Trudeau's enthusiasm as from the economic prosperity that permitted universities to overcome their conservatism and to break new ground. Latin American studies became acceptable. By 1969 there were enough scholars to form the Canadian Association of Latin American Studies (CALAS). In 1976 CALAS began publication of its journal, *N/S*. Both the association and its journal have come to depend on government or outside support. The journal receives funds from the Canada Council; an IDRC grant maintains the CALAS central office. Should this support disappear, then the organization, with its small and fluctuating (135-200) membership, would have difficulties, because Latin American studies in Canada are not expanding.[7]

For a few short years, 1971-1976, the U.S. Foreign Area Fellowship Program (FAFP) sponsored an imaginative M.A.

scholarship in Latin American Studies.[8] The program was designed to help increase Latin American expertise in the social sciences. Unfortunately the program, administered by the Canada Council, died as a result of budget alterations in Ford Foundation support for a variety of programs. At the same time, surprisingly few students applied for the scholarships. This lack of interest in pursuing graduate studies about Latin America probably reflects a normal lack of curiosity and adventurousness among undergraduates. The boom period of Third World studies in Canada is past. With decreasing enrollments, universities are sticking to more traditional paths and students, like the country as a whole, appear more inward-looking. This may not be as disappointing as it appears. There continues to be room for the imaginative young person who wants to learn another language and culture and, if there is at present virtually no future in the academic world, there are apparently opportunities in development or business for those few who will be qualified for such activities.

The Trudeau government did try its best to stimulate cultural developments as part of its policy toward Latin America. Brazilian, Mexican, and other Latin American artists performed or showed their works in Canada, mostly central Canada. Canadian artists were sent south. But this form of cultural diplomacy is, as mission diplomacy, usually ephemeral. Canada does have an advantage over Latin American countries in that it has a more permanent program. National Film Board films continue to be readily available in embassies for showing in Latin American schools and institutions. Canada also opened its first Library Centre in 1974 in Mexico City. The government planned several others in South America and even hoped to initiate a "Chair" of Canadian Studies in Brazil, just as it had done in Britain, Japan, and France. These proposals, however, have had to be shelved because of Canada's economic difficulties. Perhaps it is a good thing that this has occurred: after all, Brazil, Mexico, and Venezuela could be more curious about Canada and start their own Canadian studies program if they wanted to. However, they are rarely curious about their more immediate neighbors, or even the United States, so Canadians should not be surprised at their lack of interest. Canada, after all, was trying to spend money during a wealthy period. Canadians forget that until the thriving 1960s there was little scholarly professional interest about the United States, let alone other parts of the world outside Britain or France.

The Trudeau decade—a decade 60% of which fell in the most prosperous years Canada has experienced, indeed it may have been the apogee of Canada's standard of living—has seen the most active Canadian effort toward Latin America since the decade of 1895-1905. At that time Canadian entrepreneurs and missionaries established themselves primarly in Brazil, Bolivia, Chile, Cuba, and Mexico, countries that have had some Canadian presence since that time. But Mitchell Sharp, Trudeau's first foreign minister, was undoubtedly correct when he called the 1968 mission a "voyage of discovery." Latin America was discovered by a group of Canadians propelled there, this time, by the first Canadian Prime Minister to be truly interested in the region. Very conscious that the ways of the world had changed from the rampant exploitation of what was called the "age of imperialism," at least on the surface, the Trudeau government made it clear, and its ministers have made it clear, that Canada seeks to help stimulate trade, investment, learning, and participation on the part of both Canada and Latin America.

Brazil, Mexico, Cuba, Colombia, and Venezuela, in particular, are "discovering" Canada for their own reasons. They see Canada as a place to sell more of their increased production. Brazil even sees Canada as a place to invest.[9]

There undoubtedly will be more such initiatives because the Latin American-Canadian economic pattern is changing. Canada's exports to Latin America—outside of a technical expertise, which is itself likely to decline if the government continues to reduce its research funding--are dominated by raw or semiprocessed materials. Of Brazil's 1976 exports to Canada, 42% were manufactured while only about 11% of Canada's major exports to that country could claim to be so. The day may not be far off when Canadians will lose their sense of technical and material superiority as a so-called "advanced" country.

Trudeau and Pelletier can, thus, both look back with mixed satisfaction on this decade of Canadian-Latin American relations. Latin America still represents only about 4% in terms of Canada's international trade. Canadians have made contributions in areas of their expertise and increased Canadian funding has been made available as aid. More Canadians and more Latin Americans appear to have become aware of each other's existence. There has been a marked rise in mission diplomacy in both directions. Cultural and intellectual efforts have been made, but much of Canada's policies succeeded because the government appeared to be able to afford them. As the decade ended, there were signs that the Canadian thrust was about over, with Canadians and Latin Americans still largely distant from each other. The essential conservatism of the peoples involved and the magnet of the United States, which has an economic and cultural influence on both regions, continue to contribute to this distance. Yet it is probably not optimistic to conclude that the Trudeau decade has provided enough of an impetus that Canadian-Latin American relations have achieved their own momentum, a momentum that will not be spectacular but that will probably see Latin Americans taking more initiative in these relations. Should that occur, then it would be possible to regard the Trudeau decade as a revolutionary one. In the best Canadian tradition, that revolution would have come about in an evolutionary way.

## NOTES

1. Canada was a member of the Pan American Institute of Geography and History (a Canadian, Dr. Harold Wood, currently heads the Geography Commission); the Postal Union; the Statistical Institute; and the Radio Office. Canada was supposed, at one time, to lead the British Commonwealth Caribbean states into the OAS. But the Caribbean communities moved first, in 1967. This action received little attention in Canada (Ogelsby, 1968: 584-586), and Canadians, as a whole, continue to show virtually no interest in the activities of the Commonwealth Caribbean nations at the OAS or with their immediate

Latin American neighbors. This attitude might change should Guyana and Venezuela or Belize and Guatemala take up arms to resolve border claims. Trudeau apparently led a visiting Caribbean Parliamentary Delegation to believe that Canada would join the Commonwealth Caribbean in safeguarding Belize's independence (Private letter of Trinidadian Senator to author, 13 July and 7 August 1975). The Department of External Affairs did not view the Prime Minister's statement in as strong a light. Canadians, however, would probably be willing to have their government serve as a mediator or send a peace-keeping contingent as part of an effort to dampen the dispute.

2. For an assessment of Foreign Policy for Canadians see *International Journal* (Spring 1978). The entire volume is devoted to an analysis of "Trudeau and Foreign Policy."

3. The Canadian Broadcasting Corporation ran an hour-long documentary on the Cuban portion. *Time* (Canadian edition) and *Maclean's* featured the Cuban trip. The major dailies had ample coverage of not only the Cuban portion but also of the Mexican and Venezuelan visits.

4. Harbron (1976) and Guy (1977) have more detail on the statistical side of this activity. Harbron is especially useful for the insights his long experience as Canada's leading journalist on Latin American affairs provides.

5. It is interesting to note that Brascan has turned to the Department of National Defence as a training ground for leading executives. The General Manager of the Brazil-Canada Chamber of Commerce is a very talented retired Brigadier General with experience in public relations. More recently Brascan appointed a retired Lieutenant General to a senior administrative post within the corporation.

6. Ogelsby (1976a) has three chapters on missionary efforts up to 1973.

7. In 1978, the Donner Canadian Foundation awarded a nonrenewable five-year grant to York University, Toronto, to permit the university to establish a center for Latin American and Caribbean studies. Whether or not the center will make an impact, let alone survive in an intellectual climate not conducive to such efforts, remains to be seen (Ogelsby, 1976b).

8. The late Kalman Silvert provided the push that brought Bryce Wood and Michael Potashnik of the Social Science Research Council of the U.S. to Canada. Their visit led to the establishment of the program. Latin American specialists and others in Canada owe these men a considerable debt. Even though the FAFP-sponsored program ended, the idea of such an M.A. scholarship caught hold and special awards for study at the master's level, while not exclusively directed toward Latin America, have become part of the federal government's regular award structure.

9. In January 1977, a Brazilian firm bought into Kaiser Resources Ltd. of Vancouver (Toronto *Globe and Mail,* 20 January).

## REFERENCES

CALA (1977) Annual Report. Toronto: Canadian Association—Latin America.

Canada (1977a) "Canada's growing involvement in Latin America." Mimeograph. 31 (August).

——— (1977b) "Third meeting of Canada-Mexico joint ministerial committee November

21 and 22." Ottawa: Department of External Affairs.
——— (1976) Canada and Development Corporation, 1976-1977. Ottawa: Canadian International Development Agency.
——— (1975) CIDA Annual Review, 1974-1975. Ottawa: Canadian International Development Agency.
——— (1973) House of Commons Debates. 18 (September).
——— (1971) "First Canada-Mexico ministerial meeting, Ottawa, October 21-22. Ottawa: Department of External Affairs.
——— (1970) Latin America, Foreign Policy for Canadians. Ottawa: Information Canada.
Canadian Conference of Catholic Bishops (1969; 1978) Bulletin.
Cité Libre (1964) "Le Canada et l'OEA." XV (Octobre): 2-3.
DOBELL, P. (1972) Canada's Search for New Roles, Foreign Policy in the Trudeau Era. Toronto: Oxford.
Globe and Mail [Toronto] (1978) "Latin American gain linked to expansion of industrial nations." (18 April): B2.
GUY, J. (1977) "The growing relationship of Canada and the Americas." International Perspectives (July/August): 3-6.
HANFF, G. (1977) "Canadian foreign policy: a study of the government's decision to admit refugees from Chile." M.A. thesis. Toronto: University of Toronto.
HARBRON, J. (1976) "Canada draws closer to Latin America: a cautious involvement," pp. 109-142 in R. W. Fontaine and J. D. Theberge (eds.) Latin America's New Internationalism. New York: Praeger.
——— (1963) Canada and the Organization of American States. Montreal: Private Planning Association.
Inter-American Development Bank (1978) IDB News (April).
International Canada (1976) (January): 1-4. Toronto: Canadian Institute of International Affairs.
International Journal (1978) "Trudeau and foreign policy." XXXIII (Spring): 267-456.
MILLER, E. (1948) "Canada and the Pan American Union." International Journal (Winter): 24-38.
OGELSBY, J. (1976a) Gringos from the Far North: Essays in the History of Canadian Latin American Relations, 1866-1968. Toronto: Macmillan.
——— (1976b) "Latin American studies in Canada, 1976." CALA Review (April): 13-14.
——— (1975) "Continuing U.S. influence on Canada-Cuba relations." International Perspectives (September/October): 34-38.
——— (1968) "Canada and the Pan American Union: twenty years on." International Journal 24 (Summer): 571-589.
RANDALL, S. J. (1977) "Canadian policy and the development of Latin America," pp. 202-229 in N. Hillmer and G. Stevenson (eds.) Foremost Nation, Canadian Foreign Policy and a Changing World. Toronto: McClelland and Stewart.
SHARP, M. (1972) "Canada-U.S. relations: options for the future." International Perspectives (Autumn).
SOKOL, J. (1970) "Canada's missing the boat in the Dominican Republic." Commentator (April): 10-11.
SOLOMON, H. (1973) "Another Canada-U.S. irritant?" Financial Post 9 (June): 10.
THORDARSON, B. (1972) Trudeau and Foreign Policy, a Study in Decision-Making. Toronto: Oxford.

*J.C.M. Ogelsby is Professor of History at the University of Western Ontario, London, Canada. He teaches both Canadian and Latin American history, has served as president of the Canadian Association of Latin American Studies, and at present is preparing a study on the Cuban autonomist movement, 1865-1898. Professor Ogelsby is coordinator of the three volumes on the nineteenth and twentieth centuries in the* General History of America *sponsored by the Pan American Institute of Geography and History.*

**CHARLES D. AMERINGER**
*Department of History*
*Pennsylvania State University*

# *LEONARDO RUIZ PINEDA*
## *Leader of the Venezuelan Resistance, 1949-1952*

Tachirense heart, noble and strong.

RÓMULO GALLEGOS

A National Hero has died. In the most hideous political crime in the annals of our country, agents of the government treacherously cut down the precious life of our comrade, Dr. Leonardo Ruiz Pineda, one of the most generous and able leaders of the civil resistance commanded by our party.

ACCIÓN DEMOCRÁTICA
Caracas, October 21, 1952

It is difficult to write about a martyr. One has to contend with the keepers of the flame, who have strong personal and political reasons for preserving the hero's image. Moreover, myths usually contain elements of truth. Although Leonardo Ruiz Pineda is not known as widely as Zapata, Sandino, Che, or Camilo Torres, there are unmistakable efforts on the part of Venezuela's democratic leaders to include him in the pantheon of Latin America's recent revolutionary heroes.

In particular, the leaders of Venezuela's Democratic Action party—Acción Democrática, AD—are interested in the consecration of Leonardo. In addition to their sincere wish to honor a fallen comrade, they realize that Ruiz Pineda is a valuable political asset. In fact, ever since their return to power in 1959,

Journal of Interamerican Studies and World Affairs, Vol. 21 No. 2, May 1979, 209-232
© 1979 Sage Publications, Inc.

following the overthrow of Marcos Pérez Jiménez, they have offered Ruiz Pineda as a symbol of their resistance to tyranny. Beset by internal strife over their gradualist and pragmatic policies in a militant age engendered by the Cuban Revolution, AD's leaders need a heroic figure to give the party a mystique and a means of shaming its dissidents. None of AD's founders could perform this role because they were still alive and too much a part of the political controversy themselves, nor was AD linked to an international movement, from which it might have borrowed some great personality, such as a Lenin or Mao. Moreover, as certain elements did, indeed, break away and resort to terrorism and guerilla warfare, AD's leaders preferred a pacific hero, whose conduct did not sanctify these actions. Finally, they needed a representative of the party's sacrifice on behalf of the nation as a whole. Ruiz Pineda seemed to fulfill these needs, and AD's leaders turned to him enthusiastically.

There are no posters of Leonardo wearing bandoleras or a revolutionary cap. Pictures show him wearing a business suit, with a shirt and tie, and no firearm in view. He wears a mustache but it is well trimmed, more like that of Clark Gable than that of Emiliano Zapata. AD writers emphasize his intellectual qualities and his patient, almost gentle nature in which he eschewed violence and the extremist tactic. He was a man, they insist, "who never used any weapon other than his idealistic and vibrant pen, his electrifying oratory, and his unshakable faith in the destiny of his people" (Carnevali, 1973: 124). This is the picture which the leaders of AD have projected in contrast to the more glamorous ones of the heroes of armed revolution and structural change. This picture is worth examining in the light of Ruiz Pineda's career, in order to determine how accurate its image is.

Ruiz Pineda led the struggle against the usurper regimes of Venezuela from April 19, 1949, the day on which he was released from prison, until October 21, 1952, the day on which he was killed. A military cabal overthrew the constitutional government of Rómulo Gallegos on November 24, 1948. The colonels who made up the military junta, Carlos Delgado Chalbaud, Marcos Pérez Jiménez, and Luis Llovera Páez, held Ruiz Pineda and his party in contempt. They had supported the government of Gallegos and that of his predecessor, Rómulo Betancourt, whom they had brought to power in a coup in October 1945, but grew alarmed over what they perceived as a dangerous ideological drift on the part of the AD leaders. They accused the AD of extremism and sectarianism and asserted that its leaders sought to weaken the armed forces in order to rule the nation unchallenged. Although the colonels carried out the coup, they had sympathizers in the civilian sector, where some political leaders also objected to the AD governments. Jóvito Villalba of the Democratic Republican Union—URD—charged that the AD had exercised an "intolerable and narrow hegemony" which had "deformed" the democratic revolution, and Villalba stated that he saw no difference in principle between the coup of November 1948, and that of October 1945 (Rivas Rivas, 1961: 48-17). In time, he regretted these words, but initially the colonels were in charge.

They outlawed the Democratic Action party, imprisoning its leaders or sending them into exile. Ruiz Pineda, who occupied the post of Minister of Communications in the Gallegos cabinet, was in the first group of leaders to be rounded up, and he spent five months in the Cárcel Modelo. The junta soon discovered, however, that AD, despite its errors, represented a formidable force in Venezuelan society, which could not be overcome by edicts. AD's militants occupied influential positions in the press, trade unions, student and teacher organizations, and even in business and industry. Actions taken against these persons also affected the institutions to which they belonged, so that the repressive acts of the junta became generalized.

The junta closed AD's newspaper, *El País*, and came down hard upon any newspaper which dared to criticize it. On April 21, 1949, it closed the independent *El Nacional* for eight days because it printed the street nickname of the junta, "*los tres cochinitos*" ("the three little pigs"), and, when the Venezuelan

Association of Journalists met to protest the action, it broke up the meeting and transported 43 members of the Fourth Estate to jail (Catalá, 1974: 94).[1] Shortly afterward, the junta's Board of Censors exercised rigid control over the nation's press.

The junta acted similarly against the nation's trade unions. Because AD militants occupied most of the top posts in the country's trade unions, the junta attributed political motives to trade union activity. It dissolved the Venezuelan Confederation of Workers—CTV—and its principal affiliates in February 1949. Five months later, in response to the objections against such acts, a mission of the International Labor Organization visited Venezuela and reported that "trade union organizations in Venezuela do not enjoy freedom of action and organization" (Betancourt, 1967: 634).

These repressive acts aroused the resentment of Venezuela's youth. Students at the Central University in Caracas protested the junta's abuses. Their protests and demonstrations led to a massive student strike in October 1951 and to the junta's decision to close the university four months later. As in other cases, the junta justified its action on the basis that external forces, particularly AD militants, influenced the activities of the students.

Using the excuse that AD had penetrated virtually every sector of society, the military junta established a dictatorship under which it created the National Security police—Seguridad Nacional, SN—to help ferret out the "subversives." Under the energetic leadership of its director, Pedro Estrada, SN established a reign of terror. Without regard for civil liberties and human rights, it broke into private homes and arrested citizens suspected of antigovernmental activities. It became notorious for its third-degree methods and use of torture. For its ultimate terror, it reopened the penal colony at Guasina, an island located in the Orinoco delta, where during 1952 four prisoners died as a result of the unhealthful conditions and rigors of the camp (Abreu, 1964).[2] When the mother of a prisoner protested these conditions and expressed concern about her son, Pérez Jiménez mocked her: "Don't complain," he reportedly said. "Your son is in Guasina, with the others, enjoying his love of liberty" (Betancourt, 1967: 602).

Throughout these years, 1949-1952, the dictatorship experienced an internal dynamic of its own, which affected the fortunes of the outlawed AD and the nation at large. Within the military junta, colonels Delgado Chalbaud and Pérez Jiménez jockeyed for control. In November 1950, Delgado was assassinated under circumstances which implicated Pérez Jiménez. Because of this, Pérez Jiménez hesitated to assume power immediately and reconstituted the dictatorship as a junta of government, with Germán Suárez Flamerich, a civilian, as its nominal head. Aware of the need for legitimacy, Pérez Jiménez, acting through the junta of government, next took steps to hold elections for a constituent assembly at the end of November 1952, in order to restore constitutional government. Unable to secure the cooperation of the remaining legal parties, URD and the Social Christians—COPEI—Pérez Jiménez created the Independent Electoral Front—FEI—as his vehicle for gaining sole power. He used the resources of the government to support FEI's electoral activities, and he instructed Estrada to make certain that the outcome would be favorable. These were the circumstances under which Leonardo Ruiz Pineda led AD's resistance movement.

AD selected Ruiz Pineda to lead the resistance because he was its highest ranking member not in jail or in exile. When the struggle began, his reputation was already established. Ruiz Pineda helped to organize the Democratic Action party in 1941 and served as Secretary of the Betancourt Junta in October 1945. In 1946, he became governor of his native state of Táchira and, when Gallegos became president in February 1948, he accepted the Communications portfolio in the cabinet. He also had experience in clandestine political operations. As a founder of the National Democratic Party—PDN—in 1936, the predecessor of AD, he went underground when President/

General Eleazar López Contreras outlawed the party in the same year. Ruiz Pineda's comrades recognized him as a brilliant orator and persuasive speaker and they apparently liked him because of his good humor and ready and winning smile (Velásquez, 1973: 38-39). He had the additional advantages of being young, 32 at the time he assumed command, enjoying good health, and having an athletic build. Coming from Táchira (the native state of Juan Vicente Gómez and the other recent military dictators of Venezuela) also had significance, because Ruiz Pineda seemed to possess a mystical drive to redeem the reputation of the state and overcome the forces of regionalism generated by *andino* hegemony (D. A. Rangel, 1973: 136-137).

The principal leaders of AD in exile knew that they could count upon Ruiz Pineda as a responsible and loyal leader in the country. He had a clear understanding of and dedication to the principles of the Democratic Action party. "We are a multi-class Party," he wrote, "of the revolutionary Left, purged of violent demagoguery, and called to fulfill the democratic and antiimperialist revolution, with the aid of all political, economic, and social forces interested in the transformation of the nation. Within this task, there is a place for all Venezuelans who are eager for administrative honesty, economic and social peace, economic nationalism, agrarian democracy, industrial progress, and the exercise of public liberties and popular sovereignty" (Catalá, 1974: 18). He admired AD's president, Betancourt, who had been his political mentor since his student days. "The democratic movement respects him with passionate loyalty," Ruiz Pineda (1975: 152) declared, "because it sees in him the personification of its great national goals. The falangist Right and the communist Left combat him without quarter, in a struggle of implacable rancor, because they know that he is their most capable adversary." Ruiz Pineda's own disgust for dictatorship had been established early in life and arose from very personal circumstances. His grandfather had operated a public bathhouse in their hometown of Rubio. One day, a lieutenant of Gómez, who was in the town to supervise a public works project, came to bathe, since his hotel lacked such service. He took the "best bath" in the house—number four. "After bathing," recalled Leonardo, "instead of leaving the key with my grandfather and paying for the service, he took the key with him and left without even a thank you. From that time on, he reserved that bath for himself, arbitrarily, without explanations. . . . I learned truly to hate Juan Vicente Gómez and his government, but with a child's feeling. I hated it because it had taken from us the right to bathe in bath No. 4" (Ruiz Pineda, 1973: 19-20). There were other incidents, but the action of this one bully was enough to impress upon a young mind the nature of dictatorship.

Upon initiating the resistance, AD declared that it knew the battle would be bloody and cruel and that it would require constant sacrifice, but it pledged to persist until it had restored the public liberties (Catalá, 1974: 38). Ruiz Pineda possessed the qualities of restraint and iron will, which such a struggle demanded. Although he commented that "the Republic had never before suffered such brutal persecutions as those perpetrated by the Military Junta," he adopted as his watchword the motto of José Martí, "to fight without hatred" (Siso Martínez, 1973: 70-75). As a youth he loved poetry and literature and at 15 published his first poem, but at the same age he also played football with an intensity which made his muscles ache (Ruiz Pineda, 1973: 24). Trained in law, he fought the injustices which were the legacy of the lengthy Gómez dictatorship, but throughout his career he was known as "the poet of Táchira." Ruiz Pineda shared with the leaders of AD the conviction that there was no quick solution to the problem of the usurper government and that terrorist activities would undermine the party's popular base and provide the junta with justification for its repressions (Catalá, 1974: 19-20).

AD's National Directorate in exile, acting through party president Betancourt, confirmed Ruiz Pineda as Secretary General of the party, which placed him in charge of the National Executive Committee—CEN—the only national organ of the party existent in the country. In accordance with AD's manifesto of December 8, 1948, when it announced its decision to launch the clandestine struggle, Ruiz Pineda undertook the tasks of organization, agitation, the creation of a combative conscience, and a preperation for the recovery of power (Catalá, 1974: 108).

When Ruiz Pineda left the Modelo prison in April 1949, the AD organization was in disarray. Some of the lesser known party militants, who managed to elude the police dragnets in the wake of the coup, had tried to organize the fight but lacked the experience and authority to accomplish very much (Martz, 1966: 134). Ruiz Pineda went to work immediately. According to a comrade, Ruiz Pineda "initiated a task which seemed impossible to many and which the majority looked upon with pious skepticism." This observer continued:

> The dictatorship had managed to dismantle the structure of his party. The number of exiles increased daily and the endless chain of prisoners was growing. Leonardo proposed then to mobilize, not only his party, but the entire nation against the despotism. His mind conceived the most extraordinary measures, which his boldness then set in motion. To the embarrassment of the incredulous and in the face of the fear of the cautious, he created a machinery each time more perfect, each day more effective [Velásquez, 1973: 47-48].

This organizational task absorbed the energies of Ruiz Pineda in the initial phase of the struggle and, indeed, given the paucity of information about his daily activities, the structure which he created provides the best means for judging the effectiveness of his leadership.

Ruiz Pineda reorganized the CEN and appointed from among its membership national secretaries for organization, finance, propoganda, security, and communications, and for the labor, agrarian, and youth sectors. Later, under pressure, he created the Special Activities Committee, which became the action arm of the CEN. Ruiz Pineda also promoted the organization of regional executive committees at the sectional, district, municipal, and local levels, each with internal structures and responsibilities similar to that of the CEN. He designed this apparatus to get the job done. Because of the nature of the clandestine struggle and the danger involved in holding meetings of large numbers of persons, he made most decisions through a small Political Commission. The Political Commission had exclusive jurisdiction over contact with members of the armed forces. The CEN (or Political Commission acting under its authority) required party militants to follow its decisions "without debate or discussion" (Martz, 1966: 135).

Given understandable variations in this structure, especially at the regional levels, Ruiz Pineda had the organization working remarkably well by the end of July 1949 (Bohemia, 1949: 9). The national and regional secretaries functioned as sections of the respective executive committees and carried out their duties by organizing the party militants into a series of cells—*grupos de base*—comprised of five persons each. They performed effectively. For example, finances were never a problem. The National Secretary for Finance raised funds from the rank and file, especially the affluent, and solicited contributions from among the community at large, including the business and industrial sectors (see Abreu, 1964: 270, 303, and 315). When Ruiz Pineda was shot in 1952, he was carrying 3,600 bolivares (over a thousand dollars) in his wallet (Rivas Rivas, 1961: 52-18).

The sections for security and counterespionage instructed party members in clandestine techniques, searched for traitors and government spies in the organization, and infiltrated the police and security agencies of the dictatorship in order to be able to anticipate their activities. The security sections perfected sophisticated procedures, which governed the lives of the militants, Ruiz Pineda in particular.

Like everyone in the movement, Ruiz Pineda had a pseudonym; he used the alias Alfredo. He rarely moved about. Isolated from his wife and children, he remained in his hideout—"*concha*" —living with someone not suspected of political activity, so that necessary, nonpolitical chores, such as marketing, might be done normally and routinely. He generally used apartment dwellings for his *conchas*, because people could come and go less conspicuously. However, no one kept a rendezvous without a safe-signal visible, such as an outside light, a plant in a designated window, or a washline of clothes (Abreu, 1964: 12). When Ruiz Pineda had to travel, he did so in a private automobile with an expert driver behind the wheel. He traveled during the day, in the normal hours of vehicular traffic, changing his appearance slightly from time to time by shaving his mustache or plucking his eyebrows (Rivas Rivas, 1961: 52-18).

However, because of the high risk involved in such movement, the communications sections developed a network of mail-drops—*"estafetas"*—and couriers to facilitate the conduct of operations and the exchange of information, without personal contact. The communications section devised cipher systems, particularly for the use of clandestine radios—"*pilotos*"—which maintained contact with elements within the country, as well as with the party leaders in exile. Betancourt—"Alvárez"—in Havana and Alfredo in Caracas exchanged radio messages in cipher daily, but these were necessarily short and likely to be intercepted by the government (Ameringer, 1974: 120-121). Alfredo used couriers to send detailed information and reports abroad and to receive instructions and funds from the leaders in exile. These clandestine journeys—"*volandeos*"—followed smugglers' routes via Colombia or Trinidad, although sympathetic crewmembers of commercial airliners and merchant ships also served in the clandestine net and legitimate businesses provided cover for the importation of bulky items, such as paper stock and radio equipment (Abreu, 1964: 65).

Although the evidence indicates that the underground adhered to these security procedures rigorously, one comrade affirmed that Ruiz Pineda was not entirely isolated from Venezuelan society. His hideout occasionally had the appearance of a "presidential office," claimed Ramón J. Velásquez (1973: 48-49), where workers, bankers, military officers, and students, among others, came to confer with the clandestine chief. Velásquez stated, furthermore, that Leonardo appeared in public on occasion. He wrote that Ruiz Pineda once showed up at a gathering of a group of women, who were opposed to his cause, and totally disarmed them with his "magnaminity."

Regardless, whereas the secretaries described above provided services for the effective operation of the clandestine movement in general, that for propaganda dealt specifically with the movement's objectives of agitation and the creation of a combative will.

The clandestine AD used propaganda as a weapon for denying stability and legitimacy to the junta governments. It criticized every act and policy of the juntas and exposed their repressive measures to sow unrest and woo popular support. Without freedom of the press, the clandestine movement edited, printed, and distributed its own newspapers, to wit: *Resistencia*, *Combate*, and *Testimonios*. Under the direction of the first National Secretary for Press and Propaganda, Luis Troconis Guerrera, AD prepared and circulated these newspapers plus manifestos, handbills, occasional pamphlets, and, in 1952, a book. It used the commercial presses of sympathizers, such as José Agustín Catalá, whose Editorial Avila Gráfica printed the material during normal working hours, taking care to cover its tracks by not using its regular paper stock or typeface (Catalá, 1974: ix-xi).

The propaganda effort involved intelligence activities as well. Under Ruiz Pineda's direction, the clandestine AD collected and compiled lists of political prisoners and testimony of their treatment, which it also sent to the exile elements to marshal international opinion against the junta. When the dictatorship opened Guasina, AD denounced the act and disseminated information about the nature and regimen of the camp. The clandestine operatives gathered data about the junta's measures against labor, the press, and education, as well as the dismantling of the reforms of the AD governments, all of which they documented carefully, often using the reports of international agencies to avoid being caught in a lie. However, AD did engage in rumor-mongering.

The clandestine movement also took care to publicize the junta's assaults against persons outside its militancy, such as members of URD and COPEI, to demonstrate that the dictatorship's repression was generalized and to win popular support for the movement. AD tried especially to discredit the junta members in the eyes of the armed forces, depicting them as aberrations of the military institution and as having dishonored the uniform. The purpose, of course, was to win adherents within the armed forces and to persuade the military that it had nothing to fear if the AD returned to power.

AD sought ultimately to return to power, but the strategy for overthrowing the dictatorship was the least clear aspect of Ruiz Pineda's program, except that it was not passive in nature. Ruiz Pineda did not expect to wait for something to happen, but contemplated the creation of the bases for precipitating a governmental crisis (Catalá, 1974: 19); the only trouble was that there was no timetable. Moreover, in order to succeed, Ruiz Pineda believed in the need to mobilize popular support, which, he argued, required the rejection of the *golpista* tactic and acts of terrorism. The necessity for preparing for the ultimate violence while eschewing violent acts in the interim, created contradictions within the movement which taxed the leadership of Ruiz Pineda. He admitted that he had to win battles in the movement against "impatience, deviation, indiscipline, and anxiety" (Catalá, 1974: 28).

The situation was paradoxical. Ruiz Pineda and the AD leadership were right in that they did not possess the strength to confront the military power of the usurper government, but, in the short run, time was on the side of the junta. For example, it used its repressive apparatus to dissolve and smash the trade union movement, even though AD had advised labor leaders not to provoke the junta in the belief that if the unions remained legal, they would be a more effective weapon when the crisis came. The Seguridad Nacional scourged the clandestine movement, decimating its ranks and raising the risk of involvement to intolerable levels. Estrada's torture chambers and penal colonies threatened to reduce the clandestine organization to a shell. Although the situation was not as bad as the junta's propagandists claimed (see Ameringer, 1974: 132), there came a time when Ruiz Pineda realized that a confrontation was a lesser evil than further delay.

During 1951, AD elaborated a plan for the overthrow of the government. It planned to create a national crisis to provoke the popular uprising it had been promoting. Ruiz Pineda continued to oppose a golpe or terrorist acts in isolation. A golpe, he reasoned, would recreate the conditions of 1945, wherein the revolutionary government remained dependent upon the armed forces. He wanted a popular base, not just for the uprising, but for the future (Catalá, 1974: 19-20). He ruled out terrorism for the same reason, but also for the well-being of the party members in prison, who were, in essence, hostages of the government. At the same time, he agreed that *putchista* and terrorist tactics might accompany, indeed, might be necessary to provoke the antigovernmental movement.

The plan called for the assassination of the three members of the junta on October 12, 1951, as they reviewed the Día de la Raza—Columbus Day—parade in the Plaza Colón (Abreu, 1964: 94-95). This blow would be accompanied by uprisings in numerous cities and at various military posts across the country and by a student strike at the Central University. The CEN established the Special Activities Committee to carry out the plot under the direction of Cástor Nieves Rios. During 1951, a number of youthful action types reentered the country clandestinely, among them Alberto Carnevali and Luis Augusto Dubuc, who undertook to organize armed cadres in the labor and campesino sectors and to make contact with friends in the armed forces. The plan progressed well until almost D-day.

On October 11, two men engaged in making bombs for the plot were gravely injured in an accidental explosion. Estrada extracted their confessions on their deathbeds and within hours the SN rounded up hundreds of persons and seized stocks of explosives. The junta aborted the planned attempt in the Plaza Colón and quickly crushed uprisings in cities outside of Caracas—Puerto La Cruz, Rio Caribe, and Tunapuy. Similar assaults against several Caracas radio stations and the National Guard's Training Center collapsed. The government charged that the strike at Central University, already begun on October 1, was part of the plot and intervened in the school's administration, eventually closing it altogether and sending AD student leader Eduardo González to Guasina. The dictatorship condemned at least 76 persons implicated in the affair to the island. In its fury, it sacked Ruiz Pineda's home and forced his wife, Aurelena, and his small daughters, Magda, age 5, and Natacha, age 3, to take refuge with the underground. Llovera Páez, speaking for the junta, announced rewards for information leading to the capture of Ruiz Pineda, Carnevali, and Nieves Rios, who, he asserted, had turned to insurrection when they realized their plans to organize a clandestine political movement had failed (Rivas Rivas, 1961: 51-21).

Rómulo Betancourt (1967: 590-591) gave another version of these events. He denied any plot to assassinate the junta members and charged that the government, taking advantage of the explosion in the clandestine bomb factory, sent out "shoot-to-kill" orders against AD militants in the country. Persons in Puerto La Cruz and other places, believing they were being set up for a "St. Bartholomew's Day massacre," took up machetes, hunting rifles, and "rusty revolvers" to defend themselves. The strike at the university, he declared, had nothing to do with these events. It was necessary, of course, for Betancourt to deny this failure, but there had been, without question, a Columbus Day plot.

Ruiz Pineda's years of patient labor had been set back, but he had had to take the gamble and, having lost, now had to rebuild. The intention of the junta to hold elections in November 1952 compounded his difficulties because time was running out. If the usurper government became legitimate, AD's situation might become hopeless. Pedro Estrada, emboldened by his success in smashing the October plot, began a relentless campaign to destroy the clandestine AD once and for all. Only the action of the exile elements in arousing international public opinion against the horrors of Guasina provided some relief for the clandestine AD (Ameringer, 1974: 139-140).

Estrada began with regularity to announce the discovery of supposed terrorist plots in a systematic attempt to justify the ruthlessness of his agents. In April, he arrested a small band of militants and accused them of plotting to assassinate Pérez Jiménez. He linked this plot to events which had occurred in two crowded churches in Caracas during Holy Week, wherein a number of persons were killed in a mad rush for the exits amid cries of "fire!" He charged that the AD was attempting "to sow confusion and panic" and called Ruiz Pineda and Carnevali "common criminals." Betancourt (1967: 668) denounced this maneuver as Ruiz Pineda's "death sentence" and declared that Pérez Jiménez had given the order "for the capture of the 'cadaver' of Leonardo."

Of all the charges against him, Ruiz Pineda considered that of terrorism the most contemptible. Realizing the grave danger he now faced and scornful of Estrada's accusations, Ruiz Pineda wrote a moving letter to his father. He expressed anguish over the lies being spread about him and apologized for the pain they were causing his loved ones. "Querido papá," he wrote, "you and all my family know me and you know my spiritual and cultural formation. I am a civilized man, a normal being, a person inspired and moved by high sentiments, at odds with any attitude contrary to human decency. I follow a line of conduct which has been the standard for my entire life: to respect the opinion and property of others. It is not my intention nor that of my comrades to degrade our struggle. Our undertaking is nourished by pure ideals and honest intentions. . . . I have not wished to convert the struggle into an instrument of personal vengeance against my enemies, notwithstanding that they have destroyed my home, persecuted my family, and engulfed my loved ones in spiritual misery" (quoted in Eloy Blanco, 1973: 104-106). He explained that the calumnies were being spread to deceive the people and serve as a pretext for his murder. He declared that he would not be intimidated by this maneuver and pledged to continue the fight on the same high plane as before.

With this letter, Ruiz Pineda entered into the final phase of the combat. He knew that it was essential to develop a strategy in the face of the junta's intention to hold national elections. He knew, furthermore, that the junta was planning an electoral fraud, because he had been reading its mail. In the most striking intelligence success of the resistance, the clandestine organization had obtained government telegrams that contained instructions to state governors and other officials for assisting the FEI in voter registration and for harassing the electoral activities of the other parties. Perhaps the fact that Ruiz Pineda had been Minister of Communications enabled him to obtain telegrams and cipher keys from personnel in the telecommunications service (Abreu, 1964: 255-323).[3] Nonetheless, if Pérez Jiménez succeeded in this fraud, with even a modicum of legality, he would be extremely difficult to dislodge. Ruiz Pineda and Betancourt decided that the only way to defeat Pérez Jiménez was to refuse to take part in his election.

In September, AD prepared and circulated a pamphlet entitled *Acción Democrática ante la farsa electoral*, in which it denounced the forthcoming elections and announced its decision to abstain. It described in detail the government's use of the public power and treasury to assure its victory, including intimidation of public employees to register with the FEI, the awarding of government contracts to cooperative individuals in the private sector, and the monitoring and harrying of the campaign activities of the opposition parties. AD documented its charges by reproducing the texts of 85 confidential government telegrams containing the damaging information (Catalá, 1974: 58-84). As signatories of the document, Ruiz Pineda and Betancourt declared that if there were any chance of an honest election, AD would make the sacrifice of giving its support to one of the legal opposition parties, but that, in view of the evidence of an imminent fraud, participation in the election would only serve the purposes of the dictatorship by lulling the people and making it difficult to arouse them in the defense of their interests. They called upon all Venezuelans of every political conviction—excluding the Communists—to join AD in staying away from the polls.

Ruiz Pineda and the leaders of AD realized that the success of the abstentionist strategy required the cooperation of the other opposition parties, particularly URD and COPEI. They hoped that the AD pamphlet might help persuade them and took care to cite telegrams which exposed the government's maneuvers against their campaigns. They proposed the formation of a coalition of all forces interested in national liberation, conceding thereby AD's inability to accomplish it alone and offering all opposition elements a role in the national reconstruction (Catalá, 1974: 68). Ruiz Pineda met personally with Villalba, and an *urredista* leader described the scene: "With true, youthful emotion, we shook the hand of the great leader" (J. V. Rangel, 1973: 129). However, despite AD's overtures and these feelings of sympathy, URD and COPEI concluded that it would be "political suicide" for them to abstain (New York Times, October 1, 1952). Villalba, in fact, nourished the hope that AD would change its position and, in the end, support his candidacy (Martz, 1966: 324-326). But AD persisted in its efforts to prevent "the electoral farce."

The clandestine AD had already initiated its most ambitious propaganda effort yet. In August 1952, Captain Juan Bautista Rojas—one of several AD sympathizers within the armed forces—suggested to José Agustín Catalá that the clandestine movement collect in a single volume the "disperse denunciations" against the usurper regime. He believed that the accumulated weight of such criticism would have an "extraordinary influence" upon the inner circles of the army (Catalá, 1974: ix). Ruiz Pineda responded enthusiastically when he heard the idea: "Now more than ever we need this book in the street," he exclaimed. "It will cause an explosion" (Catalá, 1974: x). Under the general editorship of Catalá, the clandestine team of Ruiz Pineda, Carnevali, and Simón Alberto Consalvi, among others, collected data and prepared the copy. Although the book appeared under the imprimatur of a Mexican printing house and publisher, the printing was done on the presses of Catalá's Avila Gráfica, under the very noses of the Seguridad Nacional (Catalá, 1974: x-xiii). Working without rest, the clandestine AD prepared a book of over 320 pages, which it entitled, *Venezuela bajo el signo del terror, 1948-1952: Libro negro de una dictadura*, and had it ready for distribution by October.

Although the *Black Book* bore witness to the sacrifice of the AD resistance movement, it was intended to reinforce the abstentionist thesis. The book focused upon the "bloody history" of the junta rule and its generalized assaults upon the labor movement, the press, and the university, and it accused the junta governments of despoiling the nation's natural resources and wealth. The *Black Book* contained the testimony of citizens whose rights and homes had been violated and of those who had been the victims of torture. In the prologue, Ruiz Pineda admitted that AD had made errors in the past, but affirmed that it had matured in the four years of struggle in the resistance, and he reiterated the call for a coalition of national forces to restore the public liberties and the sovereignty of the people (Catalá, 1974: 30-32).

Although the legal opposition parties again rejected Leonardo's appeal, the *Black Book* evoked a violent reaction from the ruling junta. Despite the general failure of AD's strategy of abstention, Pérez Jiménez feared it. He perceived it as the only possible threat to his plans for an electoral victory. AD's September pamphlet, with its exhibits of confidential government telegrams, incensed him, and the massive indictment contained in the *Black Book* outraged him further. At this point, allegedly, he gave the order, "get Ruiz Pineda!" (Eloy Blanco, 1973: 100).

In September and October, Pedro Estrada stepped up his campaign to destroy the clandestine AD as the last obstacle to Pérez Jiménez's electoral victory. His agents arrested scores of persons, whom they brutally beat in the attempt to extract the answer to the question, "where is Ruiz Pineda?" (Abreu, 1964: 38-38 and 43-45). In their dragnet on October 4, the SN pulled in Cástor Nieves Rios, the leader of the Columbus Day plot of the year before. They subjected him to two days and nights of inhuman torture before killing him and disposing of his body in an unknown place. Ruiz Pineda realized that Estrada's campaign of terror was paying off. For the first time, he was finding the *conchas* of the top leaders. Believing that his hideout might also be compromised, Ruiz Pineda decided to move to another on October 21. By 8:30 that evening he was dead.

There are many versions of the death of Ruiz Pineda. AD claimed that he was murdered in a police ambush; the government's account said that he fired upon two SN agents from his "moving car," who returned the fire and shot him in self-defense. What did happen may have been more accidental than planned, although such an occurrence was predictable given the agitated state of affairs at the time.

In the early evening of October 21, as Ruiz Pineda and three companions were traveling in an automobile through the Plaza Pérez Bonalde in the Catía section of Caracas, two SN agents on a motorcycle picked up their trail. They followed the car for approximately 9 or 10 kilometers to the Avenida Principal in the San Agustín del Sur section, where at Pasaje Sexto a stalled schoolbus (with several children on board) blocked the way, causing a traffic snarl. When Ruiz Pineda's car stopped, the SN agents dismounted. One of them approached the car and, identifying himself as an agent of the Seguridad Nacional, declared, "give yourself up, doctor Ruiz Pineda." Ruiz Pineda, seated in the right rear seat, responded, "What is this? We are peaceful citizens." The agent asked him to identify himself, and, as Ruiz Peneda reached for his wallet, the driver of the car, David Morales Bello, got out on the driver's side, immediately followed through the same door by Segundo Espinoza, who had been seated next to Morales. Taking advantage of the agent's confusion, Leoncido Dorta, who had been next to Ruiz

Pineda, exited through the left rear door, and Leonardo moved to follow him. The agent rushed around to the left side of the car, where Espinoza scuffled with him in an attempt to seize his weapon. The agent managed to discharge his gun, and someone else also fired shots. The origin of these shots is unclear, but no one had been paying attention to the other agent, who had remained with the motorcycle. A third agent also arrived on the scene in these moments. Ruiz Pineda fell to the pavement mortally wounded, the only casualty of the encounter. He had been shot twice in the head, once from a distance and once at close range (Sánchez Rincones, 1973: 163-173).[4] To say that there was no police ambush does not exonerate the dictatorship, because it had created the circumstances for Leonardo's death. He was a hunted man, and Pérez Jiménez wanted him dead.

Under the circumstances, few persons dared display their grief publicly over the death of Leonardo/Alfredo. The SN arrested Ruiz Pineda's widow when she came to claim his body. The prisoners at Guasina, who could only be tormented so much, wore black arm bands, which they had made from an inmate's socks and shirt (Abreu, 1964: 205-206). On November 26, at its concluding campaign rally, the URD observed a moment of silence in honor of Ruiz Pineda. For the most part, however, it was up to AD's leaders in exile to pronounce his eulogies. On October 25, in the Biblioteca "Cervantes" in Mexico City, Gallegos and Andrés Eloy Blanco (1973: 103) led the ceremonies in homage to their slain comrade. "Leonardo alive was an invisible soldier," declared the poet Eloy Blanco. "Leonardo dead is an invincible soldier." These words were prophetic, because, despite the danger, Ruiz Pineda's partisans within the country found a way to express their outrage. They decided to go to the polls on November 30 and support the URD candidates.

This maneuver took the junta by suprise. Believing that the situation was completely under control, the junta planned to hold a free election. The AD gave secret instructions to its partisans to vote for the URD (Martz, 1966: 326-327). The first returns showed Villalba's party winning a stunning victory, which caused Pérez Jiménez to suspend further electoral bulletins and to oust his own junta. A few days later, the new Provisional Government of Pérez Jiménez announced that the FEI had won. Ironically, Ruiz Pineda's party abandoned his last strategy, but his death helped deny Pérez Jiménez the legitimacy he so desparately sought. Pérez Jiménez ruled for five more years, but, in the end, even though he smashed the remnants of Ruiz Pineda's clandestine apparatus, he was brought down by the very "powerful antigovernmental movement," which Ruiz Pineda had envisioned, when the people went into the streets in January 1958 and, with the aid of disaffected elements of the armed forces, toppled the dictatorship and restored "the public liberties."

It is clear that Ruiz Pineda was an extraordinary man. He was a decent person who remained civilized under cruel circumstances. By remaining true to his ideals, he strengthened them and enabled them to survive against a transitory preponderance of power. He struggled for his party's survival for four years, without taking a single innocent life, which won him the respect of the Venezuelan people. He hated dictatorship as passionately as his most violent comrades and his sense of social justice was just as keen, but his experience in the PDN taught him that nothing was impossible, despite great odds, if one persisted, just as the experience of the October 1945 coup taught him to avoid the expedient solution. He was flexible and clutched the rifle when it was necessary, but the strength of the AD party and of Venezuelan democracy was fashioned in the stoic labor of the underground and in the jails and torture chambers of the dictatorship. The comradeship established there was as powerful as that among the veterans of any army. It is essential, of course, to place Ruiz Pineda's contribution in the perspective of the full sweep of events which finally overthrew Pérez Jiménez.

Many factors contributed to the restoration of the Venezuelan democracy, and Ruiz Pineda's leadership was only one of them.

Thus, it would be enough to give Leonardo Ruiz Pineda a place in history, but the myth-makers and hagiographers have not been content to let it rest there. Because of his style of combat, Ruiz Pineda was the ideal democratic revolutionary. If he had not existed, AD would have had to invent him. When Betancourt and others returned to Venezuela after a ten-year hegira, they were the Old Guard, and the young people, who had grown up under the dictatorship of Pérez Jiménez and taken part in his overthrow, resented being replaced by "those who came from outside." When the struggle for power became violent, and the new generation adopted the Cuban model of armed struggle, AD's leaders used Ruiz Pineda's martyrdom to illustrate that 23 January 1958, Pérez Jiménez's fall, would have been just another day without the party's sacrifice (Canache Mata, 1959). They turned to him also because they needed a martyr in the style of Martin Luther King, not Malcolm X. As Domingo Alberto Rangel (1973: 139) expressed it, "He is the offering which we are able to display when anyone wants to know what sacrifices we have made for liberty."

## NOTES

1. Reprint and new edition of AD clandestine publication of October, 1952, originally entitled: Venezuela bajo el signo del terror, 1948-1952: Libro negro de una dictadura. A second edition was published in Santiago, Chile, in October, 1953.

2. There are many accounts about Guasina, but José Vicente Abreu's real-life novel is the best.

3. The pages cited contain appendices in which one finds general lists and memoranda taken from the files of the SN. These lists describe the occupations, political affiliations, activities, and alleged crimes of persons imprisoned by the SN. The author used these lists to compile data about the nature and organization of the clandestine AD. For example, see pp. 256-257 and 266-277, which reproduce the dossiers of several telegraph operators.

4. An autopsy performed on Ruiz Pineda's body showed powder burns around only one of the two wounds, which led Sánchez Rincones (1973) to charge that Ruiz Pineda had been shot first from a distance and then administered the coup de grâce.

## REFERENCES

ABREU, J. V. (1964) Se llamba S.N. Caracas: José Agustin Catalá.

AMERINGER, C. D. (1974) The Democratic Left in Exile: The Antidictatorial Struggle in the Caribbean, 1945-1959. Coral Gables: University of Miami Press.

BETANCOURT, R. (1967) Venezuela: política y petróleo. Caracas: Editorial Senderos.

BOHEMIA [Havana] (1949). Volume 41, Number 30.

CANACHE MATA, C. (1959) "La juventud de A.D." A.D. (Caracas) November 23: 4.

CARNEVALI, A. (1973) "Han asesinado a un héroe nacional," pp. 123-125 in J.A. Catalá (ed.) Leonardo Ruiz Pineda: guerrillero de la libertad. Caracas: Ediciones Centauro.

CATALÁ, J. A. [ed.] (1974) Libro negro, 1952: Venezuela bajo el signo del terror. Caracas: Ediciones Centauro.

ELOY BLANCO, A. (1973) "Testimonio," pp. 99-106 in J. A. Catalá (ed.) Lenoardo Ruiz Pineda: guerrillero de la libertad. Caracas: Ediciones Centauro.

MARTZ, J. D. (1966) Acción Democrática: Evolution of a Modern Political Party in Venezuela. Princeton: Princeton University Press.

RANGEL, D. A. (1973) "Leonardo, él de la estupenda hazaña," pp. 131-140 in J. A. Catalá (ed.) Leonardo Ruiz Pineda: guerrillero de la libertad. Caracas: Ediciones Centauro.

RANGEL, D. A. (1973) "El legado de Leonardo," pp. 127-130 in J. A. Catalá (ed.) Leonardo Ruiz Pineda: guerrillero de la libertad. Caracas: Ediciones Centauro.

RIVAS RIVAS, J. [ed.] (1961) Historia Gráfica de Venezuela (vol. 2) El mundo y la época de Pérez Jiménez. Caracas: Pensamiento Vivo, C. A.

RUIZ PINEDA, L. (1973) "Sintesis autobiográfica," pp. 3-36 in J. A. Catalá (ed.) Leonardo Ruiz Pineda: guerrillero de la libertad. Caracas: Ediciones Centauro.

——— (1975) "Betancourt, creador ideológico y constructor de Acción Democrática," pp. 149-152 in J. A. Catalá (ed.) Un hombre llamado Rómulo Betancourt. Caracas: Ediciones Centauro.

SANCHEZ RINCONES, F. (1973) "Leonardo, símbolo real del martirologío venezolano," pp. 159-175 in J. A. Catalá (ed.) Leonardo Ruiz Pineda: guerrillero de la libertad. Caracas: Ediciones Centauro.

SISO MARTINEZ, J. M. (1973) "Leonardo Ruiz Pineda, vida y epifanía," pp. 53-78 in J. A. Catalá (ed.) Leonardo Ruiz Pineda: guerrillero de la libertad. Caracas: Ediciones Centauro.

VELASQUEZ, R. J. (1973) "Leonardo Ruiz Pineda" in J. A. Catalá (ed.) Leonardo Ruiz Pineda: guerrillero de la libertad. Caracas: Ediciones Centauro.

*Charles D. Ameringer, Ph.D., the Fletcher School of Law and Diplomacy, is Professor of Latin American History at The Pennsylvania State University. Professor Ameringer has conducted research and published on Latin American historical themes, treating especially the modern Caribbean and Central America. He is the author of two books,* The Democratic Left in Exile: The Antidictatorial Struggle in the Caribbean, 1945-1959 *(University of Miami Press, 1974) and* Don Pepe: A Political Biography of José Figures of Costa Rica *(University of New Mexico Press).*

**JOHN CHILD**
*Inter-American Defense College*

# *FROM "COLOR" TO "RAINBOW": U.S. Strategic Planning For Latin America, 1919-1945*

## *Introduction*

A series of recently declassified documents in the National Archives provide striking evidence of the shift of United States military strategic thinking away from the nineteenth and early twentieth century unilateral interventionist approaches to the bilateral approaches taken in World War II under the multilateral framework of the Good Neighbor Policy.

It is also significant to note that, despite the multilateral thrust of this Good Neighbor Policy promulgated by President Roosevelt and the U.S. State Department, the U.S. Military Departments—War and Navy—made no provisions for multilateral strategic plans in World War II.

But even as U.S. military planners prepared for bilateral cooperation with Latin American allies in the war, they continued to draft and update unilateral plans for intervention and invasion of key Latin American countries if cooperative approaches should fail.

This article examines the U.S. military's transition from unilateralism to bilateralism in its approaches to Latin America, employing as primary documents both the unilateral one-nation "Color" plans and the broader World War II "Rainbow" plans. The interplay of three basic strategic concepts will first be assessed as a background setting for these plans.

---

AUTHOR'S NOTE: The views of the author do not purport to reflect the positions of the Department of the Army or the Department of Defense.

Journal of Interamerican Studies and World Affairs, Vol. 21 No. 2, May 1979, 233-259
© 1979 Sage Publications, Inc.

*Strategic Concepts*

In a broad sense, the shift in strategic plans reflected the transition from a nineteenth century unilateral concept (the "American Lake") to an early World War II bilateral concept—the "Quarter Sphere." A third concept stressing multilateralism—"Hemisphere Defense"—was also present, but was mainly a diplomatic-political idea which found no reflection in concrete U.S. military strategic plans (Child, 1976).

The unilateral American Lake concept, which did not include any cooperative military planning with any of the Latin American nations, either singly or in tandem, was the embodiment of the primary U.S. strategy toward Latin America from the days of Manifest Destiny to the coming of the Good Neighbor Policy in 1933, when politico-diplomatic multilateralism forced the abandonment of this unilateral approach. The American Lake strategy envisioned U.S. interests in Latin America almost exclusively in terms of the Caribbean, which was conceptualized as a "U.S. Lake," or the "U.S. Mediterranean." Under the maritime geopolitical vision of Admiral Mahan and Theodore Roosevelt, United States resources, diplomacy, investments, and interventions focused on the Caribbean Basin and the "soft underbelly" of the United States.

The Quarter Sphere concept expanded the American Lake geographically to encompass a defensive perimeter running from Alaska to the Galapagos to the Brazilian Bulge to Newfoundland. Developed in the late 1930s, the Quarter Sphere idea represented the broadening of the militarily realistic defensive perimeter for the continental United States in light of two technological and geopolitical realities of World War II:

(1) The line was extended to the Galapagos because Japanese aircraft operating from that point, or closer, would pose a direct threat to the Panama Canal.
(2) The Brazilian Bulge was included because of its proximity (about 1,600 miles) to Dakar in West Africa, then a French colony. When France fell in 1940, all former colonies became

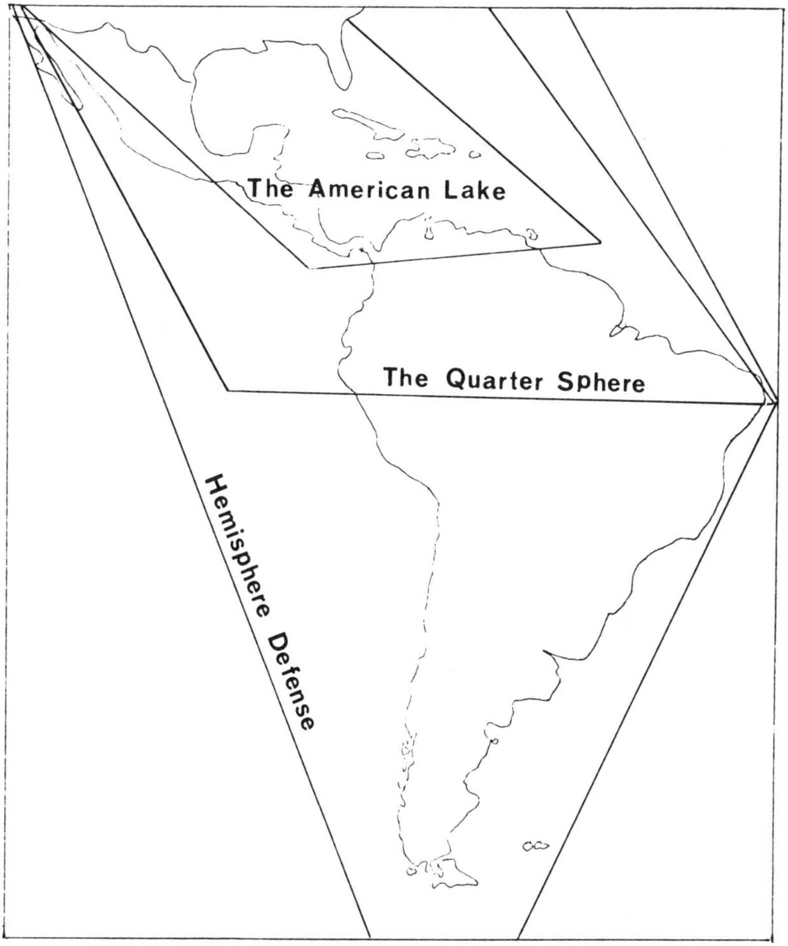


**Figure 1: Basic Strategic Concepts**

> potential Nazi bases, and those in West Africa were seen as a direct threat to eastermost South America, the logical beachhead for a move against the soft underbelly of the United States.

It should be noted that the Quarter Sphere concept was developed at a time when U.S. policies to Latin America were governed by the multilateral Good Neighbor Policy, and thus implementation of the Quarter Sphere could not rest on unilateral approaches. In order to obtain the bases it required to anchor the key points of the Quarter Sphere perimeter—Mexico, Ecuador, and Brazil—the United States would, ideally, enter into special bilateral arrangements with the key countries of the Quarter Sphere. However, as we shall see below, the U.S. military departments continued to plan for unilateral invasions, specifically of Brazil and Mexico, if bilateral approaches failed.

The third strategic concept involved was the multilateral "Hemisphere Defense" idea. Resting on the collective ideals of Bolívar and the Good Neighbor Policy, it argued that the whole hemisphere, and not just the Quarter Sphere, had to be defended, and that all the nations in the hemisphere had a responsibility and a role to play in this collective defense. The hemisphere defense concept was militarily unrealistic and was advocated by the U.S. State Department as the essential military facet of the unified diplomatic-political-economic-cultural approach to hemisphere solidarity favored by the Good Neighbor Policy in World War II. This concept was institutionalized in the form of the multilateral Inter-American Defense Board, founded for symbolic political purposes over the vehement objections of the U.S. War and Navy Departments. Thus, *no* U.S. multilateral strategic plans were reported in World War II; it was not until the Cold War in the early 1950s that the role of the Inter-American Defense Board was expanded to include a strategic planning function.

## *The Nature of Strategic Contingency Planning*

Before exploring some of the implications of the "Color" and "Rainbow" plans for the hemisphere, it would be wise to examine the nature of strategic contingency planning. Historically, military staffs devote substantial efforts in time of peace to planning for all conceivable (and some inconceivable) strategic contingencies. These contingency plans should be categorized as follows:

—those purely academic plans totally divorced from political or military reality. Frequently the product of the overly fertile imagination of an underemployed staff officer, they serve to stimulate thought and exercise subordinate staffs. They must not be taken seriously as evidence of strategic intentions.

—those which deal with possible but highly unlikely eventualities. The military feels a need to plan for these contingencies "just in case," but all concerned recognize that they do not reflect realistic strategic thinking.

—those which in fact do respond to possible or probable contingencies. Typically, these represent a response to real or likely diplomatic scenarios and are prepared in far greater detail than the two previous categories. This type of contingency planning does tend to reflect real strategic concerns from both the military and diplomatic sides.

One additional caveat is necessary before categorizing and describing the "Color" plans for the hemisphere: contingency planning is a process separate and distinct from the political and diplomatic decisions to implement any such plans, either in part or in their totality. The "Color" plans for the hemisphere can thus be classified.

In the first category, "purely academic," the best example is the 1928 "Red-Orange Coalition" (USWDGS, 1928), a "worst-case" situation in which the War Department staff was asked to evaluate a scenario in which the United States fought alone on four fronts against a coalition of "Red," Great Britain and Canada; "Orange," Japan; and "Green," Mexico. A more difficult and more unreal situation for the United States could hardly be imagined, and this was precisely the purpose of this "worst-case" approach.

In the "highly improbable" category there are two examples of two different types:

(1) The 1919 plan to invade Canada (Washington Post, 1975) is typical of those plans directed against friendly and strategically

vital neighbors. The historically amicable nature of U.S.-Canadian relations made this contingency highly improbable, but the mere fact that a hostile Canada would be a grave danger to the United States made it necessary for military strategists to prepare such a plan.

(2) The 1927-1930 "Purple" Plans (USWDWPD, 1927b; 1928a; 1928b; 1930a) for intervention in each South American country. While the South American nations could hardly be considered "neighbors" in the same strategic sense as Canada, possible political contingencies were identified which might require U.S. military intervention in South America (see detailed discussion of "Purple" below). It should be noted that "Purple" was not highly detailed or developed, and the contingency seemed far less likely than intervention in the "American Lake."

In the "possible or probable" category of "Color" contingency plans, we can cite (see Figure 2):

—"Special Plan Tan," 1924-1938, for intervention in Cuba under the Platt Amendment "due either to unsatisfactory financial conditions, to internal disorders, or to unsanitary conditions in Cuba" (USWD-WPD, 1930b: 1).
—"Strategical Plan Gray," 1927-1936, for intervention in various Central American and Caribbean countries (USWPWPD, 1927a; 1931a; 1931b; 1931c).
—Color Plan "White" ("Basic War Plan: Panama Canal Department"), 1924-1941 (USAPCD, 1924; 1941). Some portions and revisions of this and associated plans for Panama remain classified and thus unavailable.
—"Special Plan Green," for operations against Mexico, dating from the 1920s through 1940.

### *The "General Mexican War Plan" of 1919*

The principal precursor for the "Color" plans of the 1920s and 1930s appears to have been the "General Mexican War Plan" of 1919. The principal features of this plan were (USWDWPD,

**Figure 2**

1919: 1)): protection of U.S. interests along the Mexican border; seizure of the Tampico oil fields and the coal fields south of Eagle Pass; and blockade of principal Mexican ports and the cutting of the Pan American railroad near the Guatemalan border. Secondary features of the plan included an advance south from the U.S.-Mexican border along the various railroad lines and replacement of the U.S. invasion force with a native constabulary under U.S. control.

In regard to this last point, the plan envisioned that the regular Mexican Army would collapse after a short period of active operation. Following this collapse, the major threat to U.S. occupation troops would be guerrilla welfare and banditry. To counter this threat, the plan provided for the creation of a mercenary Mexican constabulary. As the 1919 memo commenting on the plan stated:

> The period of active operations will be short, as compared to the period of guerrilla operations. The early disbandment of temporary troops is highly desirable. It is the testimony of all well acquainted with Mexican character that any number of Mexicans can be hired to fight against anyone and for anyone who will regularly pay and feed them. The Mexican soldier will be cheaper and more efficient against banditry than the American and the cost can be more easily charged against the Mexican government. In addition, an Army can be established that will not be anti-American and which may, for many years in the future, exercise on the Mexican government an influence favorable to the United States (USWDWPD, 1919: 4).

## *The "Color" Plans, 1920-1940*

### *PLAN "GREEN" (MEXICO)*

"Green" was the most detailed and highly developed of all the hemisphere "Color" plans (see Figure 3). The final version of 1940 is over eight inches thick and has detailed instructions for all supporting and subordinate military units as small as separate detachments and as far away geographically as Vermont and Massachusetts (USWDGS, c1935: 33).

In concept, the various "Green" plans were very similar to the 1919 "General Mexican War Plan," and involved three phases (USWDWPD, 1940: 1-2):

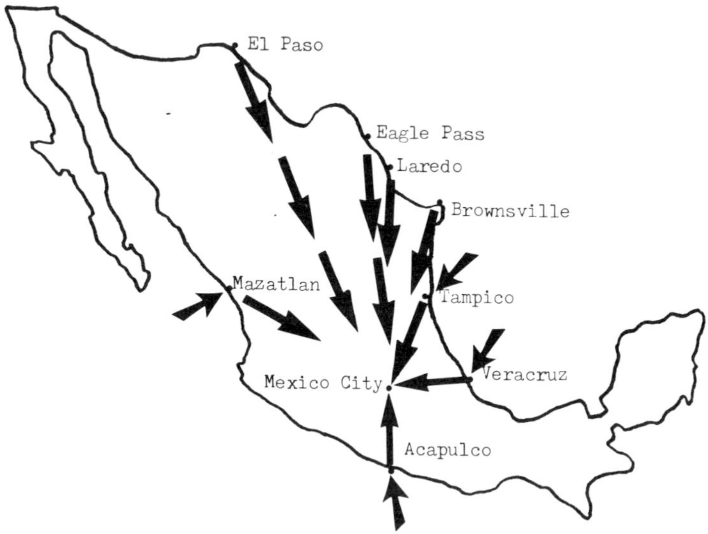


**Figure 3**

Phase 1: Protection of the U.S. southern land frontier. This was a defensive phase using regular troops only, and did not involve crossing the border. U.S. Navy units would furnish refugee protection to U.S. and other foreign nationals at various Mexican ports on both Mexican coasts.

Phase 2: Occupation of bridgeheads and seaports. If the situation deteriorated and the president so directed, the U.S. Navy would occupy one or more Mexican seaports (Veracruz, Tampico, Mazatlán, Acapulco). The Army would seize bridges and bridgeheads across the Rio Grande and relieve the U.S. Navy in port occupation duty.

Phase 3: Partial or general occupation of Mexico. This would require mobilization of the U.S. National Guard and envisioned one or more advances into Mexico and toward Mexico City along the following axis: from Acapulco, Tampico, Veracruz, El

Paso-Ciudad Juarez, and the Eagle Pass-Laredo-Brownsville area.

### *PLAN "TAN" (CUBA)*

The historic United States interest in Cuba gave rise to another detailed and specific Plan—"Tan"—whose purpose was stated in 1924 with an admirable lack of euphemism, as "Intervention in Cuba." By 1928 the rationale had been elevated to: "establish a stable and efficient Government in Cuba, with or without military support" (USWDGS, c1935: 2).

The basic assumption of "Tan" was that unsatisfactory financial conditions, internal disorder, or unsanitary conditions in Cuba would require "friendly intervention by the United States under the Platt Amendment," (USWDWPD, 1930b: 1). However, even after the Platt Amendment was abrogated in 1934, U.S. strategic planners continued to prepare plans for the unilateral occupation of Cuba. The last "Tan" on file in the National Archives is dated 1938, four years after the abrogation.

### *PLAN "WHITE" (PANAMA CANAL)*

The first "White" plan for the defense of the Panama Canal is dated 1924, and there are seven major revisions running through 1941 in the National Archives (USWDGS, 1942a).

The 1941 "White" plan, also called "Basic War Plan: Panama Canal Department," lists a range of threats to the canal (USAPCD, 1941): sabotage, air bombardment (from either carrier or land-based aviation); raids from Panamanian territory; overseas raids; bombardment from ships, major coordinated attacks; and a combination of all of these.

### *PLAN "GRAY" (CENTRAL AMERICA AND THE CARIBBEAN)*

The "Gray" plans of the late 1920s and 1930s provided for the United States intervention in those Caribbean and Central

American countries not covered by other one-country "Color" plans (i.e., Mexico, Cuba, and Panama).

The first "Gray" plan was approved on March 23, 1927 (USWDWPD, 1927a) and envisioned a Navy blockade supported by an initial Marine Corps landing force of 500 to 5,000 men followed by an Army force of not more than a division. No declaration of war was contemplated, since "this is a plan in which our forces will operate to protect American interests and very probably in support of a native faction recognized by the United States" (USWDWPD, 1927a: 1).

The "enemy" was not considered to pose a very significant threat:

> The enemy force will not be numerous—in the usual case their number will vary between 3,000 and 5,000. Their discipline will be comparatively poor and their average intelligence low. They will have no conception of modern combat and will not offer organized opposition in force [USWDWPD, 1927a: 1]

In late 1931 "there appeared to be certain indications of unrest in the countries to the south," and "Gray" received a major revision (USWDWPD, 1931b) to include more careful joint Army-Navy planning. The October 28, 1931, revised "Special Plan Gray" (USWDWPD, 1931c) envisioned operations in one or more of the following Caribbean and Central American countries: Guatemala, Honduras, Nicaragua, Costa Rica, El Salvador, Haiti, and the Dominican Republic. The minor interpositions or general interventions involving a complete occupation of the country anticipated by "Gray" could become operational due to one or more of the following factors (USWDWPD, 1931c: 1):

(1) Strategic location: that is, proximity to our own territory, to the Panama and proposed Nicaraguan Canals, and to the lines of communication between them.
(2) The Monroe Doctrine and the Roosevelt Corollary thereto.
(3) Important and growing commercial, financial, and economic interests in the countries of this region.

(4) General right under international law of the protection of life and property of our citizens in countries unable or unwilling to afford such protection themselves.

The 1931 "Gray" listed and analyzed the enemy forces in greater detail than the 1927 version and under the Nicaraguan "enemy" listed in a footnote, the 68 United States Marine Corps officers training the Nicaraguan National Guard (USWDWPD, 1931c: 2), presumably the U.S. Marine Corps "enemy" of the U.S. Army, would be evacuated before active combat operations started.

### *PLAN "PURPLE" (SOUTH AMERICA)*

As indicated previously, in the late 1920s the "Purple" color plans were drawn up for the U.S. invasion of each South American country except for Paraguay and Bolivia, which as landlocked countries were considered separately since they could not be invaded without crossing the territory of a third state.

The "Purple" plans were more of a conceptual and intellectual exercise than operational plans. They were relatively brief, closely controlled, and did not include detailed planning for subordinate units. Their life-span also was short: the planning directive was written in late 1927; the Army and Theater (i.e., joint Army-Navy) plans were written in 1928, and the last entry in the file is a thoughtful comment by an intelligence officer in 1930.

For each South American country, the basic purpose of "Purple" was to seize an important strategic area, generally the capital, and "hold it pending the outcome of a naval blockade" (USWDWPD, 1928b: cover; 3). Because of the long distances from the United States and the size of most South American countries, there was no provision for occupation or for establishing long-term U.S.-controlled native constabularies as had been the case in the "Color" plans for Mexico, Central America, and the Caribbean.

TABLE 1
Plan "Purple"

| Country | Area to be seized and held | Probable landing place | Probable operations |
|---|---|---|---|
| Argentina | Buenos Aires | La Plata | Advance along R.R. on Buenos Aires |
| Brazil | Rio de Janeiro | Copacabana and Cabo de Gavea | Occupy high ground N and NW of landing |
| Chile | Valparaiso | Quintero Bay | Advance S on Valparaiso |
| Colombia | Barranquila-Puerto Colombia | Puerto Colombia | Advance via R.R. on Barranquilla |
| Ecuador | Guayaquil | Santa Elena Bay | Advance on Guayaquil via Chongon |
| Peru | Callao-Lima | Magdalena del Mar and Chorrillos | Direct advance on Lima and Callao |
| Uruguay | Montevideo | West of Carrasco River | Advance to high ground N of Montevideo |
| Venezuela | La Guaira-Caracas | Between Macuto and La Guaira | Advance on Caracas via R.R. and trails |

The 1927 memorandum directing the preparation of the Army's "Purple" plan listed some of the contingencies which might require U.S. intervention in South America such as enforcement of the Monroe Doctrine, ill-treatment of American nationals, and the Tacna-Arica problem between Chile and Peru, in which the United States had a role as guarantor (USWDWPD, 1927b).

"Purple's" limited focus on capital cities and key ports can be seen from the summary in Table 1 (USWDWPD, 1928b: 3-4).

"Purple" included a brief assessment of the "enemy" (i.e., the military forces of each South American country) and concluded that the greatest threat was posed by the armed forces of Argentina and Chile, whose combat efficiency was rated as "good." The Brazilian and Uruguayan were listed as "fair," while the efficiency of all the others was considered "low" (USWDWPD, 1928b: 1).

In terms of the friendly forces required to accomplish "Purple's" mission, the plan estimated that the following were necessary (USWDWPD, 1928b: 2):

—Argentina, Chile, and Brazil: six divisions of infantry each;
—Uruguay and Peru: three divisions of infantry each;
—All other countries: two divisions of infantry each.

The last item in the National Archives' "Purple" plan file is a lengthy 1930 memorandum containing thoughtful comments on "Purple" by Lieutenant Colonel Charles Furlong, an intelligence officer assigned to the Army's War Plans Division (USWDWPD, 1930a). Colonel Furlong apparently had a comprehensive knowledge of the history, economy, geography, and culture of Latin America and stressed the psychological and economic factors which would vastly complicate the achievement of "Purple's" objectives. He warned that the South American nations were self-sustaining in basic needs and that "not one of the South American countries could be starved out" (USWD-WPD, 1930a: 2). He cautioned that the psychological factor was of key importance and that due to South American pride and tenacity, the seizing of a single port or city had little chance of bending these nations to the will of the U.S., as "Purple" envisioned. Colonel Furlong used his knowledge of South American history in the Argentine case to note the fate of the 1806 and 1807 British invasions of Buenos Aires, drawing obvious parallels to the "Purple" plan, and warning that despite military superiority in traditional terms, the British were demoralized (and eventually defeated) by the tenacious resistance of the civilian population of Buenos Aires (USWDWPD, 1930a: 3, 5-6).

From the beginning of "Purple" planning, all concerned realized the extraordinary political sensitivity of these plans. An August 1928 memo forwarding the first draft of "Purple" warned:

> If information should in any way leak out that the War Department is preparing a war plan of this kind, it would have a most unfortunate effect on our relations with these countries and would undo a great deal of the work that has been accomplished in the way of cultivating their friendship [USWDWPD, 1928a].

Almost 40 years later in 1967, a joint State-Defense Department declassification review recommended that these plans remain classified, not for military reasons but because of "possible adverse political consequences" (USAAG, 1967). "Purple" was not finally declassified until 1973.

## *The World War II "Rainbow" Plans*

In the late 1930s the U.S. War and Navy Departments gradually abandoned the old single-country unilateral and interventionist "Color" plans. They turned to a more global approach to strategic planning contained in a series of plans known as "Rainbow," which established the framework for U.S. strategy in World War II. The "Rainbow" plans (Conn and Fairchild, 1960; USJCS, 1952; USWDGS, 1940) had far less political sensitivity than the old "Color" plans and were analyzed in the open unclassified literature as early as 1960.

In November 1938 the U.S. Army-Navy Joint Board was directed to begin studies for appropriate U.S. plans in the face of increased power and the expansionist ambitions of Germany, Italy, and Japan (USJCS, 1952: Chapter VI, 36, 55). This directive resulted in four initial "Rainbow" plans. Their detailed provisions are beyond the scope of our interest here, but it is significant to note their implications for hemispheric military cooperation:

—"Rainbow" 1, 2, and 3 involved defending the western hemisphere only as far south as Latitude 10° south (approximately the "bulge" of Brazil), and thus embody the "Quarter-Sphere" strategic concept discussed previously.

—"Rainbow" 4 included the whole western hemisphere and provided for the sending of U.S. troops to the southern part of South America, if required. Thus, it represented the broader concept of geographic "Hemisphere Defense."

None of the four initial "Rainbow" plans recognized any need for military cooperation with the Latin American nations other than the provision of necessary bases. These included: Natal, Recife, Belem, and Bahia in Brazil; Guayaquil and the Galapagos Islands in Ecuador; the Gulf of Nicoya and the Cocos Island of Costa Rica; and various airfields in Nicaragua, Honduras, and Guatemala.

As will be brought out in discussing U.S. approaches to Mexico and Brazil, the unilateral aspects of the "Color" plans were not completely abandoned even with the advent of "Rainbow," since special unilateral "Color" plans for these two key countries were maintained through the war years.

The dramatic impact of early German successes and the subsequent first and second meetings of the Consultation of Hemisphere Foreign Ministers held in 1939 and 1940, respectively, caused U.S. strategic planners to place renewed emphasis on the problems of defending the continental United States and the hemisphere. Strategic priorities were clear (Conn and Fairchild, 1960: 159-160): first the continental United States (the "citadel"); next the Panama Canal Zone ("the most important strategic area in the Western Hemisphere"), and third, the Northeast bulge of Brazil, which was required in order to deny access to the Axis in case of an attack from Dakar in West Africa.

A specific strategic concern emerged from the "no-transfer" provision of the Second Meeting of Consultation, which foresaw the need for preemptive action to occupy the British, French and Dutch possessions in the western hemisphere, and efforts were devoted in mid-1940 to develop such plans (USJCS, 1952: Chapter IX, 26, 40).

By the time of Pearl Harbor, the U.S. military departments had developed a clear and strong preference for the Quarter Sphere approach based on realistic strategic assessments and the stark realization that very limited resources made it impossible for the United States to defend or assist the whole hemisphere. The United States's abandonment of the Southern Cone implicit in the Quarter Sphere approach was regrettable but acceptable to the United States, since the Argentine military evoked little sympathy among U.S. strategic planners. There was some concern (USOSS, 1941) among U.S. Navy planners that abandonment of the Southern Cone might make it more difficult to gain access to the Straits of Magellan if the Panama Canal were ever closed, but this was not of enough immediate significance to consider shifting away from the Quarter Sphere concept.

## *Special Plans in World War II*

As noted previously, the "Rainbow" series of plans replaced the old unilateral "Color" plans in the late 1930s. However, "Rainbow" did not prevent the U.S. military departments from developing a new series of plans aimed at key nations in the hemisphere. These will be considered as follows: unilateral and bilateral plans for Brazil and Mexico; other plans for South America; plans for Central America and the Caribbean.

### *UNILATERAL AND BILATERAL PLANS FOR BRAZIL*

Initially the United States strategic approach to Brazil was based on the need to deny bases in northern Brazil to the Axis (USDS, 1941). Subsequently, the approach was based on the value of these same bases as part of a supply route to North Africa, as well as the contribution of these bases in the naval and submarine battles of the South Atlantic. Ideally, the acquisition of these bases would be obtained by a diplomatic arrangement with the Brazilian government. However, U.S. strategic planners also prepared for other contingencies. As early as January 1939 Sumner Welles raised in the State-War-Navy Standing Liaison Committee the possibility of a German-inspired overthrow of the Vargas regime followed by an invasion across the Dakar-Natal Atlantic Narrows (USSLC, 1939: 4). Shortly afterward, the U.S. Navy employed this scenario in its Fleet Problem Exercise XX in Fall 1939 (Abbazia, 1975: 33).

The scenario of a Brazilian fascist coup was formalized in both the Navy's "Pot of Gold" plan and the Army's "Lilac" plan. "Pot of Gold" was drafted in May 1940 and envisioned the immediate dispatch of 10,000 men (Army and Marines) by air to northeast Brazil to support Brazilian government forces in the event of such a coup. This initial deployment was to be augmented by an expeditionary force of 100,000 men by sea. The Navy would also interrupt German lines of communications across the Atlantic narrows (USJCS, 1952: Chapter IX, 27-28).

The Army's "Lilac" plan, also known as "Operations Plan for the Northeast Brazil Theater," laid the problem out in greater detail. The plan parted from the fundamental assumption that bases in northeast Brazil were vital to the United States. The basic "Lilac" plan contained two variants based on two divergent scenarios (USAGH, 1941):

—under "Assumption A" the Vargas government remained in power and did not oppose U.S. occupation of the bases in the northeast. The "enemy" was limited to Nazi forces in West Africa.
—under "Assumption B" the Brazilian government would resist by force the U.S. occupation of the bases. The United States would thus be fighting two hostile powers: Germany and Brazil.

In February 1942 the supplementary plan "Lilac-Rio Sector" (also called "Lilac-RS") was approved and expanded on the 1941 "Lilac" to include the pro-German coup and the withdrawal of the deposed Vargas government to the Natal-Recife area (USAGH, 1942). The U.S. mission would be to take the northeast bases, protect the Vargas government in the northeast, and initiate offensive operations against the Brazilian armed forces, assisted by the Axis powers, in a push south to Rio. It was anticipated that the Axis stronghold would extend from Rio to the southern states of São Paulo and Minas Gerais, since this was the area of greatest concentration of persons and German extraction (see Figure 4).

The extent of U.S. concern over obtaining access to northeast Brazil is starkly illustrated by a June 1940 memo which suggested

**Figure 4**

a range of measures the United States should be prepared to use to achieve this objective:

> Lines of action for gaining admission into the vital areas.
>
> a. By means of diplomacy. . . . Provided the price is not too high, admission by this means would mark a major victory for the U.S. This means should be exploited to the maximum without delay.

> b. By subsidizing the existing regime. Before resorting to political or economic pressure, careful consideration should be given to the possibility of gaining admission by certain arrangements which would better serve our interests. . . . If we should gain admission by this means, we should quietly proceed to organize Brazil in such a way that it would serve our military and economic interests for years to come. . . . If the existing regime will not agree to these arrangements, a coup might be arranged which could be synchronized with direct political pressure and the intervention of armed forces.
>
> c. Political pressure accompanied by force. If the lines of action outlined in "a" and "b" above should fail, we should resort to political pressure and direct action to gain admission into the vital area [USWDGS, 1941].

*UNILATERAL AND BILATERAL PLANS FOR MEXICO*

In early World War II, the improbability of a close military relationship between the United States and Mexico, coupled with the fact that primary U.S. strategic concerns focused on the Brazilian bulge, meant that U.S. strategic planners paid relatively little initial attention to Mexico. U.S. wartime strategy toward Mexico was related to the over-all Quarter Sphere "Rainbow" plans, with some special aspects caused by Mexico's geographic proximity to the United States. The long Baja California coastline was considered to be a possible Japanese target, and as the Japanese threat increased, so did U.S. interest in Baja (Conn and Fairchild, 1960: 356-358).

In the Caribbean, the German submarine threat raised the value of naval and air bases on Mexican soil, especially the ones on Cozumel. A further consideration was the U.S. desire to control a string of bases in Mexico in order to have an air corridor over land to the Panama Canal. As was the case with Brazil, the United States was also deeply concerned with obtaining strategic raw materials and a Good Neighbor symbol. An additional factor not present in U.S.-Brazalian relations was the interest in Mexican manpower, especially in the Southwest. On the negative side the U.S. military departments had no illusions about the ability of the Mexican military to wage war outside of their borders (USSLC, 1942).

Uncertainty over the degree of Mexican cooperation probably contributed to continuing U.S. interest in unilateral plans for offensive action in Mexico. The old color plan "Green"—border sealing, port blockade, and a possible advance to Mexico City—was updated in 1940 (USWDWPD, 1940) and not declared obsolete until 1946. Thus, even while Mexican-U.S. military cooperation was at its closest during World War II, U.S. military planners were still preparing for possible unilateral contingencies.

The U.S. Navy was interested in obtaining access to Mexican ports, both for the immediate requirements of World War II as well as for long-term leases. The Chief of Naval Operations in mid-1940 considered the impact of taking these ports without Mexican consent:

> In case Mexico fails to cooperate in hemisphere defense, U.S. Naval Forces would be handicapped in protecting the Western Pacific, without Mexican ports. We would probably have to use the desired bases with or without consent of Mexico. Such action might militate against us in dealing with other Latin American States [USN, 1940].

Progress in the development of strategic plans for bilateral Mexican-U.S. defense was delayed by two considerations (USA-FS, 1942a; 1942b): U.S. objections to placing U.S. troops under Mexican commanders when in Mexico and Mexican objections to U.S. troops on her territory. This latter problem was a particularly thorny one, given Mexican sensitivities and historical memories, but the U.S. military presence was considered essential by U.S. military planners as ground support for the numerous air and sea bases used in the air corridor to Panama and the aircraft detector stations in Baja California. A number of ingenious subterfuges were suggested and employed at one time or another: the U.S. servicemen would not wear uniforms or carry arms; they would be assigned as assistant attachés; they would be carried on the payroll of Pan American Airways (Conn and Fairchild, 1960: 345-359; JMUSDC, 1941, 1942).

## *Other Plans for South America*

### *ARGENTINA*

Files in the National Archives reveal no U.S. strategic plans involving Argentina in World War II. U.S. military planners regarded Argentina with suspicion in World War II, and this suspicion is amply reflected in numerous memoranda and reports contained in State Department, Office of Strategic Services, and military records in the National Archives.

United States hostility to Argentina during World War II surfaced in the military sphere in various ways:

—consideration was given to forcing Argentina off the Inter-American Defense Board (USDS, 1943);

—the U.S. Joint Chiefs of Staff were asked to evaluate the strategic implications of economic sanctions against Argentina (USJCS, 1944);

—the British were asked the same question, but Churchill replied that the consequences for England would be disastrous (Churchill, 1944);

—lastly, apparently some form of direct military action was contemplated. A February 1944 letter from Admiral Leahy to the Secretary of State points out that "it is the view of the U.S. Chiefs of Staff that no action should be taken which might require the use of force, as the means for such action are not available" (USN, 1944).

### *SPECIAL PLAN FOR CHILE, PERU AND VENEZUELA*

A special 1942 plan (USWDGS, 1942b) provided for U.S. troops to be temporarily stationed in Chile, Peru, and Venezuela for the training of local troops in the use of coastal artillery. This type of weapon was considered especially important for Venezuela because of petroleum assets and for the major Pacific countries—Chili, Peru—because of their long coastlines exposed to possible Japanese attacks.

### *PLANS FOR CENTRAL AMERICA AND THE CARIBBEAN*

By 1941 the old "Gray" plan for unilateral intervention in Central America and the Caribbean had been definitely replaced with a series of bilateral "help me" plans under which the United States would come to the aid of these countries, upon their request, if they were threatened by Axis or fifth-column forces.

The abandonment of the old unilateral approach is evident in this statement of the basis for one of these 1941 plans:

> *Policy of the United States.* The United States will employ its armed forces to assist any Republic to defeat attacks on it by the armed forces of a non-American State or by fifth column groups supported by a non-American State, when requested to do so by the recognized government of the republic concerned. In other cases, the United States will employ its armed forces in accordance with decisions reached as a result of Inter-American consultation [USACDC, 1941b: 3].

The operational concept of these various plans involved the basic assumption of request for assistance by a recognized government. The United States was prepared to react to such a request with the immediate deployment of an Airborne Parachute Battalion from the Panama Canal Zone, with appropriate supporting forces to include several Navy ships and Marine detachments (USACDC, 1941a).

## *Conclusions*

Research into almost 30 years of U.S. military strategic planning files as described in this paper has produced some interesting new insights into the changing approaches taken by U.S. military strategic planners toward the hemisphere in the period between the end of World War I and the end of World War II.

In particular, these plans document the unilateral interventionist strategic approach embodied in the concept of the "American Lake"; the slow abandonment of the "American Lake" concept in the face of the multilateral Good Neighbor Policy; and the adoption of a bilateral World War II approach best described as special bilateral relationships with the key countries in the Quarter Sphere.

It is notable in this process of shifting from unilateral to bilateral strategic planning, the U.S. military departments were prepared to return to unilateral approaches, and planned for them, if the bilateral approach should fail to obtain U.S. objectives in the key nations in the Quarter Sphere—most importantlly Brazil and Mexico.

Also significant is the fact that despite politico-diplomatic adoption of the multilateral hemisphere defense concept, the U.S. military departments did *no* multilateral strategic planning in World War II. The multilateral organ, the Inter-American Defense Board, was not permitted to have a multilateral planning role until the Cold War.

These conclusions support the basic contention that in World War II multilateral military approaches were symbolic, token, and political in nature, and while the U.S. military tolerated such approaches, military realism dictated that bilateral approaches would be preferred, but that unilateral plans would be prepared for use as needed.

## REFERENCES

### *Abbreviations*

FRUS: Foreign Relation of the United States (annual State Department document, further identified by year and volume).

JBUSDC: Joint Brazil-U.S. Defense Commission.

Documents used in the National Archives of Washington, D.C., are identified by specific file, Entry Number, Record Group number (RG) and the designation NA for National Archives.

ABBAZIA, P. (1975) Mr. Roosevelt's Navy. Annapolis: Naval Institute Press.

CHILD, J. (1976) "Latin America: Military-Strategic Concepts," pp. 27-42 in Air University Review, XXVII, No. 6, September-October.

CHURCHILL, W. S. (1944) Message 552 to President Roosevelt, File CCS 091.3 Arg 1-4-44, RG 218, 23 January, NA.

CONN, S., and B. FAIRCHILD (1960) The Framework of Hemisphere Defense. Washington, D.C.: Office of the Chief of Military History, Department of the Army.

JMUSDC [Joint-Mexico-U.S. Defense Commission] (1942) Memorandum a la Sección Norteamericana. File MDC 4120, JMUSDC, RG 218, 8 May, NA.

——— (1941) Carta al General Embick. File MDC 4120, JMUSDC, RG 218, 16 December, NA.

USAAG [U.S. Army Adjutant General] (1967) Memo AGAR-S, 7100-3, Entry 365, RG 407, 4 December, NA.

USACDC [U.S. Army Caribbean Defense Command] (1941a) Plan for Support of Costa Rica. File AG 46, Entry 365, RG 407, 8 July, NA.

——— (1941b) Plan for Support of Guatemala. File AG 70, Entry 365, RG 407, August, NA.

USAFA [U.S. Army Fourth Army] (1942a) Joint Mexico-U.S. Pacific Coastal Frontier Defense Plan, File MDC 9010, RG 218, NA.

——— (1942b) Memo to the Chief of Staff, Subject: Negotiations with Mexico Concerning Defense of the West Coast. File MDC 9010, RG 218, 22 March, NA.

USAGH [U.S. Army General Headquarters] (1942) Operations Plan of Northeast Brazil Theater. Rio Sector (Plan Lilac-RS). Entry 365, RG 407, 20 February, NA.

——— (1941) Operations Plan of Northeast Brazil Theater. Entry 365, RG 407, 1 November, NA.

USAPCD [U.S. Army Panama Canal Department] (1941) Basic War Plan: Panama Canal Department. File AG 288, Entry 365, RG 407, 1 April, NA.

——— (1924) Basic War Plan: Panama Canal Department, File AG 288, Entry 365, RG 407, NA.

USDS [U.S. Department of State] (1943) Memorandum (ARA-Halle, 12 May, Decimal File 810.20 Defense 3549, RG 59, NA.

——— (1941) Memorandum, Marshall to Welles, 17 June, FRUS, 1941, Vol. VI, 498-501.

USJCS [U.S. Joint Chiefs of Staff] (1952) Evolution of Global Strategy. Prepared by Tracy Kittridge, JCS Historical Division, RG 218, NA.

——— (1944) Document JCS 652/2, Subject: Proposed Economic Sanctions with Respect to Argentina. File CCS 091.3 Arg 1-4-44, RG 218, 19 January, NA.

USN [U.S. Navy] (1944) Admiral Leahy Memo to Secretary of State Hull. File CCS 092 Argentina 2-29-44, RG 218, 29 February, NA.

——— (1940) CNO Stark Memo for the Secretary of the Navy. File MDC 4960-3, JMUSDC, RG 218, 21 August, NA.

USOSS [U.S. Office of Strategic Services] (1941) Research and Analysis Study #159: The Strategy of the Magellan Strait Area. File OSS R&A Study 159, RG 59, 8 December, NA.

USSLC [U.S. Standing Liaison Committee] (1942) Minutes for 16 November meeting. File SLC Minutes, RG 353, 16 November, NA.
——— (1939) Minutes for 21 January meeting. File SLC Minutes, RG 353, 21 January, NA.
USWDGS [U.S. War Department General Staff] (1942a) List of Registered Documents, Adjutant General's Office, RG 407, NA.
——— (1942b) Operations Plan: U.S. Troops in Chile, Peru, and Venezuela. File Reg Doc 32, RG 407, 12 February, NA.
——— (1941) Memo for the Chief of Staff, Subject: Admission of U.S. Forces into Northeast Brazil. File 5440, JBUSDC, RG 218, 14 June, NA.
——— (1940) Rainbow #1. File AG 361, Entry 365, RG 407, 11 July, NA.
——— (c1935) Classified Files List, Operations Branch, Adjutant General's Office. File 1920-1948 (AGO) Special Projects, War Plans Color, RG 407, NA.
——— (1928) Estimate of the Situation: Red-Orange Coalition. Entry 365, RG 407, 7 June, NA.
USWDWPD [U.S. War Department War Plans Division] (1940) Operations Plan Green. Entry 365, RG 407, NA.
——— (1931a) Strategical Plan Gray. File AG 71, Entry 365, RG 407. NA.
——— (1931b) Memo for the G-2, Subject: Army Strategical Plan Gray. File Gray 2877, Entry 282, RG 165, 5 May, NA.
——— (1931c) Army Strategical Plan Gray. Entry 282, RG 165, 28 October, NA.
——— (1930s) Comments on Army Strategical Plan Purple. File AG 355, Entry 365, RG 407, NA.
——— (1930b) Special Plan Tan for Intervention in Cuba. Entry 365, RG 407, NA.
——— (1928a) Memo for the Chief of Staff, Subject: Special Plan Purple. File AG 358, Entry 282, RG 165, 3 August, NA.
——— (1928b) Army Strategical Plan Purple. File AG 356, Entry 365, RG 407, 4 August, NA.
——— (1927a) Memo for the Assistant Chief of Staff, Subject: Special Service Plan (Later Plan "Gray"). File Gray 2877, Entry 282, RG 165, 3 March, NA.
——— (1927b) Memo for LTC Frazier, Subject: Plan for Intervention in South America. File AG 358, Entry 282, RG 165, 8 September, NA.
——— (1919) Memo for the Chief of Staff, Subject: General Mexican War Plan, Entry 282, RG 165, 14 July, NA.
Washington Post (1975) "1919 plan to invade Canada is disclosed." 28 October, Section A: 1.

Figure 1: Basic strategic concepts.

Figure 2: The "Color Plans," 1919-1942. Green = Mexico. Tan = Cuba. White = Panama. Gray = Haiti, Dominican Republic, Guatemala, and Nicaragua. Purple = Colombia, Venezuela, Ecuador, Peru, Chile, Argentina, Uruguay, and Brazil.

Figure 3: Plan "Green," 1920-1940.

Figure 4: World War II plans for Brazil ("Pot of Gold" and "Lilac").

*John Child, Lieutenant Colonel, U.S. Army, is on the faculty of the Inter-American Defense College, Washington, D.C. He has published several articles based on research done in connection with his doctoral dissertation, "The Inter-American Military System." His areas of research and specialization focus on hemispheric strategic and military relationships.*

**JOHN GALEY**
*3106 Iowa Street*
*Joplin, MO 64801*

# *INDUSTRIALIST IN THE WILDERNESS*
## *Henry Ford's Amazon Venture*

In the latter half of the 1920s, a half dozen North American, British, and Canadian engineers and geologists individually began secretive explorations for oil, minerals, and likely locations for rubber plantations in the Brazilian Amazon jungle. Their goal: to interest the Ford, Firestone, and Goodyear companies in land that would supply the raw materials for their product—tires. As these land speculators negotiated with the Amazonian state governments for concessions, each thought he had claimed the richest territory with virtually unlimited exploitation privileges. Several scrambled for concessions, and by July of 1927 one individual obtained 2.5 million acres on the Tapajós river in the Amazonian state of Pará. He secretively planted half a million rubber seedlings in the forest (an indication of the vastness, sparse population, and poor communications in the Amazon at that date) and left behind an armed guard to protect the land against incursions by other speculators (Winter, 1927). In a subsequent contract with Pará, Henry Ford then acquired this land to grow rubber. After these initial maneuvers, North America's pioneer car manufacturer and billionaire

---

EDITOR'S NOTE: This descriptive analysis of the Ford Motor Company's effort to develop a major rubber plantation on the Tapajós river in the Amazon drainage between 1927 and 1945 is a chronological case study of the problems of a proprietary, vertically structured, multinational industrial complex with the state of Pará and the government of Brazil under what are believed to be unique transitional circumstances for both the foreign entrepreneur and the host nation.

Journal of Interamerican Studies and World Affairs, Vol. 21 No. 2, May 1979, 261-289
© 1979 Sage Publications, Inc.

industrialist embarked on a unique social and economic experiment in the Amazon, while Brazil obtained a seemingly promising but highly controversial development project for the nation's far north.

Ford's international venture in Brazil originated as a pragmatic project for his automobile industry. In 1922 the British Stevenson Plan restricted Asian plantation rubber exports by means of cooperation between British and French planters. Thus they created an artificial rubber shortage and inflated the price of this commodity on the international market. North American industry consumed over 70% of the world's rubber supply, which came primarily from Asia, and manufacturers in the United States were forced to consider other sources beyond the cartel's control (Chalk, 1970; Costa, 1928). Secretary of Commerce Herbert Hoover urged North American industrialists to grow their own supply. In 1924 he sent a government technical mission to investigate the Amazon's rubber resources in cooperation with Brazilian authorities. Firestone eventually chose to invest in Liberian plantations, rather than Amazonian, and Goodyear planted in Sumatra and the Philippines. Henry Ford hoped to find a closer source by growing his own in the Western Hemisphere, and he expected to create a rubber autarchy from the planted seed to the tires and inner tubes on his automobiles. Ford considered the Brazilian Amazon, but first he waited until his friend and mentor, Thomas Edison, tested the possibility of growing rubber in the United States itself.

The Brazilian government and the administrations of the Amazonian states of Pará and Amazonas quickly realized that the Stevenson Plan might work to their advantage by stimulating North American capital investment in Amazon rubber. The Amazon valley was the natural habitat of *Hevea brasiliensis,* the premium species of wild rubber. This species had once dominated the world market during the valley's great rubber boom from 1890 to 1913. In this latter year, Asian cultivated rubber first overwhelmed the wild product in tonnage on the world market, and this event signaled the end of the Amazon boom.

In 1908 the Amazon basin, including non-Brazilian portions, had produced 94.4% of the world's rubber supply, but by 1918 this figure dropped to 10.9%, and later sank to a record low of 2.3% by 1928 (Filhe, 1965). During 1910 rubber from the Brazilian Amazon ranked second to coffee in the value of Brazil's major exports, but within four years rubber had declined to a negligible place. After the introduction of the Stevenson Plan, Brazilian officials hoped that a renewed demand for non-Asian rubber would warrant the revival of Amazonian production. They hoped this renewed development of rubber resources would be based eventually on the Far Eastern plantation system, for Asian plantations had clearly demonstrated that cultivated rubber could be produced more efficiently and economically than wild rubber. Theoretically, Amazonian plantations would also offer the advantage of a permanently settled work force to populate the region, rather than the seasonal, migratory, and undependable labor force involved in wild rubber harvesting. However, plantations required a substantial capital investment and produced only long-term yields. This prospect discouraged local Brazilian enterprise. Thus, the state governments of northern Brazil were prepared to offer attractive incentives in land concessions to stimulate North American investment and to rescue the region from economic stagnation (Araujo Lima, 1923).[1]

Ford decided to invest in the Brazilian Amazon in 1927 after Thomas Edison's experiments in producing domestic rubber failed. By this time, the Stevenson Plan had faltered seriously because the Dutch and native Asian growers refused to cooperate in the cartel. Despite improved rubber prices for North American purchasers, Ford persisted in planning his own independent supply as another addition to his numerous innovative and pioneering projects. After all, he had already turned a bankrupt Michigan railroad into at least a temporarily successful operation. He had improved coal-mining technology and developed revolutionary new glass-making techniques. Also by 1926 his Ford Air Transport Service had become the first private contractor to fly airmail for the United States government. Almost any new venture seemed possible for Henry Ford who confidentially accepted the challenge of growing rubber in Amazonia.

Ford's Amazon investment was preceded by a long-established foreign interest in this region for which a variety of practical projects and eccentric schemes had been planned. In the 1850s Lt. Mathew Fontaine Maury, director of the United States Naval Observatory in Washington, D.C., tried to promote the North American occupation of the Amazon drainage as a dumping ground for southern planters and their slaves at a time when Brazil forbade navigation and trade in northern Brazil by countries other than the Amazon nations (Harrison, 1955: 188-191). Brazilians rightly feared that Maury's campaign for opening the Amazon by force would inspire North American colonization of Amazonia, but the Civil War in the United States ended this inherent threat. In the 1860s, Louis and Cary Agassiz's scientific expedition to the Amazon favorably influenced Brazilian Emperor Dom Pedro II, who opened the Brazilian Amazon to all international trade and navigation in 1869. Several years later a British explorer, Henry Wickham, showed how foreign interest in this region could become predatory when he smuggled a batch of rubber tree seeds and seedlings out of Pará past unwary Brazilian customs agents. This planting material was eventually sent to the Orient where it formed the nucleus of the plantations that overwhelmed Amazonia by 1913. The problem of exploitative foreign influence erupted again at the turn of the century when the Anglo-American "Bolivian Syndicate" proposed to develop a land concession in a rich Amazon rubber territory disputed by both Brazil and Bolivia. A nationalistic Brazilian campaign against the project and a border war in the disputed area prevented the syndicate from taking control of its concession.

Still, not all foreign interest in Amazonia seemed solely exploitative to Brazilians. For example, during the rubber boom, British and North American entrepreneurs introduced some of the most modern urban public services available in the world at that time. Amazonians themselves had once hailed these works as evidence of a new era in regional progress.

Henry Ford's plantation project followed in the tradition of ambitious and sometimes controversial plans for Brazil's north, but Ford failed to realize that the severe problems associated with some of these efforts had already created an enduring stigma of failure in Amazon development. Various transportation and communications projects testified to seemingly insurmountable geographical and public health challenges in rural Amazonia. The 226-mile Madeira-Mamoré Railroad, completed in western Amazonia in 1910, typified the difficulties encountered by foreign enterprise. The death toll of 3,600 men—who perished from yellow fever, malaria, and other causes in building the line—offered sinister evidence that development in this region could exact a forbidding payment in human life (Gauld, 1964). Such projects were also financially exorbitant and frequently unprofitable. The Madeira-Mamoré cost $33 million in which European investors alone lost $10 million, and after the crash of the rubber boom in 1913 the line operated in the red (Gauld, 1964).

Amazon rubber production itself had acquired an unsavory reputation because of labor exploitation in the wild rubber forests and the failure of early plantation projects. Debt peonage in the Brazilian Amazon and outright slavery in the rubber regions of other basin nations contributed to the valley's notoriety. When European companies tried to introduce the plantation system in the Brazilian Amazon during the 1890s, poor management, labor shortages, and yellow fever epidemics ended these experiments and temporarily discouraged further plans for rubber planting. Such experiences led Latin American and European authors to portray the basin as the true heart of darkness (Cunha, 1913; Rangel, 1927; Castro, 1957; Moog, 1954; Rivera, 1971: 98-157; Tomlinson, 1964: 97-282; Baum, 1943). Amazonians themselves deeply resented their region's bad reputation and felt unjustly maligned, while in Rio de Janeiro, federal officials could only hope that one day a renewed effort in developing the north's resources would disprove Amazonia's ominous legacy.

A North American with extensive Amazon experience once wrote, "Generations of little men have nibbled like mice at the edge of the Amazon," for their accomplishments seemed insignificant in relation to the basin's sheer immensity (Schurz, 1961). The next two decades after Ford received his concession would reveal whether this billionaire industrial genius would succeed or merely nibble at the edges of the enormous valley and go down to defeat like so many of his ambitious predecessors.

When the Ford concession was publicized in early 1928, Brazilians began to question the great industrialist's intentions in Amazonia. Wary Brazilians had long feared that foreigners might seize the north for its resources and living space. This seizure allegedly might occur through the gradual alienation of land by the owners to foreign companies with extensive prerogatives and concessions. For some Brazilians the problem was particularly acute because most of the Amazon lay beyond the scrutiny and protection of national authority. The potential threat seemed magnified after the crash of the wild rubber boom when the northern states lost their main source of income from rubber export taxes. These states had borrowed heavily during the boom, but afterward they defaulted on the payment of their scandalously large foreign debts.[2] In desperation, the states' administrations then offered concessions for virtually unlimited resource exploitation in timber, potential oil or mineral deposits, rubber or any other resource.[3] Foreigners thus received exclusive exploitation rights in huge areas of national territory, as in the case of Ford whose Pará concession was about 82% of the size of Connecticut (Nevins and Hill, 1957). Some Brazilians soon wondered whether Ford might unduly exploit his contractual privileges and thus violate national and state sovereignties.

In Rio de Janeiro during 1928, a Paráense senator initiated a campaign against the Ford concession. Senator Antonio Emiliano de Souza Castro was a former governor of Pará and a former political protégé of the current governor, Dionisio Ausier Bentes, who had granted the contract. Souza Castro had left Bentes's Republican Federal Party in Pará after quarreling with Bentes over party leadership and, following this, the senator tried to politically destroy the governor by encouraging a nationalistic reaction against the Ford project. Souza Castro claimed that Bentes had concluded an agreement that abrogated Brazilian authority in Amazonia. Ford had acquired extensive privileges without reciprocal obligations.[4] The Yankee industrialist allegedly might create a private army or police force to protect his property, and his company might engage in commerce that would ruin local firms.[5] Because of the entrenched apprehensions over northern Brazil, these arguments seemed familiar and also compelling to some, even though the political motivations in the senator's accusations were well known. Nor was the senator's nationalistic appeal discredited, even when Bentes revealed that as governor of Pará in 1923, Souza Castro himself gave a 2.5 million-acre concession to a North American who tried to swindle Negroes in the United States into buying Amazon land for colonization (Correio do Pará, 1928; Barreiros, 1928: 179-181).[6]

For political reasons, other Brazilians took up the cause against Ford and as the end of the Old Republic of 1889-1930 neared, dissident politicians in 1929 capitalized on the issue by emphasizing that the source of trouble lay not in Amazonia but in Rio de Janeiro itself. Under the nation's decentralized federal system, the federal government tolerated the situation in which southern states such as Minas Gerais and São Paulo remained economically powerful and unified, while the weakened and economically stagnant northern states posed a severe liability for the union. The federation's vitiated states needed strong federal tutelage, not permissiveness, to prevent them from surrendering Brazil's patrimony for a pittance. Brazil's political system should be completely altered because only a powerful national government could bring the nation's states to heel and provide guidance for future economic development. Such, for instance, were the arguments of José Carlos de Macedo Soares, a prominent Paulista businessman, in the revolutionary movement of Getúlio Vargas, who overthrew the Old Republic and came to power in 1930.

On the other hand, Ford's supporters in the Brazilian government and the press successfully emphasized his benevolent intentions in Brazil and his image as a reformist in industry. The portrayal of Ford as the capitalist with a conscience seemed familiar to literate Brazilians who were acquainted with the homilies of the Ford philosophy after his biography, *My Life and Work,* was published in Portuguese in 1926. Ford's enlightened social and economic ideas allegedly made his investment welcome in Brazil, where other Yankee capitalists might not be so well received.[7] Ford's advocates claimed he would bring unprecedented social and economic benefits for the impoverished workers of Amazonia and for the progress of Pará. With his billions of dollars and his unfailing industrial talents, Henry Ford would begin the transformation of Amazonia, and perhaps three or four more Henry Fords would complete it (Folha do Norte, 1928; Jornal do Brasil, 1932; Jornal do Commercio, 1927; O Jornal, 1928). At least initially, such arguments seemed to reassure many Brazilians, and after 1929 the debate over Ford's intentions abated for several years.

In discussing the project, Ford himself asserted he would completely transform the world's rubber industry with his Amazon plantations. He further promised to help develop Pará and claimed he would manufacture tires and other rubber articles in Brazil (O Mundo Ford, 1928). He may also have considered a gesture of true showmanship to dramatize his Amazon venture. Rather than arrive on the *Majestic,* he reportedly considered a journey to Pará on *The Spirit of St. Louis* flown by Charles Lindberg, who was planning a 9,000-mile Latin American tour in his famous plane (Folha do Norte, 1928).[8]

Despite the effectiveness of Ford's public image, the company's relations with Brazilian officials were troubled by misunderstandings and quixotic policies that characterized the organization's relations with federal and regional Brazilian authorities during the 1930s. To begin with, intermediaries in negotiating the Ford concession received commissions totaling $125,000 from Ford representatives (Cowling, 1929: August 23). This incident particularly disturbed Henry Ford, who strongly disapproved of any transaction that even remotely involved gratuities or bribes. After this, Ford officials in Brazil strictly adhered to a policy of refusing to seek favors or special considerations through lobbying with public officials. This puritanical attitude surprised many North American businessmen in Rio de Janeiro, who made lobbying a standard practice with Congress and the ministries. In Pará during the late 1920s, Japanese entrepreneurs had openly courted favors for their jute plantation operations and then had won the support of local authorities and the Belém press. Ford's executives in Brazil were well aware of this cooperation secured by the Japanese, but Ford officials stubbornly insisted on "educating Brazil to the Ford way of thinking" (Cowling, 1929: August 20). Consequently, the company suffered much petty harassment, particularly from Paráense authorities who could not understand this attitude and Ford's unwillingness to compromise.

In negotiating the Ford concession, company representatives made a serious mistake in failing to obtain ratification of the contract by the federal government. Only the state of Pará was formally bound to fulfill the contract provisions, including one critical clause concerning import tax exemptions. This immunity from taxes involved the cooperation of the federal government, which levied the import taxes in all Brazilian states. The Ford company interpreted the exemption clause to apply to a wide variety of equipment and supplies imported for the plantation, but federal authorities claimed the exemption applied only to machinery destined for the rubber tire and inner tube plant promised by Ford. Because the contract had never received federal approval, national officials felt free to question the exemption clause. Moreover, they felt justified in delaying the tax immunity on all imports when it appeared that the Ford company was not going to build the plant. In 1929 the Minister of Agriculture, who came from Pará, was anxious to satisfy the company's needs and thus encourage the plantation project, but Brazilian President Washington Luís was uninterested in cooperating on the tax issue. By the time Getúlio Vargas became president, the exemption controversy was still unsolved.

The selection of the plantation's location was another naive mistake that seemed to defy a solution. The newly formed *Companhia Ford Industrial do Brasil* took over the 2.5 million-acre concession, which was named Fordlandia. At Ford's insistence, a company man, lacking agricultural experience, directed operations including site selection, clearing, and planting. His choice of a hilly location made rubber cultivation and erosion control difficult. If Ford had been willing to hire a professional agronomist from outside the company, these problems might have been avoided. Moreover, Fordlandia was in a wilderness far from any settlements. The company's activities thus had to start from scratch, with a massive importation of equipment and supplies.

In December 1928, Ford's freighters, the *Lake Ormoc* and *Lake Farge,* arrived at Fordlandia loaded to capacity and commanded by a large and earnest Danish sea captain, Einard Oxholm. The ships carried a complete railroad, a diesel tugboat, an entire disassembled warehouse from Detroit, and a wide variety of other equipment intended for a self-contained plantation operation. Trouble began almost immediately when the plantation manager quit and returned to the United States. This left the project in charge of Captain Oxholm, who lacked the slightest notion of how to grow rubber. Ford decided to retain Oxholm as manager, not only because of the captain's unquestioned integrity but also because of Ford's conviction that a man could rapidly acquire expertise in a field far beyond his own specialization. Oxholm was in fact so naive and scrupulously honest that he became known as a "soft touch" in Pará, where Brazilian and European entrepreneurs overcharged him for services and supplies for the plantation. For two years, the Danish captain struggled valiantly with the project, but by January of 1929 the company had already spent more than $1.5 million and had very little to show for it (Ford Motor Co., 1928). After Oxholm's replacement with another company man from Detroit, the captain remarked that the plantation was "the hardest proposition I ever tackled in my life" (Detroit News, 1930). Within one year, the company had two new additional managers each of whom quickly gave up and returned to the United States.

During this period the waste, confusion, and incompetent management at Fordlandia disillusioned Brazilian federal officials who could not reconcile Ford's reputation for efficiency with the disarray on his Tapajós property. By late 1929, 95% of the rubber tree seedlings planted to comply with the concession contract were dying or dead. The company manager admitted that half the timber cleared from the land was burned and wasted. One Ford trouble-shooter sent to Brazil wrote:

> There is a complete lack of organization at the property. No one knows what the whole picture should be. Waste is terrible. . . . I can well understand why the Minister of Agriculture in Rio should think we are crazy. . . . At present, it is like dropping money into a sewer [Cowling, 1929: September 9].

Meanwhile, because of a rivalry between the northern states of Amazonas and Pará, the Ford company was frustrated in obtaining a good seed supply for new planting attempts. Before Ford concluded the concession contract with Pará in 1927, Amazonas state officials had tried to secure his investment in their own state, and afterward they felt jealous of Pará's success. In retaliation, the governor of Amazonas embargoed a shipment of 24 cases of rubber seeds gathered in Mato Grosso for the plantation and destined for shipment to Pará by way of Manaus, Amazonas. The governor alleged that Ford planned to ship these seeds to California or the Philippines. In fact, the seeds were intended only for Pará, and the governor had apparently violated a federal Brazilian law by interfering with interstate commerce. The case eventually reached the Brazilian Supreme Court where a decision was made against Ford. The court later reversed its decision to favor Ford, but only after the company had to resort to seeds from Pará, which were inferior to the seeds from Mato Grosso.

During the early 1930s, Fordlandia's physical plant reached impressive proportions, but these elaborate facilities were a diversion from the primary business of planting rubber. Though the plantation was nominally supervised by Henry Ford's son, Edsel, in Detroit, the entire program was inspired by the elder Ford, who encouraged a diversification of plantation activities and the creation of facilities for a new social experience in Amazonia. The plantation had extensive and comfortable employee housing, a school, a hospital with modern and sophisticated equipment, a power plant, a sanitary water supply, 30 miles of road, and a sawmill with a 25,000 board foot capacity, reportedly the largest in Brazil. Plans were made to export massive quantities of lumber and to produce wooden auto parts for export. Fordlandia would also manufacture tile and brick for local use. A new plantation manager revived the early plans for a tire and inner tube factory and eventually planned for a city of 10,000 on the property.

This extensive diversification represented an unsuccessful attempt to infuse an agricultural project with the engineering expertise of Detroit. Ford himself had often emphasized the need to wed agriculture and industry on the North American farm, with mechanization to reduce the waste and drudgery of old-fashioned farming. Mechanization and the seasonal nature of most farming would then free the farmer to work in factories, while the factory worker would use his spare time in agricultural pursuits. Because of Ford's nostalgic yearnings for North

America's agrarian and small town life, he once remarked, "It was an evil day the village flour mill disappeared" (Ford and Crowther, 1923). In Amazonia, Ford inspired an effort to introduce his curious vision of an agro-industrial utopia in which employees would have "one foot in industry and one foot on the land," as the Ford Sunday Evening Hour Sermonettes expressed it for the North American public (Sward, 1972). However, in practice the wedding between industry and agriculture was difficult because expertise in the former field obviously provided no guide to the latter. Fordlandia became a complex operation with various distractions, while rubber planting itself suffered from blundering and unimaginative techniques.

Ford's plans for exporting lumber also met discouraging obstacles. In 1932, when the freighter *Boniface* docked at Hoboken, New Jersey, with a cargo of Fordlandia lumber, the Brazilian counsul general in New York hailed the event by predicting that timber from Brazil would completely revolutionize the construction industry in the United States (Jornal do Brasil, 1932). In fact, the Fordlandia export project was in deep trouble. From 1928 to 1934, nearly 9,000 acres at the site were cleared of dense forest, but some of the timber was useless because of excessive moisture absorption and the sheer hardness of some varieties. Company officials also discovered to their dismay that in Amazonia the same type of tree seldom grows together in large stands of timber; instead, a single acre usually contains dozens of different types. This problem complicated the selection and preparation of timber. Finally, the company found that Pará prohibited the export of many types of timber, and Ford officials were unable to obtain an exemption from this law until after Henry Ford lost interest in the project.

Most importantly, renewed efforts at planting failed dismally. Initially the company managers thought that all one had to do was to plant a seed or seedling and then tap it at the end of eight years to obtain the latex. Instead, they found that the trees grew slowly and the latex yield in preliminary test tappings was poor. Furthermore the Amazon had an army of insects and a variety of plant blights that attacked the young trees. The South American leaf disease, *Dothidella nisi,* and the lace bug, *Leptofarca hevea,* joined forces to riddle and defoliate the rubber trees. Other local rubber tree enemies included black crust, yellow scale, and five other fungus varieties, red mites, sauva ants, caterpillars, and hawk moths. At Fordlandia, the caterpillar problem was temporarily solved when the sauva ants ate the caterpillars as they advanced on the rubber trees, but then the ants turned their attention to the trees. As if this was not enough, white root disease and canker attacked the tree roots. Jungle underbrush also hindered tree growth and maintenance, so cover crops were planted to retard the undergrowth. These cover crops soon dried up in the Amazonian dry season and created a fire hazard. In the rainy season the cover crops absorbed water and plant foods that might ordinarily have promoted the growth of the rubber trees.

By 1933 Ford officials realized the Detroit engineering approach to rubber planting was hopeless, and for the first time the company hired a professional agronomist who was well versed in the latest rubber planting techniques. James Weir was a former plant pathologist in the U.S. Department of Agriculture who directed Goodyear's research in Sumatra and helped organize the British Rubber Research Institute in Malaya. In U.S. government circles, Weir had the reputation of a conceited crank, but even his detractors acknowledged his expertise in rubber. After inspecting Fordlandia, Weir decided the location was too hilly and sparsely planted and too much attention had been devoted to activities aside from rubber growing. He advised the company to start anew with a completely new plantation using high-yield clones from Asia—the progeny of a single tree, propagated by bud grafting—and bud grafting—placing a tree bud or clone under the bark of a seedling or young tree. Through experimentation with these methods, Weir hoped to develop a high-yield, rapid-growing, and disease-resistant strain in the Amazon.

Weir then promptly departed for Singapore where he obtained 2,046 stumped buddings from 53 of the best Asian clones. This material was the fruit of about 60 years of selected plant breeding and about 20 years of bud grafting. In a reversal of Henry Wickham's seed theft from Amazonia, Weir spirited the buddings on a ship from half way around the world back to Amazonia and had them planted only a few miles from the location where Wickham had collected his seeds 57 years previously. Belatedly, the International Rubber Commission of the British, Dutch, and French Asian colonies prohibited the export of planting material only a few months after Weir exploited the research of Asia for the apparent benefit of Amazonia.

In May 1934, the Ford company traded to Pará 703,750 acres of its Fordlandia property for an equal amount of land at a new location called Belterra, about 30 miles up the Tapajós River from its conjunction with the Amazon River (U.S. Consul, 1940). Belterra was on a broad plain about 500 feet above sea level, and it was near the Amazon's third largest city, Santarém. Tree cultivation at Fordlandia was reduced, and under Weir's direction the company began extensive clearing and seeding at Belterra using the local *Hevea brasiliensis* stock bud grafted with a high-yielding clone. Weir developed several species of rubber trees resistant to the South American leaf disease, with leaves too thick for the lace bug, but these species produced inferior latex with excessive resin. At Belterra, the various insects and diseases returned to attack the nonresistant species. The sauva ants now no longer ate the caterpillars, and so both pests had their fill of rubber plants.

These problems momentarily discouraged Edsel Ford, who considered selling the properties to Brazilian investors in 1935, but no purchasers could be found. The Brazilians complained of lacking capital, and possibly they were discouraged by the many difficulties encountered thus far at Fordlandia and Belterra. The Ford company found no alternative but to continue operations or abandon the property completely. With renewed energy and optimism, the Fords decided to expand Belterra's facilities and continue planting, with the hope that in time the trees would mature and the insect problem would be solved.

As at Fordlandia, Belterra's extensive physical plant was supposed to provide an orderly and modern environment for the workers. Henry Ford thus hoped to achieve work efficiency, though some of the provisions for the employees and their dependents had an altruistic and strictly nonprofit character. Amazonians, who had previously lived on a pittance or were impoverished and unemployed, now received a free home, free medical and dental care, recreational facilities, and a wage ranging from the equivalent of 33 to 66 cents per day. This represented at least twice the current wages paid elsewhere in the region (Bressman, 1940; Burdett, 1938). The workers bought food and supplies at low and closely controlled prices from local concessionaires and, in the case of meat and flour, the company subsidized the concessionaires so they would make a profit. Babies born on the plantations received free pasteurized milk. At Belterra the company even had a cemetery where employees were buried for free. From birth to death, the company catered to the workers with Henry Ford's vision of paternalism.

Still, Ford never succeeded in imposing his alien social philosophy on the Amazonian workers. When Ford spoke of "humanity" in industry, he meant a kind of distant and exalted benevolence and not the personal man-to-man paternalism of the patriarchical society in the Amazon. Ford could not replace the traditional Brazilian *patrão* (patron) who served as combined bossman and indulgent parent for the Amazonian working class. The *patrão* might hold the worker in debt servitude, but he also served as godfather, advisor, and protector. In contrast, Ford's approach was characterized by his remark that "A great business is really too big to be human. It supplants the personality of man" (Ford and Crowther, 1923). Ford would thus have criticized the *patrão*'s services as coddling and unsuited to modern employer-employee relations, but obviously Amazonia was not Detroit, nor were the region's ingrained cultural and economic traditions easily replaced or altered.

Even less so could the plantation workers adjust to Ford's obsession with timesaving and efficiency on the job. At the Henry

Ford Hospital in Detroit, Ford had once required that physicians punch time clocks, but the doctors silently refused. When Ford tried to impose rigid work schedules in the Amazon, the workers became violent. Tension over the issue of rigid work regimes mounted to the point where a riot erupted when the company attempted to introduce the cafeteria system as a means of reducing lunchtime breaks at Fordlandia. As the workers filed down the serving line with trays for the first time, one of them suddenly stopped and irately shouted, "I'm a worker, not a waiter!" Others grumbled that they were not "dogs" and they wanted to be waited on when they ate (Morgan, 1931; Ostenfeld, 1930). The foremen became angry when they realized they would have to eat in the same manner as the workers. The men proceeded to wreck the cafeteria, and then they armed themselves with shotguns, rifles, and machetes for a destructive rampage through the plantation. The North American staff barely escaped on company boats and remained in the middle of the Tapajós River until Brazilian troops arrived to subdue the riot.

Company authorities felt the trouble had been caused by professional agitators, but in any case they pursued a lenient policy in continuing the employment of most workers. Brazilian officials who arrived at the plantation after the riot were surprised at the good working conditions and the permissive attitude of the company. For example, Pará Interventor Joaquim de Maghalaes Barata, a federally appointed governor who had previously been hostile to the company, inspected Belterra for the first time and decided the workers enjoyed better working conditions here than elsewhere in Brazil. He sternly berated the rioters, and in fact he reportedly told them, "You'd better get down on your knees and thank God for the benefits the Ford company has brought you" (Ford, 1940). The interventor also threatened drastic action if he heard of any more riots on the property.

Indeed, the company achieved an excellent record in promoting public health and good sanitary and dietary standards for the workers in a region of Brazil where these conditions were frequently absent. The company carried out strict sanitary precautions against malaria and yellow fever and maintained a well-staffed 120-bed hospital at Belterra. In a program reflecting Ford's back-to-the-earth philosophy, workers were encouraged to grow their own vegetables for a healthy and well-rounded diet. Lessons were given in vegetable garden cultivation and annual prizes were offered, including one for the best "school boy garden." Belterra and Fordlandia were virtually free of botulism and diet-related diseases such as beri beri, while hookworm and other endemic Amazon scourges were also absent. However, the company was much less successful in trying to impose a regulation by Henry Ford, who prohibited the consumption of alcoholic beverages on the property. Many workers continued to drink their customary *cachaca,* a raw alcoholic drink, and could not understand why a teetotaler in distant Detroit had forbidden it.

While some of Ford's provisions seemed eccentric and unsuited to the locale, the plantations were not influenced by the colonialist mentality that so often characterized North American company camp life abroad. Fordlandia and Belterra never became exclusive foreign enclaves that abrogated national authority as some Brazilians had feared. In 1941, for example, the North American staff at Belterra numbered only six compared with 2,042 other employees, most of them Brazilian, including personnel in key supervisory capacities (U.S. Consul, 1941). The plantations' schools employed Brazilian teachers using Portuguese according to Brazilian educational regulations, and national holidays were always celebrated. The company catered to Brazilian sports with no less than five soccer fields. Ford officials turned criminal and disciplinary cases over to local Brazilian authorities. Workers were free to come and go as they pleased: sometimes they quit the company on a whim, and were later rehired without question.

Despite these conditions, some Brazilians were never completely satisfied that the Ford company would not override or usurp national authority in Pará. In part these suspicions reflected the continuing sense of unease about Amazonia's vulnerability and economic stagnation. The misgivings also derived from the occasional awkwardness in reconciling two trends in the government of Getúlio Vargas, who sought a nationalistic developmental policy for the nation but still accepted foreign enterprise. The Brazilian sensitivity over maintaining national authority in the north was evident in the prolonged disputes between government ministries and the Ford company over minor but symbolic issues, such as the right of the company to operate a wireless station in Pará. In other instances during the 1930s, the Ford project was attacked outright by nationalistic military officers influenced by geopolitical doctrines and Integralism—Brazilian fascism. Military geopoliticians emphasized the dangers of tolerating foreign influence in Brazil's demographic vacuums and unintegrated geographical regions such as Amazonia (Verissimo, 1935; Cidade, 1940). These concerns were publicized through the nationalistic "Society of the Friends of Alberto Tôrres," which served as a forum for the discussion of national security risks in Brazil. Integralists criticized Ford's project by associating his plantations with other alien influences in Amazonia, such as the Japanese agricultural colonies in Pará (Carvalho, 1937). Such condemnations stemmed from the amalgamation of anti-Oriental, anticapitalist, and antiimperialist doctrines used to denounce the foreign presence in Brazil's north during the 1930s.

These criticisms, though, were only annoying irritants for Ford, compared with the chronic labor problems that plagued the plantations through the decade. The basic problem was the lack of a sufficient work force, for recruitment within and outside Amazonia proved extremely difficult. With its low population density, the Amazon region itself could not supply sufficient workers for expanding Ford's plantations. After importing blacks from Barbados to work on the property, the company found they were inexperienced and unable to adjust to life in Amazonia. Ford officials then considered recruitment in the Brazilian northeast, from where many workers had come during the great rubber boom. But during the 1930s most northeastern workers preferred to migrate to the industrial and farming centers of southern Brazil. By the late 1930s the company resorted to a plan for importing thousands of workers from Portugal, but this project was interrupted by the outbreak of World War II.

On the plantations, the workers' various grievances remained outstanding when the company and Brazilian authorities were unable to cooperate in solving altercations over workers' rights and labor laws. Ford's opposition to labor unions influenced his plantation managers, who insisted on an open shop. The laborers on the Tapajós properties never did try to form their own union, but in the early 1930s a local labor arbitration board, known as the Conciliation Junta, began to represent disgruntled workers who had complaints against the company. The number of these workers remained small, but these were symbolic and exasperating test cases that were never satisfactorily settled. The company had no representatives on the Conciliation Junta to defend its position, and the Brazilian Ministry of Labor tended to side with the junta. Many of the grievances against the company involved claims for the 15-day paid vacation that Brazilian industrial workers were entitled to by law. Ford representatives argued that this industrial legislation did not apply to plantation workers, for 19% of these laborers were employed in agriculture, while only 10% were in skilled trades (Johnston, 1939). Since even this 10% worked for an agricultural firm, the Ford company argued that they were not entitled to paid vacations or other provisions of national industrial laws. The company further claimed that its entire operation should be overseen not by the Ministry of Labor but by the Ministry of Agriculture, which happened to be more sympathetic to the company. Meanwhile, the two ministries debated their jurisdiction over the Ford plantations, and by the beginning of World War II they still had reached no decision on the status of Ford's workers.[9]

Despite the example of the Ford company's difficulties in Amazonia, both the United States and Brazilian governments became interested in rubber planting possibilities in this region during 1940, when it appeared that the West's continued access to Asian supplies might be severed by the war. At this time, the problems at Fordlandia and Belterra did not discourage Washington officials from considering more extensive rubber projects in Amazonia and elsewhere in Latin America. Thus, the United States might eventually develop an independent source of rubber in the Western Hemisphere. In response to this renewed interest, the Brazilian government again considered the possibilities of Amazon cultivated rubber, for North American technological and financial resources could assist Brazil in starting new plantations. The Brazilians also hoped for United States aid in reviving the wild rubber industry for potential wartime needs. In October 1940, Getúlio Vargas promised the economic recovery of the Amazon, with the expectation that North American and Brazilian interests might coincide in this region during the war. Vargas's regime later insisted on full Brazilian participation and control in the United States-Brazilian Amazon development program initiated in 1942, but Vargas was clearly willing to use foreign aid in this region.

Edsel Ford and other company officers were encouraged by this renewed interest in rubber, and they hoped they would now receive Brazilian cooperation in solving such thorny issues as the labor problems. In particular, they welcomed a personal visit by President Vargas as a good beginning. In a holiday mood during an Amazon tour, Vargas arrived in Santarém after flying the presidential plane part way from Belém, Pará. As the presidential motorcade approached Belterra, the plantation workers asked that the motor in Vargas's car be shut off so they could pull the car into the plantation, as an act of homage to the president. Wearing the baggy white linen suits of the era and white pith helmets, the presidential party went on a mosquito hunt inside the plantation's screened buildings to ascertain whether Ford's project really deserved its reputation as a prime example of tropical hygiene and sanitation. Here was a test to determine whether a prerequisite for efficient Amazon development had really been achieved, and Vargas felt elated when they failed to find even a single mosquito. As for the various labor problems, these were not mentioned because the plantation manager felt it would be indiscreet to thus confront the president during his goodwill tour.

After Vargas's visit, a naive North American proposal and renewed Brazilian suspicions frustrated plans for United States-Brazilian cooperation in rubber planting experiments. Initially, the U.S. Department of Agriculture hoped to develop a disease-resistant and high-yield strain of rubber tree using basic Amazonian stock. This experiment was intended to benefit not only Brazil but also other Latin American rubber producing nations. For this plan, a mission of Goodyear representatives in Brazil proposed to ship 8 to 10 tons of rubber tree seeds from Amazonia to the Department of Agriculture (Donneley, 1940; Blandin and Ingle, 1941). Brazilian authorities immediately suspected this project because it reminded them of Wickham's notorious seed theft. Evidentally the United States wanted to exploit the Brazilian Amazon for the benefit of competitor nations and under these conditions, Brazil refused to cooperate. The Amazonians themselves discounted the possibility of planting rubber in the early 1940s because it was much easier to exploit the existing wild rubber supply. North American officials also eventually became discouraged about planting possibilities when they realized that planted rubber might help to meet future Allied war needs only if the world conflict continued into the 1950s. Meanwhile, by 1941 the United States needed an immediate rubber supply because Asian shipments had almost ceased. Thus, North American authorities changed their plan for Amazonia by concentrating solely on prospects for exploiting the region's wild rubber supply.

During the war, the Ford company found compelling reasons for abandoning the project on the Tapajós. To begin with, in 1942 the company sold the River Rouge Tire Plant in Michigan to Soviet Russia: this indicated the Fords had lost interest in manufacturing tires and other rubber products. Then in 1943, the development of synthetic rubber in the United States relieved much of the pressure to obtain natural rubber in the Western Hemisphere. During this same year, Belterra was assaulted by the greatest army of caterpillars ever seen in Pará, and this was followed by the worst attack of leaf disease in the plantation's history. Company officials wondered whether the defoliated trees would ever recover. Two years later, when Henry Ford II, Edsel's son, became president of the Ford Motor Company, he began a cost-cutting campaign that eliminated the unprofitable plantations. Belterra and Fordlandia were sold to the Brazilian government for the pittance of $500,000. In total, the Fords had invested over $9 million in these properties, which had failed to produce any rubber for large-scale commercial use (Ford Motor Co., 1945a; 1945b).[10]

The end of the wartime demand for all Amazon rubber discouraged the Brazilian government from attempting further major experimentation with rubber planting on the Tapajós locations. The plantations were then turned over to the Brazilian Agronomy Institute of the North for livestock and agricultural projects. Brazil thus lost all hope that Amazon planted rubber would one day compete with the Asian product. Fordlandia and Belterra joined the legacy of failures facing Brazilians as the nation embarked on other ambitious Amazon ventures in future decades.

Some of the problems encountered during Ford's Amazon experiment later reoccurred during the Brazilian government's Amazon development projects initiated since the revolution of 1964. In particular, the road construction program and agro-pastoral colonization has led conservationists to question whether large-scale forest clearing may not destroy the delicate ecological balance of Amazonia. While some authorities claim that reforestation will be easy and that the conservationist's concerns are unwarranted, the Ford experience has clearly demonstrated the contrary. Nearly two decades of planting on cleared land failed to create mature, much less commercially productive, trees. Other experiences in forest clearing and planting, such as the agricultural colonies' farms along Pará's Belém-Braganza Railroad, have resulted in a conservationist's nightmare of sandy leached soil and useless secondary scrub growth. The poor agricultural techniques and ignorance about Amazonia's ecology evident in the Ford project and other regional experiments thus serve as warnings for more cautious and experienced future use of this land.

As in the case of the Ford project, Brazilians have found it difficult to achieve a consensus on the issue of foreign influence in Amazonia after 1945. In general, projects that allowed for little or no national participation were rejected outright. Other plans for development involving some form of partnership or cooperation were more favorably received, but not without misgivings. Nationalist campaigns defeated three major postwar projects that seemed to threaten national sovereignty in Brazil's north, but in the 1970s the Brazilian military regime has welcomed North American enterprise in large-scale Amazonian mining, cattle-raising, and timber projects.[11] While following this policy, Brazil's ranking officers have recognized the popularity and mystique inherent in the nationalist position that emphasizes self-reliance and Brazilian capabilities in developing Amazonia. Lip service has thus been paid to the nationalist doctrine. While not all officers are comfortable with the notion of massive foreign influence in the north, the extent of current North American investment in this region indicates the government's willingness to rely heavily on technological and financial resources from abroad.[12]

International cooperation in the Amazon basin seems warranted by the region's formidable challenges to development, but the nagging suspicions and apprehensions that troubled the Ford project will likely persist in any international ventures. The love-hate attitude toward United States economic influence in Amazonia, as elsewhere in South America, is long-established and ingrained. Moreover, the Amazon basic nations themselves mistrust each other's intentions. For example, some of the eight member nations of the Brazilian-inspired "Amazon Pact" of 1977 seem to fear Brazilian expansionism in the north and west of the continent, and consequently they disagree over the creation of an organization for future economic and political cooperation in the development of the basin.[13] The next few decades may reveal whether the world's need for natural resources may encourage a settlement of such problems and stimulate a multinational effort to finally open the valley for the benefit of its owners.

## NOTES

1. Less than a year after the Stevenson Plan was initiated, the Brazilian Minister of Agriculture urged the government to attract North American capital investment in Amazonia by discontinuing export taxes levied by the northern states, funding the states' budgets, and servicing the states' foreign debts. These measures would allegedly solve some of the Amazon's critical problems and would help to create stable conditions sought by investors in the United States (Araojo Lima, 1923). From New York, the Brazilian consul wrote Henry Ford in 1923 to inform him of the favorable terms offered by the Brazilian Minister of Agriculture for rubber cultivation in Pará. The consul later went to Detroit for a personal meeting with Ford in early 1925, and he forwarded a letter from Pará's governor Diomisio Ausier Bentes, who also offered favorable conditions.

2. During the period of negotiations for the Ford concession in Pará, U.S. consular officials in Belém considered the possibility of Ford's funding of the state's debt to create a favorable impression for the concession itself. The vice consul estimated that $7.5 million would purchase the outstanding principle on Pará's loans plus the accrued interest. The state's internal funded and floating debts amounted to approximately $5.5 million, which could be settled at less than half its book value. Thus, for about $10 million Ford could bail out Pará from its onerous indebtedness (U.S. Consul, 1927: July 22). Ford never seriously considered the proposal because of his moralistic scruples against such transactions. Moreover, the plan would have involved a foreign intrusion in the internal affairs of a Brazilian state.

3. For example, Amazonas gave three North American corporations affiliated with Sinclair Oil all mineral rights, including petroleum, in three enormous sections of the state during September 1930 (U.S. Chargé d'Affairs, 1930). After the Brazilian revolution of 1930, the new government of Getúlio Vargas refused to recognize these agreements and revoked the contracts.

4. The subsoil rights on the Ford property remained unclarified by the concession contract of 1927, and rumors soon circulated in Brazil that Ford was interested in petroleum exploration and development on the land. The U.S. ambassador in Rio de Janeiro warned that Ford's alleged side interest in oil might create "international complications" in the future because foreign petroleum exploration in Brazil was an explosive issue that might arouse the opposition of Brazilian nationalists (U.S. Consul, 1930; 1927). In the Ford Motor Company archive, this researcher has found no documentary evidence of Ford's alleged interest in petroleum in Amazonia.

5. Souza Castro's attacks on the Ford concession were published in the *Gazeta de Noticias* of Rio de Janeiro during May 1928. In May and June of 1928, *O Imparcial* and *A Manhã* also carried anti-Ford editorials. Other Rio de Janeiro dailies such as *O Globo* were hostile to the Bentes administration in Pará because of the governor's repression of opposition journalists who wrote for *Belém Nôva* and *O Estado do Pará*. These newspapers in Brazil's capital also attacked the Ford concession.

6. In 1921 the American-Brazilian Colonization Syndicate proposed locating North American Negro colonies in Mato Grosso by selling land at $3 per hectare. Nationalistic congressmen from Minas Gerais and other southern states defeated this project by alarming congress with the claim that a great "Amazon Negro Empire" with 15 million North American Negroes would soon engulf Brazil. In 1923 the syndicate's agent in Brazil then obtained a land concession in Pará for another attempt at Negro colonization.

7. For example, Ford believed the obsession with profits fostered the evils of business, including labor exploitation. He alleged that the concern for service should always come before profits and that the working man should receive the just rewards of his work with an adequate salary. Big business was a "sacred trust" in which the employer was responsible for the welfare of thousands of lives and the future of families and whole communities. "What this generation needs," Ford said, "is the belief in the practibility of righteousness, justice, and humanity in industry" (Ford and Crowther, 1923: 105).

8. In fact, Ford made his first and only air flight during a short hop on Lindberg's plane at the Ford Airport in Dearborn. Despite his pioneering role in air transportation, Ford then decided he disliked flying, and he never journeyed to Amazonia.

9. In November 1941, the Federal Council of Foreign Commerce finally decided that Ford's Tapajós plantations were agricultural and that therefore the Brazilian Ministry of Agriculture would review the company's activities, including labor relations.

10. The $9 million was a very conservative estimate of the loss, based on an exchange rate of Cr. 20.475 to the U.S. dollar. Actually, the Ford Company had invested dollars at lower rates of exchange, including one rate of Cr. 12.000 to the dollar. Thus, the company's total loss was considerably higher than $9 million.

11. From 1946 to 1949, UNESCO sponsored a project called the International Intitute of the Hylean Amazon, which was supposed to carry out scientific research in the ecology of the Amazon basin. Brazilian nationalists regarded the plan as a prelude to economic exploitation and "internationalization" of the Brazilian Amazon by the world's super powers. A campaign launched by the nation's leading economic nationalist, Artur Bernardes, defeated the project by 1950. In 1966 and 1967, U.S. citizens purchased large quantitites of northern and central Brazilian land through fraudulent land deals. A Brazilian parliamentary commission of enquiry disclosed this scandal, and the government subsequently revoked most of the purchases. At this same time the Hudson Institute of New York planned a great Amazon lake with dams for hydroelectric power. The lake would have permanently submerged part of the basin. A nationalistic campaign in Brazil repudiated the plan and influenced a government rejection of the proposal.

12. During the last 10 years, the Amazon forest planting project of the North American billionaire, Daniel K. Ludwig, has far exceeded Ford's Tapajós plantations in expenditures, scope, and physical size. In 1967 Ludwig purchased a 3 million-acre tract, about the size of Connecticut, on the Jari River in Amapá. After clearing the land, he planted fast-growing *Gemelina arborea* trees, used in making wood pulp. Like Ford, Ludwig started from scratch in the jungle with a crash program involving a high initial overhead expenditure with primarily long-term yields. He built a new town, Monte Dourado, with

340 homes, a sawmill, slaughterhouse, pulp plant, a school, hospital, social club, and other amenities for the workers. As in the Ford venture, mistakes due to inexperience seemed inevitable: by 1975, 175,000 acres had been cleared, but some of the soil was unsuitable for *Gemelina* trees. The company used jungle-clearing bulldozers that destroyed the fragile Amazonian top soil, and the crews had to resort to machetes for jungle clearing. But unlike the Ford experience, diversification of production in the project seems to have paid off: the company has made substantial profits on the export of rice and kaolin, a clay used for pottery and high-gloss paper finishes. By late 1976 Ludwig had already spent about $200 million on the various projects, and he planned to sink a total of one billion dollars into his Jari property by 1983. Until most of the *Gemelina* trees mature, the success of this part of his project remains as problematical as Ford's venture in the early 1930s, but certainly Ludwig has obtained more sustained federal Brazilian cooperation than his predecessor in Amazon planting. Ludwig shrewdly hired ranking Brazilian military officers as company executives during the late 1960s and thus avoided opposition fro Brasília. To some degree, regional criticism from Amazonians and occasionally hostile press articles about Ludwig's project may derive from the fact that he has generally bypassed local officials in dealing directly with federal authorities in Brasilia.

13. The eight member nations of the Amazon Pact are Brazil, Venezuela, Colombia, Bolivia, Peru, Ecuador, Surinam, and Guyana.

# REFERENCES

ARAUJO LIMA, J. G. (1923) A situacão econômica do Amazonas especialmente em face das pretençoẽs Americanas: conferencia realizada pelo Dr. Araujo Lima na Sociedade Nacional de Agricultura em 19 de julho de 1923. Rio de Janeiro: Imprensa Nacional.

BARREIROS, T. L. [ed.] (1928) A concessão Ford e o governador Dionisio Bentes, collectanea de artigos publicados em defesa do governador Dionsio Bentes, sôbre a entrevista concedida a Gazeta de Noticias, do Rio de Janeiro, pelo senador Souza-Castro, em torno da concessão Ford. Belém: Oficinas Graphicas do Instituto Lauro Sodre.

BAUM, V. (1943) The Weeping Wood. Garden City, N.Y.: Doubleday, Doran & Co.

BLANDIN, J. J., and J. B. INGLE (1941) Memorandum of conversation, January 9. 810.6176/86, RG 59, NA.

BRESSMAN, E. H. (1940) Memo to Secretary of State, March 25. 832.6176/86, RG 59, NA.

BURDETT, W. C. (1938) Memo on Ford Rubber Plantations, June 5. 832.6176 F75/76, RG 59, NA.

CARVALHO, A. de (1937) O Brasil não e dos Brasileiros. São Paulo: Edição Revista Panorama.

CASTRO, J.M.F. de (1957) A selva. Lisbon: Guimarães.

CHALK, R. F. (1970) "The United States and the international struggle for rubber, 1914-1941." Ph.D. dissertation. Madison: University of Wisconsin.

CIDADE, F. de P. (1940) Notas de geografia militar sul Americana. Rio de Janeiro: Bedeschi.

Correio do Pará [Belem] (1928) May 18: 1.

COSTA, A. (1928) A Amazônia e a borracha: necessidade de capitaes que explorem suas riquezas. Manaus: Oficinas Typograficas do Servico de Informaçoẽs do Ministro de Agricultura..

COWLING, W. C. (1929) South America letters from Cowling to Ford: en route to Pará, August 20; no city cited, August 23; Belém, September 9. 1929 Folder, Box 15B, Accession 74, FMCA.

CUNHA, E. da (1913) A margem da história. Porto: Chardson de Lelo e Irmão.

Detroit News (1930) March 25: 1.

DONNELEY, W. J. (1940) Memo to Secretary of State, July 25. 810.6176/46, Decimal file 1940-1944, RG 59, NA.

FILHO, C. F. (1965) Porque perdomes a batalha da borracha. Manaus: Ediçoẽs do Estado do Amazonas.

Folha do Norte [Belem] (1928) June 5: 1.

FORD, H., and S. CROWTHER (1923) My Life and Work. Garden City, N.Y.: Doubleday, Page & Co.

Ford Motor Co. (1945a) Deed of Sale for Fordlandia and Belterra, December 28. Box 1, Accession 301, FMCA.

——— (1945b) Minutes of the General Planning Commission, November 5. Box 4, Accession 134, FMCA.

——— (1940) Exposição que o gerente da Ford Motor Co. Export Inc. fez na sessão da Câmara da Produção, Consumo e Transportes em 28 de maio. Procedding 1061, Folio 5, Box 83, Proceedings of the Federal Council of Foreign Commerce, Arquivo Nacional (AN), Rio de Janeiro.

——— (1928) Report of the Directorate of the Companhia Ford Industrial do Brasil, September 12. Box 1, Accession 301, FMCA.

GAULD, C. (1964) The Last Titan: Percival Farquhar, American Entrepreneur in Latin America. Stanford: Stanford University Press.

HARRISON, J. P. (1955) "Science and politics: origins and objectives of mid-nineteenth century government expeditions to Latin America." Hispanic American Historical Review 35, 2 (May): 175-202.

JOHNSTON, A. (1939) To H. Braunstein, Rio de Janeiro, February 9. R. I. Roberge Folder, Box 12, Accession 74, Ford Motor Co. Archive (FMCA).

O Jornal [Rio de Janeiro] (1928) February 28: 4.

Jornal do Brasil [Rio de Janeiro] (1932) July 8: 10.

Jornal do Commercio [Rio de Janeiro] (1927) November 12: 10.

MOOG, C. V. (1954) Bandeirantes e pioneros: paralelo entre duas culturas. Rio de Janeiro: Editora Globo.

MORGAN, E. V. (1931) Rio de Janeiro to Secretary of State, October 9. Enclosure: Report by the U.S. Naval Attaché, September 18. 832.6176 F 75/76, RG 59, NA.

O Mundo Ford [Rio de Janeiro] (1928) May: 20.

NEVINS, A., and F. E. HILL (1957) Ford: Expansion and Challenge, 1915-1933. New York: Scribners.

OSTENFELD, K. (1930) Report on riot of December, December 22. 1930 Folder, Box 2 (Accounting File 1), Accession 74, FMCA.

RANGEL, A. (1927) Inferno verde, scenas e scenarios do Amazonas. Tours: Typographia Arrault.

RIVERA, J. E. (1971) La voragine. Buenos Aires: Editorial Losada, S. A.

SCHURZ, W. L. (1961) Brazil, the Infinite Country. New York: Dutton.
SWARD, K. (1972) The Legend of Henry Ford. New York: Atheneum.
TOMLINSON, H. M. (1964) The Sea and the Jungle. New York: Time Inc.
U.S. Chargé d'Affairs (1930) Ad interim; memo to Secretary of State, September 27, enclosing contracts between state of Amazonas and the Amazon Corporation, the American-Brazilian Exploration Corp., and the Canadian Amazon Co. Ltd. 832.63 Amazon Corp., RG 59, NA.
U.S. Consul [Belém] (1941) To Secretary of State, August 5. 832.6176 F 75/90, RG 59, NA.
——— (1940) To Secretary of State, March 25. 832.6176 F 75/90 PS/RK, RG 59, NA.
——— (1930) To Dr. Munro, June 27. 832.6175 F 75/62, RG 59, NA.
——— (1927) To Secretary of State, July 5, July 22, December 12. Microcopy No. 519, Roll 43, NA.
VERISSIMO, I. J. (1935) A concessão Ford no Pará. Rio de Janeiro: Imprensa Nacional.
WINTER, J. R. (1927) Correspondence from U.S. Consul Winter, Belém, July 5 to December 12. Microcopy No. 519, Roll 43, NA.

*John Galey spent his early life in Venezuela, where he also taught at the Institute Universitario Pedagogica in 1978 following the receipt of his Ph.D. in history at Stanford University in 1977. His current research interest is in the history of economic development of the Brazilian Amazon during the twentieth century.*

# BOOKS RECEIVED

## *GENERAL AND REGIONAL LATIN AMERICA*

Booth, John A. and Mitchell A. Seligson, eds. POLITICAL PARTICIPATION IN LATIN AMERICA. Volume 1: Citizen and State. New York: Holmes & Meier, 1978. Collected bibliography, notes on contributors, index. ix, 258 pp. $19.75 cloth, $8.95 paper.

Deal, Carl W., ed. LATIN AMERICA AND THE CARIBBEAN: A DISSERTATION BIBLIOGRAPHY. Ann Arbor: University Microfilms International, 1978. 164 pp. Paper.

Erasmus, Charles J., Solomon Miller and Louis C. Faron. CONTEMPORARY CHANGE IN TRADITIONAL COMMUNITIES OF MEXICO AND PERU. Volume III, Contemporary Change in Traditional Societies, edited by Julian H. Steward. Urbana: University of Illinois Press, 1978. Index. ix, 302 pp. $4.95 paper.

Frei, Eduardo. LATIN AMERICA: THE HOPEFUL OPTION. Maryknoll, New York: Orbis Books, 1978. Notes. xii, 271 pp. $7.95 paper.

Frenkel, Roberto, and Guillermo O'Donnell, LOS PROGRAMAS DE ESTABILIZACION CONVENIDOS CON EL FMI Y SUS IMPACTOS INTERNOS. Vol. 1, No. 1. Buenos Aires: CEDES, 1978. Anexo. 62 pp. Paper.

IDB. ECONOMIC AND SOCIAL PROGRESS IN LATIN AMERICA: 1977 REPORT. Washington, D.C.: Inter-American Development Bank, 1977. Statistical appendix. 450 pp. Paper.

Newton, Wesley Phillips. THE PERILOUS SKY: U.S. AVIATION DIPLOMACY AND LATIN AMERICA, 1919-1931. Coral Gables, Florida: University of Miami Press, 1978. Appendices, glossary, notes, bibliography, index. 457 pp. $20.00.

OAS, AMERICA EN CIFRAS, 1977. Tomo I and II. Situación Económica. Washington, D.C.: OAS, 1978. Bibliografía, índice analítico. Tomo I: xv, 244 pp. Tomo II: xi, 172 pp. Paper.

Journal of Interamerican Studies and World Affairs, Vol. 21 No. 2, May 1979, 291-296
© 1979 Sage Publications, Inc.

Pease Garcia, Henry, Marcial Rubio Correa and Laura Madalengoitia U. MITOS DE LA DEMOCRACIA. Lima, Peru: DESCO, 1978, praxis No. 12. Epilogo. 189 pp. Paper.

Swift, Jeannine. ECONOMIC DEVELOPMENT IN LATIN AMERICA. New York: St. Martin's Press, 1978. Notes, index. vii, 154 pp. $12.95 cloth, $5.95 paper.

Wirth, John D. and Robert L. Jones, eds. MANCHESTER AND SÃO PAULO: PROBLEMS OF RAPID URBAN GROWTH. Stanford, CA: Stanford University Press, 1978. Index. 234 pp. $17.50.

Wynia, Gary W. THE POLITICS OF LATIN AMERICAN DEVELOPMENT. New York: Cambridge University Press, 1978. Preface, maps, appendix, index. xiii, 335 pp. $21.95 cloth, $8.50 paper.

*ARGENTINA*

Walter, Richard J. THE SOCIALIST PARTY OF ARGENTINA 1890-1930. Austin: Institute of Latin American Studies, Latin American Monographs No. 42, University of Texas, 1977. Appendices, notes, bibliography, index. xx, 284 pp. $14.95 cloth, $5.95 paper.

*BOLIVIA*

Koster, Gerrit. SANTA CRUZ DE LA SIERRA (BOLIVIEN); ENTWICKLUNG, STRUKTUR UND FUNKTION EINTER TROPISCHEN TIEFLANDSTADT. AGA Heft 12. Aachen: Geographisches Institut der RWTH Aachen, 1978. Text in German with a summary in Spanish, English, and French. List of figures and tables. xiii, 272 pp. Paper.

*BRAZIL*

Fonyat, Bina. CARNAVAL. Rio de Janeiro: Editoria Nova Fronteira, 1978. Fotografias de Bina Fonyat. 72 pp. Paper.

Ministério da Educação e Cultura. ANAIS DO II ENCONTRO INTER-REGIONAL DE CIENTISTAS SOCIAIS DO BRASIL. Série Cursos e Conferencias, 2. Recife: Instituto Joaquim Nabuco de Pesquisas Sociais, 1977. 232 pp. Paper.

Ministério da Educação e Cultura. ICONOGRAFIA DE JOAQUIM NABUCO. Série Documentas, 2. Recife: Instituto Joaquim Nabuco de Pesquisas Sociais, Convênio IJNPS-MEC-DAC, 1975. 81 pp. Paper.

Tavares Bastos, Aureliano Cândido. CORRESPONDENCIA E CATALOGO DE DOCUMENTOS DA COLEÇÂO DA BIBLIOTECA NACIONAL. Brasília: Senado Federal, 1977. 246 pp. Paper.

Tavares Bastos, Aureliano Cândido. DISCURSOS PARLAMENTARES. Brasilia: Senado Federal, 1977. 612 pp. Paper.

Universidade Federal de Minas Gerais. I, SEMINARIO DE PROFESSORES DE DIREITO ECONOMICO. Belo Horizonte, Brazil: Ediçoès do Cinquentenário da UFMG, 3; Universidade Federal de Minas Gerais, 1977. Crônico do Seminário. 277 pp. Paper.

*CENTRAL AMERICA*

Helms, Mary W. MIDDLE AMERICA: A CULTURE HISTORY OF HEARTLAND AND FRONTIERS. Englewood Cliffs, New Jersey: Prentice-Hall, 1975. Suggested readings, index. xiv, 367 pp. Paper.

*CHILE*

Gigueroa, Gonzalo, ed. DERECHO Y SOCIEDAD. Santiago: CPU, 1978. 289 pp. Paper.

Gil, Federico G., Ricardo Lagos E. and Henry A. Landsberger. CHILE, 1970-1973: LECCIONES DE UNA EXPERIENCIA. Madrid: Editorial Tecnos, 1977. 470 pp. Paper.

*COLOMBIA*

Poveda Gomez, Nuria. TESAURO COLOMBIANO DE LA EDUCACION: VERSION PRELIMINAR. Bogotá: ICFES, 1978. ix, 173 pp. Paper.

Rezazadeh, Reza and Joseph McKenzie. POLITICAL PARTIES IN COLOMBIA: CONTINUITY IN POLITICAL STYLE. Ann Arbor: University Microfilms International, 1978, published for University of Wisconsin—Platteville. Appendix, bibliography, list of tables and figures. 89 pp. $13.75.

Torres, Rosa Elvia. TERMINOLOGIA DE LA EDUCACION. Bogotá: ICFES, 1978. Apéndices. iii, 210 pp. Paper.

Wogart, Jan Peter. INDUSTRIALIZATION IN COLOMBIA: POLICIES, PATTERNS, PERSPECTIVES. Tubingen, Germany: Mohr, 1978. List of tables and figures, appendix, bibliography, xiii, 176 pp.

*MEXICO*

Banco Nacional de Comercio Exterior, S.A. MEXICO 1976: FACTS/FIGURES/TRENDS. México, D.F.: Banco Nacional de Comercio Exterior, S.A., 1977. Bibliography, illustrations. 400 pp. Paper.

Cole, Garold. AMERICAN TRAVELERS TO MEXICO, 1812-1972: A DESCRIPTIVE BIBLIOGRAPHY. Troy, NY: Whitston Publishing Co., 1978, x, 139 pp. $12.50.

Feder, Ernest. STRAWBERRY IMPERIALISM: AN ENQUIRY INTO THE MECHANICS OF DEPENDENCY IN MEXICAN AGRICULTURE. México, D.F.: Editorial Campesina, 1978. Appendices. 156 pp. Paper.

Meyer, Jean, con la colaboración de Enrique Krauze y Cayetano Reyes. ESTADO Y SOCIEDAD CON CALLES, Historia de la Revolución Mexicana, Periodo 1924-1928, No. 11. México, D.F.: El Colegio de México, 1977. Bibliografía, índice de nombres. ix, 371 pp. Paper.

Meyer, Lorenzo, con la colaboración de Rafael Segovia y Alejandra Lajous. LOS INICIOS DE LA INSTITUCIONALIZACION. LA POLITICA DEL MAXIMATO. Historia de la Revolución Mexicana, Período 1928-1934, No. 12. México, D.F.: El Colegio de México, 1978. Bibliografía, índice analítico. ix, 314 pp. Paper.

Salamini, Heather Fowler. AGRARIAN RADICALISM IN VERACRUZ 1920-1938. Lincoln and London: University of Nebraska Press, 1978. List of tables and maps, notes, bibliography, acknowledgments, index. xviii, 239 pp. $15.00.

Shapira, Yoram. MEXICAN FOREIGN POLICY UNDER ECHEVERRIA. The Washington Papers, No. 56. Beverly Hills: Sage Publications. Sage Policy Paper published for the Center for Strategic and International Studies, Georgetown University, 1978. Notes, bibliography. 84 pp. Paper.

Walker, Ronald G. INFERNAL PARADISE: MEXICO AND THE MODERN ENGLISH NOVEL. Berkeley: University of California Press, 1978. Appendix, notes, bibliography, index. xvi, 391 pp. $14.95.

*PARAGUAY*

Warren, Harris Gaylord. PARAGUAY AND THE TRIPLE ALLIANCE: THE POSTWAR DECADE, 1869-1878. Austin: Institute of Latin American Studies, Latin American Monographs, No. 44, University of Texas, 1978. Notes, bibliography, index. 376 pp. $17.95 cloth, $7.50 paper.

*PERU*

Escobar, Alberto. VARIACIONES SOCIOLINGUISTICAS DEL CASTELLANO EN EL PERU. Lima: Instituto de Estudios Peruanos, Peru Problema 18, 1978. Equivalencia de los signos, bibliografía. 179 pp. Paper.

Riofrio Benavides, Gustavo. SE BUSCA TERRENO PARA PROXIMA BARRIADA: ESPACIOS DISPONIBLES EN LIMA 1940-1978-1990. Lima: DESCO, 1978. Anexos, post scriptum. xiv, 171 pp. Paper.

Rubio Correa, Marcial, César Luna Victoria Leon and Francisco Eguiguren Praeli. CONSTITUCION: QUE Y PARA QUE? Lima: DESCO, 1978. Praxis No. 11. 152 pp. Paper.

Universidad Nacional de San Cristobal de Huamanga. UNIVERSIDAD SAN CRISTOBAL DE HUAMANGA, 1677-1977. Libro Jubilar en Homenaje al Tricentenario de su Fundación 3-VII-1977. Ayacucho, Peru: UNSCH, 1977. x, 271 pp. Paper.

*URUGUAY*

Novaes, Paulo. THE CITY AND HUMAN RESOURCES. Studies and Monographs No. 32. Montevideo; CINTERFOR, 1978. 75 pp. Paper.

*VENEZUELA*

Briceño-Iragorry, Mario. TAPICES DE HISTORIA PATRIA: ENSAYO DE UNA MORFOLOGIA DE LA CULTURA COLONIA. Caracas: Cultural Venezolana, 1978. 197 pp. Paper.

Carreño, Eduardo. VIDA ENECDOTICA DE VENEZOLANOS: PROLOGO DE SANTIAGO KEY AYALA. 5th edition (1st in 1941). Caracas: Concejo Municipal del Distrito Federal, 1978. 229 pp.

Lameda, Ali. GALERON Y VIDALITA: DECIMAS DE PAMPA Y LLANURA. A la memoria de Francisco Lazo Martí y Alfredo Arvelo Larriva. Caracas: Concejo Municipal del Distrito Federal, 1978. Portfolio. 32 pp. Paper.

Stewart, Bill. CHANGE AND BUREAUCRACY: PUBLIC ADMINISTRATION IN VENEZUELA. Chapel Hill: University of North Carolina Press, 1978. The James Sprunt Studies in History and Political Science, Vol. 56 Notes, bibliography, index. xiii, 140 pp. $10.00.

*MISCELLANEOUS*

Aronson, Jonathan David. MONEY AND POWER: BANKS AND THE WORLD MONETARY SYSTEM. Vol. 66, Sage Library of Social Research. Beverly Hills: Sage Publications, 1978. Bibliography, index, selected books. 220 pp. $14.00 cloth, $6.95 paper.

Choucri, Nazli and Thomas W. Robinson, eds. FORECASTING IN INTERNATIONAL RELATIONS: THEORY, METHODS, PROBLEMS, PROSPECTS. San Francisco: W. H. Freeman & Co., 1978. Bibliography, index. xii, 468 pp. $29.95.

ICFES. CATALOGO COLECTIVO NACIONAL DE PUBLICACIONES PERIODICAS. Ciencias Naturales Salud y Agropecuarias. Volumenes I y II. Bogotá: ICFES, Instituto Colombiano para el Fomento de la Educación Superior, 1977. Vol. I: xlix, 282 pp. Vol. II: 232 pp. Paper.

Joshi, Nandini. THE CHALLENGE OF POWER: THE DEVELOPING COUNTRIES IN THE NEW INTERNATIONAL ORDER. New Delhi: Birla Institute of Scientific Research, 1978. List of tables, selected bibliography, structure of the world economy, index. ix, 101 pp.

Minar, Zdravko and Henry Teune, ed. THE SOCIAL ECOLOGY OF CHANGE: FROM EQUILIBRIUM TO DEVELOPMENT. Beverly Hills: Sage Publications, 1978. Sage Studies in International Sociology, Vol. 15. 296 pp. Paper.

OECD. TRILATERAL COOPERATION. Volume II: Proceedings and Background Papers on the Conference organized by OECD on January 26-27, 1977, on "Special Approaches to Trilateral Cooperation." Paris: OECD, Development Centre Studies, 1978. 241 pp. $12.50 paper.

Pillado Matheu, Armando. ACUMULACION, CRISIS, ESTADO Y SOCIALISMO: EL ORDENAMIENTO DE LA ECONOMIA POR EL CAPITAL. Lima: DESCO, 1978. Notas. 169 pp. Paper.

Ramm, Hartmut. THE MARXISM OF REGIS DEBRARY: BETWEEN LENIN AND GUEVARA. Lawrence: The Regents Press of Kansas. Notes, bibliographical note, sources, index. xi, 240 pp. $13.50.

Romo, Ricardo and Raymund Paredes. NEW DIRECTIONS IN CHICANO SCHOLARSHIP. Chicano Studies Monograph Series. La Jolla: University of California, San Diego, Chicano Studies Program, 1978, viii, 268 pp. $5.95 paper.

Rondinelli, Dennis A. and Kenneth Ruddle. URBANIZATION AND RURAL DEVELOPMENT: A SPATIAL POLICY FOR EQUITABLE GROWTH. New York: Praeger, 1978. List of tables and figures, bibliography, index. xi, 221 pp.

Scharf, Traute. TRILATERAL COOPERATION. Vol. 1: Arab Development Funds and Banks: Approaches to Trilateral Cooperation. Paris: OECD, Development Centre Studies, 1978. 271 pp. $14.50 paper.

Teune, Henry and Zdravko Mlinar. THE DEVELOPMENTAL LOGIC OF SOCIAL SYSTEMS. Beverly Hills: Sage Publications, 1978. Sage Library of Social Research No. 60. 208 pp. $14.00 cloth, $6.95 paper.

U.S. Arms Control and Disarmament Agency. WORLD MILITARY EXPENDITURES AND ARMS TRANSFERS 1967-1976. Washington, D.C.: U.S. Arms Control & Disarmament Agency, 1978. Foreword, highlights, essays, statistical notes, and tables. ii, 168 pp. Paper.

# Advertising Supplement: Journal of Interamerican Studies and World Affairs

This supplement has been prepared especially for our readers to bring them information and announcements of professional interest. By placing advertisements in the pages of this journal, our advertisers have indicated a desire to communicate with our readers. We hope our readers will acknowledge their indirect support of the journal and its purposes by mentioning the journal in correspondence with advertisers.


SOCIAL FORMATIONS AND POWER IN LATIN AMERICA

edited by **JORGE GRACIANRENA and ROLANDO FRANCO,**
*United Nations Economic Commission for Latin America, Santiago, Chile*

Two perspectives are presented concerning the political development of Latin America over the last three decades—the political process in relation to inherent values and ideological frames of reference, and as it has been reflected in the social sciences—through a discussion of regional contributors.

**A special issue of CURRENT SOCIOLOGY, Spring 1978**
**266 pages / Individual $4.00 / Institutional $7.50**

**SAGE PUBLICATIONS, INC.**
**275 South Beverly Drive**
**Beverly Hills, California 90212**

**SAGE PUBLICATIONS LTD**
**28 Banner Street**
**London EC1Y 8QE, England**

# LATIN AMERICA AND WORLD ECONOMY: A Changing International Order

edited by **JOSEPH GRUNWALD**

How do nations of Latin America interact with other countries in the world community? This anthology approaches the region's relations with the outside world from both an economic and a political perspective, examining Latin America's desire to integrate with the world economy, as well as its struggle for self-reliance. Latin American and non-Latin American contributors discuss a range of subjects including the character of the "special relationship" between Latin America and the United States, and the ambiguous nature of Latin America's relations with other countries of the Third World.

**CONTENTS**


Preface

1. Reflections on Latin America in the World Economy, JOSEPH BRUNWALD

**Part I. Economic Relations with Industrial Countries**

2. The Mature Neighbor Policy: A Proposal for A United States Economic Policy for Latin America, ALBERT FISHLOW
3. Britain's Economic Relations with Latin America, LAURENCE WHITEHEAD
4. The Economic Relations between Germany and Latin America and the significance of the European Community, ALBRECHT von GLEICH
5. Latin America's Opening to the Pacific, CLAUDIO VELEZ

**Part II. Mexico and Brazil**

6. The External Sector of the Mexican Economy, LEOPOLDO SOLIS
7. The Determinants of Brazil's Foreign Economic Policy, WERNER BAER, CARLOS von DOELLINGER

**Part III. Regional Integration and Economic Relations with the Third World**

8. The Andean Pact: A Model of Economic Integration for Developing Countries, RICARDO FFRENCH-DAVIS
9. Fissures in the Volcano? Centeral American Economic Prospects, CLARK W. REYNOLDS
10. Latin America and the Third World, FELIPE HERRERA

**Part IV. Two Major Issues: Financing Development and the Multinational Corporation**

11. Problems of External Financing in Latin America, LUIS ESCOBAR
12. Mexico and Multinational Corporations: An Explanation of State Action, DOUGLAS BENNETT, MORRIS J. BLACHMAN, KENNETH SHARPE

**Part V. Commentary**

**The Good Neighbor Policy Revisite**

**Part V. Commentary**

The Good Neighbor Policy Revisited, BRYCE WOOD

Notes on SELA, GABRIEL VALDES S.


*"As long as the notion persists that Latin America is unimportant for the United States and other developed countries, it will be difficult to persuade Latin American countries that they are living in an interdependent world. One-sided importance creates a one-sided dependency relationship. Such a perseption results in demands, not cooperation. Cooperation for development becomes meaningful only when there is a recognition of interdependence on both sides of the North-South relationship."*

*—from Chapter 1*


***Sponsored by the Center for Inter-American Relations**

**Latin American International Affairs, Volume 2**

| | | | |
|---|---|---|---|
| **1978** | **ISBN 0-8039-0864-4** | **hardcover** | **$18.50** |
| **320 pages** | **ISBN 0-8039-0966-7** | **softcover** | **$ 8.95** |

**SAGE** PUBLICATIONS, INC.
275 South Beverly Drive
Beverly Hills, California 90212

**SAGE** PUBLICATIONS LTD
28 Banner Street
London EC1Y 8QE, England

# University of Texas Press

### Political Attitudes in Venezuela
**Societal Cleavages and Political Opinion**
By Enrique A. Baloyra and John D. Martz

In providing a definitive portrait of the political Venezuelan, this book breaks new ground in quantitative research methods. The authors interviewed over 1,500 voters to determine relationships between class, status, community, context, religion, ideology, and partisanship on the one hand and political attitudes and preferences on the other.
*336 pages, 22 tables, 27 figures, $19.95*

### Brazil and the Quiet Intervention, 1964
By Phyllis R. Parker

It has become apparent, largely through government documents declassified during the course of research for this book, that the United States had an invisible but pervasive part in the overthrow of Brazilian President João Goulart in 1964. Relying principally on documents from the Johnson and Kennedy presidential libraries, Phyllis Parker unravels the events of the coup in fascinating detail.
*120 pages, $9.95*

### Contemporary Portugal
**The Revolution and Its Antecedents**
Edited by Lawrence S. Graham
and Harry M. Makler
Foreword by Juan J. Linz

This volume brings together for the first time the majority of the leading social science experts on Portugal. The result is a comprehensive collection of essays discussing in detail the events leading up to the Portuguese Revolution of 1974, the causes of the military coup, and the movement of a society on the brink of upheaval toward open, democratic parliamentary elections.
*400 pages, $7.95, paper; $24.95, cloth*

# Distributed by Texas Press Services

### The Perilous Sky
**U.S. Aviation Diplomacy and Latin America, 1919–1931**
By Wesley Phillips Newton

This study examines in detail the aviation rivalry between various European competitors, principally the French and Germans, and the United States in Latin America following World War I.
*457 pages, $20.00*

**University of Texas Press**
Post Office Box 7819
Austin, Texas 78712

·ase mention Journal of Interamerican Studies and World Affairs when writing advertisers.

# LEADERS OF REVOLUTION

by **MOSTAFA REJAI** with **KAY PHILLIPS**

*"Professor Rejai's* Leaders of Revolution *is a comprehensive report of a major research undertaking. It is the first general comparative study of revolutionary elites; no one to my knowledge has tried anything so broad in scope and historical depth. The empirical work is solid, given the limitation of the sources. The comparative evidence on the life experiences and ideological orientations of revolutionary leaders is a particularly valuable contribution. The 'situational theory' of revolutionary leadership is plausible, especially in the light of the evidence which gives it substance. The clarity of style is exemplary. A distinguished addition to the empirical literature on revolutionary movements."*

*— Ted Robert Gurr, Northwestern University*

*"LEADERS OF REVOLUTION fills a long-standing void in the literature of revolution and violence. The study presents a remarkable and ingenious comparative analysis of revolutionary elites, using quantified data. At times I had thought it impossible to get any quantifiable comparability between leaders. LEADERS OF REVOLUTION has changed my mind. A bold and pioneering venture."* *- James C. Davies, University of Oregon*

**PART I. THEORY**
1. The Psychoanalytic Approach
2. The Psychohistorical Approach
3. The Sociological Approach
4. The Situational Approach

**PART II. ANALYSIS I.: CHARACTERISTICS OF REVOLUTIONARY ELITES**
5. General Characteristics of Revolutionary Leaders
6. Demographic and Situational Correlations
7. Ideological and Attitudinal Correlations
8. The Configuration of Personalities

**PART III. ANALYSIS II: EMERGENCE OF REVOLUTIONARY LEADERS**
9. Patterns of Radicalization
10. Psychological Dynamics

**PART IV. SYNTHESIS**
11. A Situational Theory of Revolutionary Leadership

Appendices / Bibliography / Index / About the Authors

**Sage Library of Social Research, Volume 73**

| | | | |
|---|---|---|---|
| February 1979 | **ISBN 0-8039-1139-4** | **hardcover** | **$15.00** |
| 248 pages | **ISBN 0-8039-1140-8** | **softcover** | **$ 7.95** |

**SAGE PUBLICATIONS, INC.**
**275 South Beverly Drive**
**Beverly Hills, California 90212**

**SAGE PUBLICATIONS LTD**
**28 Banner Street**
**London EC1Y 8QE**

# handbook of INTERCULTURAL COMMUNICATION

Edited by: **MOLEFI K. ASANTE, EILEEN NEWMARK,**

**and CECIL A. BLAKE**, *all at SUNY– Buffalo*

The *Handbook of Intercultural Communication* is a state-of-the-art review of theoretical and methodological findings in the field of communication studies. The original essays in the collection—contributed by an interdisciplinary assemblage of psychologists, anthropologists, and communication specialists—set out ground rules designed to direct research on intercultural communication into a unified field of inquiry. Illuminating both the similarities that enhance, and the differences that impede communication across cultural boundaries, the *Handbook* will find applications in the areas of diplomacy, immigrant education and counseling, training for service abroad, and the improvement of both interpersonal and international relations.

*"We present this work as a foundation upon which to build. It is interdisciplinary and innovative. Because our intention has been to create a volume which practices what it preaches, we have included manuscripts from differing cultural as well as disciplinary views. It is not enough to discuss the theory of intercultural communication; we must begin to act on the basis of our theory. A book on intercultural communication that presents views from a single perspective indicts itself. Consequently, we have tried scrupulously to avoid that posture. It is to be hoped that other scholars will find instructive value in the structure and substance of this work."*

*— from the Preface to the Handbook of Intercultural Communication*

**March 1979** **496 pages (tent.)**
**ISBN 0-8039-0954-3** **hardcover** **$25.00**

**SAGE PUBLICATIONS** • **The Publishers of Professional Social Science**
275 South Beverly Drive / Beverly Hills, California 90212
St George's House / 44 Hatton Garden / London EC1N 8ER

Please mention Journal of Interamerican Studies and World Affairs when writing advertisers.

# INTERNATIONAL NEWS: FREEDOM UNDER ATTACK

**edited by Congressman Dante B. Fascell, U.S. House of Representatives**

Freedom of the press and the free flow of news and information is under attack around the world today. The conflict over media access and independence has developed on several levels: from attempts by a growing number of countries to bar American reporters to restrictive resolutions in UNESCO; from calls for redistributing radio bands to movements toward creating government monopolies on the distribution of information.

Four specialists on these questions have written timely studies touching on every aspect of contemporary international media affairs. Topics include the politics of international broadcasting, the Third World challenge to Western news services, the quality of American foreign coverage, and the ways in which various states are trying to censor news. This is an important and unique book which should be of vital interest to all who make and write the news, as well as the millions of Americans who depend on the media for their knowledge of global events.

**March 1979 320 pages ISBN 0-8039-1129-3 hardcover $15.00**

**SAGE PUBLICATIONS, INC.**
**275 South Beverly Drive**
**Beverly Hills, California 90212**

**SAGE PUBLICATIONS LTD**
**28 Banner Street**
**London EC1Y 8QE, England**

Please mention Journal of Interamerican Studies and World Affairs when writing advertisers.

Vol. 21 No. 3
August 1979

# JOURNAL OF INTERAMERICAN STUDIES

# and WORLD AFFAIRS

A Publication of the Center for Advanced International Studies,
The University of Miami

SAGE PUBLICATIONS

*Journal of INTERAMERICAN STUDIES and WORLD AFFAIRS*

**EDITORIAL STAFF:**

John P. Harrison—Editor
Jan Peter Wogart—Associate Editor
Gerry Machovec—Editorial Assistant

**BOARD OF EDITORS:**

Orlando Albornoz, Universidad Central de Venezuela
D. A. Brading, Cambridge University
David Chaplin, Western Michigan University
Tom E. Davis, Cornell University
Malcolm Deas, St. Antony's College, Oxford, England
Rosario Green, El Colegio de Mexico
Elizabeth Jelin, Centro de Estudios de Estado y Sociedad
Isaac Kerstenetzky, Instituto Brasileiro de Geografia e Estatistica, Brazil
Celso Lafer, Universidade de São Paulo
Vaughan A. Lewis, University of the West Indies, Mona, Jamaica
Abraham Lowenthal, Woodrow Wilson International Center for Scholars
Robert McNicoll, University of Miami, emeritus
Carmelo Mesa-Lago, University of Pittsburgh
James J. Parsons, University of California, Berkeley
Clark Reynolds, Stanford University
Richard Schaedel, University of Texas, Austin
Hanns-Albert Steger, Universitat Erlangen-Nurnberg, Germany
Alfred Stepan, Yale University
Evelyn P. Stevens, Case Western Reserve University
Victor L. Urquidi, El Colegio de Mexico

The editors and publisher wish to acknowledge with gratitude the assistance and encouragement of the Center for Advanced International Studies, University of Miami, in providing ancillary services and support for this journal.

*Journal of*
INTERAMERICAN
STUDIES
*and* WORLD AFFAIRS

Vol. 21
No. 3
August
1979

# CONTENTS

*Ten Years of Change in the Church: Puebla and the Future*
ALEXANDER WILDE 299

*Early Peronism and the Post-Liberal Argentine State*
PETER RANIS 313

*Allende's Chile and the Soviet Union: A Policy Lesson for Latin American Nations Seeking Autonomy*
JOSEPH L. NOGEE
JOHN W. SLOAN 339

*Society, Politics, and the Press: An Interpretation of the Peruvian Press Reform of 1974*
DENNIS GILBERT 369

*The State, Elite, and Export in Nineteenth Century Peru: Toward an Alternative Reinterpretation of Political Change*
STEPHEN M. GORMAN 395

**BOOKS RECEIVED** 419

**SAGE PUBLICATIONS** / *Beverly Hills* *London*

**Policy:** The **JOURNAL OF INTERAMERICAN STUDIES AND WORLD AFFAIRS** reflects the interests of the scholarly community and interested public concerned with the social, economic, political, and cultural aspects of life in Latin America (including the Caribbean), particularly in those instances where the subject is of concern to more than one of the traditional disciplines. As these concerns change, so will the content of the journal.

**Articles** which have special relevance for interrelationships between American nations and of those nations with the rest of the world will be given special consideration. An effort will be made to include occasional articles that state an unusual or even discordant position on a subject of broad interest to be supplemented by critical comments of authorities representing differing positions on the topic. The editors continue to welcome articles by scholars from all parts of the world.

**Manuscripts** should be submitted in duplicate to: Editor, **JOURNAL OF INTERAMERICAN STUDIES AND WORLD AFFAIRS,** Box 24-8134, University of Miami, Coral Gables, Florida 33124. Manuscripts should be typewritten, double-spaced, with footnotes, references, tables, and charts on separate pages, and should follow the current journal style. A brief biographical paragraph describing each author's current affiliation, research interests, and recent publications should accompany the manuscript.

**Correspondence** regarding book reviews should be sent directly to: Book Review Editor, **JOURNAL OF INTERAMERICAN STUDIES AND WORLD AFFAIRS,** Box 24-8134, University of Miami, Coral Gables, Florida 33124.

---

**JOURNAL OF INTERAMERICAN STUDIES AND WORLD AFFAIRS** is published four times annually—in February, May, August, and November. Copyright © 1979 by Sage Publications, Inc. All rights reserved. No portion of the contents may be reproduced in any form without written permission of the publisher.

**Subscriptions:** Regular institutional rate $32.00 per year. Individuals may subscribe at a one-year rate of $16.50. Add $1.00 for subscriptions outside the United States. Orders from the U.K., Europe, the Middle East, and Africa should be sent to the London office (address below). Noninstitutional orders **must** be paid by personal check.

Second class postage paid at Beverly Hills, California. ISSN 0022-1937

This journal is abstracted or indexed in **Historical Abstracts, Human Resources Abstracts, Sage Urban Studies Abstracts, International Political Science Abstracts, Public Affairs Information Service, Current Contents, Social Sciences Citation Index, Social Sciences Index, ABC POL SCI,** and **United States Poltical Science Documents.**

**Back Issues:** Information about availability and prices of back issues may be obtained from the publisher's order department (address below). Write to London office for sterling prices.

**Inquiries:** Address all correspondence and permissions requests to SAGE PUBLICATIONS, Inc., 275 South Beverly Drive, Beverly Hills, California 90212. Inquiries and subscriptions from the U.K., Europe, the Middle East, and Africa should be sent to SAGE PUBLICATIONS Ltd, 28 Banner Street, London EC1Y 8QE, England. Other orders should be sent to the Beverly Hills office.

**Advertising:** Current rates and specifications may be obtained by writing to the Advertising Manager at the Beverly Hills office (address above).

**Claims:** Claims for undelivered copies must be made no later than three months following month of publication. The publisher will supply missing copies when losses have been sustained in transit and when the reserve stock will permit.

**Change of Address:** Six weeks' advance notice must be given when notifying of change of address. Please send old address label along with the new address to insure proper identification. Please specify name of journal.

---

**ALEXANDER WILDE**
*Research Associate*
*The Wilson Center*
*Smithsonian Institution Building*
*Washington, D.C. 20560*

# *TEN YEARS OF CHANGE IN THE CHURCH*

## *Puebla and the Future*

The Puebla meeting of the Latin American bishops in early 1979 capped a decade of far-reaching and surprising change in the Catholic Church. A new, local-level unit—the "ecclesial base community"[1] or CEB—has given Catholicism a vitality in society it has not known for centuries. At the same time, the Church has achieved an unprecedented integration as an institution nationally and regionally, in Latin America as a whole. It has found itself, through an unexpected historical dynamic, increasingly committed to the cause of the poor in deed as well as word, And it has been thrust into political confrontations with state authority throughout the region with an intensity and scope unmatched since the nineteenth century.

The meeting at Puebla faithfully reflected both the state and the direction of the Latin American Church.[2] The text of the final document, and the process by which it was produced, showed clearly the coexistence within the Church of divergent and at times directly opposed points of view. At the same time, however, the meeting demonstrated a surprising consensus in the Church—remarkable in view of the rapid changes it has

AUTHOR'S NOTE: I am grateful for the suggestions of Abraham Lowenthal and Laurel Lucey on a draft of this article.

Journal of Interamerican Studies and World Affairs, Vol. 21 No. 3, August 1979 299-312
© 1979 Sage Publications, Inc.

undergone in the last 10 years—about its past experience, its present context, and its future direction.

The Puebla document endorsed the fundamental lines set out at Medellín in 1968, which marked such an innovative departure at the time:[3] (1) an identification with the poor and oppressed; (2) a sociological analysis of "structural sin," of "institutionalized injustice" and "institutionalized violence," of poverty produced by "mechanisms of oppression"; and (3) the need for rapid "structural change." When Puebla departed from Medellín, it frequently went beyond earlier positions. This was particularly true of its political analysis, which was notably clearer and more specific in its condemnation of dictatorial regimes.[4]

Puebla, much more than Medellín, was a product of the collective experience of the Latin American Church. Medellín was a kind of manifesto for the Church produced by its more progressive sectors (although the radical Catholic Left was disappointed with it at the time). But Puebla, despite early efforts to manage the outcome, turned into an encounter quite representative of different forces found in the Church today. The final document records their efforts to make sense of their experience in the last decade. It is significant for both the consensus and the divisions it reports.

This essay is an analysis of the 10 years of change that preceded and produced Puebla. It is an interpretation of the conditions and forces—outside as well as within the Church—that brought the Church to the state reflected there. And it offers a way of thinking about what this broad process of change signifies for the future.

What was it, first, that gave the ideas of Medellín such deep resonance in the Church? Why have they so significantly oriented what it has done, rather than remaining, as so many other Church documents have, statements of good intentions? Second, how much does a socially progressive posture characterize the Church as a whole? Will this stance be a source of growing consensus in the future, or of increasing division? Third, very much related to the previous question, what kind of a role is the Church likely to play in the future in society and politics as a whole? What are the factors that will shape its direction and influence?

*I*

The new theological directions marked out by Medellín had the impact on Church action they did because of their congruence with the particular historical setting in which they emerged. In a longer line of theological change, they built upon Vatican II and anticipated the Theology of Liberation. At Medellín the bishops were attempting to adapt the ideas and insights of the Council to Latin American reality. But they built better than they knew. Dynamic forces in Latin American societies and within the Church itself reinforced new theology to push change toward consequences they did not foresee.

Although students of the Church frequently see new theology at the root of institutional change, doctrinal positions are hardly ever fully implemented merely because they are directives from recognized authority. If they resonate within the institution the way that Medellín did, there must be other factors at work. The Church's new commitment to the poor, for example, or its confrontation with the state would not have taken place in the way it did without the texts of Medellín. But the depth of the change that has occurred is due also to the context of authoritarian military regimes, within which the meaning of new theological formulations (of, for example, "institutionalized violence") has been defined by experience and struggle. The depth of the Church's new social commitments in different countries closely parallels the harshness of their regimes. Where there have not been institutional military governments (e.g., in Colombia, Venezuela, and Mexico), the Church has changed its social stance much less, in spite of exposure to the same progressive theology.

On the other hand, however, authoritarian conditions alone were not sufficient to have "forced" the Church into the social and political roles it has assumed. When other associations in society have been repressed, some of their functions have undoubtedly been displaced onto the Church (about which, more below). But the Church certainly could have chosen to fight much less than it has; it often so chose in the past. That it has begun to put itself on the line in the last decade is the result of courage and leadership—sometimes from the hierarchy, often from priests, nuns, and lay people at local levels (Smith, 1979; compare Vallier, 1970). Their courage has been fortified and enlightened by the new theology of the last 10 years. Under conditions of the authoritarian regimes, concepts, such as "structural sin," Christian "liberation," *concientización*, and "human rights" have helped them make sense of their environment and their responsibilities in it.

Without important organizational changes, however, the Church would have lacked the institutional resources to resist authoritarian regimes. At the grass roots, it has created a variety of structures—many of them called *comunidades de base*—that are smaller, more informal, and more personal than the traditional parish. It has tried through these groupings to engender more authentic religious commitment among its faithful by speaking to their human problems. Thus it has taken up its fundamental pastoral task in just the way signaled by Medellín, rooting its religious purposes in concrete social situations. The Church is an unquestionably more vital presence in society where these new units have taken hold at the local level (Bruneau, 1978; Della Cava, 1978). At Puebla the bishops gave them a ringing endorsement, recognizing them as a key to the Church's most basic task (CELAM, 1979: 477-478).

The comunidades de base (CEBs) have been sustained under repressive conditions by a complementary strengthening of Church structures at higher levels. National episcopal conferences have made each country's bishops aware of a common agenda of national and international issues, and CELAM and CLAR (for the Religious Orders) have gone a long way toward accomplishing that for Latin America as a whole.[5] The new specialized commissions, such as those for Peace and Justice, have used new permanent staff to monitor and respond to situations (such as human rights violations) in an ongoing way, within individual nations and across the region. The Church's institutional capacity to know what is going on, and to utilize its linkages abroad for support, has become a critical resource for protecting its social and pastoral initiatives at the local level (Smith, 1979: 116).

*II*

A "Latin American Church" exists today in several senses it did not a decade ago. As the previous section makes clear, political environments are more similar, theological understandings are more shared, institutional integration is more established. To close observers 10 years ago, the differences between various national Churches seemed more important than their similarities; change in them suggested a variety of distinctive "profiles" of Church development (Vallier, 1970: 121-147). Today Churches formerly as disparate as those of Brazil and Paraguay, Bolivia and Chile, and Ecuador and El Salvador are using the same arguments to fight similar battles and are comparably committed, in their pastoral missions, to social change (Smith, 1979: 92-111).

The great degree to which a truly regional Church has developed, despite important internal divisions, was established by Puebla. With greater confidence than its Medellín counterpart, Puebla's final document plunged into analysis of different facets of the general regional context—cultural, economic, political—that shapes the Church's mission despite local variations. The document is also willing, with some specificity, to characterize the broad—and as the Church sees them, frequently deteriorating—trends of the region's recent history (CELAM, 1979: 16-27). Even among bishops who evaluated the situation differently, there was widespread acceptance of a regional perspective and sociological method. The Pope, too—symbol of universality in the Church—seemed pleased rather than threatened by regional solidarities. After expressing cautions in his opening statement at Puebla, his subsequent behavior suggested that he was confident of the Latin American bishops' fidelity in adapting universal truths to regional realities.

The Church's overall position represents a relative triumph for the Catholic Left of a decade ago (Dodson, 1979: 20). (Although different from what those on the Left would have wished, the Church has become more socially committed than they believed possible.) But this position is the outcome of an interplay of forces within the institution. It is a point of balance for a complex coalition more than a uniform conversion to a point of view. To maintain a religious institution encompassing divergent perspectives, the Church hierarchy seeks the position that engenders greatest unity. That position has shifted over the course of the last 10 years toward a "structural" understanding of social problems and a widening "pastoral" commitment to the poor and suffering. The dynamic of the Church's historical situation since 1968 has pulled the institution as a whole in the direction of its most progressive social sectors.

The presence of authoritarian military governments has been crucial. As the bishops reemphasized with great clarity at Puebla, the Church has come increasingly to view these regimes in regional terms. Whereas formerly it might have distinguished between national cases as different as Paraguay, Chile, and Brazil, it now looks on them all as manifestations of a common economic model (CELAM, 1979: 26) and common National Security ideology (Calvo, 1979; CELAM, 1979: 407-408). The recent political situation of the region has fit the new theological directions of the Church with particular aptness. That congruence has effectively moved the point of unity which the Church seeks (CELAM, 1979: 383, 387, 547) to the left during this period.

In the future, that political environment could become less uniform. There may be openings in some regimes which allow some degree of political participation and open partisan activity. Even where such openings do not develop into the full political democracy the Church endorses (CELAM, 1979: 1024), the changed situation will create difficulties within particular national Churches and among them. To the extent that regimes in the region become more different from one another, the Latin American Church will find it more difficult to interpret them within a common framework.

Politics—political developments in the region and the Church's involvement in them—is likely to be the central issue challenging the consensus that existed at Puebla. The position reached there (which is analyzed in the next section) distinguishes partisan political activity, which is not appropriate for the Church, from prophetic and pastoral social activism, which is fundamental to its purposes. The difficulties of making this distinction in practice may well prove as great for the Church in "decompressing" systems in the future as they did in populist situations in the past (most strikingly in Chile in the late '60s and early '70s). Brazil, whose bishops played such an important part in achieving the progressive consensus at Puebla, is likely to be the key test of Church unity in this regard in the years to come.

The most surprising element of the bishops' consensus at Puebla—their enthusiastic support for ecclesial base communities—will also be tested in the future (and very likely in Brazil, where more CEBs have been created than anywhere else). The bishops were clearly impressed with the promise of the CEBs for religious renewal at the grass roots. The Puebla document designates them as a major instrument for the Church in its fundamental task of evangelization. But the proliferation of CEBs also poses real problems of authority for the Church. The bishops made clear their concerns (CELAM, 1979: 478, 489) that these small groupings be linked institutionally with clerical authority (hence their description as "ecclesial base communities," and not "base communities" alone, as they have frequently been called in practice). Balancing clerical authority over the CEBs with those qualities that give them such promise for evangelization—their responsiveness to personal concerns, their authenticity, their spontaneity—will be a significant challenge to the Church in the future, as the next section analyzes in more detail.

## *III*

Puebla made it obvious that the Church will be deeply involved in politics in the future. Its broad understanding of its prophetic and pastoral responsibilities will draw it into basic issues of freedom, equality, justice, participation, and power (Levine and Wilde, 1977). Whether its involvement will be a source of unity and consensus—and will have significant effects on society as a whole—will depend on the nature of its political context. It will also depend on the Church's success in evangelization, the kindling of a genuine religious renewal among Latin America's people.

The Church's involvement in politics is both a paradox and a problem. It is a paradox because that involvement exists in the face of a sincere desire to stay out of politics. The Puebla document was explicit and adamant that the institution must avoid any partisan activity. It echoed the opening message of Pope John Paul II in asserting that the Church is a mystery and not a political party, a position that seems in particular to reflect the experience of the Chilean Church. The Church has a problem, as Levine (1979: 8-9; 24, 25) writes, with politics. It would be torn apart from within if it allowed partisan factions to claim its universal truths for their particular programs and politics (CELAM, 1979: 388-389).

Authoritarian regimes, however, make it almost inevitable for the Latin American Church, as it now understands its purposes, to become politically involved. This involvement occurs in several ways, with implications which vary in different *coyunturas* of the regimes:

(1) The efforts of dictatorships, first, to repress or strictly control manifestly political activity has the effect of displacing pressures and participation into structures which the Church defends as "religious" and its own. To the extent that competition among manifestly political groups is not legitimate, social activists in the Church are freed from easy identification with particular parties or programs. Church unity can more easily be maintained and a pastoral commitment to "the poor" become more significant when it does not operate among different partisan movements claiming to represent them.

(2) The repressive extremes of authoritarian regimes, second, have moved the Church to explicit political statements about the desirability of democracy. The Puebla document is eloquent about the qualities that should characterize the good polity—equal protection under the law, an independent judiciary, more equitable distribution of wealth and opportunity, a guaranteed

right for workers and peasants to organize themselves, and, repeatedly, widespread popular participation (CELAM, 1979: 924-929; 998-1014). The bishops see all this as falling within the Church's larger pastoral mission, a "Mother and Teacher of all." They expect resistance but express confidence that the Church will pursue it to its "ultimate consequences" (CELAM, 1979: 93-94; 381, 385).

(3) Particularly in an authoritarian setting, third, the Church has become an advocate of political pluralism and social "space" for institutional as well as theological reasons (CELAM, 1979: 967-1014). In a society of demobilized organizations and intervened institutions, the Church is determined to insist on autonomy in its own religious sphere (CELAM, 1979: 381). As the Chilean bishops said in 1976, "To define the limits of our pastoral competence, we recognize the authority only of the Roman Pontiff" (Roncagliolo and Reyes Matta, 1978: 177).[6] In condemning the "totalitarian" implications of National Security Doctrine, the Church both rejects many of the policies that the ideology is used to justify and affirms its own Social Doctrine, which stresses the importance of intermediary bodies between the individual and the state. But even more fundamentally, the Church rejects the presumption of National Security Doctrine that its values have some overriding primacy in society (Roncagliolo and Reyes Matta, 1978: 45-62). The Church, "expert in humanity" (CELAM, 1979: 379, 1028), asserts a right autonomous of the state, any state, to articulate social values and goals.[7]

As Puebla made clear, the Church sees this mission as quite distinct from politics and does not intend to be deterred from pursuing it, in both its pastoral and prophetic faces. But beyond its possible confusion with politics, there is a further difficulty the Church will face with its broad sense of its pastoral responsibilities. The basic image of the shepherd, the *pastor*, and his flock evokes a relationship of leader and followers of a more traditional kind than seems to be evolving in the contemporary Church. *Lo pastoral* involves clerical solidarity with the poor and suffering (*compartir las angustias*: CELAM, 1979: 16-20) as well as their "formation" under clerical tutelage, and pastors seem to undergo *concientización* as well as their flocks. Both sides of pastoral action are reflected in the Puebla document.

Although individual bishops will undoubtedly draw different lines about what is legitimately pastoral, observers at Puebla were impressed by their sincerity about pastoral concerns. The fact that they made them as central as they did, and accepted the basic direction of change since Medellín, suggests that the Church will become still more socially active in the future.

Whether that activity will have a significant effect depends on how firmly the Church's role is rooted in religious commitment at the local level. Ultimately its impact will turn on the efficacy and the extent of initiatives such as the new "base communities." Although they have proliferated rapidly in some areas (Della Cava, 1978; Bruneau, 1978), we do not know yet how widespread these communities are or may become (estimates run to 100,000 and more for Latin America as a whole). But we can already make some preliminary observations about the effects of those that do exist.

As a fundamental unit of the Church, the base communities differ from the parish in several ways. They are smaller and typically involve much more active lay participation, both in liturgical ceremonies and in religious study. Characteristically, they have much more uniform social membership than the parish, permitting greater face-to-face communication. As a more informal kind of grouping, they have made most progress among those for whom the previous institutional existence of the Church was least established—that is to say, among the poor (Bruneau, 1978). They have tried to reach new social groups by addressing the concrete realities of their social situations in religious terms: this is the ground to the Church's pastoral commitment to authentic "liberation."

In cases such as Chile and Brazil, these local communities—sheltered under the Church's institutional shield—have provided a "surrogate" for otherwise repressed associational life (Smith, 1979: 93-95; Della Cava, 1978). Where there had previously been political polarization, they have played a specific role in bringing Marxists and Catholics together. They have provided the sites for shared experience, which have given new meaning to their old concepts of "dialogue" and "praxis." It has been a process not so much of one side convincing the other as of both old antagonists realizing they had much more to learn from the other (Smith, 1979: 94).

It is interesting in this connection to see how the authoritarian setting changes the implications of the Church's role. A fundamental element of its position on social change since 1968 has been the insistence of its centrist hierarchy on consensus rather than coercion. The Puebla document systematically balances its denunciation of dictatorial repression with condemnation of revolutionary violence (CELAM, 1979: 393-394). In the more open environment of polarized populist politics, this emphasis on consensus was viewed by both Left and Right as deceptive and divisive. But in the authoritarian regime, in which the decisive balance of violence lies with the state, to foster consensus among popular forces may be a contribution that progressive forces view much more positively (but see Krischke in Della Cava, 1978).

It is difficult to know yet whether the Church's new base communities will affect social consciousness on a large scale or, by giving their members experience in participation in one setting, facilitate a participatory society more broadly.[8] In a significant case of political "opening" recently, in Brazil, one observer attributed great importance to the Church's grass roots initiatives among the working class of São Paulo, a "vast mobilization . . . in silence, without fanfare, and with all deliberation required for schooling men in a way of life" (Della Cava, 1978: 10). Whether the Church will more generally play that sort of role remains to be seen.

It is difficult, also, to know how well the CEBs will be able to balance their two sides, as "centers of evangelization and engines of liberation and development" (CELAM, 1979: 56) or, to put it differently, how well they can reconcile loyalty to the ecclesiastical institution with commitment to their particular small community. We do know that the bishops see them as the "hope of the Church" (CELAM, 1979: 477) and will attempt to create more of them, impelled by falling clerical vocations and a genuine "option" for the poor. On the basis of the authoritarian experience of the last 10 years, we also know, as Levine puts it so well, that these communities will at least be "keeping alive hope for a different kind of future" (1979: 23).

Puebla was a kind of photograph that captured a highly dynamic collectivity at a particular point in time. The final document produced by the bishops, shot through with compromises and contradictions, faithfully reflected the current state of the Church. That the document is as progressive as it is tells us more about the past than the future. It demonstrates that the changes of the past 10 years are real—that they have been written into the lives of those that are the Church and cannot be reversed by the intentions of some ecclesiastical elites. But what Puebla will come to mean in the future cannot be extrapolated from the words of the document or from past experience. It will be shaped above all by the political context of particular national churches and the degree to which unity and momentum can be maintained around the central purposes of evangelization. Much of that will depend on the leadership of the bishops and their ability to foster a pastoral authority for new times, within the Church and for society as a whole.

## NOTES

1. The Spanish "eclesial" has been translated to "ecclesial," a word now returning to English usage, rather than "ecclesiastical" because the latter would imply inclusion in the canonical structures of the Church.

2. Bouvy (1978), IDOC International (1978), and MacEoin (1978) all provide useful collections of articles on the background to Puebla.

3. See the articles by Poblete (1979: 35-36) and Levine (1979: 12-15). This essay will draw particularly upon articles in the February 1979 special issue of the *Journal of Interamerican Studies and World Affairs* and on other papers given originally at a workshop on the Church and Politics in Latin America held at the Woodrow Wilson Center in Washington, D.C., in May 1978.

4. See paragraph 379 in CELAM (1979). References to paragraphs in the provisional Puebla document will be given in the text as, for example, CELAM, 1979: 379.

5. One should not overemphasize the degree to which continental consensus could be produced by these newly institutionalized regional organizations. The secretariats of the bishops' CELAM and the Orders' CLAR have had significant differences for several years, a conflict which came into the open just before the CELAM meeting in Puebla.

6. The statement by the Permanent Committee of the Chilean Episcopate was made in reaction to the Riobamba incident in Ecuador in August 1976. A meeting in Riobamba to "exchange pastoral experiences" was denounced as "subversive" and forcibly broken up by dozens of heavily armed police. The priests and bishops involved, from throughout the hemisphere, were summarily deported by the Ecuadorian authorities. Roncagliolo and Reyes Matta (1973) provides useful documentation.

7. Those who would assert the autonomy of Christian values fight, in effect, for political pluralism in any authoritarian setting. The situation of reformist elements of the Catholic Church in Cuba, who would like to support the revolution but on their own Christian grounds, is an interesting parallel (see Crahan, 1979: 175, 177).

8. It is worth noting, as Crahan (1979: 174-178) does for the Cuban case, that active participation by lay people in a religious setting by no means precludes their holding conservative social views. Whether such experience has "progressive" implications for a wider environment depends greatly on the character of that setting.

## REFERENCES

BOUVY, J. [ed.] (1978) "Latin America: approaching the Puebla conference." Lumen Vitae 33: 3.

BRUNEAU, T. (1978) "Notes toward the study of popular religiosity and strategies of change in church: evidence from eight Brazilian dioceses." Presented at the Workshop on Religion and Politics in Latin America, Woodrow Wilson International Center for Scholars, Washington, D.C.

CALVO, R. (1979) "The church and the doctrine of national security." J. of Interamerican Studies 21: 69-88.

CELAM [Consejo Episcopal Latinoamericano] "La evangelización en el presente y en el futuro de América Latina." Provisional document. Puebla de los Angeles, México: III Conferencia General del Episcopado Latinoamericano.

CRAHAN, M. E. (1979) "Salvation through Christ or Marx: religion in revolutionary Cuba." J. of Interamerican Studies 21: 156-184.

DELLA CAVA, R. (1978) "Short-term politics and long-term religion in Brazil" (with a critique by Paulo Krischke). Latin American Program Working Paper No. 12. Washington, D.C.: Woodrow Wilson International Center for Scholars.

DODSON, M. (1979) "The Christian left in Latin American politics." J. of Interamerican Studies 21: 45-68.

IDOC International (1978) The Church at the Crossroads: Christians in Latin America from Medellin to Puebla, 1968-1978. IDOC Europe Dossier 6. Rome: IDOC International.

LEVINE, D. [ed.] (1979) "Religion and politics, politics and religion: an introduction." J. of Interamerican Studies 21: 3-29.

——— and A. WILDE (1977) "The Catholic church, 'politics,' and violence: the Colombian case." Rev. of Politics 39: 220-239.

MacEOIN, G. [ed.] (1978) "Puebla: moment of decision for the Latin American church. Cross Currents 28, 1.

POBLETE, R. (1979) "From Medellin to Puebla: notes for reflection." J. of Interamerican Studies 21: 31-44.

RONCAGLIOLO, R. and F. REYES MATTA (1978) Iglesia, Prensa y Militares: El Caso Riobamba y los Obispos Latinoamericanos. México, D.F.: Instituto Latinoamericano de Estudios Transnacionales.

SMITH, B. H. (1979) "Churches and human rights in Latin America: recent trends in the subcontinent." J. of Interamerican Studies 21: 89-127.

VALLIER, I. (1970) Catholicism, Social Control, and Modernization in Latin America. Englewood Cliffs, NJ: Prentice-Hall.

*Alexander Wilde is Research Associate in the Latin American Program at the Woodrow Wilson International Center for Scholars in Washington, D.C. He is the author of a forthcoming book on politics and the Church in Colombia and has written on the Latin American Church for general as well as scholarly audiences.*

**PETER RANIS**
*Department of Political Science*
*York College*
*City University of New York*
*150-14 Jamaica Avenue*
*Jamaica, New York 11432*

# *EARLY PERONISM AND THE POST-LIBERAL ARGENTINE STATE*

Perón and the Peronista party and movement have been interesting from at least two crucially important perspectives: first, Perón's ability to keep Argentina hostage for three decades in his roles as twice-elected "lider," as exiled "caudillo," and president once more (I say "hostage" in the sense that he remained the pivotal political force in all the crucial coalition bargains struck among the major power contenders since 1943); second, his ability to forge an intellectual and political clientele that spanned several generations and encompassed various, but unique, ideological views. Perón had the leadership capability not only of touching many people but also of striking a common political resonance among vastly differing sets of values.

The purpose of this article is to present Perón in the light of his country's overall development struggle to gain a better idea of the arena in which his political skills were exercised and the climate in which his political thought had its genesis. The antecedent conditions to the Peronist state are noteworthy in that they not only describe the generation in which Perón himself

AUTHOR'S NOTE: Research for this article was made possible by a grant from the Organization of American States. I also would like to express my personal gratitude to Geulio Steinbach for his kindness in making available the many facilities of the Instituto de Desarrollo Economico y Social of Buenos Aires.

Journal of Interamerican Studies and World Affairs, Vol. 21 No. 3, August 1979 313-338
© 1979 Sage Publications, Inc.

became politicized but also forecast much of the character and direction of Perón's initial administration.

## *The Antecedents*

Though the 1930s have been characterized as the "infamous decade" of political fraud and imposed elections in Argentina, this was also a time in which the country experienced significant social and economic changes as well as shifts in the arena of ideological perceptions. The precipitating event was the worldwide depression. It not only ushered in the conservative civil and military governments which guided the state during that decade but also forced those governments to take steps to industrialize Argentina to produce the goods no longer readily available from the European continent.

The initiation of import substitution policies—with its emphasis on light industries such as food and beverages, textiles, and metallurgy (Murmis and Portantiero, 1972: 11, 91; Camillo et al., 1973; Peralta Ramos, 1972; Jorge, 1973)—had important consequences. For one thing, differences between the interests of the emerging new industrial class and the agrarian investments in those same sectors were conciliated. The most powerful agrarian interests supported these light industry plans expressly because they foresaw the need for ancillary and complementary industries related to the processing of their own production of meat, wheat, and other agricultural raw materials destined for the domestic market. As the president of the Argentine Rural Society said in 1933:

> We find ourselves in agreement with the necessity of helping organize industries that can prosper transforming the various and numerous quantities of raw materials that our land produces and offers so generously [Murmis and Portantiero, 1972: 24].

Thus, as import substitution policies became more universal, not only did the industrial interests become ever more important but the agrarian interests also began to invest heavily in the industrial sector after 1930. When Jacinto Oddone listed the top 50 landowners in Buenos Aires Province during the 1930s—those with more than 30,000 hectares—he found that approximately half had industrial interests in both national and foreign enterprises (Llach, 1972: 22). Between 1935 and 1943 the gross product of industry grew by 35%, profits grew by 44% (Llach, 1972: 25-26), and large-scale factories appeared, though light industry still predominated.

Another consequence of the import substitution industrialization process was the growth of the urban proletariat class. The newly urbanized industrial proletariat flowed into greater Buenos Aires at a rate calculated from 72,000 to 117,000 between 1934 and 1947 (Van Hove, 1970; Jorge, 1973: 151-152). From 1935 to 1943, employment in the industrial labor sector experienced an 81% growth, while the real wage scale decreased by 10% (Llach, 1972: 25-26). These two factors gave strong momentum to the trade union movement. According to Murmis and Portantiero (1972: 61), these newly arrived workers were distinguishable from older workers in three ways which were to make them susceptible to future populist appeals: (1) they tended to share a value system oriented toward personal economic advantages; (2) they shared a sense of belonging to a primary group, as opposed to feelings of class solidarity based on ideological principles; and (3) they expressed their social consciousness in terms of being "poor," not in terms of class. To further emphasize their point, the authors show that of the 113 strikes which took place in 1942, almost 90% were based purely upon salary claims and readjustments (1972: 91). This trade union movement was itself divided into two important currents: one was the tendency to maintain the independence of the unions as a working class pressure group while the other urged union with the parliamentary parties of the left, subordinating the workers' purely domestic preoccupations to the international crusade against fascism (Peralta Ramos, 1972: 94).

These two consequences fed a third. The role of the state became increasingly complex, as it no longer solely represented the interests of the landed oligarchy, its prime mission since the

1880s, but had to expand to encompass the interests of the newly emergent industrial bourgeoisie as well. The government became more like a mediator between these two capitalist classes, which, from the late 1930s, would move ever closer to a position of balanced equilbrium. While the Argentine state became step by step more paternalistic and interventionist (as evidenced by the Pinedo Plan for governmental stimulation of industry in 1940), the military establishment reinforced this trend. It did so both through the political potential it had acquired through its increased autonomy (Panaia et al., 1973; Díaz Araujo, 1970; Potash, 1969; García Lupo, 1963) as well as through its strong support of the developing industrial sector. The military command was the first organized interest to advocate outright heavy industrialization. Its prime motivation was the development of an independent armaments industry second to none in South America.

All these trends accelerated after the outbreak of World War II. The equilibrium between the agricultural and industrial sectors began to teeter, with the industrial mobilization of the new working class and the growing strength of the state itself exemplied by the increased role of the military in its decisions. In 1941, the latter was responsible for the creation of the General Administration for Military Production, which was assigned such tasks as projecting the industrial capabilities of Argentina related to war materiel, explorations for key mineral deposits (such as iron, copper, manganese, aluminum, and others used for weaponry), and the construction of military factories (Panaia, et al., 1973: 105). The military felt the

> management of necessary violence in order to maintain order required capabilities that the industrial sector is not able to provide. Because of this it is necessary to reorient the course of the economy and, at the same time, establish a considerable war industry [Panaia et all., 1973: 98].

These activities intruded the military into the political economy, from which they have seldom thereafter absented themselves. It resulted in an ever more interventionist role for the military by 1943 and legitimized their interest in the management of the economy.

### *The Politicization of Perón*

Juan Perón was a product of this period and a reflection of its concerns. Along with other army officers under General Uriburu, Perón had participated in the 1930 coup against the civilian president, Irigoyen. Reporting on the behind-the-scenes preparation for the first modern military intervention of 1930, Perón described his thoughts in January of 1931:

> we all thought that the worst thing that we would do was to enthrone a military dictatorship which would be absolutely opposed by the entire nation. . . . we tried to convince the General [Uriburu] of the importance of interesting the people in the revolution. . . . It was all arranged by the following day as we looked for supporters, and reached . . . 300; this proves that the officers were convinced by the logic of the ideas that emerged on the fringe of those who wanted a dictatorship divorced from the people of the country, that would have made the military hateful and would have encountered great resistance from the populace [1963: 63-65].

Perón then described Uriburu's strategem—having the military junta represented before the civil junta of the revolution—so that "in this way the people and the army marched hand in hand in expelling from the government those men who were exploiting it." Perón was to repeat this procedure against greater odds 15 years later.

From 1930 to 1931 Perón was a lecturer at the Superior War College and in 1932 published some of his lectures under the title *Notes on Military History,* which forecasts the thinking repeated in many of his later books. In the realm of ideas, Perón's study is a compilation of doctrinal propositions without internal rigor, systematization, or apparent ideological content. Early in the book he warns that it is the *variable application* of certain principles that constitutes objective rational behavior at any given moment in history:

> To understand the principles, but not be able to apply them, produces nothing. In war the deed predominates over the idea, action over the word, and execution over theory [1932: 33].

Crucial to his thinking is his definition of the role and importance of the leader and his notion of the function of the state. For Perón, the great geniuses of military history were those very rare men who were able to apply instinctively the theory of war to changing conditions; thus, the linchpin of his theory was the leader who creates and applies the precepts, rules, and principles in "the great experimental field of historic reality" (Perón, 1932: 41). In his definition:

> Military art and leadership are two inseparable elements. All operations depend upon them in their entirety.
>
> The first represents the theory of the art, and the second, the artist. The leader is destined to give life and practical form to that theory. On him depends the totality of the work achieved. In essence, the leader is the primordial and fundamental element of leadership [1932: 237].

The first incipient statement of Peronist ideological "verticality" and political movement discipline is also revealed in these published lectures:

> The true strategic leadership begins by transmitting the idea of Command to the army. The leader will say: "This is my conception. It is transformed into reality." From that moment on, the principal task of the Command consists of reaching the point where *one single thought dominates the whole army. This thought is that of the Commander-in-Chief* [Perón, 1932: 245].

From his treatise, Perón seemed to be opting for a Spartan view of society and a militarized orientation of the state. In fact, Perón's notion of the function of the state at this time was preeminently military and political. The economy ought to be geared to potential war efforts or, as he called it using the phrase of the Bismarck era in Germany, a "Nation of Arms." The press and propaganda ought to be supportive of the political initiatives and undermine those of the enemy. Military and political objectives ought to serve and complement each other:

> The politician serves the military man during peace-time, creating the best political conditions in case of war. The military man serves the politician in war by annihilating the enemy, so that the politician is able to impose his political objectives, which is the nation itself [Perón, 1932: 144].

At the same time, Perón was not unaware of the need for economic resources and organization, and he spoke of the "aspiration of new nations which will continue to be externally dependent for many years." Yet it was mainly the ability of the economy to supply military needs that made it crucial, as politicians similarly supplied popular support for the army.[1]

Given these perspectives, it is not at all unusual that Perón could join his destinies with military conspiracies and populist aspirations, as he did later on. In the meantime, however, he pursued a strictly military career, serving as military attaché in Chile from 1936 to 1938, then traveling to Mussolini's Italy in 1939 on a study mission which lasted until 1941, when he returned to Argentina to serve as an instructor in a Mendoza military alpine school and as an inspector for the army Chiefs of Staff.

However, these positions coincided with the beginning of the war years, and to set the scene for Perón's access to full power it is appropriate to define the environment of that time. First, the onset of the war marked the end of British dominance and monopoly over Argentine affairs, concomitant with the slow decline of the agrarian sector's hold over decision making. At the same time, it ushered in the authentic beginnings of serious industrialization proposals and initiatives as countermeasures to the absence of industrial imports from the belligerents and former trading partners. Socially, this industrialization brought with it consequential internal mobilization,[2] as rural to urban migration swelled the ranks of the new industrial working classes in the large metropolitan centers, particularly greater Buenos Aires and Rosario, affording the workers potential social cohesiveness and political power. Furthermore, the military, of which Perón was a part, increased its participation in the management of the economy.

In 1943 the famous secret Task Force for Unity (GOU)[3] was founded, its initial goals being to defend the army against corruption from within, from certain civilian sectors, from politicians, and from communist influence. Like Perón, almost all the officers of GOU had participated in the 1930 coup of Uriburu. The group was well established when Perón joined its ranks and used this military lodge as a vehicle to propel himself to political power (Díaz Araujo, 1970; Potash, 1969). According to Potash (1969: 187), the 1943 coup was a preemptive strike to avoid the imposition of a pro-British, conservative candidate, Patrón Costas, and to prevent an accommodation with the United States which would make Argentina eligible for lend-lease military equipment.

The June 1943 coup was certainly not Perón's doing, but he supported its goals, added a new moral and social content to its policies, and eventually rode it to power against the old system, the old parties, and the precapitalist mentality still dominant in the Argentina of World War II. Perón had characterized the coup as a revolution:

> By my way of thinking the June 4th revolution is not just another revolution. It is not a revolution destined to change men and parties, but it is moving to change the system and to do what is necessary so that in the future these unhappy circumstances don't repeat themselves, which necessitate our taking direction of the State. It aspires, therefore, to be profoundly transforming, especially in the moral and humanistic sense. Revolutions have never escaped those two fundamental phenomena [1963: 86].

In June 1943 after the coup, he was named head of the First Army Division Chiefs of Staff.

A major turning point for Perón was the meatpackers' strike of 1943, in which the unions demanded a salary increase, the potential of working 60 hours per week, equal conditions for women, and the reinstatement of laid-off and fired workers. At the urging of the community party, the union leader, José Peter, advocated that the workers should return to work with their demands unmet because the Anglo-American packing houses were contributing by their exports to the Allied war effort against nazism (Puiggros, 1969: 55-56; González, 1974: 26). Perón, on the other hand, intervened from the offices of the Ministry of War on behalf of the workers and forced a favorable settlement. He won the workers' unfailing support and moved quickly to consolidate this situation by recognizing the autonomous meatpackers' unions unaffiliated with the socialist and communist parties. Perón learned his lesson well and was to repeat these strategies with increased vigor up to, and following, his election to the presidency.

Following the settlement of this strike, Perón was named director of the National Department of Labor, and thence began his rapid ascension to power (Luna, 1969):

October 27, 1943: Director, National Department of Labor
December 10, 1943: Secretary of Labor; also Chief of Civil Aeronautics Administration (Air Force)
May 4, 1944: Minister of War
June 7, 1944: Vice-President (under President Edelmiro Farrell)
August 25, 1944: President, Post-War National Council.

Perón's rise was so rapid that by October 1945 the military command was sufficiently alarmed to make a belated attempt to curb his growing power by placing him under house arrest and forcing his resignation. Perón's response was equivocal. He acceded to the military's demands, on the one hand, but on the other gave the green light to his labor union supporters to mobilize on his behalf. On October 10, 1945, he also presented a farewell address over the national radio, an emotional recital of his triumphs and achievements on behalf of the workers:

> Workers, I have just finished speaking with the employees and functionaries of the Secretary of Labor. I have asked them as my last wish as Secretary of Labor that no one leave his post, because

> I have received numerous resignations. I consider that in this hour that work within the Ministry is not an administrative post, but a combat post, and one does not resign one's combat post; one dies in them.
>
> Stripped of my office, I speak today to my friends, the workers, expressing to them, for the last time from this house, all that my heart feels toward them and all that is left in my life to do for their well-being.
>
> If the revolution [June 1943] is satisfied in holding free elections, it will have made only a gesture on behalf of one of the political parties. This could not have been, cannot be, and will not be the exclusive goal of the revolution. That is what some politicians would want in order to return; but the revolution embodies in itself the fundamental reforms that have been proposed in the economy, in politics and in the social area. That trilogy represents the conquests of this revolution on the march and nothing that happens will be allowed to drain it of its fundamental content. These social programs accomplished have such a firm consistency that they will give way before no one, and those who appreciate them are not those who denigrate them, but the workers who feel them. This social work that only the workers appreciate in its true value must also be defended by them in every sphere.

After spelling out many of the social gains, Perón continued:

> I have also left signed a decree of extraordinary importance to the workers. It is one that refers to an increase in salary and wages, implementation of a sliding, living and basic wage and a profit-sharing measure.
>
> And now, as citizen, in leaving my public function, in leaving this house that has had for me such pleasant memories, I wish to show once more the firmness of my faith in a perfect democracy, as we understand it here. Within that democratic faith we affirm our incorruptible and indomitable position against the oligarchy. We believe that the workers must have confidence in themselves and remember that the emancipation of the working class is within the worker himself. We are engaged in a battle that we shall win because it is the world that is marching in that direction. We must have faith in that strugggle and in that future. We shall triumph in one year or we shall triumph in ten, but we shall triumph (Venceremos) [1973b].

Within a week of the farewell address, a massive concentration of workers before the presidential palace (La Casa Rosada) obtained Perón's release from custody through its incontrovertible demonstration of his political power to the government. Simultaneously it provided the impetus for the organization of the labor party shortly thereafter, with Perón as its presidential candidate. Its program defined as enemies:

> the minority made up of large landowners, landowning industrialists, businessmen, bankers and landlords, and every variety of large national and foreign capitalism. . . . Against them they find the working class made up of laborers, employees, and peasants, along with professionals, artists and intellectuals, as well as small merchants, industrialists and farmers [Peralta Ramos, 1972: 115].

While Perón's formal support came from the newly formed labor party, he also received aid from several dissident nationalist groupings within the radical party—FORJA and UCR Junta Renovadora—military sectors, and the Catholic Church.[4] When Argentine elections were held in late February 1946, the Peronist coalition won the day with 55% of the vote.

The 1946 election culminated a noteworthy evolution of Perón's own perception of Argentina's socioeconomic process since his days as captain and major in the 1930s.

### *Perón's Political Thought*

It is interesting to note that Perón's immense popularity from 1943 to 1946 came chiefly from his socioeconomic positions and policies, rather than because of his political orientation. His political victory solidified the developing national bourgeois alliance with the urban proletariat, both new and old, and augmented the role played by the military in this basic triple alliance. The defeat of the Democratic Union marked the end of the era of liberal politics with its (1) emphasis on a limited state role, (2) basic satisfaction with parity of agriculture and industry in decision making, and (3) national income being skewed in favor of the middle and upper classes.

Let us examine Perón's thinking as it matured during this brief but consequential interlude in Argentine history, the two years between his assumption of the labor post until his election in February 1946. These are the years of a man, not yet 50 years old, still speaking and writing without the shackles of the prime responsibilities of executive office, without needing to develop a political doctrine to explain his perceptions, and without the encumbrances of representing a unified administration.

In the ideological context one is struck by Perón's usage of Marxist terminology, but within a nonsocialist framework of understanding. He speaks of the "proletarians," the "exploitation of man by his fellow man," the "dehumanization of capital." At the same time, Perón (1973b: 38-39) expresses fears of foreign ideological penetration and continually reiterates the need to avoid class conflict between capital and labor:

> Once again I exhort that there be peace between the bosses and the workers, because I wish for my country that the class struggle be replaced by harmony between them [Perón, 1973b: 76, 93].

His critique of Marxism centers around what he calls humanist and Christian attitudes which, if applied, render class struggle irrelevant.

> The historical materialists, like all one-dimensional thinking, believed that warlike conflicts which drain humanity have as their basic and ultimate reason inevitable economic divergence and dissension. . . . Fortunately over and above these fictions, arises the human spirit, eternal foundation of light and fire, in which are harbored the most excellent sentiments and most disinterested aspirations [1973b: 76].
>
> I know those who separate the vindications of workers in the economic and social sphere, from those who aspire for the domination of the proletariat [1973b: 93].

Perón's corporativist scheme already was one of class collaboration under the auspices and direction of the state.

> Instead of understanding that the old Marxist maxim of the "class struggle" has fallen, defeated in the dawn of this century by the more humane and courageous "class collaboration," which permits cordial relations between capital and labor under State tutelage, they resist all calls for understanding which would permit the government to expand throughout the nation a little more social justice which our people, gently and long-suffering, come to claim with humility, without letting themselves be tempted by the examples of other lands where these fruits have been snatched away from them [1973b: 166].

Speaking of the collaboration of the conservatives and the left in the Democratic Union, Perón said at a speech announcing his candidacy on February 12, 1946:

> It is not insignificant that oligarchic groups disguised as democrats, unite their shouts and their conduct with those same Communists which before were (by the terror they inspired) the cause of their fervor, and to whom now they dedicate their best smiles. It is equally funny, to observe the eagerness with which those Communist leaders proclaim their democratic faith, forgetting the Marxist doctrine of the dictatorship of the proletariat and its practice in the Soviet Union [1973b: 191].

Perón's (1973a: 114) political vision and vocabulary in those traditional days emphasized such ideals as "virtue," "morality," "higher interest," "humanizing capital," "honesty," "unity of the Argentine people," "great will," "sure instinct," "Catholic character." "We don't need ideological protectors or leaders," Perón had said, "our mass of workers is conscious and capable; it can and must lead itself without interference." What Perón was offering was not the individual consciousness of the unreconstructed liberal, nor the class consciousness that he identified with foreign and alien alternatives, but unified, communitarian, social consciousness that would assauge class warfare, avoid the contamination of international socialism, and organize society to transcend the old liberal state conceptions.[5]

Perón spoke of the need to utilize certain class and group differences in projects of national collaboration with each group doing its share for the general welfare (1973a: 150). But the principal underlying ideological notion present in Perón's thinking at that time was a kind of vague Christian communitarianism with state leadership to intervene on behalf of *perceived* disadvantaged groups. For example, Perón speaks continually in this period of "God, country, and home" or "God, country, and social justice." When these values are discarded or "When there is an abandonment of Christian solidarity, a direct cause of this neglect is insensitive and dehumanized super-capitalization which uses the individual as a thing, taking better care of tools than of human beings" (1973b: 34).

Socially, Perón spoke of the abolition of privileges; politically, of the institutionalization of an "authentic democracy" equidistant from oligarchic and totalitarian systems and economically, of the harmonious relationship between capital and labor "organically" institutionalized.

In an interesting footnote to history, Perón at this time likened his struggle in Argentina to President Franklin Roosevelt's struggle in the United States. He eulogized Roosevelt often in 1945, particularly after his death, and considered the New Deal similar to the kind of "national restoration" he was supporting for Argentina. Perón considered Roosevelt's struggle against the left and right parallel to his own particular position. In one speech after Roosevelt's death in April 1945, Perón said:

> I couldn't express any better the words of President Roosevelt when he answered the attacks which adversaries from distinct and diametrically opposite angles were directing against him with equal passion. Roosevelt said this: "Certain timid people, who are afraid of progress, try to describe with new and exotic words the work we are doing. Sometimes they label it fascism, other times communism, still other times interventionism or socialism. They try by this to make something difficult or *theoretical* out of something that is in reality simple and *practical*" [emphasis added; 1973b: 87].

Perón has often been called a fascist. Certainly from his writings it is obvious that, though he does not espouse the doctrine, he apparently uses enough of the symbolic vocabulary of Franco Spain and Mussolini Italy to be so confused. For example, speaking to various worker groups in late 1943 and 1944, he rails against the absence of a "superior collective ideal" (1973a: 30), the need for "the organizational imperative" (1973a: 31), "the mystique of duty" and "the happiness of mass action" (1973a: 61), and "the two greatest attributes of humanity: The Gospel and arms. . . . The Gospel, a Catholic grouping equivalent to peace, harmony and a mystical sense, without which the world would have social anarchy" (1973a: 100). Finally, he speaks of serving the nation "because we have one and only one ideology: the fatherland" (1973b: 18).

But a much more ubiquitous strain in Perón's speeches and writings was his talent at pragmatic improvisation (1973a: 100, 108, 135, 148, 160, 205). This can be seen in his early strategic war studies, as discussed above, and is often reiterated in these years prior to his assumption of power.

> Better to do than to say; better to bring about than to promise.
>
> The practical effects of a revolutionary work determines the conduct one must follow.
>
> I don't tie myself to the ridiculous prejudices of any particular ideology. I look for the truth wherever it may be.
>
> I make decisions in accord with the necessities and rhythm of the hour.
>
> I haven't gone to the labor agreements, nor to workingman's laws, nor to the theories which speak to labor. I have gone to the workplace.
>
> We are working in a constructive sense, which may be slow but which will be accomplished, distinct from the imaginary theories that are never carried out.
>
> The merit is in accomplishing things. The concept in itself is worthless.

## *The Post-Liberal State*

On the political level, Perón's concept of the state has consistently focused on a tripod system of official representation, namely the industrial interests, the state, and the labor unions

(1973a: 161). The state maintains for itself the authority to decide all conflicts between capital and labor. The state in its capacity as arbiter has the obligation to defend each association of interests from the other because an equilibrium or a balance of organized forces would be easier to control and/or lead. Perón's fear was complementary: that unorganized and "inorganic" forces would escape the state's direction and control.

While the state's responsibility is to promote the general welfare, Perón's perspective did not allow for interference in essential "economic liberties" nor should these liberties be compromised when the state takes a leadership role in the economy. Under his model of the state, it would regulate the major social and economic functions and goals of the society without intervening directly into the areas of individual prerogatives which constitute the inalienable rights of, for example, individuals, businessmen, and consumers. As Perón said at one point, "The modern state is more a social problem than a political problem.... The objectives of this social policy are minimum salaries, social assistance, organization and regulation of work and rest. . . . We defend the supreme dignity of work. We want each man to earn what is necessary to eat, to dress and to live with dignity. The rest is up to private social activity and the state social action" (1973a: 183-184).

By private social activity, Perón was referring to private and cooperative insurance and assistance plans and business compensatory plans for their salaried workers. By state social action, Perón had in mind the state's obligation to the sick, in case of accident, and to the indigent.

And the army, what role has it in the state apparatus? Perón once summarized the military's function as a dual one: to support the legitimate aspirations of the worker and safeguard private property. In addition, Perón saw nothing incompatible between the military forces' repressive function and its revolutionary qualities. As will be recalled, his analysis of the 1943 coup established its revolutionary credentials. In addition, Perón's military lecture themes of 1931 are reiterated and made more comprehensive during this period. As in his *Notes on Military*

*History,* "the concept of a 'Nation in arms or total war' as developed by Marshall von de Goltz in 1883 is, in a certain sense, the most modern theory of national defense by which nations use peace and war alike, up to the ultimate productive capacity of the State, to gain their political objectives . . . ." To sustain this type of military leadership in the name of national defense, the armed forces must take the lead in creating wealth, industries, diversifying production, and multiplying the means of transport and communications (Perón, 1973a: 71-79).

His definitions of what constitutes a genuine revolution, pronounced to various groups in mid-1944, regardless of where the 1943 coup fits in, is one of Perón's more thorough evaluations. To follow his criteria, a revolution must first have a social content or risk being completely inconsequential in impact. Second, it must have a binding ideological point of view, or it may find itself alone and without followers (1973a: 116). Third, if the revolution is well conceived, it passes through three stages: preparation, coup, and the revolution itself. If the revolution is well planned and executed, "it avoids unnecessary struggle and loss of blood" (1973a: 123). It is clear that Perón felt that the people should *not* be involved in the preparation or coup phases, but only integrated into its third phase—the revolution. What Perón meant by revolution were the changes instituted and policies derived *after* a shift in the power constellation had occurred. As Perón said, "a revolution of the army converts itself into a revolution of the people" (1973a: 172).

In Perón's terms, a revolution with a social content requires the changing of the life of the citizenry by inculcating new social-judicial structures and new attitudes. Yet, Perón felt this could all be done without violence and without societal ruptures and lesions. Substantively, the revolution was aimed at producing greater national industrial wealth and elevation of the workers' standard of living. In his thinking, these were tied together. It was essentially a welfare-capitalist revolution meant to end economic underproduction and complementarily to strengthen the political power of the Argentine state. Third, these benefits were to be distributed to the major force that creates new wealth—the laboring class.

In the international politics arena, Perón fastened most heavily onto two concepts: that of national power and that of dependency. True political sovereignty, he believed, depended upon a sufficient defensive posture and a productive self-sufficiency that did not require a nation to undertake foreign adventures. Perón recognized that the independence movements in Latin America were basically political and did not guarantee later economic independence (1973a: 125). Only industrialization would avoid a colonial relationship with the advanced countries (1973b: 44). Nevertheless, his "dependency" understanding is limited at this time to such nominal characteristics as the existence of foreign debts or the absence of choice in formulating independent political diplomacy.

At the level of social stratification and class structure, Perón saw four groupings: working class, middle class, capitalist class, and the state. The state's relationship to the working class, however, is special since it provides a vindication against past wrongs. Though the social structure remains the same, the working class is given relief from its relatively impoverished position vis-à-vis the other classes. This should help not only the working class as such but also productivity generally. Meanwhile, Perón hoped for the continual growth of the middle class, upon whom any nation's greatness depends. And he would defend their interests at all costs against the oligarchy that had kept Argentina backward.

Between the working and middle classes, Perón sought to establish an indelible bond of common interests and sentiments. As he told a group of visiting bank employees:

> The workers who use their muscles, those who use their brains, the poor, the rich, must achieve a national harmony, because we believe that human institutions are not founded on divisions and hatred but on collaboration and love. By this we conceive of an *organized society* . . . [emphasis added]. We begin with the most needy classes. After that we shall convoke the financiers, bankers, cattlemen and industrialists [1973a: 145].

Not two weeks after this speech, Perón made what is certainly the most significant speech of his early career. It was presented to the Buenos Aires Chamber of Commerce in August 1944. In it he attempted to assuage the suspicions of the business community as to his role as governmental strongman—Vice-President, Minister of War, and Secretary of Labor. He spoke of his belief in the Papal Encyclical of Leo XIII and its promulgation of social justice and Christian democracy. Perón warned that the only dangerous working class is the unorganized and dissatisfied one. Only as an unorganized mass are they susceptible to foreign ideologies and subversive forces. With the state giving strong direction to the organization of workers' unions, communist and socialist trade unions can be subordinated to these new entities, which will be stronger and more active under governmental auspices.

Perón paints a spectre of communist victories and influence in the world since 1917 and the loss of Russia by the capitalist world. He warns of the dangers of the Spanish Civil War. He went on to say:

> Better to give 30% on time than to lose everything later. . . . In order to avoid that the masses, once having received the necessary social justice, attempt to go beyond this, the first remedy is the organization of these masses. . . . That will be our insurance, the organization of the masses . . . because the state has the instruments that, if it is necessary, by force can put things in their proper place and not let them run amok.
>
> It has been said, gentlemen, that I am an enemy of capital, and if you observe what I have just finished saying you will not find a more determined defender than I, *because I know that the defense of businessmen, of industrialists, of merchants is the defense of the State itself* [Emphasis added; 1973a: 157-166].

On the other hand, Perón meant to establish a minimum standard of life for these selfsame masses.

> Those that find themselves under this line [basic life's necessities] are the "submerged" . . . whose privations and poverty affect their physical and spiritual health.

> Those that one finds above this line are the "emerged," those that fortune has favored and who, in many cases, waste the excess to satisfy other excesses.
>
> The task of government in its social policy is to try to assure that no one, or at least the lowest number of workers, finds themselves in the condition of being "submerged" [1973b: 22].[6]

Concerning the small farmer, Perón had another solution: to give the land to those who work it. He envisioned a class of property-owning peasant-farmers. He said:

> The Argentine problem is in the land: Give a farmer a rock in property and he will turn it into a garden; Give a farmer a rented garden, not his own, and he'll return it as a rock [1973b: 24].

Thus, Perón's reactions to the plight of the proletariat and peasant-farmer are well within the capabilities of a modified welfare capitalist system, and his positions do imply a considerable adherence to many of the standard liberal norms: the profit motive, material incentives, puritanism, the potential for individual upward mobility, and the inherent positive features of private property.

Moving to the connected questions of social relations, social conflict, and the alliance of classes, Perón follows a similar course. Here, as has been mentioned earlier in another context, he supports a class alliance between the proletariat and the bourgeoisie which will raise the standards of both proportionally. Perón felt that without interclass agreement on the basic values concerning capitalism, the wealth of the middle and capitalist classes would never be secure. Unless the workers and the weaker elements of the middle class were able to share somewhat in that wealth, the equilibrium would be very tenuous.

Perón's attitude toward the working class is highly paternalistic. In his same speech at the Chamber of Commerce he said:

> If I were the owner of a factory, it wouldn't cost me anything to gain the affection of my workers with some social programs handled with intelligence. Many times it is achieved with a doctor

> who goes to the house of a worker whose son is sick, with a little gift on a particular day; the boss who passes by and slaps his workers on the shoulder and speaks to them once in a while, like we do with our soldiers. So that the workers be more efficient, one has to control them by the heart. Man is more receptive to commands when commands are directed at his heart, not his head. In the same way workers can be managed. It is only necessary that men who have workers at their disposal, reach them by these means, in order to dominate them, to make them true collaborators [1973a: 167].

Perón is quite convinced that the workers' class consciousness as a revolutionary prerequisite can be watered down with a form of wise incrementalism. He perceives the relationship to capital as not necessarily antagonistic because of the worker's basic personal concerns for his family and his children's future.

The guiding role in offering policy palliatives is in the hands of the Secretary of Labor. This assures a peaceful evolution as Argentina undertakes the task of industrialization (Perón, 1973b: 119). Under the strains of industrialization, the state is able, by its skillful tutelage, to reduce any mass revolutionary propensities. By integrating the working class into the industrial rhythm, one gives it a stake in its success while at the same time the social stratification system and the class system remain virtually unaltered.

The tangible benefits for working class accommodation to the existing system were, according to Perón, in the political power to be given the workers' unions in a potential governing coalition. More explicitly, the workers benefited from social policies in areas of social security, health, auxiliary services, housing, working conditions, retirement benefits, protection against firings, equal opportunity for women, minimum wage for each type of work, insurance plans, the creation of labor tribunals to oversee and defend employee and worker prerogatives, maternity law, hours, minimum salary scale for a family, union hotels and resort discounts, and, lastly, the rights to organize under the aegis of a paternal but benign state.

It is in the area of workers' organization into unions that labor received its most lasting benefit during the early Perón years.

Each occupation within industry could have only one union representing the worker. This allowed Perón greater leverage for control, but without question it also gave the mass of workers a more powerful, unified interest in Argentine politics both then and since. It was this reform under Perón that was most jealously prized by the bulk of labor and most thoroughly missed when future governments were to abrogate its provisions.

Lastly, what was Perón's thinking and impact on economic matters, admittedly the area which intuitively least interested him? Nevertheless, it will be remembered, that Perón as Vice-President was named president of the Post-War National Council. This body was organized to plan for Argentine economic and social adjustments in the post-war period. Its meetings, often presided over by Perón himself, commenced in September 1944 and produced at least two important position papers in May and August 1945. The more important contribution was entitled *Regulating the Social Economy*. The second was called *Employment and Unemployment in Argentina.*

The overall objectives of the council were to plan for the impact of the war's end on the Argentine economy and to study the potential and capacity of the Argentine economy to meet this threat. The relative strengths and weaknesses of its public and private sectors were studied in order to project long-range growth possibilities.

The orientation of Perón (1973a: 174-185) toward these tasks was circumscribed by several basic Keynesian economic assumptions: (1) the end of the war will breed certain dislocations in the Argentine economy, but whatever government initiatives are taken, the private sector will continue to play a major, if not dominant, role; (2) the state's major role is to stimulate the private sector to greater productivity; and (3) the government must be responsible for overall economic and social measures predicated on bringing the Argentine society through the transitional years from war to peace.

The more important of the two documents, *Regulating the Social Economy,* makes very important recommendations, particularly in light of subsequent policies under Peronist governments from 1946 to 1955. The recommendations were for full employment, the establishment of a comprehensive system of social security, the maintenance of economic liberties in the private sector, and the delineation with precision of the field of action of the state in the social economy. To achieve these goals, the council advocated the diversification of industry, reeducation of laborers for the new technical requirements of an industrial economy, and the creation of new industries (Vicepresidencia de la Nación, 1945b: 37-39).

Secondary recommendations (Vicepresidencia de La Nación, 1945b: 40-57) included (1) the termination of noncompetitive industries, which needed high tariffs from foreign imports, and replacing them with new competitive ones; (2) massive attempts to raise national income but *not* at the expense of social welfare requirements; (3) reduction and stabilization of prices of basic food and household items; and (4) avoidance of depopulation of the country's interior.

In social terms, a major recommendation of Perón's council was the need to "humanize capital as the supreme aspiration of social justice that the Argentine State wishes to implant" (1945b: 57). It meant creating a minimum level of social conditions for all workers.

The council also recommended the organization of *both* workers and businessmen into entities more easily accessible to governmental leadership and coordination. In the agricultural sector, a five-year plan was recommended which focused on guarding against increasing speculation of underutilized land, self-sufficiency in key agricultural production, aggressive international commercialization of major agricultural products, and improvements in rural housing and education.

The council's tariff recommendations were devised to protect only industries that employ national raw materials and are destined to supply the domestic market and industries that partially or totally process raw materials semiproduced abroad, if they were of prime necessity or essential to national defense. All other enterprises had to depend upon their international and/

or local competitiveness. The rationale for these tariff policies was to protect national industries and to avoid hurting industries that provide major sources of employment.

The paper *Employment and Unemployment in Argentina* (Vicepresidencia de la Nación, 1945a) had two significant recommendations: (1) development of local industries to absorb unemployment due to diminishing exports after World War II and (2) state stimulation of employment through public works, housing starts, and the creation of state and mixed industries. Thus, the council would prove to have had a unique impact on Perón's socioeconomic policies during his first presidency.

## *Conclusion*

Perón's major contribution in this early phase of Argentine Peronism was his ability to mobilize society from a unique vantage point. As the major figure in the administrative, economic, labor, and military hierarchies, he was able to shape the future of his country and affect its norms and values. His move to reorganize the role of the state in economic development, his propensity to have labor recognized, and his ability to gain labor and bourgeoisie acceptance of each other's roles were instrumental achievements in the development of a national capitalist system of some consequence. The direction of post-war Argentina has been charted. The twilight of the liberal political system was at hand, the dual-class social system in which the proletariat class was virtually ignored had been undermined, and an economic system had been launched which had its most fervent reformist champion in the future president, Juan Perón. As the major post-war Argentine figure, Perón was nevertheless dwarfed by the economic and structural realities of Argentine capitalist development and can best be seen within this framework. Within such a context one receives a clearer idea of Perón's later socioeconomic initiatives and retrenchments and his political strategies and tactics. His political skills were considerable, but they were severely conditioned by enduring domestic and international economic forces.

## NOTES

1. In fact, Perón's vision of military preparedness takes him to quite an early liberal conception of the state. He said, "The art of governing and giving laws and regulations is for the purpose of maintaining public tranquillity and security and to preserve order and good habits and customs" (1932: 162).

2. Jorge (1973) found that during the war years, 25,000 business and industrial establishments were founded, many developed by national capital and aimed solely at the growing domestic market.

3. It has been translated many times by many people. The original Spanish name of the group was Grupo Obra de Unificación—GOU.

4. Navarro Gerassi comments: "Perón also counted on the appreciable help of the Catholic Church. On November 16, 1945, a pastoral letter urged Catholics to vote against those parties that promoted the separation of Church and State, lay education, and divorce. Even if the letter simply defined the ecclesiastical position, it attacked without naming the Democratic Union candidates and supported Perón because of his identification with the (1943) regime that had established obligatory religious education" (1968: 189).

5. Speaking in Junín, Buenos Aires, on October 15, 1944, Perón said: "The requirements of the Nation will not be exaggerated individualism, nor will there be State collectivization, which kills the individual and buries him in a prison" (1973a: 214).

6. This speech was delivered to 250,000 business and trade employees.

## REFERENCES

CAMILLO, E., et al. (1973) Acumulación y Centralización en la Industria Argentina. Buenos Aires: Tiempo Contemporaneo.

DIAZ ARAUJO, E. (1970) La Conspiración del 43, El GOU: Una Experiencia Militarista en la Argentina. Mendoza: Universidad Nacional de Cuyo.

GARCIA LUPO, R. (1963) La Rebelión de los Generales. Buenos Aires: Jamcana.

GONZALEZ, E. (1974) Qué Fué y Qué Es el Peronismo. Buenos Aires: Ediciones Pluma.

JORGE, E. (1973) Industria y Concentración Económica. Buenos Aires: Siglo XXI.

LLACH, J. J. (1972) "Intereses económicos dominantes y origenes del Peronismo." Unpublished manuscript.

LUNA, F. (1969) El 45: Crónica de un Año Decisivo. Buenos Aires: Jorge Alvarez.

MURMIS, R. and J. C. PORTANTIERO (1972) Estudios Sobre los Origenes del Peronismo (Vol. 1). Buenos Aires: Siglo XXI.

NAVARRO GERASSI, M. (1968) Los Nacionalistas. Buenos Aires: Jorge Alvarez.

PANAIA, M., et al. (1973) Estudios Sobre los Origenes del Peronismo (Vol. 2). Buenos Aires: Siglo XXI.

PERALTA RAMOS, M. (1972) Etapas de Acumulación y Alianzas de Clases en Argentina. Buenos Aires: Siglo XXI.

PERON, J. D. (1973a) El Pueblo Quiere Saber de Que se Trata. Buenos Aires: Editorial Freeland.

——— (1973b) El Pueblo Ya Sabe de Que se Trata. Buenos Aires: Editorial Freeland.

——— (1963) Tres Revoluciones Militares. Buenos Aires: Editorial Escorpian.
——— (1932) Apuntes de Historia Militar. Buenos Aires: Ediciones de la Reconstrucción.
POTASH, R. (1969) The Army and Politics in Argentina. Stanford: Stanford Univ. Press.
PUIGGROS, R. (1969) El Peronismo: Sus Causas. Buenos Aires: Ediciones Cepe.
VAN HOVE, P. J. (1970) "Working-class crowds and political change in Buenos Aires." PhD. dissertation. Albuquerque: University of New Mexico.
Vicepresidencia de la Nación, Consejo Nacional de Postguerra (1945a) "Occupación y desocupación en la Argentina." Buenos Aires.
——— (1945b) "Ordenamiento económico-social." Buenos Aires.

*Peter Ranis is Associate Professor of Political Science at York College, City University of New York. He is author of* Five Latin American Nations: A Comparative Political Study, *published by Macmillan in 1971, and continues research on both Argentine Peronism and Cuban revolutionary institutions.*

**JOSEPH L. NOGEE**
**JOHN W. SLOAN**
*Department of Political Science*
*University of Houston*
*Central Campus*
*Houston, Texas 77004*

# *ALLENDE'S CHILE AND THE SOVIET UNION*

## *A Policy Lesson for Latin American Nations Seeking Autonomy*

The fall of Salvador Allende's government on September 11, 1973, has given rise to debates over many issues, such as the role of the United States in bringing about the conditions that led to a military coup, the feasibility of a peaceful road toward socialism, and the existence or nonexistence of a democratic and national bourgeoisie in Chile (Valenzuela and Valenzuela, 1975).[1] One issue remains relatively unexplored, however, namely, how much was the Soviet Union willing to aid the Popular Unity (UP) government in its quest for autonomy from the United States? This quest for autonomy was a paramount foreign policy goal because the basic program of Allende's coalition government, approved by the Communist, Socialist, Radical, Social Democratic, Movement for Unitary Popular Action, and Independent Popular Action parties, stated that the basic cause of Chile's poverty and inflation was their intimate economic ties with the United States. The resulting dependence brought about the underdevelopment of Chile and prevented the Chilean bourgeoisie from being truly nationalistic. These dependent ties with the United States would have to be broken for Chile to be capable of autonomous development.

Journal of Interamerican Studies and World Affairs, Vol. 21 No. 3, August 1979 339-368
© 1979 Sage Publications, Inc.

Because the Soviet Union encourages Latin American countries to reduce their economic and political bonds with the United States, Allende believed that Moscow would significantly aid Chile in ending this traditional dependence. Yet, given Russia's limited resources, her global commitments, her expensive experiences in helping Cuba achieve autonomy from the United States, and her aspirations for detente with the United States, the qustion arises as to how much aid the Soviet Union would be willing to extend to countries such as Chile.

To answer that question, we must find some measure of the extensive foreign aid required by the UP government as it attempted to solidify and expand its internal political support and reduce its dependence upon the United States. Then we must examine the relationship between Allende's government and the Soviet Union to see if the Kremlin could or would meet such foreign aid requirements. To measure Chile's foreign aid needs, we shall analyze, first, the consequences of Allende's distributive policies and, second, the costs UP incurred in reducing Chile's dependence upon the United States. Finally, we shall explore Chilean-Soviet relations. We conclude that Allende's road to socialism—and the United States' reactions to it—engendered enormous financial needs that could not be satisfied internally. The Soviet Union was willing to satisfy only a portion of those needs and was not willing to subsidize the Chilean experiment to the same degree it aided the early years of Castro's regime.

## *Allende's Distributive Policies*

Before the coup led by General Augusto Pinochet Ugarte, Chile had been governed by eight successive elected civilian governments. Chile was generally considered to be the most democratic nation in Latin America with institutionalized political parties, a strong bicameral Congress, a directly elected president, a tradition of competitive elections, and well-organized bourgeois, working-class, and peasant interest groups. For decades, however, the economy had experienced economic stagnation and inflation and an overreliance on the export of copper owned, for the most part, by Kennecott and Anaconda. The Christian Democratic leader, Eduardo Frei, elected president over Allende in 1964, had tried to break this impasse but his limited reforms had only succeeded in whetting more appetites than they satisfied. When Allende won a plurality of the vote, 36.3%, in the 1970 presidential election against his Christian Democratic and National Party opponents, he inherited the responsibility for an economy whose middle class, representing about 30% of the 9 million Chileans, had sophisticated consumer tastes and whose lower class, with the exception of a few highly unionized industries such as the copper mines, was poverty-stricken. To satisfy the consumer appetites of the middle class, previous Chilean governments had encouraged virtually every kind of industry, but the relatively small national market meant that most industries after an initial period of growth to satisfy the demand for a new product had stagnated, cut production, raised prices, and demanded governmental protection and subsidies. The consequences of these industrial policies, the stagnation of agricultural production, and the limited growth of the copper industry meant that Chile was stuck in a frustrating, chronic stagflation.

In combating this situation, Allende had four short-term advantages: Chilean industry operating considerably below full capacity; idle manpower; large inventories of consumer goods; and a large reserve of foreign currency. The UP believed that these advantages would provide a cushion to soften the inflationary effect of policies that emphasized the distribution of wealth instead of the accumulation of wealth. The political rationale for this thinking was candidly admitted by the Minister of Economy, Pedro Vuskovic, who stated that the government's "economic policy is subordinate, in its content, shape and form, to the political needs of increasing Popular Unity's support. . . . It is not possible to make deeper changes without broadening the Government's political support, and economic reactivation and income redistribution will provide an impulse to these fundamental changes" (1973: 50).

The UP strategy called for the lower classes to increase their private and social consumption through policies of income redistribution and increased employment. To achieve these goals, the Allende government quickly raised wages, froze prices, took control of the banking system and expanded credit, nationalized the copper industry, increased the pace of land expropriations based on Frei's 1967 agrarian reform law, distributed daily a half liter of milk free to each child under the age of 16, took charge of all legal foreign trade transactions, and developed five alternative procedures for taking over private business (de Vylder, 1976: 142). The economists in Allende's administration predicted that these policies would change the impetus for development from the luxury demands of the wealthy few to the consumption needs of the popular classes. In 1971 Allende's distributive policies met with success: the share of national income received by wage and salary earners rose from 51% to 59%; the gross national product increased by over 8%; industrial production was up 12%; employment dropped from 8% to a record low of 3.8%; 80,000 houses were built; and 48 million liters of milk were distributed to school children (Sigmund, 1976: 121-122). What is even more striking is that in 1971 the inflation for Chile was a relatively modest 22% as against 34% the year before.

However, beneath these statistics were signals of future economic problems. The foreign reserves that Allende inherited from Frei were used up. Gross capital formation declined from 15.7% to 13.3% of the gross domestic product. Total public expenditures rose by 80%, and bank credits, now controlled by the state, increased by more than 200% in one year (de Vylder, 1976: 58, 63). Allende had already "spent" his four short-term advantages. The UP government was now constrained by a shortage of foreign exchange and by its promise to the popular classes that they would not lose the benefits their government had won for them because of inflation. Since most of the unemployed were now working, future growth would have to come from increased investment. But Allende's policies had scared off foreign and private investors, and his distributive policies had placed higher income in the hands of the poor who, because of their consumption needs, had no propensity to save. Here the obstacle to future success was the "economism" of the Chilean working class. Valenzuela and Valenzuela (1976: x-xi) stress that the Chilean labor movement, mobilized to a great extent by the socialist and communist parties, had institutionalized a pattern which combined "an almost exclusive union concern with the pursuit of greater socioeconomic benefits with a multifaceted reliance upon the parties of the left in order to obtain them. The characteristics of the labor movement made it virtually impossible for the UP government not to increase the worker's capacity to consume, which, in the absence of an effective system of rationing and/or dramatic increases in production, contributed to economic dislocations." Allende himself conceded:

> It is not easy to persuade workers who have acquired certain habits to give them up or to explain to them that they are no longer striking against those who exploit but against a government representing their own interests. But we have undertaken an intense effort of political education. Its results have been mixed so far, and this problem remains our Achilles heel. . . . Many Chileans are convinced that a socialist government is supposed to make each citizen a lottery winner [de Vylder, 1976: 228].

Before coming to power, the UP had predicted that the decline in foreign and private investment would be more than compensated for by incorporating all the large, high profit, monopolistic enterprises into the public sector. However, most of the nationalized industries, instead of generating profits, lost money because they tended to keep their prices too low in order to fight inflation, hired too many workers, raised wages, were frequently poorly run by government administrators, had difficulty in getting spare parts from overseas, and were sometimes sabotaged by right-wing elements.

Lacking majority control of Congress, the UP could not pass a law to increase taxes to dampen inflation, and so the executive printed more and more currency to meet its financial obligations. The result of these combined pressures was spiraling inflation. Between July 1972 and July 1973 the Consumer Price Index rose by 320% (Boorstein, 1977: 204). The accelerating rate of inflation increased class tensions and wrecked the political strategy of the UP coalition. Before coming to power Allende had predicted that only foreign capitalists, domestic monopolists, and large landowners had anything to fear from the UP program. In de Vylder's words:

> The strategy behind the whole "Chilean road" to socialism was based on the underlying assumption that it was possible to divide the bourgeoisie into two separate and well-defined parts: one monopolistic sector, which should be fought and expropriated, and one nonmonopolistic sector, which in no way should feel threatened . . . but which instead should and could be won over to the side of the "popular forces" (or at best "neutralized") [1976: 84].

These plans were destroyed. Allende's policies, the inflation, the rhetoric of the extreme left, the illegality of expropriations of industries and commercial establishments, and the propaganda of Chilean conservatives, some of which was sponsored by the CIA, all contributed to the growing cohesion and mobilization of the bourgeoisie against the Allende government. The failure of the UP strategy to appeal to the petty-bourgeoisie is best demonstrated by the behavior of the many small, nonmonopolistic trucking firms in Chile who, fearing nationalization, launched nationwide strikes on October 11, 1972, and July 26, 1973.

In summary, the UP government had initial success by first emphasizing consumption but was not able to shift gears to win the equally necessary battle of production. Political factors prevented Allende from winning this battle internally. The UP controlled only a minority of the seats in each chamber of the Congress, which meant that Allende could not pass a bill to raise taxes and thus reduce inflation and obtain investment funds. Moreover, the UP was constrained by its commitment to winning elections. The UP had obtained control over the presidency through elections, and now they were determined to extend their control over Congress by increasing the welfare of the bulk of the population without imposing any substantive sacrifices. But as three sympathetic observers of the UP point out:

> winning the approval of the majority meant, among other things, maintaining a high level of economic output and satisfaction; and

> no transition to socialism has occurred without short and medium-term dislocations and without threatening those who had previously benefited from the unjust economic system [Farnsworth et al., 1976: 367].

Allende clearly stated that, "The political model towards socialism that my government is applying requires that the socio-economic revolution take place simultaneously with an uninterrupted economic expansion" (de Vylder, 1976: 53). Given the political situation in Chile, the enormous capital necessary to maintain the victories won in the battle of consumption and to finance the new battle of production could not be mobilized internally; it would have to be raised externally.

### *Allende's Quest for Autonomy from the United States*

The ideology of the UP government blamed the economic dependence of Chile upon the United States as the fundamental factor responsible for the nation's poverty, stagnation, inflation, and balance-of-payments difficulties. Now having the responsibility of power, they wanted to reduce this dependence, but slowly; a sudden break—which is often advocated by those out of power—was seen as being too costly. The UP's intentions are reflected in the words of Allende's Director of Planning:

> The old model of export oriented growth is being replaced, and with it the slogan of "export or die." The link between the peripheral Chilean system and central capitalism will no longer be the source of development as in previous models based on the need to increase copper exports. That is to say, it involved exporting more in order to obtain dollars and to import technology, machinery, equipment etc. This does not deny the convenience of maintaining links with the rest of the world, but the emphasis must be on internal dynamic forces [Martner, 1973: 72].

However, since the emphasis of Allende's policies was distributive rather than productive, the cost of reducing Chile's dependence upon the United States was a totally unforeseen increase in external dependence.

In 1970 the economic ties between Chile and the United States were strong. The United States had invested $1.1 billion in Chile, out of an estimated total foreign investment in Chile of $1.7 billion. Most important, Anaconda and Kennecott controlled the production of 80% of Chile's copper, which accounted for almost four-fifths of Chile's foreign exchange earnings. U.S. political support for the previous two governments is reflected in the fact that "between 1962 and 1969 Chile received well over a billion dollars in direct, overt U.S. aid, loans and grants both included. Chile received more aid per capita than any country in the hemisphere. Between 1964 and 1970, $200 to $300 million in short-term lines of credit was continuously available to Chile from private American banks" (U.S. Senate, 1975: 4, 32).

Recognizing that Allende would pose a threat to U.S. interests, the CIA had tried to prevent his coming to power in the elections of 1958, 1964, and 1970. President Nixon and Henry Kissinger attempted to block Allende's induction to the presidency, and when that failed they issued National Security Decision memorandum 93 which was designed to "destabilize" the Chilean economy by cutting off all new bilateral and multilateral aid (U.S. Senate, 1975: 33). Exceptions to these guidelines were made for allowing aid to the Chilean military and Catholic University. The Nixon policy of destabilization had two objectives: "an informal blockade to disrupt the Chilean economy, and assistance and encouragement to Chilean internal opposition to Popular Unity in order to create a mass basis for a military intervention" (O'Brien, 1976: 230).

As for Allende's policy of achieving autonomy from the United States, his first priority was the nationalization of the copper mines, a goal which was quickly achieved when the Chilean Congress unanimously passed an enabling constitutional amendment in July 1971. The UP government decided that because Anaconda and Kennecott had made "excess profits" since 1955, Chile would not pay these companies the book value of their investments. Allende's second policy priority was to negotiate

Chile's foreign debts. In November 1971, Allende declared a moratorium on foreign debt repayments. Since coming to power, the UP government had spent most of the $500 million in foreign exchange the Frei government had left in the treasury, and the total foreign debt had almost doubled to nearly $4 billion, half of which was owed to the United States. Chile was scheduled to pay about $400 million annually to her foreign debtors over the next three years, a figure that represented 37% of anticipated yearly foreign exchange earnings (Farnsworth et al., 1976: 359). In spite of the opposition of the United States, Chile negotiated an agreement in Paris in which her creditors granted her a 70% moratorium on payments due in 1972 and six years of grace for the balance (de Vylder, 1976: 104). No agreements were made with the United States. By 1973 the economic chaos in Chile meant the UP could no longer live up to the Paris agreement and service its foreign debts. Allende called for a new renegotiation, but he was overthrown before a meeting on this matter could take place.

Both friendly and unfriendly critics of the UP have asked why Allende was so severely damaged by what appears to be predictable U.S. policies. Surely, the UP, given its ideology, could not have been surprised that the Nixon administration was determined to use its economic strength to cut off bilateral and multilateral aid. The answer to this question appears to be that the UP miscalculated a number of crucial factors. First, they did not foresee that the United States would cut Chile off from nearly all U.S. short-term bank credits. One study reports that, "when the Allende government came to power, 78.4% of the total short-term credit available to Chile came from the U.S. suppliers and banks" (Farnsworth et al., 1976: 357). This meant the UP had to use cash from the rapidly dwindling supply of foreign reserves to buy such necessities as spare parts and machinery for the newly nationalized copper mines and other industries in Chile. Second, the UP did not anticipate the decline in copper prices from 64 cents a pound in 1970 to 48 cents a pound in 1972. Since each penny decline in the price of copper cost Chile about $15 million a year in foreign exchange, the impact of this price fall was enormous. Chilean officials estimated that the marked fall in prices cost Chile $500 million in foreign exchange in 1971 and 1972. By the time the price rose to 66 cents a pound in 1973, the combination of strikes and economic chaos meant it was too late to save the Allende government. Third, the UP underestimated the effects of its distributive policies on Chile's balance of payments, especially in terms of food imports. Allende had not foreseen that the lower classes would spend a significant portion of their extra income on imported food.

> Chile's degree of self- sufficiency in agricultural products dropped from about 80 percent in 1965-70 to 74 percent in 1971 and 67 percent in 1972. This took place despite a significant rise in Chile's own production and was, then, a . . . reflection of the virtual explosion of demand for foodstuffs (stimulated not only by the wage increases and income redistribution but also by the UP's exchange rate policy which made imported foodstuffs very cheap). In 1973, when domestic production did fall off, the dependence on imports rose further [de Vylder, 1976: 201].

By the end of 1972 about half of export earnings were being used to import agricultural goods.

Fourth, the UP underestimated the costs of diversifying their dependence. The dependence theorists have so emphasized the negative consequences of economic ties with the United States that they create the expectation of rapid and significant benefits for the nation that attains increasing autonomy from the United States. What is generally not understood is the fact that Chile did succeed in reducing its dependence upon the United States but the results were disappointing. For example, U.S. private investments in Chile which had totalled about $1 billion in 1970 were under $70 million by September 1973. The U.S. share of total Chilean imports was reduced from 37% in 1970 to 10% in 1972. Moreover, Allende did manage to circumvent the U.S. blockade by obtaining credits from the Soviet Union, China, several countries of Eastern Europe, Argentina, France, Spain, Mexico, Brazil, Japan, Sweden, Holland, West Germany, Finland, and the International Monetary Fund. Sigmund stressed that, "on August 30, 1973, Allende had more short-term credits available to him ($574 million) than at the time of his election to office ($310 million)" (1974: 336). In a postcoup analysis, one Chilean communist official wrote, "The economic blockade caused much damage. And there can be no doubt that the problems posed by "destabilization" made things easier for the *putschists*, enabling them, among other things, to rely on certain sections of the population. Nonetheless, the blockade was, in the main, foiled" (Cantero, 1977: 51).

But the UP was discouraged to find that most of this aid was tied to purchases in the creditor country and that there was frequently no economical substitute for U.S. machinery, spare parts, and technology. By the end of 1972 "almost one-third of the diesel trucks at Chuquicamata Copper Mine, 30 percent of the privately owned city buses, 21 percent of all taxis, and 33 percent of state-owned buses in Chile could not operate because of the lack of spare parts or tires" (U.S. Senate, 1975: 32). Another study reported that "in 1972, Chile paid cash ($5.5 million) for a Boeing 727, even though the U.S.S.R. made credits available for buying Soviet-made *Ilyushins*. Switching to Soviet made aircraft would have necessitated retraining Chilean crews, setting up expensive new maintenance facilities and stockpiling new parts, all of which Chile wanted to avoid" (Farnsworth et al., 1976: 365). This technological dependence was most obvious in the copper industry, in which 95% of the capital equipment had been made in the United States.

In brief, Allende succeeded in reducing Chile's dependence upon the United States by finding alternative sources of supplies and credits. However, the consequences of this policy were not what the dependence theorists would predict. The results were increasing balance-of-payments problems, accelerating inflation, and continuing reliance upon U.S. technology. The Allende government was as dependent upon outside aid as the preceding Alessandri and Frei regimes. In de Vylder's words, "The overall volume of credits—and imports—rose markedly, and if the amount and commodity composition of Chilean imports nevertheless turned out to be inadequate, it was because of the domestic economic situation which made Chile's import requirements virtually insatiable" (1976: 106). Allende and the Chilean Communist Party (Sandri, 1976: 200) recognized that the impact of the U.S. economic blockade could be softened by increasing the efficiency of domestic production as evidenced by their espousal of the slogan, "Winning the battle of production is crucial for lifting the imperialist siege." However, the battle for production could not be won, so the UP was forced to rely on external sources of help. Only the Soviet Union could have provided the external subsidies necessary to offset the consequences of Allende's policies and U.S. countermeasures.

### *Allende and the Soviet Union*

Allende had good reason to expect support from his Soviet comrades. Cuba illustrated the possibilities of Soviet largesse once the Kremlin decided to make the commitment. Between 1967 and 1972, some $4.14 billion in economic aid had been extended by the Soviet Union to Cuba (Tansky, 1973: 776). When Allende came to power, the Soviet Union was subsidizing the Cuban economy by roughly a half billion dollars a year. Khrushchev made the original commitment to Castro largely because of the strategic value of Cuba to the Soviet Union, but also because of the ideological obligations of proletarian internationalism. The Soviets accepted Cuba as a socialist state, albeit with some reluctance, and Cuba became a member of the socialist camp in 1972.[2] When the Soviets recognized Cuba as a socialist state, Moscow was obliged to guarantee Cuba's survival as a socialist state. To do otherwise might undermine one of the most sacrosanct of communist principles, the irreversibility of socialist construction.

Thus the question of Soviet-Chilean relations was linked with the Kremlin's doctrinal assessment of where in Chile's revolutionary development Allende's government was located. According to Marxist-Leninist theory, Third World nations—i.e., the underdeveloped countries of Asia, Africa, and Latin America—must go through two stages of development before they can achieve socialism. The first is referred to by several names, most commonly "the noncapitalist road of development," or the stage of "national democracy," or sometimes the "antiimperialist" stage. The second is the stage of "socialist construction" or the "building of socialism." Cuba and the peoples' democracies of Europe are considered to be in the second stage. The stage of "noncapitalist development" is not a universal law, but it does constitute the phase through which Soviet leaders see the countries of the Third World moving.

One of the Soviet Union's leading specialists on the Third World, Ulyanovsky, published a comprehensive description of the theory of noncapitalist development in the journal *International Affairs* about a year after Allende's accession to power. Ulyanovsky noted that many nations in Latin America had already attained a middle-level of capitalist development, so that, for them, the stage of noncapitalist development "is taken to mean national-democratic, antiimperialist, antifeudal and antimonopoly transformation and the direct preparation for the transition from the democratic to the socialist stage of the revolution." In this stage, political power is wielded by a coalition of forces including both working class and bourgeois elements. A progressive domestic policy is pursued which involves strengthening the state sector through nationalization of industry. The state gradually takes over running the economy by concentrating in its hands the nation's mineral and fuel resources, the means of communication, the banks, and wholesale internal trade. In foreign policy this stage is characterized by resistance to the economic exploitation of imperialist states and by cooperation with socialist countries.

The question arises: what economic obligations do the socialist countries have to countries in the democratic revolutionary stage of development? Ulyanovsky answered in part this way:

> The material and technical support of the socialist countries furthers the development of the young independent countries and serves them as a socio-political guarantee of the success of their progressive reforms and as a safeguard against the encroachments

> of imperialism. In effect, assistance from the socialist community which actively opposes imperialism, is the foundation of non-capitalist development and the factor making this development possible. [However] assistance from the socialist countries necessarily bears the character of mutually beneficial cooperation, because the resources of one side obviously cannot satisfy the acute and growing requirements of the countries that have taken or are prepared to take the road of non-capitalist development [1971: 28].

In these words the Soviets are ideologically freeing themselves from the obligation to provide sizable economic aid to developing countries. This point was made explicitly in an issue of *New Times,* an authoritative Soviet journal, which rejected the idea that the socialist countries should increase their material assistance to thc developing countries even if that meant lowering their own standards of living. Smith quotes the *New Times*: "Let it bc said in this connection, that to strengthen the economic might of their own country and raise the welfare of its working people is the supreme internationalist duty for communists in power. As for assistance to the Third World, it is rendered on such a scale as will not impede the progress of the socialist community" (1972: 1,136). In brief, the Soviets will engage in "mutually beneficial" relations with Third World nations, but they are not ideologically committed to subsidize the movement toward socialism at the material expense of their own population.

If Chile were in the second stage, the stage of socialist construction, then the wealthier socialist states would have a much greater obligation. So where did Chile fit in the revolutionary picture? Chile and most of Latin America were placed in the first stage which must precede the transition to socialism. In the words of Victor Volsky, editor of the journal *Latinskaia Amerika,*" the road to socialism on the continent of [Latin America] lies basically through a people's democratic revolution" (Smith, 1972: 1,130). Those who have claimed that Latin America is now ready for a full transition to socialism are condemned as radicals, guilty of what Lenin called "left-wing infantilism." The orthodox Soviet position is that a higher level of industrialization and capital accumulation must be attained so that the countries of Latin America are able to stand on their own feet and—not incidentally—so that they will not make exorbitant demands on the Soviet Union. Soviet theorists do not believe that the Cuban model, or one-step leap into socialism, can be repeated in Latin America.

It is thus clear that Moscow never regarded the Allende government as a "socialist" regime requiring an economic or military guarantee of survival. The Kremlin took pains to avoid the kind of ideological ensnarement that Castro imposed upon them. Generally, Soviet references to Allende and socialism were vague. Thus, Leonid Brezhnev, in his address to the 24th Party Congress in March 1971, described the Allende victory as follows:

> Great changes have been taking place in a number of Latin American countries. The victory of the Popular Unity Forces in Chile was a most important event. There, for the first time in the history of the continent, the people have secured, by constitutional means, the installation of a government they want and trust. This has incensed domestic reaction and Yankee imperialism, which seek to deprive the Chilean people of their gains. However, the people of Chile are fully determined to advance along their chosen path [Novosti Press Agency, 1971: 25].

In short, the Kremlin was pleased with the Allende victory, but was not ideologically committed to guarantee the survival of the Popular Unity government in any decisive way.

While Moscow may not have been prepared to underwrite Allende's economic program, the Soviet Union was willing to provide the Popular Unity government with substantial economic assistance. Indeed, until his overthrow in September 1973, Allende was the second largest beneficiary of Soviet aid in Latin America, exceeded by a considerable margin only by Fidel Castro. The exact amount of Soviet aid is uncertain. Data provided by the U.S. Department of State (1976: 23-25) put the total sum from 1971 through 1973 at $183 million, with an additional $115 million from Eastern Europe and $65 million from China.[3] Soviet and Chilean Popular Unity sources claim a total of $620 million from socialist countries—$156.5 million in short-term credits and $463.5 million in project aid and supplier credits—of which the Soviet Union alone gave $260.5 million—$98.5 million in short-term credits and $162 million in economic aid (Theberge, 1974: 77).[4] Some reports claim that Moscow's aid commitments to Allende went as high as $340 million (Sigmund, 1977: 194).[5] Adding to the uncertainty about the amount of aid given is the fact that much of the credit was never utilized.

The parameters of the bulk of Soviet assistance to Allende's government were formalized in the intergovernmental agreements signed in May 1971 and June 1972. At the invitation of the Kremlin, in May 1971 Chilean Foreign Minister Clodomiro Almeyda Medina visited Moscow where a trade, cultural, and technical agreement was signed. A credit of approximately $55 million previously extended to the Frei government, but unused, was renegotiated on more favorable terms. Additional credits were given for Chile to purchase Soviet machinery and equipment. Trade missions were established and a joint Soviet-Chilean trade commission was created to work out some of the details of future trade. The Soviet Union committed itself to the construction of a basic oils plant and a housing construction combine. Chile asked for Soviet assistance in the construction of chemical industrial facilities and aid in the building of a fishing port, both of which Moscow promised to consider. It was agreed on both sides that there would be an expansion of scientific and technical cooperation (Current Digest of the Soviet Press, 1971b: 2).[6]

During 1971, Moscow fleshed out the May agreement with several technical assistance projects. In July, at Chile's request 20 Soviet specialists were sent to work in the copper industry. In August, an agreement on assistance to the fishing industry was signed. This led to a Soviet commitment to aid in the construction of one or more fishing ports and to furnish a number of fishing trawlers and fishing vessels. "The flotilla," said Radio Moscow, "will be lent to Chile on mutually advantageous conditions (USSR and the Third World, 1972d). Equipment which the Soviet Union agreed to supply Chile included road-building machinery, tractors, and electric trains. On the occasion of Allende's first year in office, *Pravda* congratulated the successes of his administration in nationalizing the nation's copper and expropriating the large landed estates (Current Digest of the Soviet Press, 1971a: 16). At the same time, it cautioned against too radical a leap forward. It endorsed the Popular Unity commitment to maintain a mixed economy, state and private, "for a long time to come."

As the Allende government passed into its second year, economic difficulties increased. By early 1972, the Chilean debt had passed the $2 billion mark (New York Times, 1972). In January, a high level Soviet mission visited Chile to consider questions of economic aid and trade. Foreign Minister Almeyda apparently sought Soviet assistance in hard currency to finance badly needed imports from the United States. There is no confirmation that the request was met, though he was promised an additional credit of $50 million (USSR and the Third World, 1972d).

In the spring and summer of 1972, a variety of agreements were negotiated between the Soviet Union and Chile. On March 6, both countries agreed to initiate weekly air flights between Moscow and Santiago. On March 3, a program was signed for Soviet-Chilean exchanges in athletics, science, health, art, radio, television, and films. In June, a Chilean trade delegation headed by socialist party leader C. Altamirano went to Moscow for more aid. Received by Brezhnev himself, Altamirano was promised more credits, particularly for the purchase of machinery and equipment for the copper industry. As with all Soviet credits, these had to be repaid by Chilean exports. In July, an agreement was reached for the Soviet purchase of 130,000 tons of Chilean copper over a three-year period. In addition, the Kremlin agreed to buy $87 million worth of copper products (USSR and the Third World, 1972c). An additional loan of $103 million in short-term credits was reported in November 1972 by Chilean Finance Minister Millas (Sigmund, 1974: 336). This money was presumably released to finance urgent imports, especially food. When Allende visited Moscow in December, economic issues continued to dominate Soviet-Chilean relations. A joint communiqué of December 9, 1972, declared that Moscow would give further aid in building industrial enterprises, in developing power production, and for agriculture and fishing, but no mention was made of new credits.[7]

There is evidence that the Soviet leaders were aware of and concerned about the state of Chile's economy in 1973. Their concern, however, did not move them to supply the massive dose of aid that clearly was necessary. Chile needed untied convertible currency for food and spare parts. When his regime collapsed, Allende was importing about $700 million a year in food alone (Theberge, 1974: 77-78). Soviet aid in 1973 was marginal: building a fishing institute and a fishing port at Colcura, expanding the Topcopilla Electric Plant, and constructing a wheat mill in Valparaiso.

What this survey of Soviet aid to Allende reveals is that Moscow, while willing to give all-out political support and a moderate amount of economic aid, was unprepared to give massive economic aid to save a faltering leftist government and was certainly unwilling to intervene militarily.[8] More than once the Kremlin made it clear to Allende that the responsibility for Chile's economy rested with the Chileans. As the Soviet journal *New Times* commented: "Money for [the Popular Unity] reforms would have to come from the nationalization of the copper industry, banks and foreign companies" (USSR and the Third World, 1971b).

How does one explain Moscow's policy toward the Popular Unity government? Quite clearly the ideological question discussed above was not definitive. If nothing else, the experience with Cuba demonstrated the flexibility Soviet leaders have in establishing ideologically defined historical stages. Castro's revolution could have been defined as "national democratic," instead of socialist, and the Popular Unity government could have been viewed as "constructing socialism," instead of being only antiimperialist.

To understand Soviet policy in Chile, one must begin with a general look at Soviet policies (1) regarding Latin America and (2) regarding economic aid. To begin with, Latin America has never had a high priority for the Kremlin. This can be demonstrated in the figures for all Soviet economic aid to the Third World from 1954, when it began, through 1975. It breaks down by region as follows: Africa—$1,435 million; East Asia—$156 million; Latin America—$602 million; Near East and South Asia—$8,666 million (Cooper, 1976: 194). Latin America received 5% or less of the aid that was given to Pakistan alone. The bulk of Soviet assistance—about 80%—has gone to a narrow band of nations extending from the Mediterranean to China's southwestern borders. Despite year-to-year fluctuations, the general picture has been consistent. Foreign aid is a political-economic instrument that is used in conjunction with other techniques to gain power and influence in strategically vital areas. By and large Latin America has not been a part of the USSR's vital zone militarily or economically. It supplies the Soviet Union with no vital materials or important markets. The Kremlin has tended to recognize the primacy of American interests and power in the continent. Cuba, of course, is an exception. But the Cuban experience may well have reinforced the Kremlin's basic inclinations to move cautiously in Latin America. The missile crisis in 1962, along with the abortive maneuver in 1970 to establish a submarine base at Cienfuegos, demonstrated that the United States might be willing to accept a communist state but not a hostile military base in the Caribbean.

In addition, Soviet economic aid is dispensed more cautiously than it used to be. Nikita Khrushchev, who invented Soviet aid, believed that lavish expenditures, well placed, could exert a powerful political influence. Khrushchev believed that the newly independent countries of the Third World could be moved along the noncapitalist path of development and, incidentally, toward a pro-Soviet posture by such largesse. Developments in the 1960s tended to disprove many of the Khruschevian assumptions about foreign assistance. Soviet influence did not always follow the ruble. Within a period of just a few years, four Third World leaders in whom the Soviet Union had invested large sums of money were overthrown: Ben Bella in Algeria, 1965; Sukarno in Indonesia, 1965; Nkrumah in Ghana, 1966; and Keita in Mali,

1968. Indeed, in the mid-1960s Soviet money in the Third World might have seemed like the kiss of death.

Khrushchev's successors have adopted more conservative foreign aid policies (Cooper, 1976; Valkenier, 1974: 218-224). The practice of making lavish expenditures for largely political purposes is now abandoned. Commitments made by the Brezhnev administration now require careful study and are made for economically viable projects. Furthermore, an increasingly important consideration is the compatibility of aid programs with domestic economic plans. Almost all Soviet aid is tied to the purchase of Soviet equipment or services. Approximately 95% of all aid consists of credits which must be repaid. Thus, there is an integral link between aid and trade. Aid has become in large part an alternative to domestic investment. Prime Minister Kosygin virtually acknowledged as much when he told the 24th Party Congress:

> Our trade and economic cooperation with many [developing nations of Asia, Africa, and Latin America] are entering a stage at which one can begin to speak of stably founded, mutually advantageous economic relations. Our cooperation with them is based on the principles of equality and respect for mutual interests . . . and is acquiring the character of stable distribution of labor. . . . At the same time, by expanding trade with the developing countries, the Soviet Union will gain the opportunity of satisfying more fully the requirements of its own national economy [*Valkenier, 1974: 220*].

This introduces another explanation for the relative Soviet disinterest in Latin America. Because the Soviet Union has little need for Latin America's raw materials and foodstuffs, there is little incentive for trade or aid. Indeed, many of the commodities exported by Latin America are also exported by the USSR. Nor is there a great demand in Latin America for Soviet products. Many potenial importers are put off by the inferiority of Soviet manufactured goods, by the inefficiency of its state bureaucracy, and by high prices. Between 1958 and 1965, the Third World countries paid generally a 15% to 25% higher price for commodities purchased from the Soviet Union than did the Western nations for the same commodities (Theberge, 1974: 19-20). Except for Cuba, the Latin American countries generally enjoy a favorable balance of trade with the Soviet Union, but the level tends to remain low.

Finally, Soviet policy toward Chile reflected some of the special characteristics of Chilean society, the Popular Unity government, and its leader, Salvadore Allende. Moscow realized that Chile was not ready for a full-scale socialist revolution. Chile had a large middle class and a long tradition of bourgeois democratic politics. Sizable elements of Chile's well-developed middle class derived too much benefit from American "imperialism" to permit an assumption of power by the proletariat. Further impeding the revolutionary process in Chile, as viewed by Soviet theorists, was the strength of that segment of the bourgeoisie known as the *comprador*—the middleman between foreign imperialism and native business. This distinctly Latin American type stands not only in opposition to the working class but also to those elements of the nationalistic and patriotic bourgeoisie who, resentful of the domination of Yankee imperialism, are inclined to unite politically with left-wing working class elements. Some Soviet theorists argue that the *comprador* class is so strong in Latin America generally that the transition to socialism there may well take even longer than in more economically backward regions such as Africa (Dinerstein, 1967: 85). In addition, the Chilean military showed no inclination to accept a proletarian dictatorship. It seems very clear that Soviet objectives in Chile, as throughout the continent generally, were not to introduce communism nor to achieve any direct control over the government and people of that country. They were to bring to power an "anti-imperialist" administration so as to reduce United States influence in Chile. The most effective vehicle for that goal is the indigenous radical nationalism which cuts across class lines and is intensely antiforeign and anti-United States (Dinerstein, 1967: 88-89).

This objective dictated relatively cautious and moderate tactics. There could be no monopoly of political power in the hands of a communist party which represented only one class.

Power would have to be shared by a coalition of parties representing a broad spectrum of Chilean opinion, united fundamentally by a nationalistic, anti-Yankee set of impulses. Left-wing adventurism was as much an anathema as right-wing reaction.

The communist party of Chile was well suited for the tactics desired by Moscow. As long ago as the "United Front" days of the 1930s, the Chilean communists had been supporters of the strategy of broad-based political coalitions with limited aims. Chile's communist party was not only one of the strongest and best organized in Latin America but it was also one of the most staunchly pro-Soviet parties. Thus it is not surprising that the Chilean communist party played a major role in the formation of the Popular Unity government. The Soviets were prepared to support Allende's drive for power even though he was one of the founders of the socialist party in the 1930s as a rival to the communists in the struggle for power. In the mid-1960s, a conference of leftists in Santiago, attended by high Soviet officials, endorsed Allende's leadership in a coalition effort to win the presidency.[9]

For many reasons, Allende's election in October 1970 was even preferable to a communist victory. It brought a revolutionary government to power without directly obligating the Soviet Union. Moscow was particularly concerned that a Marxist government in Santiago not produce a violent reaction in the United States. Before Allende's confirmation by the Chilean Congress, the Soviet press maintained a very low key posture toward events in Chile and, even at Allende's inauguration, the Soviet delegation was of a fairly low level (Duncan, 1971: 653-654; Hamburg, 1974: 196).

In reality, Moscow's relations with the Popular Unity government were complex because the circumstances which confronted Chile in the early 1970s were conflicting and contradictory. A major dilemma of the Popular Unity government was how to build a socialist infrastructure without alienating a vital source of capital necessary for that construction. One can see the extent of Allende's dilemma by examining Table 1 which indicates the amount of economic aid provided by the United States to Chile from 1953 to 1973.

TABLE 1
Foreign Aid to Chile from U.S. Government, 1953-1973
(in millions of dollars)

| FISCAL YEARS | TOTAL U.S. ECONOMIC AID |
|---|---|
| 1953-1961 | 339.7 |
| 1962 | 169.8 |
| 1963 | 85.3 |
| 1964 | 127.1 |
| 1965 | 130.4 |
| 1966 | 111.9 |
| 1967 | 260.4 |
| 1968 | 97.1 |
| 1969 | 80.8 |
| 1970 | 29.6 |
| 1971 | 8.6 |
| 1972 | 7.4 |
| 1973 | 3.8 |

SOURCE: U.S. Senate, 1975: 34.

The Soviets, while encouraging Allende's domestic reforms and efforts to extricate the country from the dominance of American capital, realized that Chile would continue to need foreign capital, spare parts from the United States, and Western markets for its copper. During the life of the Popular Unity government, the Chilean communist party constituted one of the more moderate elements in the coalition. Some of its leaders even attempted to encourage friendly relations between Chile and the United States (U.S. House of Representatives, 1977: 364).

Soviet propaganda came down hard against the extremist elements within the Popular Unity coalition who wanted to move faster than Allende. Radio Moscow (USSR and the Third World, 1972b: 483) condemned left-wing elements in Chile "who make the air tremble with pseudo-revolutionary phrases" but who in fact aid the cause of the reactionaries while *Pravda* blasted "provocateurs who hide behind all sorts of ultra-leftist masks" (Current Digest of the Soviet Press, 1971a). On the occasion of Allende's state visit to the Soviet Union in December 1972, Soviet President Podgorny counseled moderation to his guest. "We understand your difficulty and concerns," he said, "but we also know from our own experience that, if a people's power knows how to draw to its side and unite all democratic and genuinely patriotic forces—the working class, the peasantry, the middle classes—and if it is consistent and purposeful in realizing its proclaimed programme no reactionary force will be able to stop the working people from following its chosen role" (USSR and the Third World, 1973b). According to U.S. intelligence sources, while in Moscow Allende was advised by his hosts to negotiate his differences with the United States (U.S. Senate, 1975: 47). The military coup which overthrew the Popular Unity government was, of course, bitterly condemned by the Soviet Union, but in a retrospective analysis, Allende himself did not escape censure. He was accused of failing to heed Soviet advice and of alienating important segments of the population including the middle class.[10]

It is possible that Allende's character and temperament put off the Russians. According to testimony before the House Subcommittee on Inter-American Affairs (U.S. House of Representatives, 1977: 303), some people in Eastern Europe claimed that the Soviets did not regard Allende as sufficiently reliable or as a sufficiently malleable instrument for their purpose. Perhaps the experience of Fidel Castro alerted the Soviets to the risks of dealing with a temperamental Latin. Laurence Birns noted before the House Subcommittee, "Allende was even more unplausible than Castro. After all, he wore elegant suits and he engaged in a variety of bourgeois practices, so they never effectively comprehended Allende and thus were not inclined to make a massive commitment" (U.S. House of Representatives, 1977: 364).

One last thought: The Popular Unity government came to power in a very critical period of Soviet foreign policy. Domestic crises and problems with China were forcing Moscow to re-examine Soviet relations with the major powers. In the fall of 1970, Leonid Brezhnev had decided to undertake a major effort to transform Soviet relations with the United States. As much as anything else, Allende and the Popular Unity government may have become a victim of detente.

## *Conclusion*

Allende's Chile has been called "the Spain of the 1970s—a socialist dream transformed into a fascist nightmare" (Winn, 1976: 7). In this ideologically charged atmosphere, it is difficult to sort out the realities from the polemics and all too easy to be misunderstood. It should be clear that our analysis does *not* blame the Soviet Union for the overthrow of the Allende regime. What we are saying is that Allende's distributive policies and his quest for autonomy from the United States brought about a situation in which Chile unexpectedly found herself more externally dependent than ever. The UP government won the battle of distribution but was not able to shift gears to win the battle of production. To have won this second battle would have required the holding down of consumption, an increase in agricultural production, and increasingly efficient administration of the nationalized industries. None of this was accomplished because Allende was tied to an electoral strategy that imposed only a minimal amount of sacrifice on the majority of the electorate in order not to antagonize their vote. Allende was determined that only the monopolistic sector of the bourgeoisie and foreign investors would be hurt by the UP program. Allende did not foresee that the expansion of domestic demand brought about by his distributive policies would produce shortages, inflation, and the increasing alienation and mobilization of the petit bourgeoisie. These problems were exacerbated by the fall in copper prices, the enormous sums of foreign exchange that had to be used to import food, the increasing foreign debts, and the hostility of the United States government and several multinational corporations. In 1972 and 1973 Chile was burdened by an economy that was neither capitalist nor socialist; it was simply chaotic and suffering from skyrocketing inflation. More escudos were printed in 1972 and 1973 than in all the previous years of the Chilean republic combined. In some ways Allende in power was more of a populist than a socialist.

Allende understandably looked to the Soviet Union for help. But instead of socialist brotherhood, he found that the Soviet Union was interested in "mutually beneficial" economic relations. The Soviets made it clear that they would support Allende's "noncapitalist road of development" but not at the expense of their own working people. Cuba had already taught the Kremlin how expensive and dangerous the construction of socialism can be in Latin America. The Soviets were cautious because Latin America and the geographically remote Chile are not high priority areas in their foreign policy. Moscow's commitment to detente may also have inhibited the Soviet Union from becoming more active in a nation generally conceded to be within the United States' sphere of influence. Finally, the Soviet Union's ideological commitments to Allende's regime were not sufficient to overcome the Kremlin's cautious pragmatism brought about by the facts: the Chilean communist party was a minority party in a minority coalition government headed by a non-communist, the existence of a powerful anti-Marxist military, the ineptness of Allende's economic policies, and the strong possibility that the United States would use its political and economic power to destabilize the UP government. From Allende's perspective it must have been discouraging that Frei's bourgeois government received more help from the United States than the UP government received from the Soviet Union.

The policy lesson that is suggested by the Allende experience is that Latin American nations that aspire to achieve socialism and/or autonomy from the United States cannot expect decisive aid from the Soviet Union. Russia will subsidize a socialist revolution in Latin America to a very limited degree. A socialist regime would need to understand that its revolution would have to depend primarily on *internal* sources.

## NOTES

1. For an excellent review of the literature on Allende's Chile, see Valenzuela and Valenzuela (1975).

2. Cuba, however, is not a member of the Warsaw Pact and did not join Comecon until 1972. For a description of the evolution of Fidel Castro to the cause of communism and his eventual embrace by the Soviet Union, see Dinerstein (1976: 118-183).

3. A distinction must be made between Soviet aid which was promised and assistance delivered. The bulk of Soviet aid to Chile, as in Latin America generally, consisted of credits or commitments of intent to provide goods or services. Not all such credits resulted in a delivery of goods or services. Soviet press sources do not provide a country-by-country breakdown of the economic aid committed and delivered for each year. The most authoritative source in English of data on Soviet aid to the developing countries during the Allende period is U.S. Department of State (1972, 1973, 1974; see also Gouré and Rothenberg, 1975: 140-144). Gouré and Rothenberg, citing the Department of State source, erroneously credit the USSR with offering Allende aid credits totaling $238 million. That figure includes $55 million which was given to the Frei government in 1967. Similarly, they give a figure of $120 million for Eastern European aid to Allende, but $5 million of that sum was given in 1968 (see also U.S. House of Representatives, 1977: 123-235).

4. In addition, Soviet sources report that the Popular Unity government was granted $103 million in short-term credits to finance urgent imports, especially food (Gouré and Rothenberg, 1975: 140).

5. Sigmund cites reports that, at the time of Allende's visit to Moscow in December 1972, Soviet aid totaled $293 million and that on the occasion of that visit additional credits of $47 million were promised.

6. In March 1971 an agreement on scientific and technical cooperation was signed in Santiago, but this concerned primarily an exchange of information between scientific academies (USSR and the Third World, 1971a).

7. Newspaper reports credit the Soviet Union with granting Allende $27 million in medium-term credits for the purchase of wheat, pork, butter, and cotton and a $20 million increase in earlier short-term loans during his Moscow visit (Sigmund, 1977: 194).

8. The Soviet Union gave no military assistance to Chile, but there almost certainly were negotiations for Chilean purchase of arms. In May 1973 General Carlos Prats, Commander in Chief of the Chilean ground forces, made an official visit to Moscow during which he and Soviet Marshall Grechko discussed the possible purchase of Soviet arms and equipment. The Chilean military probably vetoed the idea (USSR and the Third World, 1973a).

9. Among the Soviet leaders were Politburo member A. P. Kirilenko and Central Committee member V. G. Korionov (Jordan, 1971: 334).

10. Allende was also criticized when in power. In 1972 *New Times* published an article by Joaquin Gutierrez, a Cuban journalist, critical of some aspects of Popular Unity

policies. The government's economic experts, Gutierrez wrote, had believed that by redistributing the national wealth and thus increasing the purchasing power of the population, industrialists would make greater investments in the consumer industries. This was not to be, however. "Partly to blame for this was irresponsible left extremist action against medium and small businessmen. Why spend money, the latter thought, to acquire new machinery if it would be expropriated anyway. After 1971 there were less goods to meet the heightened purchasing capacity, inflation spiralled, prices climbed, and such negative side-effects as profiteering erupted. Shortages began to be felt.... The difficulties encountered in supplies are largely responsible for the unsympathetic attitude towards the government to be observed even among women of working-class families" (USSR and the Third World, 1972a).

## REFERENCES

BOORSTEIN, E. (1977) Allende's Chile: An Inside View. New York: International Publishers.

CANTERO, M. (1977) "Chile: the role and character of external factors." World Marxist Rev. 20 (August): 42-53.

COOPER, O. (1976) "Soviet economic aid to the third world." Soviet Economy in a New Perspective, Joint Economic Committee, Congress of the United States, 94th Congress, Second Session.

Current Digest of the Soviet Press (1971a) "Allende's first year in Chile hailed." Volume 23, 44 (November 3): 16, 31.

——— (1971b) "Chile's foreign minister visits Moscow." Volume 23, 22 (June 29): 1-3.

de VYLDER, S. (1976) Allende's Chile: The Political Economy of the Rise and Fall of the Unida Popular. London: Cambridge Univ. Press.

DINERSTEIN, H. (1976) The Making of a Missile Crisis. Baltimore: Johns Hopkins Univ. Press.

——— (1967) "Soviet policy in Latin America." Amer. Pol. Sci. Rev. 61: 80-90.

DUNCAN, R. W. (1971) "Soviet policy in Latin America since Khrushchev." Orbis (summer): 643-669.

FARNSWORTH, E., R. FEINBERG and E. LEENSON (1976) "The invisible blockade: the United States reacts," pp. 338-374 in A. Valenzuela and J. S. Valenzuela (eds.) Chile: Politics and Society. New Brunswick, NJ: Transaction Books.

GOURE, L. and M. ROTHENBERG (1975) Soviet Penetration of Latin America. Coral Gables, FL: Center for Advanced International Studies, Univ. of Miami.

HAMBURG, R. (1974) "The Soviet Union and Latin America," pp. 179-213 in R. Kanet (ed.) The Soviet Union and the Developing Nations. Baltimore: Johns Hopkins Univ. Press.

JORDAN, D. (1971) "Marxism in Chile." Orbis (spring): 315-337.

MARTNER, G. (1973) "The Popular Unity government's efforts in planning," pp. 69-75 in J. ZAMMIT (ed.) The Chilean Road to Socialism. Austin: Univ. of Texas Press.

New York Times (1972) January 27: 5.

Novosti Press Agency (1971) 24th Congress of the Communist Party of the Soviet Union, March 30-April 9. Documents Moscow: Novosti Press Agency Publishing House.

O'BRIEN, P. (1976) "Was the U.S. responsible for the Chilean coup?" pp. 217-244 in P. O'Brien (ed.) Allende's Chile. New York: Praeger.

SANDRI, R. (1976) "Chile: analysis of an experiment and a defeat." Science and Society 40 (summer): 194-219.

SIGMUND, P. E. (1977) The Overthrow of Allende and the Politics of Chile, 1964-1976. Pittsburgh: Univ. of Pittsburgh Press.

——— (1976) "Three views of Allende's Chile," pp. 115-135 in A. Valenzuela and J. Valenzuela (eds.) Chile: Politics and Society. New Brunswick, NJ: Transaction Books.

——— (1974) "The invisible blockade and the overthrow of Allende." Foreign Affairs 52 (January): 322-340.

SMITH, W. S. (1972) "Soviet policy and ideological formulation for Latin America." Orbis XV: 1122-1147.

TANSKY, L. (1973) "Soviet foreign aid: scope, direction, and trends," in Joint Economic Committee, Congress of the United States, 93rd Congress, First Session. Soviet Economic Prospects for the Seventies: June 27: 766-776.

THEBERGE, J. D. (1974) The Soviet Presence in Latin America. New York: Crane, Russak.

ULYANOVSKY, R. (1971) "The 'Third World'—Problems of Socialist Orientation." International Affairs 9 (September): 26-35.

U.S. Department of State (1976) Communist States and Developing Countries: Aid and Trade in 1974. Bureau of Intelligence and Research. Report 298, January 27.

——— (1974) Communist States and Developing Countries: Aid and Trade in 1973. Bureau of Intelligence and Research. INR RS-20, October 19.

——— (1973) Communist States and Developing Countries: Aid and Trade in 1972. Bureau of Intelligence and Research. RECS-10, June 15.

——— (1972) Communist States and Developing Countries: Aid and Trade in 1971. Bureau of Public Affairs, RECS-3, July 10.

U.S. House of Representatives (1977) "The Soviet Union and the Third World: watershed in great power policy?" Report to the Committee on International Relations. 95th Congress, First Session. Washington, DC: U.S. Government Printing Office.

U.S. Senate (1975) Covert Action in Chile: 1963-1973. Staff Report of the Select Committee to Study Governmental Operations with Respect to Intelligence Activities. 94th Congress, First Session. Washington, DC: U.S. Government Printing Office.

USSR and the Third World (1973a) Volume 3, 5: 370.

——— (1973b) Volume 3, 1: 59.

——— (1972a) Volume 2, 10: 622.

——— (1972b) Volume 2, 8: 483.

——— (1972c) Volume 2, 7: 415.

——— (1972d) Volume 2, 2: 133.

——— (1971a) Volume 1, 4: 211.

——— (1971b) Volume 1, 1: 38.

VALENZUELA, A. and S. VALENZUELA [eds.] (1976) Chile: Politics and Society. New Brunswick, NJ: Transaction Books.

——— (1975) "Visions of Chile." Latin American Research Rev. 10, 3: 155-175.

VALKENIER, E. (1974) "Soviet economic relations with the developing nations," pp. 215-236 in R. Kanet (ed.) The Soviet Union and the Developing Nations. Baltimore: Johns Hopkins Univ. Press.

VUSKOVIC, P. (1973) "The economic policy of the Popular Unity Government," pp. 49-57 in J. Zammit (ed.) The Chilean Road to Socialism. Austin: Univ. of Texas Press.
WINN, P. (1976) New York Times Book Rev. May 9: 7.

*Joseph L. Nogee, Professor of Political Science at the University of Houston, is the author of* Soviet Policy Toward International Control of Atomic Energy *and coauthor of* The Politics of Development. *He is currently researching Soviet policy toward nuclear proliferation.*

*John W. Sloan is Associate Professor of Political Science at the University of Houston. He is author of numerous articles on Latin American politics, inter-American relations, and regional integration. He is presently writing a book on comparative public policy in Latin America.*

**DENNIS GILBERT**
*Department of Sociology*
*Hamilton College*
*Clinton, New York 13323*

# *SOCIETY, POLITICS, AND THE PRESS*
## *An Interpretation of the Peruvian Press Reform of 1974*

In the early morning hours of July 27, 1974, the military government of Peru employed riot police to seize control of the country's principal daily newspapers. The government announced that the newspapers were being transferred to independent organizations representative of broad sectors of Peruvian society. Peru's "Revolutionary Government of the Armed Forces," which came to power in 1968, had already surprised students of the Latin American military with a series of radical measures which included an extensive land reform, the expropriation of a number of foreign companies, reorganization of the financial sector, and the creation of a system of worker control for industry. Now President Juan Velasco Alvarado presented the press takeover as an integral part of a fundamental reordering of the existing society along progressive nationalist lines. "The reform responds to the principles of the Peruvian revolution and is in the same line as the revolution's other great transformations. . . . Faithful to its democratic and participatory goals, the revolution transfers [the power of the press] to the social organizations of the nation. . . . The law seeks to create for the first time in Peru an authentically independent press, the expres-

AUTHOR'S NOTE: I wish to thank Terry McCoy, who collaborated on an earlier draft (1974), Steve Morrow, and Bill LeoGrande for their help with this article.

Journal of Interamerican Studies and World Affairs, Vol.21 No. 3, August 1979 369-393
© 1979 Sage Publications, Inc.

sion and reflection of great social sectors and varied tendencies" (Velasco Alvarado, 1974: 52-53).

The government's critics were unconvinced. The move, which was greeted with several nights of occasionally violent demonstrations in Lima's wealthier suburbs, was widely condemned in the Western world. The Inter-American Press Association, speaking for the newspaper publishers of the hemisphere, predictably attacked the moves as "an arrogant abuse of power based mainly on the persuasive use of guns," while the New York *Times* solemnly editorialized that, "The men in uniform who rule Peru by fiat have finally acted to silence the country's only surviving voices of independence and criticism" (New York *Times*, 1974c, 1974d).

This paper attempts to place the 1974 press reform in historical and sociological perspective. An examination of the old press suggests that the implicit premise of the law's critics is incorrect: the Velasco regime did not destroy freedom of the press in Peru; it had never really existed there. The old press had been constrained by the repressive tactics of right-wing governments, by a pattern of ownership by a small circle of wealthy families, and the oligopsonistic power of a few major advertisers. It reflected, in other words, the economic and class arrangements of the Peruvian status quo. On the other hand, the new press, like the government itself, had no clear social base. The promised transfer to representatives of the organized sectors of the corporative society was aborted. The new press—even in the initial period when it displayed disarming vitality and independence—was rooted only in the shifting politics of the regime itself.

## *The Press Under the Old Regime*

Few Peruvian governments in the twentieth century have failed to harass the press. Even the dramatic 1974 seizures were not unprecedented. In September 1919, for instance, *El Comercio* and *La Prensa*, Lima's principal dailies, were attacked by government-orchestrated mobs. At *El Comercio*, the attackers were driven off by gunfire, but they were successful in burning down the publisher's nearby home (Basadre, 1964: viii, 3591; Miró Quesada Sosa, 1945: 289-300). Two years later *La Prensa* was taken over by the government and for nearly a decade it was operated as a semiofficial organ of the regime of Augusto B. Leguía. The succession of dictatorial governments which ruled Peru for most of the period from 1919 to 1956 kept the press under control through devices ranging from closure to deportation or imprisonment of journalists (*La Prensa*, 1973).

If measures against the major dailies seldom assumed such spectacular proportions, it is because they voluntarily stayed within the limits imposed by right-wing regimes with which their conservative publishers were, after all, generally sympathetic. The antiestablishment press was less fortunate, as can be seen in the examples of *Amauta* and *La Tribuna*. The former, 29 issues of which were edited and published from 1926 to 1930, was the intellectual journal of J. L. Mariátegui. It was the principal literary and artistic outlet of the Peruvian left at that time. It was closed once by the government because of its association with Alianza Popular Revolucionaria Americana (APRA) and was closed permanently after it had become specifically the forum for socialized thought. *La Tribuna*, the official organ of the APRA party, was shut down on 13 separate occasions and was, in fact, legally banned during most of the period from 1931 to 1956 (Garguervich, 1972: 44-47; Miró Quesada Laos, 1957: 239). Only after the party allied itself with conservative elements in 1956 was the paper able to publish freely.

There have been brief periods when press freedoms were respected in Peru, such as from 1945 to 1948 during the liberal presidency of José Luis Bustamante (Miró Quesada Laos, 1957). Under the last two civilian governments of Manuel Prado from 1956 to 1962 and Fernando Belaúnde from 1963 to 1968, the press enjoyed freedom from direct restraint. However, Prado's government was never above using such devices as tax audits and pressure on advertisers and advertising agencies to subdue offending publications. Similar tactics were employed, though infrequently, by the Belaúnde government.[1]

The external constraints on Peruvian journalism have by no means been limited to those imposed by governments. In Peru, as elsewhere, the survival of a newspaper is generally dependent on advertising. If a paper cannot sell at least 50% of its space to advertisers, it can exist only with substantial subsidies from a sympathetic source. Two facts stand out about advertising in Lima: (1) advertising revenues are disproportionately distributed among papers and (2) a relatively small number of advertisers buy most of the space. In 1968 *El Comercio* and *La Prensa* received 71% of the advertising paid to 9 Lima newspapers, most of which were in the same circulation class of the two advertising leaders. *La Tribuna* was receiving less than a quarter of 1% of such income. Seven of *La Prensa*'s 256 commercial advertisers provided 50% of its advertising income; at *El Comercio*, 19 of 320 firms accounted for 42% of advertising revenue (Garguervich, 1972: 59-62; Espinosa Urirarte and Osorio, 1971: 260-270).[2]

The effect of such concentration is clearly heavy financial dependence on a small group of major, frequently foreign, companies. For the less favored publications, this means a precarious existence indeed. *La Tribuna* was closed in 1970 because it could not afford to pay its taxes (Alisky, 1976: 662). However, even the advertising leaders are vulnerable, given their dependence on a small number of major companies. The political relevance of this situation was demonstrated by the economic pressures brought to bear against the Miró Quesadas, owners of *El Comercio*, in an effort to force them to give up an editorial campaign against the International Petroleum Company. Certain advertisers and advertising agencies withheld business from *El Comercio* and other media owned by the family. While the Miró Quesadas, an aristocratic clan with a strong sense of family pride, refused to yield to the boycott, they did sustain serious financial losses because of it (Zimmerman, 1968; Garguervich, 1972: 151; Gilbert, 1977: 296-297). Another publisher might have lacked the determination or the financial capacity to resist. If such countercampaigns have been infrequent, it is because dependence on advertisers has created what economists call a "barrier to entry" against potential publishers who are ideologically undependable.[3]

The most serious constraint on press freedom in Peru was neither government repression nor advertiser pressure, but the structure of ownership in the newspaper publishing industry itself. If the notion of freedom of the press has any substantive significance at all, it is the creation of a free marketplace of ideas through the printed word. However, the spectrum of political and economic interests represented by the publishers of the Lima dailies prior to 1968 was so narrow that nothing approaching this liberal ideal was conceivable.[4]

Throughout the twentieth century, newspaper publishing in Peru has been dominated by a small circle of wealthy and powerful families. Consider the five major dailies on the eve of the 1968 revolution.[5] *La Prensa* was run by Pedro Beltrán, member of a planter family, political leader of Peruvian export interests, and holder of key political offices in several conservative regimes. Since the early 1930s, the paper had been the principal organ of coastal planter interests. *El Comercio* belonged to the powerful Miró Quesada family, important actors in Peruvian politics since the turn of the century when several of its members had been leaders of the dominant Civilista Party.

The Prados, who controlled an extensive financial empire centered on the Banco Popular, Peru's second largest bank, were owners of *La Crónica.* On four separate occasions, members of the family had served in the presidency. Even out of office, the Prados were known in Peru as key behind-the-scene political manipulators. *Expreso* was controlled by Manuel Ulloa, member of a prestigious Lima family; Ulloa had made a considerable fortune abroad in association with United States capital. The paper supported the Belaúnde government in which Ulloa served as finance minister. *El Correo* was the head of a chain of papers owned by the fishing magnate Luis Banchero, one of the wealthiest Peruvians of the day. In the 1960s Banchero's recently accumulated fortune was gaining him rapidly expanding political influence (Garguervich, 1972; Espinosa Urirarte and Osorio, 1971; Gilbert, 1977: 184-186, 353-358).

What is particularly striking in the foregoing is the fact that the publishers were deeply involved in the political and economic developments their papers reported and editorialized about. In most cases, the newspaper was not even the primary economic interest of the publishers, although *El Comercio* was a clear exception. Typically it was some combination of political ambition and the need to defend property which led wealthy Peruvians into publishing. The process is well illustrated in the history of *La Prensa*. In the early 1930s, when the Peruvian ruling class faced a severe political and economic crisis, the paper was kept alive through secret subsidies from members of the planter-dominated National Agrarian Society. "We are," wrote one of the planters to his son, "interested in the life of *La Prensa*, its circulation, its political program of order and, above all, service to national agriculture and other influential national interests" (Gilbert, 1977: 186). In 1945 control of the then-moribund paper passed to a group led by Pedro Beltrán, who had the financial backing of his close friends and political associates Augusto and Juan Gildemeister, Peru's wealthiest sugar planters. The reasons behind the decision to purchase *La Prensa* were discussed in an exchange of letters between Beltrán and the Gildemeisters. National political power was about to pass from an upper-class-dominated conservative regime to Bustamante's liberal National Democratic Front government, and Beltrán was afraid that the new government might "move too far to the left." He was particularly disturbed by what the new president was saying "in the economic field.". Beltrán proposed the purchase of a major daily through which, he argued, significant "power" could be exercised over a sensitive political situation (Gilbert, 1977: 354-355).

For the powerful men who controlled the Lima dailies, the political uses of the press were both tactical and strategic. Tactically, the press could be employed to "destabilize" hostile regimes and shore up friendly ones. In 1948, for instance, a stream of attacks on the Bustamente government from *El Comercio* and *La Prensa* contributed to the volatile political atmosphere that led to a military coup. Their subsequent support for the right-wing dictatorship of General Manuel Odría helped the new regime consolidate itself politically (Bustamente y Rivero, 1949; Payne, 1968: 21; Villanueva, 1962: 121-125; Gilbert, 1977: 121-124).

In strategic terms, the press was a vehicle for the propagation of a concept of Peruvian society and politics which tended to legitimize the privileges of the dominant class and delegitimize the efforts of its critics and political enemies. Analysts of Peruvian politics have stressed the importance of Beltrán's efforts through *La Prensa* to justify the laissez-faire political economy which served the major export interests while dismissing developmentalist and socialist alternatives as dangerously impractical (Bourricaud, 1970: 194-202; Jaquette, 1971: 64-67). The virulent campaigns against APRA carried on by *El Comercio* and, until 1956 when a political pact brought APRA into the Peruvian establishment, by the rest of the Lima press may help explain the party's failure to attract a substantial middle-class following outside its principal geographic strongholds.

Velasco Alvarado saw the old press as one of the "bastions of the old traditional power, a political instrument" (1974: 56). The foregoing demonstrates that the press was indeed an essential supporting element in the structure of the established order, a crucial means of class rule. It was this power aspect of the press which made its transformation a fundamental project for the Peruvian revolution.

To argue that the Peruvian press has served upper-class interests is by no means to deny that there have been substantial differences among the papers at certain historical junctures. By far the most significant case in recent years was the protracted debate between Beltrán's *La Prensa* and the Miró Quesadas's *El Comercio* (Miró Quesada Caceres, 1974; Gilbert, 1977: 294-305) over strategies of social and economic development.

While *La Prensa* continued to defend the exporter-oriented laissez-faire political economy with which it had long been identified, *El Comercio* moved from a relatively conservative stance to a liberal modernizing position. *El Comercio* called for the state to take a more active role in planning and promoting economic growth and championed such policies as agrarian reform and nationalist control of foreign investment in the economy. When the Velasco regime appeared in 1968 and began to pursue such policies, it received *El Comercio*'s backing.

The shift was not *El Comercio*'s first important editorial transformation. Early in the century the paper had reflected the politics of the family's younger members, who were identified with the reformist branch of the Civilista Party. However, by the early thirties when the established order faced a serious challenge from the left, the paper retreated to an cxtremely reactionary position. In those years the family published editorials praising Adolph Hitler (a practice later quietly abandoned) and were among the leaders of their class in promoting the repressive right-wing dictatorship of Colonel Luis Sánchez Cerro. From this point until the late 1950s *El Comercio* did not represent a distinctive political alternative among the dailies, except with respect to certain rather specific issues (Gilbert, 1977: 288-294).

It has been argued that *El Comercio* of the 1960s was the organ of a modernizing national industrial bourgeoisie in its struggle with dominant export interests represented by *La Prensa*.[6] The Miró Quesadas had no industrial interests of their own. (They were, in fact, unique among the Lima publishers in having no investments outside the newspaper, with the exception of some other media investments held briefly around 1960.) They were, however, anxious to encourage such a dynamic and politically conscious class of entrepreneurs. But no such class emerged. The smaller industrialists remained disorganized and powerless, overshadowed by a pattern of industrial development dominated by foreign interests. The few families with major industrial interests (often in partnership with foreign capital) such as the Berckemeyers and the Ferreyroses did not come to *El Comercio*'s side in debates over development questions. The paper was, as one of the family's leaders later expressed it, "spokesman for the silent." The Miró Quesadas, aristocrats and intellectuals, did not even typically associate with the entrepreneurs they admired in the abstract. *El Comercio* thus presents a rather striking contrast to *La Prensa* which was so directly linked to the interests it defended.

The considerations which led the Miró Quesadas to shift political ground in the late 1950s were rather idiosyncratic (Gilbert, 1977: 295-305). But in the long run the positions they took and the reasons they did so proved to be less important than the broader class interests that united them with the other publishers. Just as the crisis of the 1930s found them backing reaction, so in the 1970s they joined the opposition to Velasco as his government's politics moved threateningly to the left. (It will be suggested below that *El Comercio*'s defection was one of the factors precipitating the 1974 press reform.)

As the confrontation between *El Comercio* and *La Prensa* suggests, the old press did not speak with a single voice. But if there was debate among the Lima dailies, the range of that debate was fairly narrow and certainly never faithfully expressed the diversity of national political interests and opinion. If *El Comercio* and *La Prensa* came to argue for different patterns of capitalist development, where was the daily partisan of socialist development? If *La Prensa* spoke for planter interests, *La Crónica* for the bankers, and *Correo* for the fishing industry, which paper represented industrial workers, or the peasants, or the inhabitants of Lima's shanty towns? These were precisely the questions that were being raised by the Velasco government and its supporters on the eve of the 1974 press reform.

## *Initiating the Press Reform*

The Velasco government's early relations with the press were generally cordial, but they deteriorated rapidly after the first year as the government demonstrated its inability to brook journalistic criticism of its policies. Initially the regime had the crucial support of *El Comercio*, Lima's most prestigious daily, along with that of *El Correo* and *La Crónica*. Beltrán's *La Prensa* was unfriendly, as was Ulloa's *Expreso*, which had been closely identified with the deposed regime.

At the end of 1969, the military government issued a new press law which, among other things, provided that a publisher could be fined or jailed for libeling a private citizen, public official, or government entity. The strongest provisions related to attacks on the government. The statute, which proved to be an apt instrument for legal harassment of the press, was uniformly denounced in the Lima dailies (Garguervich, 1977: 165-167). The most dramatic application of the law resulted in the removal of Pedro Beltrán as publisher of *La Prensa* under a controversial interpretation of the residency requirements which the legislation imposed on publishers. (Beltrán was replaced by a less able nephew.)

In March 1970 the government expropriated *Expreso* and turned it over to a communist-dominated cooperative of the paper's employees (Garguervich, 1972: 195-226). Under this new arrangement the paper became a staunch supporter of government policy. *Expreso* took a vanguard role, consistently pushing for more radical legislation and attacking conservative and moderate opposition.

After these early press control measures, the regime's attention shifted to *El Comercio*, whose editorialists had recoiled from their early support of the government. The Miró Quesadas now found in the revolution a threat to "fundamental values of Western Christian Civilization." Among those values were "the necessity of private property under law" (*El Comercio*, 1970). The enormous prestige of *El Comercio*, its early identification with the cause of modernization, initial support of the revolution, and the paper's traditional following within the military itself made its defection all the more threatening to certain sectors of the government. In response, *El Comercio* was attacked in public statements of high government officials and through the columns of the government press, most notably *Expreso.* Government sources privately informed the Miró Quesadas that they were running the risk of losing the paper. Beginning in 1971, the Miró Quesadas' enemies in the government helped promote a series of damaging labor conflicts at *El Comercio.*

By 1973, when bitter charges and countercharges were being traded on an almost daily basis by *El Comercio* and its antagonists in the regime, it had become apparent that there was a serious division within the government over the treatment of the paper. This internal controversy reflected division over the direction of the revolution itself as it entered its most radical phase. In August 1973 and again in May 1974, shortly before the promulgation of the press reform measure, rare public debate broke out among members of the cabinet over questions of freedom of expression in general and the situation of *El Comercio*, in particular. The 1974 exchanges culminated in the forced resignation of Navy Minister Luis Vargas Caballero, *El Comercio*'s main defender, along with two other Admirals in the government. The navy was the most conservative sector of the government, and the removal of Vargas despite the unanimous support he received from the navy high command represented a decisive triumph for the left within the government. It also cleared the way for the reorganization of the press (DESCO, 1974: II, 579-590; DESCO, 1975: III, 842, 855; Oiga, 1973).

The manner in which the entire press debate revolved around the Miró Quesadas suggests that their break with the government helped precipitate the reform. However, the legislation did have roots in the sociological critique of the old press, outlined above, and in the emerging ideology of the revolution.

The Velasco regime's ideologues conceptualized the press reform as consonant with their emphasis on finding a Peruvian third way, "Neither capitalist nor communist." Announcing the measure Velasco said, "We reject, therefore, a model of the press based entirely on private property, as well as one based wholly on state property. We defend pluralism in press property forms, with a clear preference for social property modes" (Velasco Alvarado, 1974: 52). The 1974 press decree, D.L. 20680, establishes a distinction between "dailies of national distribution" and other publications. The latter could continue to be published privately. The former were defined as daily newspapers with circulations exceeding 20,000 or encompassing over half the departmental capitals. Such publications were reserved for "entities representative of the organized sectors of the population of the new society," with the exception that the state could have its own organs "designed to explain, disseminate and defend" national policy.

Under the 1974 law, six Lima dailies were expropriated and assigned to specific "organized sectors." *El Comercio* went to rural organizations including the various cooperative enterprises established by the agrarian reform; *La Prensa* to the "labor communities" which had been set up in manufacturing, mining, and the fishing industry; *Correo* to professional organizations such as the colleges of physicians, lawyers, and engineers; *Ojo* to associations of workers in culture and the fine arts; and *Ultima Hora* to organizations in the service sector of the economy. Even *Expreso*, which had earlier been cooperativized, was now expropriated and turned over to educational organizations. *La Crónica* remained in the hands of the government.

The papers were not, however, to be immediately turned over to sector representatives, largely because in several sectors the national organizations which were to receive the dailies still did not exist. The agricultural cooperatives had not, for instance, been united in a single organization. This problem had been considered at some length by the commission which had been quietly set up in early 1974 to consider the press legislation.[7] According to one of the civilian participants, the final determination was made by General Velasco. The press reform would itself be used as an instrument to promote sectoral organization. For the first year the papers would be placed under interim editors appointed by the government. These editors would work closely with sector representatives who had been elected to a "Civil Association" in each paper. At the end of the first year, ownership and control of the papers were to pass to the civil association.

The editors who were appointed in 1974 were generally men of recognized talent and independence, such as Walter Peñalosa of *La Prensa*, a university philosopher and diplomat, and Héctor Cornejo Chávez of *El Comercio*, Christian Democratic leader, former senator, and presidential candidate (Garguervich, 1977). They took their positions with assurances from the government of total independence. However, all were known to be sympathetic to the government and this situation raised questions about the relationship between the new press and the regime which had created it. Velasco had tried to meet this problem head on in his address; he emphasized that the government had avoided nationalizing (*estatización*) the press because it had no intention of creating a press which was "servile, regimented and laudatory." Instead, the government's objective was "a press which was authentically independent, the expression and reflection of great social sectors and diverse tendencies" (Velasco Alvarado, 1974: 52-53). However, the language of the decree itself is somewhat equivocal on this point. The papers should express the "aspirations, necessities, appreciations, criticisms, and points of view of the respective sector. . . . They should encompass, in an attitude which is pluralist and open to dialogue, the ideological viewpoints which *fall within the parameters of the Peruvian Revolution*" (emphasis added).

## *Corporatist and Class Interpretations of the Reform*

The ambiguity evident in this formulation is part of a general lack of clarity concerning the goals of the "participatory" institutions (agrarian cooperatives, labor-management communities, the mobilization agency SINAMOS, and so on) the Peruvian military has set up since 1968. Cotler comments, "The organizations sponsored by the government with the purpose of achieving the 'full participation' of the population are, in fact, designed to encourage the segmentary incorporation of the lower class through the establishment of strong vertical, hierarchical linkages. This results in depolitization of the dominated population" (1975: 76). This viewpoint is common to a significant literature which characterizes the emerging society in Peru as "corporatist" (Middlebrook and Palmer, 1975; Lowenthal, 1975a, 1975b; Malloy, 1974). These authors find in the revolution an emphasis on "top-down" initiatives, a pattern of localization of citizen influence to the workplace or residence, an effort to eliminate mobilization structures (e.g., major unions and political parties) which cannot be directly integrated into the regime, and an affinity for institutions which diffuse class conflict through hierarchical organization along sectoral lines. In short, the insistence on participation provides a facade for a sophisticated form of authoritarian control. The experience of the press reform would appear to reinforce this evaluation.

Although the press reform was justified in terms of the regime's "democratic and participatory" goals (Velasco Alvarado, 1974: 52), the manner in which sectors to be served by individual dailies were defined had, from the outset, the effect of withholding media representation from much of the population. *La Prensa*, for instance, was reserved for the "labor communities," which is to say a privileged minority of workers employed in the most modern industrial, mining, and fishing concerns (Middlebrook and Palmer, 1975: 30). This situation might have been remedied in part by the expedient of assigning one paper to the urban shantytown population, a well-defined sector seemingly worthy of access to the press. On the other hand, certain sectors were so inclusively defined as to render them meaningless in terms of any advocacy function. The educational organizations, which were assigned *Expreso*, formally included all groups concerned with education: instructors, students, and parents from primary school to the universities. The service sector, represented by *Ultima Hora*, encompassed everything from transportation to banking, on both labor and management levels.

Once sectors were defined, the appropriate sector representatives had to be designated. In at least two cases the government opted to deny access to the new press to important organizations which were hostile to the government. The Sole Union of Education Workers of Peru, which represents a majority of Peruvian teachers, was not represented at *Expreso*. In the agrarian sector, the National Peasant Confederation was defined as the only legal representative. This meant that the competing Confederation of Peasants of Peru would have no influence at *El Comercio*.

In the first two years of the reform's operation, relations between the papers and the organizations they were supposed to represent varied considerably. At *El Comercio*, Alex Noriega, a peasant leader and president of the board of the Civil Association, had significant influence on editorial policy in agrarian matters. (For a short time after the resignation of Cornejo Chávez in 1975, he served as acting editor.) Noriega's position was all the more impressive given that the National Peasant Confederation which he represented was demonstrating unanticipated independence of the government. For *La Prensa*, matters were complicated by a struggle between leftist and antileftist factions for control of the National Congress of Industrial Communities which, like the National Peasant Confederation, was proving difficult for the government to control. Walter Peñalosa, the government-appointed editor, worked endlessly to reconcile the two factions while the leftists who controlled the paper's new labor supplement were clearly favoring the left in the controversy. According to sources at *La Prensa*, the leaders of the Civil Association were taken seriously by the editors and interim publisher during the first year. After that they were largely ignored. The situation at *Correo* was, in the words of one journalist there, "a manipulated thing" from the beginning. The reason for this was that most of the conservative professional organizations were hostile to the government and its press reform. Open warfare developed between the association at *Ultima Hora* and the paper's second appointed editor, who severely limited the association's influence.

Thus, although there were early indications (most notably in the important case of *El Comercio*) that the representative press promised by the 1974 legislation might emerge, by late 1976 any pretense that this might happen had been abandoned. A crucial point was reached at the end of the first year when the government went through the motions of transferring the papers to the Civil Associations, as had been planned, but reserved to itself for another year the right to appoint editors. The following year the government again deferred the final devolution of control, only this time indefinitely.

By August 1977, when research for this paper was carried out, there was no evidence whatever that the Civil Associations had any influence on the newspapers. At one of the most important dailies the editor privately commented, "the Civil Association has no duties, no function. . . . They collect their salaries regularly." An older journalist at the same paper said, "They don't come around much any more." At *El Correo*, the association had formally declared itself in suspension. The other associations were reportedly in a similar state. Moreover, public statements of government spokesmen on the future of the press no longer mentioned representation of organized sectors.[8]

In one sense, the failure to carry out the transfer of the papers could be interpreted as evidence confirming the corporatist conception of the revolution outlined above. Having sensed the danger that the new press could not be dependably directed from above, the government was unwilling to relinquish its formal control.

Given the evidence of this failure to create a corporatist press, how is the relationship of the new press to state and society to be understood? One possibility is that the new press, like the old press, is an instrument of class rule, only now mediated through the state. This thesis would assume that a new class had come to power through the revolution. It runs into the difficulty that the regime lacks any clearly discernible social base outside the armed forces and the government itself.

Students of the revolution generally agree that the military government failed to secure a significant lower-class following, despite measures such as the agrarian reform designed to attract such support (Fitzgerald, 1976; Cotler, 1975; Philip, 1976; Kendall, 1974). Behind this failure may be the fears of mass mobilization which corporatist interpretations have stressed. This orientation would seem to place the military on the side of a broad middle-class and upper-class constitutuency which shares such fears, but it hardly suggests a political base. Two recent writers (Lowenthal, 1975b; Fitzgerald, 1976) do find one source of support for the regime among these strata: the technocratic elite which has filled the planning bureaucracies which have grown so rapidly since 1968. However, events immediately after the press takeover indicate that the military are certainly in no position to claim extensive upper-middle and upper-class support. The reaction in Lima's elite suburbs of San Isidro and Miraflores left no doubt about the population's hostility toward the regime. There was violent antigovernment rioting in Miraflores. In San Isidro, an endless stream of cars flowed past the Miró Quesada mansion on Avenida Javier Prado honking to indicate support of the family. In movie theatres, the government's newsreels were greeted with derisive hooting.

Dore, Weeks, and Bollinger have argued in recent articles[9] that the Peruvian revolution represents the triumph of a national industrial bourgeoisie whom the Peruvian military now serves as "loyal agents" (Dore and Weeks, 1977: 4). It does appear that development policy under Velasco was initially predicated on the notion that Peru's traditionally weak industrial bourgeoisie could play a more dynamic entrepreneurial role (Velasco Alvarado, 1974: 127-150; Cotler, 1975; Quijano, 1971). The government attempted to promote industrial expansion by offering exceedingly generous economic incentives to local industrialists. However, the revolution simultaneously frightened investors with labor policies which they perceived as tending toward socialism (Fitzgerald, 1976; Abusada Salah, 1977). In general, the Peruvian bourgeoisie has responded hostilely to the government's major industrial policies (Lowenthal, 1975b; Cotler, 1975; Philip, 1976; Fitzgerald, 1976; DESCO, 1974: I, 192; II, 548, 664). For instance, a survey conducted by the Banco de Credito of 400 companies in 1972 found 76% of them opposed to the key Industrial Community Law.[10] In 1972 the government felt compelled to remove legal recognition from the National Industrial Society, which had turned into a persistent critic (Lowenthal, 1975b: 9). Perhaps the most telling indicator of the attitude of industrialists toward the regime was the drop in private investment in industry, which forced the state to increase its own rate of investment (Fitzgerald, 1976: 62-63). In his speech on the press measure, Velasco noted the failure of the old press to represent "the authentic national entrepreneurs" (Velasco Alvarado, 1974: 56), but the regime's distrust of this group is clearly revealed in the failure to place one of the expropriated newspapers in the hands of the industrial bourgeoisie.

## *The New Press and the Politics of Revolution*

The new press, then, is tied to neither corporate sectors nor a dominant class. Instead, it is rooted in nothing more substantial than the changing politics of the regime itself. This would, in any event, seem to be the most economical explanation of the transformations of the Lima press since July 1974. It is possible to discern two phases in the development of the press in this period, corresponding roughly to the two phases of the revolution itself.

In the initial phase, which lasted through the first year of the reform, the press could be characterized as relatively pluralist, tending toward the left, and unexpectedly independent of the government. Although the papers have been formally assigned to organized social sectors, they tended to fall into the hands of specific political groups. *El Comercio*, for instance, reflected the politics of the party of its new editor, Christian Democratic leader Cornejo Chávez. *Expreso* maintained a leftist line, sympathetic to the communist party (Moscow), which had characterized it since it was cooperativized in 1970. *Correo* followed the "participation" politics associated with Carlos Delgado's group at SINAMOS. *La Prensa* was similar to *Expreso*, though perhaps more diverse in editorial content. *Ultima Hora* leaned toward the conservative group within the regime associated with Fishing Minister General Javier Tantalean Arbulú.

Typically these situations were created by the government-appointed editors, who filled top editorial positions with their political allies. The Lima dailies were suddenly invaded by a small army of intellectuals with strong political convictions (generally leftist) and little or no journalistic experience. One of them later commented, "I am not a professional journalist. My objectives were political . . . to maintain a line within the government."

Given the presence of these ideologues, it could be argued that the new press was, at least implicitly, based on class. This interpretation makes the most sense in connection with *Expreso* and *La Prensa*. Leftists at these papers seem to have developed ties to Moscow-communist sectors of the labor movement. It seems less compelling in the case of those papers which were tied only to cliques within the government. Moreover, an emphasis on the new press's dependence on the politics of the military government would seem to be justified by the pattern which emerged of moving such men in and out of the Lima dailies as political shifts occurred within the regime.[11]

The infusion of these politically motivated intellectuals into the Lima papers produced one of the most interesting periods in the history of Peruvian journalism. The ideological diversity of the papers gave rise to frequent political debates among the papers. The editorialists at *Correo*, for instance, carried on a running exchange with their counterparts at *Expreso* over the role of mass parties in revolutionary change. Although such debates were often arid and totally esoteric to many of the newspapers' readers, they were significant in that they reflected heated discussion within the regime over the direction of the revolution. In fact, as the editor's comment above suggests, the intended audience of the new press was quite frequently the government itself.

The political commitment of the new journalists encouraged investigative journalism aimed at both private enterprise and the government itself. Observers were struck with the independence of the regime demonstrated by the new press. New York *Times* correspondent Marvine Howe wrote in September 1974, "Never before in recent times has the Peruvian press appeared so free, publishing political debates, sharp attacks on the government's press policy and even a campaign charging police torture" (New York *Times*, 1974b). The following month the *Times* sent Marvine Howe's colleague, Jonathan Kendall, to Lima for another look. Kendall noted the papers' strong progovernment bias, but confirmed the earlier assessment, saying, "Under the new directors, papers have published articles, editorials, and letters considerably more critical of the government than the papers published under previous governments. . . . Some articles have included remarks by peasant groups impatient with agrarian reform measures" (New York *Times*, 1974a).

This spirit was lost in the second phase of the history of the new press, which began sometime between July 1975 and March 1976. In this period the government shifted decisively to the right, followed by the press. At the same time the government perfected its mechanism for controlling the newspapers.

This trend to the right was clearest in the purging of the leftist journalists from the papers and the appointment of editors less independent of the government. The first purge came in July 1975, but a more extensive campaign in March 1976 eliminated all evident leftist influence in the newspapers. These ideological housecleanings were justified by government spokesmen with the notion that the papers had been infiltrated by subversives (*infiltrados*). The 1975 law which suspended labor legislation for this purpose (D.L. 21204) is prefaced by the observation that there was an "infiltration of the majority of the papers by persons of ideologies different from the defined ideology of the Revolutionary Government for the purposes different from those which inspired the socialization of the press." These purges took place as the government faced a mounting political and economic crisis which helped precipitate the fall of Velasco in August 1975 and resulted in the removal of the most radically inclined generals from the cabinet (Werlich, 1977; DESCO, 1977).

The government now controls the Lima papers through the Central Information Office, a bureaucracy which has expanded considerably in the second phase of the new press. It holds weekly meetings with the editors of the Lima dailies at which general lines of editorial policy are laid out. While such meetings were held in the first phase, they were less frequent and poorly attended. One first-phase editor indicated that he never participated. Now they are apparently taken quite seriously. In addition to such meetings, the Central Information Office periodically provides editors with memoranda indicating recommended lines of editorial page commentary.

Associated with this office is the Empresa de Servicio de Información, an official news agency which feeds the government's version of national events to the papers. Its presence often places editors in the difficult position of having to reconcile the reporting of their own newsmen with Empresa de Servicio de Información copy. According to the bureau manager of a foreign news agency, the tendency has been for the papers to make increasing use of the service's material, especially for sensitive political events. Recently it has become clear that some papers are rewriting the service's material without indicating the source.

In general, the reformed press in its second phase has become more conservative and less varied, reflecting the transformation of the government it serves. "Some papers," observes a foreign journalist in Lima, "are more likely than others to run ladies in bikinis on the front page. Other than that, they're all the same."

## *Epilogue*

The Peruvian press has moved from domination by an established ruling class to domination by the shifting politics of a military regime, via an abortive corporatist press reform. Could the process come full circle?

In July 1978, the government published a complicated decree providing for the return of the papers to private ownership. Under its provisions, the former owners would be compensated in cash for the 1974 expropriation and offered first rights to purchase 25% of the paper's stock. The employees of each paper would have the opportunity to purchase another 25%. The remaining 50% would be sold on the Lima stock exchange. In an apparent attempt to prevent the reemergence of publishers as powerful political figures, the law prohibits any individual from holding more than 5% of a newspaper's outstanding stock.

The plan quickly floundered. It was rejected by the publishers who insisted on total and direct devolution of their property. It was unattractive to investors because all the dailies, with the exception of *El Comercio*, were in de facto bankruptcy after four years of careless quasi-public management. Political groups initially intrigued by the prospect of obtaining newspapers as propaganda organs were restrained by fears that any transfer of newspaper stock would be subject to legal challenge in the event of a return to civilian rule.

In March 1979, the law remains on the books but is not being applied. The government, struggling with a protracted political and economic crisis, now appears reluctant to allow the press to slip out of its immediate control. In the long run, however, restoration of the old press is likely, especially if the traditional political forces which sustained it continue to reassert themselves in Peru. For the moment, the Lima dailies remain in the limbo created by the failure of the 1974 reform.

## NOTES

1. This and certain other information used in this paper were developed through interviews with journalists and politicians in Lima in 1974 and 1977.

2. These data do not appear to include classified advertising, which might dilute financial dependence somewhat. *El Comercio* is the classified leader.

3. Oddly enough, political pressure from advertisers did not cease with the 1974 reform, although the framers of the new press law anticipated that it would. As long as the papers were in any degree ideologically differentiated and remained unsubsidized, advertisers had a political wedge. These conditions held in the new press's first year of operation when, for reasons which will be explained below, *La Prensa* moved sharply to the left, while *El Comercio* took a relatively conservative stance within the revolution. As a result, *La Prensa* experienced a sharp decline in revenues; *El Comercio* did not.

4. I have identified these families, sometimes called "the oligarchy," and demonstrated their connection with the press (see Gilbert, 1977).

5. For reasons of economy this discussion will not treat the lesser tabloids associated with the major dailies.

6. This position has been most ably developed by Roberto Miró Quesada Caceres (1974), a distant cousin of the newspaper Miró Quesadas. His work is based on an analysis of *El Comercio* editorials.

7. The commision was composed of Fishing Minister Tantalean, Minister of Industry Jiménez de Lucio, Augusto Zimmerman, presidential press secretary, Ismael Frias, Gilberto Escudero, and Héctor Cornejo Chávez (DESCO, 1974: III, 893).

8. See, for example, remarks by General César Vinatea, chief of the government information agency SINADI, in *El Comercio* and other papers on August 4, 1977.

9. See special number of *Latin American Perspectives* on Peru 4 (Summer 1977): No. 14.

10. *Business Latin America*, February 8, 1973, cited in Philip (1976). Philip notes that the large sample size is an indication that many medium-sized companies must have been included.

11. This is not to deny that such shifts themselves were related to underlying class realities.

## REFERENCES

ABUSADA SALAH, R. (1977) "Industrialization policies in Peru, 1970-1976." Presented at National Meetings of LASA, Houston, November 2-5.

ALISKY, M. (1976) "Government-press relations in Peru." Journalism Q. 53: 661-665.

BASADRE, J. (1964) Historia de la República del Perú. Lima: Ediciones Historia.

BOURRICAUD, F. (1970) Power and Society in Contemporary Peru. New York: Praeger.

BUSTAMANTE Y RIVERO, J. (1949) Tres Años de Lucha por la Democracia en el Perú. Buenos Aires: no publisher.

El Comercio (1970) Luis Miró Quesada. Lima: El Comercio.

COTLER, J. (1975) "The new mode of political domination in Peru," pp. 44-78 in A. Lowenthal (ed.) The Peruvian Experiment. Princeton: Princeton Univ. Press.

DESCO (1974, 1975, 1977) Perú: Cronología Política, 1968-1973; 1968-1974; 1975; 1976. 4 volumes. Lima: DESCO.

DORE, E. and J. WEEKS (1977) "Class alliances and class struggle in Peru." Latin American Perspectives 4 (Summer): 4-17.

ESPINOSA URIRARTE, H. and J. OSORIO (1971) "El poder económico en el sector de medios de comunicación de masas," pp. 231-272 in Espinosa et al. (eds.) Dependencia Económica: Caso Peruano. Lima: Centro de Investigaciones Económicas y Sociales de la Universidad Nacional Villareal.

FITZGERALD, E.V.K. (1976) "Perus: the political economy intermediate regime." J. of Latin Amer. Studies 8 (May): 53-71.

GARGUERVICH, J. (1977) Introducción a la Historia de los Medios de Comunicación. Lima: Editorial Horizonte.

——— (1972) Mito y Verdad de los Diarios de Lima. Lima: Editorial Gráfica Labor.

GILBERT, D. (1977) The Oligarchy and the Old Regime in Peru. Latin American Studies Program Dissertation Series 33. Ithaca: Cornell University.

JACQUETTE, J. S. (1971) The Politics of Development in Peru. Latin American Studies Program Dissertation Series 69. Ithaca: Cornell University.

KENDALL, J. (1974) "Peru's junta, after 6 years, still has little support." New York Times, November 8.

LOWENTHAL, A. (1975a) The Peruvian Experiment. Princeton, NJ: Princeton Univ. Press.

——— (1975b) "Peru's ambiguous revolution," pp. 3-43 in A. Lowenthal (ed.) The Peruvian Experiment. Princeton, NJ: Princeton Univ. Press.

MALLOY, J. (1974) "Authoritarian corporatism and mobilization in Peru." Rev. of Politics 36 (January): 52-84.

MIDDLEBROOK, K. and D. S. PALMER (1975) Military Government and Political Development: Lessons from Peru. Beverly Hills, CA: Sage Publications.

MIRO QUESADA CACERES, R. (1974) "Contradicciones al interior de la burguesía peruana a través del análisis de los diarios 'El Comercio' y 'La Prensa,' 1956-1962." B.A. thesis. Lima: Universidad Católica.

MIRO QUESADA LAOS, C. (1957) Historia del Periodismo Peruano. Lima: Librería Internacional del Perú.

MIRO QUESADA SOSA, A. (1945) Don José Antonio Miró Quesada, 1845-1930. Lima: Torres Aguirre, S.A.

New York Times (1974a) October 21.

——— (1974b) September 6.

——— (1974c) August 11.

——— (1974d) July 30.

Oiga [Lima] (1973) August 17.

PAYNE, A. (1968) The Peruvian Coup d'Etat of 1962. Washington, DC: Institute for the Comparative Study of Political Systems.

PHILIP, G. (1976) "The soldier as radical: The Peruvian military government, 1968-1975." J. of Latin Amer. Studies 8 (May): 29-51.

La Prensa (1973) September 23.

QUIJANO, A. (1971) Nationalism and Capitalism in Peru. New York: Monthly Review Press.

VELASCO ALVARADO, J. (1974) Plan Inca. . . . Mensaje a la Nación. Lima: Editorial Inti-Kallaw.

VILLANUEVA, V. (1962) El Militarismo en el Perú. Lima: Empresa Gráfica T. Scheuch.

WERLICH, D. (1977) "The Peruvian revolution in crisis." Current History 72 (February): 61-64; 81-82.

ZIMMERMAN, A. (1968) La Historia Secreta de Petróleo. Lima: Editorial Gráfica Labor.

*Dennis Gilbert is Assistant Professor of Sociology at Hamilton College and currently Visiting Assistant Professor of Sociology at Cornell University. His doctoral dissertation, "The Oligarchy and the Old Regime in Peru," is now being translated for publication in Lima.*

**STEPHEN M. GORMAN**
*Department of Political Science*
*North Texas State University*

# *THE STATE, ELITE, AND EXPORT IN NINETEENTH CENTURY PERU*
## *Toward an Alternative Reinterpretation of Political Change*

In a recent reinterpretation of political change in Peru between independence and World War I, Berg and Weaver (1978) suggest that the rise of guano export beginning in the 1840s led to important changes in socioeconomic relations within the country. In consequence, a centralized and powerful state emerged which asserted its authority over the formerly dominant provincial elites. On this point, Berg and Weaver's analysis is not inconsistent with existing literature on the period (Basadre, 1963; Pike, 1967; Bonilla, 1974).[1] But their argument that by retaining control over guano export the state acquired the financial resources with which to establish its independence from newly emerging urban elites does not seem completely valid. By assigning to the state an autonomy during the middle decades of the century which was never achieved, the authors miss the nexus between government, urban elites, and export which came to dominate political-economic behavior in subsequent generations. In the present discussion, the intention is to place the rise of state power within a broader political and economic context which will allow a better

AUTHOR'S NOTE: I would like to acknowledge the helpful comments made by David Scott Palmer and J. Mark Ruhl on an earlier draft of this paper. Naturally, they hold no responsibility for any errors of fact or interpretation which may remain in this final version.

Journal of Interamerican Studies and World Affairs, Vol. 21 No. 3, August 1979 395-418
© 1979 Sage Publications, Inc.

understanding of the transitionary process between the generally recognized periods of Peruvian history in the nineteenth century.

Three major periods stand out: postindependence, 1824-1845; the Guano Age, 1845-1869; and the consolidation of urban political and economic power, 1869-1919.[2] The first was a period in which no effective central administration existed within the country and power resided in the provinces with the landed aristocracy. Although anarchy prevailed at the national level, it was primarily an intraelite affair while the masses in the provinces were held in check by the age-old technique of the mailed fist. During the second period, the caudillos—who had rotated in control of the presidency during the first period in line with their military fortunes and political backing from one or more of the major provincial power centers (such as Trujillo and Arequipa)—found themselves in control of new wealth with which to assert their independence from provincial patrons. The way in which guano earnings financed the consolidation of state power, however, gave rise to a new urban elite to which the government eventually became captive. The final period involved a transformation in the political organization of the urban elite intended to bring about its direct control of the state. The way in which the urban elite utilized state power to further its economic interests precipitated a war with Chile from 1879 to 1884, followed by a decade of military rule. By 1895, however, the urban elite reassumed control of the state, but under significantly changed economic circumstances brought about by its own abuse of state finances.

It is not difficult to recognize that the Guano Age represented a transitionary period between the earlier system of provincial hegemony and the later system of urban hegemony. But the supposed powerful and independent state that arose during this historical juncture should not be anthropomorphized into an entity acting on its own volition to undermine the foundations of provincial power and establish the prerequisites of an urban elite. Rather, the state was an instrument employed by influential groups to further their particularistic interests—often to the detriment of the interests of other elites or the nation at large. The *manner* in which provincial-based elites acquired access to, and derived benefits from, the state throughout the first period continued along a new axis during the Guano Age and proved to be the decisive factor in the economic collapse which helped configure the postguano society that emerged. Indeed, had the state been powerful and independent during the Guano Age it is doubtful that Peru would have experienced economic collapse, military defeat, and foreign economic penetration in the immediate postguano period.

## *I*

The war for independence in Peru, as in most of the other Spanish colonies, was a political, and not a social, revolution (Burns, 1977: 81-85; Matos Mar, 1969: 30-31). The Viceregal administration apparatus had managed Peru in the interest of the Crown, but otherwise endeavored to maintain a *modus vivendi* with the creole elite which was firmly ensconced in the provinces (Fisher, 1966). The provincial elite had long since codified its propertied and political privileges in the countryside (Stein and Stein, 1970: 30-31; Larson and Bergman, 1969: 31) and enjoyed the status of a landed aristocracy.[3] Its dealings with Lima were primarily concerned with either protecting those privileges from transient threats or obtaining sinecures by which to add liquid fortune to propertied wealth (Bronner, 1977). The demise of the Spanish colonial bureaucracy precipitated a struggle between rival provincial power centers for control of the state apparatus for the purpose of guaranteeing a perpetuation of the status quo against the *excesses* of the liberalism of the urban intelligentsia (Pike, 1967: 53-55). Naturally, control of the state was also desirable because it provided access to patronage, limited as it was in the debilitated state of government during the period.

It was a period of "National Determination" (Basadre, 1963: 77-78) in which the constant state of war between provincial elites seeking to capture Lima and legitimize their power gave rise to the caudillo (Alberti and Sánchez, 1974: 32-33). The social institution of caudillismo provided upward mobility to mestizos who achieved respectability within the so-called white aristocracy in proportion to their military successes. Although individuals from even the highest stratum of the aristocracy played at being caudillos and capturing Lima (for instance, Manuel Vivanco), the arch-type caudillos normally came from a lower station in life.[4] According to Villanueva (1973: 23-31), the typical caudillo was a petty-bourgeois entrepreneur who could afford to finance his own start in the profession of arms, assumed the title of colonel, and then sought a political-military base of operations in one of the provincial centers of the interior. Ramón Castilla is accepted as the most outstanding of the caudillos, and his provincial base of Arequipa during this period was the strongest of the aristocratic provincial centers (Markham, 1892: 338-339; Werlich, 1978: 78-79). Castilla was a first-generation mestizo from a merchant family in Tarapaca. He consolidated his ties in Arequipa with an advantageous marriage, and upon his ascension to power in 1845 provided access to high office for his family and supporters from Arequipa and elsewhere. Only the wealthiest members of the wealthiest provincial centers regularly succeeded in backing successful military campaigns to capture Lima. Hence, as a rule only this upper stratum was transplanted to Lima upon the success of their candidate where, so long as their man held power, they availed themselves of the public treasury (Belaúnde, 1960).

The prevailing attitude was that politics was a business and that, upon capturing the state, a just profit was in order. To the extent that the monetary resources of the state were limited, its legislative and judicial functions were abused to facilitate the acquisition of land and other resources from which wealth and power could be derived (Mariátegui, 1968: 58-59). Simultaneously, a process of intermarriage occurred between the recently transplanted aristocracy—with its status grounded in landed property—and the wealthy merchant families—with their liquid fortunes. Intermarriage across caste lines to wed status with money had been a relatively common practice since early in the colonial period (Bronner, 1977), but the tempo seems to have increased after independence (MacLean y Estenós, 1959; Gilbert,

1977: 25). With new family and business interests in Lima, many of the aristocrats did not return to the provinces on the fall from power of their caudillo, but rather continued on in the capital waiting for the winds of political fortune to shift once more in their favor. With the advent of the Guano Age, the conceptualization of politics as a business did not change, but the stakes increased dramatically and the strategies to participate in the new wealth began a gradual transformation. The axis of interaction between elites and the state shifted slowly in favor of those already residing in Lima over those remaining in the provinces, yet no new institutionalization of the relationship emerged comparable with that of caudillism in the first period. Indeed, caudillism appeared to persist, but with entirely altered consequences.

*II*

Guano is a natural fertilizer formed by bird droppings which have accumulated over centuries on a number of small islands off the southern Peruvian coast. Beginning in the 1840s, roughly parallel with the rise to power of Peru's most prominent nineteenth century soldier-politician, Ramón Castilla, it became a major source of export earnings. The new source of revenues endowed the state under Castilla with patronage power far beyond earlier capabilities (Gilbert, 1977: 27) and thus made possible the consolidation of political power on the basis of expanded employment and public works contracts (Werlich, 1978: 104; Bourricaud et al., 1969: 99; Dobyns and Doughty, 1976: 214). The exploitation of guano was originally begun under an exclusive state concession to a legislative politician who then attracted foreign capital to set the industry in motion (Yepes del Castillo, 1971: 57-58; Esteves, 1971: 105-114). In subsequent years the state grant under which guano was exported underwent numerous revisions with the primary objective of securing a larger state share of earnings (Yepes del Castillo, 1971: 59-61; Mathews, 1972).[5] This was understandable since the early concessions allowed only a very restricted circle of Peruvians (in conjunction with powerful foreign capitalists) to benefit directly from the industry, while others were required to share in the wealth primarily through the intermediation of the state's share of earnings.

According to Berg and Weaver, the state exercised control over the guano industry in such a fashion as to provide itself with

> a source of immense revenues whose collection and expenditure were independent of the action and influence of even the most powerful domestic groups and which was based on an economic activity that did not strengthen domestic economic elites [1978: 73].

Yet, in the first instance, the state itself was in the hands of influential domestic elites who, at first, were content to share in guano earnings indirectly—through the state's percentage—in the form of sinecures and public contracts, not to mention graft (Mariátegui, 1968: 20; Pike, 1967: 113-114; Mathews, 1972: 607). Just as important, influence in government was used to obtain import franchises from which the leading merchant families prospered as the consumption of imported luxuries increased in line with the new prosperity (Gilbert, 1977: 29). Also, as Mathews (1977: 36-39, 56-57) shows, a few landowners reaped sizable profits from guano loading contracts secured from friends in government, while a small class of native speculators became rich by joining with foreign capital in loaning large sums to the government against its projected guano income. As the financial resources of the merchant class increased and its familiarity with foreign markets became more intimate, pressure was exerted on the government to surrender direct control of the guano trade to a consortium of Lima businessmen in 1851. Although this initial arrangement failed for want of capital and managerial skill, by 1862 the industry came under the complete control of the Lima plutocracy (Bonilla, 1974: 42-43). Control of guano would again be lost in 1869, from which Berg and Weaver (1978: 75) conclude that the plutocracy had never exercised considerable influence in the state during this period. But this assessment neglects the reality that the rift that emerged between the state and plutocracy in 1869 signified the end of the urban elite's influence through anachronistic structures and the beginning of its reestablishment along new institutional lines (Mariátegui, 1972: 16-17).

One example of how the emerging urban elite prospered from its influence in government was the consolidation of the national debt in 1850 (Gilbert, 1977: 24; Dobyns and Doughty, 1976: 160; Marett, 1969: 97). Using their influence in government to full advantage, elites presented unsubstantiated or poorly substantiated claims for financial endemnity for losses incurred in assisting the struggle for independence or quelling civil rebellions thereafter. Gilbert (1977: 24-30) points out that this major transfer of state wealth to the private sector enabled the Lima elite to consolidate the capital necessary to eventually take over direct management of the guano industry. As Pike (1967: 100) comments, the consolidation of the internal debt "gave rise to some of the most monumental graft and peculation that Peru had experienced." Cotler (1978: 95-96) observes that the consolidation of the internal debt was intended to insure that "the money received by the government would benefit the dejected [*decaída*] class of national land owners" who would then to be able to "invest in haciendas and mines, promoting employment and social peace." But in practice, it only brought about the "enrichment of a small group of land owners" and the impoverishment of the remainder. This process was instrumental in the formation of the plutocracy (Cotler, 1978: 101).

During the plutocracy's direct, and hence more profitable, control of guano trade, vast amounts of capital were accumulated with which Peru's first national banks were established (Pike, 1967; Dobyns and Doughty, 1976: 151). These financial institutions were capitalized in the early 1860s with the profits from guano and remained under the direct control of the major plutocratic families thereafter (Bourricaud et al., 1969: 30-31). The expanding fortunes of the plutocracy, consolidated within the new banking structures, allowed for a centralized control over an expanding web of economic interests (Bourricaud, 1970: 41-47). Land, in particular, became an especially attractive investment, both because of the social status attached to landed property and because of the new earning opportunities of agro-export brought on by the advent of steamship transport and the California gold rush (Gilbert, 1977: 33; Engelsen, 1977). Coastal estates to the north of Lima were especially attractive investments because of their comparatively easy communications with Lima and their proximity to port facilities (Larson and Bergman, 1969: 355-356; Bourricaud, et al., 1969: 100). Klarén explicitly ties the growth of agro-export on the northern coast during the 1870s to the profits from guano:

> important for the resurgence of coastal Agriculture during this period . . . was the guano boom of the 1840s and 1850s, which for the first time since independence produced large amounts of capital for reinvestment in the agrarian sector. Profits from this "new industry" rapidly soared, *enriching in the process the old creole families and parvenue landholders* of the independence period—many of whom now turned to the problem of reorganizing and revitalizing coastal agriculture [emphasis added; 1973: 4].

The Peruvian-owned banking houses that had been capitalized with guano profits played an important role in this process by extending easy credits to the large sugar and cotton producers of the northern coast (Klarén, 1973: 7).

The finishing touch to the rise of the Lima plutocracy was the founding of exclusivistic social clubs during the 1860s which solidified the new lines of social demarcation and promoted class cohesion within the urban elite (MacLean y Estenós, 1959: 130-137). Cotler (1978: 101) clearly reveals the role of the state in the formation of this dominant class when he observes that "the 'plutocracy' was born thanks to the favors of the military chiefs and developed on the basis of the benefits obtained from the state."[6] It therefore seems hard to sustain the contention that during the Guano Age no new elites were created, nor existing elites strengthened, through government policies.

There are, similarly, qualifications to be made concerning Berg and Weaver's (1978) argument that during the height of the Guano Age the state established its hegemony over the provincial elite. In fact, this was achieved only at the close of the period between 1869 and 1872. Castilla, who rose to power through the institution of caudillism, enhanced the wealth and power of the state, but in no way rendered it immune to the decisive role of competition between provincial elites by which presidential successions were decided. Castilla himself twice resorted to provincial uprisings after his first term as president to overthrow the constitutional authority in Lima (Pike, 1969: 98-119). In 1854 Castilla overthrew President Echenique with strong support from Arequipa and assistance from Ayacucho and Huancayo; and in 1865 Castilla's brother-in-law, General Canseco, joined forces with Colonel Mariano Ignacio Prado in Arequipa to bring down the government of President Pezet (Pike, 1967: 105-120; Gorman, 1977: 50-52). In 1867-1868, during a provincial rebellion against Lima in which Castilla died (of poor health), the elites of Arequipa and Trujillo declared against the central government and installed Colonel José Balta in the presidency (Markham, 1892: 363-365). It would seem clear, then, that the central government remained vulnerable to provincial putschs up to 1868, at which point Balaúnde (1960) tells us that power shifted definitely in favor of Lima. As Henri Favre (Bourricaud et al., 1969: 99) has concluded, *money* succeeded in consolidating *Lima's* control over the country (which is not the same as government control). The Balta administration was the last to be installed in power by provincial rebellions, and itself helped to diminish irreversibly the potency of the provincial elite by the construction of railroads into the interior which penetrated the political-economic isolation on which aristocratic power had reposed (Belaúnde, 1960; Markham, 1892: 366-370). According to Flores-Galindo (1977: 83), however, the impact of the railroads was not entirely negative, since in spite of allowing outside political-economic penetration of the Andean south it also facilitated a consolidation of Arequipa's hegemony *within* this region. But Flores-Galindo (1977: 90-91) likewise emphasizes that Arequipa *did not* participate in the guano earnings of the period, which transformed the agriculture of the central and northern coast where the influx of investment stimulated capitalist production techniques and the adaption of technology. Flores, like Cotler, then, acknowledges a relationship between guano earnings and the growth of the coastal sugar and cotton estates under plutocratic control

The financial malfeasance of governments during the Guano Age included not only mismanagement of guano revenues but also the squandering of the large foreign loans secured by those revenues which were used to support the partonage on which government stability rested (Gilbert, 1977: 29; Cotler, 1978: 93-97). The process terminated in an unserviceable foreign debt. Berg and Weaver (1978: 76) note that the government was caught short by the early 1870s as guano prices fell while the foreign debt continued to rise. But they do not explain how the government arrived in such dire straits after having taken in so much revenue in the previous three decades. As Owens recounts, however:

> Between 1840 and 1867 Peru had sold 7 million tons [of guano] and earned over 218 million soles. Yet the national debt amounted to 45 million soles and the budget had a 15 million deficit. The *guaneros* had made fortunes, while the Government's share had melted away in suppressing revolts and in minor wars [1966: 41].

Balta's solution in 1869 was to rescind the guano concession held by the Lima plutocracy and return it to foreign capitalists in exchange for a partial cancellation of the foreign debt. This represented a frontal attack on the economic base of the Lima elite and signified an *end to* (and not the previous *absence of*) its influence in government. The plutocracy, under the leadership of Manuel Pardo, then organized itself politically in order to restructure its relationship with the state.

Because it required three years after the loss of the guano concession for the plutocracy to capture direct control of the government, Berg and Weaver (1978: 75) conclude that the urban elite did not exercise much influence in the state before 1872. But this neglects the reality that between 1869 and 1872 the elite was not engaged in *establishing* its influence in government, but was moving to *reestablish* its influence. As Larson and Bergman (1969: 259) have observed, the measures which the government was forced to adopt as guano prices began to decline forced the elite to realize that "to defend itself, the newly formed plutocracy needed to *regain* control of the government that *for the first time* was showing some autonomy" (emphasis added). In 1872 the plutocracy brought to a close the era of caudillism and inaugurated a new political system in which political parties and restricted elections became the instruments by which the state was controlled (Villanueva, 1973: 90-97; Basadre, 1963: 119-120; Yepes del Castillo, 1971: 106).

It should be understood that the economic difficulties faced by the government toward the end of the Guano Age arose directly from the plutocracy's parasitic relationship to the state. With the end of prosperity, a wedge was driven between the caudillo and the plutocracy. The caudillo's political amibitions could no longer be reconciled with the financial demands of the plutocracy, forcing both parties into open competition. The struggle proved an unequal one. With increasing regularity throughout the Guano Age, caudillos who had risen to power with the support of the provincial elite shortly came to rely on the plutocracy in Lima to establish their political independence from the interior, Colonel Mariano Ignacio Prado being the most representative of this phenomenon. When the institution of caudillism came into open conflict with the plutocracy, the caudillos discovered too late that the provincial elite no longer constituted an adequate counterweight to the demands of the Lima elite. The very measures (public works, railroads, expanding bureaucracies) which caudillos had sponsored in the interests of the urban elite had undermined the foundations of provincial power. By institutionalizing its power in the Partido Civil, the plutocracy assumed direct control of the state in 1872, discarding the anachronistic traditions of caudillism.

## *III*

During the first period, from 1824 to 1845, the provincial aristocrats had relied on caudillos to promote their interests within the state while controlling the caudillos through social co-optation into their own ranks. During the height of the Guano Age, 1845-1869, the provincial aristocracy continued to promote caudillos, but invariably found that once a soldier-politician established himself in the presidency, he came increasingly under the sway of the Lima plutocracy—which had been formed by the very process of provincial caudillism. But the avarice of the plutocracy debilitated state finances and rendered an open clash between caudillism and its retainers inevitable. Under the leadership of Manuel Pardo, the plutocracy not only organized itself politically for the direct control of the state but also began to formulate a political ideology to legitimize the new regime.

The two principal features of the Civilista program of government were democracy and modernization (Bonilla, 1974: 69-72; Pike, 1969: 127-130). By democracy the elite meant "an aristocratic republic in which the great families would have kept under their tutelage the inert peasant masses, the soldiery and the Lima proletariat" (Bourricaud, 1970: 52). Accordingly, Civilista presidents even after 1895 were not infrequently elected with votes equal to as little as 1.5% of the total population which, Villanueva (1973: 140) tells us, "they called a popular triumph." By this restricted enfranchisement, the state was held as an elitist preserve. "Modernization" within the plutocratic lexicon meant an expansion of export and its supporting infrastructure (ports and railroads) together with the establishment of industries to process export products and increase their prices (Yepes del Castillo, 1971: 95-106). The declining price of guano and the diminishing control over the industry by the plutocracy as a consequence of the foreign debt intensified efforts to develop alternative export industries. Finally, the sine qua non of the plutocratic state was the absolute subordination of the military to civilian authority. This was accomplished not so much through the professionalization of officers as by the emasculation of the army. Troop levels were cut and military budgets reduced, while the Partido Civil assumed control of the paramilitary Guardia Civil which became the armed wing of the plutocratic political organization (Villanueva, 1973: 99-102; Cotler, 1978: 109).

One of the first moves of the plutocracy after regaining control of the state was an attempt to transfer to itself control of the hitherto-neglected nitrate industry, which had been developed by Chilean and British capital. The industry was to be nationalized and turned over to a consortium composed of Manuel Pardo's close associates (Yepes del Castillo, 1971: 117), but the attempt eventually precipitated the War of the Pacific from 1879 to 1883. Peruvian defeat and Chilean occupation of Lima not only destroyed the plutocratic government but also discredited civilian rule which, as opinion had it, was responsible for Peru's low order of military preparedness. In the following decade the military controlled the state and General Andrés Avelíno Cáceres dominated national politics. Although the plutocracy recaptured power in the Revolution of 1895, major economic transformations had occurred as a result of Cáceres's measures to contend with the national debt which had been aggravated by the recent war. In exchange for the cancellation of Peru's foreign debt of over 51 million pounds, Cáceres granted to an association of Peru's creditors far-reaching economic concessions, including control of the national railroad network, free port facilities, annuities from Callao customs, and the right to invest in mining and coastal agriculture (Markham, 1892: 436; Yepes del Castillo, 1971: 136-140; Klarén, 1973: 10-20). Consequently, the plutocracy reassumed control of a country which had been thrown open to foreign economic penetration (Mariátegui, 1968: 22).[7] As such, many of the business advantages of political influence, like the acquisition of state-supported monopolistic control over economic activities, had become diluted.

Still, as far as possible the Lima elite returned to the political formula advocated by Pardo in 1872 (Cotler, 1978: 120). The military was subordinated to civilian authority and measures were enacted to professionalize the officer corps, in preference to destroying the army as an effective force. The export sector was supposedly modernized through investments in ancillary industries, and new export industries were encouraged—including petroleum and rubber (Werlich, 1978: 120-127). But the ability of the plutocracy to protect itself from economic competition through its control of the state had been irretrievably lost, so that foreign capital displaced native capital in much of the coastal agro-export sector (Larson and Bergman, 1969: 355-356; Klarén, 1973: 20-23) and gained nearly exclusive control over newly emerging industries such as petroleum (Pinelo, 1973: 3-25). Foreign control of the central railway network posed a special problem since it facilitated the consolidation of foreign control over mining. The railway's adaptation to the needs of mining impeded utilization of the railroad to transport agricultural goods from the Mantaro valley to the Lima markets, with the result that Australian wheat sold more cheaply in Lima than Mantaro wheat due to railroad tariffs (Miller, 1976: 34-38). The overall effect, nevertheless, was a tremendous expansion in foreign commerce. Between 1895 and 1904 the value of exports increased by almost 190%, while imports increased by over 200% (Yepes del Castillo, 1971: 146). As Thorp and Bertram (1976: 54) point out, this was also a period of industrialization in the country under the leadership of the native elite, thanks principally to the protection offered by a falling exchange rate, import tariffs, and increasing domestic demand. But the return of prosperity did not bring with it a dramatically revitalized state.

The plutocracy institutionalized its hegemony after 1895 in the form of a praetorian republic. The presidency rotated in a more or less orderly fashion among members of the urban elite (Gilbert, 1977: 54; Werlich, 1978: 127-132) while a societal-wide amalgamation of sectoral elites constrained government action through parliamentary politics (Marett, 1969: 129-133). From the very outset, however, the formal structures of authority proved weak and tenuous as they were increasingly challenged by extralegal maneuvers from political cliques too impatient and ambitious to promote their interests through established channels. After 1903 the military was brought back into the political system (Gilbert, 1977: 54; Villanueva, 1973: 140), sometimes as a coconspirator to coerce government, sometimes as an ally of government in resisting coercion. By 1914 the military also became instrumental in protecting the restricted political system from popular pressure (Blanchard, 1975: 268-269), and in return began pressing its own institutional interests on the state (Villanueva, 1973: 140-142). Berg and Weaver (1978: 80) rightly observe that "competing groups . . . brought a new complexity to Peruvian politics" during this period, and inaugurated the contemporary practice of coalition politics. But their explanation for this political transformation requires some modification.

Berg and Weaver (1978: 79) contend that the critical quality of guano export was that it represented an economic enclave with only minimal linkages to other sectors of the society. Hence, the state prospered during the Guano Age from an industry which produced few unsettling social dislocations and did not bring about social mobilization or the formation of new social groups. I have already suggested that, in fact, guano led directly to the rise of the plutocracy and that guano revenues together with foreign loans secured against guano earnings financed the construction of railroads into the interior as well as set in motion the agro-export industry of the northern coast. But aside from these important qualifications, Berg and Weaver are partially correct in arguing that the "enclave"[8] nature of guano export limited its immediate impact on the bulk of the population. The expansion and diversification of export industries after 1895 involved many activities which were not enclaves, but which were instead closely linked with existing social structures and groups, such as rubber collection and mining. Consequently, new and distinct elites emerged in the various export sectors and competed for influence in the state, while new social groups such as urban workers and provincial miners came into existence and confronted government with popular demands (Blanchard, 1975: 253-254). Berg and Weaver see this expansion and diversification of export activity, along with the closer linkage of export industries to national life, as the key to understanding the transformation of the state after the guano era. The society became more integrated and mobilized, the political sphere widened, and competing demands on the state inhibited policy freedom. Nevertheless, they observe:

> Peruvian politics did not preclude a powerful, centralized state, but such a state was possible only so long as it could successfully

> mediate the interests of frequently conflicting groups. The *oncenio* of Augusto Leguía's dictatorship (1919-1930) is a prime example of this process [Berg and Weaver, 1978: 78].

They are, of course, right. But why? If their conclusion were taken to its extreme, it would mean that certain Latin American political systems can contend with competing demands (pluralism?) only by establishing dictatorships. To understand why this statement is uncomfortably close to the truth in the case of Peru requires that we return briefly to a discussion of the formative influence of guano on the Lima plutocracy.

## *IV*

The plutocracy was nurtured by concessionary state policies which allowed the Lima elite to transform the earnings of an export enclave into privately controlled financial institutions. These institutions in turn functioned as the core of expanding investment activities in coastal agriculture, mining, and other export-related activities (Gilbert, 1977; Klarén, 1973). When the interests of the elite came into conflict with the institution of caudillism through which the state had been controlled, a new political formula was elaborated between 1869 and 1892. The new regime resembled a democracy only in its more overt features: party politics, civilian leaders, and supposedly open elections. Meaningful access to government remained, nevertheless, highly restricted (Blanchard, 1977: 252). The intimate relationship between political influence and economic success persisted, even after 1895, so that access to government policy making remained the primary means for minimizing the risk taking normally associated with entrepreneurship. But the multiplication of sectoral elites after 1895 engaged in heterogeneous industries demanding particularistic policies to guarantee their success began to overtax the patronage resources of the state. When the appearance of popular pressures was added to this intraelite competition in 1912 with the election of President Billinghurst, the democratic facade began to disintegrate.

Thus, the weakness of the state after the Guano Age resolves itself into the weakness of the democratic system on which it reposed. Naturally, there is nothing inherent in a restricted democracy which precludes an adept and viable elite from protecting and promoting its own interests over those of the wider society. Mexico demonstrates quite clearly how the careful manipulation of political rules can stabilize a society of vast income inequality and diverse economic interests. But it requires unique talents on the part of elites which were lacking in the plutocracy between 1895 and 1919. The plutocracy under the leadership of Manuel Pardo inaugurated a democratic regime at a time in Peruvian history when other social groups were not in a position to avail themselves of its opportunities. Put another way, a grand bourgeoisie emerged as the dominant class in a country "still predominantly precapitalist" in its economic and political relations (Bollinger, 1977: 32). Adherence to the new rules was, in consequence, relatively cost free. Later, the multiplication and diversification of export activities factionalized the elite, and newly integrated social groups began to appropriate the rules of the system to promote popular demands (Blanchard, 1977: 261-263). The aptitudes and attitudes of export elites which had been molded in an earlier and less competitive era handicapped the plutocracy's efforts to manipulate the system to its own advantage.

It is helpful to conceptualize the plutocracy during the late Guano Age as a proto-bourgeoisie. On the surface, its members promoted political-economic programs supportive of a modern urban-industrial society and elaborated a somewhat progressive political reorganization of the state (Bollinger, 1977: 33-34). But because the economic base of the plutocracy was an export enclave and because economic success depended ultimately on the favoritism of the state, the proto-bourgeoisie never acquired the skills for dealing with labor on any large scale or dealing effectively with a state less than completely compliant with its wishes. In short, the proto-bourgeoisie emerged without acquiring the aptitudes which would be demanded by the very socio-economic system it set out to achieve in 1872 and which it finally established in 1895. The export-oriented economy and praetorian political system advocated by Pardo were predicated on conditions which changed immensely with the decline of guano, the loss of nitrate deposits to Chile, and the major foreign economic penetrations made possible by the Grace Contract of 1889 which retired the foreign debt. The plutocracy had learned to depend on state concessions and export industries and continued to rely on this basic formula of success after 1895 even when it began to produce dangerous contradictions. The scramble for alternative export industries to replace those which had declined or been lost did not restrict itself to enclave activities. The growth of export-related industries in urban centers further accentuated the new tendency of export activity to mobilize formerly marginal sectors of the population, who in turn entered the political system as competitors. It then became essential for the plutocracy to make effective use of the political party, which it had introduced, as an instrument to adjust interests within its own ranks and recruit and control new elements within the polity. It failed absolutely in this regard and became increasingly disadvantaged in its access to the state on whose policies it remained critically dependent for its economic well-being. The inability of the plutocracy to formalize its power in the party, together with its inability or unwillingness to reduce its dependency on the state, made even the restricted democracy of the period threatening.

It needs to be stressed that the interpretation offered here does not assume that the underlying ill of post-guano Peruvian society derived from the failure of the national bourgeoisie to realize its historical role within the nation's development. Such arguments are vague in identifying causal relationships and presume a deterministic course of social evolution which expects a particular class to arise at a given historical juncture and behave in a predetermined fashion (Bollinger, 1977: 36). On the contrary, I have identified specific relationships between a nascent bourgeoisie and the state created by caudillism which transformed guano wealth into the financial foundations of a hegemonic class. The so-called contradictions of this class are given a precise content: The overextension of state finances brought about by the system of patronage that joined the caudillos to the urban elite destroyed the basis of cooperation between the two groups and precipitated the direct ascendency of the plutocracy in 1872.

Berg and Weaver (1978) correctly emphasize the enclave nature of guano export during this period, but mistakenly see the state as the primary beneficiacy of the industry. When it is recognized that the plutocracy was the primary recipient of guano wealth, then their arguments respecting the special impact of guano revenues take on a different meaning. The apparent stability and independence of the state during the guano period stemmed from the unity of the plutocracy, which was able to aggregate its interests on the common denominator of a dominant enclave industry and present the government with coherent and manageable demands.

From 1895 to 1919 the economic activities of the plutocracy undermined the cohesion of export elites and created new political actors within the system. To counteract the centrifugal forces within its own class and counterbalance the potential power of popular classes, the plutocracy needed to strengthen the political party as its axis of influence in the state. Instead, increasing reliance was placed on the military, first as the arbiter between conflicting elite factions, then between the elitist state and the larger public (Villanueva, 1973: 139-149). Unable to prevent the election of the reformist Billinghurst to the presidency in 1912, the plutocracy began its retreat from the democratic system which culminated in the August B. Leguía dictatorship from 1919 to 1930.[9] In place of an upper-class political alliance centered in a modern political party which could control the state, there emerged an informal and amorphous societal-wide coalition of sectoral elites united in a common desire: the exclusion of popular influence from state authority. The amalgamation of diverse and heterogeneous elites included the core of the Civilista plutocracy, new export elites, high-ranking military officers, and the stronger remnants of the provincial aristocracy. Far from possessing the unity of interests requisite to forge a political party capable of capturing and holding state power in an open political system, the oligarchy that emerged from this loose confederation of elites limited itself to passively supporting strongmen who could retain power. The minimum demands of the oligarchy from such autocratic governments was a tacit recognition that sectoral elites would be allowed vetos over state actions affecting their special interests (Bourque, 1971).

The twentieth century Peruvian state became weak because the leading economic class could not formalize its power in the political party and take firm control of the state. Yet, by forming a wider social alliance with other elites, the plutocracy was able to prevent the representatives of emerging classes from acquiring direction of the state. The oligarchy that was forged by the degeneration of the proto-bourgeoisie (plutocracy) was too weak to give direction to government but strong enough to prevent other social classes from providing that leadership (Bourque, 1971; Gorman, 1977). The weakness of contemporary Peruvian politics can be understood in terms of the noncompetitive conditions under which democracy was first introduced and the betrayal of democracy by the elite once political-economic competition from below threatened elite control of government. The shift from a single dominant enclave export industry to a society of multiple export industries closely associated with the internal economy greatly contributed to the social mobilization which allowed lower classes to penetrate the praetorian political system.

## NOTES

1. Other important but unconsulted works include Hunt (1973), Caravedo Molinari (1976), Blanchard (1975), Bertram (1974), and Thorp (1974). Other works by Blanchard (1977) and Thorp and Bertram (1974) which draw upon the above titles have been consulted and included in the present paper.

2. Periodization in history is never precise. The dates chosen here reflect an emphasis on political rather than economic events: 1845 marks the ascendency of Ramón Castilla to the presidency, 1869 marks the political split between native guaneros and the presidency of Colonel Balta. The Guano Age proper extended from 1840 to 1889, marking the dates of its earliest commercial development and the eventual transfer of the industry to foreign creditors a half century later.

3. Three generic terms are employed in this work to designate different configurations of elites in Peruvian history. All of them have been used by Peruvian historians

and intellectuals, but not in the precise manner adopted here. By "aristocracy" is meant a provincially based landed elite whose primary economic interests were associated with the hacienda; by "plutocracy," an essentially urban elite, sharing many social customs and closely integrated through private clubs, intermarriage, and financial-commercial economic interests, by "oligarchy," a loose societal-wide confederation of heterogeneous elites with diverse social settings and economic interests, unified only through their common desire to keep the lower classes from achieving political power and threatening established economic interests.

4. It is generally accepted that the majority of successful caudillos were mestizos of mixed Spanish-Indian blood. In fact, a basis may exist for disputing this assumption. A review of the caudillos who became presidents between 1824 and 1865 indicates that perhaps half were from prominent families and were as close as upper-class Peruvians of the period came to being "pure" whites. I hope to pursue this question more fully in a manuscript I am now working on, *The Rotation of Elites in Peru: From Creole Liberals to Revolutionary Corporatists.*

5. Mathews shows that the Peruvian government improved its bargaining position with foreign merchants involved in the guano industry in each of three successive contracts between 1840 and 1842, pointing to a relatively strong state vis-à-vis *external* forces. He does not demonstrate a strengthening of the state's position in relation to domestic elites, however. On the contrary, Mathews (1972: 601-607) makes repeated references to the influential role of native elites in contract negotiations, the liberal use of bribes, and the participation of Peruvians (in conjunction with foreign capital) in the guano concessions. Particularly supportive of the position presented in the present article is Mathews's (1972: 260) observation that "by being able to raise with facility such large sums of money in a period when their grasp of the levers of power was unusually uncertain, when they were obliged through expediency to give financial and other rewards to their supporters, Peruvian Governments dissipated the funds they acquired" from guano.

6. The fact that guano wealth created a national financial network in the hands of a small elite had ramifications for subsequent efforts at industrialization. As Thorp and Bertram (1976: 62) have noted: "Some of the most influential industrialists of the time [turn of the century] were also export producers, import merchants, or leading members of the financial community, with direct access to the inner councils of government, but with no strong reason to press for policies favoring industry against other sectors when they could shift their interests from sector to sector. The well-developed banking system provided a channel through which resources from one sector could be readily transferred to other sectors when profit opportunities offered." Since it was guano money that capitalized the dominant Peruvian banks in the 1860s, this is yet another direct impact of the guano industry.

7. In truth, only a fraction of the plutocracy formed by guano export survived the War of the Pacific (in which many of the younger generation died in the defense of Lima) and the subsequent years of economic stagnation. Thus, the plutocracy was a numerically diminished class when it returned to power in 1895, but those that remained were extremely wealthy and set in motion the political-economic associations with other social groups which eventually gave rise to the oligarchy.

8. Mathews states that "The inadequacy of the guano export sector as a stimulating force within the Peruvian economy, it must be stressed, lies not in the fact that it was an enclave but in the crudity of its organisation . . . far too much of the income generated by guano was directed into Peruvian hands for the classic enclave model to be applicable" (1977: 57). Nevertheless, it is possible to accept Berg and Weaver's central argument,

specifically, that the industry did not directly affect the bulk of the population. Of course the counterthesis presented here is that it did affect the country greatly indirectly through the formation of the plutocracy.

9. Blanchard (1977: 256, 269) notes the inability of the elites' political parties to compete with Billinghurst and their resulting complicity in the conspiracy to overthrow him with military support. This is consistent with my interpretation of elitist political parties presented in the present work. On the nature of the Leguía regime, however, Blanchard (1977: 272) suggests that "Leguía wanted to destroy the power of the old oligarchy." The opposing view presented here is that he endeavored to *restructure* the elite system to relieve the oligarchy of political pressures to which it was unequal. This conclusion is supported by Villanueva (1973) and Bains (1972). As Pike states, Leguía tried to "modify" the system by fostering an assertive middle class, but "What actually occurred was that part of the middle sector, rather than acting as a countervailing power to the traditional aristocracy, joined with it in supporting Leguía" (1967: 218).

## REFERENCES

ALBERTI, G. and R. SANCHEZ (1974) Poder y conflicto social en el valle del Mantaro. Lima: Instituto de Estudios Peruanos.

BAINS, J. (1972) Revolution in Peru: Mariátegui and the Myth. Tuscaloosa: Univ. of Alabama Press.

BASADRE, J. (1963) Historia de la Republica del Peru (Vol. 3). Lima: Ediciones Historia.

BELAUNDE, V. A. (1960) Arequipa de mi infancia. Lima: Imprenta Lumen.

BERG, R. H. and F. S. WEAVER (1978) "Toward a reinterpretation of political change in Peru during the first century of independence." J. of Interamerican Studies and World Affairs 20: 69-83.

BERTRAM, G. (1974) Development Problems in an Export Economy: A Study of Domestic Capitalists, Foreign Firms and Government in Peru, 1919-1930. Ph.D. dissertation. Oxford: Oxford Univ. Press.

BLANCHARD, P. (1977) "Populist precursor: Guillermo Billinghurst." J. of Latin American Studies 9: 251-273.

——— (1975) The Peruvian Working Class Movement, 1883-1919. Ph.D. dissertation. London: Univ. of London.

BOLLINGER, W. (1977) "The bourgeois revolution in Peru: conception of Peruvian history." Latin American Perspectives 4: 18-65.

BONILLA, G. (1974) Guano y burguesía en el Perú. Lima: Instituto de Estudios Peruanos.

BOURQUE, S. C. (1971) "Cholification and the campesino: a study of three Peruvian peasant organizations in the process of social change." Ph.D. dissertation. Ithaca: Cornell Univ. Dissertation Series.

BOURRICAUD, F. (1970) Power and Society in Peru. New York: Praeger.

——— (1969) La oligarquía en el Perú. Lima: Moncloa-Campodonico.

BRONNER, F. (1977) "Peruvian encomenderos in 1630: elite circulation and consolidation." Hispanic Amer. Historical Rev. 57: 633-659.

BURNS, E. B. (1977) Latin America: A Concise Interpretive History. Englewood Cliffs, NJ: Prentice-Hall.

CARAVEDO MOLINARI, B. (1976) Burguesía e industria en el Perú, 1933-1945. Lima: Instituto de Estudios Peruanos.

COTLER, J. (1978) Clases, estado y nación en el Peru. Lima: Instituto de Estudios Peruanos.

DOBYNS, H. F. and P. L. DOUGHTY (1976) Peru: A Cultural History. New York: Oxford Univ. Press.

ENGELSEN, J. R. (1977) Social Aspects of Agricultural Expansion in Coastal Peru, 1825-1878. Ph.D. dissertation. Los Angeles: Univ. of California.

ESTEVES, L. (1971) Apuntes para la historia económica del Perú. Lima: Centro de Estudios de Poblacion y Desarrollo.

FISHER, L. E. (1966) The Last Inca Revolt, 1780-1783. Norman: Univ. of Oklahoma Press.

FLORES-GALINDO, A. (1977) Arequipa y el sur andino: ensayo de historia regional (siglos XVIII-XX). Lima: Editorial Horizonte.

GILBERT, D. L. (1977) The Oligarchy and the Old Regime in Peru. Ph.D. dissertation. Ithaca: Cornell Univ. Dissertation Series.

GORMAN, S. M. (1977) Creole Liberalism and Revolutionary Corporatism in Peru: A Socio-historical Analysis of the Revolution of 1968. Ph.D. dissertation. Riverside: Univ. of California.

HUNT, S (1973) "Growth and guano in nineteenth century Peru." Princeton, NJ: Princeton Univ., Woodrow Wilson School. Research Program in Economic Development discussion paper 34.

KLAREN, P. F. (1973) Modernization, Dislocation, and Aprismo: Origins of Peruvian Aprista Party, 1870-1932. Univ. of Texas: Latin American Research Monograph 32.

LARSON, M. and A. E. BERGMAN (1969) Social Stratification in Peru. Berkeley, CA: Institute of International Studies.

MacLEAN Y ESTENOS, R. (1959) Sociología del Perú. México, DF: Universidad Autónoma de México.

MARETT, R. (1969) Peru. New York: Praeger.

MARIATEGUI, J. C. (1968) Siete ensayos de interpretación de la realidad peruana. Lima: Biblioteca Amauta.

MARKHAM, C. (1892) A History of Peru. Chicago: C. H. Sergel.

MATHEWS, W. M. (1977) "Primitive export sector: guano production in mid-nineteenth century Peru." J. of Latin Amer. Studies 9: 35-57.

——— (1972) "Peru and the British guano market, 1840-1870." Economic History Rev. 23: 112-128.

MATOS MAR, J. (1969) Perú problema, 5 ensayos. Lima: Instituto de Estudios Peruanos.

MILLER, R. (1976) "Railways and economic development in central Peru, 1890-1930," pp. 27-52 in R. Miller, C. T. Smith and J. Fisher (eds.) Social and Economic Change in Modern Peru. Liverpool: Univ. of Liverpool, Center for Latin American Studies, Monograph Series 6. Papers from a conference held at the center, 1974.

OWENS, R. J. (1966) Peru. New York: Oxford Univ. Press.

PIKE, F. B. (1967) A Modern History of Peru. London: Weidenfeld and Nicolson.

PINELO, A. J. (1973) The Multinational Corporation as a Force in Latin American Politics: A Case Study of the International Petroleum Company in Peru. New York: Praeger.

STEIN, S. J. and B. H. STEIN (1970) The Colonial Heritage of Latin America. New York: Oxford Univ. Press.

THORP, R. (1974) Industrialización en una economía abierta: el caso del Perú en el período 1890-1940. Lima: CISEPA, No. 23.

——— and G. BERTRAM (1976) "Industrialisation in an open economy," pp. 53-86 in R. Miller, C. T. Smith and J. Fisher (eds.) Social and Economic Change in Modern Peru. Liverpool: Univ. of Liverpool, Center for Latin American Studies, Monograph Series 6.

VILLANUEVA, V. (1973) Ejército peruano: del caudillaje anárquico al militarismo reformista. Lima: Juan Mejía Baca.

WERLICH, D. P. (1978) Peru: A Short History. London: Feffer and Simos.

YEPES DEL CASTILLO, E. (1971) Perú, 1820-1920: un siglo de desarrollo capitalista. Lima: Instituto de Estudios Peruanos.

*Stephen M. Gorman is currently Visiting Assistant Professor in the Department of Political Science, Purdue University. He has completed research projects in Peru between 1974 and 1976. Recent publications include "Peru before the Elections for a Constituent Assembly" in* Government and Opposition, *"Corporatism with a Human Face?" in* Inter-American Economic Affairs, *and articles on the Beagle Channel Islands dispute and proliferation dangers in the southern cone in* Parameters: Journal of the U.S. Army War College.

# BOOKS RECEIVED

## *GENERAL AND REGIONAL LATIN AMERICA*

Cardosa, Fernando Henrique and Enzo Faletto. DEPENDENCY AND DEVELOPMENT IN LATIN AMERICA. Translated by Marjory Mattingly Urquidi. Berkeley: University of California Press, 1979. Conclusions, post scriptum, name and subject indices. xxv, 227 pp. $18.50 cloth, $4.50 paper.

CEDAL. LA BANCA DE INTERES SOCIAL EN AMERICA LATINA. San José, Costa Rica: Colección Seminarios y Documentos, CEDAL, 1977. Indice. 141 pp. Paper.

CEPAL. STATISTICAL YEARBOOK FOR LATIN AMERICA, 1976. Santiago, Chile: United Nations Economic Commission for Latin America, CEPAL, 1977. Explanatory notes, sources. xcviii, 716 pp. Paper.

Ducci, Maria Angelica and Ligia Chang. TEMAS SOBRE LA FORMACION PROFESSIONAL DE LA MUJER. San José: Seminarios y Documentos, Centro de Estudios Democraticos de América Latina, CEDAL, 1978. Indice. 105 pp. Paper.

ECLA. ECONOMIC SURVEY OF LATIN AMERICA, 1976. Santiago, Chile: United Nations, 1977. 448 pp. Paper.

Henderson, James D. and Linda Roddy Henderson. TEN NOTABLE WOMEN OF LATIN AMERICA. Chicago: Nelson-Hall Publishers, 1979. Glossary, selected bibliography, index. $15.95 cloth, $7.95 paper.

Linz, Juan J. and Alfred Stepan, eds. THE BREAKDOWN OF DEMOCRATIC REGIMES. Baltimore: Johns Hopkins University Press, 1979. Biographical notes, indices. 168 pp. $35.00 cloth. As separate paperback volumes: Vol. 1, CRISIS, BREAKDOWN, AND REEQUILIBRATION, Juan J. Linz, $2.95; Vol. 2, EUROPE, Juan J. Linz and Alfred Stepan, eds., $3.95; Vol. 3, LATIN AMERICA, Juan J. Linz and Alfred Stepan, eds., $3.95; Vol. 4, CHILE, Arturo Valenzuela, $3.95.

Mesa-Lago, Carmelo. SOCIAL SECURITY IN LATIN AMERICA: PRESSURE GROUPS, STRATIFICATION, AND INEQUALITY. Pittsburgh, PA: University of Pittsburgh Press, 1978. Pitt Latin American Series. List of figures and tables, appendices, notes, index. xix, 351 pp. $19.95.

OAS. AMERICA EN CIFRAS 1977. Tomo III, Situación Demográfica, Social, Cultural. Washington, DC: OAS, 1979. Notas generales, notas explicativas, bibliografía, índice analítico. xi, 175 pp. Paper.

Oszlak, Oscar. FORMACION HISTORICA DEL ESTADO EN AMERICA LATINA: ELEMENTOS TEORICO-METODOLOGICOS PARA SU ESTUDIO. Vol. 1, No. 3. Buenos Aires: CEDES, 1978. 46 pp. Paper.

Padua, Jorge. EL ANALFABETISMO EN AMERICA LATINA: UN ESTUDIO EMPIRICO CON ESPECIAL REFERENCIA A LOS CASOS DE PERU, MEXICO Y ARGENTINA. México, D. F.: El Colegio de México, Jornadas 84, 1979. Bibliografía, lista de mapas y cuadros. vi, 192 pp. Paper.

Roy, Joaquín, ed. NARRATIVA Y CRITICA DE NUESTRA AMERICA. Madrid, Spain: Editorial Castalia, 1978. Bibliografía anotada. 414 pp. Paper.

Portantiero, Juan Carlos. ESTUDIANTES Y POLITICA EN AMERICA LATINA, 1918-1938: EL PROCESO DE LA REFORMA UNIVERSITARIA. México, D. F.: Siglo veintiuno editores, S. A., 1978. Colección América Nuestra No. 17, caminos de liberación. Indice de nombres. 461 pp. Paper.

Raposo Cordeiro, Daniel, ed. A BIBLIOGRAPHY OF LATIN AMERICAN BIBLIOGRAPHIES: SOCIAL SCIENCES & HUMANITIES, Volume I. Metuchen, NJ: Scarecrow Press, 1979. Subject, author index. 280 pp. $12.00.

Sable, Martin H. A GUIDE TO NONPRINT MATERIALS FOR LATIN AMERICAN STUDIES. Detroit: Blaine Ethridge-Books, 1979. Author, title, and geographic subject and form index, institution and firm directory. iv, 141 pp. $15.00.

Wilkie, James W., ed. STATISTICAL ABSTRACT OF LATIN AMERICA, Volume 19. Los Angeles: UCLA Latin American Center Publications, University of California, 1978. List of tables, maps, explanation of terms, index. xxiv, 424 pp. Paper.

*ARGENTINA*

Solberg, Carl E. OIL AND NATIONALISM IN ARGENTINA: A HISTORY. Stanford, CA: Stanford University Press, 1979. Notes, bibliography, index. xiv, 245 pp. $15.00.

Sourrouille, Juan V. LA PRESENCIA Y EL COMPORTAMIENTO DE LAS EMPRESAS EXTRANJERAS EN EL SECTOR INDUSTRIAL ARGENTINO. Buenos Aires: CEDES, 1978, Vol. 1, No. 2. 76 pp. Paper.

Wright, Ione S. and Lisa M. Nekhom. HISTORICAL DICTIONARY OF ARGENTINA. Latin American Historical Dictionaries, No. 17. Metuchen, NJ: Scarecrow Press, 1978. Historical chronology, suggested readings, maps. x, 1,113 pp. $35.00.

Wynia, Gary W. ARGENTINA IN THE POSTWAR ERA: POLITICS AND ECONOMIC POLICY MAKING IN A DIVIDED SOCIETY. Albuquerque: University of New Mexico Press, 1978. Notes, bibliography, index. x, 289 pp. $15.00 cloth, $6.95 paper.

*BRAZIL*

Agudelo Mejía, Santiago. INDIVIDUAL TRAINING: SYSTEM USED BY SENAIR OF RIO DE JANEIRO. Studies and Monographs, No. 33. Montevideo: CINTERFOR, 1978. Bibliography, annexes. 136 pp. Paper.

IBGE. ANUARIO ESTATISTICO DO BRASIL: 1977, v. 38. Rio de Janeiro: Fundaçao Instituto Brasileiro de Georgrafia e Estatistica, Secretaria de Planejamento da Presidencia da Republica, 1977. Legislacao, indice, relacao das fontes. 847 pp. Paper.

Levine, Robert M. HISTORICAL DICTIONARY OF BRAZIL. Latin American Historical Dictionaries, No. 19. Metuchen, NJ: Scarecrow Press, 1979. Bibliography, table of contents, key to frequently cited journals. ix, 297 pp. $12.50.

*CARIBBEAN*

Gastmann, Albert. HISTORICAL DICTIONARY OF THE FRENCH AND NETHERLANDS ANTILLES. Latin American Historical Dictionaries, No. 18. Metuchen, NJ: Scarecrow Press, 1978. Bibliography: General, French Antilles, Netherlands Antilles. xiii, 162 pp. $7.50.

Gleijeses, Piero. THE DOMINICAN CRISIS: THE 1965 CONSTITUTIONALIST REVOLT AND AMERICAN INTERVENTION. Baltimore: Johns Hopkins University Press, 1979. Acronyms, notes, bibliographical essay, index of names. xiii, 460 pp. $22.50.

Grabendorff, Wolf. KUBAS ENGAGEMENT IN AFRIKA. Ebenhausen, West Germany: Stiftung Wissenschaft und Politik, Forschungsinstitut fur Internationale Politik und Sicherheit, 1978. 107 pp. Paper.

Pérez, Louis A., Jr. INTERVENTION, REVOLUTION, AND POLITICS IN CUBA, 1913-1921. Pittsburgh: University of Pittsburgh Press, 1978. Notes, bibliography, index. xv, 198 pp. $12.95s.

Sariola, Sakari. THE PUERTO RICAN DILEMMA. Port Washington, NY: Kennikat Press, 1979. National University Publications. Notes, index. 200 pp. $15.00.

*CENTRAL AMERICA*

Ameringer, Charles D. DON PEPE: A POLITICAL BIOGRAPHY OF JOSE FIGUERES OF COSTA RICA. Albuquerque: University of New Mexico Press, 1979. Notes, bibliography, index. x, 324 pp. $16.50.

CEDAL. EL SECTOR DE ECONOMIA LABORAL. San José: Colección Cuadernos CEDAL, Centro de Estudios CEDAL, 1978. Anexos, índice. 126 pp. Paper.

Martz, Mary Jeanne Reid. THE CENTRAL AMERICAN SOCCER WAR: HISTORICAL PATTERNS AND INTERNAL DYNAMICS OF OAS SETTLEMENT PROCEDURES. Athens: Ohio University Press, Papers in International Studies, Latin America Series No. 4, 1978. References. 113 pp. $6.00 paper.

*CHILE*

Donoso Loero, Teresa. LOS CRISTIANOS POR EL SOCIALISMO EN CHILE. Santiago: Editorial Vaitea, 1976. Tercera edición aumentada. 314 pp. Paper.

Leggett, John, Deborah Vidi de James, Joe Somma and Tom Menendez. ALLENDE: HIS EXIT AND "OUR TIMES." Seven Stages: The Natural History of a Counter Revolutionary News Story: Human Rights, Overseas Fascism and the New York Times. New Brunswick, NJ: New Brunswick Cooperative Press, 1978. Footnotes, appendix A. xiii, 79 pp. Paper.

Romero, L. A. LA SOCIEDAD DE LA IGUALIDAD: LOS ARTESANOS DE SANTIAGO DE CHILE Y SUS PRIMERAS EXPERIENCIAS POLITICAS, 1820-1851. Buenos Aires: Instituto Torcuato Di Tella, 1978. Serie Histórica, Cuaderno No. 101. 73 pp. Paper.

Stallings, Barbara. CLASS CONFLICT AND ECONOMIC DEVELOPMENT IN CHILE, 1958-1973. Stanford: Stanford University Press, 1978. List of tables and figures, abbreviations, statistical appendix, notes, index. xviii, 295 pp.

*COLOMBIA*

Arrubla, Mario, et al. COLOMBIA, HOY. 2a Edición. Bogotá, Colombia: Siglo XXI Editores de Colombia, 1978. 403 pp. Paper.

Bergquist, Charles W. COFFEE AND CONFLICT IN COLOMBIA, 1886-1910. Durham, NC: Duke University Press, 1978. List of figures, maps, and tables; bibliography of sources cited; index. x, 227 pp.

Marzahl, Peter. TOWN IN THE EMPIRE: GOVERNMENT, POLITICS, AND SOCIETY IN SEVENTEENTH CENTURY POPAYAN. Austin: University of Texas, 1979. Institute of Latin American Studies, Latin American Monographs No. 45. Maps, tables, appendices, notes, glossary, bibliography, index. xxiv, 218 pp. $14.95 cloth, $5.95 paper.

*ECUADOR*

Drekonja, Gerhard, et al. ECUADOR: HOY. Bogotá: Siglo XXI Editores de Colombia, 1978. Anexo documental, los autores, siglas, 381 pp. Paper.

Lutchman, Harold Alexander. FROM COLONIALISM TO CO-OPERATIVE REPUBLIC: ASPECTS OF POLITICAL DEVELOPMENT IN GUYANA. Caribbean Monograph Series No. 9. Río Piedras, Puerto Rico: Institute of Caribbean Studies, University of Puerto Rico, 1974. Appendices, select bibliography. xi, 291 pp. Paper.

*MEXICO*

Brading, D. A. HACIENDAS AND RANCHOS IN THE MEXICAN BAJIO: LEON 1700-1860. New York: Cambridge University Press, Cambridge Latin American Studies 32, 1979. Tables, figures and maps, measures and money, glossary, archival abbreviations, notes, index, bibliography. xviii, 258 pp. $29.50.

Corwin, Arthur F., ed. IMMIGRANTS—AND IMMIGRANTS: PERSPECTIVES ON MEXICAN LABOR MIGRATION TO THE UNITED STATES. Westport, CT: Greenwood Press, 1978. Maps, illustrations, appendix, index. xiii, 378 pp.

Garza, Gustavo and Martha Schteingart. LA ACCION HABITACIONAL DEL ESTADO EN MEXICO. México, D. F.: El Colegio de México, Centro de Estudios Económicos y Demográficos, Colección VI, 1978. Bibliografía citada. x, 245 pp.

Rangel Guerra, Alfonso. LA EDUCACION SUPERIOR EN MEXICO. México, D. F.: El Collegio de México, Jornadas 86, 1979. Apendice, bibliografía. vii, 146 pp. Paper.

Taylor, William B. DRINKING, HOMICIDE AND REBELLION IN COLONIAL MEXICAN VILLAGES. Stanford: Stanford University Press, 1979. Notes, bibliography, index. 242 pp. $16.50.

Vellinga, Menno. ECONOMIC DEVELOPMENT AND THE DYNAMICS OF CLASS: INDUSTRIALIZATION, POWER AND CONTROL IN MONTERREY, MEXICO. Assen, The Netherlands: Van Gorcum, Studies of Developing Countries No. 24, 1979. List of tables and figures, appendices, bibliography. xv, 213 pp. Dfl. 37.50 paper.

*PANAMA*

OAS. REPORT ON THE SITUATION OF HUMAN RIGHTS IN PANAMA. Washington, DC: OAS, 1978. Appendix. 122 pp. Paper.

*PERU*

Basadre, Jorge. PERU: PROBLEMA Y POSIBILIDAD. Segunda edición. Reproducción facsimilar de la Primera Edición de 1931, con el apéndice: "Algunas Reconsideraciones Cuarentisiete Años Después." Lima: Banco Internacional del perú, 1978. Indice onomástico. xxii, 425 pp. Paper.

Díaz Rementería, Carlos J. EL CACIQUE EN EL VIRREINATO DEL PERU: ESTUDIO HISTORICO-JURIDICO. Sevilla: Seminario de Antropología Americana, Universidad de Sevilla, 1977. Apendice Documental, Fuentes, bibliografía. 260 pp. Paper.

Isbell, Billie Jean. TO DEFEND OURSELVES: ECOLOGY AND RITUAL IN AN ANDEAN VILLAGE. Latin American Monographs No. 47. Austin: Institute of Latin American Studies, University of Texas, 1978. Appendix, glossary, bibliography, index, guide to the pronunciation of Quechua, list of figures, tables, plates and maps. xv, 289 pp.

Long, Norman and Bryan R. Roberts, eds. PEASANT COOPERATION AND CAPITALIST EXPANSION IN CENTRAL PERU. Austin: Institute of Latin American Studies, University of Texas, 1979. Latin American Monographs No. 46. Bibliography, index, maps. xii, 349 pp. $19.95 cloth, $7.95 paper.

*VENEZUELA*

Banco Central de Venezuela. INFORME ECONOMICO 1977. Caracas: BCV, 1979. Síntesis de la Economía Venezolana, anexo estadístico. 773 pp. Paper.

Carlisle, Douglas H. VENEZUELAN FOREIGN POLICY: ITS ORGANIZATION AND BEGINNING. Washington, DC: University Press of America, 1979. Appendices, bibliography. v, 208 pp.

*MISCELLANEOUS*

Centro de Estudios Humanísticos de la Universidad Autónoma de Nuevo León. HUMANITAS: ANUARIO DEL CENTRO DE ESTUDIOS HUMANISTICOS. Monterrey Mexico: Centro de Estudios Humanísticos, Universidad de Nuevo León 1978. 642 pp. Paper.

Granger, John V. TECHNOLOGY AND INTERNATIONAL RELATIONS. San Francisco: W. H. Freeman & Co., 1979. List of acronyms, index. xi, 202 pp. $15.00 cloth, $6.50 paper.

Kanter, Arnold. DEFENSE POLITICS: A BUDGETARY PERSPECTIVE. Chicago: University of Chicago Press, 1979. Notes, references, index. viii, 152 pp. $12.50.

Laqueur, Walter, ed. FASCISM: A READER'S GUIDE. Analyses, interpretations, bibliography. Berkeley: University of California Press, 1979. Index. x, 478 pp. $22.50 cloth, $6.95 paper.

OECD. INVESTING IN DEVELOPING COUNTRIES. Fourth revised edition. Paris: OECD, 1978. List of text and annex tables. 121 pp. Paper.

Williams, Maurice J. DEVELOPMENT CO-OPERATION: EFFORTS AND POLICIES OF THE MEMBERS OF THE DEVELOPMENT ASSISTANCE COMMITTEE. 1978 Review. Paris: OECD, 1978. Statistical annex. 278 pp. Paper.

Sunseri, Alvin R. SEEDS OF DISCORD: NEW MEXICO IN THE AFTERMATH OF THE AMERICAN CONQUEST, 1846-1861. Chicago: Nelson-Hall Publishers, 1979. Epilogue, notes on sources, bibliography, index, chronology. xvii, 195 pp. $14.95.

3.00
ach

QUANTITATIVE
APPLICATIONS
IN THE
CIAL SCIENCES

*A SAGE UNIVERSITY PAPER SERIES*

**SPECIAL OFFER:**
4 or more
for $2.50 each
(prepaid only)

meets the need for brief, clear explanations of methodological techniques—for those with limited knowledge of statistics and mathematics

improves the quality of data analysis in the social sciences

ideal for use as classroom supplements

SAGE PUBLICATIONS
Beverly Hills · London

ORDER CARD

# Quantitative Applications in the Social Sciences

*(A Sage University Papers Series)*

NAME ______________________

ADDRESS ______________________

CITY ______________ STATE ______________ ZIP ______

☐ I want to take advantage of your **Special Offer.** Please send me the following 4 or more titles at $2.50 each. My check or money order is enclosed.

- ☐ **ANALYSIS OF VARIANCE** (Iversen/Norpoth 407001)
- ☐ **OPERATIONS RESEARCH METHODS** (Nagel/Neef 407002)
- ☐ **CAUSAL MODELING** (Asher 407003)
- ☐ **TESTS OF SIGNIFICANCE** (Henkel 407004)
- ☐ **COHORT ANALYSIS** (Glenn 407005)
- ☐ **CANONICAL ANALYSIS & FACTOR COMPARISON** (Levine 407006)
- ☐ **ANALYSIS OF NOMINAL DATA** (Reynolds 407007)
- ☐ **ANALYSIS OF ORDINAL DATA** (Hildebrand/Lang/Rosenthal 407008)
- ☐ **TIME SERIES ANALYSIS:** Regression Techniques (Ostrom 407009)
- ☐ **ECOLOGICAL INFERENCE** (Langbein/Lichtman 407010)
- ☐ **MULTIDIMENSIONAL SCALING** (Kruskal/Wish 407011)
- ☐ **ANALYSIS OF COVARIANCE** (Wildt/Ahtola 407012)
- ☐ **INTRODUCTION TO FACTOR ANALYSIS** (Kim/Mueller 407013)
- ☐ **FACTOR ANALYSIS** (Kim/Mueller 407014)

☐ Please send me the Sage Papers checked above at the regular price of $3.00 each.

☐ Payment enclosed $________

☐ Please bill me $__________*
*plus postage & shipping

ORDERS FOR $10.00 OR LESS MUST BE PREPAID

*(California residents add 6% sales tax)*

☐ **Please add my name to your mailing list for announcements of new titles in this series.**

SAGE Publications, Inc.
P. O. Box 5024 / Beverly Hills, CA 90210

# Quantitative Applications in the Social Sciences

(A Sage University Papers Series)

**$3.00 each**

PLACE
STAMP
HERE

SAGE PUBLICATIONS, INC.
P. O. Box 5024
BEVERLY HILLS, CALIF. 90210

# Advertising Supplement:

# Journal of Interamerican Studies and World Affairs

This supplement has been prepared especially for our readers to bring them information and announcements of professional interest. By placing advertisements in the pages of this journal, our advertisers have indicated a desire to communicate with our readers. We hope our readers will acknowledge their indirect support of the journal and its purposes by mentioning the journal in correspondence with advertisers.

## PUBLIC POLICY AND PUBLIC CHOICE

Edited by **Douglas W. Rae**, *Yale University*

**Theodore J. Eismeier**, *Hamilton College*

How do citizens form judgments on political matters? How do they react at the ballot box to the use of their tax monies by their elected representatives? What can we learn by applying a "public choice perspective" to the study of policy making under democratic institutions and processes? The original essays in this volume analyze the choices of citizens and politicians --the consumers and producers of public policy. By focusing on "public choice", the editors and authors have created a rigorous examination of costs and benefits as perceived by the various actors in the political decision process.

**Contents**: Series Editor's Introduction *Stuart S. Nagel* Volume Editor's Introduction *Douglas Rae and Theodore J. Eismeier* **Part 1** Citizen's Policy Judgments (1) Issue Voting: What Counts as Evidence *Christopher Achen* (2) Redistributing Wealth; Positions, Payments and Attitudes *Jennifier L. Hochschild* **Part II** Elections as Referenda on Government Policy Performance (3) Popular Votes for the President; Economic and Fiscal Effects *William A. Niskanen* (4) Budgets and Ballots: The Political Consequences of Fiscal Choice *Theodore J. Eismeier* **Part III** Institutional Arrangements and Policy Decisions (5) Election Expectations and Outcomes: A Theory of Nominating Convention Conflict, 1896-1976 *W. Ross Brewer and Garrison Nelson* (6) Rational Allocation of Congressional Resources: Member Time and Staff Use in the House *Thomas E. Cavanagh* (7) Creating a Policy Equilibrium: The Role of Institutional Structure *Kenneth A. Shepsle* About the Contributors

**Sage Yearbooks in Politics and Public Policy, Vol. 6**

| | | | |
|---|---|---|---|
| **May 1979** | **ISBN 0-8039-0725-7** | **hardcover** | **$18.50** |
| **284 pages** | **ISBN 0-8039-0726-5** | **softcover** | **$ 8.95** |

**SAGE** PUBLICATIONS, INC. **SAGE** PUBLICATIONS LTD

275 S. Beverly Dr. Beverly Hills, CA 90212 28 Banner Street, London EC1Y 8QE, England

Please mention Journal of Interamerican Studies and World Affairs when writing advertisers.

# REVIEW

A JOURNAL OF
THE FERNAND BRAUDEL CENTER
FOR THE STUDY OF ECONOMIES,
HISTORICAL SYSTEMS,
AND CIVILIZATIONS
of the State University
of New York at Binghamton

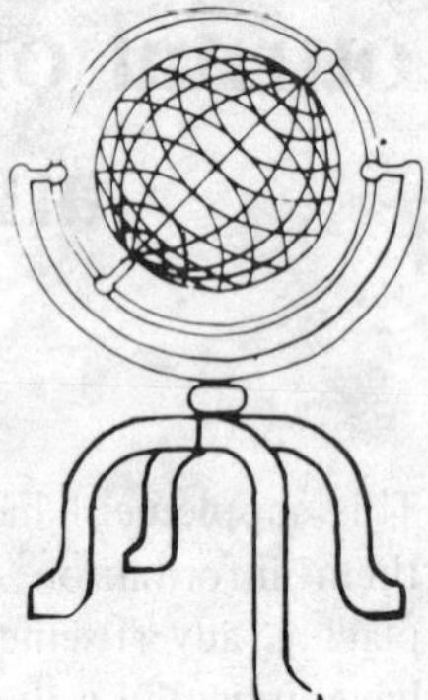

Editor:

**IMMANUEL WALLERSTEIN**

*State University of New York, Binghamton*

**REVIEW is committed to the pursuit of a perspective which recognizes the primacy of analyses of economies over long historical time and large space, the holism of the socio-historical process, and the transitory, heuristic nature of theories.**

Contributors to recent issues include

KARLY POLANYI
FERNAND BRAUDEL
IMMANUEL WALLERSTEIN
M. I. FINLEY
GEORGES HAUPT
N. D. KONDRATIEFF
ANDRÉ GUNDER FRANK
EMMANUEL LEROY LADURIE

. . . and others

**Recent and Forthcoming Special Issues:**
* **The Impact of the *Annales* School on the Social Sciences**
* **Trends and Cycles**
* **Incorporation of Southern Africa into the World-System, 1800-1940**

**SAGE Publications, Inc.**
**275 South Beverly Drive**
**Beverly Hills, California 90212**

**SAGE Publications LTD**
**28 Banner Street**
**London EC1Y 8QE, England**

# CITIES OF PEASANTS

## The Political Economy of Urbanization in the Third World

by **BRYAN ROBERTS,**
*Professor of Sociology, University of Manchester*

This book is about the expansion of capitalism in the Third World. It is one of the few accounts linking contemporary differences in the political and economic structure of underdeveloped countries to the historically specific way in which these have become part of the world economy. Focusing on the most securely capitalist of all underdeveloped regions of the continent of Latin America — the author traces the growth of urban-based industrialism and its impact, both externally and internally. He shows how it has transformed the economy and produced new political and social pressures, whose significance can be seen in the daily economic activities, social relationships and even religious behavior of people in Third-World cities. This analysis explains and uses the concepts of dependent development and core periphery: there is also a critical review of current theories about urbanization in the third world and, in particular, a discussion of the debate on marginality.

The nature of the urban working class in underdeveloped countries, with its potential for organization and collective aspirations, will be a crucial factor in the future. This book conveys both the flavor of life in the cities of the Third World and the immediacy of their problems.

**CONTENTS**

1. Urbanization and underdevelopment
2. Urbanization and underdevelopment before the modern period
3. Urbanization and industrialization
4. Migration and the agrarian structure
5. The urban economy and social stratification
6. Urban poverty and coping with urban life
7. Urbanization and marginality in underdevelopment

Explorations in Urban Analysis, Volume 1

| | | | |
|---|---|---|---|
| **June 1979** | **ISBN 0-8039-1290-0** | **hardcover** | **$17.50** |
| **216 pages** | **ISBN 0-8039-1291-9** | **softcover** | **$ 8.95** |

**SAGE** PUBLICATIONS, INC.
275 South Beverly Drive
Beverly Hills, California 90212

**SAGE** PUBLICATIONS LTD
28 Banner Street
London EC1Y 8QE, England

# USING EVALUATIONS:

## DOES EVALUATION MAKE A DIFFERENCE?

**Marvin C. Alkin / Richard Daillak / Peter White**

*Graduate School of Education, UCLA*

From many quarters, the answer to the question, "Is evaluation working?" has been a sad, disillusioned "No." This timely study, however, offers an altogether different perspective, one largely unheralded in the literature, which concludes that evaluations *already* influence social intervention programs in important and useful ways. The authors present the results of five extensive case studies of school programs and their evaluations, examining the influence of the evaluations upon program decision making and program operation. In each case the authors attempt to explain why and how evaluation did or did not have an impact on program decisions.

By adopting a broader definition of utilization, the authors have made a strong case for the inherent usefulness of evaluation. Their conclusions will make fascinating reading for anyone concerned with the present status and future direction of evaluation research.

| | | | |
|---|---|---|---|
| 1979 | ISBN 0-8039-1177-7 | hardcover | $15.00 |
| 272 pages | ISBN 0-8039-1178-5 | softcover | $ 7.95 |

**SAGE** PUBLICATIONS, INC
275 South Beverly Drive
Beverly Hills, California 90212

**SAGE** PUBLICATIONS LTD
28 Banner Street
London EC1Y 8QE, England

# EVALUATION
## A Systematic Approach

**Peter H. Rossi  Howard E. Freeman**
**Sonia R. Wright**

**EVALUATION: A Systematic Approach** is the first comprehensive text in the field. Its organization allows the reader to gain an understanding of the role of evaluation research in planning, design and implementation of both established and innovative social programs and projects. Contemporary technical procedures for planning interventions, target population selection, program monitoring and impact assessment are provided. A unique feature of the book is its detailed treatment of cost-benefit and cost-effectiveness techniques.

The authors of the volume bring to bear their broad and practical experience in discussing the uses and prospects of evaluation research. The use of social science methods and concepts are stressed in this unique applied social research text. Throughout the volume, "case modules" (exhibits) are used to provide valuable and pragmatic illustrative information.

**EVALUATION: A Systematic Approach** is designed for social researchers, policy and planning specialists and practitioners in health care, community education, psychiatry, public safety and criminal justice, urban development, social welfare and other human service fields. Students of research methods in all social science disciplines and in professional schools will find this volume the essential text and reference work in evaluation research.

**April 1979  336 pages  ISBN 0-8039-1179-3  hardcover  $14.95**

**SAGE** PUBLICATIONS, INC.
275 South Beverly Drive
Beverly Hills, California 90212

**SAGE** PUBLICATIONS LTD
28 Banner Street
London EC1Y 8QE, England

lease mention Journal of Interamerican Studies and World Affairs when writing advertisers.

# INTERNATIONAL NEWS: FREEDOM UNDER ATTACK

**edited by Congressman Dante B. Fascell, U.S. House of Representatives**

Freedom of the press and the free flow of news and information is under attack around the world today. The conflict over media access and independence has developed on several levels: from attempts by a growing number of countries to bar American reporters to restrictive resolutions in UNESCO; from calls for redistributing radio bands to movements toward creating government monopolies on the distribution of information.

Four specialists on these questions have written timely studies touching on every aspect of contemporary international media affairs. Topics include the politics of international broadcasting, the Third World challenge to Western news services, the quality of American foreign coverage, and the ways in which various states are trying to censor news. This is an important and unique book which should be of vital interest to all who make and write the news, as well as the millions of Americans who depend on the media for their knowledge of global events.

**March 1979  320 pages  ISBN 0-8039-1129-3  hardcover  $15.00**

**SAGE** PUBLICATIONS, INC.
275 South Beverly Drive
Beverly Hills, California 90212

**SAGE** PUBLICATIONS LTD
28 Banner Street
London EC1Y 8QE, England

# THE WORLD SYSTEM OF CAPITALISM: Past and Present

Edited by **Walter L. Goldfrank,**
*University of California, Santa Cruz*

**The "world-system approach," formulated by Immanuel Wallerstein, series editor of these POLITICAL ECONOMY OF WORLD-SYSTEM ANNUALS, serves to unify the contributions included in this volume. The social scientists who are published here have rejected the traditional ahistorical approach of Western social research in favor of this interdiciplinary, historicallyoriented. often radical approach to the study of the capitalist worldsystem. Contributions include theoretical articles and case studies from both the seventeenth and twentieth centuries. Notable is a tantalizing preview of Wallerstein's forthcoming second volume of THE MODERN WORLD-SYSTEM, dealing with stagnation in seventeenth century Europe and its effects.**

**Political Economy of the World-System Annuals, Volume 2**

| | | | |
|---|---|---|---|
| **1979** | **ISBN 0-8039-1105-X** | **hardcover** | **$18.50** |
| **312 pages** | **ISBN 0-8039-1106-8** | **softcover** | **$ 8.95** |

SAGE PUBLICATIONS LTD
28 Banner Street
London EC1Y 8QE

SAGE PUBLICATIONS, INC
275 South Beverly Drive
Beverly Hills, California 90212

# CHALLENGES TO AMERICA

UNITED STATES FOREIGN POLICY IN THE 1980s

Edited by: **CHARLES W. KEGLEY, JR.**, University of South Carolina
**PATRICK J. McGOWAN**, University of Southern California

In the selected "case-for-analysis" – the United States– the outstanding contributors explore the relationship between enviromental change and foreign policy response by examining long term secular trends which are likely to present special problems to U.S. society and foreign policy into the 1980's. Topics covered include the strategic arms balance, foreign perceptions of the United States, and the probable nature of the future relations between the United States, Europe, and Japan.

This, the fourth volume of the Sage International Yearbooks of Foreign Policy Studies, marks the inauguration of a new format for the series – the present and all subsequent volumes will each focus on a specific aspect of foreign policy. *Challenges to America* sets a high standard for all future Yearbooks in considering two important theoretical questions: How is foreign policy shaped by the environmental changes encountered by national actors? What are the linkages which exist between a state's foreign policy and its domestic and international environments?

**CONTENTS** / CHARLES W. KEGLEY, Jr. and PATRICK J. McGOWAN **Part I: AMERICA'S RESPONSE TO CHANGES IN THE INTERNATIONAL SYSTEM: THEORIES AND EVIDENCE** / FRANK L. KLINGBERG, FARID ABOLFATHI, JOHN J. HAYES, AND RICHARD E. HAYES **Part II: SOME EMERGENT GLOBAL CHALLENGES TO THE UNITED STATES** / MELVIN SMALL , J. DAVID SINGER, CHARLES F. DORAN, JAMES A. CAPORASO , MICHAEL D. WARD, WERNER J. FELD, ALVIN RICHMAN **Part III: SOME SOURCES OF AMERICAN FOREIGN POLICY ADAPTION** / OLE R. HOLSTI , JAMES N. ROSENAU, CHARLES F. HERMAN **Part IV: BIBLIOGRAPHY** / MARK W. DELANCEY , THOMAS H. JOHNSON

**Sage International Yearbooks of Foreign Policy Studies, Volume 4**

| | | | |
|---|---|---|---|
| **February 1979** | **ISBN 0-8039-1121-1** | **hardcover** | **$18.50** |
| **312 pages** | **ISBN 0-8039-1122-X** | **softcover** | **$ 8.95** |

**SAGE** PUBLICATIONS, INC
275 South Beverly Drive
Beverly Hills, California 90212

**SAGE** PUBLICATIONS LTD
28 Banner Street
London EC1Y 8QE, England

Please mention Journal of Interamerican Studies and World Affairs when writing advertise

Vol. 21 No. 4
November 1979

# JOURNAL OF INTERAMERICAN STUDIES

# and WORLD AFFAIRS

A Publication of the Center for Advanced International Studies,
The University of Miami

SAGE PUBLICATIONS

*Journal of INTERAMERICAN STUDIES*
*and WORLD AFFAIRS*

**EDITORIAL STAFF:**

John P. Harrison—Editor
Jan Peter Wogart—Associate Editor
Gerry Machovec—Editorial Assistant

**BOARD OF EDITORS:**

Orlando Albornoz, Universidad Central de Venezuela
D. A. Brading, Cambridge University
David Chaplin, Western Michigan University
Tom E. Davis, Cornell University
Malcolm Deas, St. Antony's College, Oxford, England
Rosario Green, El Colegio de Mexico
Elizabeth Jelin, Centro de Estudios de Estado y Sociedad
Isaac Kerstenetzky, Instituto Brasileiro de Geografia e Estatistica, Brazil
Celso Lafer, Universidade de São Paulo
Vaughan A. Lewis, University of the West Indies, Mona, Jamaica
Abraham Lowenthal, Woodrow Wilson International Center for Scholars
Robert McNicoll, University of Miami, emeritus
Carmelo Mesa-Lago, University of Pittsburgh
James J. Parsons, University of California, Berkeley
Clark Reynolds, Stanford University
Richard Schaedel, University of Texas, Austin
Hanns-Albert Steger, Universitat Erlangen-Nurnberg, Germany
Alfred Stepan, Yale University
Evelyn P. Stevens, Case Western Reserve University
Victor L. Urquidi, El Colegio de Mexico

The editors and publisher wish to acknowledge with gratitude the assistance and encouragement of the Center for Advanced International Studies, University of Miami, in providing ancillary services and support for this journal.

*Journal of*
INTERAMERICAN
STUDIES
*and* WORLD AFFAIRS

Vol. 21
No. 4
November
1979

# CONTENTS

*Oil and U.S.-Mexican Relations*
GEORGE W. GRAYSON 427

*Party Development in Revolutionary Cuba*
WILLIAM M. LeoGRANDE 457

*Belief Systems of Colombian Political Party Activists*
GARY HOSKIN 481

*Origins of the "New Professionalism" of the Brazilian Military*
FRANK D. McCANN, Jr. 505

*Modernization and Rural Population Movements: Western Puerto Rico*
JANICE J. MONK
CHARLES S. ALEXANDER 523

*Index* 551

**SAGE PUBLICATIONS** / *Beverly Hills* *London*

**Policy:** The **JOURNAL OF INTERAMERICAN STUDIES AND WORLD AFFAIRS** reflects the interests of the scholarly community and interested public concerned with the social, economic, political, and cultural aspects of life in Latin America (including the Caribbean), particularly in those instances where the subject is of concern to more than one of the traditional disciplines. As these concerns change, so will the content of the journal.

**Articles** which have special relevance for interrelationships between American nations and of those nations with the rest of the world will be given special consideration. An effort will be made to include occasional articles that state an unusual or even discordant position on a subject of broad interest to be supplemented by critical comments of authorities representing differing positions on the topic. The editors continue to welcome articles by scholars from all parts of the world.

**Manuscripts** should be submitted in duplicate to: Editor, **JOURNAL OF INTERAMERICAN STUDIES AND WORLD AFFAIRS,** Box 24-8134, University of Miami, Coral Gables, Florida 33124. Manuscripts should be typewritten, double-spaced, with footnotes, references, tables, and charts on separate pages, and should follow the current journal style. A brief biographical paragraph describing each author's current affiliation, research interests, and recent publications should accompany the manuscript.

**Correspondence** regarding book reviews should be sent directly to: Book Review Editor, **JOURNAL OF INTERAMERICAN STUDIES AND WORLD AFFAIRS,** Box 24-8134, University of Miami, Coral Gables, Florida 33124.

---

**JOURNAL OF INTERAMERICAN STUDIES AND WORLD AFFAIRS** is published four times annually—in February, May, August, and November. Copyright © 1979 by Sage Publications, Inc. All rights reserved. No portion of the contents may be reproduced in any form without written permission of the publisher.

**Subscriptions:** Regular institutional rate $32.00 per year. Individuals may subscribe at a one-year rate of $16.50. Add $1.00 for subscriptions outside the United States. Orders from the U.K., Europe, the Middle East, and Africa should be sent to the London office (address below). Noninstitutional orders **must** be paid by personal check.

Second class postage paid at Beverly Hills, California. ISSN 0022-1937

This journal is abstracted or indexed in **Historical Abstracts, Human Resources Abstracts, Sage Urban Studies Abstracts, International Political Science Abstracts, Public Affairs Information Service, Current Contents, Social Sciences Citation Index, Social Sciences Index, ABC POL SCI,** and **United States Poltical Science Documents.**

**Back Issues:** Information about availability and prices of back issues may be obtained from the publisher's order department (address below). Write to London office for sterling prices.

**Inquiries:** Address all correspondence and permissions requests to SAGE PUBLICATIONS, Inc., 275 South Beverly Drive, Beverly Hills, California 90212. Inquiries and subscriptions from the U.K., Europe, the Middle East, and Africa should be sent to SAGE PUBLICATIONS Ltd, 28 Banner Street, London EC1Y 8QE, England. Other orders should be sent to the Beverly Hills office.

**Advertising:** Current rates and specifications may be obtained by writing to the Advertising Manager at the Beverly Hills office (address above).

**Claims:** Claims for undelivered copies must be made no later than three months following month of publication. The publisher will supply missing copies when losses have been sustained in transit and when the reserve stock will permit.

**Change of Address:** Six weeks' advance notice must be given when notifying of change of address. Please send old address label along with the new address to insure proper identification. Please specify name of journal. Send change of address to: Journal name, c/o 275 South Beverly Drive, Beverly Hills, CA 90212.

---

**GEORGE W. GRAYSON**
*Department of Government*
*College of William and Mary*

# *OIL AND U.S.-MEXICAN RELATIONS*

## *Oil and Gas Reserves*

The Aztecs discovered petroleum in Mexico and used it before the arrival of the Spanish in 1519. They burned it in tribute to their gods, caulked their canoes with it, smeared it on their bodies as a medicine, and utilized it as a dye and a glue. Over three centuries elapsed before an effort was made to turn black gold into cash. Ten years after Edwin L. Drake drilled his famous well near Titusville, Pennsylvania, in 1859, a group of Mexicans unsuccessfully attempted to produce oil on the "Furbero" hacienda near Papantla in Vera Cruz state. It was not until May 1901 that Edward L. Doheny, a wily product of the rough-and-tumble American oil industry in which he had amassed a fortune, struck oil in Ébano, a jungle region of San Luis Potosí. Another pioneer in the development of Mexico's petroleum industry was Weeman Pearson, later Lord Cowdray, a Yorkshire entrepreneur who formed the fabulously profitable Mexican Eagle (Aguila) Company after discovering the "Golden Lane" fields in 1908 (Bermúdez, 1963; Sampson, 1975: 83-85; Grayson, 1978a).

Production soared from 10,000 barrels in 1901 to 13 million barrels in 1910 and reached a peak output of 193.4 million barrels in 1921. In that year, the ancient Aztec nation became the world's

AUTHOR'S NOTE: This article has profited from thirty confidential personal and telephone interviews with individuals on congressional staffs, in the Export-Import Bank, and in the Departments of Energy, State, and Treasury. Also interviewed were officials of *Petróleos Mexicanos* and the Ministry of Patrimony.

Journal of Interamerican Studies and World Affairs, Vol. 21 No. 4, November 1979 427-456
© 1979 Sage Publications, Inc.

principal oil exporter, accounting for one-quarter of global supplies. Although the rate of well drilling more than doubled from 1921 to 1926, production declined (Powell, 1972: 15). As assertive nationalism grew in Mexico, the foreign firms—responsible for the bulk of investment—steadily shifted their activities to Venezuela and, later, to the Middle East and Indonesia. President Lázaro Cárdenas's expropriation decree of March 18, 1938, drove them from Mexico. Domestic demand, sharpened by increased industrial development and a rising birth rate, expanded more rapidly than yields of oil and gas, now completely in the hands of *Petróleos Mexicanos* (PEMEX). Beginning in the 1960s, imports exceeded exports.

This situation changed dramatically with the discovery of a new hydrocarbon province in Mexico's Southeast. In the mid-1960s, the national company began serious exploratory work in the deeper strata of Tabasco and Chiapas. This effort, which benefited from more sophisticated seismic methods and improved deep-drilling equipment and techniques, paid handsome dividends in 1972 when oil started flowing from the rich Reforma trend. The vertiginous rise in crude oil prices after the 1973 Yom Kippur war gave a fillip to the venture.

High-quality crude and exceptional productivity characterized wells in the Reforma. Yields surged from 71,000 barrels per day (bpd) in December 1972 to 1,018,518 bpd in December 1978. This area, now known as "little Kuwait," furnished 76.6% of Mexico's 1978 production of 485.3 million barrels (Petróleos Mexicanos, 1979: 5).

Mainly as a result of the Reforma output, Antonio Dovalí Jaime, director general of PEMEX from 1970 to 1976, announced that, as of December 31, 1975, Mexico's proven reserves totaled 6.338 billion barrels—just over 1 billion barrels higher than the proven reserves a decade before. President-elect López Portillo, curious as to how reserves had expanded only 20% while production had nearly doubled in the course of a decade, named a task force to investigate the size of Mexico's holdings. This group of experts concluded that proven reserves actually stood at 11.160 billion barrels, an amount that Jorge Díaz Serrano—the chairman of the task force and López Portillo's choice to head PEMEX —made public in December 1976.

PEMEX has subsequently announced several increases. At the end of 1978, it placed "proven reserves" of oil and gas at 40.194 billion barrels, "probable reserves" at 44.612 billion barrels, and "possible reserves" at 200 billion (Petróleos Mexicanos, 1979: 5).

A number of factors bolster the optimism concerning holdings in Mexico, where only 15% of the country's geologically promising structures have been explored. *First,* PEMEX continues to find new oil in the Reforma area, which yields the bulk of the country's total output. In 1978 the success ratio—70% for production wells and 25% for exploratory wells—was high, and 7.7 billion barrels had been proven here by year's end. Only 19 of the 100 seismically promising structures were producing as of March 18, 1979. Exploratory work has also revealed the presence of oil near Tuxtla Gutiérrez, as well as in the area of Lacantun on the Guatemalan border (Díaz Serrano, 1979).

*Second,* Díaz Serrano has announced that the Campeche Sound embraces deposits closer to shore and in shallower water than those of the North Sea. Two of the first wells drilled, Akal and Nohoch, contained oil-impregnated rock approximately 1,000 meters in thickness compared to cores of 100 meters in the North Sea. Cantarel, the principal field, may prove larger than the 58-square mile A. J. Bermúdez configuration in Reforma. Wells thus far have varied in depth from 8,200 to 13,000 feet. Nonetheless, prospects are also good in shallower areas. PEMEX plans for 1979 and 1980 call for the installation of 25 drilling platforms and seven production units at depths of not greater than 230 feet. A 1979 production target of 200,000 bpd was set for the Campeche fields, whose high-density oil has a low gas-oil ratio (World Oil, 1979). The "blowout" of a test well, which spewed 30,000 bpd into Campeche Bay in June 1979, may impede achieving this goal.

*Third,* the newly publicized Chicontepec basin covers 1,275 square miles between Tampico and Poza Rica along the Gulf of Mexico, north of the "Golden Lane" where the country's first major oil wells were found. This deposit, called by Díaz Serrano "one of the bigger hydrocarbon accumulations in the Western hemisphere," could contain up to 100 billion barrels. But low porosity and permeability will necessitate the sinking of 16,000 wells, as many as PEMEX has drilled in its entire history. With each well lifting but 50 or 100 bpd, it will be a decade before this area makes a significant contribution to output. The need to construct such support facilities as roads, rail spurs, gathering lines, and production facilities further complicates the picture (Excelsior, 1978b).

*Fourth,* PEMEX has verified the presence of major new gas fields in the Sabinas basin of Nuevo Leon (Lampazos) and Coahuila (Moncloya and Ulua), thus permitting the commercial production of hydrocarbons outside the Gulf Coastal Plain for the first time in the country's history. *Fifth,* the Miralejos well in the Paploapan River basin near Totaxtla, Vera Cruz, produces gas and condensates in geological formations similar to those of the Copite and Mata Pionche fields, with which it joins to form a productive strip of more than 15 miles. *Sixth,* serious work is just beginning in Chihuahua, Sonora, Durango, Nuevo Leon, and Baja California, where the Bombas well confirms the occurrence of hydrocarbons on this western peninsula. However, as of late 1978, Baja California had proved a major disappointment: The two offshore holes turned out to be dry, while the onshore wells lacked commercial quantities of oil.

On the basis of PEMEX's "proven" reserves of 40.194 billion barrels, Mexico ranks sixth in the world in petroleum deposits, surpassed only by Saudi Arabia, the Soviet Union, Kuwait, Iran, and the United States. If the "possible" reserve estimate turns out to be accurate, Mexico's hydrocarbon wealth would exceed that of Saudi Arabia.

The 200 billion barrel amount is highly speculative and will remain so until scientifically verified. Talk of surpassing Saudi Arabia's 165.7 billion known barrels is, to say the least, premature; recent years have seen little exploration in the Croessus kingdom. Still, a medley of reasons inspire the state enterprise to advance the highest figure possible. In fact, key members of Dovalí Jaime's administration contend that the reserve figures have been inflated by failure to observe industry-sanctioned norms in calculating them.[1] Domestically, the prospect of massive holdings strengthens the monopoly's position with respect to bureaucratic competitors, bolsters the pride of a highly nationalistic people who for four decades have viewed the oil industry as a symbol of national dignity, and enhances public confidence in an economy plagued by mounting inflation, debt, and unemployment. A prestigious journal of finance reports that the oil discoveries have contributed to the recovery of the Mexico City stock market (Barron's, 1978). Large reserve figures also justify the rapid exploitation of individual wells—a tendency which alarms petroleum engineers conversant with the excesses of the 1920s and the 1958-1964 period. An accelerated flow of oil gives rise to more contracts that all too often involve sub rosa "commissions" for executives in PEMEX, where opportunities for graft and corruption have never been greater. Similarly, leaders of the venal Oil Workers Union have profited from the boom atmosphere. Internationally, the possession of major reserves lofts a country's standing within the community of nations, improves its position with the World Bank and other financial agencies, and increases its attractiveness to private foreign lenders from whom Mexico has succeeded in extracting lower interest rates (Economist, 1978). Mexican officials no doubt anticipate that impressive reserve figures will also expand their leverage in negotiations with the United States.

### *Bilateral Energy Policy*

The United States and Mexico have vastly different means of formulating foreign policy. The U.S. Constitution confers authority in this area on both the executive and legislative branches, but the judiciary, regulatory bodies, intelligence agencies, state governments, mass media, and a bewildering array of special interests often play a key role—a fact that confuses both domestic and foreign observers. Generally speaking, the State Department and other agencies charged with fashioning policy prefer to deal with issues individually, reducing them to their technical aspects.

Mexico's political system is highly centralized despite formal separation of powers and a federal structure. This centralization pervades and influences the formulation of domestic and foreign policy. Naturally, the President consults his advisers and appropriate leaders inside and outside the government. But once he or the high-level official to whom he has delegated authority reaches a decision, it is rarely criticized, much less reversed by Congress, party officials, or interest group spokespeople.

Centralized decision-making contributes to what has been called "closet diplomacy" (Ronfeldt and Sereseres, 1978). In the foreign policy field, Mexicans prefer to establish personal contacts with high-level American officials. Their goal is to nurture a mutual confidence, engage in unpublicized, informal discussions, and seek solutions to a number of issues affecting bilateral relations. Former Foreign Minister Santiago Roel García even retained a private Washington attorney, who operated independently of the Mexican embassy, to collect information, prepare reports, and establish contacts with key figures in the bureaucracy and on Capitol Hill.

Mexico's style stands in sharp contrast to the fragmented, bureaucratic approach of the Americans and lends itself to the linking of issues, a concept favored by López Portillo when he proposed examining the "total picture" and considering a "package" approach to resolving problems of mutual concern (Ronfeldt and Sereseres, 1978).

Linkage poses enormous difficulties whether attempted in U.S.-Soviet or U.S.-Mexican relations. The most intractable problem is assigning weights to various issues to help determine the feasibility of tradeoffs. For instance, can oil and gas sales by PEMEX compensate for American flexibility on border and trade questions? If so, how many barrels of crude must be placed on the scale to balance the annual entry of, say, 200,000 undocumented aliens? How many tons of tomatoes must be admitted at reduced tariffs to justify a 20-year supply contract for natural gas?

Inextricably bound to the "weighting" problem is that of authority: namely, determining the individual or group assigned responsibility for bargaining once weights have been calculated. During the Nixon presidency, Dr. Henry Kissinger played this role and has been sharply criticized for it in recent years. No one currently involved in fashioning American foreign policy enjoys a similar position of power and confidence. National Security Adviser Zbigniew Brzezinski has often shown enthusiasm for linkage, but this tactic enjoys little support from Secretary of State Cyrus R. Vance, who prefers careful, methodical negotiations on individual matters. Of course, the two presidents could meet to strike bargains. But this is a dangerous way to conduct diplomacy unless each has a comprehensive command of the outstanding issues.

López Portillo's rather vague notion of "package" negotiations may entail attempting to resolve one outstanding problem to improve the climate for addressing another—and, upon settling that one, still another. In any case, he attempted to develop ties with his American counterpart that might foster personal diplomacy. Three months before donning the red, white, and green presidential sash, he visited Washington where he was courteously received by then President Gerald R. Ford, both in a private family dinner and in a White House meeting. The Mexican leader skillfully presented the agenda of issues between the two countries. In reply, President Ford made a pro forma suggestion that these matters be taken up with the appropriate cabinet members. After the President-elect and his party returned to Mexico, the Republican administration made no attempt to follow up on questions raised at the White House session.

Jimmy Carter took a different tack in dealing with Mexico. In addition to a 12-member delegation headed by Secretary Kissinger, Mrs. Rosalyn Carter attended López Portillo's December 1, 1976, inauguration as a private guest of the new chief executive and his wife. She brought a message of "special friendship" for Mexico from her husband, who would himself take office on January 20, 1977.

Once in the White House, President Carter invited López Portillo to become the first foreign head of state to visit Washington during his administration. Upon welcoming his guest on February 14, Carter pledged to work closely on a personal and official basis to bind the two countries in a "continual demonstration of common purpose, common hope, common confidence and common friendship" (Facts on File, 1977).

The two men, although extremely different, share a moderate political philosophy, a penchant for administrative reform, and election to the presidency with relatively few debts to traditional power brokers. López Portillo gained his party's banner thanks to the endorsement of Echeverría, a friend since law school years. Carter won his nomination by strong showings in primary contests held throughout the country. Mrs. Carter claims a longstanding interest in Latin America and the American President has worked exceedingly hard to learn Spanish.

The chief executives reportedly got along quite well. In a White House meeting with several staff and cabinet members, Carter acted quite differently than had Ford six months earlier. He took charge of the session, expressed a keen interest in Mexican affairs, and promised to follow up on matters of mutual concern. Energy, immigration, trade, narcotics, tourism, and the like were identified as matters of mutual interest; however, no in-depth discussions were held. Instead, President Carter proposed the creation of a consultative mechanism to focus on outstanding issues and lay the groundwork for future high-level meetings between representatives of the two countries. During a visit by ranking Mexican officials on May 26, 1977, this mechanism took shape in the establishment of three working groups to concentrate on (1) politics, (2) social matters, and (3) finance.

These groups compiled a mixed record of achievement. With the exception of the political group, they were large, unwieldy, ad hoc bodies with a changing cast of characters who, on each side, had competing interests and sometimes rather indefinite agendas. In the absence of a commitment by either nation to settle major disputes, the groups often lavished attention on peripheral matters. Generally speaking, the participants lacked authority to set policy. One of the most important bilateral issues —the terms for the shipment of Mexican gas to the United States —was largely taken up outside the consultative framework.[2] The groups did enable bureaucrats from a number of agencies to make trips abroad for meetings. However, regularly assigned embassy personnel might well have handled such talks—at least in the preliminary stages—with appropriate civil servants of the host government. But many U.S. agencies would not permit the Department of State to serve as their spokesman. Thus, the mechanism provided an interagency forum for discussing selected issues among representatives of both countries who gained familiarity with each other. It fostered the exchange of information and research and actually helped resolve several problems, such as cooperation against smugglers, known as "coyotes," who assist illegal aliens entering the United States.

The activities of the working groups could not stem an erosion of U.S.-Mexican relations. This deterioration resulted from the collapse of negotiations over the sale of natural gas and efforts by the Carter Administration to secure new legislation on illegal immigration. The natural gas "deal" lies beyond the scope of this article.[3] Suffice it to say that six American gas transmission firms signed a "letter of intent" in August 1977 to import Mexican gas at a price equivalent to the BTU composition of no. 2 fuel oil or $2.60 per thousand cubic feet (Mcf). The memorandum called for initial deliveries of 50 million cubic feet per day to reach 2 billion cubic feet per day by 1979—an amount equal to 4% of U.S. consumption. The Export-Import Bank, a U.S. agency, was expected to provide credits for a 1,183-kilometer gas line to convey the fuel from the Reforma fields to the Texas border.

This accord coincided with congressional consideration of the Carter Administration's natural gas bill, which promised to boost the price to at least $1.75 per Mcf. Paying Mexicans $2.60 per Mcf seemed unfair to many observers when domestic producers could look forward to just two-thirds of this amount. Moreover, the Department of Energy resisted the tie to no. 2 fuel oil, whose price is strongly influenced both by OPEC manipulation and the gyrations of the spot market. But this was only half the problem.

It was feared that Canadians, who at that time received $2.16 per Mcf for gas shipped to the upper Midwest, might increase their price in the face of a Mexican deal. In a pre-Christmas 1977 meeting between Díaz Serrano, Santiago Roel, and then Secretary of Energy James P. Schlesinger, the Mexicans again pressed for the link to no. 2 fuel oil. The Secretary, in a manner perceived by the visitors as abrupt and arrogant, rejected this demand. The ensuing impasse prompted PEMEX to announce on December 22 that it would not renew the letter of intent, scheduled to expire at the end of the year.

Mexican columnists, professors, labor leaders, and government officials lashed out at the United States—and especially Schlesinger, whom officials vilified as a "liar"—for refusing to pay the "world price" for their country's patrimony. Meanwhile, López Portillo announced that the *gasoducto* would extend only to San Fernando, 75 miles below the U.S. border, and that PEMEX would divert the fuel to domestic needs.

This issue quickly became entangled with illegal immigration. President Carter submitted an Illegal Alien Control Bill to Congress in August 1977. His plan contemplated permanent legal alien status for those who had lived continuously in the United States since January 1, 1970, and temporary legal alien status for individuals who had entered the country between that date and January 1, 1977. All persons covered by the legislation would have to register with the government, and the status after five years of the "temporary aliens" was left unclear. The bill also specified increased border surveillance, as well as civil penalties for employers who knowingly hired illegal immigrants. The number of unlawful aliens residing in this country may fall midway among estimates that range from 2 million to 10 million. The Immigration and Naturalization Service apprehended approximately 1 million such aliens in 1978, and many observers contend that at least that many gain entrance to the country each year. The legislation failed because of opposition in the Senate Judiciary Committee and because of growing concern on both ends of Pennsylvania Avenue that a resolute border program would offend Hispanic-American leaders in pivotal, vote-rich states.

President Carter visited Mexico in this climate of recrimination and suspicion. Ironically, his talks with López Portillo began on February 14, 1979—St. Valentine's Day. If the American leader expected bouquets, he was in for a surprise. López Portillo treated his guest to frank, even bristling, lectures. Typical of the tone was an allusion to the breakdown in natural gas negotiations, embedded in a luncheon toast: "Among permanent, not casual neighbors," he said, "surprise moves and sudden deceit or abuse are poisonous fruits that sooner or later have a reverse effect" (New York Times, 1979c).

Carter soldiered on despite fatigue, scorching comments, and the strain of keeping abreast of developments in Iran and Afghanistan. He spoke Spanish to school children, lunched on tacos and beans with farmers in Ixtlilco el Grande, and attempted to reassure every audience that the United States had no imperialist designs on Mexico's hydrocarbons. Private conversations between the two men reportedly proceeded more amicably. Moreover, in a lengthy airport press conference after Carter's departure, López Portillo softened his language toward the President and the United States and attempted to give a more positive interpretation to the joint meeting. Nonetheless, the chief executive forcefully articulated the message that interdependence and mutual respect should replace paternalistic and patronizing attitudes in relations between the two countries. "For Mexico, a country deeply conscious of its past, this public airing of long-held grievances was almost obligatory before resentment toward the United States could be buried" (New York Times, 1979a). It remains to be seen what will happen. Yet if President Carter's visit had a cathartic effect on Mexican leaders, perhaps it will usher in a new period of bilateral ties. The leaders did agree to a resumption of negotiations over natural gas. They also urged a strengthening of the consultative mechanism to infuse it with "more dynamism, cohesion and flexibility for its more effective operation."[4]

What changes have been made in the consultative mechanism? According to a plan developed by the Mexican Affairs desk of the State Department, the three original working groups have given way to eight, each co-chaired—on the U.S. side—by one State Department official and an appropriate representative of another agency. A new "multilateral working group," consisting of Vance and Foreign Minister Jorge Castañeda, replaces the political group. An official at the assistant secretary level will head each of the other seven. These, including the agency working in tandem with the State Department, are: trade (Office of the Special Trade Representative); energy (Department of Energy); finance (Treasury); industry (Commerce); migration (Justice); border (Commerce); law enforcement (Justice); and tourism (Commerce). Representatives of U.S. and Mexican agencies that have an interest in the subject matter constitute the full membership of the seven bodies.

President Carter has proposed a Special Coordinator for Mexican Affairs to serve as the executive secretary for the U.S. side of the consultative mechanism. The name of Ambassador Patrick J. Lucey, envoy to Mexico, surfaced as the likely candidate for this assignment. After an article criticising the governor-turned-diplomat appeared in the Los Angeles *Times* (1979b), Carter warmly praised Lucey, emphasized that he was needed in Mexico City, and selected instead Robert C. Krueger, a 43-year-old former congressman from Texas who has good contacts on Capitol Hill and in the executive branch. This mandate may permit him to cut across bureaucratic fiefdoms to fashion policy in a comprehensive, rather than a fragmented, manner—an approach strongly favored by Ambassador Lucey. He may even be in a position to explore linkages. In making decisions, Krueger can solicit the counsel of a senior interagency advisory group whose composition varies according to the issue at hand.

### *Group Interests*

Governmental and private groups have shown a keen interest in U.S.-Mexican energy relations. A great deal of activity has occurred on Capitol Hill. Senators and representatives from southern, Sun Belt, and eastern states—served by the six transmission companies which have negotiated with PEMEX—generally favor buying Mexican gas. Senators Lloyd Bentsen (D-Tex.), Richard Stone (D-Fla.), and Jacob K. Javits (R-N.Y.) most vocally attacked Secretary Schlesinger for vetoing the original agreement. In contrast, many legislators from the upper Midwest and Northwest, whose constituents depend on Canadian supplies, opposed the terms of the original agreement. An exception has been Senator Frank Church, chairman of the Senate Foreign Relations Committee, who, despite the use of Canadian gas by his Idaho electorate, has suggested agreeing to the higher price as a kind of American aid program for Mexico (Washington Post, 1979a). While the Export-Import Bank was considering a $590 million credit to Petróleos Mexicanos to finance goods and services related to the gasline, Senator Adlai E. Stevenson, III (D-Ill.) introduced a resolution disapproving the $2.60 price as "unreasonable" and a possible "dangerous precedent." Bentsen excoriated the legislation as an act of "economic coercion," stressing that oil and gas revenues were crucial to a "stable, secure and prosperous Mexico" (Excelsior, 1977a). The measure, though never passed, sent a shock wave through the Export-Import Bank, because Stevenson chairs the Senate subcommittee that oversees the agency's activities. The Bank, which needed congressional approval to extend and renew its charter, announced postponement of final action on the loans pending an "indefinite additional review." Despite the eventual approval of both loans, this blatantly political move aroused widespread opposition in Mexico City.

Senator Edward M. Kennedy (D-Mass.) has included Mexican affairs among the many questions that his more than 150 committee and office staff members focus on. Kennedy, who chairs the Subcommittee on Energy of the Joint Economic Committee, became interested in Mexican energy questions on March 21, 1978, when Dr. Bernard Grossling, a scientist at the U.S. Geological Survey, told his subcommittee that Mexico's holdings might be 20 times greater than its proven reserves, then totaling 17 billion barrels (Congressional Research Service, 1978: vii). The Senator requested that the Congressional Research Service

(CRS) conduct an in-depth study of Mexico's energy prospects. If Mexico did embrace large hydrocarbon reserves, he was anxious to pursue a "package deal," a comprehensive agreement in the mold of the SALT and Middle East settlements that covered trade, immigration, and energy.

The analysis, which underlines the potential importance of PEMEX's oil and gas to the United States, reinforced Kennedy's belief that the Carter Administration was badly handling bilateral relations. He berated Schlesinger for having "spurned the opportunity for negotiations with the Mexicans on price."

A great deal of Mexico's gas is associated with oil and must be injected, consumed at home, or exported to prevent loss through flaring. "Unless we encourage long-term gas supplies from Mexico," he warned, "Mexico will never maximize oil production" (Washington Post, 1979d). In his view, increased Mexican output will enable consuming nations, if not the United States, to shift "reliance away from the Middle East" (Congressional Research Service, 1978: vii). Even more important, sale of oil and gas will stimulate the economic growth required to solve the immigration problem to which the Massachusetts Democrat must now pay special attention as chairman of the Senate Judiciary Committee. With respect to Mexico as with a half-dozen other issues, Kennedy has painstakingly put distance between himself and the administration, while cultivating an important constituency—in this case, Mexican-Americans, who are well disposed toward the Catholic *político.*

Also concerned about relations with Mexico is the Hispanic Caucus in the House of Representatives. The caucus, organized in late 1976, named its three-member staff in 1977 and held its first fund-raising dinner in September 1978. Its purpose is to establish an identity for Hispanic-American political leaders and sharpen the country's awareness of the needs of their people in housing, bilingual education, immigration, and employment. Energy forms a component of a comprehensive policy proposal on Mexico that was being elaborated in mid-1979. Caucus members, along with other Hispanic-American leaders, have made a bid for greater influence with the Carter Administration. They met with the President, at his request, on the eve of his February 1979 visit to Mexico, and, later, advanced candidates to succeed Lucey when it appeared that he would leave his ambassadorial post. A confluence of factors—newness, small size, lack of resources, and divisions with its constituency—militate against the Hispanic Caucus's playing a role for Mexico that Jewish and Greek leaders play, respectively, for Israel and Greece. The Mexican government has kept a polite distance between itself and the Hispanic-American community. Still, López Portillo, well aware of the importance of ethnic politics in the United States, has met with a number of Chicano leaders, whose political influence can be expected to increase.

Dozens of U.S. legislators have become acquainted with their Mexican counterparts through annual meetings held under the auspices of the Mexico-United States Interparliamentary Group.[5] This group, formed in 1961, was led for many years by former Senate Majority Leader Mike Mansfield, who developed an expertise in Mexican affairs. The American delegation, chaired by Senator Bentsen and Representative de la Garza in 1979, may consist of as many as 12 senators and 12 representatives, although it has sometimes been difficult to fill the U.S. quota. The binational sessions, held alternately in Mexico and the United States, are essentially opportunities for travel, social contacts, and exchanges of views. For example, the Americans were well acquainted with Enrique Olivares Santana appointed Minister of Gobernación (Interior) in mid-May 1979 because he had served for several years as a leader of the group.

That U.S. state governments, which enjoy much greater autonomy than their Mexican counterparts, endeavor to shape policy further complicates bilateral relations and confuses opinion-makers below the Rio Grande. For example, Texas Governor William P. Clements has argued publicly that a sensible energy strategy entails deregulating oil and gas, tumbling regulatory barriers, spurring the construction of nuclear plants, and acquiring Mexican hydrocarbons at the price fixed by PEMEX. To facilitate the last objective, he has proposed a conference of governors from adjoining U.S. and Mexican states. "The United States must not compromise its position as a world power," he said. "This is the moment that the United States must get off its knees and stand tall" (Proceso, 1979). Mexico City's leading weekly magazine, *Proceso,* interpreted this forceful statement as a threat that "one of the most influential governors in the North American power structure" was prepared, if necessary, to dispatch armed forces to secure Mexico's oil and gas. Other Mexican elites, whose familiarity with their own political system makes it difficult for them to comprehend the plurality of American politics and who are convinced that the U.S. Marine Corps eagerly awaits a return to the Halls of Montezuma, immediately assumed that the governor was acting in concert with the White House and the Pentagon.

Thc Alaska state government, also acting independently of Washington, figured prominently in an initiative to send Prudhoe Bay crude oil to Japan in exchange for the shipment of Japanese-purchased Mexican oil to the U.S. Gulf Coast. Proponents claim the "swap" would save from 60¢ to $2.00 per barrel in transportation costs, help diminish the 400,000 bpd glut on the Pacific Coast, and provide additional incentives for major oil firms to increase Alaskan production and enlarge the capacity of the 800-mile trans-Alaskan pipeline (Washington Post, 1979b). The Carter Administration, wary of public reaction to the export of U.S. oil, has exhibited coolness toward this proposal, which would require congressional approval before implementation.

Nongovernmental interest groups have also attempted to influence U.S.-Mexican policy. The American Federation of Labor/Congress of Industrial Organizations (AFL-CIO) has been particularly active in recent years. It has lobbied for (1) the termination of the Bracero program, (2) an aggressive plan to halt the flow of illegal aliens, and (3) tariff protection against Mexican imports, including the products of the assembly plants along the border which the Mexican government has encouraged with special tax advantages. Organized labor has not yet taken an active part in energy-related issues.

Banks with a stake in the development of Mexico's hydrocarbons have been more visible in this regard. The International Monetary fund reported that Brazil and Mexico were responsible for 44% of the identifiable outstanding debt owed by non-OPEC nations to private banks in 1976. Loans to Mexico totaled $10.75 billion. Three years later, the two countries accounted for 70% of the $100 billion in foreign debt of Latin American countries (Excelsior, 1979b). The banks have excellent contacts on Capitol Hill. They also communicate their interests through the Treasury Department and various chambers of commerce devoted to business activity in Mexico.

The Mexican-U.S. Chamber of Commerce, composed of equal numbers of members in both countries, is an important voice of private business with access to leading policy makers on both sides of the border. In October 1978 this organization, in cooperation with Petróleos Mexicanos, sponsored a tour of Mexico's oil and gas facilities for ten members, including Caterpillar Tractor Co., Rockwell International, and W. R. Grace and Co., which provide equipment, parts, and service to Mexico's oil industry. Ostensibly designed to give the firms an overview of Mexican operations, the activity may also have been intended to gain grass-roots support for closer energy relations.

The chamber has also cultivated senators and representatives. In January it made a PEMEX-prepared slide presentation to members and staff of the Senate Energy and Natural Resources Committee. Later in the year, it developed plans for a second Mexican oil tour, especially for key legislators and staff committee aides.

A number of corporations have individually attempted to influence the course of U.S.-Mexican affairs. For example, the gas transmission companies fought hard to gain congressional and bureaucratic support for their deal with PEMEX.

Articles appearing in influential industry-oriented publications reflect the business community's disenchantment with U.S. policy vis-à-vis Mexico. A typical commentary, entitled "A Perplexing U.S. Coolness toward Mexican Oil," stated:

> Washington has . . . done very little to boost development in southern Mexico, with one of the world's biggest non-OPEC oil reserves. In some ways, the U.S. has even hampered the Mexican effort by feeding political ammunition to opponents of rapid development and early sale to American buyers. Washington policy has been neutral at best [Business Week, 1978].

Ironically, friends of Israel who excoriated Mexico's vote for a 1976 "Zionism is racism" resolution in the United Nations now see in that country's black gold an opportunity to reshape American foreign policy. Most vociferous has been *The New Republic,* whose publisher, Martin Peretz, is one of the leading advocates and financial backers of Israel's cause in the United States. In an August 19, 1978, editorial, his magazine identified Mexican reserves at between 150 and 200 billion barrels and accused the U.S. government of concealing this fact from the American public and Congress "apparently to avoid undermining energy policies premised on scarcity and foreign policies based on nuzzling the Arabs." It reserved special criticism for the "Mexico can't" school which contends that "PEMEX can't produce more than four or five million barrels a day by 1985." While denying acceptance of conspiracy theories, the piece states that "both the Ford and Carter administrations seem to have made deliberate decisions to discount Mexican oil in charting U.S. energy and foreign policy."

Leaders of Hispanic-American organizations also wish to help shape their country's relationship with Mexico. To date, theirs has been but a weak voice in an interest group chorus dominated by unions, banks, corporations, and Jewish spokesmen. As mentioned above, the Hispanic-American community suffers from internal divisions, disagreement over strategy and objectives, internecine struggles, low educational and income levels, and limited political experience. In contrast to attitudes toward Jews and Greek-Americans in Jerusalem and Athens, officials in Mexico City view Mexican-Americans, who are caught between two cultures, with noticeable misgivings.

*Mexico's Petroleum Policy*

While the Carter Administration and Congress wrestled over an energy program, the López Portillo government had to make hard choices concerning its own petroleum policies. Should Mexico affiliate with the Organization of Petroleum Exporting Countries (OPEC)? Should it concentrate on selling crude or refined products? Should it attempt to diversify its market? Should a pipeline for gas be built to connect the southeastern fields to the U.S. border?

Although at least one of Luis Echeverría's ministers voiced interest in OPEC membership as a part of a strategy of nonalignment, López Portillo has rejected affiliation with the cartel.[6] Every government spokesman has echoed this position, including the director-general of PEMEX, who said there was no need to join the organization "neither in the short, medium, or long run" (Excelsior, 1977b). What accounts for this emphatic position? To begin with, Mexico differs from most of the 13 cartel members. The majority of these countries export one principal item—oil—whereas Mexico also earns substantial foreign exchange from tourism, silver, coffee, manufactures, and farm products. In comparison with the 90% of hard currency which it ordinarily generates for most OPEC members, oil and petrochemicals accounted for 49% of the value of Mexico's exports in 1979 (Díaz Serrano, 1979: 27).

Even more significant, the cartel sprang up in 1970 in reaction to price manipulation by multinational corporations on which OPEC nations depended for the exploitation, refining, transportation, and marketing of their oil. In contrast, Mexico freed itself from similar foreign influence four decades ago by expropriating the companies that dominated its industry. Unlike the OPEC countries, Mexico boasts a national oil firm that has gained invaluable experience and knowhow since 1938. While all OPEC members have now created state companies, these tend to specialize in the lifting of crude oil as compared with the fully integrated structure of PEMEX. Further, the Mexican Petroleum Institute, a research center and think tank, employs 3,000 people, has 90 patents to its credit, and performs a high percentage of the industry's engineering and design work.

Joining OPEC would expose Mexico to both anticartel criticism and the loss of export preferences under the 1974 U.S. Trade Reform Act. Washington has already imposed this sanction on OPEC members, including two Latin American states, Venezuela and Ecuador. Developed countries can cushion the impact of higher energy costs through their pricing of manufactured goods; however, most less-developed nations enjoy no such hedge, and the sharp rise in oil prices since 1973 has ravaged their economies. Mexico would do well to remain outside the body responsible for this increase, especially if it wants to gain influence at the expense of Venezuela in Central America and the Caribbean, where OPEC prices have exacerbated economic problems. Mexico, which remains aloof from many international bodies, jealously safeguards its freedom of action. Díaz Serrano has cited a desire to preserve its commercial flexibility as a reason for staying out of OPEC (Daily Report, 1978a). In view of the increasing supply of oil on world markets, OPEC could shift from coordinating prices to setting production quotas. This possibility, though remote, makes the cartel even less attractive to a new exporter such as Mexico, which, if a member, could play but a minor role in influencing policy until its exports approach those of the key members.

Saudi Arabia and some other Arab members are reportedly cool to Mexican membership in view of its present modest export level of 672,000 bpd in 1979 and its vigorous courting of Israel, as exemplified by PEMEX's readiness to supply 50,000 of the 70,000 barrels consumed by Israel in mid-1979. An interest in attracting American Jews as tourists and the encouragement of the U.S. State Department help explain closer Mexican-Israeli ties.

As a result, Mexico has kept a sharp eye on OPEC deliberations and charged prices somewhat higher than those of the cartel in June 1979 ($17.10 per barrel versus $14.54). Reduced ocean shipping costs and a surtax because of the quality of Mexican crude oil contribute to the higher price.

Will Mexico sell mostly crude or refined products? Pressures are building for PEMEX to stimulate the economy and demonstrate its advanced status and technological machismo by exporting products. But López Portillo, who makes the final decisions, has emphasized the urgent need to move crude to galvanize his country's economic growth.

The imperative to earn hard currency springs from difficult economic conditions that include the growing import of corn, wheat, and other basic foodstuffs. In view of the huge investment required for refineries and the current worldwide surplus of refining capacity, more money can be made quickly by exporting crude. Consequently, PEMEX's six-year investment program calls for a relative diminution in outlays for refining, while expenditures for drilling, production, and transportation rise (Petróleos Mexicanos, 1978).

Where will Mexico sell the bulk of its hydrocarbons? Every oil-related official document carries a de rigeur paragraph about the maximum diversification of purchasers, and a key cabinet member has emphasized that "Mexico will not commit itself to supplying the United States with petroleum." Yet, several factors strongly favor a "sell-America" policy.

To begin with, Mexico is used to doing business with the United States, which accounts for the bulk of its trade. Financing from American banks, holders of over half of the Mexican government's foreign debt, is crucial to PEMEX's $15 billion six-year development program. Moreover, despite the bitter expropriation struggle four decades ago, American firms—often with Mexican partners—have provided invaluable exploration, geological, and engineering assistance to PEMEX. Finally, because of high production costs and geographic propinquity, Mexico can most profitably sell oil and natural gas to the United States, which will continue to receive a majority of its exports.

López Portillo's petroleum policy has not encountered the impediments suffered by Carter's energy plan because of the centralized, authoritarian nature of Mexico's political system. In theory an Energy Commission, composed of relevant agency heads, including the Secretary of National Patrimony under whose jurisdiction Petróleos Mexicanos falls, advises the President in this important area. More often than not, he seems to make decisions after consulting PEMEX's director-general and, possibly, his key advisers in energy matters—Rafael Izquierdo and Jaime Corredor. Still, there has been more opposition than usually confronts programs of the Mexican executive. Although it eventually passed overwhelmingly, a constitutional amendment to facilitate construction of the Cactus-Reynosa gas line excited sharp criticism within Mexico's usually docile congress. Deputy Victor Manzanilla Schaffer, a member of the governing party's peasant sector, denounced the measure, which permits PEMEX to occupy or expropriate land deemed necessary for investigation, exploration, or exploitation, as unconstitutional and contrary to the spirit of the Mexican revolution's sacred agrarian reform (Proceso, 1978). Only four days before, Senator Jorge Cruickshank García, leader of the left-leaning Popular Socialist Party, criticized a government-sponsored mining bill, which also fell under article 27, as heightening the possibility that foreign firms could exploit the nation's newly discovered uranium deposits (Latin America Political Report, 1978).

A National Front for the Protection of Natural Resources, composed of a score of small Marxist organizations, emerged in March 1978 to protest the "massive and indiscriminate" exploitation of Mexico's mineral wealth. Herberto Castillo, head of the small but vocal Mexican Workers Party and one of the most articulate adversaries of López Portillo's program, said that current policies would not only exhaust the country's energy resources but exacerbate Mexico's dependence on the United States. The National Front demanded an energy policy that would benefit the neglected members of the populace (Daily Report, 1978b). Recently adopted political reforms which give minority parties greater access to media and congressional seats will no doubt facilitate increased criticism of governmental energy policy.

Mexican presidents often use foreign policy to bolster their domestic standing, reaffirm a commitment to the country's revolution, and disarm critics (Pellicer de Brody, 1972: 124). In the face of desultory attacks, López Portillo adopted this strategy so often employed by his predecessors. *First,* his ministers emphasized that only "surplus" gas would be shipped to the northern neighbor and then only at Mexico's price. Failure to attain that price would lead to domestic consumption of the fuel.

*Second,* even though the chief executive flew to Panama to witness the June 16, 1978, exchange of instruments of ratification of the new Panama Canal Treaties, he made clear his disfavor over clauses that allow the United States to intervene militarily in Panama should the canal be closed for any reason. He manifested this disapproval by declining to attend a dinner for other Latin American leaders at the ratification ceremony, thereby forcing cancellation of the evening event.

*Third,* to assert his nation's independence in foreign affairs and defuse carping from Marxist-oriented groups, López Portillo in mid-May 1978 made a 15-day visit to Eastern Europe. He spent the bulk of his time in the Soviet Union, praised for signing the "Tlaltelolco Treaty" prohibiting nuclear arms in Latin America. As a goodwill gesture, the Russians—who run a massive intelligence-gathering operation from their Mexico City embassy—pledged to share sophisticated fishing techniques and advanced petroleum technology. Thus, he put Washington on notice that the United States is not the only superpower with which Mexico can have working relations on energy matters.

## *Prospects*

The United States will no longer be the only star in Mexico's international firmament. Until the 1970s foreign affairs for Mexico meant, in essence, relations with its northern neighbor. Echeverría's move to change that failed as economic difficulties made his country even more dependent on American financial help. Mexico's vulnerability was especially evident when North American Jews launched a boycott of tourist facilities in the wake of the UN vote equating Zionism with racism. Yet, despite his many problems, Echeverría whetted Mexican aspirations for a new, more assertive role on the world stage.

The role that Echeverría couldn't secure with breathless globe-trotting and stentorian speeches, López Portillo is assuming thanks to his country's massive oil supplies. The former president scurried from continent to continent in search of diplomatic support and recognition for his country. Now the presidents, premiers, and foreign ministers of major nations flock to Mexico City. As Jorge Díaz Serrano expressed it: "We are frankly as inundated with buyers as with oil" (Washington Post, 1979c).

Political turmoil in Iran enhanced Mexico's attractiveness to energy-starved Japan. Two loan accords were signed in 1978: One committed a consortium of private banks to nearly $600 million, the largest credit without strings ever granted a foreign borrower by Japanese banks; the other amounted to $460 million. These funds will help finance a petrochemical complex, ports in Tabasco and Oaxaca, and the Alpha Omega road, rail, and pipeline link across the Isthmus of Tehuantepec. No long-term oil agreement existed in mid-1979, but port and transport facilities are of particular concern to the Japanese, who hope to purchase regular 220,000 bpd shipments (Latin American Economic Report, 1978). The high Mexican price has thus far proved an obstacle to significant hydrocarbon sales to the oriental nation.

Mexico and Sweden have explored the possibility that petrochemical plants in the Scandanavian country could process PEMEX crude and distribute it in Europe. The countries have also discussed collaborative efforts in nuclear energy, tourism, and shipbuilding (Daily Report, 1979b). Canada has announced plans to exchange "Candu" nuclear generators for Mexican crude oil beginning in 1980. One reactor costs about $1 billion and will probably command a year's supply of oil at the rate of 150,000 bpd (Daily Report, 1979e). Meanwhile, Mexico has publicized its intention to furnish Spain 5 million tons of crude oil over a 5-year period (Daily Report, 1979d). Also under study is the possibility of building PEMEX refineries in this Iberian nation to facilitate the sale of Mexican petroleum products within the European Economic Community (Daily Report, 1978c). Even before Giscard d'Estaing's highly successful visit, France had signed a contract, effective January 1, 1980, to buy 100,000 bpd of Mexican oil (Daily Report, 1979a).

Over a dozen countries have entered into agreements with Mexico, and by January 1979 it had committed all of that year's production and most of the output for 1980. This activity formed part of an "export diversification plan" whereby the U.S. share of purchases will fall from 85% in 1978 to 80% in 1979 to between 60% and 66% in 1980 (Washington Post, 1979c).

Even as it picks and chooses among deals proposed by European nations and Japan, Mexico has lent a helping hand to sister Latin American republics. Cooperation has been impressively close with Brazil which, with Mexican aid, anticipates self-sufficiency in petroleum by the early 1980s. To achieve this goal, the Brazilian state oil company, Petrobras, concluded a working agreement with PEMEX and the Mexican Petroleum Institute in 1977 (Excelsior, 1977c). Mexico has also discussed providing both 20,000 barrels of oil and technical assistance to El Salvador (Daily Report, 1979c). López Portillo has also promised oil to Costa Rica in 1980, although he refused the Central American nation's request for a special price (Excelsior, 1979a). The attention lavished on Mexico has increased the confidence and asssertiveness of its governmental leaders.

Media reports have stressed the negative aspects of U.S.-Mexican relations. Newspaper, magazine, and television commentaries have paid inordinate attention to prickly toasts, artless references to "Montezuma's revenge," and recriminations over the natural gas negotiations. Largely ignored has been the remarkable degree of cooperation in energy matters between Mexico and private and public groups in the United States. PEMEX buys millions of dollars worth of equipment, parts, and supplies from U.S. manufacturers each year; it relies on American firms for drilling rigs and crews for offshore exploration and development; and it hires American scientists and technicians for important geological and seismological work. Symbolic of this need for U.S. expertise was the decision to have DeGoyler and MacNaughton, an internationally respected Dallas consulting firm, certify the larger reserve estimates announced early in the López Portillo administration.

Exports to the United States will continue to grow in volume as they decrease as a percentage of Mexico's sales abroad. In addition, some of the oil sold to other countries winds up in the United States because of exchanges and swaps that characterize the international oil business. Little attention has been given to Mexico's readiness to sell crude oil to the Department of Defense for the National Strategic Petroleum Reserve. This reserve, projected to reach 1 billion barrels, is stored in western salt mines and will be used in case of a national emergency. PEMEX's one sale to date for this purpose was made in June 1978 and totaled 1.4 million barrels at a price of $19 million (Excelsior, 1978a).

The Pentagon purchases emphasize the advantages of Mexican oil supplies in terms of proximity, quality, and security.[7] A draft of a presidential review memorandum (PRM-41), prepared by the National Security Council, reportedly refers to Mexico as "the most promising new source" of oil in the 1980s and suggests a serious upgrading in the country's priority among U.S. foreign interests. The document, yet to be published, much less translated into policy, suggests that a redirection in bilateral relations might include U.S. concessions to Mexico on trade and illegal immigration (Washington Post, 1978).

If this is true, the memorandum epitomizes the tendency of some decision makers to overreact in the face of new circumstances. Mexico's oil is important. But it is questionable whether access to these hydrocarbons at the price, for instance, of continuing to absorb hundreds of thousands of unlawful workers each year would enhance the overall security and well-being of the U.S. population. This is not the forum for analyzing the migration problem. However, Mexico has opted for capital-intensive rather than labor-intensive industrialization, and the number of new people in the labor force outstrips the creation of jobs. Most evidence, including an accelerating rate of inflation, points to an expansion in the current flood of *indocumentados*—with marked political, economic, and environmental consequences for the United States. Even a Spanish-speaking Quebec, activated by the drum-beat of secession, could emerge in the Sun Belt by the end of the century. By that time, the T-shirts now on sale in San Antonio, which proclaim, "YOU ARE NOW IN OCCUPIED MEXICO," may not appear so facetious. And quite apart from the illegal alien question, growing dependence on Mexico would make this country vulnerable to pressures exerted by future governments that might not be as moderate as the existing one. Easy access to a new oil cornucopia would also delay long overdue efforts in conservation and the development of alternative energy sources.

Oil is fungible. And the important thing about Mexican crude is not who buys it but that it is sold. Its availability on the world market will not shatter OPEC, but it should relieve the pressure on North Sea and Persian Gulf sources. A backyard reserve would be most useful to the United States in case of a Mideast explosion, world war, or interdiction of the shipping lanes. Yet, in the event of an international crisis, Mexico might also find it convenient to have a contiguous market for its exports. Even then, the United States would be treaty bound to share available supplies with its allies.

Higher prices and energy may combine to hold U.S. oil imports to 10 or 11 million bpd in the mid-1980s when Mexican exports will have reached 1.8 to 2.5 million. Assuming the United States purchases 60% of these shipments, Mexico would supply 10% to 15% of its neighbor's imports. This figure would exceed 25% if President Carter manages to hold imports to their 1977 level, as announced in July 1979. Although not the subject of this article, it is interesting to note that the imperative to buy an increasing volume of basic farm products abroad may pose as serious a problem for Mexico as energy does for America. This complementarity, replete with linkage opportunities, further illuminates a growing coincidence of interests that means that neither country will again have to approach the other with hat in hand.

## NOTES

1. Several reasons lead Francisco Viniegra, former manager of exploration for PEMEX, and others to doubt the reserve figures: (1) unlike any other country, Mexico places natural gas, which constitutes 35% of the total, in its reserves; (2) "probable" reserves may have been included in "proven" reserves; and (3) the recoverable potential of the Chicontepec fields has been greatly exaggerated. When the senior vice president for DeGolyer and MacNaughton, the U.S. firm hired by PEMEX to certify its oil discoveries, was asked if Mexico's proven oil reserves might be as high as, perhaps, 28 billion barrels, he exclaimed, "Oh, no. Oh, no" (Los Angeles, Times, 1979a).

2. Discussions on the gas transactions took place at the highest levels, culminating in a confrontation between Foreign Minister Santiago Roel and PEMEX Director General Díaz Serrano, on one hand, and then Secretary of Energy James R. Schlesinger, on the other (Latin America Economic Report, 1978).

3. For an analysis of the gas deal, see Fagan and Nau (1978) and Grayson (1978b).

4. Excerpts from the joint communique by the presidents appeared in the New York *Times* (1979b).

5. Thc activities of the congressional interchange are described in Mansfield (1976).

6. For analyses of Mexico's relation to the cartel, see Williams (1978) and Grayson (1979).

7. Richard R. Fagan (1978) explores the security implications of Mexican oil.

## REFERENCES


Barron's (1978) October 9: 43.

BERMUDEZ, A. J. (1963) The Mexican National Petroleum Industry: A Case Study in Nationalization. Stanford: Institute of Hispanic and Luso-Brazilian Studies.

Business Week (1978) May 29: 50.

Congressional Research Service (1978) "Mexico's oil and gas policy: an analysis." Prepared for the Committee on Foreign Relations, U.S. Senate and the Joint Economic Committee, Congress of the United States.

Daily Report [Foreign Broadcast Information Service, Latin America] (1979a) March 1: M-1.

——— (1979b) February 7: M-2.

——— (1979c) January 23: M-2.

——— (1979d) January 15: M-1.

——— (1979e) January 12: M-1.

——— (1978a) June 20: M-1.

——— (1978b) March 21: M-1.

——— (1978c) February 3: M-1.

DIAZ SERRANO, J. (1979) "Informe del director general de Petróleos Mexicanos, 18 de marzo 1979." Mexico, D.F.: Petróleos Mexicanos.

Economist (1978) September 23: 125.

Excelsior (1979a) May 21: 15-A, 21-A.
——— (1979b) May 20: 1-A, 8-A.
——— (1978a) June 6: 1-A, 14-A.
——— (1978b) March 14: 23-A.
——— (1977a) November 4: 17-A.
——— (1977b) September 10: 4-A.
——— (1977c) May 29: 34-A.
Facts on File (1977) February 26: 136.
FAGAN, R. R. (1978) "El petroleo mexicano y la seguridad nacional de Estados Unidos." Foro Internacional 19 (October-December): 216-230.
——— and H. R. NAU (1978) "Mexican gas: the northern connection." Prepared for conference on the United States, U.S. Foreign Policy and Latin America and the Caribbean Regimes, Washington, DC, March 27-31. (unpublished)
GRAYSON, G. W. (1979) "Mexico, the United States and OPEC." Presented at Symposium on Mexican-U.S. Economic Relations held at Universidad Metropolitana Xochimilco, Mexico City, May 23-25.
——— (1978a) "Mexico's opportunity: the oil boom." Foreign Policy 29 (winter): 67-71.
——— (1978b) "Mexico and the United States: the natural gas controversy." Inter-American Economic Affairs 32 (Winter): 3-27.
Latin America Economic Report (1978) November 10: 346.
Latin America Political Report (1978) January 6: 7.
Los Angeles Times (1979a) May 18: 1,6.
——— (1979b) March 24: 1.
MANSFIELD, M. (1976) The Mexico-United States Interparliamentary Group: A Sixteen-Year History. Washington, DC: Government Printing Office.
New York Times (1979a) February 19: A-5.
——— (1979b) February 17: A-5.
——— (1979c) February 16: A-16.
PELLICER DE BRODY, O. (1972) Mexico y la Revolucion Cubana. Mexico, D.F.: El Colegio de Mexico.
Petróleos Mexicanos (1979) Memoria de labores 1978. Mexico, D.F.: Instituto Mexicano del Petroleo.
——— (1978) Memoria de labores 1977. Mexico, D.F.: Institute Mexicano del Petroleo.
POWELL, J. R. (1972) The Mexican Petroleum Industry: 1939-1950. New York: Russell & Russell.
Proceso (1979) March 19: 10-11.
——— (1978) January 2: 6 ff.
RONFELDT, D. and C. SERESERES (1978) "Immigration issues affecting U.S.-Mexican relations." Presented to Brookings Institution-El Colegio de Mexico Symposium on Structural Factors Contributing to Current Patterns of Migration in Mexico and the Caribbean Basis, Washington, D.C., June 28-30. (unpublished)
SAMPSON, A. (1975) The Seven Sisters. New York: Viking.
Washington Post (1979a) February 14: D-8.
——— (1979b) February 7: A-17.
——— (1979c) January 14: K-2.
——— (1979d) January 11: P-3.
——— (1978) December 15: 1, 26.

WILLIAMS, E. J. (1978) "Mexico, oil and OPEC." Latin American Digest 11, 12 (Fall-Winter): 4-6.

World Oil (1979) February 1: 40.

*George W. Grayson, whose Ph.D. is from Johns Hopkins University, is Professor of Government at the College of William and Mary. His research on Mexican oil, with four trips to Mexico since 1976, has resulted in articles in several journals and a forthcoming book to be called* The Politics of Mexican Oil.

**WILLIAM M. LeoGRANDE**
*School of Government and Public Administration*
*American University*

# *PARTY DEVELOPMENT IN REVOLUTIONARY CUBA*

During the Cuban revolution's first decade, Fidel Castro's charismatic authority and predominant position eclipsed the significance of the new institutions created to replace the prerevolutionary political order. The "institutionalization" under way in Cuba since 1970, however, has strengthened and formalized the political structure to the extent that the island's institutions can no longer be regarded as peripheral to the dynamics of Cuban politics. This is particularly true of the Communist party of Cuba, which has emerged from the 1970s as the central political institution. The way in which the party has developed not only highlights some of the problems inherent in the process of creating a new political order, but is also essential for understanding contemporary Cuban politics.

## *Building a New Party Apparatus*

### *THE ORI: THE ABORTIVE ATTEMPT TO BUILD A PARTY*

Most socialist revolutions undertake the process of forming new political institutions with the Communist party at center stage. Forged during the struggle for state power, the party con-

---

AUTHOR'S NOTE: This article is a revised and updated version of *The Development of the Party System in Revolutionary Cuba,* a monograph published by the Northwestern Pennsylvania Institute for Latin American Studies. The author wishes to express his appreciation to Professor Edward Gonzalez for his comments and suggestions on the manuscript's first draft.

Journal of Interamerican Studies and World Affairs, Vol. 21 No. 4, November 1979 457-480
© 1979 Sage Publications, Inc.

stitutes the organizational core around which the new political system is erected; other institutions are constructed under its guidance and at its direction. The Cuban revolution, however, was the first socialist revolution to succeed without a Leninist party in the vanguard of the revolutionary struggle. The victory over Batista's dictatorship was won instead by a loose coalition of political groups, foremost among them Fidel Castro's 26th of July Movement, hereinafter referred to as M-26-7. Shortly after victory, the anti-Batista coalition began to disintegrate over the issue of what the future course of the revolution should be, and even the M-26-7 divided into warring factions. Always more a movement than an organization, the M-26-7 was by 1961 so atrophied from disuse and so riddled by defections that the meager infrastructure it had possessed initially no longer existed. Thus, as the revolutionaries turned to the task of creating a new Cuba, there was no party apparatus through which to govern.

In order to provide such a political apparatus and perhaps to convince the Soviet Union that Cuba's revolution was authentically socialist, the creation of a new vanguard party was begun in early 1961 with the merger of the only three groups remaining in the political arena: the M-26-7, minus its right wing; the Revolutionary Directorate (Directorio Revolucionario—DR), essentially a student group; and the Popular Socialist party (Pardito Socialista Popular—PSP), the old Communist party. In July 1961, Castro formally announced the merger of these three organizations into the Integrated Revolutionary Organizations (Organizaciones Integradas Revolucionarias—ORI; see Castro, 1961).

Since only the PSP had cadres with both the requisite organizational experience and a long history of commitment to the revolution's newly adopted socialist goals, construction of the ORI was entrusted to veteran leaders of the PSP. Under the direction of Aníbal Escalante, former PSP Executive Secretary, the development of the ORI proceeded rapidly. Within a few months, hundreds of ORI members had been selected and appointed to key governmental posts, giving the ORI tremendous influence over the most fundamental policies and programs of the revolution.

The process of building the ORI did not proceed without friction, however. On July 26, 1961, Castro had implied that the ORI would be a transitional institution through which the M-26-7, DR, and PSP would cooperate in the creation of a unified party—the United Party of the Socialist Revolution (Partido Unido de la Revolución Socialista—PURS). He reaffirmed this view explicitly on December 2, 1961, when he declared himself a Marxist-Leninist. Aníbal Escalante's view (1961), however was that the ORI would *be* the new party. In September 1961, he called the ORI "the backbone of the revolutionary state" and implied that a simple change in name would constitute the change from the ORI to the PURS.

Behind these disparate conceptions of the ORI was a growing controversy over how its construction was being handled. Lauded as the organization which would structurally integrate the three major revolutionary groups, the ORI was, in fact, nothing but the apparatus of the PSP under a new name. Escalante used his dominant position to pack the new party with his old comrades from the PSP, to the virtual exclusion of veterans from the M-26-7 and DR. In fact, as ORI members were appointed to posts in the government and mass organizations, hundreds of M-26-7 and DR veterans lost their positions in those institutions because of their "low political level" (Castro, 1962a).

Given the relatively marginal role played by the PSP in the struggle against Batista, such practices engendered much bitterness. Equal in seriousness to the aggravation of divisions within the revolutionary leadership caused by the PSP's capture of the ORI was the manner in which the party undertook its role of directing the revolutionary process. In order to attain hegemony over the other institutions of the political system, the vast majority of newly selected ORI members were appointed to administrative posts in these other institutions, leaving virtually no membership among rank and file workers. As a result, the ORI was neither capable of perceiving the degree of support or opposition among the people for various policies nor of mobilizing the people in support of policy. When resistance was displayed toward ill-conceived policy, the ORI responded with coercion. The popular reaction to this arbitrary and sometimes illegal repression was disillusionment, intensified by the appearance of special privileges for those in the ORI hierarchy.

The ORI's response to the 1961 agrarian problem offers, in microcosm, an excellent picture of the dimensions of the political crisis then brewing. The 1959 agrarian reform expropriated only the largest of the private estates, leaving some 57% of the cultivable land outside the public sector in the form of small and medium-sized farms. In the fall of 1961, resistance developed among the remaining private farmers to the regulations compelling them to sell their produce solely to the government at fixed rates. The ORI's response was to crack down on the private farmers indiscriminantly; produce was seized, people arrested, and some lands were even confiscated, although the Council of Ministers had passed no law authorizing the expropriation of medium-sized farms. The farmers defended their interests in classic fashion—they planted only enough for their own consumption, so that by 1962 the regime was faced with a critical shortage of food, resulting in considerable popular discontent and several overtly antigovernment demonstrations. In the first major test of its ability to guide the revolution forward, the ORI proved to be a miserable failure—alienating en masse the private farmers, and provoking such privation that general support for the revolution was jeopardized. For Castro, who had resolved in December to institutionalize his "one-man rule" in the collective wisdom of the party, the result could not have been more disturbing. Perhaps it is not coincidental that Castro's first public intimation that significant changes in the ORI were required came on March 12, 1962, when he announced the need to ration food (Castro, 1962b).

The following day, at a ceremony commemorating the DR's assault on the presidential palace and the death of the DR's founder José Antonio Echevarría, a student leader reading Echevarría's political testament omitted a passage referring to God. Outraged at the alteration of the text, Castro (1962c) denounced such rewriting of history as foreign to Marxism. Such attitudes were turning the revolution into a tyranny, he said; a struggle had to be waged against them and also against vagrants and privileged persons who had esconsed themselves in the ORI. Speaking five days later at the Conrado Benítez School of Revolutionary Instruction, Castro (1962d) escalated his attack on the ORI; it had lost touch with the masses, he charged, and had imposed on the nation a despotism "almost indistinguishable from Batista and his henchmen." It was necessary, he continued, to wholly reorganize the party, doing away with sectarianism and privilege once and for all.

On March 22, the National Directorate of the ORI met and created the apparatus for conducting this reorganization—the National Secretariat of the ORI (Cuba Socialista, 1962). Only one of the Secretariat's six members, Blas Roca, was a PSP veteran, and his assignment to edit the newspaper *Hoy* effectively removed him from the reorganization of the ORI. To undertake the reorganization, the Secretariat created an Organizational Commission composed of M-26-7 veterans Osvaldo Dorticós and Emilio Aragones, formerly the M-26-7's National Coordinator. Aníbal Escalante was removed from the National Directorate and went into exile in Czechoslovakia shortly thereafter.

Finally, in a televised address to the nation on March 26, Castro (1962a) presented a detailed criticism of Escalante and the ORI. The party had, he said, degenerated into a pervasive sectarianism—"the sectarianism of believing that the only revolutionaries . . . who could hold positions of trust . . . had to be old Marxist militants." This attitude had created not a political apparatus, but "a nest of privilege, toleration, favoritism, a system of immunities and favors," the authority of which "came from the fact that from it one might expect a favor, some dispensation, or some harm or good." Through its appointees, the ORI had reduced the government to an appendage by directing even the day-to-day operations of state agencies. The result of these deficiencies was "the destruction of the prestige of the Revolution."

Castro's criticism alone destroyed the political influence of the ORI. It halted all operations after March 26 and was completely dismantled within months; but the political aftershocks of the sectarianism of the ORI reverberated through the Cuban political system long after the party's dissolution. The most significant long-term effect was to retard severely the institutional development of a political apparatus capable of assuming the central role of directing the political system. The building of the ORI was the first major attempt at institutionalization undertaken by the revolution, and its disastrous effects upon both the fragile unity of the revolutionary leadership and upon the regime's mass support resulted in a marked reluctance to resume the institutionalization process even after the reorganization of the ORI. Castro's charisma proved to be vastly superior to the experience of institutionalization provided by the ORI. The coalition of organizations which composed the ORI was, from its inception, an uneasy one held together primarily by Castro's demand for unity. Rather than systematizing the integration of revolutionary forces in an institutional framework that could outlast Castro personally, the ORI had so inflamed antagonism that only a reassertion of Castro's prestige prevented an explosion of the coalition.

The loss of popular support engendered by the ORI also reinforced Castro's charismatic role, retarding the process of institutionalization. The revolution's overwhelming support among the Cuban people was, in the early years, primarily support for and faith in Fidel Castro. This support was one of the revolution's greatest strengths. Rather than institutionalizing the support held by Castro personally, the ORI began to dissipate it, withdrawing from the people and becoming a haven for a privileged few.

Castro's criticism of the ORI represented a clear reassertion of the charismatic authority against that of the developing party apparatus. In effect, he stepped outside the new institutional framework to condemn the manner and direction in which it was evolving. That his charismatic authority remained intact was demonstrated by the ease with which Escalante was deposed and the ORI discredited. The catastrophic results of the attempt to institutionalize that authority in the ORI discredited the process of institutionalization in Cuba before it had hardly begun. The ORI had been a "straitjacket, a yoke" binding the revolution rather than advancing it, and the fear of freezing the political system prematurely in an inadequate set of political institutions continued to weigh upon the development of the party throughout the decade.

### *THE PURS AND THE TRIAL OF MARCOS RODRIGUEZ*

In the wake of Castro's denunciation, the party apparatus which had been built up over the preceding months was completely dismantled, and the ORI's control over the other institutions of the political system was liquidated with the wholesale dismissal of Escalante's appointees. In many localities, popular feeling ran so high against the ORI that meetings convened spontaneously to purge the nuclei from the bottom up (Suárez, 1967: 152). This practice was discouraged, however, in favor of a systematic process of "reorganization and purification" supervised by the National Directorate and implemented by Dorticós's Organizational Commission. Whereas previously, ORI officials had merely appointed, sometimes secretly, whomever they pleased to form a party nucleus, members of the PURS were chosen by the "mass method" designed by Castro (Cuba Socialista, 1963). The "mass method" gave the workers themselves the power to nominate and ratify the people in their work places who would become party members. This procedure began with the ORI commission calling an assembly (asamblea de selección) in the work place and soliciting nominations for prospective party members. If, after discussing the merits of a nominee, the assembly voted its approval of the nomination, the individual became an "exemplary worker." The commission would then conduct an investigation of the candidate and decide whether to admit him/her to the new United Party of the Socialist Revolution. This mass method of party recruitment continues to be employed today.

The "reorganization and purification" of the ORI was a long and difficult process, both because the mass method was extremely time-consuming and because of the mutual distrust sown within the revolutionary leadership by the sectarianism of the ORI. It took over a year just to reorganize the nuclei originally created by the ORI. Even then, the PURS stood in marked contrast to the ORI in terms of political influence. Whereas the ORI under Escalante had firmly asserted its primacy over the other political institutions, the PURS had no discernible influence at all with regard to policy. It was not until mid-1963 that newly constituted PURS nuclei began to undertake any political work. The party then concentrated on stimulating productivity, aiding socialist emulation, and mobilizing voluntary work brigades at the work-place level; it had no responsibilities beyond those until 1965. Its apparatus remained too limited in terms of the number of work places covered and too weak in terms of the capabilities of intermediate bureaus to act effectively in any other capacity. Thus, the new Communist party of Cuba was an institution still in gestation when, in March 1964, it was rocked by a political crisis nearly as severe as that which destroyed its predecessor.

In the aftermath of the Revolutionary Directorate's 1957 assault on the presidential palace, four of the DR's surviving leaders took refuge in an apartment at 7 Humboldt Street. Betrayed by an informer, they were murdered by Batista's police. The DR long suspected one Marcos Rodríguez of being responsible for the massacre and had him arrested in 1959. However, the PSP, of which Rodríguez had become a member, protested his innocence, and since the DR could furnish no evidence against him, Rodríguez was freed. When Rodríguez was arrested again in 1961 on an unrelated charge, the earlier investigation was reopened, and he continued to receive the support of Joaquin Ordoqui, a founding member of the PSP, member of the National Directorate of PURS, and Vice Minister of the Armed Forces. In 1963, Rodríguez finally confessed his guilt and, more importantly, rclaimed he had confided his treachery to Ordoqui as early as 1958, thus implicating Ordoqui in a cover-up of the crime.

In March 1964 Rodríguez was tried, convicted, and condemned to death. The veterans of the DR, however, used the trial to attack all the old communists. Faure Chomón, Echevarría's successor as president of the DR, charged the PSP as an organization with responsibility for Rodríguez's action. *Revolución* featured his charges on page one, and in the days that followed mimeographed copies of his testimony were distributed in Havana. Faced with mounting attacks on their revolutionary credentials, the former members of the PSP in the revolutionary leadership began mobilizing their defense, demanding a full hearing and an opportunity to refute the charges against them. The National Directorate took up the matter and ordered an appeals trial for Rodríguez before the Supreme Court. Rodríguez, of course, was not the real subject of the new trial; his guilt had been sealed by his own confession. Broadcast live on radio and fully covered by the press, the trial was a public airing of the charges made by Chomón against the PSP. Chomón repeated his accusations, albeit in less virulent prose, and the former members of the PSP, one by one, took the stand to defend their pasts.

On the fourth day of the trial, Castro (1964) himself spoke for nearly five hours, rendering, in effect, the political verdict. He called for unity among the already formally unified revolutionary groups, observing that the Rodríguez trial had been "unexpectedly converted into a trial of political character." He criticized Chomón for exacerbating divisions within the revolutionary leadership, thereby "giving arms to the enemy," and he accused *Revolución* and *Bohemia* of irresponsibility in their coverage of the affair. The PSP as an organization was thus vindicated, although Ordoqui's behavior was described as negligent, and he was stripped of his leadership positions.

The Marcos Rodríguez affair demonstrated that the fragility of the formal unity between the M-26-7, DR, and PSP had improved little since 1961. Their merger had not wiped out memories of old antagonisms, and the ease with which these erupted in bloody infighting, threatening to rend the party before it was even fully constructed, did not bode well for the process of institution-building in the new Cuban political system. As had happened so many times previously, Fidel Castro was obliged to step in and, asserting his overwhelming personal authority, rescue the revolution from a debilitating political crisis.

*BUILDING THE NEW COMMUNIST PARTY OF CUBA*

Prior to 1965, the construction of the party's base organizations was given first priority and as a result the middle-level leadership bureaus of the PURS remained only skeletal. Consequently the party could not function in a coordinated fashion and its responsibilities were restricted to the work-place level. During 1965, however, a major effort was begun to strengthen the party's provincial, regional, and municipal organs. This involved the expansion of these intermediate party committees, increases in their staffing, a clearer delineation of their responsibilities, and the formalization of a mechanism for selecting their members (Hart, 1965). In October the National Directorate and National Secretariat of PURS were replaced by a Political Bureau, Central Committee, and Secretariat, and the name of the party was changed to the Communist Party of Cuba (Partido Comunista de Cuba—PCC).

By 1965, the PCC's initial recruitment drive, begun in 1962, had been completed and its chain of command had been strengthened in anticipation of the party taking on major responsbilities in the supervision of production and in the struggle against bureaucracy. As the party undertook its new duties, however, it rapidly became apparent that the problem of forging a political apparatus capable of playing the central role in the political system had not yet been solved.

Foremost among the difficulties which plagued the party from the time it began nationwide tasks in 1965 through the end of the decade was the fact that it remained a severely underdeveloped quasi-institution. Twice during the decade, first in 1967 and then again in 1969, the founding Congress of the PCC, which would have given the party a set of statutes and a program, was scheduled and then postponed.

The most compelling indication of the party's underdeveloped character was its size, with the resultant shortage of competent cadres and disorganization of operations (Table 1). If we take the prevailing size of other Communist parties as a measure, the PCC was tremendously undersized throughout the 1960s. Not only was

TABLE 1
Party Membership in Cuba, 1962-1965

| YEAR | MEMBERS AND CANDIDATES | NUCLEI | MEMBERS AND CANDIDATES AS % OF POPULATION |
|---|---|---|---|
| 1962 | 2,109 | 331 | .03 |
| 1963 | 16,002 | 2,209 | .2 |
| 1964 | 35,558 | 4,819 | .4 |
| 1965 | 50,000 | na | .5 |
| 1966 | 50,000 | na | .5 |
| 1969 | 55,000 | na | .6 |
| 1970 | 100,000 | na | 1.2 |
| 1971 | 101,000 | na | 1.2 |
| 1972 | 122,000 | na | 1.4 |
| 1973 | 153,000 | 14,360 | 1.7 |
| 1974 | 186,995 | 16,000 | 1.9 |
| 1975 | 202,807 | na | 2.2 |

SOURCE: LeoGrande (1978d).

it by far the smallest ruling Communist party (only one-fifth the per capita size of the next smallest party, the Albanian Labor party), but it was also smaller than nonruling parties in Italy, Finland, Cyprus, and Indonesia. The underdevelopment of the PCC was also apparent from the party's incomplete coverage of Cuban society. In the late 1960s no more than 16% of Cuba's work centers had PCC organizations. Though the party was organized primarily in the island's larger work places, data from the 1966 Industrial Efficiency Plan suggests that less than half the Cuban working class were employed in places that had a party nucleus (Domenech, 1966).

Another symptom of the party's low level of institutional development was the emergence of serious organizational difficulties when the party began work on its newly assigned tasks in 1965. Part of the reason for this was the persistent shortage and poor quality of party cadres. The general shortage of qualified personnel generated an intense competition among various bureaucratic structures for the talents of the few skilled people who were available. Paralyzed for over a year by the purge of the ORI, the party became a hunting ground for the state administration in its search for good leaders. Government agencies had considerable success hiring away the party's best activitists; the problem became so severe that Castro (1963) was finally moved to condemn the practice publicly, warning that such "piracy" would lead to the "progressive anemia" of the party. Protecting the party apparatus from the state bureaucracy's recruiters could not, however, solve the more serious problem of the general shortage of qualified personnel. By 1966, the low educational level of party members had become a recurrent theme in public discussions of the party's performance.

After over a year of working at various national projects, the weaknesses in the party organization had become all too clear. At a PCC meeting in Oriente, Organizational Secretary Armando Hart (1966a) surveyed them candidly: "Our party organization," he began, "is extraordinarily weak." He described virtually every area of party activity as deficient, blaming poor organization and a shortage of skilled cadres. Party organs were characterized by "the absence of aggressiveness" and a "contemplative attitude in the face of problems." Summing up his report, Hart (1966a) lamented, "There are so many tasks we could move forward on and we do not because of the weakness of our organizational structures! . . . We have a revolution which is greater than the organization of our party."

These weaknesses led in 1967 to a campaign for the "construction and amplification of the party." This involved accelerating the building of party nuclei in sectors where there were few or none, as well as improving operations in existing nuclei, coordination among different levels of the party, and relations between the party and the state (PCC, 1967).

Despite these concerted efforts, most of the problems outlined by Hart in 1966 persisted through the end of the decade. The educational level of party members improved hardly at all. In 1969, 79% of the party's membership still did not have even a sixth-grade education, and only 29% were studying (Hart,

1969b). Disorganization within the party apparatus also remained pronounced. José Machado (1969), Political Bureau delegate to Matanzas province, acknowledged that a shortage of party members and poor organizational work had left many key work centers without any party nucleus. In some factories, Machado said, party members were not even functioning together as a nucleus because things were so disorganized.

The 1960s produced in Cuba a nominally Marxist-Leninist political system in which the Communist party, beset by organizational weakness and intraelite conflict, was incapable of truly directing the other institutions of the polity. It remained one of Cuba's "provisional institutions," more an extension of Castro's charisma than an independent base of political authority. When the party finally began to function in 1965, its attempts to exert control over other institutional centers of political power were met with resistance.

### *Party-State Relations, 1965-1970*

The first year in which the party was assigned nationwide duties was 1965; it was mandated to launch a fight against bureaucracy, and it was given responsibility for aiding economic development by overseeing the administration of key economic sectors and by mobilizing the work force to increase productivity.

The primary importance of the struggle against bureaucracy was that it graphically demonstrated the basic weakness of the party apparatus. Bureaucratic inefficiency was by no means a new problem to Cuba, but the advent of socialism had done little to ameliorate the problem. The chaotic fashion in which the state apparatus developed after 1959 and the shortage of trained personnel had, in some instances, made matters worse. As early as 1963 Guevara (1968: 220-225) had warned of the spread of "bureaucratism," and called for the party to lead a "war" against this malady. Between 1963 and 1965, Castro devoted several speeches to the pernicious effects of bureaucracy, but it was not until the party had installed its strengthened chain of command that a program for eradicating bureaucratism was presented.

On January 2, 1965, Castro (1965) devoted a major portion of his annual report on the state of the revolution to the problem of bureaucratism and how to combat it. The solution Castro proposed was to freeze the number of office jobs and to introduce a system of "labor control boards" in every locality to enforce the freeze and to begin reducing the number of administrative employees. The formation of these boards, later christened the "Commissions for the Fight Against Bureaucracy," was delegated to the party. This battle, Castro emphasized, required concerted and organized effort, perhaps explaining why it had not been launched before the party apparatus was in a position to undertake it.

In its first two years the campaign against bureaucracy was not very successful because the PCC proved unequal to the task of overseeing the government administration. Still extremely small, the party apparatus was simply unable to keep track of what the state apparatus was doing; government bureaucrats showed little hesitance to ignore both the hiring freeze and the commissions designed to enforce it. A 1967 survey by a special PCC committee created to evaluate the campaign discovered that 75% of the administrative units surveyed were in violation of the directives on personnel reduction (Granma Weekly Review, 1967a). During 1965 and 1966, the Commissions for the Fight Against Bureaucracy eliminated 21,066 administrative posts, either reassigning the personnel to other jobs or sending them to school. By the end of 1966, however, nearly half these people were back in jobs "similar to their old ones." Bureaucracy had gone "back on the offensive," and Castro (1966) declared that the Commissions for the Fight Against Bureaucracy had themselves become bureaucratized.

A renewed and intensified campaign against bureaucracy ensued. New regulations on the hiring and transfer of personnel were promulgated, and bureaucrats were warned that violators would be punished this time. In the first eight months of 1967 as many administrative jobs were "rationalized"—i.e., eliminated—as in the first two years of the antibureaucracy campaign (Granma Weekly Review, 1967a).

In its new phase, however, the campaign against bureaucracy focused upon the central agencies of the state. Since the party had not yet been organized in the central agencies, the campaign had to be handled directly by the national leadership of the party through directives restructuring administrative operations. This, of course, required little reliance upon the party apparatus. In fact, the party organization found itself among the targets of the new antibureaucracy drive; over 1,000 PCC officials from Havana alone were dispatched to the countryside for three years to do agricultural work (Granma Weekly Review, 1967b).

In addition to the struggle against bureaucracy, the PCC's other principal mission after 1965 was to advance the economic development of the nation. Prior to 1965, the activities of the PURS were almost exclusively in the economic sphere—i.e., stimulating production by political agitation and mobilizing voluntary labor campaigns. When the party expanded operations nationally in 1965, the PCC's responsibilities in the economic field increased dramatically (Hart, 1966b). The PCC was assigned to supervise the administration of production in key work centers and in the economically strategic sugar industry. In 1966, the first Plan for Industrial Efficiency was introduced, systematizing both the PCC's mobilization and supervisory duties in the economy. The plan left no doubt as to the preeminence accorded to this area of party work by asserting that the only yardstick for measuring overall party performance was the level of production (PCC, 1967).

The PCC's two major projects during the 1960s—the struggle against bureaucracy and assistance to the economy—led to political conflict which, in the long run, proved to be critically important in molding the development of the PCC's role in the Cuban political system. Fighting bureaucracy and supervising production were both tasks which posed the party as an institutional rival and threat to the government bureaucracy. Conflict was engendered because, in both projects, the party was mandated to seek out and expose government inefficiency, corruption, and noncompliance with policy directives. Moreover, this supervision was imposed suddenly; until 1965 the government had not been faced with any systematic external review of its operations.

The political conflict stemming from the initiation of party supervision of the state was severe and persistent, lasting until the subordination of both institutions to the armed forces at the end of the decade (LeoGrande, 1978b, 1978c). The government bureaucracy resisted party supervision by meeting disagreeable directives with passive noncompliance, and the party routinely ignored the prohibition against issuing directives to administrators. Relations between the two institutions progressively deteriorated (Hart, 1966a).

Something of a stalemate existed until 1967; the state apparatus was unable to challenge openly the supervisory role of the party since that role had been assigned to the party by the Political Bureau and by Castro himself. On the other hand, the weakness of the party apparatus prevented it from adequately overseeing the bureaucracy's operations or putting a halt to noncompliance. We have already reviewed the government's disregard of the directives on personnel reduction during the first phase of the antibureaucracy campaign. In January 1967, President Dorticós (1967) revealed that similar resistance had been encountered with regard to the voluntary labor campaigns. There was opposition within the state apparatus because, so it was argued, the campaigns disrupted administrative operations. Perhaps so, Dorticós conceded, but that could not justify the erection of procedural roadblocks to thwart the mobilizations. Some officials, he warned, were verging on a "criminal stance." The renewal of the antibureaucracy campaign in early 1967 marked the end of this stalemate between the party and state organizations, not by increasing the strength of the party, but by overcoming the centers of resistance in the state bureaucracy.

This left the problem of party interference in administration unsolved, however. Subdued by the attacks on bureaucracy, the government apparatus was easily dominated, even in some instances supplanted, by the party apparatus. With many party officials also filling administrative positions, the party's supervision of production gradually evolved into the administration of production, thus collapsing the distinction between state and party functions. By 1969, the party had once again become an "administrative party" neglecting its "political work."

Conflict within the revolutionary leadership concerned not only party-state relations, but also the general development policies advanced in the late 1960s. This conflict was highlighted by the 1968 trial of the "microfaction"—a group of 43 state and party officials charged with treason for their organized, clandestine opposition to the leadership's economic policy. The microfaction's admitted intent was to convince the USSR and other socialist countries to exert economic pressure on Cuba, forcing a change in policy and even a change in leadership. To this end, they were in contact with foreign diplomats (R. Castro, 1968).

Led by none other than Aníbal Escalante, who had returned from exile in 1966 to manage a state poultry farm, the microfaction was composed primarily of PSP veterans. They were, however, second- and third-echelon officials; only two junior members of the Central Committee were among the 43, and their involvement was peripheral. Thus the microfaction itself posed no serious threat to the leadership of the revolution.

Its members were so obscure and so few as to be inconsequential, not even really constituting a faction—only a microfaction. Yet the incident was regarded seriously because its political significance transcended the individuals involved. The trial served as a warning to potential dissidents that opposition to prevailing policies was, in itself, counterrevolutionary. Thus it had a chilling effect on PCC and state officials critical of the deteriorating economic situation at a time when the ranks of those critics were expanding (F. Castro, 1968).

## *The Communist Party of Cuba in the 1970s*

Cuba's failure to produce ten million tons of sugar in 1970—a goal upon which Castro had staked both his personal prestige and the prestige of the revolution—catalyzed a thorough reassessment of the political system created over the previous decade. As a result of this reassessment, the Cuban revolution entered a "new phase" in which "institutionalization" and "democratization" became the watchwords of a far-reaching reorganization of the entire political process.

The institutionalization of Cuban politics since 1970 has had a profound effect on the Cuban Communist party: The size of the party has been greatly expanded, internal coordination and control have been systematized, institutional functions have been specified, and individual roles have been codified. Moreover, the functional boundaries *between* the party and other institutions are, for the first time, clearly delineated and enforced, and the subordination of the PCC to Fidel Castro's charismatic authority has been reduced.

By 1969, even before the beginning of the new phase, it had become clear that the PCC was too small to fulfill even the purely administrative duties to which it had been assigned during the 1960s. Consequently, in the middle of 1969, a campaign of "construction and growth" was begun in order to expand overall party membership and to increase the number of nuclei (Hart, 1969a). After 1970, the policy of increasing party membership continued to be an important aspect of the overall campaign to strengthen the PCC. By September 1975 membership had reached 200,000—nearly four times the 1969 membership. The average size of the nuclei also increased by nearly 50%—from 7.4 members per nuclei in 1964 to 10.6 in 1974—and by 1974 nearly half the nation's work centers—that is, almost all the medium-sized and large work centers—had party organizations. Another aspect of the drive to strengthen the PCC was the policy of increasing the percentage of rank and file workers in the party (Mesa-Lago, 1978: 71; PCC, 1976a).

Improving internal coordination and information flow became a concern after 1970. The first stage of this process was the convening of evaluation meetings at various levels of the party apparatus in order to evaluate past work, adopt plans for future work, and elect delegates to higher-level meetings.

Once the system of evaluation meetings had been established and the information on party operations which they provided had been analyzed, the next step in strengthening the PCC was the full-scale reorganization of its apparatus in 1972. The most important results included the establishment of a routine reporting system from lower to higher party bodies, something which had not existed previously; a specific delineation of the PCC's relationship to the government administration and the mass organizations; the beginning of regular scheduled meetings of PCC organs which heretofore had met only sporadically; and the expansion of the national Secretariat from 7 to 11 members to facilitate a wider division of responsibilities. Toward the end of 1973 and in the early months of 1974, the annual evaluation meetings were accompanied by the election of PCC officers from the nuclei up through the provincial level.

In December 1975, fully ten years after the party's founding and seventeen years after the victory over Batista, the Communist party of Cuba held its First Congress. Lauded as the most important event in the history of the revolution since the party's founding in 1965, the First Congress marked the culmination of the "institutionalization" of the PCC. Formal statutes and a preliminary party program were adopted, thus giving the party, for the first time, coherent operational and policy guidelines (PCC, 1976b, 1976c; Castro, 1976). In the years since the First Congress, the PCC has further codified its procedures with a series of regulations on the operation of various party organs, and in 1978 its organizational structure was finally completed with the creation of the National Commission for Control and Revision to oversee adherence to party regulations (Machado, 1978; Granma Weekly Review, 1978, 1977).

The strengthening of the PCC in the years since 1970 was also reflected in the composition of the Central Committee elected at the First Congress. In 1965, only 12% of the committee's members held positions in the party apparatus; in the 1975 Central Committee, this figure rose to 29%, indicating the growing influence of the PCC in the political system as a whole (LeoGrande, 1978a).

The composition of the new political elite also suggests that the intraelite conflict between PSP veterans and other revolutionary leaders, which plagued the party during the 1960s, has diminished considerably. The Political Bureau of the 1965 Central Committee did not contain any veterans of the old Communist party, whereas the new Political Bureau contains three out of a total membership of thirteen. This increasing integration of the elite is mainly attributable to the fact that policy differences between the old communists and the veterans of the M-26-7 have been considerably reduced since 1970. Also, the mere passage of time may be partially responsible for the reduction of hostilities. Along with the strengthening of the PCC, there has been a subtle but discernible shift in its relationship to its First Secretary. During the 1960s the party was an extremely weak institution, dependent upon Fidel Castro personally for its cohesion, its legitimacy, and its direction. Meetings of its national bodies were rare and directives from them were rarer still. Important policy decisions were made by Castro and his inner circle of trusted advisers, and if Castro's opinion contradicted a decision of the Central Committee, then the Central Committee was overruled.

Now, however, the party is becoming a cohesive and legitimate institution in its own right, capable not only of directing its own organs but also of giving direction to the other institutions of the political system. It is no longer true that without Castro the whole edifice would fall apart, as one Cuban official indicated it would in 1965 (Lockwood, 1969: 329). Castro has also begun to treat the party as if he were responsible to it, rather than vice versa. This shifting relationship between Castro and the PCC is but one aspect of the ongoing process of institutionalizing his charismatic authority. As Castro (1973) himself observed, "Men die, but the Party is immortal."

One of the major criticisms leveled against the PCC's performance during the late 1960s was its usurpation of the administration of the economy and the consequent fusion of state and party functions. In the early 1970s the distinction between state and party was redrawn and reinforced (Granma Weekly Review, 1974). The first step taken to reverse the fusion of these two institutions was the stricture that the roles of plant manager and Party Secretary in a plant could no longer be held by the same person, a practice which had become almost universal in the late 1960s. Such a division of functions was seen as necessary if the party was to supervise adequately the work of the administration and report on its deficiencies (Castro, 1970).

In the long run, of course, personnel changes could not by themselves resolve the problem of state-party relations; that required a clear delineation of the respective duties of the two institutions and their relationship to one another. After more than a year of study, the necessary guidelines were spelled out in a document entitled "The Structure, Mechanisms, and Means of the Party to Direct and Control the State and Society as a Whole," adopted by the Political Bureau of the party in January 1973 (Castro, 1974).

The restructuring of the Cuban political system since 1970 has also involved the creation of an entirely new set of institutions—the Organs of People's Power. These elected assemblies, which now exist at all administrative levels, are analogous to soviets in the USSR. The relationship between the PCC and the People's Power assemblies typifies the new relationship between the party and government in Cuba. The PCC leads the state through its right to nominate the executive committees of the People's Power assemblies, its right to introduce proposals, and through party members who sit on the assemblies. The party is proscribed, however, from issuing directives to People's Power or intervening in routine administrative matters (Castro, 1974; PCC, 1975).

In the event of disagreement between a party organization and an organ of People's Power, which mutual consultations cannot resolve, the party must refer the matter to the next higher party organization which will then take up the matter in consultation with the next higher Organ of People's Power. If a solution still cannot be reached, the matter continues to be referred upward, to the national level if necessary. Though this is similar to the consultation process outlined in 1965-1966, both the party and the state are more clearly defined now then they were a decade ago and the prohibition on party interference in administrative affairs has been advanced much more adamantly. Thus the prospects for this consultation process succeeding are better now, but whether it will actually operate as designed is something that is still too early to evaluate.

## *Conclusion*

The absence of a Leninist party in the leadership of the struggle against Batista meant that when the dictatorship was overthrown and the old political system was swept away, there was no party organization around which to build a new set of political institutions. The dynamics of Cuban politics in those early years of the revolution revolved around the military as the only institution with any significant degree of cohesion and capacity and, moreover, around the charismatic leadership of Fidel Castro.

Early attempts to institutionalize Castro's charismatic authority were largely unsuccessful. Despite its purported "leading role," the Cuban Communist party did not develop the organizational capacity to direct the political process during the 1960s. This was due, in part, to the intense distrust and hostility among veterans of the M-26-7, DR, and PSP, feelings that repeatedly threatened to fragment the revolutionary leadership. The experiences of the ORI and the Marcos Rodríguez affair demonstrated that elite cohesion could not be maintained in Cuba by institutional means. Only Castro's preeminent authority was able to hold this fragile coalition together.

The experience of the ORI also revealed how easily new and untried institutions might dissipate the regime's popular support and legitimacy rather than institutionalizing it. The ORI brought to reality all the hypothetical dangers inherent in the process of transferring authority from a charismatic to an institutional foundation. The failure of the ORI instilled in the leaders of the revolution a distrust of institutions, with the result that Cuba's political structures remained "provisional" until 1970. The ORI's successor, the Communist party of Cuba, did not even begin operating nationally until 1965, and by 1970 it was still small, disorganized, and incapable of directing the political process. Its relations with the government bureaucracy were more conflictual than cooperative, partly because neither structure had a clearly defined functional domain.

After the failure to produce ten million tons of sugar in 1970, the basic institutional relationships in the Cuban political system began to shift considerably with the campaign to "institutionalize" the revolution. For the first time, internal coordination and control were systematized, institutional functions were specified, and the boundaries between institutions were clearly demarcated. The military, which had been a dominant force in politics during the 1960s and had literally taken over the administration of the economy in 1969-1970, was in the 1970s separated from political and administrative tasks unrelated to national security policy.

The focal point of the "institutionalization" process has been the strengthening of the Communist party. Its expanded size, its improved cohesion and coordination, and its increasingly important role in the routinization of Castro's charismatic authority have all combined to make the PCC the dominant institution in post-1970 Cuba. It is no longer possible to view the PCC simply as an organizational extension of its First Secretary's charismatic authority, and therefore it is no longer possible to understand Cuban politics without analyzing the central, leading role played by the Communist party of Cuba.

## REFERENCES


CASTRO, F. (1976) "Report of the central committee to the first congress," pp. 16-279 in First Congress of the Communist Party of Cuba: Collection of Documents. Moscow: Progress Publishers.

——— (1973) "Speech on the 20th anniversary of the attack on Moncada." Granma Weekly Review (August 5): 2-5.

——— (1970) "Speech on the 17th anniversary of the attack on Moncada." Granma Weekly Review (August 2): 2-6.

——— (1968) "Speech on the 11th anniversary of the attack on the presidential palace." Granma Weekly Review (March 24): 2-8.

——— (1966) "Speech to the 5th national plenary of the FMC." Granma Weekly Review (December 18): supplement.

——— (1965) "Discurso . . . en la concentración conmemorativa del VI aniversario de la revolución." Obra Revolucionaria 1: 5-34.

——— (1964) "Declaración del Primer Ministro . . . en el juicio contra el delator de los mártires de Humboldt 7." Obra Revolucionaria (March 27): 5-47.

——— (1963) "El PURS, espina dorsal de la revolución." Cuba Socialista 19 (March): 1-32.

——— (1962a) Fidel Castro Denounces Sectarianism. Havana: Ministry of Foreign Relations.

——— (1962b) "Reparto equitativo de alimentos sin privilegios." Obra Revolucionaria 7: 7-21.

——— (1962c) "Hay que crear en la juventud un mayor espíritu comunista." Revolución (March 14): 1, 6, 9-10.

——— (1962d) "Ahora damos a los trabajadores las cosas que antes tenían los burgueses." Bohemia (March 23): 36-39, 89-90.

——— (1961) "La revolución no será tolerante con los traidores." Revolución (July 27): 3-5, 7, 13-14.

CASTRO, R. (1974) "Speech to the delegates to People's Power." Granma Weekly Review (September 8): 2-5.

——— (1968) "Report to the central committee on the activities of the microfaction." Granma Weekly Review (February 11): 7-11.

Cuba Socialista (1963) "La selección del trabajador ejemplar." 9 (May): 129-132.

——— (1962) "Integración del secretario y de comisiones de la dirección nacional de las ORI." 8 (April): 136-137.

DOMENECH, J. (1966) "Activity of the party nuclei in the plan for industrial efficiency." Granma Weekly Review (October 16): 2.

DORTICOS, O. (1967) "We base the future of our homeland on revolutionary honor, dignity and enthusiasm." Granma Weekly Review (January 29): 5.

ESCALANTE, A. (1961) "Las ORI son la vanguardia." Bohemia (October 8): 72-73.

Granma Weekly Review (1978) "Communist party of Cuba holds 6th plenary meeting."

June 11: 1.

——— (1977) "Central committee of Cuba holds 5th plenary meeting." December 25: 1.

——— (1974) "The party, the state, and the mass organizations in the dictatorship of the proletariat." January 27: 10.

——— (1967a) "General offensive against bureaucracy is stepped up." March 2: 4.

——— (1967b) "One thousand party militants." April 23: 8.

GUEVARA, E. (1968) Venceremos: The Speeches and Writings of Che Guevara. New York: Simon & Schuster.

HART, A. (1969a) "The process of building and developing the party has tremendous importance." Granma Weekly Review (May 5): 3-4.

——— (1969b) "Production's first need is technical and cultural improvement... of party cadres and members." Granma Weekly Review (July 20): 10-11.

——— (1966a) "Debemos elevar la organización del partido a la altura de nuestra revolución." Granma Weekly Review (September 19): 2-3.

——— (1966b) "How should the party units perform their role in the revolution's tasks of production?" Granma Weekly Review (March 6): 2.

——— (1965) "Intervención del compañero Armado Hart sobre organización." Cuba Socialista 51 (November): 42-52.

LeoGRANDE, W. (1978a) "Continuity and change in the Cuban political elite." Cuban Studies 8, 2 (July): 1-31.

——— (1978b) "A bureaucratic approach to civil-military relations in communist political systems: the case of Cuba," pp. 201-218 in D. Herspring and I. Volyges (eds.) Comparative Communist Civil-Military Relations. Boulder, CO: Westview.

——— (1978c) "The politics of revolutionary development." J. of Strategic Studies 1, 3 (December): 260-294.

——— (1978d) The Development of the Party System in Revolutionary Cuba. Erie: Northwestern Pennsylvania Institute for Latin American Studies.

LOCKWOOD, L. (1969) Castro's Cuba, Cuba's Fidel. New York: Vintage.

MACHADO, J. (1978) "The party leadership has confidence in the work you will be doing." Granma Weekly Review (October 8): 4.

——— (1969) "In the face of all difficulties we will not forget the fundamental factor." Granma Weekly Review (June 29): 5.

MESA-LAGO, C. (1978) Cuba in the 1970's. Albuquerque: Univ. of New Mexico Press.

PCC [Partido Comunista de Cuba] (1976a) "Sobre la vida interna del partido: tesis y resolución," pp. 13-54 in Tesis y Resoluciones: Primer Congreso del Partido Comunista de Cuba. La Habana: Departamento de Orientación Revolucionaria.

——— (1976b) Estatutos del Partido Comunista de Cuba. La Habana: Departamento de Orientación Revolucionaria.

——— (1976c) Plataforma Programática del Partido Comunista de Cuba. La Habana: Departamento de Orientación Revolucionaria.

——— (1975) Constitution of the Organs of People's Power. New York: Center for Cuban Studies.

——— (1967) "Acerca de las tareas y los métodos de dirección del partido." Granma Weekly Review (October 26): 2.

SUAREZ, A. (1967) Cuba: Castroism and Communism, 1959-1966. Cambridge, MA: MIT Press.

*William M. LeoGrande is Assistant Professor of Political Science in the School of Government and Public Administration of the American University and has contributed several articles on Cuban politics to journals. His current research concerns Cuban foreign policy and international economic relations.*

**GARY HOSKIN**
*Department of Political Science*
*State University of New York at Buffalo*

# *BELIEF SYSTEMS OF COLOMBIAN POLITICAL PARTY ACTIVISTS*

## *Introduction*

The relationship between ideas and political action represents a continuing, albeit frustrating, point of contention among political analysts. Referring to the literature on ideology, Robert Putnam reflects this sentiment by noting, "Few concepts in social analysis have inspired such a mass of commentary yet few have stimulated the production of so little cumulative knowledge about society and politics. The lack of cumulation is due, above all, to recurrent confusion of empirical with definitional issues and of both with normative concerns" (Putnam, 1971: 651). The proliferation of definitions, measurement techniques, and frameworks for analyzing the concept should not be surprising because "for the political scientist the term ideology points to a cluster concept, i.e., belongs to the concepts that bracket a variety of complex phenomena about which one tries to generalize" (Sartori, 1969: 398). The scope of the concept ranges from a

---

AUTHOR'S NOTE: This article uses data gathered for a larger project on Colombian political parties executed in the Political Science Department of the Universidad de los Andes in Bogotá, with financial assistance from the SUNY Research Foundation. I want to thank my Colombian colleagues at los Andes for their gracious support and encouragement, along with the Colombian politicians who agreed to placate the whims of still another intrusive social scientist. For their assistance in preparing the study, I want to extend my appreciation to John Sinclair, who did the scaling work, and to Marilyn Hoskin and Javier Torres for portions of the level and party analyses.

Journal of Interamerican Studies and World Affairs, Vol. 21 No. 4, November 1979 481-504
© 1979 Sage Publications, Inc.

complex of ideas that seeks to maintain the existing order—or modify it in the case of utopias[1]—to the belief systems of political elites and mass publics.

In addition to the ambiguities associated with the breadth of the concept, further complications arise because studies of ideology may focus upon one or more of the following dimensions: (1) determinants, or what Sartori labels ideology of knowledge (Sartori, 1969: 398);[2] (2) intensity or affect; (3) substantive content; (4) structure or interrelatedness; (5) centrality; and (6) the relationship between ideology and political action. In view of its multiple uses, it is not unexpected that "the growing popularity of the term—ideology—has been matched, if anything, by its growing obscurity" (Sartori, 1969: 398).

Recent research in political science has attempted to avoid some of the thorny conceptual problems associated with ideology by focusing upon political belief systems, "the set of beliefs according to which individuals navigate and orient themselves in the sea of politics" (Sartori, 1969: 400). For Converse, a belief system consists of "a configuration of ideas and attitudes in which the elements are bound together by some form of constraint or functional interdependence" (Converse, 1964: 207). Such constraints, if they are present, need not be logical in nature; they may stem from either psychological or social characteristics of individuals and the society. The degree of constraint may vary directly with the location of an individual in the social hierarchy, the extent of political involvement—interest and/or activity—and formal education (Dahl, 1967: 4).[3]

Utilization of belief systems rather than ideology as a focus of inquiry has not, however, resulted in a tradition marked by research that is perfectly cumulative. Within Converse's conceptualization, ideology assumes meaning only if belief systems have abstract objects of centrality, wide scope, and are highly constrained. For Sartori, "It is not sufficient to say . . . that ideology is the political slice, or part of, a belief system. . . . I assume that ideology indicates a particular state, or structure, of political belief systems. By definition, then, not all political belief systems are ideological" (Sartori, 1969: 400). In this formulation, an ideologue is one whose political beliefs are closed in a cognitive sense and strongly held in terms of effect. The opposite of an ideologue is a pragmatist, whose beliefs display a cognitive openness and are weakly held. In contrast to Converse, who is called an "empiricist," the "rationalists" do not look for unidimensional constraint—left-right based—in explaining voting behavior of mass publics, but rather focus upon multidimensional belief systems (Stimson, 1975: 394-395). Thus, for the "rationalists," an interrelated set of political beliefs is not the crucial variable in explaining the behavior of mass publics. Consequently, the literature on political belief systems is not immune from charges of conceptual, operational, and normative differences from one analyst to another; the problems, nontheless, appear less formidable than is the case with the concept of ideology.

Following the Converse tradition, this article is concerned with the belief systems of Colombian political party activists. The data are derived from interviews with a population of party leaders in the metropolitan area of Bogotá, drawn from four political groups (Liberal, Union Conservative, Independent Conservative, and *Alianza Nacional Popular*—ANAPO) and from three levels of their respective party hierarchies (national, district, and neighborhood or *barrio*). The survey, conducted in 1969 and 1970, includes interviews with 412 party leaders who held office at that time. We shall be concerned primarily with the derivation and explanation of six political belief dimensions as derived from a series of Likert items administered to the respondents: (1) religiosity, (2) procommunism, (3) political party efficacy, (4) political party orientation, (5) class conflict, and (6) antisystem orientation.

During most of the present century, political parties have been free to operate within an environment of electoral competition and have been situated structurally at the center of the political system, in the sense that parties, in one way or another, have constituted the locus of political activity.[4] Since the latter part of the nineteenth century, Colombia's two traditional parties, Liberal and Conservative, have contributed significantly to the formation and consolidation of an oligarchical structure of power in the society, monopolizing political activity throughout this period, with the exception of a brief interlude—1953-1957—when the military, under General Gustavo Rojas Pinilla's leadership, governed the country. The military, acting in accordance with the desires of leaders representing both the Liberal and Conservative parties, ousted Rojas Pinilla in 1957, and a coalition government emerged which returned control of the government to the traditional parties.

The National Front was a bipartisan pact designed to curb interparty rivalries through *alternación* in the presidency and *paridad* between the two traditional parties in all legislative and administrative posts from the local to national levels of government.[5] Although electoral participation was restricted to the two traditional parties, this did not prevent diverse factions, foremost among them ANAPO, from utilizing the Conservative and Liberal labels to elect government officials. The electoral restrictions associated with the National Front were removed at all levels of the political system by 1974 and the parity provisions expired in 1978, although President Turbay has extended the coalition by appointing Conservatives to the bureaucracy under provisions of Article 120 of the Colombian constitution.

Very divergent views abound in the literature with respect to the role that Colombian parties discharge in the political system and, more specifically, with respect to the importance of ideology in explaining party behavior.[6] Some studies adopt an expansive view of ideology—a complex of ideas that seeks to maintain the existing order—which is reflected in their assessment that both traditional parties defend oligarchical interests and, therefore, are similar (Fals Borda, 1969; Montaña Cuéllar, 1977; Fluharty, 1957; Leal Buitrago, 1973). While emphasizing that parties represent faithfully oligarchical interests of the society, another view stresses that ideological distinctions separating the parties are reflected among party activists but that structural obstacles impede their expression in the political system (Hoskin and Swanson, 1974).

Working within a different research tradition—that of pluralism—Robert Dix observes that ideological differences between the traditional parties have not been erased as a result of the National Front but that the gap separating them has narrowed and points of similarity are emphasized (Dix, 1967: 253). Likewise, Harvey Kline suggests that there are and have been ideological differences between the parties, but these differences are moderate today (Kline, 1979: 3-6). In contrast, James Payne finds no major interparty differences with respect to ideology: "In thinking about Colombian politics, then, we must discard labels of 'left' and 'right,' of 'progressive reformers' and 'regressive reactionaries.' These labels do not identify or explain the major political cleavages" (Payne, 1968: 94).[7] In summary, propositions about the role of ideology in Colombian party politics range between those who view it as quite significant, although for very different reasons, to those who maintain its irrelevance.

In the next section of the article, we shall discuss the derivation and construction of the scales designed to tap various belief dimensions of Colombian party leaders, along with an examination of the interrelationships between the six belief dimensions, focusing upon Converse's concept of constraint. The interdependence of the dimensions will be analyzed for the entire group of activists as well as for each level in the party hierarchy—national, district, and barrio. In the second section, attention turns to differences between political parties on the one hand and party hierarchies on the other with respect to the six belief dimensions. These comparisons are drawn on the basis of an analysis of variance model, not only by comparing parties and levels but assessing which explains a greater proportion of the variance. The concluding section summarizes the findings and interprets them within the context of the extensive but often noncumulative literature on Colombian political parties.

### *Scale Construction and Constraint Levels*

Individual items in each of the six belief dimensions are presented in Table 1; they are based upon a series of Lickert items that were included in the questionnaire administered to party activists. The items were pretested on students, upper-level business executives, and congressmen. As a result, several items were discarded or rewritten and new ones added in accordance with criteria for Thurstone and Lickert scaling. In the process of scaling the responses, the original 48 items administered in the survey were reduced through factor analysis to the 28 that appear in Table 1.

Turning now to the individual attitudinal syndromes shown in Table 1, the religiosity scale consists of five items measuring support for the political role of the Church in Colombian society, a traditional source of interparty cleavage in the party system dating from the nineteenth century. The second belief dimension deals with the respondents' attitudes toward the Communist party; the three items, in terms of face validity, relate to what might be called a traditional political liberalism scale, but the word "Communist" constitutes such a powerful stimulus for the respondents that this scale, as shown below, is more related to religiosity than to political liberalism. While the party efficacy scale (3 items) taps party leaders' beliefs as to whether they can influence decision-making within their respective parties, the party orientation scale (4 items) measures a more general dimension of affect toward a member's political party. The last two attitudinal syndromes relate to a traditional left-right political continuum, with those scoring high on each scale presumably falling on the left of the political spectrum. The five-item class conflict scale measures the attitudes of party activists with respect to social and economic inequities separating social classes in Colombia. Finally, the antisystem scale consists of eight items that emphasize problems associated with present Colombian political structures or, more generally, the orientation of party leaders toward the political system. This scale appears to represent a more inclusive theoretical construct than the class con-

TABLE 1

INDIVIDUAL ITEMS AND FACTOR STRUCTURE OF SIX BELIEF DIMENSIONS FOR PARTY ACTIVISTS*

| SCALE | FACTOR LOADING** |
|---|---|
| RELIGIOSITY | |
| 1. Divorce should not be legalized in Colombia. | .631 |
| 2. Religious communities should not pay taxes. | .515 |
| 3. The Church does not play a favorable role in the country's development. | .545 |
| 4. Publication of school texts is a function of the church and not of the state. | .608 |
| 5. Religious instruction should be eliminated from the schools. | .648 |
| Eigenvalue 1.75 (N=391)*** | |
| PRO-COMMUNISM | |
| 6. The communist party should be recognized in the constitution. | .808 |
| 7. Colombia should not trade with communist countries. | .638 |
| 8. The government should not fail to recognize communist labor unions. | .769 |
| Eigenvalue 1.65 (N=386) | |
| PARTY EFFICACY | |
| 9. I am not interested in working hard for my party because very little can be accomplished. | .681 |
| 10. Considering my party organization, my opinion often does not count for much. | .702 |
| 11. At times I feel it is necessary to resign my position as leader. | .789 |
| Eigenvalue 1.58 (N=400) | |
| PARTY ORIENTATION | |
| 12. It is not difficult for me to be heard by leaders of my party. | .481 |
| 13. I always follow the orientations of my political party. | .720 |
| 14. My party offers advantages for those who work in good faith. | .773 |
| 15. In the selection of presidential candidates, barrio leaders are listened to. | .654 |
| Eigenvalue 1.78 (N=364) | |
| PRO-CLASS CONFLICT | |
| 16. The state should not permit more petroleum concessions to foreign companies. | .562 |
| 17. Participation of the upper class in Colombian politics should be less. | .664 |
| 18. The state has an obligation to see that workers participate in the profits of an enterprise. | .640 |
| 19. Large businessmen do not pay enough taxes. | .703 |
| 20. More cooperatives should be established to eliminate the middlemen in commerce. | .506 |
| Eigenvalue 1.92 (N=385) | |
| ANTI-SYSTEM, POLITICAL CHANGE ORIENTATION | |
| 21. There is considerable internal democracy in political parties. | .473 |
| 22. Foreign economic interests in Colombia are favorable to national development. | .495 |
| 23. A violent revolutionary change in this country would mean the ruin of the nation. | .410 |
| 24. We do not have a popular democracy given the existence of political repression. | .635 |
| 25. Political parties do not represent the needs of the popular classes. | .644 |
| 26. The governing class never has sought to benefit the country. | .552 |
| 27. The rebel priest movement represents the Church that we need. | .502 |
| 28. The traditional political parties have been the basis of national progress. | .676 |
| Eigenvalue 2.47 (N=362) | |

* The item wording in this table, for reasons of brevity, does not follow exactly the Spanish construction in the questionnaire.

** These are unrotated principal factor loadings, as the program called for one factor.

*** Cases with missing values were deleted from the analysis.

flict dimension and is more powerful statistically, as reflected in the percentage of the variance explained by the items in each scale.

This scaling exercise deviated somewhat from our original theoretical notions, in large part because of the social and political heterogeneity of the respondents as one moves across the party hierarchies; that is to say, the political cosmology of upper- and lower-level leaders may differ considerably depending upon the dimension involved. Consequently, the factor loadings for the entire sample may be relatively low for some items, but they are retained not only because they contribute to an explanation of the variance in the scales but also because they are quite salient for a sizable proportion of the group, either upper- or lower-level activists.

The correlation matrix shown in Table 2 reveals a fairly high degree of constraint among the diverse attitudinal syndromes; lack of interscale constraint is the exception rather than the rule. If the levels of interscale correlations are examined, three sets of relationships are apparent, that between (1) religion and procommunism, (2) party efficacy and party orientation, and (3) social conflict and antisystem orientation. This observation is confirmed by the results of a factor analysis of the six scales, as revealed in Table 3. The scales load heavily on three underlying dimensions: The first factor favors a traditionalism dimension—religiosity and procommunism—the second reflects party orientation—efficacy and orientation—and the third relates to a left-right dimension—social conflict and antisystem.

As suggested by the emerging factor structures, correlations between those scales that load heavily on the same factor are relatively high, but other interscale relations likewise are fairly high. For instance, those activists who score high on the religiosity scale tend to be positively oriented toward their respective parties and negatively oriented toward the political system. While their orientations toward social conflict run in the same direction as toward the political system, a high religiosity orientation does not imply a significant adherence to the belief that social inequi-

TABLE 2

INTERRELATIONSHIPS AMONG BELIEF DIMENSIONS FOR COLOMBIAN PARTY ACTIVISTS

| DIMENSION | RELIGIOSITY | PRO-COMMUNISM | PARTY EFFICACY | PARTY ORIENTATION | SOCIAL CONFLICT |
|---|---|---|---|---|---|
| Religiosity | - | | | | |
| Pro-Communism | -.40 | - | | | |
| Party Efficacy | .02* | .03* | - | | |
| Party Orientation | .19 | -.13 | .26 | - | |
| Social Conflict | -.06* | .01* | -.19 | .14 | - |
| Anti-System | -.20 | .18 | -.16 | -.11 | .40 |

NOTE: The correlation coefficients are Pearson's r. Strictly speaking, levels of statistical significance are not appropriate for analyzing this data set because it consists of a population of party leaders. However, I shall report significance levels in order to facilitate the reader's interpretation of the analysis. If respondents failed to complete every item in a scale, they were declared as missing values on that scales. However, respondents were assigned the mean score of a scale if they had scores on at least four of the six scales. Consequently, six interviewees were excluded from the analysis of the scales, leaving 406 with scores on the belief dimensions. Unless otherwise stated, the group size for the subsequent tables is 406.

* Not significant at the .05 level.

ties in the system are rampant. Or, put differently, religiosity explains very little about an activist's beliefs about social inequalities. Likewise, religiosity is not related to efficacy.

The party scales show that leaders who are highly efficacious tend to score low on both the social conflict and antisystem dimensions. This is expected because of the conservatism represented by the political parties; that is, those who are the most efficacious are the most conservative—score low on both social conflict and antisystem scales. Left-leaning party activists are not likely to display a pronounced sense of efficacy in Colombian parties, excepting the *Anapistas*, for reasons that will become apparent later. Leaders oriented positively toward their respective parties tend to be favorably inclined toward the system but display attitudes that reflect their desire to reduce social inequities, which is to say that they have not lost faith in the ability of their respective parties to reduce social injustices in the country. Finally, the party activist who relates negatively to the system will favor reducing social inequities, score low on religiosity, relate positively to the procommunism scale, and is characterized by both a low sense of efficacy and party orientation.

TABLE 3

FACTOR LOADINGS OF THE ATTITUDINAL SCALES*

| DIMENSION | FACTOR 1 | FACTOR 2 | FACTOR 3 |
|---|---|---|---|
| Religiosity | -.795 | -.099 | .099 |
| Pro-Communism | .820 | .042 | .029 |
| Party Efficacy | .183 | -.318 | .768 |
| Party Orientation | -.267 | .202 | .808 |
| Social Conflict | -.063 | .880 | .063 |
| Anti-System | .289 | .732 | -.153 |

* Varimax Rotations, with eigenvalues greater than 1.0 (70.6% of the variance explained by the three factors).

Constraint levels among idea elements in belief systems are linked closely to the location of individuals in the social hierarchy. Converse suggests that as one moves downward from elite sources of belief to the mass publics, constraint declines across the universe of idea elements (Converse, 1964: 213).[8] In operational terms, this means that those individuals who score higher on measures of political information, education, and political involvement will display more highly constrained belief systems. Thus it seems to follow from Converse's argument that one might expect to find higher levels of constraint among those Colombian party activists at the top of their respective party hierarchies than those at the base, particularly in view of the fact that we are referring not only to stratification by party but by social positions as well.[9]

This postulated relationship between level of constraint and location in the social hierarchy is tested in Table 4, which compares upper-echelon and barrio politicans with respect to factor communalities on each belief dimension. Higher communalities supposedly reflect higher constraint levels.[10] Upper-level leaders do not uniformly manifest more constrained belief systems, as operationalized here. In fact, the communalities for the upper level are higher on three dimensions (religiosity, party orientation, and social conflict), and lower on the remaining three (procommunism, party efficacy, and antisystem). As shown in Table 4, these mixed results likewise are reflected by the similar pro-

TABLE 4

BELIEF DIMENSION COMMUNALITIES FOR PARTY LEADERS ACCORDING TO LEVEL*

| DIMENSION | LEVEL IN PARTY HIERARCHY UPPER (N=126) | LOWER (N=282) |
|---|---|---|
| Religiosity | .695 | .664 |
| Pro-Communism | .656 | .680 |
| Party Efficacy | .520 | .751 |
| Party Orientation | .764 | .692 |
| Social Conflict | .690 | .608 |
| Anti-System | .490 | .764 |
| Variance explained | 72.1% | 69.4% |

* Principal factor rotation, with eigenvalues greater than 1.0.

portion of the variance explained by the factors for each group of party leaders—72.1% vs. 69.4%. Moreover, the number of factors —two—required to explain the variation for upper-echelon activists is less than that for the lower-level—three—which according to one writer suggests a higher level of constraint operative at the upper levels (Stimson, 1975: 410). To summarize, the foregoing evidence leads to the conclusion that upper-level leaders do not display belief systems that are markedly more constrained than lower-echelon activists.

Failure to discover that the belief systems of upper-level party activists are consistently more constrained than their lower-level counterparts does not necessarily resolve the wider question as to whether constraint varies directly with social status. Even though Colombian party leaders mirror the social heterogeneity of the wider social system, the entire group represents, nonetheless, a political elite and, consequently, may be expected to manifest more constrained beliefs than mass publics because of their levels of political information, political activity and, to a lesser extent in this case, education (Dahl, 1967: 4). Referring to political elites, Dahl observes "Because they are more involved in, concerned with, and articulate about politics, they invest more time and effort in elaborating a consistent ideology" (Dahl, 1961: 320). Thus, this analysis lends support to the argument that the political stratification system is not coterminous with more general patterns of social stratification, at least with respect to belief systems.[11]

*Variations in Belief Systems: Party Affiliation and Level in Party Hierarchy*

Considering the important historical role that parties have discharged in the Colombian political system and the highly intense partisanship associated with the traditional party labels, it is not unreasonable to expect that party membership constitutes an important determinant of party leaders' belief systems. Table 5 offers ample support for the proposition that political party affiliation constitutes a significant determinant of political beliefs: The variation on each belief dimension according to party membership is statistically significant.

Turning first to the religious dimension, the two Conservative groups are the most religiously oriented, followed by the Anapistas, then the Liberal party. These findings conform to the historical cleavage patterns for the two traditional parties; the Liberal party has been associated with anticlerical policies and the Conservative party has defended Church prerogatives. Because the religiosity and procommunism scales load heavily on the same dimension, not surprisingly the party differences on the latter scale parallel those on the former, allowing for a shift in the rank ordering of the Anapistas and the Independent Conservatives. If party differences by level are scrutinized, the principal deviation from the general pattern revolves around the Independent Conservatives, whose upper-level leaders score considerably higher on religiosity than either their followers or the upper-rung leaders of the other party groups.[12]

Party differences related to party efficacy and party orientation highlight the similarities of the coalition parties (Liberals and Union Conservatives), in comparison with those in the opposition (Anapistas and Independent Conservatives). How-

TABLE 5
VARIATION IN BELIEF SYSTEMS ACCORDING TO POLITICAL PARTY AFFILIATION OF ACTIVISTS*

| | MEAN SCORE BY PARTY | | | | | |
|---|---|---|---|---|---|---|
| DIMENSION | LIBERAL | UNION CONSERVATIVE | ANAPO | INDEPENDENT CONSERVATIVE | GRAND MEAN | ETA |
| Religiosity | 12.57 | 15.52 | 14.45 | 15.36 | 14.19 | .33 |
| Pro-Communism | 10.84 | 9.57 | 10.16 | 10.40 | 10.24 | .18 |
| Party Efficacy | 10.51 | 10.39 | 11.25 | 9.66 | 10.59 | .18 |
| Party Orientation | 14.64 | 15.24 | 16.26 | 13.88 | 15.18 | .28 |
| Social Conflict | 20.08 | 19.89 | 21.42 | 18.36 | 20.21 | .29 |
| Anti-System | 22.14 | 21.24 | 27.58 | 22.14 | 23.48 | .47 |
| N= | (126) | (112) | (118) | (50) | (406) | |

* Using a one-way analysis of variance test, the differences between parties on each dimension are significant at the .01 level.

ever, participation in government explains neither the degree of efficacy nor the direction of party orientation because the opposition parties anchor both ends of each scale. Thus, we must turn to organizational characteristics of ANAPO and the Independent Conservative faction to explain their respective party positions on each dimension.

ANAPO clearly deviates from the traditional parties, resembling what Di Tella (1962) labels a national populist movement. In contrast to the Liberal and Conservative parties, ANAPO enjoyed a formidable populist base of support and a well-developed organizational apparatus, especially in the major metropolitan areas of the country. Since its inception, ANAPO had opposed the National Front and espoused a program designed to appeal to marginal groups in the society. At the same time, the fit with a national popular movement was not extremely close because of ANAPO's highly personalist leadership, a network of clientele held together by personal relations, and pronounced commitments to the existing political system. ANAPO's electoral success can be traced precisely to National Front agreement in that the movement capitalized on the popular discontent with *Frente* governments. But after ANAPO abandoned its designation as a political movement bridging both traditional party labels and assumed the status of an official political party on June 13, 1971, the group, for all practical purposes, ceased to be a significant political force in Colombia.[13]

As shown in Table 5, the Anapistas obviously manifest a more positive orientation toward their party as well as being more efficacious than activists of the traditional parties. This is somewhat ironic, for the efficacy dimension in view of ANAPO's highly centralized party decision-making apparatus—before his death, General Rojas and his daughter María Eugenia Rojas de Moreno Díaz, completely dominated the group. ANAPO's antiestablishment, populist orientation clearly evoked a pronounced sense of affect toward the movement from its followers. In contrast, the Independent Conservatives display relatively little positive affect toward their party or feel that they can accomplish much within it, a reflection of the tenuous electoral base of the group, particularly in Bogotá. The Liberals and Union Conservatives fall between ANAPO and the Independent Conservatives on both party dimensions. Controlling for level, upper-echelon Liberal leaders are more efficacious than other upper-level activists, including the Anapistas.

The principal conclusion that emerges from Table 5 in terms of the left-right dimension (social conflict and antisystem scales) is that the Anapistas are considerably further to the left than activists in the traditional parties, which helps explain the coalescent behavior of the traditional parties, who perceived ANAPO as a threat to their hegemony (Hoskin and Swanson, 1973: 335-336). The traditional parties differ more on the social conflict dimension than on the antisystem dimension, with the Liberals scoring higher on the social conflict scale than the *Unionistas*, followed by the Independent Conservatives. This rank-ordering corresponds to both scholarly assessments and journalistic accounts of the left-right spectrum in Colombian politics. Controlling for level in the party hierarchy, upper-rung Liberal leaders are the *most* conservative on the antisystem scale, clearly revealing their commitment to the political system; barrio leaders in the Liberal party are not so conservative. Contrary to expectations, Unionista activists rank second, behind ANAPO as a group, on the social conflict scale, testimony to their association with the "progressive bourgeois" segment of the party. Although the Anapistas obviously represent the ideological deviates in the Colombian party system, their removal from the political spectrum, as has progressively occurred since 1970, would restrict the scope of ideological cleavage but would not eliminate interparty differences; the traditional parties still would reflect different belief systems with respect to religiosity, procommunism, efficacy, party orientation, and social conflict.

Because of the *policlasista* bases of Colombian parties, along with highly stratified, closed leadership structures, those leaders at the same level in party hierarchies might be expected to manifest common belief systems. Thus upper-level *políticos* dedicated to the prevailing power structure may share more similar ideological orientations with their cohorts in other parties than with barrio leaders within their respective party structures, most of whom are from the lower class. This supposition assumes special significance if the traditional parties are conceptualized as instruments of oligarchical interests in the society. Consequently, the belief systems of Colombian party activists are analyzed in Table 6 in accordance with the level a respondent occupies in party structures. The hypothesis that level constitutes an important determinant of belief systems is confirmed with respect to each belief dimension, excepting political party orientation. Barrio leaders score higher on religiosity, party orientation, social conflict and antisystem orientation than middle- and upper-rung políticos. In contrast, middle- and upper-echelon leaders score higher on procommunism and party efficacy. This is not surprising considering the traditional political liberalism interpretation of the procommunism scale for the top leaders, compared with the religiously based fear of communism for the lower-level leaders. Because of the concentration of power at the apex of party structures, the discovery that middle- and top-rung leaders are more efficacious than barrio activists likewise is predictable. Note that middle-level leaders always score between upper- and lower-rung leaders, except on the party orientation scale.

TABLE 6

VARIATION IN BELIEF SYSTEMS ACCORDING TO POSITION IN PARTY HIERARCHIES*

| DIMENSION | MEAN SCORE BY LEVEL UPPER | MIDDLE | LOWER | GRAND MEAN | ETA |
|---|---|---|---|---|---|
| Religiosity | 13.23 | 13.94 | 14.44 | 14.19 | .12 |
| Pro-Communism | 11.28 | 10.70 | 9.92 | 10.24 | .19 |
| Party Efficacy | 11.35 | 11.08 | 10.32 | 10.59 | .15 |
| Party Orientation | 14.95 | 14.70 | 15.35 | 15.18 | .09 |
| Social Conflict | 17.23 | 18.79 | 21.08 | 20.21 | .42 |
| Anti-System | 21.74 | 22.09 | 24.16 | 23.48 | .18 |
| N= | (57) | (67) | (282) | (406) | |

* Using a one-way analysis of variance test, the differences between levels on each dimension are significant at the .05 level, with the exception of party orientation which is not significant.

The most notable interlevel difference shown in Table 6 consists of the location of barrio leaders on the left-right dimension (social conflict and antisystem scales); barrio activists are considerably more leftist than their middle- and upper-level counterparts. In short, the left-right belief dimensions of those at the bottom differ markedly from those at the top, which represents a potentially significant source of political cleavage, particularly if upper-echelon leaders are unable to control their followers, as was the case during *la violencia.* Controlling for party affiliation, the gap separating ANAPO leaders and followers on the left-right dimensions is significantly narrower than that for the other three groups. The same generalization holds for party efficacy, underscoring the "uniqueness" of ANAPO in the party system.

From the foregoing analysis of belief systems according to party affiliation and level in the party hierarchy, it is apparent that both party and level are important variables in the structuring of the belief systems of Colombian party activists. We still do not know, however, which is the more significant, party or level. Utilizing information gathered from the same survey but a different data set than employed here, it has been argued elsewhere that level constitutes a more forceful determinant than party affiliation in explaining the perceptions of Colombian party leaders, because respondents' locations in party hierarchies, closely reflecting their positions in the class structure, produce a homogeneity of perceptions. In contrast, party affiliation represents a weak source of constraint for reasons of the social heterogeneity within each party organization (Hoskin and Swanson, 1973: 340). The analysis of preference order data confirms the salience of level over party affiliation in explaining the derived spatial configurations that reflect political cleavages based upon ideology and government affect. Level is *not*, however, a more important determinant than party affiliation in explaining the belief systems of Colombian party activists, as revealed below.

Two-way analysis of variance is an appropriate procedure for assessing whether the relationship between two independent variables and a dependent variable is statistically significant, but it will not tell you whether one variable contributes more than another in explaining the relationship, as does the Multiple Classification Analysis.[14] Table 7 summarizes the contributions of both party affiliation and level in the party hierarchy in explaining the belief systems of Colombian party leaders. The "eta" coefficient indicates the impact of utilizing one variable *alone*; the "beta" weight represents the additional explanatory power derived from considering a second variable as well, and the "multiple R" assesses the joint impact of both variables in explaining the dependent variable. In terms of the religiosity scale shown in Table 7, the eta coefficient of party affiliation in explaining religiosity is .33; adding level to party affiliation raises the beta weight only slightly to .35. Relying solely upon level produces an eta of .12, and injecting party into the analysis produces a beta of .17. The multiple R is .37. Thus, political party affiliation is a more potent predictor of religiosity than level (the eta coefficient is larger for party than level, and adding level in the analysis—beta weight—contributes little to explaining religiosity).

TABLE 7

VARIATIONS IN BELIEF SYSTEMS ACCORDING TO BOTH PARTY AFFILIATION AND LEVEL IN PARTY HIERARCHY*
(MULTIPLE CLASSIFICATION ANALYSIS)

| DIMENSION | | ETA | | BETA |
|---|---|---|---|---|
| Religiosity | Party | .33 | | .35 |
| | Level** | .12 | | .17 |
| | Multiple R = | | .37 | |
| Pro-Communism | Party | .18 | | .20 |
| | Level | .19 | | .20 |
| | Multiple R = | | .27 | |
| Party Efficacy | Party | .18 | | .23 |
| | Level | .15 | | .21 |
| | Multiple R = | | .27 | |
| Party Orientation | Party | .28 | | .27 |
| | Level | .09 | | .04 |
| | Multiple R = | | .28 | |
| Social Conflict | Party | .29 | | .23 |
| | Level | .42 | | .38 |
| | Multiple R = | | .47 | |
| Anti-System | Party | .47 | | .47 |
| | Level | .18 | | .15 |
| | Multiple R = | | .50 | |

* The significance levels for all the relationships in this table are $P < .01$, except the relation between party orientation and level.

** This table reflects a level analysis based upon three leadership strata, upper, middle, and barrio.

Thus, Table 7 reveals that party affiliation predicts more accurately the belief systems of party activists than the level they occupy in party hierarchies. This generalization holds with respect to religiosity, party efficacy, party orientation, and antisystem orientation. In contrast, level is more important than party affiliation in explaining the procommunism and social conflict scales. Thus, as Converse argues, the centrality of the belief dimension for a party activist is an important determinant of whether level or party contributes most to the structuring of a belief system. These findings suggest that the political socialization patterns associated with Colombian political parties contribute to the formation of political beliefs that do not correspond closely with the location of an individual in the social or political hierarchy.

The multiple correlation coefficients for religiosity, social conflict, and system orientation are relatively high, indicating that party affiliation and party level are critical variables, but the role of both party and level is less significant for the procommunism, party orientation, and party efficacy scales, all of which reflects the contribution of other variables not considered here; personality attributes and background characteristics of the activists might well be important in structuring these belief dimensions.

## *Conclusions*

This study supports the position that ideological differences remain salient for Colombian party activists. Although comparable data on the belief systems of party leaders are lacking, little additional evidence exists which would suggest that this generalization is less valid today than during the height of the National Front period. The same upper-level politicans dominate their respective parties, the coalition agreement between the two traditional parties continues, and the electoral returns since the restoration of open electoral competition do not deviate significantly from the National Front period, excepting the virtual demise of ANAPO as a viable party organization (Hoskin, 1979; Ruhl, 1978).

Because of the important historical role played by Colombian political parties, the highly intense partisanship associated with traditional party labels, and the pronounced interparty competition (except during periods of coalition government), it should not be startling to discover that the belief systems of Colombian party activists differ markedly in terms of their partisan attachments. Generally speaking, the position of party leaders on each belief dimension conforms to historical cleavage patterns in the party system.

The combination of poly-class composition of Colombian parties and their highly stratified leadership structures makes it reasonable to expect similarities of belief systems according to the level a leader occupies in the party hierarchy. This supposition is sustained for all the belief dimensions analyzed except party orientation. While the degree of constraint manifested in a belief dimension fluctuates according to the location of a leader in the party hierarchy, upper-echelon activists, unexpectedly, do not *uniformly* display higher constraint levels than lower-rung leaders. In comparison to those at the top, barrio politicians are considerably more leftist, which represents a potential source of political instability, essentially class-based, particularly if upper-level leaders lose control of their followers. The leader-follower gap on the left-right spectrum is quite pronounced in the traditional parties but not in ANAPO.

Analysis of the belief domains by party affiliation and party level clearly indicates that both are important variables in structuring the belief systems of party activists. Contrary to a thesis developed elsewhere (Hoskin and Swanson, 1973, 1974), party emerges in this study as a more potent predictor of belief systems than level in the hierarchy. These findings underscore the importance of political socialization patterns associated with the parties and reveal that the formation of belief systems does not necessarily correspond closely with a person's social position.

This article has demonstrated, unmistakably, that the belief systems of Colombian party activists differ significantly according to party affiliation and level in the hierarchy. These beliefs supposedly do not remain encapsulated within party leaders but are reflected in their political behavior. As Fred Greenstein argues, "Behavior . . . is a factor of both the environmental situations in which actors find themselves and the psychological predispositions they bring to those situations" (Greenstein, 1969: 7). Our findings should not, however, be interpreted to suggest that ideological conflict is rampant in the Colombian political system; situational factors weigh heavily in the Colombian context. Interparty conflict stemming from divergent belief systems—as well as cleavages derived from social and political hierarchies that cut across party lines—is not easily translated into political action. This is because structural features of the political system, most notably the coalescent behavior of the traditional party elites when confronted with threats from below, reflecting their commitment to the prevailing structure of power.

## NOTES

1. This conceptualization of ideology obviously resembles Marxian analysis, as well as that of Mannheim (1936).

2. For an excellent critique of Mannheim, see the classic article by Geertz (1964).

3. For a convincing argument that party membership and activity are functional equivalents of formal education in the Italian Socialist party, see Barnes (1966).

4. For overviews of the Colombian party system, consult Dix (1967), Fluharty (1957), Payne (1968), Martz (1962), Leal Buitrago (1973), Latorre Rueda (1974), Hoskin and Swanson (1973), and Hoskin (1975).

5. For the best treatment of the formation and early years of the National Front Coalition, see Williams (1972). An excellent overview of the National Front is contained in Kline (1979).

6. For a superb review of the different conceptions and evaluations of Colombian political parties that prevail in the literature, see Peeler (1976).

7. For a good critique of Payne's analysis, both theoretically and empirically, see Kline (1973).

8. For an argument that constraint among mass publics is not lower than for elites, see Luttbeg (1974).

9. See Hoskin and Swanson (1974), for a table relating a respondent's level in party hierarchies to his socioeconomic status; the relationship is significant at the .001 level.

10. Luttbeg (1974: 338) notes that "a communality is the sum of the squares of the loadings on the various factors for a given issue [belief dimension in our case]. Moving the decimal point two places to the right, the communality may be viewed as the percentage of variation in opinions on a given issue that is accounted for by the factors. If it is high, this would mean that little other than the five [three in our case] factors is necessary to completely account for the variation in opinion on that issue; there is a great deal of constraint."

11. For a discussion of the theme that political stratification does not correspond with social stratification in the pluralist literature, see Jackman (1974).

12. The Independent Conservatives had a skeletal organization when these data were collected, at least in the Bogotá metropolitan area. Consequently, the total size for this group is 52, with only 23 of them drawn from barrio organizations, and even these tend to be predominantly middle class.

13. For analyses of ANAPO, see Costa Pinto (1971), Premo (1977), Melman (1977), and Dix (1978). Among the explanations offered for the demise of ANAPO, the following appear relevant: (1) the frustrations for Anapistas associated with their perceptions of having won the presidential elections in 1970, then being denied the office by government vote fraud; (2) organizational stress related to the transfer of leadership from Rojas Pinilla to his daughter, María Eugenia; (3) ideological cleavages among ANAPO's upper-level leaders; (4) assuming a distinct political party label in 1971; and (5) the resurgence of traditional interparty competition after the electoral restrictions expired.

14. See the Statistical Package for the Social Sciences Manual for a description of the Multiple Classification Analysis Program. There are interaction effects between party affiliation and party level in only two of the scales, religiosity and social conflict, which undermines, to some extent, the validity of the Multiple Classification Analysis. The conclusion that party is more important than level probably is not in jeopardy because one of the variables showing interaction, social conflict, relies heavily upon level to explain the variance, while the other variable, religiosity, is more affected by party affiliation.

## REFERENCES

BARNES, S. (1966) "Participation, education, and political competence: evidence from a sample of Italian socialists." Amer. Pol. Sci. Rev. 60 (June): 348-353.

CONVERSE, P. (1964) "The nature of belief systems in mass publics," in D. Apter (ed.) Ideology and Discontent. New York: Free Press.

COSTA PINTO, L. (1971) Voto y Cambio Social. Bogotá: Tercer Mundo.

DAHL, R. (1967) "Ideology, conflict and consensus: notes for a theory." Presented at Seventh World Congress of the International Political Science Association, Brussels, September.

——— (1961) Who Governs? New Haven: Yale Univ. Press.

DI TELLA, T. (1962) "Monolithic ideologies in competitive party systems: the Latin American case." Presented at Fifth World Congress of Sociology, Washington, D.C., September.

DIX, R. (1978) "The varieties of populism: the case of Colombia." Western Pol. Q. 31 (September): 334-351.

——— (1967) Colombia: The Political Dimensions of Change. New Haven: Yale Univ. Press.

FALS BORDA, O. (1969) Subversion and Social Change in Colombia. New York: Columbia Univ. Press.

FLUHARTY, V. (1957) Dance of the Millions: Military Rule and the Social Revolution in Colombia. Pittsburgh: Univ. of Pittsburgh Press.

GEERTZ, C. (1964) "Ideology as a cultural system," in D. Apter (ed.) Ideology and Discontent. New York: Free Press.

GREENSTEIN, F. (1969) Personality and Politics. Chicago: Markham.

HOSKIN, G. (1979) "Post-national front trends in the Colombian political party system: more of the same?" Presented at Seventh National Meeting of the Latin American Studies Association, Pittsburgh, April.

——— (1975) "Dimensions of conflict in the Colombian national legislature," in G. Boynton and C. Kim (eds.) Legislative Systems in Developing Countries. Durham, NC: Duke Univ. Press.

——— and G. SWANSON (1974) "Political party leadership in Colombia: a spatial analysis." Comparative Politics 6 (January): 395-423.

——— (1973) "Inter-party competition in Colombia: a return to la violencia?" Amer. J. of Pol. Sci. 17 (May): 316-350.

JACKMAN, R. (1974) "Political elites, mass publics, and support for democratic principles," in N. Luttbeg (ed.) Public Opinion and Public Policy: Models of Political Linkage. Homewood, IL: Dorsey.

KLINE, H. (1979) "The national front: historical perspective and overview," in A. Berry et al. (eds.) Politics of Compromise: Coalition Government in Colombia. New Brunswick, NJ: Transaction.

——— (1973) "Las ideologias en la politica colombiana." Razón y Fábula 31 (enero-marzo): 46-58.

LATORRE RUEDA, M. (1974) Elecciones y Partidos Políticos en Colombia. Bogotá: Universidad de los Andes.

LEAL BUITRAGO, F. (1973) Estudio del Comportamiento Legislativo en Colombia, Tomo I. Bogotá: Universidad de los Andes.

LUTTBEG, N. [ed.] (1974) Public Opinion and Public Policy: Models of Political Linkage. Homewood, IL: Dorsey.

MANNHEIM, K. (1936) Ideology and Utopia. New York: Harvest.

MARTZ, J. (1962) Colombia: A Contemporary Political Survey. Chapel Hill: Univ. of North Carolina Press.

MELMAN, R. (1977) "Populist mass mobilization Latin America." Ph.D. dissertation, Columbia University.

MONTANA CULLAR, D. (1977) Colombia: País Formal y País Real. Bogotá: Editorial Latina.

PAYNE, J. (1968) Patterns of Conflict in Colombia. New Haven: Yale Univ. Press.

PEELER, J. (1976) "Colombian parties and political development: a reassessment." J. of Interamerican Studies and World Affairs 18 (May): 203-225.

PREMO, D. (1977) "Gustavo Rojas Pinilla and the national popular alliance: a study of personalist leadership and populism in Colombia, 1961-1976." Presented at Seventh National Meeting of the Latin American Studies Association, Houston, November.

PUTNAM, R. (1971) "Studying elite political culture: the case of 'ideology.'" Amer. Pol. Sci. Rev. 61 (September): 651-681.

RUHL, M. (1978) "Party system in crisis? an analysis of Colombia's 1978 elections." Inter-American Econ. Affairs 32 (Winter): 29-45.

SARTORI, G. (1969) "Politics, ideology and belief systems." Amer. Pol. Sci. Rev. 63 (June): 398-411.

STIMSON, J. (1975) "Belief systems: constraint, complexity and the 1972 election." Amer. J. of Pol. Sci. 19 (August): 393-417.

WILLIAMS, M. (1972) "El frente nacional: Colombia's experiment in controlled democracy." Ph.D. dissertation, Vanderbilt University.

*Gary Hoskin is Director of graduate studies in political science at the State University of New York at Buffalo. The author of a number of articles on recent Colombian politics and administration, he is author of a forthcoming book,* Colombian Political Parties: A Structural Analysis, *with Francisco Leal Buitrago and Harvey Kline.*

**FRANK D. McCANN, Jr.**
*Department of History*
*University of New Hampshire*

# *ORIGINS OF THE "NEW PROFESSIONALISM" OF THE BRAZILIAN MILITARY*

In 1973 Alfred Stepan published an article with the descriptive title "The New Professionalism of Internal Warfare and Military Role Expansion." In this article, he used the cases of Brazil and Peru to discuss "how the ideology of new professionalism arose and how it contributed to the expansion of the military's role in politics." He proposed to do this by identifying "some of the institutional and political variables that are peculiar to Brazil and that help account for some of the special characteristics of the present military regime" (1973). He then set out the paradigms of the "old professionalism" as formulated in the carefully constructed analysis of Samuel P. Huntington (1957) and compared these to the stated missions and observed activities of the Brazilian army in the 1960s. This comparison led him to conclude that because the army's missions and activities were clearly different from those in the Huntington model they must flow from a different definition of the military profession rather than merely being lapses from the "old professionalism" (Stepan, 1973: 48). Further, he argued that "the *content* and *consequences* of the two forms of professionalism are quite distinct" (Stepan, 1973: 51). Table 1 contrasts the two professionalisms.

---

AUTHOR'S NOTE: The author wishes to acknowledge that grants from the American Philosophical Society, the University of New Hampshire, the Fulbright program, and the SSRC-ACLS supported research for this article as part of a larger project on the history of the Brazilian army.

Journal of Interamerican Studies and World Affairs, Vol. 21 No. 4, November 1979 505-522
© 1979 Sage Publications, Inc.

TABLE 1
Contrasting Paradigms: The Old Professionalism of External Defense, the New Professionalism of Internal Security and National Development

| | OLD PROFESSIONALISM | NEW PROFESSIONALISM |
|---|---|---|
| FUNCTION OF MILITARY | External Security | Internal Security |
| CIVILIAN ATTITUDES TOWARD GOVERNMENT | Civilians accept legitimacy of government | Segments of society challenge government legitimacy |
| MILITARY SKILLS REQUIRED | Highly specialized skills incompatible with political skills | Highly interrelated political and military skills |
| SCOPE OF MILITARY PROFESSIONAL ACTION | Restricted | Unrestricted |
| IMPACT OF PROFESSIONAL SOCIALIZATION | Renders the military politically neutral | Politicizes the military |
| IMPACT ON CIVIL-MILITARY RELATIONS | Contributes to an apolitical military and civilian control | Contributes to military-political managerialism and role expansion |

SOURCE: Stepan (1973: 52).

Stepan pyramided his assumptions in such a fashion and marshaled his data so adroitly that one nearly forgets to ask if the first premise is correct. Does Huntington's description of the "old professionalism" apply to the Brazilian army? Does the army of the 1970s function with a different definition of what a soldier does or what the army is to do from that which it used in previous decades? In a piece published five years after his classic *The Soldier and the State* (1957), Huntington observed that if an army's focus were on domestic conflict rather than interstate warfare, a pattern of civil-military relations different from that which he had described earlier could emerge (1962: 19-22).

Did the Brazilian army fit Huntington's idea of an external defense force? It is my contention that it did not. Clearly, since 1964 Brazil's system of civil-military relations functions differently from before, but that is not to say that the military has a completely new self-definition, rather that they are applying their usual one in a more direct and forceful manner. The problem is one of point of view. If you study the Brazilian military's role in politics from the perspective of the post-1964 political arena, Stepan's "new professionalism" seems reasonable. If you approach it from a historical analysis of the military institution, it begins to lose its newness and the situation of the last fifteen years appears as the logical outcome of long-range evolution.

Though various definitions of a professional soldier might be employed, a common feature of any definition must portray him as a manager or exerciser of controlled violence. Beyond that, the national context will determine what missions are assigned to the military. In turn, though, armies everywhere will have certain like characteristics; the professionalism of a particular army is relative to its missions and the manner in which it carries them out.[1]

In the course of Brazilian military history, since at least the beginning of the century, there have been debates and even violence revolving ultimately around questions of self-definition. Why have an army? What was it for? The answers as to what the army's missions were and hence what it meant to be an officer and a soldier varied across time; the variance produced conflict within the institution. This resulted from the deliberate ambiquity of the military's constitutional status. The constitutions of the Empire (1824) and the Republic (1891, 1934, 1937, 1946) specified that the military were to defend the country against foreign attack and, as the constitution of 1891 phrased it, to "maintain the laws in the interior."[2] The political leaders wanted the military squarely between the two poles of external and internal security, so not surprisingly some officers defined their profession in terms of an exclusive external or internal orientation, while others mixed the two. Clearly such men as the Duke of Caxias in the Empire, Marshals Deodoro da Fonseca, Floriano Peixoto, Hermes da Fonseca, Pedro A. de Góes Monteiro, and Eurico Dutra fall into the latter category because they exercised both external defense and internal political roles. There appear to have been relatively fewer officers who were totally external defense oriented and therefore apolitical in the Huntington sense. A few who do come to mind are José Caetano de Faria, Estevão Leitão de Carvalho, and João B. Mascarenhas de Morais because these adhered to the legalist position that the army must obey the lawful orders of the government and because they were concerned with shaping the army into a fighting force of European quality. Yet, though their orientation was basically professional in the Huntington sense, they were drawn into internal affairs because of their desire for a modern, European-style, external defense army.

Perhaps it is best not to seek hard and fast definitions of professionalism but to examine currents of thought that mix and blend over time. José Murilo de Carvalho discerned three currents: that of the citizen-soldier, the professional soldier, and the corporative soldier (1974: 154-162). The first made its appearance in the 1880s serving as a means of unifying the officer corps for reformist intervention to replace the tottering monarchy with a renovating republic.

## *The Citizen Soldier*

The officer corps had been split since the Paraguayan war into two antagonistic groups, the *tarimbeiros* and the *doutores*, who nevertheless shared a common disdain for the political elite. The tarimbeiros were those who had come up from the ranks without attending the military school. The term referred to the *tarimba*, the hard wooden soldier's bunk that was common in old forts and barracks. They favored intervention only to strengthen the military institution, that is to say their own positions vis-à-vis the civilian elite. Their desires revolved almost exclusively around power and prestige. The doutores were the graduates of the military school, who glowed with the light of Colonel Benjamin Constant's positivist teachings. In their view soldiers should be regarded as armed civilians, rather than as a separate caste, because industrial progress would retire armies and their weapons of destruction to the museums and pages of history (Carvalho, 1974: 155). The distinction between the concepts of citizen and soldier should be extinguished in favor of a broadened view of citizenship. But they acknowledged that a weakened army could not bring about political reform and so before it could disappear, the army had to be strengthened. Given the generational fissures of the era and the differences between tarimbeiros and doutores, simultaneous reformist intervention and institutional strengthening were incompatible. The first decade of the republic did little to improve the army's martial abilities until the rude awakening of the Canudos campaign of 1897, and efforts to secure the Amazon during the Acré affair (1903-1904) forced a reassessment of values.

The interventionist sentiment that flowed from, or perhaps even created, the concept of the citizen-soldier was based on resentment against an elite that ignored the officer corps, keeping salaries low, promotions slow, and arms scarce, while seeking to minimize the army's political power via increases in police and National Guard forces in and around Rio de Janeiro (Lyra, 1964: II, 29-30). Lieutenant Sebastião Bandeira, Captain Antônio Adolfo de Mena Barreto and General Tibúrcio de Sousa were typical of officers convinced that not only was the imperial government hostile to the army but, in a broader sense, all civilian politicans were the enemy (Lyra, 1964: II, 31).

Psychologically, the officers compensated for their inferior status by counterposing it with a belief in their spiritual superiority. "There was a generalized conviction that the men in uniform were *pure*, were *vigorous*, were *patriots*; whereas the civilians were *corrupt*, were *vice-ridden*, without any public sentiment" (Lima, n.d.: II, 33). The officers saw themselves as "saviors of the *patria*," with the obligation not only to defend their own rights and interests, but to rescue the fatherland from the civilian politicians who corrupted it. Floriano Peixoto wrote that a military dictatorship was necessary because only a "government of the sword" could "purify the blood of the social body" (Piexoto, 1887: 126). The vision of the officer corps as a priesthood of national purification blended with republican terminology to give form and substance to the citizen soldier and his role in Brazilian society. But after overthrowing the imperial government, the officers discovered that running a country was not as easy as it looked from the barracks window. The civil war, the continued disagreements between tarimbeiros and doutores, resurgent regionalism, and the Canudos affair shook the officers' self-assurance, and they stepped aside for civilians (Hahner, 1969).

## *The Professional Soldier*

In the first two decades of the new century, the professional soldier embraced the citizen-soldier idea as a vehicle to reform the army. This reform in turn would lead to a widening of the army's influence, power, and roles. The professionals, whose family backgrounds and premilitary education were apparently similar to the more politically involved citizen-soldier and corporative soldier types, desired a European-style army. Nineteenth-century Brazilian history demonstrated little need for such an army. The major experiences had been internal affairs in which officers either fought against government forces as rebels or battled to suppress rebellion. The list is impressive: uprisings in Rio de Janeiro in 1831 and 1832; the *Cabanagem* in Pará from 1835 to 1840; the *Sabinada* in Bahia in 1837-1838; the *Balaiada* in Maranhão in 1831-1841; the Alagôas revolt of 1844; the *Praieira* revolt of 1848-1850 in Pernambuco; and, of course, the *Farroupilha* in Rio Grande do Sul from 1835 to 1845. By comparison, the foreign combat had been against the United Provinces of the Rio de la Plata, 1825 to 1828; Buenos Aires' Rosas in 1852; and Paraguay's Solano Lopez from 1865 to 1870.

This last was "The War" for the senior officers who commanded the army at the turn of the century. The experience left its mark in a distrust of politicians who would declare war without providing adequate means or forces to fight with, and who would ignore and deprecate the victors, the wounded, the widowed, and the orphaned. Officers came to believe that only they were concerned about Brazil's defense. Another legacy of the war was a lingering bitterness between the former Argentine and Brazilian allies regarding the treaty arrangements. In the years before World War I, as Buenos Aires modernized its forces with German equipment and instructors, the Brazilian army held up their southern neighbor's energetic activities as a warning against complacency (Tasso Fragoso, 1910). To make matters more nerve-wracking, the undefended Amazon, with all its supposed riches, seemed a likely target for a repetition of what the powers had done to Africa and Asia. Even the great republic of the north had recently acquired an overseas empire and the nightmare of the powers sitting around a table in some faraway chancellery dividing the Amazon and the underpopulated interior seemed possible if the nation did not create a sufficiently martial façade.

In 1904, Minister of War Marshal Francisco de Paula Argollo complained that Brazilians placed too much faith in "the principles of international jurisprudence and the efficacy of diplomatic notes" to protect their territory. But without military force—the *ultima ratio*—the diplomats would not be able, he argued, to make their logic prevail. "The weak countries lived condemned to the degrading tutelage of the strong, who feel that they possess the right to counsel them, direct them, and even to admonish them, transforming, de facto, their independence and autonomy into a true fiction." Japan was treated with respect, he observed, because it had demonstrated military prowess. Brazil must do likewise. But how? Civilian and military enthusiasm for army reform rose and fell with equal speed. "The army is in the condition it finds itself," he lamented, "not because we ignore its necessities . . . but only because of the lack of firmness, resolution and courage on our part to realize that which we recommend and avow to be indispensable" (Argollo, 1904: 3-5).

So the military problem of the new century was twofold: A European-style army would have to be created because the likely enemy would employ such a force; and basic attitudes inside and outside the army would have to change. The professionals knew that Brazil was too poor to maintain a large standing army and so they placed their hopes in developing a cadre army with large trained reserves. The easily expandable force was convincing on paper, suited the economic realities, and did not appear to threaten the political power of the regional elites.

Because the past did not provide the models that they needed for the future, the professionals did tours of duty as junior officers in the imperial Prussian army (1910-1912) and later accepted a French Military Mission (1919-1939) to organize and teach their advanced officer and general staff courses. Since their geopolitical views were shared by Foreign Minister Rio Branco and his diplomats, they had support for obtaining new foreign-made armament. But how to alter the attitudes of civilian society?

Here the professionals found ready allies in the growing urban middle class. These people were appalled at the stunning ignorance, poverty, and filthiness of the masses, and burned with resentment at the rural landowners, or *coroneis*, whose armed hangers-on and elaborate alliance system kept the masses and the central government subservient. If the middle class could control an invigorated army they might be able to impose their vision of Brazil. But they lacked the will for conflict and knew from experience in the civil war of 1893-1895 that they would suffer from such internal warfare. And because they had little ability, or perhaps taste, for unified political action, they sought to reform the prevailing system from within: in historian Edgard Carone's phrase, "instead of struggle, collaboration; in place of its own ideology, the vague glorification of citizenship (*civismo*)" (Carone, 1972: 162).

Through spokespersons such as the patriotic poet Olavo Bilac, the middle class supported the establishment of a national draft lottery in 1916 to provide annual levies of recruits to be given a year of training and then returned home as reservists to spread the good work of citizenship (McCann, 1977: 211-243). Bilac saw the lottery as "a promise of salvation" for Brazil. Reflecting the prevalent middle-class view that Brazil was not a cohesive, unified nation, he saw the privileged classes wanting only self-pleasure and prosperity, the lower classes living in "inertia, apathy, and superstition," and the foreign immigrants isolated from others by language and custom. The "militarization of all civilians" was the way to impart middle-class virtues to society

BILAC, O. (1965) A Defesa Nacional (Discursos). Rio de Janeiro: Biblioteca do Exército. (a reissue of the 1917 edition)

CAETANO DE FARIA, J. (1917) Relatório apresentado ao presidente do república dos Estados Unidos do Brasil. Rio de Janeiro: Imprensa Nacional.

CALOGERAS, J. P. (1920) Relatório apresentado ao presidente da república dos Estados Unidos do Brasil. Rio de Janiero: Imprensa Militar, Estado-Maior do Exército.

CARONE, E. (1972) A República Velha, Instituições e Classes Sociais. São Paulo: Difusão Européia do Livro.

CARVALHO, J. M. de (1974) "As fôrças armadas na primeira república: o poder desestabilisador." Cadernos do Departamento de Ciência Política (Universidade Federal de Minas Gerais) 1 (March): 154-162.

COELHO, E. C. (1976) Em Busca de Identidade: O Exército e a Política na Sociedade Brasileira. Rio de Janeiro: Forense-Universitária.

DUTRA, E. G. (1941) O Exército em Dez Anos de Governo do Presidente Vargas. Rio de Janeiro: Departamento de Imprensa e Propaganda.

——— (1940) Relatório apresentado ao presidente da república dos Estados Unidos do Brasil. Rio de Janeiro: Imprensa do Estado-Maior do Exército.

GOES MONTEIRO, P. A. de (1935) Relatório apresentado ao presidente da república dos Estados Unidos do Brasil. Rio de Janeiro: Imprensa do Estado-Maior do Exército.

——— (n.d., c. 1931) A Revolução de 30 e a Finalidade Política do Exército. Rio de Janeiro: Adersen Editores.

HAHNER, J. (1969) Civil-Military Relations in Brazil, 1889-1898. Columbia: Univ. of South Carolina Press.

HUNTINGTON, S. P. (1962) "Patterns of violence in world politics," in S. P. Huntington (ed.) Changing Patterns of Military Politics. New York: Free Press.

——— (1957) The Soldier and the State: The Theory and Politics of Civil-Military Relations. Cambridge, MA: Harvard Univ. Press.

KLINGER, B. (1950) Narrativas Autobiográficas. Rio de Janeiro: Emprensa Gráfica "O Cruzeiro."

——— (1930) "Os militares e a politica." A Defesa Nacional [Rio de Janeiro] 18 (October-December): 15-17.

——— (1913) Editorial. A Defesa Nacional 1 (October): 1.

LIMA, M. D. OLIVEIRA (n.d.) "O ocaso do imperio," as quoted in Heitor Lyra (1964) História da Queda do Império. São Paulo: Editôra Nacional.

LOVE, J. L. (1971) Rio Grande do Sul and Brazilian Regionalism, 1882-1930. Stanford: Stanford Univ. Press.

LYRA, H. (1964) História da Queda do Império. São Paulo: Editôra Nacional.

McCANN, F. D. (1977) "The nation in arms: obligatory military service during the old republic," in D. Alden and W. Dean (eds.) Essays Concerning the Socioeconomic History of Brazil and Portuguese India. Gainesville: Univ. Presses of Florida.

OLIVEIRA, E. R. de (1976) As Fórças Armadas: Política e Ideologia no Brasil, 1964-1969. Petrópolis:L Editôra Vozes.

PEIXOTO, F. (1887) "Communication to João Neiva, July 10," in A. V. Peixoto (1939) Floriano, Memórias e Documentos, Volume 1, Biografia. Rio de Janeiro: Ministério da Educação.

PIKE, F. B. (1973) Spanish America, 1900-1970: Tradition and Innovation. New York: Norton.

POTASH, R. A. (1977) "The impact of professionalism on the twentieth century Argentine military." Occasional Papers Series No. 3. University of Massachusetts, Program in Latin American Studies.

SILVA, E. M. DE CASTRO (n.d., c. 1961) A Margem do Ministério Calógeras: Memorias, I. Rio de Janeiro: Editôra Melso.

STEPAN, A. [ed.] (1973) Authoritarian Brazil: Origins, Policies, and Future. New Haven: Yale Univ. Press.

——— (1971) The Military in Politics, Changing Patterns in Brazil. Princeton: Princeton Univ. Press.

TASSO FRAGOSO, A. (1910) "Conjecturas sobre o plano de operações da Argentina contra Brasil," in A. Tasso Fragoso to Emygido Dantas Barreto, Communição do adido militar na República Argentina, Buenos Aires, November 25. (unpublished)

TAVARES, A. L. (1965) Exército e Nação. Recife: Imprensa Universitária.

*Frank D. McCann, Jr., is Associate Professor of History at the University of New Hampshire. He is the author of* The Brazilian-American Alliance, 1937-1945 (Princeton University Press, 1973) *and is currently writing a history of the Brazilian army in the republican period. He has also contributed numerous articles to periodicals.*

**JANICE J. MONK**
**CHARLES S. ALEXANDER**
*Department of Geography*
*University of Illinois at Urbana-Champaign*

# *MODERNIZATION AND RURAL POPULATION MOVEMENTS*
## *Western Puerto Rico*

In geographic studies of modernization, attention has tended to focus on the processes of urbanization and the characteristics of urban areas rather than on rural areas. The latter have been included in macro-scale studies such as those of Gould and Soja in Africa investigating the spatial diffusion of modernization.[1] In their studies of change in the Pacific, Brookfield (1973) and his associates also worked in rural communities, concentrating on the micro-scale. In research dealing with change in rural Latin America, emphasis has been on colonization studies and rural-urban migration (Parsons, 1973; Preston, 1974; Stouse, 1971), but study of the effects of urbanization on change within a traditional rural areas has been neglected. Further, there have been few attempts in research on modernization to integrate macro and micro studies or to work at an intermediate scale.

The present study attempts to complement existing research by working with these neglected themes. It focuses on the effects of modernization in rural Puerto Rico, considering population distribution, settlement patterns, and mobility, and attempts to understand both the patterns of change and the processes shaping these patterns. We shall examine not only the recognized process of rural to urban migration, but also the considerable migration occurring within the countryside, the recent emergence of migration from urban to rural residences, and the development of substantial circulation between town and country. Unlike other

Journal of Interamerican Studies and World Affairs, Vol. 21 No. 4, November 1979 523-550
© 1979 Sage Publications, Inc.

studies of internal migration in Puerto Rico (Boswell, 1976; Lewis, 1969; Stone, 1965) we shall be concerned with three decades, 1940-1970, rather than a single intercensal period. We shall deal briefly with islandwide changes to provide a macro-scale framework, but will concentrate on the western region, including the city of Mayagüez and surrounding rural uplands. At the micro-scale, we shall study a sample of nine rural *barrios* within these uplands, with the data drawn from census materials, a sample survey in the nine rural barrios, field observations, and local interviews conducted outside the survey.[2]

To set our research in a larger context, our results will be compared with the model of the mobility transition developed by Zelinsky (1971) and elaborated by Pryor (1975). Zelinsky (1971: 221-222) proposed: "There are definite patterned regularities in the growth of personal mobility through space-time during recent history, and these regularities comprise an essential component of the modernization process." He defines five social phases in the mobility transition—preindustrial traditional, early and late transitional, the advanced society, and a future superadvanced society. Each phase has a characteristic set of migration and circulation patterns, changing from a base of minimal residential migration and circulation in the traditional society through increasing rural-urban migration and circulation in the transitional phases to an eventual emphasis on inter- and intraurban moves and major amounts of circulation. Pryor (1975) expands Zelinsky's model to categorize migration between traditional and modern sectors as either innovative or conservative. The former implies movement to a more modern space and the latter, movement within a status space or to one less modern.

## *Islandwide Changes in Population Distribution*

During the twentieth century, the population of Puerto Rico increased from approximately 953,000 in 1899 (U.S. Bureau of the Census, 1973) to 2,951,000 in 1973 (U.S. Bureau of the Census, 1975: 826). The rate of growth has been relatively steady

Figure 1: Barrios in the Municipios of Anasco, Rincon, and Mayaguez, Puerto Rico

(Figure 2) except for the decade 1950-1960, when it was dampened by a substantial migration to the United States.

The impact of this population growth has varied over the island. Most obvious has been a change from a predominantly rural population to one which had become 58% urban by 1970. The urban growth rate has been irregular, with marked increases in the proportion of urban residents between 1920 and 1930, 1940 and 1950, and major growth from 1960 to 1970. In the fifties, only San Juan and Ponce showed any substantial growth. Of the other urban areas with populations greater than 5,000 in 1950, four

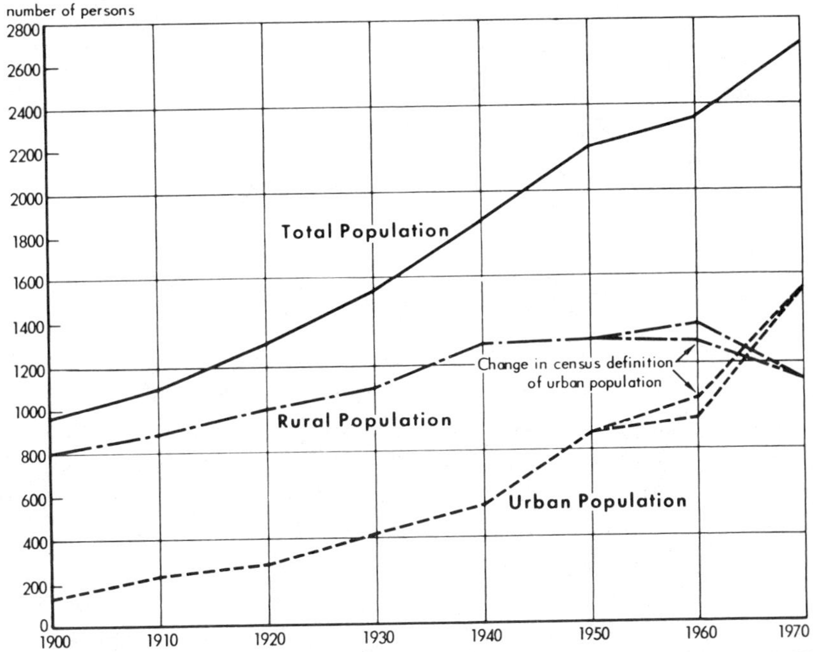


Figure 2: Population Changes in Puerto Rico, 1900-1970

remained relatively stable and ten actually lost population, showing that movement to the United States at that time was affecting the urban areas (Blume, 1974). During the sixties, however, all these towns grew rapidly. In fact, the number of places over 2,500 increased from 55 to 84. Despite the trend toward urbanization and emigration, rural population continued to grow in absolute numbers through much of the period 1900-1970 (Vásquez, 1968), though it began to stabilize after 1940 and showed its first decline after 1960 (see Figure 2).

In addition to the shift of people from rural to urban areas, there have been changes in the regional distribution of Puerto Rico's population. Growth has been concentrated in the North and East, both of which experienced urban-industrial development and agricultural growth. By contrast, western hill areas began losing population before 1910. This decline continued as the coffee industry lost world markets and the region suffered hurricane damage on several occasions (Bothwell, 1937; Gulick, 1955; Stone, 1965). A study based on the 1960 census showed this same area to have the lowest rates of population growth and mobility on the island (Lewis, 1969). Data from the 1970 census show the coffee areas to have the highest rates of net outmigration on the island (Boswell, 1976).

### *Traditional Patterns of Settlement and Mobility*

Entry of the United States in 1898 stimulated a variety of social and economic changes affecting the numbers and distribution of people on the island. Especially important were improved public health, which fostered population growth, and expansion of the sugar industry on the lowlands, which resulted in changes in population distribution. However, the most pronounced changes have occurred since 1940, initiated under the regime of Muñoz Marín. Accordingly, we shall concentrate on the latter period. During these years there have been concerted, government-sponsored development efforts, including rural electrification, road building, land reform, industrial expansion, and programs in public health, housing, and education.

To examine the effects of this modernization on population distribution, settlement patterns, and mobility we chose the rural uplands in the municipios of Mayagüez, Añasco, and Rincón. The region was selected because it appears to illustrate the island-wide trends of change and because it is small enough to permit a manageable field study (see Figure 1).

Before analyzing the changes, we shall describe the population distribution, patterns of settlement, and mobility as they existed prior to intensive modernization. Fortunately, detailed geographic and anthropological field studies made in the late 1940s make such a task feasible (Augelli, 1955; Imus, 1951; Lounsbury, 1955; Gulick, 1955; Wolf, 1956).

In 1940 the population of the three municipios of Mayagüez, Añasco and Rincón totalled 101,444—46% rural and 54% urban.

In the rural areas, the physical setting and agricultural occupation of the uplands favored a dispersed settlement pattern. In the eastern part of the region, coffee was the predominant crop. On the larger holdings, or *haciendas,* the workers lived in small clusters of dwellings near the owner's or manager's house. The operators of smaller *fincas* lived on their holdings, their employees occupying scattered small plots of land allowed them by the landowners. Toward the western side of the region, sugar cane cultivation extended from alluvial lowlands up the lower slopes. Larger field patterns maximizing use of land resulted in some settlement concentration, though in small clusters of houses rather than in agricultural villages. In the far western portion of the area, to the east and south of Rincón, subsistence farming predominated on steep, eroded land. A high-density population was dispersed on ridge tops, slopes, and in narrow valleys and ravines.

The urban population was divided among the three towns of Mayagüez, Añasco, and Rincón, of which Mayagüez was dominant, having a population of 50,376 or 91% of the area's urban residents. Añasco ranked second, with a population of 3,286, and Rincón, third, with 1,678 persons. Each of these towns was fairly compact in form, although some ribbon development may have occurred along the main roads out of Mayagüez.

Most of the rural population had little opportunity or reason for travel. Rugged terrain and poor roads in both the coffee and subsistence cultivation areas restricted movement. In the cane area, the roads were better, but focused on the mill. The country people made a few trips to town during the year for clothing, hardware, some dry goods, and various celebrations. Food was produced on a subsistence basis, or there were opportunities to trade with traveling salesmen or in hacienda stores. Rural stores were rare and more important in providing liquor and as recreational centers than in meeting the need for other goods in a situation where relatively little cash circulated.

## *Population Changes in Western Puerto Rico, 1940-1970*

Although analysis of population change over the entire island shows western Puerto Rico to have experienced severe and continuous population decline in this century, detailed study reveals more complex patterns. The movement of population is not simply decline of rural and growth of urban areas. In the three municipios studied, total population increased by 13% between 1940 and 1970. The urban proportion grew from 54% to 65%, with most growth around Mayagüez, which increased by 37% and retained its overwhelming urban dominance. The town of Añasco increased at about the same rate, but the small center of Rincón declined by 9%. Much of the urban growth occurred around the peripheries of the towns. Most of the areas included in the boundaries of the city of Mayagüez in 1940 actually lost population by 1970, although some sections did increase—for example, where high-density public housing projects were constructed.

Though the total rural population of the three municipios declined by 14%, this may not be a clear indication of rural population loss. The Mayagüez municipio lost a little over one-third of its rural inhabitants, but this is largely attributable to annexations of rural barrios by the city of Mayagüez after 1960. The number of rural people increased by one-fifth in Añasco and remained essentially stable in Rincón.

Figures 3 through 6 show several patterns of population change at the barrio level in the three municipios between 1940 and 1970. Ten barrios gained each decade, nine lost steadily, and thirty experienced fluctuations in population.[3] Some reasons for the changes are urban growth around Mayagüez, government policy, and the nature of highway access to urban centers. Several, but not all, of the barrios of steady growth are near the city of Mayagüez and represent suburban developments. Those to the south and southeast of the city show the greatest percentage gain in population. However, the pattern of growth is irregular, both spatially and temporally, as witness the changes in the barrios of Sábalos, Guanajibo, and Miradero (Figures 3-6).[4]

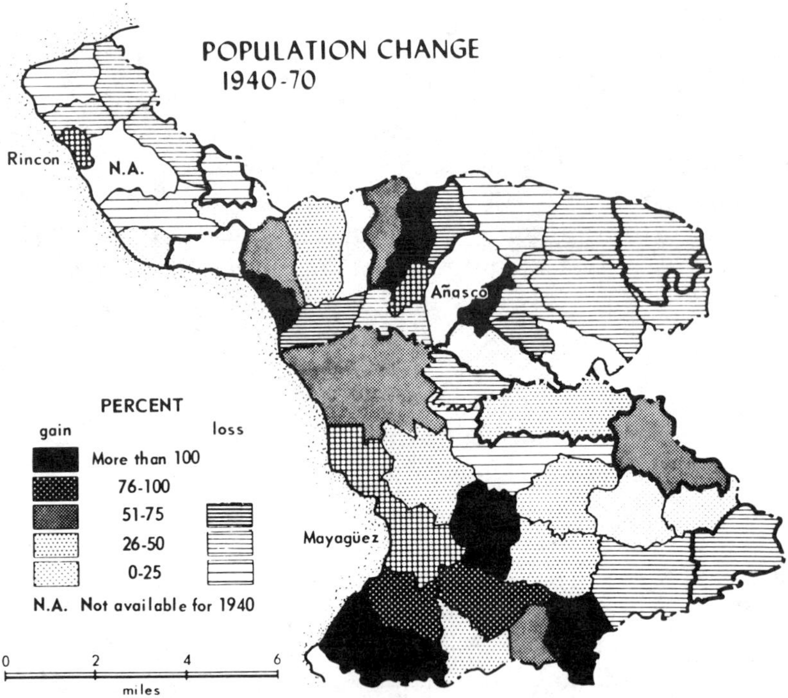


Figure 3: Population Changes, 1940-1970

Some of the population growth in rural barrios may be explained by movement to planned rural communities constructed under the auspices of the Social Programs Administration in the Department of Agriculture. These communities provided new housing and access to social services for rural people who neither owned farmland nor participated in the Commonwealth's program under which family-sized farms were distributed (Picó, Marías, and Espino) in the municipio of Añasco.

Barrios which lost population steadily are difficult to characterize. They include several, such as Rio Arriba in Añasco or Cruces in Rincón, which are remote from the urban areas of Mayagüez and Añasco. Others showing marked decline have poor highway accessibility, for example, Casey Abajo in Añasco and Rio Cañas Abajo in Mayagüez.

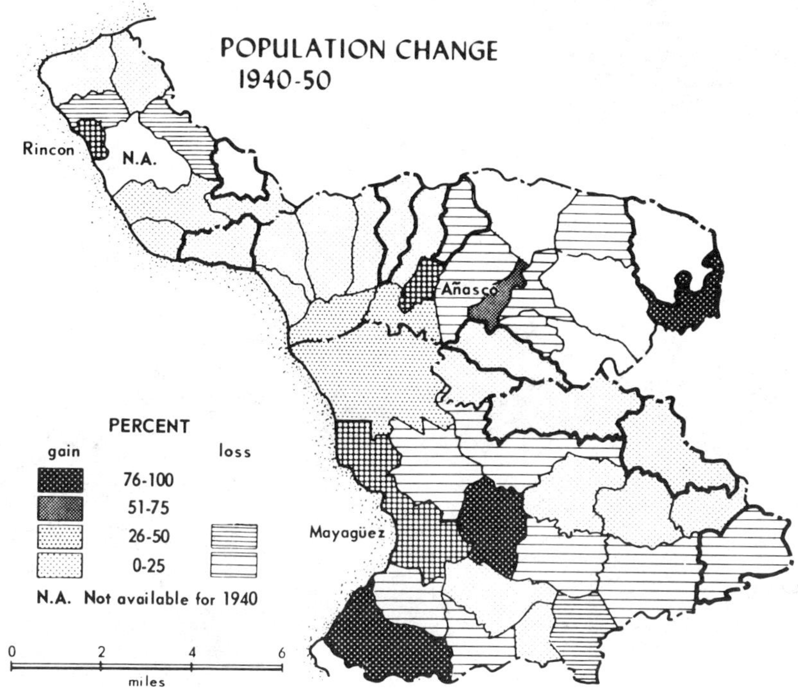


Figure 4: Population Changes, 1940-1950

These initial explanations for the changes in barrio population illustrated in Figures 3-6 are incomplete or speculative. To obtain more definitive information about the impact of modern change on settlement patterns and mobility, we made a general field study in the uplands of the three municipios. To support this study we conducted a more detailed survey in nine rural barrios to investigate the residential history and mobility of their populations. By including these micro-level data, we can comment on intrarural population movements which have hitherto been discussed in a speculative fashion in work dependent on census data (Boswell, 1976).

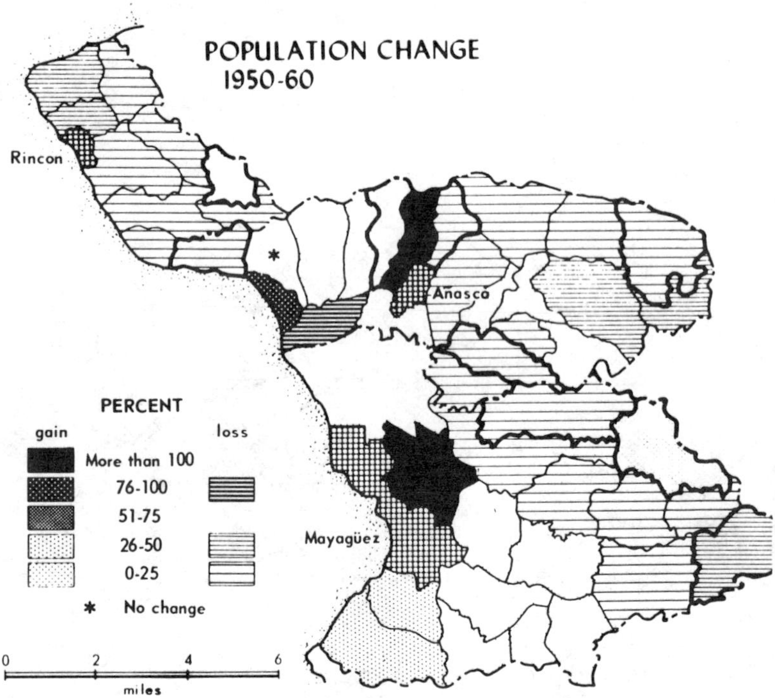


Figure 5: Population Changes, 1950-1960

## *Field Sampling Techniques*

In selecting barrios for field study, we excluded those closest to the Mayagüez urban area, where growth was clearly related to suburban expansion.[5] Thirty-nine rural barrios remained in the hill areas of the three municipios.[6] We selected barrios with growth or decline of similar magnitudes and those with approximately the same population in 1970 as in 1940, a total of nine in all. Table 1 shows the population characteristics of the barrios selected for study. Of these, two, Quebrada Larga and Rio Cañas Arriba, experienced steady gains in population; two, Corcovada and Daguey, continuing losses; and the remaining five fluctuated. One of these, Leguisamo, was characterized by overall gain; one, Montoso, by overall decline; and the remaining three by little aggregate change.

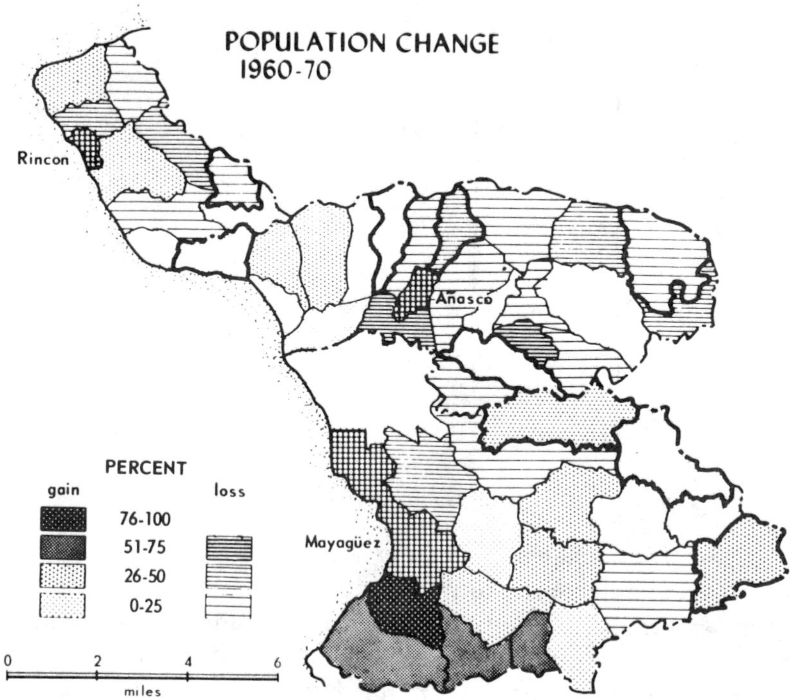


Figure 6: Population Changes, 1960-1970

To select homes for interview we employed a two-stage sampling procedure to include a 5% random sample of households. Initially a random selection of half-mile road segments was made, followed by a random choice of occupied houses within the road segments. This method excluded dwellings accessible only by foot trail, but on the basis of field observation and comparison of our field data and house counts from the 1970 census, we judge this number to be small. When the occupant was unavailable, we replaced the house with another selected at random. In all, 68 households were included in the sample.

TABLE 1
Population Characteristics of Nine Sample Barrios in the Mayaguez Area

| BARRIO | POPULATION 1940 | POPULATION 1950 | POPULATION 1960 | POPULATION 1970 | PERCENTAGE CHANGE 1940-1970 |
|---|---|---|---|---|---|
| Quebrada Larga | 504 | 609 | 673 | 797 | 58.1 |
| Ovejas | 571 | 705 | 548 | 610 | 6.8 |
| Corcovada | 576 | 579 | 476 | 404 | -29.9 |
| Río Cañas Arriba | 641 | 798 | 827 | 911 | 57.7 |
| Caguabo | 655 | 755 | 675 | 679 | 3.1 |
| Daguey | 706 | 621 | 532 | 319 | -54.8 |
| Leguisamo | 906 | 1091 | 946 | 1224 | 35.0 |
| Jaguey | 768 | 801 | 811 | 681 | -11.3 |
| Montoso | 852 | 680 | 427 | 563 | -34.0 |

SOURCE: U.S. Bureau of Census (1972).

## *Barrio Population Changes*

Apart from changes resulting from births and deaths, the increases and decreases of population in an area are the product of migration. Such change is frequently explained as a function of economic development, especially that associated with industrial expansion. This generalization has been verified at the regional and municipio levels in Puerto Rico (Boswell, 1976; Macisco, 1967; Stone, 1965). However, when western Puerto Rico is studied at the barrio level, the relationship is less clear. In analyzing population growth and decline among the nine barrios, we recognize that the number of sample households from any one barrio is small and statistical testing cannot be applied. However, the survey data are supplemented by field observations and interviews with storekeepers, realtors, agricultural operators, and government officers in the area. In addition, we have compared the field data with 1970 census data where possible. Information from these various sources confirms the generalizations derived from the survey data.

In the household interviews, questions were asked on such topics as housing (age, ownership, financing of construction), residential moves (year, previous location, reasons for moving), occupation, workplace, journey to work (means, length of journey), trips to urban areas (frequency, means, purposes), and places of obtaining food. Tabulation of responses to these questions and analysis of the supporting data on conditions in the barrios of population growth, decline, and fluctuation can shed light on the factors consistently associated with each type of change.

Quebrada Larga, the barrio with the greatest and most consistent growth, has the strong urban orientation and economic characteristics one might expect. Our sample survey shows it to have a high rate of employment, with over 60% of those employed working in town and virtually no one engaged in agriculture. It also has the highest percentage of all inmigrants among the barrios, including people from urban areas and return migrants from the United States. Residents travel to town regularly for most of their needs.

The other two barrios, Rio Cañas Arriba and Leguisamo, which have experienced gains over their 1940 populations, show less consistent growth, and the greatest gains were made in the earlier decades. In contrast to Quebrada Larga, they lack a clear urban orientation and have maintained stronger ties with agriculture and the local community. In these barrios the inmigrants include a higher proportion of people with rural origins, and the dependence on urban employment is less. Urban travel is low in Rio Cañas Arriba and modest in Leguisamo.

Turning to the barrios which have declined, there is some reversal of the Quebrada Larga circumstance. In Corcovada, participation in the workforce is low, most of those interviewed being elderly, incapacitated, or unemployed. None is working in an urban area. There has been little inmigration, and urban travel is less than in any of the other sample barrios. In Montoso, urban employment is also unimportant, but a number are engaged in agriculture. However, it is evident from field observation that this barrio is changing. Finca operators are experiencing difficulty obtaining labor, and some are offering their land for sale in residential lots. Housing construction is appearing along a new highway. The population increase noted in the 1970 census of the barrio seems to be continuing, with people moving out from town likely to be making an important contribution.

Those barrios which have similar population numbers in 1970 as in 1940 have attributes associated with both gaining and losing barrios. For example, in Ovejas, the people interviewed had a high urban orientation in their employment and shopping habits, but the barrio had attracted few inmigrants, either from rural or urban sources. In Caguabo and Jaguey, inmigration was also low and urban orientation low to modest. Most of the barrios with fluctuating and declining numbers were also affected more severely than the gaining barrios by population losses in the 1950s, when Puerto Rican migration to the United States was at its peak.

Variations in population changes between barrios may also have been influenced by a number of other variables. One of the more important is accessibility to urban areas. The three gaining barrios have direct, well-established main road connections to Mayagüez. In comparison, the three declining barrios are either more distant (Corcovada and Montoso) or have poorer road development within the barrio (Daguey). Of the fluctuating barrios, Ovejas has good access to Añasco and Mayagüez, but the highest transportation costs. The main links of the remaining two, Caguabo and Jaguey, are with the small town of Rincón rather than with the larger centers. Rincón provides fewer opportunities for urban employment, and this may account for the lower attractiveness of these two barrios to migrants.

We have not been able to investigate in detail why some areas obtain more road improvements than others, but political factors are certainly involved. For example, the mayor of Añasco has been a resident of Quebrada Larga which has a good road network, reputedly the result of his initiative. Two of the barrios, Rio Cañas Arriba and Montoso, have been the sites of planned rural settlements which contribute to changes in population distribution. Political considerations were doubtlessly involved in the locational decisions for these settlements.

The nature of land ownership is another factor bearing on population change. If owners of large holdings cease their opera-

TABLE 2
Changes in Population and Dwelling Units in the Study Barrios

| BARRIO | NET POPULATION CHANGE FOR EACH BARRIO 1950-1970 | | DWELLING UNIT CHANGES ALONG SAMPLED ROAD SEGMENTS 1950-1975 | |
|---|---|---|---|---|
| | Number | Percent | Number | Percent |
| Quebrada Larga | 188 | 23.6 | 46 | 309 |
| Leguisamo | 133 | 12.4 | 73 | 304 |
| Río Cañas Arriba | 113 | 10.9 | 111 | 252 |
| Caguabo | - 76 | -13.5 | 58 | 171 |
| Ovejas | - 95 | -10.0 | 29 | 91 |
| Jaguey | -120 | -15.0 | not available | |
| Montoso | -117 | -17.2 | 21 | 525 |
| Corcovada | -175 | -30.2 | 4 | 13 |
| Daguey | -302 | -48.2 | 37 | a |
| Net Change[b] | -331 | - 5.67 | 379 | 211.73 |

SOURCES: U.S. Bureau of Census (1972); 1950 dwelling unit counts taken from land-use maps prepared by Jones (1950, 1951). We appreciate the help of Professors M. F. Dacey and J. Hudson of Northwestern University in providing us access to these maps.
a. No houses on sample road segments in 1950.
b. Excluding Jaguey.

tions, but retain the land, as in Daguey, population loss follows. If they hold out for high prices, growth may be diverted to other areas. This appears to have been the case on the flat lands near Mayagüez.[7] Where small holdings have existed, as in Quebrada Larga, or where operators will subdivide, as in Montoso, there is more opportunity for residential expansion.

One more factor which seems relevant is the attractiveness of one rural setting versus another, especially where growth is associated with inmigration. Wooded highland sites in Leguisamo, Rio Cañas Arriba, and Montoso are cooler and more pleasant than the lower, more open areas in Ovejas, Caguabo, and Jaguey.

TABLE 3
Housing Construction in the Rural Barrios

| AGE OF DWELLING (YEARS) | PERCENTAGE OF DWELLINGS N = 68 |
|---|---|
| 0 - 5 | 27.9 |
| 6 - 10 | 26.5 |
| 11 - 15 | 19.0 |
| 15 - 20 | 9.0 |
| 21 and over | 14.6 |
| not available | 3.0 |

SOURCE: Field Survey.

*Modernization and Rural Settlement Patterns*

Marked changes have occurred in rural settlement patterns over the last 25 years. Most notable has been a substantial increase in the number of houses along paved roads both in areas of population growth and in those where population is relatively stable or declining. The extent of increase in housing units is indicated in Table 2. A consequence of the change has been the emergence of a strongly linear settlement pattern, in marked contrast to the dispersed housing distribution characteristic prior to 1950.

Building has been far from uniform along the roads. There are numerous stretches, even on main roads, where dwellings are absent. The greatest expansion has occurred on the main highways leading to Mayagüez and Añasco. Housing development of the last ten years also extends along short stretches of paved roads tributary to the main highway. Clusters of houses are common, containing as few as four or five residences or as many as fifty or more. The larger and more closely spaced clusters, which began to appear on main highways before 1950, tend to be closer to Mayagüez. Further from the city, the clusters are often associated with elementary schools built during the last thirty years.

The evidence in Table 2 might be interpreted as showing the increase in the number of roadside houses to be associated with population growth since the 1970 census. However, the rate of housing development has been relatively constant over the last decade (Table 3). In addition, inspection of topographic maps dated 1964 and 1966 (U.S. Geological Survey) shows substantial gains in the number of houses along roads by those years. Census data for the rural portions of all barrios in the Mayagüez Standard Metropolitan Statistical Area indicate relatively low rates of building in the fifties, but a substantial increase in the 1960s with 43% of all 1970 housing being built during that decade (U.S. Bureau of the Census, 1972: Table H-2).

The construction of houses along paved roads has improved access to town for rural residents, although the motives for initiating construction are not necessarily directly associated with accessibility. The most frequent primary reason cited in the sample for building (26% of houses) was to improve the quality of residence. Governmental programs encourage new housing by providing materials through low-interest loans with easy repayment conditions if homeowners will supply mutual construction assistance (Picó, 1974). Changing family status (17%) and moving to be near relatives (16%) are also reasons for building houses. In both cases, family assistance with construction is likely. A result is that family neighborhoods develop. In some barrios these take the form of small family compounds with two or three houses built on one lot. Other important reasons for moving are associated with changes in employment (13%), desire to obtain access to water and electricity (12%), and preference for a rural environment (13%). The latter attracts new residents who have rejected the urban setting because of cost, or perceived pollution and crime, or those who see the country as a suitable retirement haven.

The data suggest a new movement from town to country within the last ten years which may become more important in the future. It is being encouraged by the division of coffee fincas into one to five *cuerda* (.39 to 1.97 ha.) lots, advertised along the highways and sold directly by owners or through real estate companies. The prices of these lots are influenced by their distance from town. A five-cuerda lot within ten kilometers of Mayagüez might sell for $3,000, with the price beyond that distance dropping to $2,000. Such high prices assure that country people account for only a small percentage of the buyers of these lots. The most numerous purchasers are industrial workers from Mayagüez, though a notable portion of the sales are also made to migrants returning from the United States.[8]

The settlement pattern in the rural areas thus appears to be changing as a result of migration related to modernization. People are leaving isolated dwellings for roadside locations, though the move may be initiated by a variety of motives, and some outmigration from urban centers is occurring. From our data, we are able to identify the significance of these components in rural change and also to note some additional contributing elements. Among the sample population, 57% of all residents made only short moves and were occupying houses in the same general location as their previous residence.[9] This leaves a surprisingly high number of inmigrants to the study barrios—43% of all sampled residents. Such an amount of inmigration does not fit the commonly held impression of flight from rural to urban areas.

Tracing the origins of inmigrants, we find that equal numbers have come from other rural barrios or urban areas in western Puerto Rico (41% from each) and 17% have returned from the United States.[10] Interviews with rural storekeepers, as well as data from our sample, indicate that many of those returning have brought skills and capital which allow them to build some of the more expensive houses or to establish themselves in business. Others have come back because of personal and economic difficulties in the United States, anticipating cheaper living and familial security in Puerto Rico.

Regardless of their origins, respondents to our survey hold common perceptions about the desirability of country life. Only 3% of the sample population expressed discontent with their residential location. The dominant impression is one of rural *"tranquilidad."* Other perceived advantages are lower living costs, whether for housing or because of the possibility of having a garden. In addition, rural residents like the cool, fresh air in the hills, compared with the heat and noise of town. These attractions alone might not be sufficient to retain and attract a rural population. However, they are reinforced by the provision of urban services including electricity, water, in some cases mail delivery, and by generally easy access to town. Given these services, people who remain in the country see no disadvantages to living there.

*Modernization and Mobility*

Rural people in western Puerto Rico today travel readily within rural areas and between their homes and town. This is in marked contrast to the limited mobility of rural residents in the late 1940s. To investigate the extent of mobility, we measured the frequency of trips to urban areas using a minimum monthly trip index in which each round trip of a household member is recorded as one point. Thus daily trips to work would have a value of twenty points per person per month; a shopping trip twice a week would be eight points. This index is regarded as a measure of minimum movement per household because we assume that in some cases additional family members accompany the person reporting.

The mean index value for survey households is 13.7. This represents more than three urban trips per week made from the average household. However, variation between households is considerable. Daily urban travel by at least one person is reported for 32% of the households; two or more trips per week are recorded in 19%, one or more per week in 27%, and less than weekly trips are made by 22%. Only three households visit town less than once a month, in marked contrast to the traditional patterns when most people made only a few trips per year.

By far the greatest number of urban trips are destined for Mayagüez (61%), with decreasing numbers to the urban centers of smaller sizes—27% to Añasco, 9% to Rincón, and 3% to Las Marías and San Sebastián combined. In the course of a year, virtually everyone visits Mayagüez. The smaller centers are visited by residents of the nearby barrios, though some of these bypass Añasco and Rincón for Mayagüez.

Such extensive rural-urban travel is possible because of both the improved highway network and readily available transportation in private cars or *públicos.* Cars are owned by at least one member of 44% of the rural households surveyed.[11] Públicos travel a number of times daily between numerous rural points and the urban areas. They are large cars which follow regular routes, picking up and setting down passengers virtually anywhere along the way. Fares range from about 60 cents to $2.00, and travel time is as little as 30 to 45 minutes, though if the traveler has to wait for a car, the total time for the journey may increase to an hour or an hour and a half. Whatever the means of transport used, rural residents generally find it easy to get to town.

The reasons for travel are quite varied, giving a good indication of how rural Puerto Rican life has changed in thirty years. The frequency of urban trips shows extensive participation in the modern economy. Almost half the survey group does general and food shopping in town. Over 40% rely on small local *colmados* (grocery stores), and the remainder shop regularly in both. Home gardens provide a supplement for some, but subsistence cultivation, hacienda stores, and traveling vendors are no longer important sources of food. The medical services, social security system, and high schools all draw people to town regularly and make a new contribution to rural welfare.

Although road construction and improved transportation give country people more employment choices and services, they also contribute to the decline in agriculture, thus reducing available rural employment opportunities. Among the adults in the sample households (excluding women primarily engaged in home and child care), urban employment provides the main opportunity. Almost half of all the employed work in town. Another 27% are in rural nonagricultural jobs, for example, as carpenters, in public works, or as small businessmen. These kinds of employment require considerable daily travel. Only 25% remain working in agriculture, where wages are considerably lower than in town.[12] These are the least mobile of all workers, although some even move between holdings to obtain relatively constant work. Because they pay low wages, producers find it difficult to secure workers and maintain their operations. Consequently, agricultural decline is continuous, and rural job opportunities lessen. Agricultural workers who have few skills appear to face continuing poverty so long as they remain in their rural homes.

Besides agricultural workers, there are other groups with low mobility, including the unemployed, the retired, and the incapacitated. Excluding women occupied at home, these people make up slightly over 40% of the adults in the sample. As a final analysis, we would like to note the variations between barrios in travel behavior. Using the Kruskal-Wallis method of analysis of variance to compare minimum trip index values in the nine barrios, find the difference between them to be significant ($p < .01$, 8 d.f.). Important factors which explain the variation are the percentages of car ownership and of inmigrants in the barrio populations. A high incidence of each is associated with high trip index values.

## *Some Theoretical Implications*

We would now like to compare the patterns of population change and mobility observed in Puerto Rico with the model developed by Zelinsky (1971) and elaborated by Pryor (1975). Though the model fits much of our information, some modifications are evident. Rural Puerto Rico in the 1940s can be clearly identified as possessing the minimal circulation characteristics of Zelinsky's Phase 1 (Traditional Society), although Phase 2 (Early Transitional) urban growth was under way and the declining population of some rural barrios was indicative of some outmigration. Emigration from the island was also heavy in the early 1950s, another Phase 2 characteristic.

By the 1970s, some of the Phase 4 (Advanced Society) attributes emerged in the Puerto Rican population. Circulation reached quite a high level and moves which appear to be intraurban can be observed when the island is studied at a local scale. Urban growth in Mayagüez concentrated in the inner-city barrios in the 1940s has shifted to outer areas, and the inner-city barrios have begun to lose population.

There is no clear evidence in the data of Phase 3 (Late Transitional) conditions, such as slackening rural to urban migration and declining emigration. This may be partly a function of the data we have been able to collect. We do not have the same detail for the years between 1950 and 1975 as for each of these years. However, statistics on emigration and census data do suggest some differences in aspects of Phase 3 in the Puerto Rico case. Changes in emigration rates appear to respond not only to modernization in Puerto Rico but to conditions in the destination. Emigration, which was high in the early 1950s when employment conditions in the United States were favorable, declined in the later 1950s and early 1960s (Picó, 1974).

In general, our study suggests urban growth rates in Puerto Rico have been tied partly to changing rates of emigration rather than following the phases outlined by Zelinsky (1971). Urban growth was rapid in the 1940s when emigration was modest, then in the 1950s most towns lost population when emigration was high but began to grow rapidly in the 1960s as emigration declined. While these conditions may be peculiar to Puerto Rico, it seems important to recognize that emigration rates will be a function of conditions in receiving areas, not only of transitions associated with internal modernization. Analysis of the changes observed may also lead to the speculation that modernization in Puerto Rico has been so rapid that the passage of each phase is telescoped compared to transitions noted by Zelinsky, who draws on examples covering several centuries of history.

Another modification to the model which our local study suggests is the prospect of urban decline, which we have noted in the smallest of our three towns, Rincón, and in some of the central areas of Mayagüez. Again, this is a phenomenon not restricted to Puerto Rico, and to an extent it contradicts the generalization of increasing urbanization with modernization, albeit that such a modification may not belong in a macro-scale model.

Turning to Pryor's (1975) work, we can identify at least three and perhaps five of the migration types he postulates. There has certainly been rural to urban migration in the study area, indicated by the growth of Mayagüez and Añasco. This migration would generally involve a transition from a traditional to a modern environment. Intrarural movement has been marked, and again this involves modernization for the migrant. Both of these types could be regarded as innovative migrations. Within the last decade, urban-rural movement has begun, and this might be considered a conservative move, in that the migrants could be leaving a modern urban setting for a more traditional rural residence. Pryor was uncertain how to classify urban-rural migrants, but chose conservative. Our study suggests that while the residential move may appear conservative, the level of circulation exhibited by these migrants might allow them to be classified as innovative. Our data are not sufficient to elaborate on a fourth type, intraurban moves, but the spatial patterns of growth observed in the city of Mayagüez suggest that movement from the central areas of the city to peripheral suburbs could be regarded as innovative. In addition, there is a small but continuing migration from outside the current rural-urban system, with migrants returning from the United States to rural Puerto Rico. These migrants probably include those who could be described as innovative, in that they bring capital and skills to improve their living circumstances, as well as those who could be regarded as conservative, because they have returned after unsuccessful experiences in the United States.

### *Summary*

When viewed from an islandwide perspective, the changes in population distribution in Puerto Rico since 1940 confirm the widely held generalization of urban growth and rural decline. Studies of regional and local scales in western Puerto Rico question this stereotype by indicating substantial movement of people within the rural areas and even into the countryside. Areas of continuous rural population decrease are actually less prevalent than those which have experienced population fluctuation or increase. Some of the rural growth has been stimulated by government settlement schemes, but most has resulted from self-initiated migration. The migrants come from three sources: other rural areas in the western part of the islands, Puerto Rican towns, and the United States.

It is difficult to establish commonalities between the rural growth areas, other than that they have shed their dependence on agricultural employment. Some are characterized by a high urban orientation, with residents making frequent trips to town for their work and most of their needs. In others, the people retain a more local outlook. These tend to be areas which increased in population earlier in the period under investigation, rather than later. The declining areas have more dependence on agricultural employment and considerable numbers of elderly, incapacitated, and unemployed persons who are generally less mobile.

Although there have been variations in the nature of population change within the rural areas, the life of all the rural people has altered markedly in the last thirty years. There has been a substantial shift in their residential locations with a dramatic change from a dispersed settlement pattern to a strongly linear concentration along main highways and nearby sections of tributary roads. Virtually all have access to electricity, water, and good transportation. Education and social welfare services have brought even the most remote into the urban and national orbit.

Even though their lives have in a sense become more urbanized, people living in rural areas exhibit a strong preference for the country and have no hesitation in describing themselves as country people. Their feelings are coming to be shared by some migrants from the Puerto Rican towns. This preference reflects an appreciation of the rural ambience, especially its tranquility. For many, it also reflects a strong maintenance of traditional family ties and support, demonstrated by patterns of residential location, assistance in building of houses, and support in times of economic stress.

In conclusion, we would like to reflect on some implications of the changes we have observed for the future of Puerto Rico. Government efforts have stimulated industrial expansion on the island and the widespread diffusion of modern health, education, and living amenities to rural people, and many have benefited. However, there has been a simultaneous and related decline in agriculture. As a consequence, there is quite high unemployment in rural areas and associated immobility. Even though their living conditions have improved, many people have restricted prospects for the future. Further attention should be paid to their needs. In addition, the interroad rural land is being abandoned, with seemingly little chance that it will be brought back to productivity. While much of the abandoned land is badly eroded and of marginal capacity, some may have productive potential. However, present abandonment does not reflect any assessment of differential land quality. More attention should be directed to planning the use of this land, particularly when one considers that the island is becoming largely dependent on expensive imported food.

## NOTES

1. For a review of geographic work on modernization, see de Souza and Porter (1974).

2. Assistance with field expenses was provided by the Center for Latin American and Caribbean Studies, University of Illinois. We also wish to thank Susan Taylor of the University of Illinois for the use of her car in much of our field work.

3. The three urban areas, Mayagüez, Añasco, and Rincón, as defined by their 1970 boundaries, have been excluded from this analysis.

4. Sábalos and Miradero, adjacent to the city, lost population in the 1940s and gained in the 1950s. Sábalos expanded even more rapidly in the 1960s but Miradero lost. Guanajibo, further from the city, gained population in each decade. We can only speculate why the population increase in Guanajibo began earlier. It may be related to the ease of building on flat land there, rather than on hilly sites in the other barrios. Alternatively, land further from the city may have been cheaper. Augelli (1955) explains similar growth around San Lorenzo in terms of land cost.

5. The barrio of Pueblo adjoining the town of Rincón on the south was also excluded because 1940 data were not available.

6. Two lowland barrios in Añasco were excluded, one because it was mainly in cane fields and contained very few people throughout the period, the other because it was made up mainly of cane fields and its population was clustered on the outskirts of Añasco.

7. Information obtained by interviews with personnel of the Puerto Rican Real Estate and Mortgage Company, Mayagüez.

8. The source is data from the Puerto Rican Real Estate and Mortgage Company.

9. Boswell (1976), in his study of population change between 1960 and 1970, noted that the highest rates of residential mobility within municipios occurred in the central highland coffee areas characterized by net outmigration. This reinforces our observation of substantial intrarural movement.

10. A high rate of movement and diversity of origins also characterizes the rural portions of the Mayagüez Standard Metropolitan Statistical Area (SMSA). The 1970 census indicates that 46% of all residents over five years of age had moved since 1965. Migration from the central city was quite marked (averaging 35% in the rural tracts, though varying between them), with about the same number coming from other parts of the SMSA and smaller but still consequential numbers coming from other parts of Puerto Rico, 17%, and returning from the United States, 7% (U.S. Bureau of the Census, 1972: Table P-2).

11. Census data for 1970 for the rural portions of the Mayagüez SMSA indicate that 35% of all workers drove their own cars to work, 30% used públicos, and 9% rode as passengers in privately owned cars. Only 16% walked to work (U.S. Bureau of the Census, 1973: Table 79).

12. Census data show that in 1970 agriculture provided employment for only 19% of the rural farm and nonfarm employed population over 16 years of age in the three municipios. Manufacturing accounted for 31%, while wholesale and retail trade, construction, and professional and related services accounted almost equally for most of the remainder (U.S. Bureau of the Census, 1973: Tables 106 and 108).

## REFERENCES

AUGELLI, J. P. (1955) "Rural settlement types of interior Puerto Rico: sample studies from the Loiza Basin," pp. 325-336 in C. F. Jones and P. Picó (eds.) Symposium on the Geography of Puerto Rico. Rio Piedras: University of Puerto Rico.

BLUME, H. (1974) The Caribbean Islands (J. Maczewski and A. Norton, trans.). London: Longman.

BOSWELL, T. D. (1976) "Net migration on a municipio scale in Puerto Rico, 1960-1970," pp. 75-82 in R. J. Tata (ed.) Latin America: Search for Geographic Explanations. East Lansing, MI: C.L.A.G.

BOTHWELL, L. D. (1937) "The geographic factor in the distribution, trends, and peaks of population of Puerto Rico, 1900-1930." Michigan Academy of Sci., Arts and Letters 22: 321-27.

BROOKFIELD, H. [ed.] (1973) The Pacific in Transition. New York: St. Martin's Press.

DE SOUZA, A. and P. W. PORTER (1974) "The underdevelopment and modernization of the third world." Commission on College Geography, Resource Paper 28. Washington, DC: Association of American Geographers.

GULICK, L. H. (1955) "Occupance summary of rural Utuado and Jayuya," pp. 369-401 in C. F. Jones and R. Picó (eds.) Symposium on the Geography of Puerto Rico. Rio Piedras: University of Puerto Rico.

IMUS, H. R. (1955) "The sugar cane economy of the Mayagüez area," pp. 155-183 in C. F. Jones and R. Picó (eds.) Symposium on the Geography of Puerto Rico. Rio Piedras: University of Puerto Rico.

——— (1951) "The Mayagüez area of Puerto Rico: a study in farm economy analysis." Ph.D. dissertation, Northwestern University.

JONES, C. F. (1950-1951) "Programa de clasificación de terrenos rurales; mapas de utilización terrenos rurales." Issued by Universidad de Puerto Rico and Northwestern University.

LEWIS, L. A. (1969) "The spatial properties of population mobility within Puerto Rico." J. of Tropical Geography 29: 33-38.

LOUNSBURY, J. F. (1955) "Types and patterns of rural settlements in the Aguas-Buenas-Naranjito-Comerío-Corozal area," in C. F. Jones and R. Picó (eds.) Symposium on the Geography of Puerto Rico. Rio Piedras: University of Puerto Rico.

MACISCO, J. J. (1967) "Internal migration in Puerto Rico, 1955-1960." Dissertation Abstracts, Humanities 28: 303A-304A.

PARSONS, J. J. (1973) "Latin America," pp. 16-46 in M. Mikesell (ed.) Geographers Abroad: Essays on the Problems and Prospects of Research in Foreign Areas. Chicago: University of Chicago Department of Geography.

PICO, R. (1974) The Geography of Puerto Rico. Chicago: Aldine.

PRESTON, D. A. (1974) "Geographers among the peasants: research on rural societies in Latin America," pp. 143-178 in C. Board et al. (eds.) Progress in Geography. International Review of Current Research, Volume 6. London: Edward Arnold.

PRYOR, R. J. (1975) "Migration and the processes of modernization," pp. 23-28 in L. A. Kosinski and R. M. Prothero (eds.) People on the Move: Studies on Internal Migration. London: Methuen.

STONE, L. O. (1965) "Population redistribution and economic development in Puerto Rico, 1950-1960." Social and Econ. Studies 14: 264-271.

STOUSE, P.A.D. (1971) "Settlement geography in Latin America," pp. 95-103 in R. L. Carmin et al. (eds.) Geographic Research on Latin America: Benchmark 1970.

Carmin et al. (eds.) Geographic Research on Latin America: Benchmark 1970.

Muncie, IN: Ball State University.

U.S. Bureau of the Census (1975) Statistical Abstract of the United States, Washington, DC: Government Printing Office.

——— (1973) Census of the Population, 1970, Volume 1: Characteristics of the Population. Washington, DC: Government Printing Office.

——— (1972) Census of Population and Housing, 1970: Census Tracts, Final Report PHC (1)-239, Mayagüez, Puerto Rico, SMSA. Washington, DC: Government Printing Office.

U.S. Geological Survey (1966) "Rincón quadrangle." Commonwealth of Puerto Rico. Washington, DC: Government Printing Office.

——— (1964) "Central La Plata quadrangle; Rosario quadrangle." Commonwealth of Puerto Rico. Washington, DC: Government Printing Office.

VASQUEZ, J. L. (1968) "El crecimiento poblacional de Puerto Rico 1493 al presente." Revista de Ciencias Sociales 12: 5-22.

WOLF, E. R. (1956) "San José: subcultures of a 'traditional' coffee municipality," pp. 171-264 in J. H. Steward (ed.) The Peoples of Puerto Rico. Urbana: Univ. of Illinois Press.

ZELINSKY, W. (1971) "The hypothesis of the mobility transition." Geographical Rev. 61: 219-249.

*Janice J. Monk is Assistant Professor of Geography at the University of Illinois at Urbana-Champaign. Her interests include social change, and her recent research deals with the implications of sexual differences in migration patterns in Puerto Rico and with changing rural land use in the Caribbean.*

*Charles S. Alexander is Professor of Geography at the University of Illinois at Urbana-Champaign. He has long-term interests in peasant agriculture in the Caribbean and is studying the impact of land-use changes on the physical environment. His research in physical geography also includes Caribbean shoreline studies.*

# INDEX

## to

## JOURNAL OF INTERAMERICAN STUDIES

## AND WORLD AFFAIRS

## VOLUME 21

**Number 1 (February 1979) pp. 1-184**
**Number 2 (May 1979) pp. 185-296**
**Number 3 (August 1979) pp. 297-424**
**Number 4 (November 1979) pp. 425-552**

**Authors:**

ALEXANDER, CHARLES S., see Monk, Janice J.
AMERINGER, CHARLES, "Leonardo Ruiz Pineda: Leader of the Venezuelan Resistance, 1949-1952," 209.
CALVO, ROBERTO, "The Church and the Doctrine of National Security," 69.
CHILD, JOHN, "From 'Color' to 'Rainbow': U.S. Strategic Planning for Latin America, 1919-1945," 233.
CRAHAN, MARGARET E., "Salvation through Christ or Marx: Religion in Revolutionary Cuba," 156.
DODSON, MICHAEL, "The Christian Left in Latin American Politics," 45.
GALEY, JOHN, "Industrialist in the Wilderness: Henry Ford's Amazon Venture," 261.
GILBERT, DENNIS, "Society, Politics, and the Press: An Interpretation of the Peruvian Press Reform of 1974," 369.
GILFEATHER, Sr. KATHERINE ANNE, M.M., "Women Religious, the Poor, and the Institutional Church in Chile," 129.
GORMAN, STEPHEN M., "The State, Elite, and Export in Nineteenth Century Peru: Toward an Alternative Reinterpretation of Political Change," 395.
GRAYSON, GEORGE W., "Oil and U.S.-Mexican Relations," 427.
HOSKIN, GARY, "Belief Systems of Colombian Political Party Activists," 481.
LeoGRANDE, WILLIAM M., "Party Development in Revolutionary Cuba," 457.
LEVINE, DANIEL H., "Introductory Note" (Introduction to Special Issue on The Church and Politics in Latin America), 3.
——— "Religion and Politics, Politics and Religion: An Introduction," 5.
McCANN, FRANK D., Jr., "Origins of the 'New Professionalism' of the Brazilian Military," 505.
MONK, JANICE J. and CHARLES S. ALEXANDER, "Modernization and Rural Population Movements: Western Puerto Rico," 523.
NOGEE, JOSEPH L. and JOHN W. SLOAN, "Allende's Chile and the Soviet Union: A Policy Lesson for Latin American Nations Seeking Autonomy," 339.

OGELSBY, J.C.M., "A Trudeau Decade: Canadian-Latin American Relations 1968-1978," 187.
POBLETE, RENATO, S.J., "From Medellín to Puebla: Notes for Reflection," 31.
RANIS, PETER, "Early Peronism and the Post-Liberal Argentine State," 313.
SLOAN, JOHN W., see Nogee, Joseph L.
SMITH, BRIAN H., S.J., "Churches and Human Rights in Latin America: Recent Trends in the Subcontinent," 89.
WILDE, ALEXANDER, "Ten Years of Change in the Church: Puebla and the Future," 299.

## Articles:

"Allende's Chile and the Soviet Union: A Policy Lesson for Latin American Nations Seeking Autonomy," Nogee and Sloan, 339.
"Belief Systems of Colombian Political Party Activists," Hoskin, 481.
"The Christian Left in Latin American Politics," Dodson, 45.
"The Church and the Doctrine of National Security," Calvo, 69.
"Churches and Human Rights in Latin America: Recent Trends in the Subcontinent," Smith, 89.
"Early Peronism and the Post-Liberal Argentine State," Ranis, 313.
"From 'Color' to 'Rainbow': U.S. Strategic Planning for Latin America, 1919-1945," Child, 233.
"From Medellín to Puebla: Notes for Reflection," Poblete, 31.
"Industrialist in the Wilderness: Henry Ford's Amazon Venture," Galey, 261.
"Introductory Note," Levine, 3.
"Leonardo Ruiz Pineda: Leader of the Venezuelan Resistance, 1949-1952," Ameringer, 209.
"Modernization and Rural Population Movements: Western Puerto Rico," Monk and Alexander, 523.
"Oil and U.S.-Mexican Relations," Grayson, 427.
"Origins of the 'New Professionalism' of the Brazilian Military," McCann, 505.
"Party Development in Revolutionary Cuba," LeoGrande, 457.
"Religion and Politics, Politics and Religion: An Introduction," Levine, 5.
"Salvation through Christ or Marx: Religion in Revolutionary Cuba," Crahan, 156.
"Society, Politics, and the Press: An Interpretation of the Peruvian Press Reform of 1974," Gilbert, 369.
"The State, Elite, and Export in Nineteenth Century Peru: Toward an Alternative Reinterpretation of Political Change," Gorman, 395.
"Ten Years of Change in the Church: Puebla and the Future," Wilde, 299.
"A Trudeau Decade: Canadian-Latin American Relations 1968-1978," Ogelsby, 187.
"Women Religious, the Poor, and the Institutional Church in Chile," Gilfeather, 129.

## Books Received:

291, 419.

# Advertising Supplement:

# Journal of Interamerican Studies and World Affairs

This supplement has been prepared especially for our readers to bring them information and announcements of professional interest. By placing advertisements in the pages of this journal, our advertisers have indicated a desire to communicate with our readers. We hope our readers will acknowledge their indirect support of the journal and its purposes by mentioning the journal in correspondence with advertisers.

**Supplement to A Bibliography of United States-Latin American Relations Since 1810**

*compiled and edited by Michael C. Meyer*

There is no competitive volume for this bibliography as, together with the original volume (*A Bibliography of United States-Latin American Relations Since 1810*), it is the only comprehensive research tool for the study of U.S.-Latin American relations. Chapter subsections have been added to accommodate newly important hemispheric trends and diplomatic events. The chronological sections of the original bibliography have been updated to include the series of inter-American conferences that have occurred in the last decade.
xxvi, 193 pages. **$19.50**

**University of Nebraska Press**
901 North 17th Street Lincoln 68588

# CITIES OF PEASANTS

## The Political Economy of Urbanization in the Third World

by **BRYAN ROBERTS,**
*Professor of Sociology, University of Manchester*

This book is about the expansion of capitalism in the Third World. It is one of the few accounts linking contemporary differences in the political and economic structure of underdeveloped countries to the historically specific way in which these have become part of the world economy. Focusing on the most securely capitalist of all underdeveloped regions of the continent of Latin America — the author traces the growth of urban-based industrialism and its impact, both externally and internally. He shows how it has transformed the economy and produced new political and social pressures, whose significance can be seen in the daily economic activities, social relationships and even religious behavior of people in Third-World cities. This analysis explains and uses the concepts of dependent development and core periphery: there is also a critical review of current theories about urbanization in the third world and, in particular, a discussion of the debate on marginality.

The nature of the urban working class in underdeveloped countries, with its potential for organization and collective aspirations, will be a crucial factor in the future. This book conveys both the flavor of life in the cities of the Third World and the immediacy of their problems.

**CONTENTS**

1. Urbanization and underdevelopment
2. Urbanization and underdevelopment before the modern period
3. Urbanization and industrialization
4. Migration and the agrarian structure
5. The urban economy and social stratification
6. Urban poverty and coping with urban life
7. Urbanization and marginality in underdevelopment

**Explorations in Urban Analysis, Volume 1**

| | | | |
|---|---|---|---|
| **June 1979** | **ISBN 0-8039-1290-0** | **hardcover** | **$17.50** |
| **216 pages** | **ISBN 0-8039-1291-9** | **softcover** | **$ 8.95** |

**SAGE PUBLICATIONS, INC.**
**275 South Beverly Drive**
**Beverly Hills, California 90212**

**SAGE PUBLICATIONS LTD**
**28 Banner Street**
**London EC1Y 8QE, England**

Please mention Journal of Interamerican Studies and World Affairs when writing advertiser

# Scarcity and Survival in Central America

## Ecological Origins of the Soccer War

*William H. Durham.* Looking at both population and land tenure dynamics in their historical context, this study challenges the view that the 1969 conflict between El Salvador and Honduras was primarily a response to population pressure. The author demonstrates that land scarcity, a principal cause of the war, was largely a product of the concentration of land holdings. The analysis focuses on the emigration of 300,000 Salvadoreans to Honduras in the years before the war, inquiring into the reasons for the emigration, its impact on local agricultural economies, and its relation to the conflict. In addition to its value as a case study in human ecology, this book gives a clear account of the nature and origins of ecological pressures in rural Central America. Illustrated. $14.50

# Capitalism and the State in U.S.-Latin American Relations

*Edited by Richard R. Fagen.* Why does the United States respond as it does to political and economic events in Latin America? How does the United States condition events in Latin America, and how is it in turn conditioned by the results of its influence? This volume presents ten papers which seek the answers to these questions by exploring the deep sources of U.S. foreign policy toward the hemisphere. Part I deals with general aspects of U.S. foreign policy. Part II is a collection of case studies of relations between individual Latin American countries and the United States. Cloth, $22.50; paper, $6.95

**Stanford University Press**

lease mention Journal of Interamerican Studies and World Affairs when writing advertisers.

# WORLD LEADERS:
## A Study of Heads of Government in the Postwar Period

by **JEAN BLONDEL**, *University of Essex*

WORLD LEADERS is the first volume in a series of three books entitled Political Executives in Comparative Perspective: A Cross-National Empirical Study, which will attempt to fill a serious gap in the study of political leadership by providing a comprehensive study of the world's heads of state. This volume includes a comparison of leaders of brief duration with those whose rule has extended over decades, and of military rulers with chief executives of western democracies. It provides, in addition, analyses of leaders of the Communist world, and indeed even of the world's few remaining monarchs. The study emphasizes the contrast between the few leaders -- particularly those in newly independent and Communist countries -- who hold office for long periods of time, and the vast majority of political executives for whom "charisma" is rather a remote question due to the relatively short time in which they are in power. Further, this volume examines the significance of the current development of forms of "dual" leadership. WORLD LEADERS will make fascinating reading for political scientists, specialists in comparative government, and their students.

**1979** **ISBN 0-8039-9830-9** **hardcover** **$17.50**
**250 pages (tent.)** **ISBN 0-8039-9831-7** **softcover** **$7.95**

**SAGE** PUBLICATIONS, INC
275 South Beverly Drive
Beverly Hills, California 90212

**SAGE** PUBLICATIONS LTD
28 Banner Street
London EC1Y 8QE, England

# EVALUATION
## A Systematic Approach

**Peter H. Rossi   Howard E. Freeman**
**Sonia R. Wright**

**EVALUATION: A Systematic Approach** is the first comprehensive text in the field. Its organization allows the reader to gain an understanding of the role of evaluation research in planning, design and implementation of both established and innovative social programs and projects. Contemporary technical procedures for planning interventions, target population selection, program monitoring and impact assessment are provided. A unique feature of the book is its detailed treatment of cost-benefit and cost-effectiveness techniques.

The authors of the volume bring to bear their broad and practical experience in discussing the uses and prospects of evaluation research. The use of social science methods and concepts are stressed in this unique applied social research text. Throughout the volume, "case modules" (exhibits) are used to provide valuable and pragmatic illustrative information.

**EVALUATION: A Systematic Approach** is designed for social researchers, policy and planning specialists and practitioners in health care, community education, psychiatry, public safety and criminal justice, urban development, social welfare and other human service fields. Students of research methods in all social science disciplines and in professional schools will find this volume the essential text and reference work in evaluation research.

**April 1979   336 pages   ISBN 0-8039-1179-3   hardcover   $14.95**

**SAGE** PUBLICATIONS, INC.
275 South Beverly Drive
Beverly Hills, California 90212

**SAGE** PUBLICATIONS LTD
28 Banner Street
London EC1Y 8QE, England

Please mention Journal of Interamerican Studies and World Affairs when writing advertisers.

# INTERNATIONAL NEWS: FREEDOM UNDER ATTACK

**edited by Congressman Dante B. Fascell, U.S. House of Representatives**

Freedom of the press and the free flow of news and information is under attack around the world today. The conflict over media access and independence has developed on several levels: from attempts by a growing number of countries to bar American reporters to restrictive resolutions in UNESCO; from calls for redistributing radio bands to movements toward creating government monopolies on the distribution of information.

Four specialists on these questions have written timely studies touching on every aspect of contemporary international media affairs. Topics include the politics of international broadcasting, the Third World challenge to Western news services, the quality of American foreign coverage, and the ways in which various states are trying to censor news. This is an important and unique book which should be of vital interest to all who make and write the news, as well as the millions of Americans who depend on the media for their knowledge of global events.

**March 1979 320 pages ISBN 0-8039-1129-3 hardcover $15.00**

**SAGE** PUBLICATIONS, INC.
275 South Beverly Drive
Beverly Hills, California 90212

**SAGE** PUBLICATIONS LTD
28 Banner Street
London EC1Y 8QE, England

Please mention Journal of Interamerican Studies and World Affairs when writing advertisers.

# THE WORLD SYSTEM OF CAPITALISM: Past and Present

Edited by **Walter L. Goldfrank,**
*University of California, Santa Cruz*

The "world-system approach," formulated by Immanuel Wallerstein, series editor of these POLITICAL ECONOMY OF WORLD-SYSTEM ANNUALS, serves to unify the contributions included in this volume. The social scientists who are published here have rejected the traditional ahistorical approach of Western social research in favor of this interdiciplinary, historicallyoriented. øften radical approach to the study of the capitalist worldsystem. Contributions include theoretical articles and case studies from both the seventeenth and twentieth centuries. Notable is a tantalizing preview of Wallerstein's forthcoming second volume of THE MODERN WORLD-SYSTEM, dealing with stagnation in seventeenth century Europe and its effects.

Political Economy of the World-System Annuals, Volume 2
1979 ISBN 0-8039-1105-X hardcover $18.50
312 pages ISBN 0-8039-1106-8 softcover $ 8.95

SAGE PUBLICATIONS LTD
28 Banner Street
London EC1Y 8QE

SAGE PUBLICATIONS, INC
275 South Beverly Drive
Beverly Hills, California 90212

Please mention Journal of Interamerican Studies and World Affairs when writing advertisers.

# CHALLENGES TO AMERICA

UNITED STATES FOREIGN POLICY IN THE 1980s

Edited by: **CHARLES W. KEGLEY, JR.**, University of South Carolina
**PATRICK J. McGOWAN**, University of Southern California

In the selected "case-for-analysis" – the United States– the outstanding contributors explore the relationship between enviromental change and foreign policy response by examining long term secular trends which are likely to present special problems to U.S. society and foreign policy into the 1980's. Topics covered include the strategic arms balance, foreign perceptions of the United States, and the probable nature of the future relations between the United States, Europe, and Japan.

This, the fourth volume of the Sage International Yearbooks of Foreign Policy Studies, marks the inauguration of a new format for the series – the present and all subsequent volumes will each focus on a specific aspect of foreign policy. *Challenges to America* sets a high standard for all future Yearbooks in considering two important theoretical questions: How is foreign policy shaped by the environmental changes encountered by national actors? What are the linkages which exist between a state's foreign policy and its domestic and international environments?

**CONTENTS** / CHARLES W. KEGLEY, Jr. and PATRICK J. McGOWAN **Part I: AMERICA'S RESPONSE TO CHANGES IN THE INTERNATIONAL SYSTEM: THEORIES AND EVIDENCE** / FRANK L. KLINGBERG, FARID ABOLFATHI, JOHN J. HAYES, AND RICHARD E. HAYES **Part II: SOME EMERGENT GLOBAL CHALLENGES TO THE UNITED STATES** / MELVIN SMALL , J. DAVID SINGER, CHARLES F. DORAN, JAMES A. CAPORASO , MICHAEL D. WARD, WERNER J. FELD, ALVIN RICHMAN **Part III: SOME SOURCES OF AMERICAN FOREIGN POLICY ADAPTION** / OLE R. HOLSTI , JAMES N. ROSENAU, CHARLES F. HERMAN **Part IV: BIBLIOGRAPHY** / MARK W. DELANCEY , THOMAS H. JOHNSON

**Sage International Yearbooks of Foreign Policy Studies, Volume 4**

| | | | |
|---|---|---|---|
| **February 1979** | **ISBN 0-8039-1121-1** | **hardcover** | **$18.50** |
| **312 pages** | **ISBN 0-8039-1122-X** | **softcover** | **$ 8.95** |

**SAGE** PUBLICATIONS, INC
275 South Beverly Drive
Beverly Hills, California 90212

**SAGE** PUBLICATIONS LTD
28 Banner Street
London EC1Y 8QE, England

# Evaluation Studies Review Annual

## Volume 4

Edited by

**Lee Sechrest**

**with STEPHEN G. WEST, MELINDA A. PHILLIPS, ROBIN REDNER, and WILLIAM YEATON**

Today, more than ever evaluation research is concerned with the internal, external and construct validity of social investigation. These concerns, coupled with a full awareness of the monetary and political pressure associated with social intervention programs, have spawned the issues on which this volume is based: adequacy of treatment and outcome as opposed to the purely technical concerns of research design. Volume 4 of EVALUATION STUDIES REVIEW ANNUALS, with its emphasis on the planned strength and integrity of treatment, has focused attention on the ideals of evaluation research as opposed to the actual circumstances in which they are put into practice. This gap between aspiration and achievement, and the related ethical and policy concerns of social experimentation -- all factors with crucial implications for evaluation research -- are illuminated here by many of the finest minds in applied social science.

Like its predecessors, Volume 4 of EVALUATION STUDIES REVIEW ANNUALS is a "must" for the library of every evaluation specialist.

1979 Volume 4 768 pages ISBN 0-8039-1329-X hardcover $32.50

**SAGE** PUBLICATIONS, INC.
275 South Beverly Drive
Beverly Hills, California 90212

**SAGE** PUBLICATIONS LTD
28 Banner Street
London EC1Y 8QE, England

A New Journal! First Issue in September, 1979

# KNOWLEDGE

## Creation ◦ Diffusion ◦ Utilization ◦

RECEIVED NOV 1979 Hartwick College Library

edited by ROBERT RICH, Princeton University

associate editors:

JAMES DANZIGER, CAROLE GANZ, JUDITH K. LARSEN

### Our Purpose

Individuals have tended to think of themselves as working, or at least concentrating on knowledge creation, knowledge diffusion or knowledge utilization. As a result, these three subfields studying knowledge have evolved independently of each other. KNOWLEDGE: CREATION, DIFFUSION, UTILIZATION will provide the first forum for communication among individuals in these divergent areas as well as a context in which to develop research, methodology, and practices which establish much-needed linkages between them.

### editorial board

Henry Aaron
Bernhard Badura
Vincent P. Barabba
Martin Blumer
Donald T. Campbell
Nathan Caplan
Thomas D. Cook
Howard E. Davis
Irwin Feller
Joel Goldhar
Ronald Havelock
Irving Louis Horowitz
Melvin Kranzberg
Thomas Kiresuk
Karin Knorr
Fritz Machlup
Ian Mitroff
Serge Moscovici
Dorothy Nelkin
Carnot Nelson
Kenneth Prewitt
Derek de Solla Price
Everett M. Rogers
Nathan Rosenberg
Jean-Jacques Salomon
Carol H. Weiss
Gerald Zaltman

| Subscription rates | Introductory (1yr.) | Charter (3yr.)* |
|---|---|---|
| Individuals | $15.00 (save $1.50) | $45.00 (save $4.50) |
| Institutions | $30.00 (save $3.00) | $90.00 (save $9.00) |

*Your name will appear on the list of Charter Subscribers published in one issue of each of the first three volumes.

SAGE Publications Ltd
28 Banner Street
London EC1Y8QE

SAGE Publications Inc
275 South Beverly Drive
Beverly Hills, California 90212